D1097859

NEIL GAIMAN'S
MR HERO
THE NEWMATIC MAN™

Based on a concept created by NEIL GAIMAN

JAMES VANCE
Writer

TED SLAMPYAK
Penciler

BOB McLEOD
MIKE WITHERBY
ART NICHOLS
JOHN COULTHART
DAVE HUNT
TERRY BEATTY
Inkers

With special TEKNOPHAGE sequences drawn by
BRYAN TALBOT
Penciler and Inker
ANGUS McKIE
Inker

SUPER
GENIUS

NEW YORK

GRAPHIC NOVELS AVAILABLE FROM SUPER GENIUS

COMING SOON

NEIL GAIMAN'S
LADY JUSTICE
Volume One

NEIL GAIMAN'S
TEKNOPHAGE
Volume One

NEIL GAIMAN'S
MR. HERO
Volume One

WWE SUPERSTARS
#1
"Money in the Bank"

WWE SUPERSTARS
#2
"Haze of Glory!"

WWE SUPERSTARS
#3
"Legends"

WWE SUPERSTARS
#4
"Last Man Standing"

NEIL GAIMAN'S MR. HERO THE NEWMATIC MAN™ VOLUME ONE
Copyright © 1995 BIG Entertainment, Inc. (Assigned to Overline Capital, LLC.) All rights reserved. Neil Gaiman's MR. HERO THE NEWMATIC MAN™, including all characters featured and the names and distinct likenesses thereof, are trademarks of Overline Capital, LLC. Published under license from Overline Capital, LLC.

Dawn Guzzo – Design & Production
Ed Polgardy – Original Editor
Julie Riddle – Original Assistant Editor
Dr. Martin Greenberg – Original Senior Editor
Ben Spoont – Associate Producer
Albert Rodriguez – Original Production Director
David Silvers – Associate Producer
Mitchell Rubenstein – Co-Founder of Tekno•Comix
Laurie Silvers – Co-Founder of Tekno•Comix
Jeff Whitman – Production Coordinator
Bethany Bryan – Associate Editor
Dan Berlin – Editorial Intern
Jim Salicrup
Editor-in-Chief

ISBN: 978-1-62991-435-0 Paperback Edition
ISBN: 978-1-62991-436-7 Hardcover Edition

Printed in China, February 2016 by WKT Co. Ltd.
3/F Phase 1 Leader Industrial Centre
188 Texaco Road, Tseun Wan, N.T. Hong Kong

Super Genius books may be purchased for business or promotional use. For information on bulk purchases please contact Macmillan Corporate and Premium Sales Department at (800) 221-7945 x5442.

DISTRIBUTED BY MACMILLAN
FIRST SUPER GENIUS PRINTING

Table of Contents

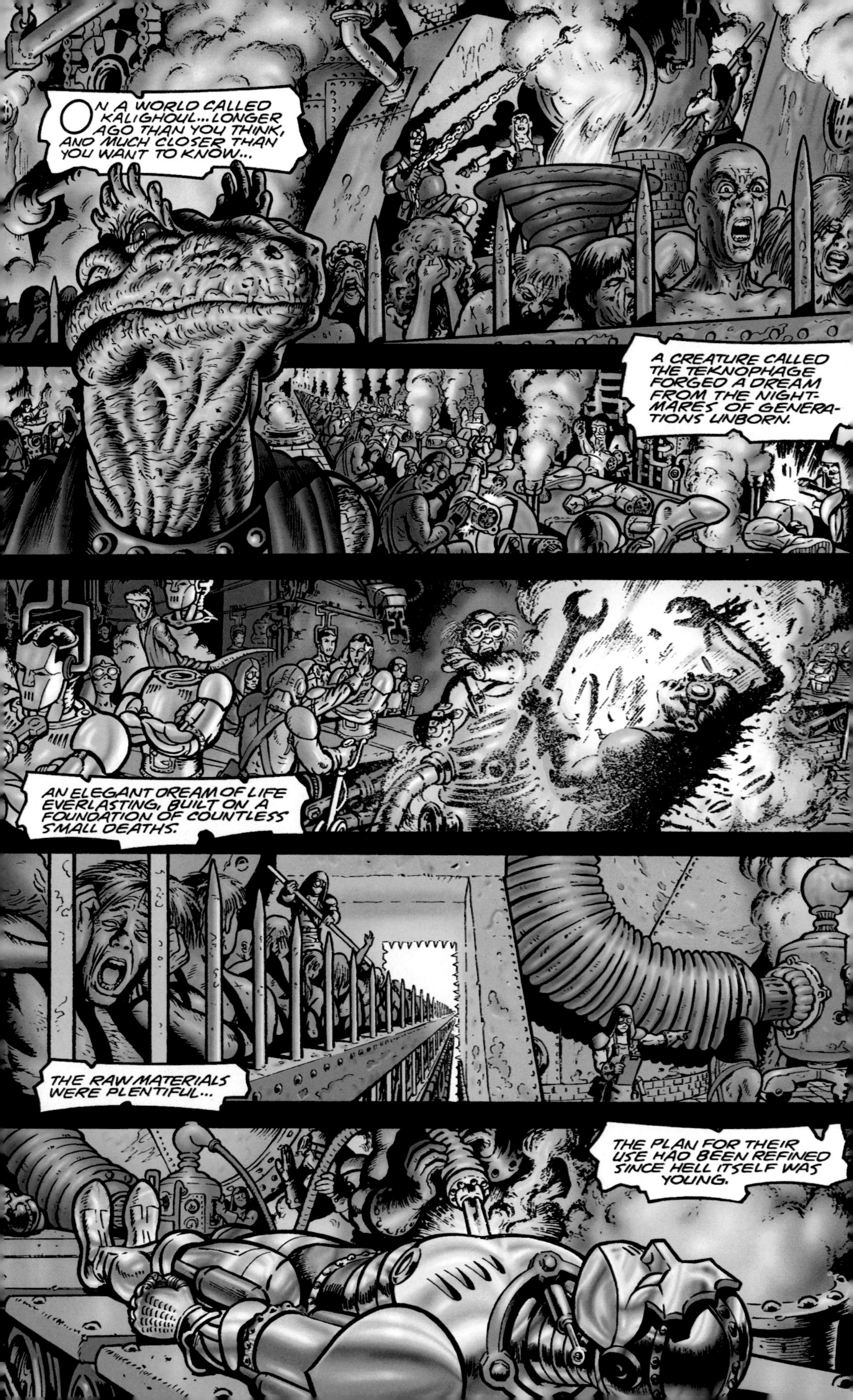
ON A WORLD CALLED KALIGHOUL... LONGER AGO THAN YOU THINK, AND MUCH CLOSER THAN YOU WANT TO KNOW...
A CREATURE CALLED THE TEKNOPHAGE FORGED A DREAM FROM THE NIGHT-MARES OF GENERA-TIONS UNBORN.
AN ELEGANT DREAM OF LIFE EVERLASTING, BUILT ON A FOUNDATION OF COUNTLESS SMALL DEATHS.
THE RAW MATERIALS WERE PLENTIFUL...
THE PLAN FOR THEIR USE HAD BEEN REFINED SINCE HELL ITSELF WAS YOUNG.

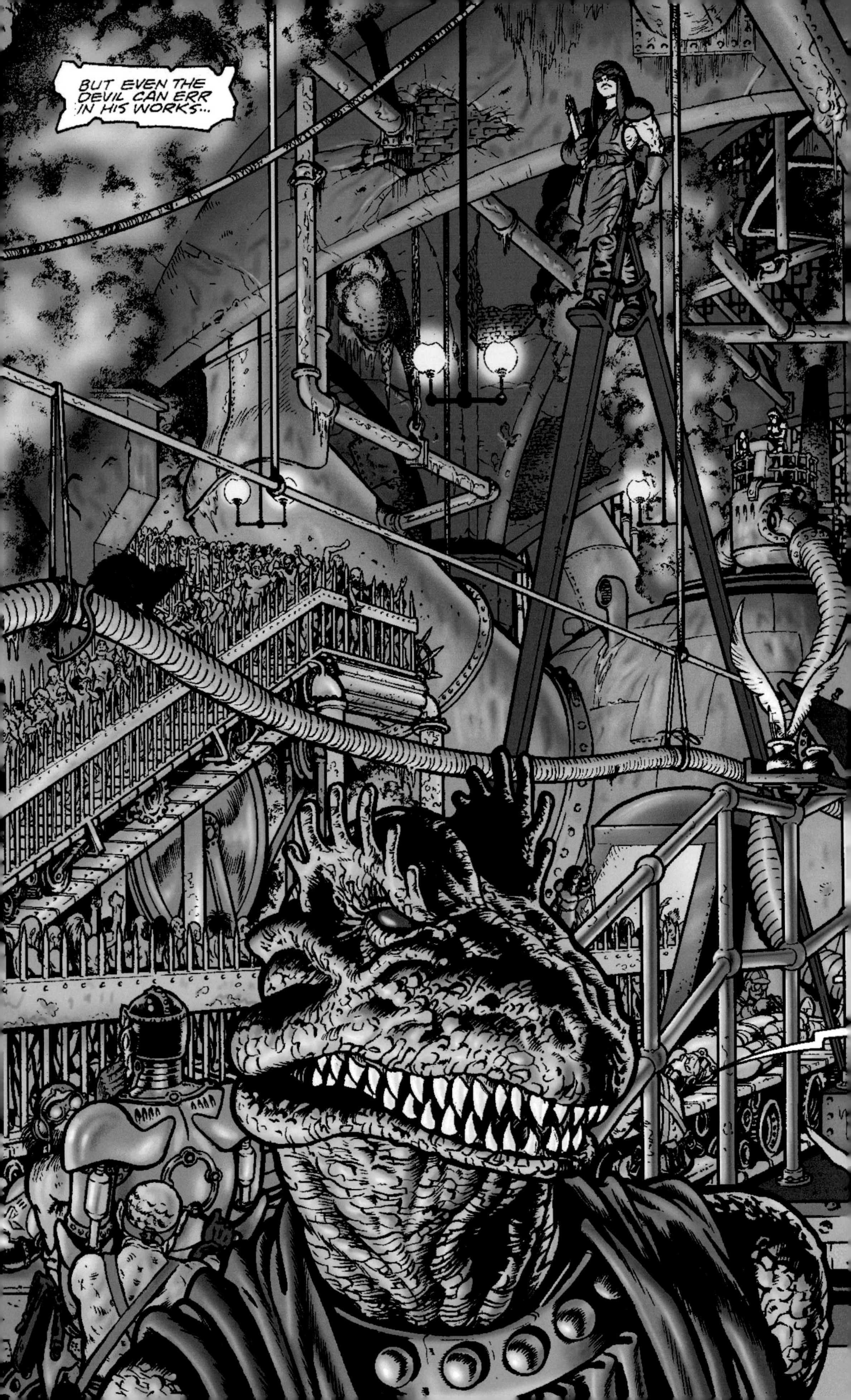
BUT EVEN THE DEVIL CAN ERR IN HIS WORKS...

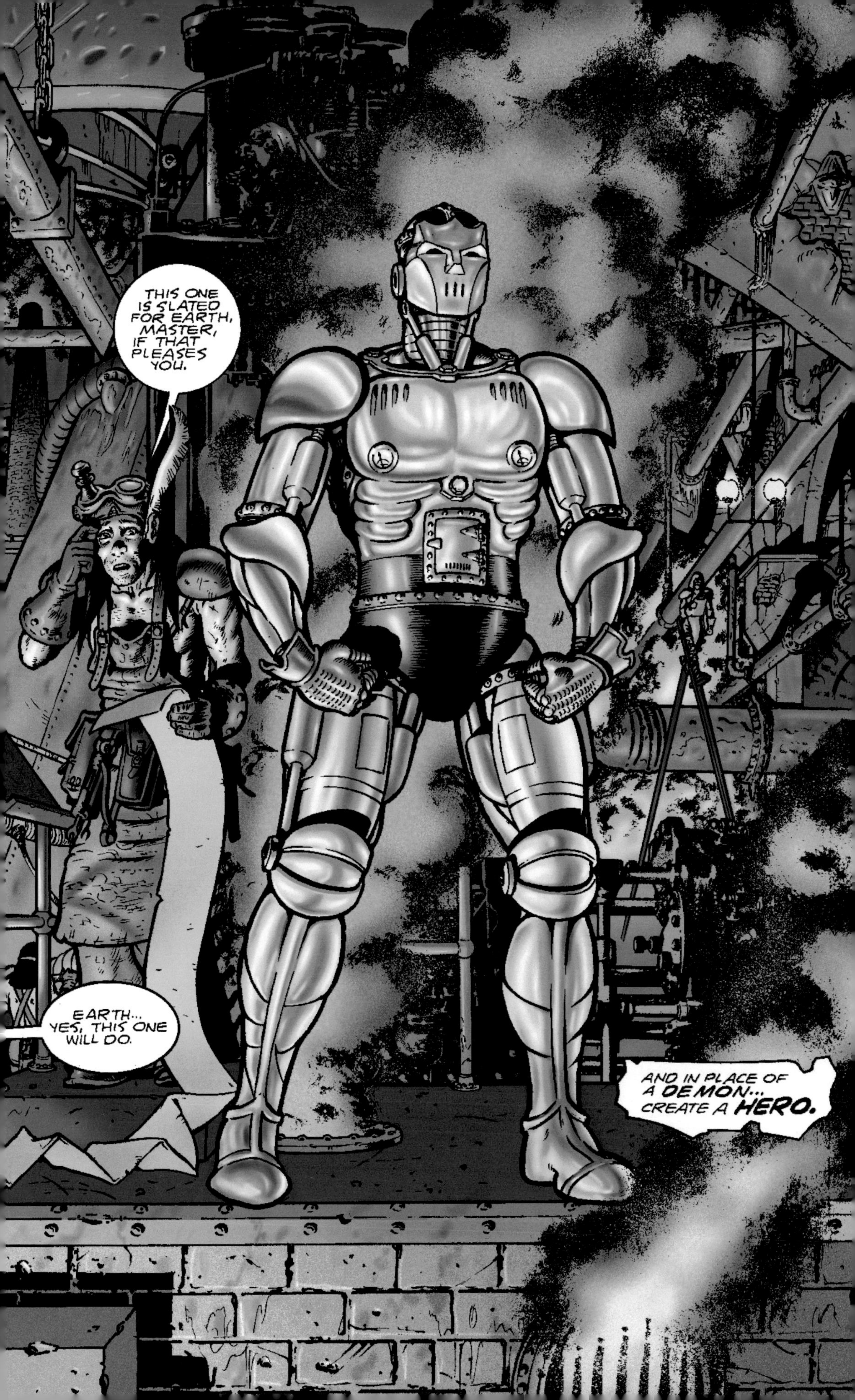
THIS ONE IS SLATED FOR EARTH, MASTER, IF THAT PLEASES YOU.
EARTH... YES, THIS ONE WILL DO.
AND IN PLACE OF A DEMON... CREATE A HERO.

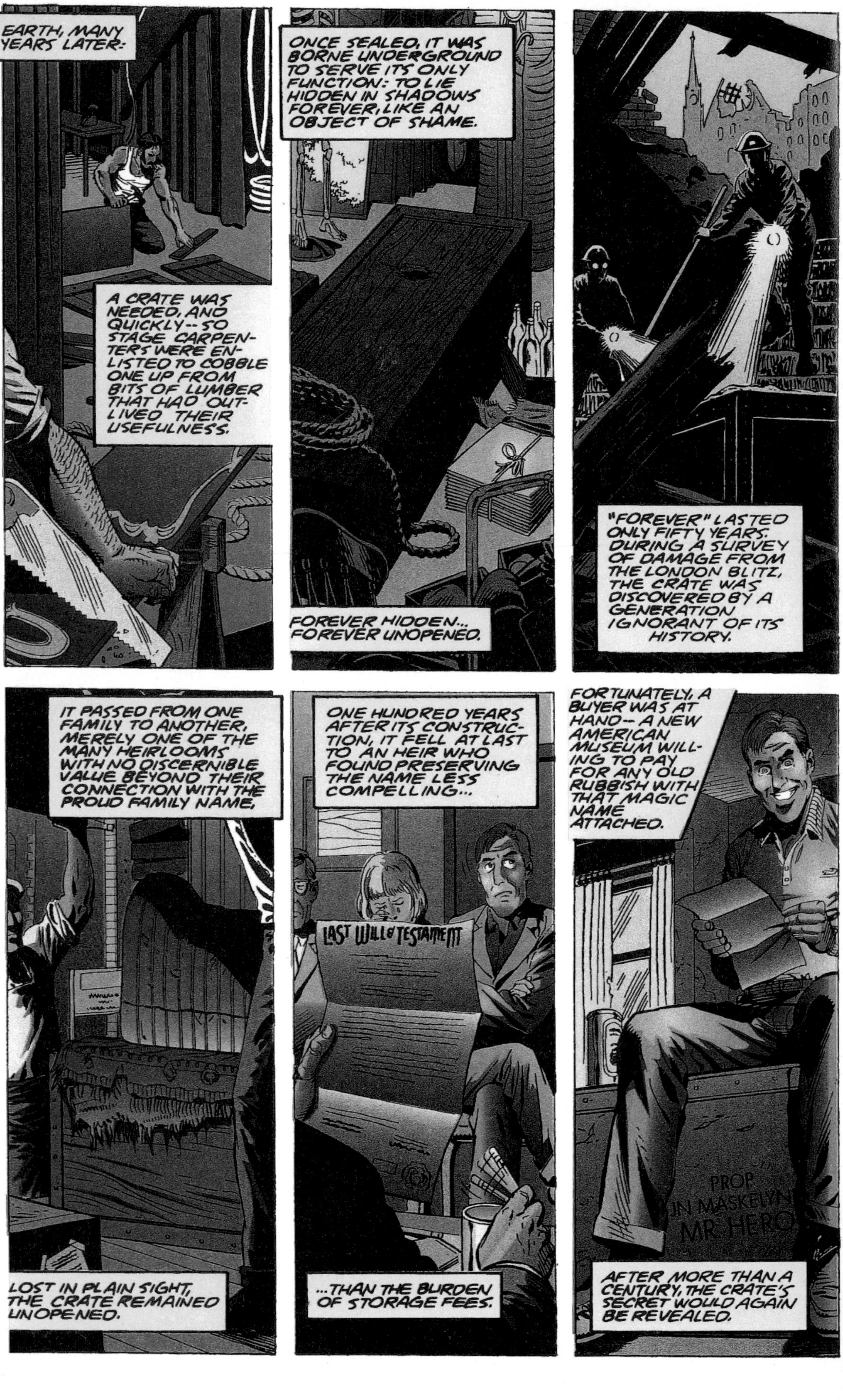
EARTH, MANY YEARS LATER-
A CRATE WAS NEEDED, AND QUICKLY-- SO STAGE CARPENTERS WERE ENLISTED TO COBBLE ONE UP FROM BITS OF LUMBER THAT HAD OUTLIVED THEIR USEFULNESS.
ONCE SEALED, IT WAS BORNE UNDERGROUND TO SERVE ITS ONLY FUNCTION: TO LIE HIDDEN IN SHADOWS FOREVER, LIKE AN OBJECT OF SHAME.
FOREVER HIDDEN... FOREVER UNOPENED.
"FOREVER" LASTED ONLY FIFTY YEARS. DURING A SURVEY OF DAMAGE FROM THE LONDON BLITZ, THE CRATE WAS DISCOVERED BY A GENERATION IGNORANT OF ITS HISTORY.
IT PASSED FROM ONE FAMILY TO ANOTHER, MERELY ONE OF THE MANY HEIRLOOMS WITH NO DISCERNIBLE VALUE BEYOND THEIR CONNECTION WITH THE PROUD FAMILY NAME.
LOST IN PLAIN SIGHT, THE CRATE REMAINED UNOPENED.
ONE HUNDRED YEARS AFTER ITS CONSTRUCTION, IT FELL AT LAST TO AN HEIR WHO FOUND PRESERVING THE NAME LESS COMPELLING...
LAST WILL & TESTAMENT
...THAN THE BURDEN OF STORAGE FEES.
FORTUNATELY, A BUYER WAS AT HAND-- A NEW AMERICAN MUSEUM WILLING TO PAY FOR ANY OLD RUBBISH WITH THAT MAGIC NAME ATTACHED.
PROP
MR. HERO
AFTER MORE THAN A CENTURY, THE CRATE'S SECRET WOULD AGAIN BE REVEALED.

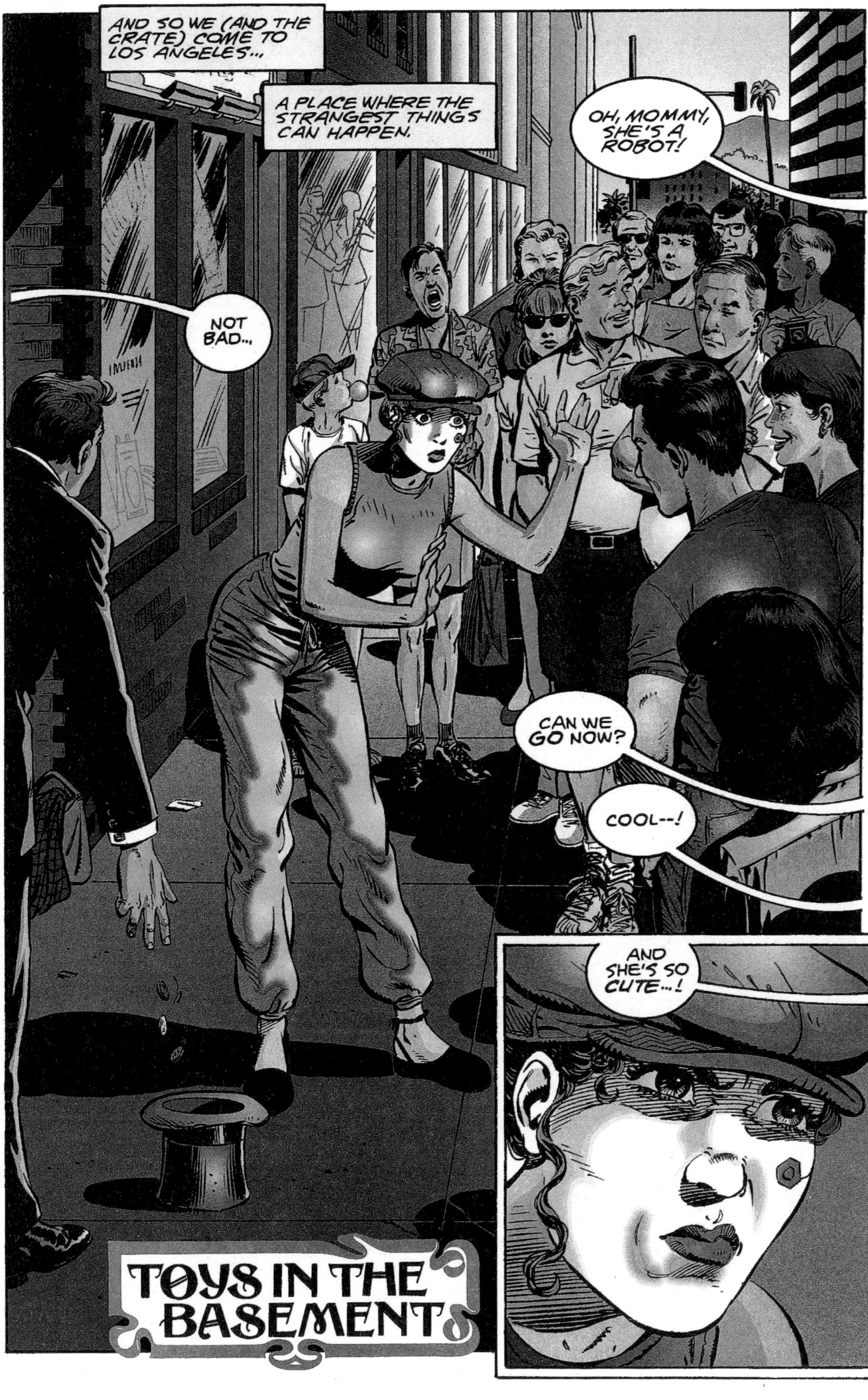
AND SO WE (AND THE CRATE) COME TO LOS ANGELES...
A PLACE WHERE THE STRANGEST THINGS CAN HAPPEN.
OH, MOMMY, SHE'S A ROBOT!
NOT BAD...
CAN WE GO NOW?
COOL--!
AND SHE'S SO CUTE...!
TOYS IN THE BASEMENT

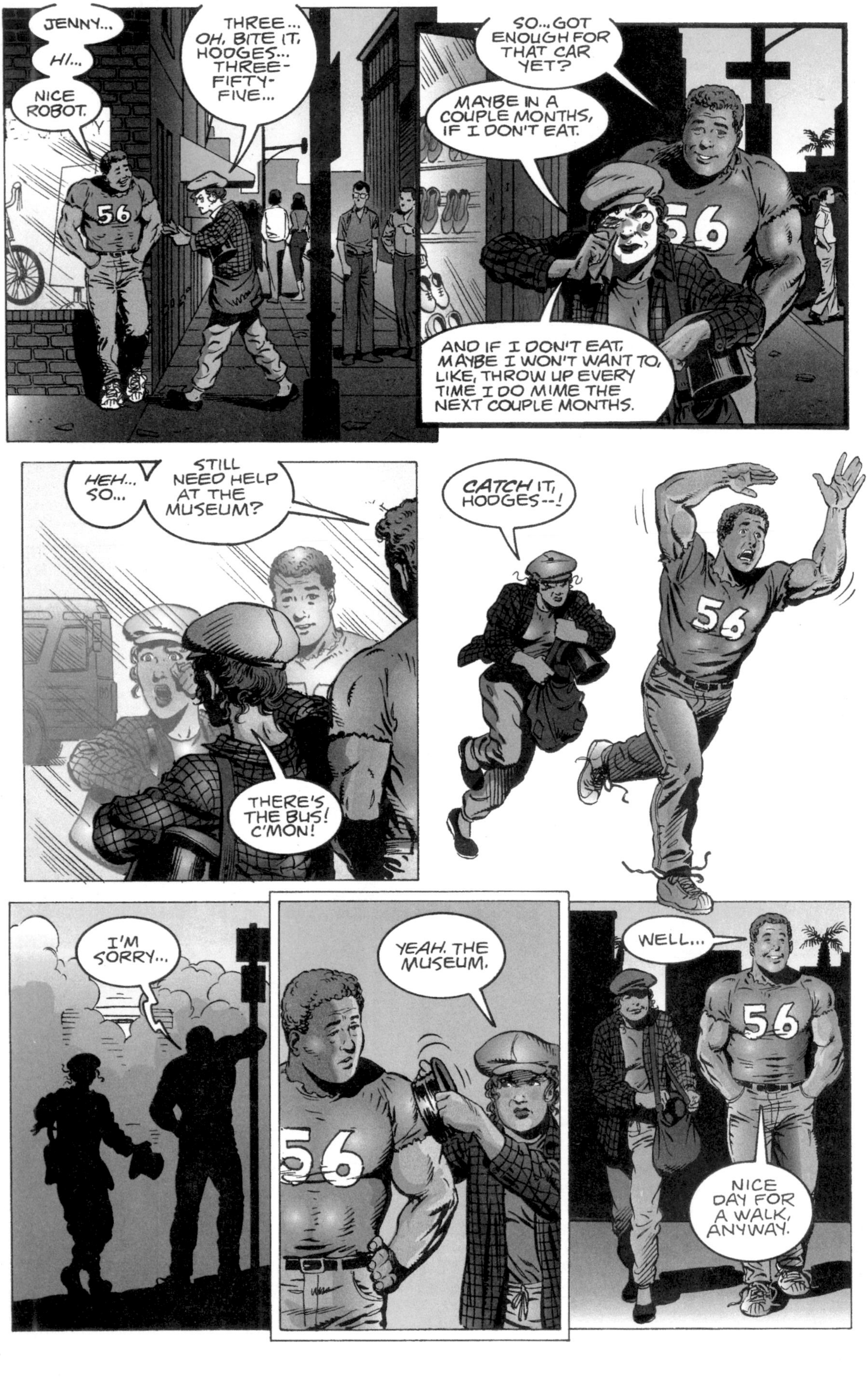

JENNY...
HI...
NICE ROBOT.
THREE... OH, BITE IT, HODGES... THREE-FIFTY-FIVE...
SO... GOT ENOUGH FOR THAT CAR YET?
MAYBE IN A COUPLE MONTHS, IF I DON'T EAT.
AND IF I DON'T EAT, MAYBE I WON'T WANT TO, LIKE, THROW UP EVERY TIME I DO MIME THE NEXT COUPLE MONTHS.
HEH... SO...
STILL NEED HELP AT THE MUSEUM?
THERE'S THE BUS! C'MON!
CATCH IT, HODGES--!
I'M SORRY...
YEAH. THE MUSEUM.
WELL...
NICE DAY FOR A WALK, ANYWAY.

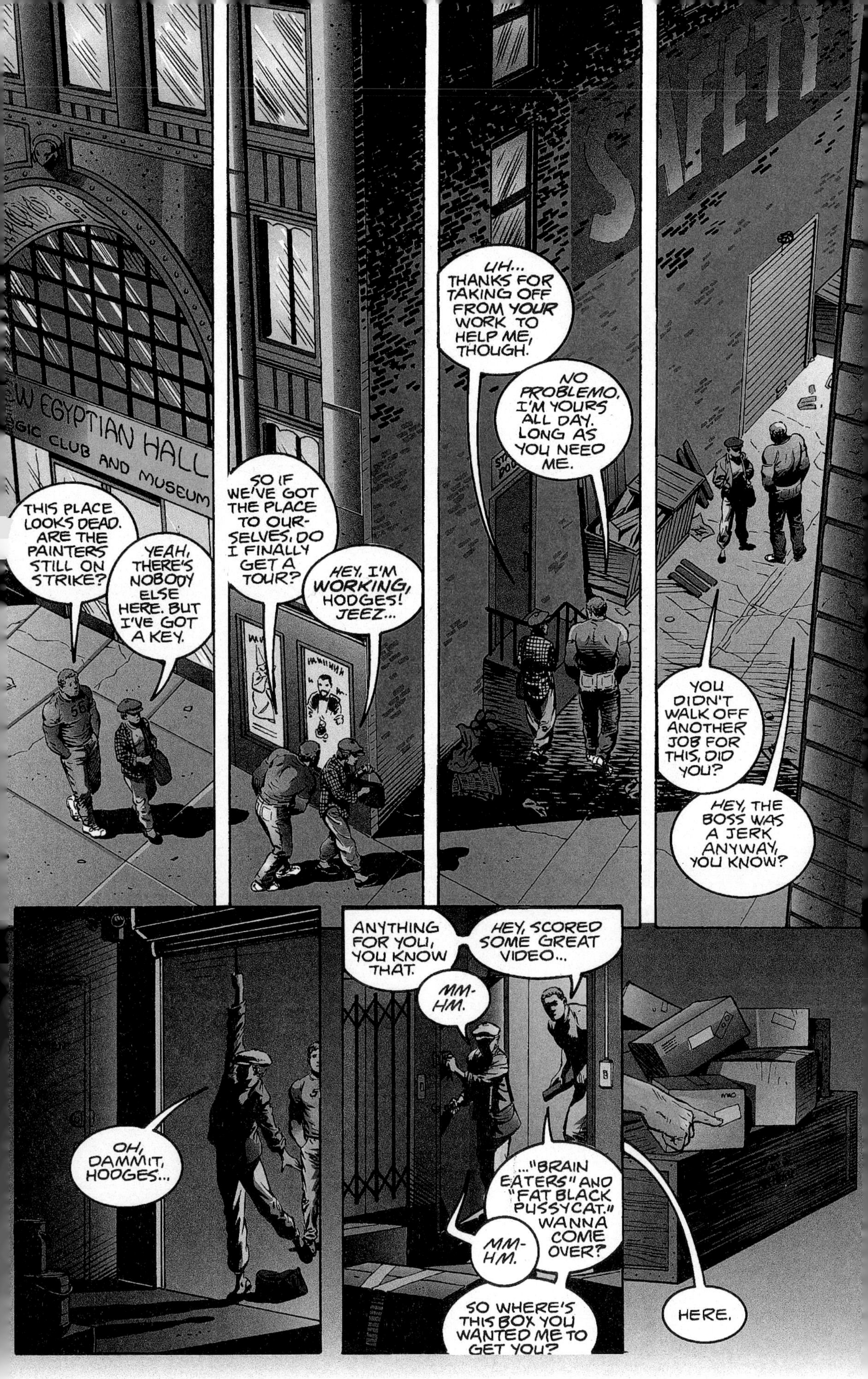
NEW EGYPTIAN HALL
MAGIC CLUB AND MUSEUM
THIS PLACE LOOKS DEAD. ARE THE PAINTERS STILL ON STRIKE?
YEAH, THERE'S NOBODY ELSE HERE. BUT I'VE GOT A KEY.
SO IF WE'VE GOT THE PLACE TO OURSELVES, DO I FINALLY GET A TOUR?
HEY, I'M WORKING, HODGES! JEEZ...
UH... THANKS FOR TAKING OFF FROM YOUR WORK TO HELP ME, THOUGH.
NO PROBLEMO. I'M YOURS ALL DAY. LONG AS YOU NEED ME.
SAFETY
YOU DIDN'T WALK OFF ANOTHER JOB FOR THIS, DID YOU?
HEY, THE BOSS WAS A JERK ANYWAY, YOU KNOW?
OH, DAMMIT, HODGES...
ANYTHING FOR YOU, YOU KNOW THAT.
HEY, SCORED SOME GREAT VIDEO...
MM-HM.
..."BRAIN EATERS" AND "FAT BLACK PUSSYCAT." WANNA COME OVER?
MM-HM.
SO WHERE'S THIS BOX YOU WANTED ME TO GET YOU?
HERE.

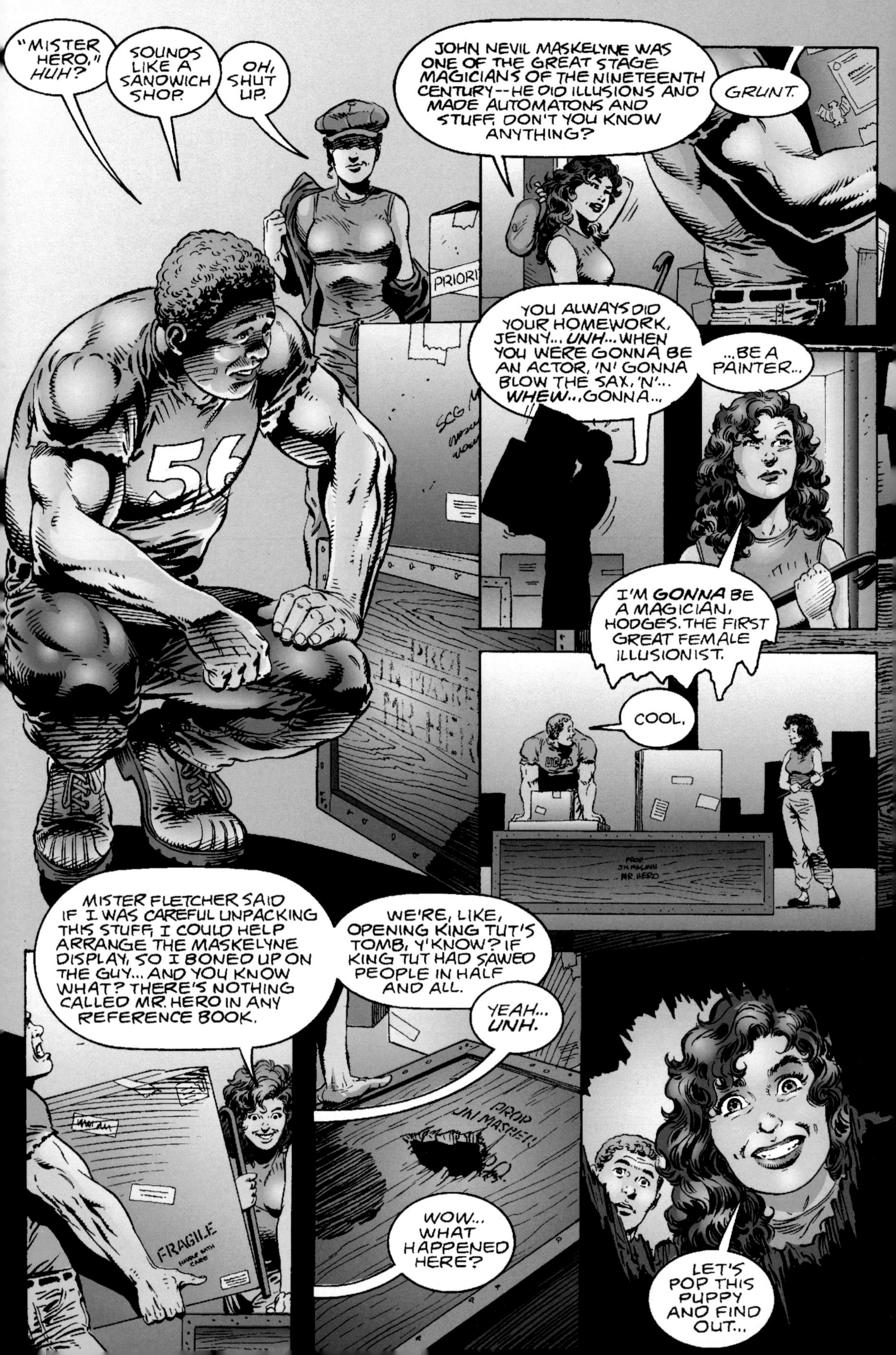
"MISTER HERO," HUH?
SOUNDS LIKE A SANDWICH SHOP.
OH, SHUT UP.
JOHN NEVIL MASKELYNE WAS ONE OF THE GREAT STAGE MAGICIANS OF THE NINETEENTH CENTURY--HE DID ILLUSIONS AND MADE AUTOMATONS AND STUFF. DON'T YOU KNOW ANYTHING?
GRUNT.
YOU ALWAYS DID YOUR HOMEWORK, JENNY... *UNH*... WHEN YOU WERE GONNA BE AN ACTOR, 'N' GONNA BLOW THE SAX, 'N'... *WHEW*... GONNA...
...BE A PAINTER...
I'M **GONNA** BE A MAGICIAN, HODGES. THE FIRST GREAT FEMALE ILLUSIONIST.
COOL.
MISTER FLETCHER SAID IF I WAS CAREFUL UNPACKING THIS STUFF, I COULD HELP ARRANGE THE MASKELYNE DISPLAY, SO I BONED UP ON THE GUY... AND YOU KNOW WHAT? THERE'S NOTHING CALLED MR. HERO IN ANY REFERENCE BOOK.
WE'RE, LIKE, OPENING KING TUT'S TOMB, Y'KNOW? IF KING TUT HAD SAWED PEOPLE IN HALF AND ALL.
YEAH... *UNH.*
FRAGILE
WOW... WHAT HAPPENED HERE?
LET'S POP THIS PUPPY AND FIND OUT...

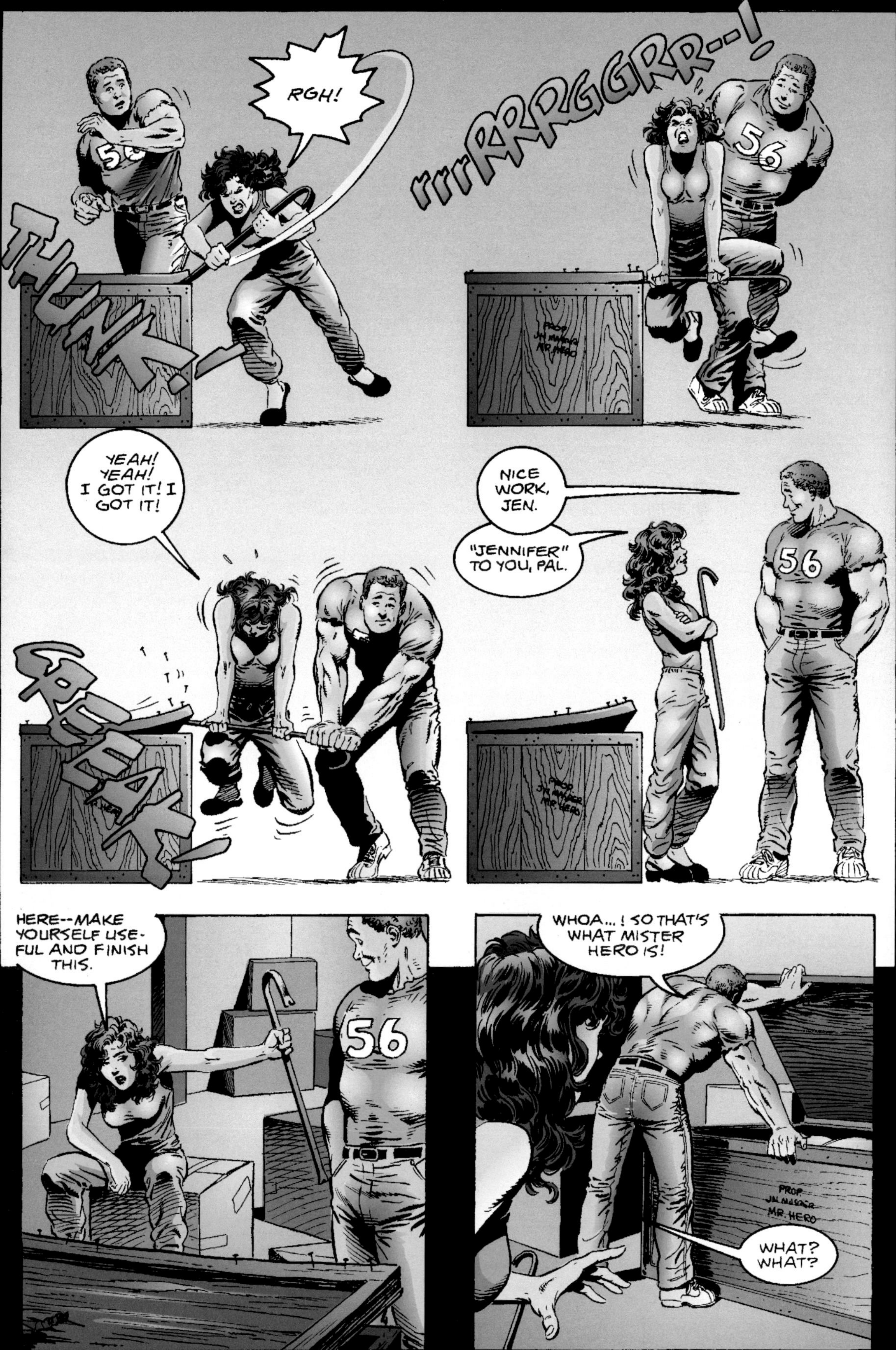
RGH!
THUNK!
rrrRRRGGRR--!
YEAH! YEAH! I GOT IT! I GOT IT!
CREAK!
NICE WORK, JEN.
"JENNIFER" TO YOU, PAL.
HERE--MAKE YOURSELF USE-FUL AND FINISH THIS.
WHOA...! SO THAT'S WHAT MISTER HERO IS!
WHAT? WHAT?

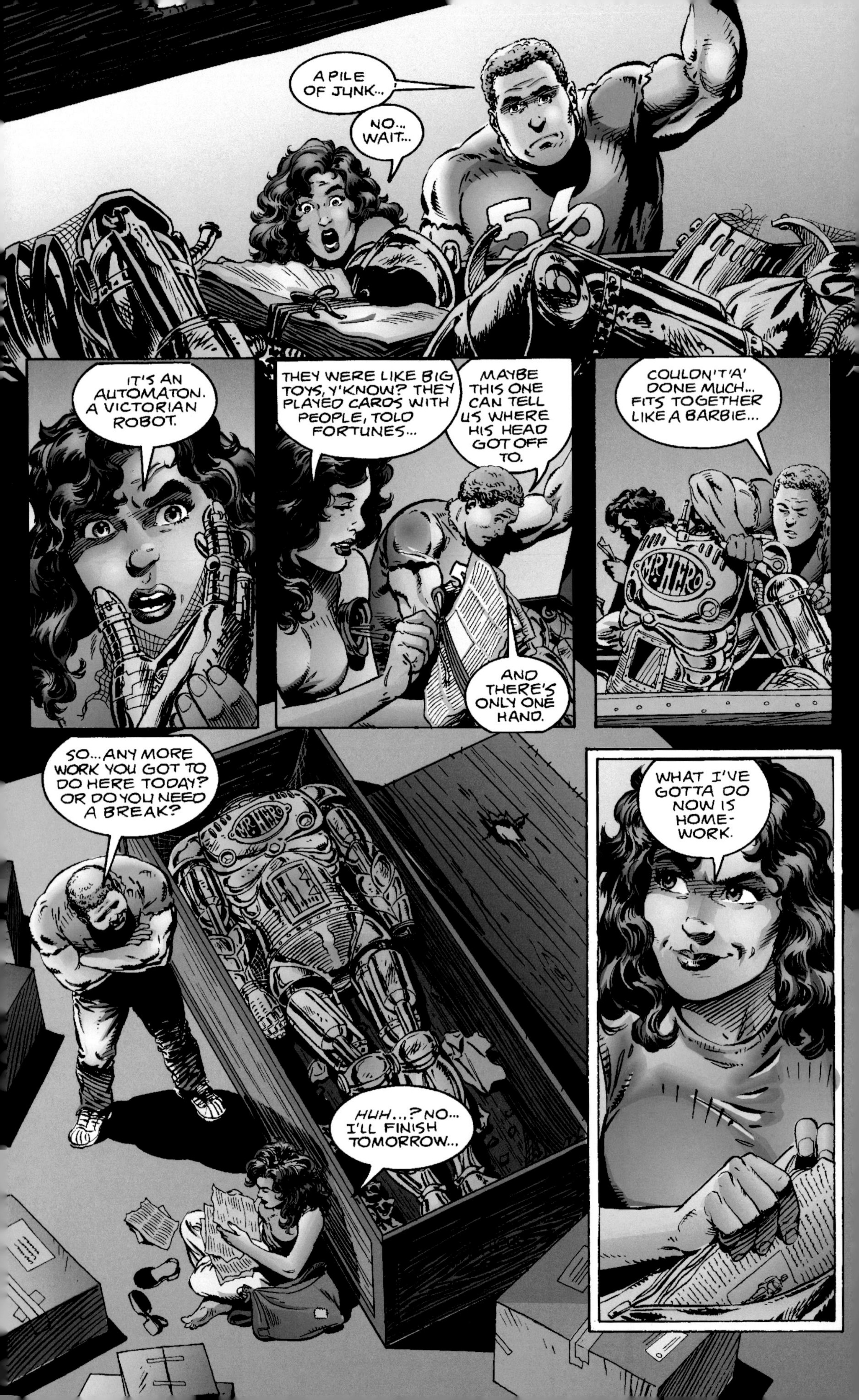

A PILE OF JUNK...
NO... WAIT...
IT'S AN AUTOMATON. A VICTORIAN ROBOT.
THEY WERE LIKE BIG TOYS, Y'KNOW? THEY PLAYED CARDS WITH PEOPLE, TOLD FORTUNES...
MAYBE THIS ONE CAN TELL US WHERE HIS HEAD GOT OFF TO.
AND THERE'S ONLY ONE HAND.
COULDN'T'A' DONE MUCH... FITS TOGETHER LIKE A BARBIE...
SO... ANY MORE WORK YOU GOT TO DO HERE TODAY? OR DO YOU NEED A BREAK?
HUH...? NO... I'LL FINISH TOMORROW...
WHAT I'VE GOTTA DO NOW IS HOME-WORK.

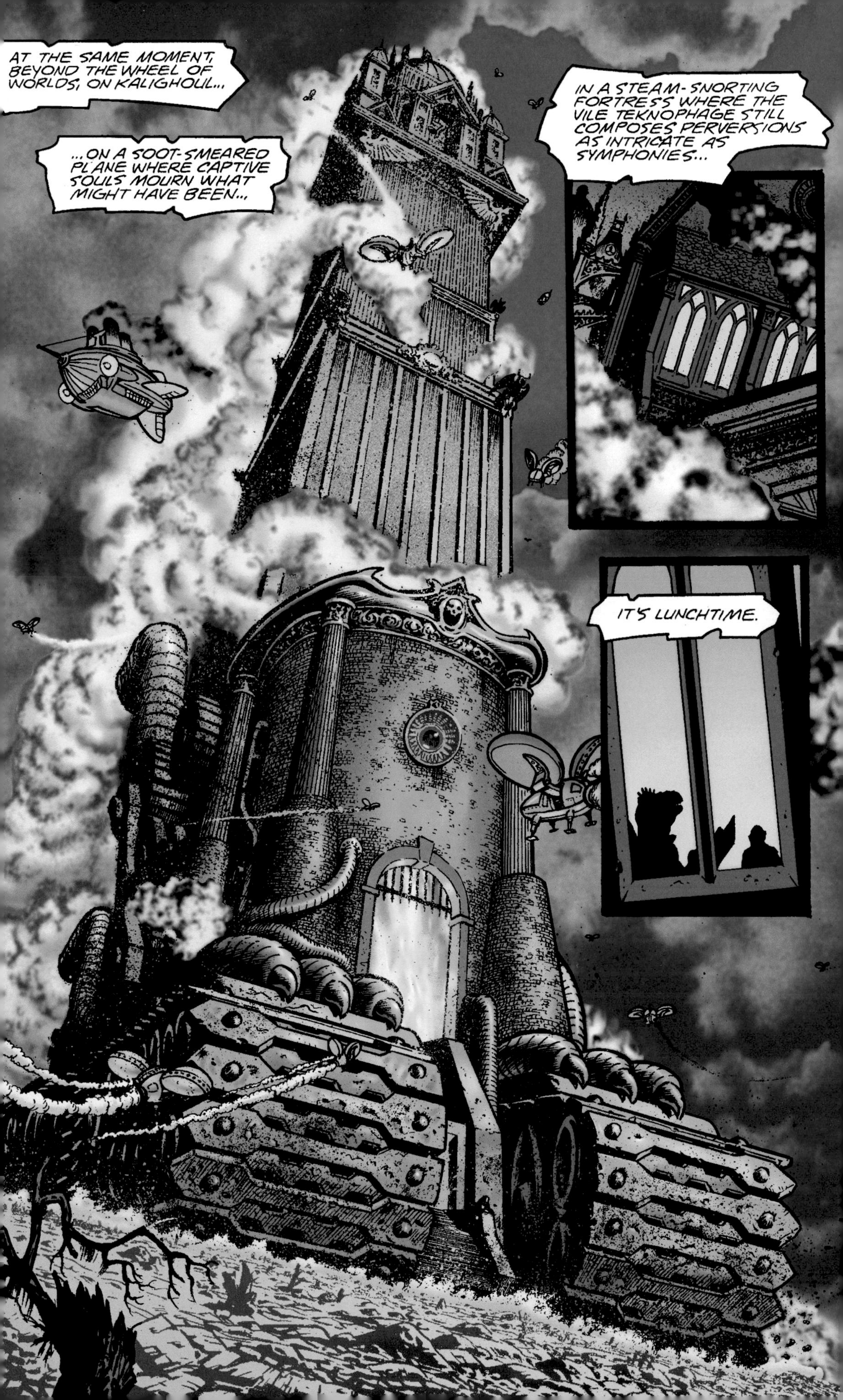
AT THE SAME MOMENT, BEYOND THE WHEEL OF WORLDS, ON KALIGHOUL...
...ON A SOOT-SMEARED PLANE WHERE CAPTIVE SOULS MOURN WHAT MIGHT HAVE BEEN...
IN A STEAM-SNORTING FORTRESS WHERE THE VILE TEKNOPHAGE STILL COMPOSES PERVERSIONS AS INTRICATE AS SYMPHONIES...
IT'S LUNCHTIME.

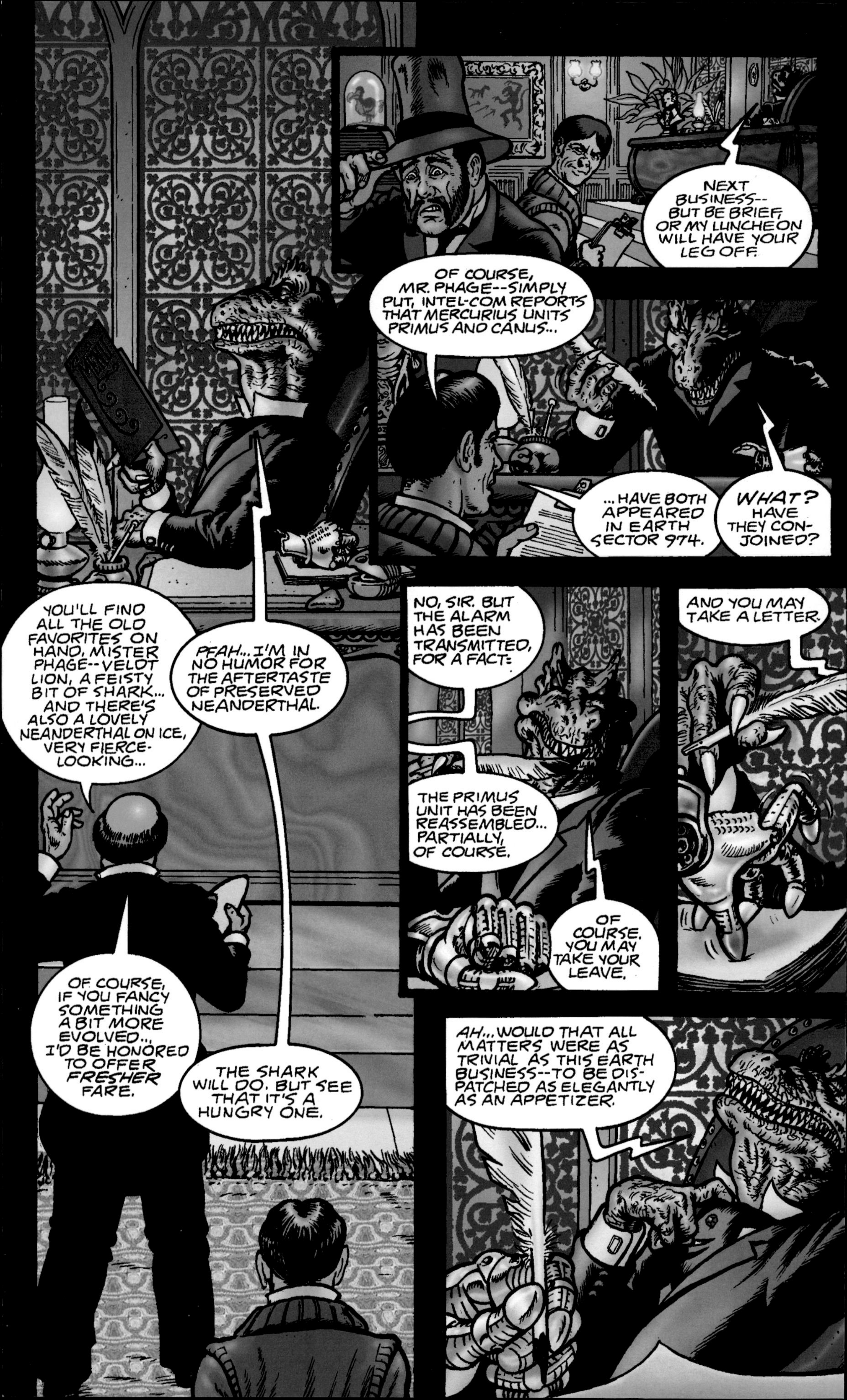
YOU'LL FIND ALL THE OLD FAVORITES ON HAND, MISTER PHAGE--VELOT LION, A FEISTY BIT OF SHARK... AND THERE'S ALSO A LOVELY NEANDERTHAL ON ICE, VERY FIERCE-LOOKING...
PFAH... I'M IN NO HUMOR FOR THE AFTERTASTE OF PRESERVED NEANDERTHAL.
OF COURSE, IF YOU FANCY SOMETHING A BIT MORE EVOLVED... I'D BE HONORED TO OFFER FRESHER FARE.
THE SHARK WILL DO. BUT SEE THAT IT'S A HUNGRY ONE.
NEXT BUSINESS-- BUT BE BRIEF, OR MY LUNCHEON WILL HAVE YOUR LEG OFF.
OF COURSE, MR. PHAGE--SIMPLY PUT, INTEL-COM REPORTS THAT MERCURIUS UNITS PRIMUS AND CANUS...
...HAVE BOTH APPEARED IN EARTH SECTOR 974.
WHAT? HAVE THEY CONJOINED?
NO, SIR. BUT THE ALARM HAS BEEN TRANSMITTED, FOR A FACT:
THE PRIMUS UNIT HAS BEEN REASSEMBLED... PARTIALLY, OF COURSE.
OF COURSE. YOU MAY TAKE YOUR LEAVE.
AND YOU MAY TAKE A LETTER.
AH... WOULD THAT ALL MATTERS WERE AS TRIVIAL AS THIS EARTH BUSINESS--TO BE DISPATCHED AS ELEGANTLY AS AN APPETIZER.

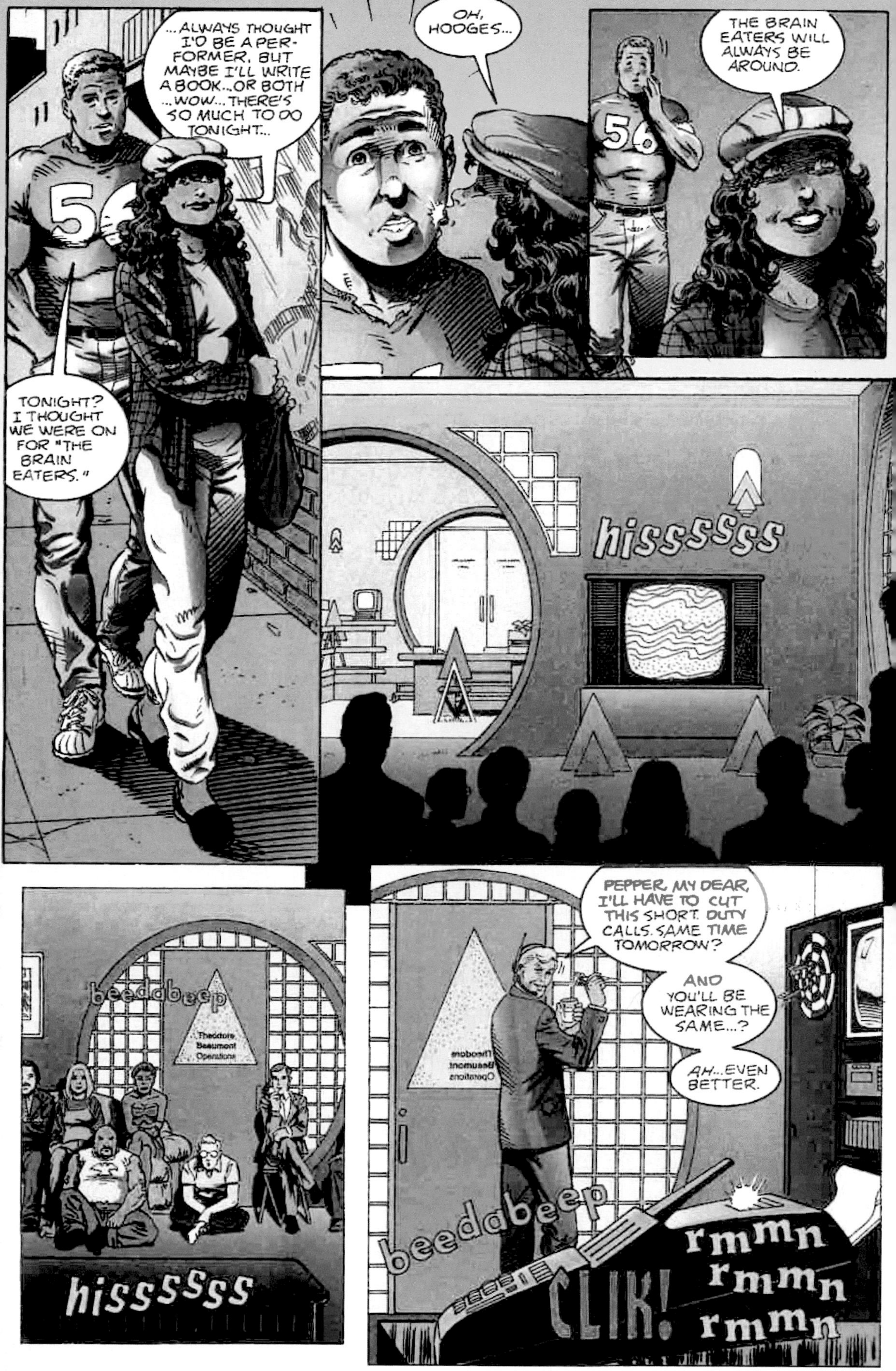
...ALWAYS THOUGHT I'D BE A PERFORMER, BUT MAYBE I'LL WRITE A BOOK...OR BOTH ...WOW...THERE'S SO MUCH TO DO TONIGHT...
TONIGHT? I THOUGHT WE WERE ON FOR "THE BRAIN EATERS."
OH, HOOGES...
THE BRAIN EATERS WILL ALWAYS BE AROUND.
hissSSSS
beedabeep
Theodore Beaumont Operations
hissSSSS
PEPPER, MY DEAR, I'LL HAVE TO CUT THIS SHORT. DUTY CALLS. SAME TIME TOMORROW?
AND YOU'LL BE WEARING THE SAME...?
AH...EVEN BETTER.
beedabeep
CLIK!
rmmn
rmmn
rmmn

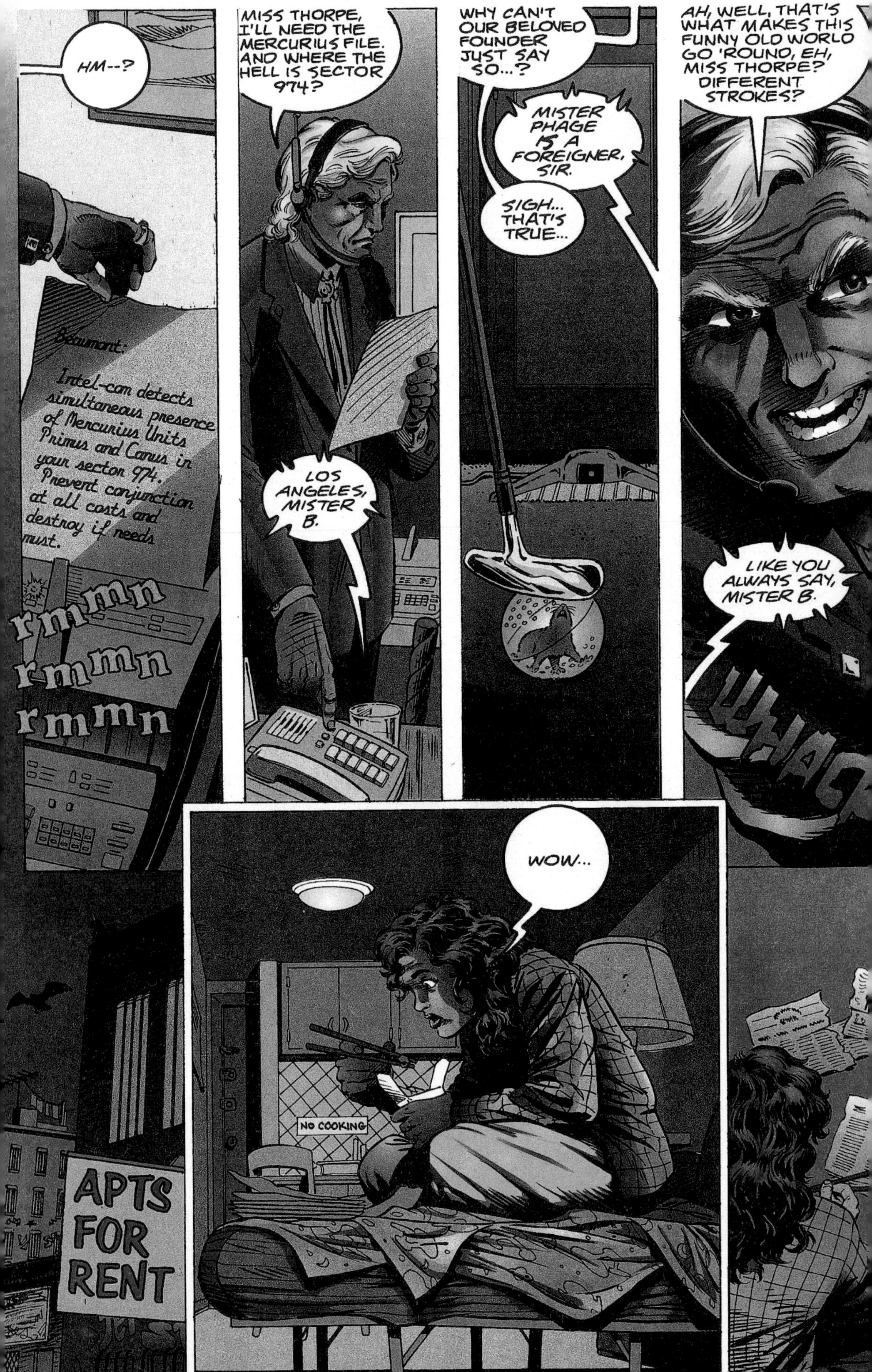
HM--?
Beaumont:
Intel-com detects simultaneous presence of Mercurius Units Primus and Canus in your sector 974. Prevent conjunction at all costs and destroy if needs must.
rmmn
rmmn
rmmn
MISS THORPE, I'LL NEED THE MERCURIUS FILE. AND WHERE THE HELL IS SECTOR 974?
LOS ANGELES, MISTER B.
WHY CAN'T OUR BELOVED FOUNDER JUST SAY SO...?
MISTER PHAGE IS A FOREIGNER, SIR.
SIGH... THAT'S TRUE...
AH, WELL, THAT'S WHAT MAKES THIS FUNNY OLD WORLD GO 'ROUND, EH, MISS THORPE? DIFFERENT STROKES?
LIKE YOU ALWAYS SAY, MISTER B.
APTS FOR RENT
WOW...
NO COOKING

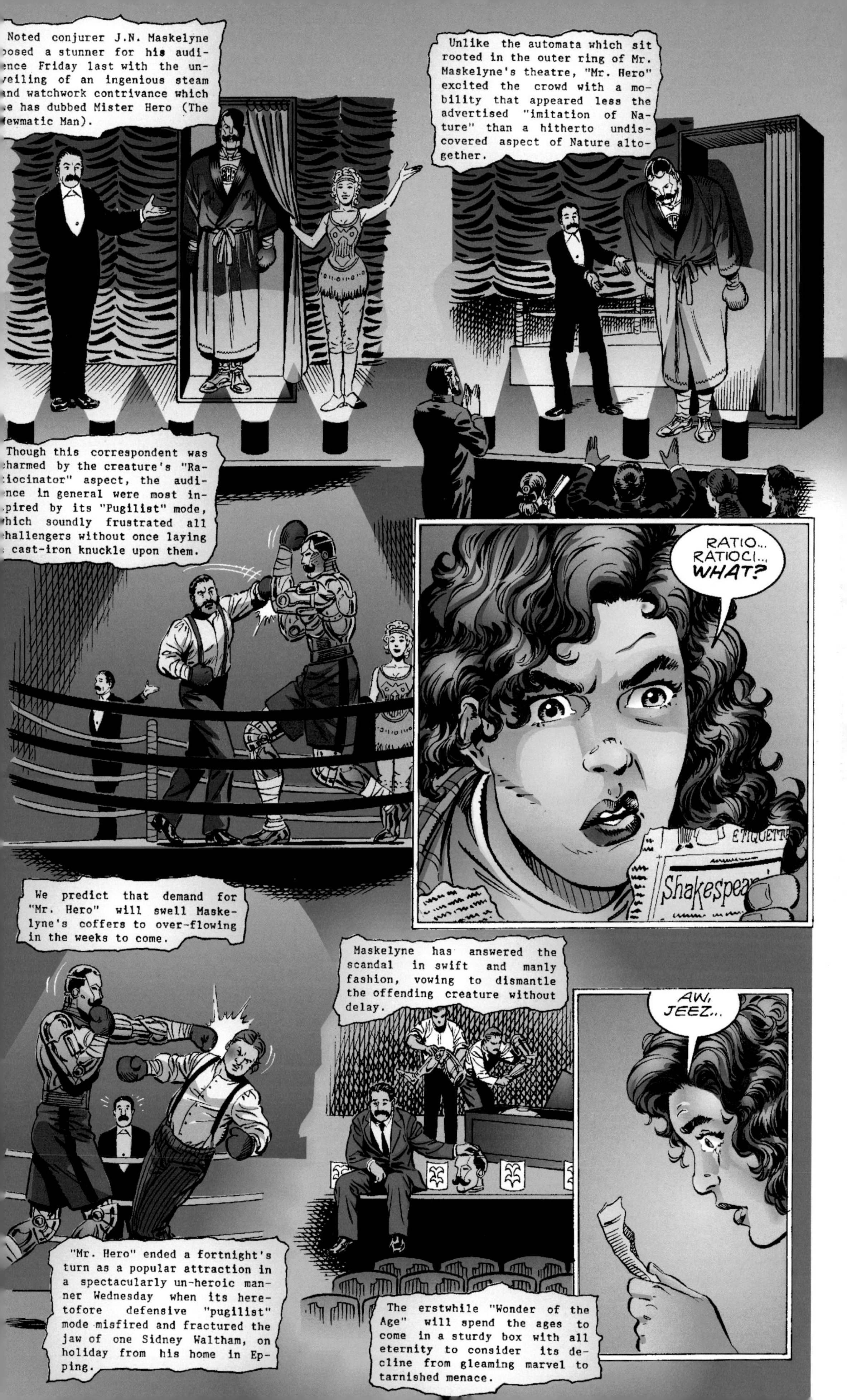

Noted conjurer J.N. Maskelyne osed a stunner for his audi-nce Friday last with the un-eiling of an ingenious steam nd watchwork contrivance which e has dubbed Mister Hero (The ewmatic Man).
Unlike the automata which sit rooted in the outer ring of Mr. Maskelyne's theatre, "Mr. Hero" excited the crowd with a mobility that appeared less the advertised "imitation of Nature" than a hitherto undiscovered aspect of Nature altogether.
Though this correspondent was harmed by the creature's "Raiocinator" aspect, the audi-nce in general were most in-pired by its "Pugilist" mode, hich soundly frustrated all hallengers without once laying cast-iron knuckle upon them.
RATIO... RATIOCI... WHAT?
We predict that demand for "Mr. Hero" will swell Maskelyne's coffers to over-flowing in the weeks to come.
"Mr. Hero" ended a fortnight's turn as a popular attraction in a spectacularly un-heroic manner Wednesday when its heretofore defensive "pugilist" mode misfired and fractured the jaw of one Sidney Waltham, on holiday from his home in Epping.
Maskelyne has answered the scandal in swift and manly fashion, vowing to dismantle the offending creature without delay.
The erstwhile "Wonder of the Age" will spend the ages to come in a sturdy box with all eternity to consider its decline from gleaming marvel to tarnished menace.
AW, JEEZ...

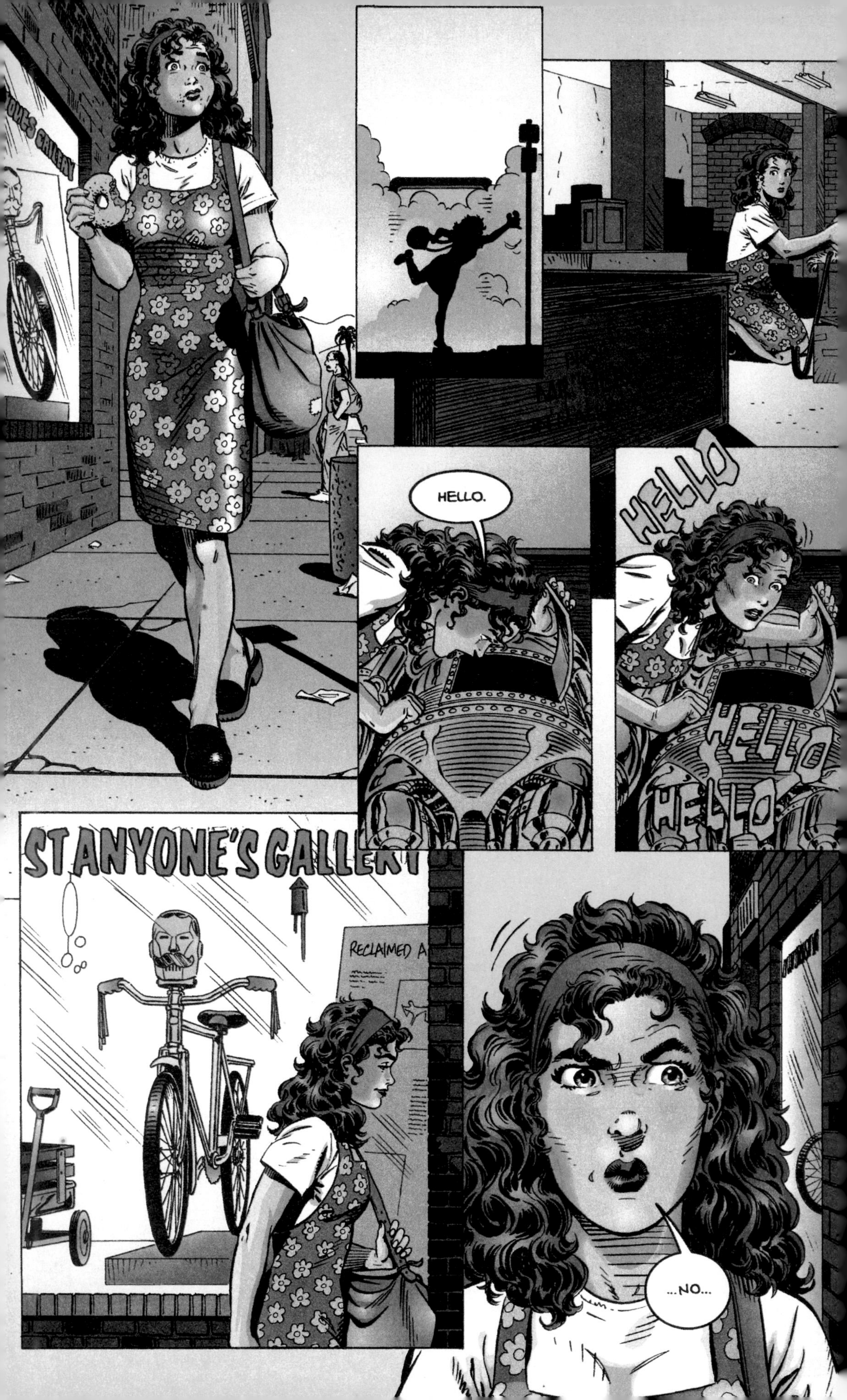

ONE'S GALLERY
HELLO.
HELLO
HELLO
HELLO
ST ANYONE'S GALLERY
RECLAIMED A
...NO...

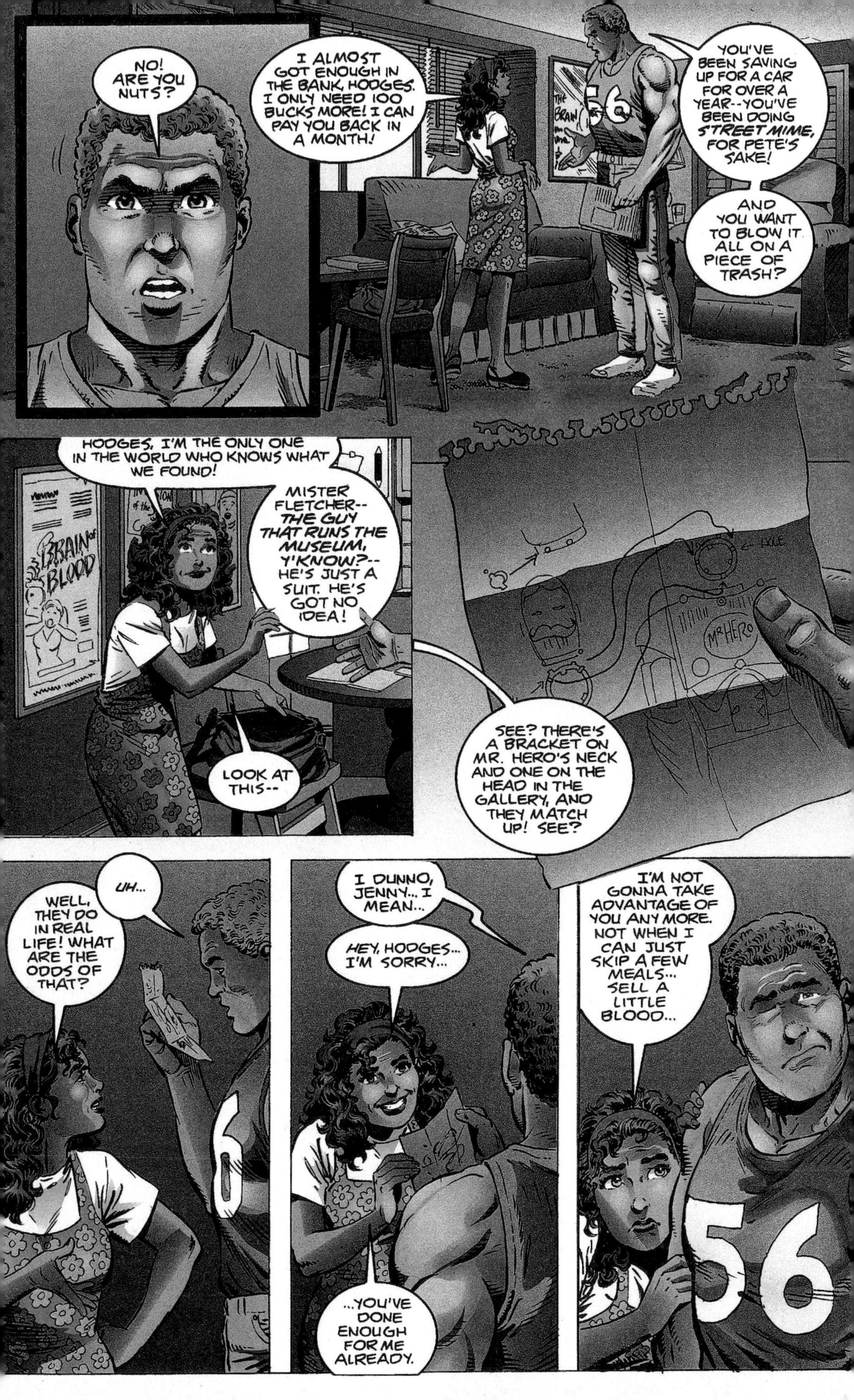
NO! ARE YOU NUTS?
I ALMOST GOT ENOUGH IN THE BANK, HODGES. I ONLY NEED 100 BUCKS MORE! I CAN PAY YOU BACK IN A MONTH!
YOU'VE BEEN SAVING UP FOR A CAR FOR OVER A YEAR--YOU'VE BEEN DOING STREET MIME, FOR PETE'S SAKE!
AND YOU WANT TO BLOW IT ALL ON A PIECE OF TRASH?
HODGES, I'M THE ONLY ONE IN THE WORLD WHO KNOWS WHAT WE FOUND!
MISTER FLETCHER-- THE GUY THAT RUNS THE MUSEUM, Y'KNOW?-- HE'S JUST A SUIT. HE'S GOT NO IDEA!
LOOK AT THIS--
BRAIN of BLOOD
MR HERO
SEE? THERE'S A BRACKET ON MR. HERO'S NECK AND ONE ON THE HEAD IN THE GALLERY, AND THEY MATCH UP! SEE?
UH...
WELL, THEY DO IN REAL LIFE! WHAT ARE THE ODDS OF THAT?
I DUNNO, JENNY... I MEAN...
HEY, HODGES... I'M SORRY...
...YOU'VE DONE ENOUGH FOR ME ALREADY.
I'M NOT GONNA TAKE ADVANTAGE OF YOU ANY MORE. NOT WHEN I CAN JUST SKIP A FEW MEALS... SELL A LITTLE BLOOD...

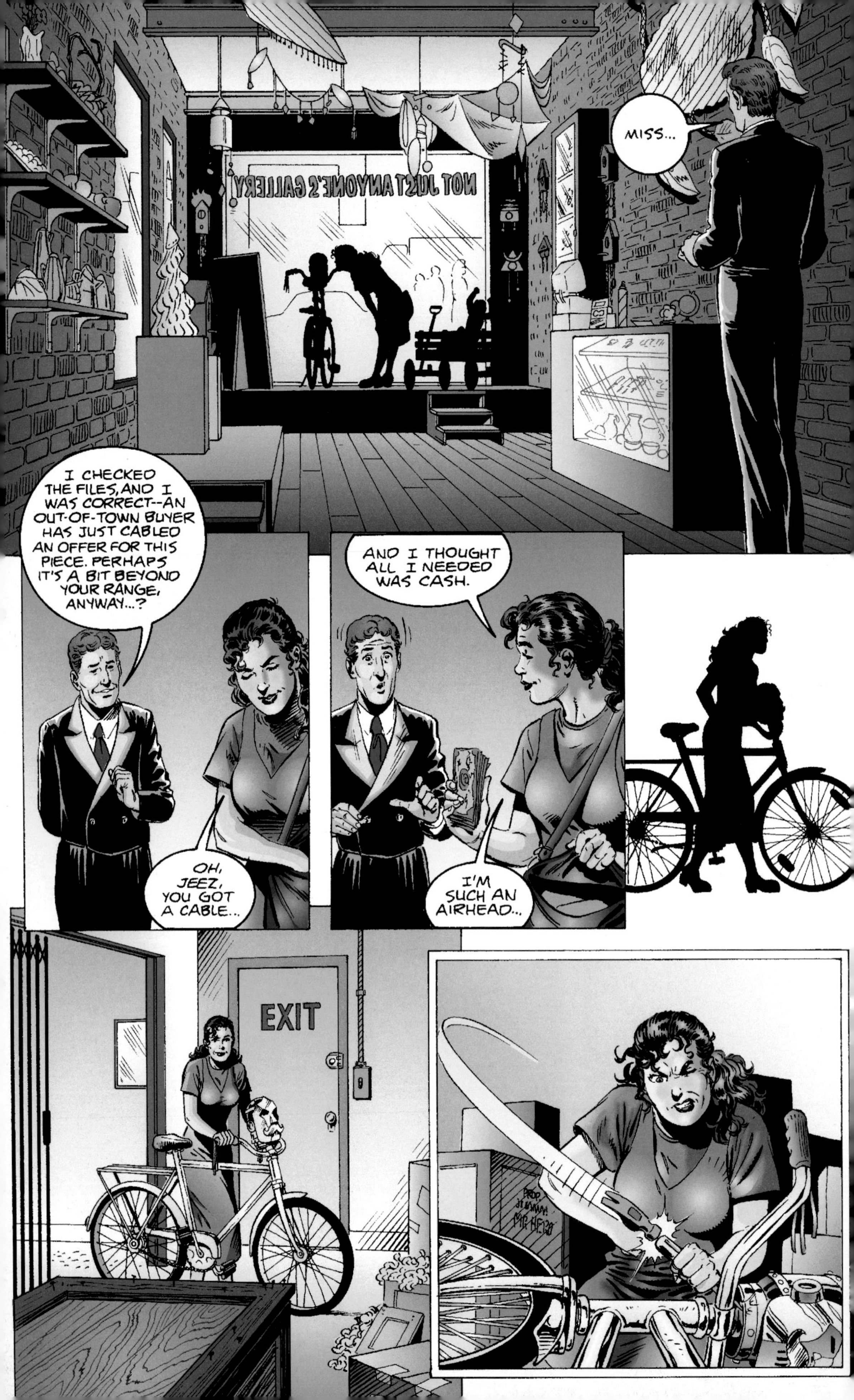
NOT JUST ANYONE'S GALLERY
MISS...
I CHECKED THE FILES, AND I WAS CORRECT--AN OUT-OF-TOWN BUYER HAS JUST CABLED AN OFFER FOR THIS PIECE. PERHAPS IT'S A BIT BEYOND YOUR RANGE, ANYWAY...?
OH, JEEZ, YOU GOT A CABLE...
AND I THOUGHT ALL I NEEDED WAS CASH.
I'M SUCH AN AIRHEAD...
EXIT

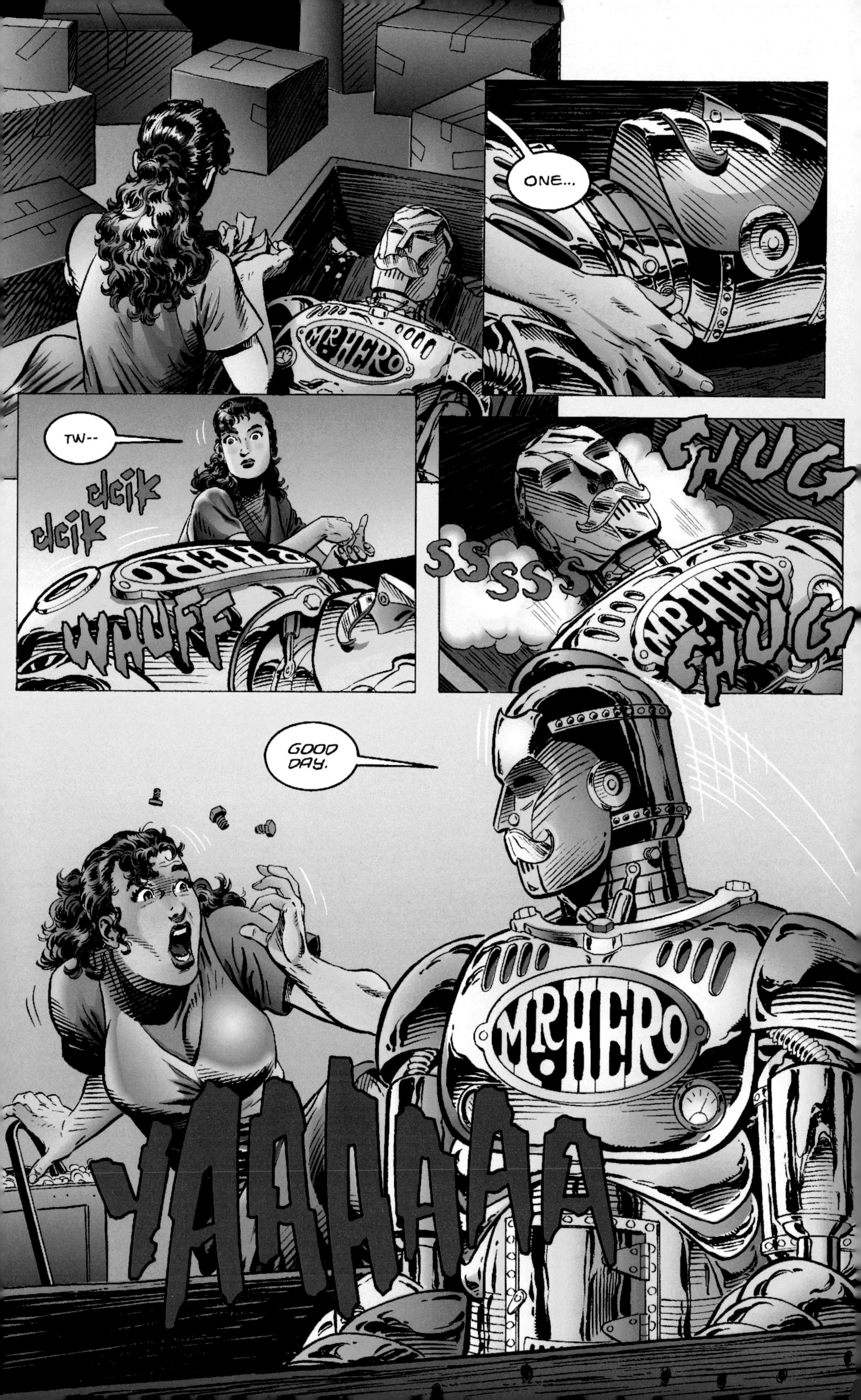
ONE...
TW--
clcik
clcik
WHUFF
CHUG
SSSSS
CHUG
CHUG
GOOD DAY.
YAAAAAA

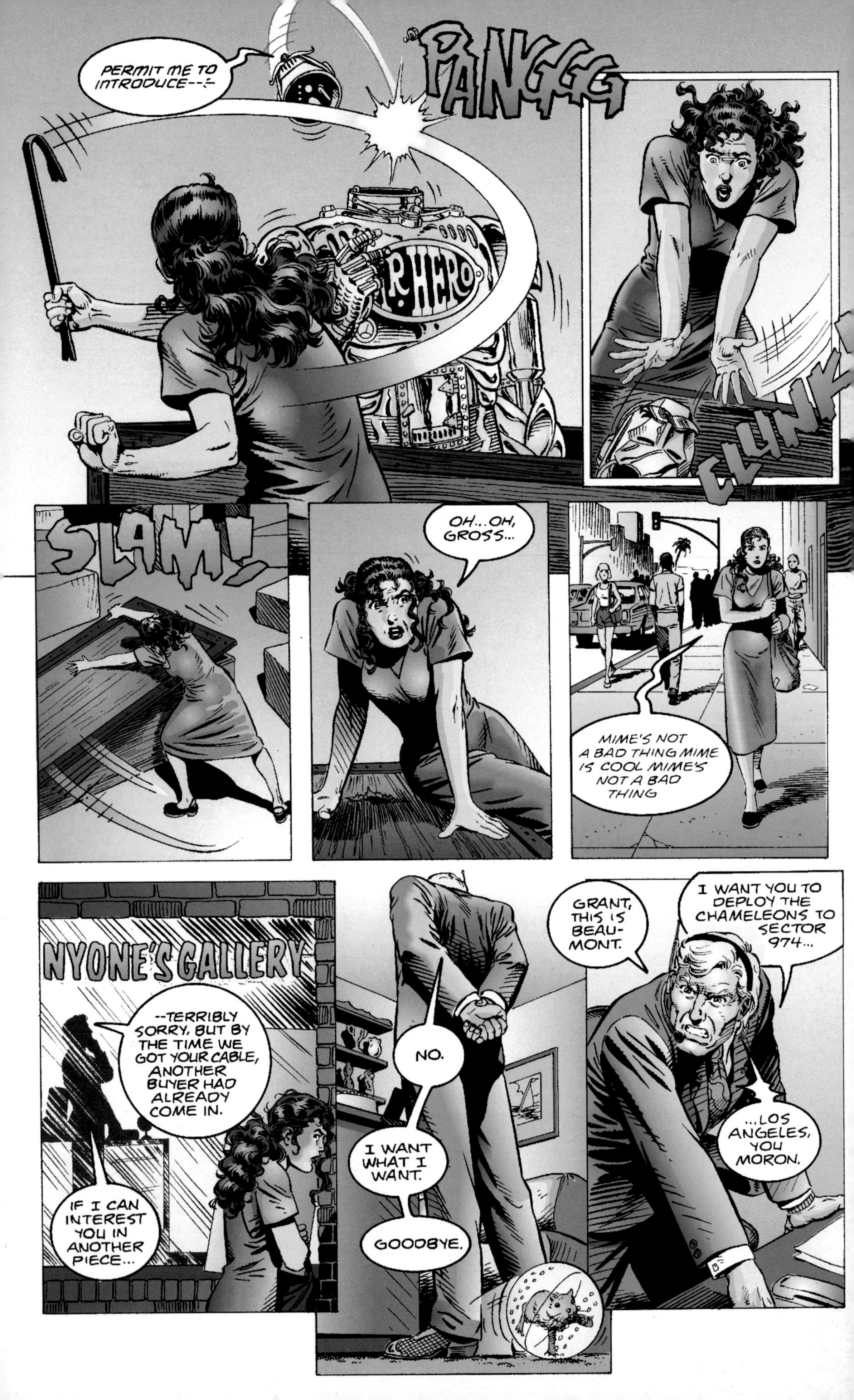
PERMIT ME TO INTRODUCE--:-
PANGGG
CLUNK!
SLAM!
OH...OH, GROSS...
MIME'S NOT A BAD THING MIME IS COOL MIME'S NOT A BAD THING
NYONE'S GALLERY
--TERRIBLY SORRY, BUT BY THE TIME WE GOT YOUR CABLE, ANOTHER BUYER HAD ALREADY COME IN.
IF I CAN INTEREST YOU IN ANOTHER PIECE...
NO.
I WANT WHAT I WANT.
GOODBYE.
GRANT, THIS IS BEAU-MONT.
I WANT YOU TO DEPLOY THE CHAMELEONS TO SECTOR 974...
...LOS ANGELES, YOU MORON.

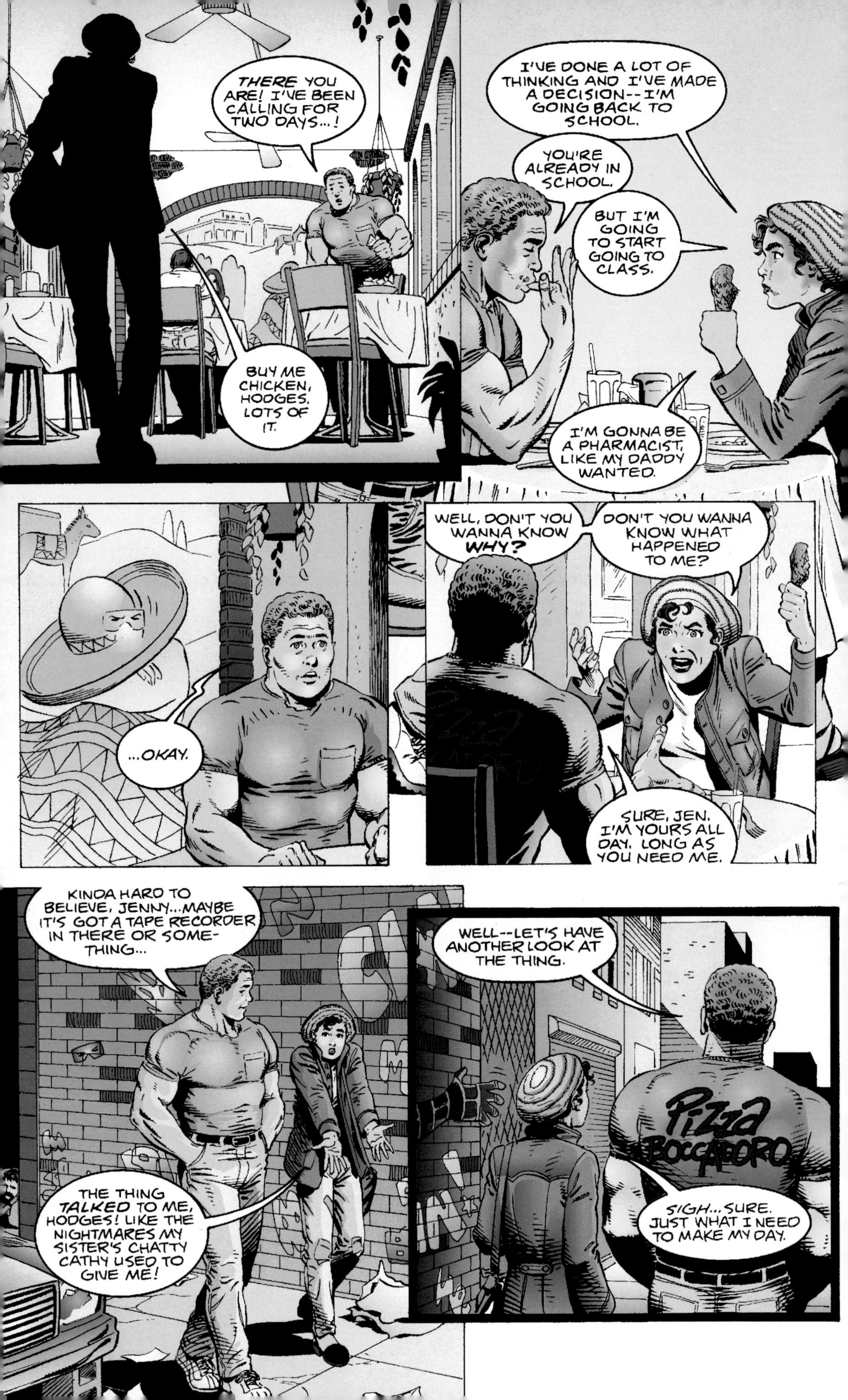
THERE YOU ARE! I'VE BEEN CALLING FOR TWO DAYS...!
BUY ME CHICKEN, HODGES. LOTS OF IT.
I'VE DONE A LOT OF THINKING AND I'VE MADE A DECISION--I'M GOING BACK TO SCHOOL.
YOU'RE ALREADY IN SCHOOL.
BUT I'M GOING TO START GOING TO CLASS.
I'M GONNA BE A PHARMACIST, LIKE MY DADDY WANTED.
...OKAY.
WELL, DON'T YOU WANNA KNOW WHY?
DON'T YOU WANNA KNOW WHAT HAPPENED TO ME?
SURE, JEN. I'M YOURS ALL DAY. LONG AS YOU NEED ME.
THE THING TALKED TO ME, HODGES! LIKE THE NIGHTMARES MY SISTER'S CHATTY CATHY USED TO GIVE ME!
KINDA HARD TO BELIEVE, JENNY...MAYBE IT'S GOT A TAPE RECORDER IN THERE OR SOMETHING...
WELL--LET'S HAVE ANOTHER LOOK AT THE THING.
SIGH...SURE. JUST WHAT I NEED TO MAKE MY DAY.
PIZZA BOCCADORO

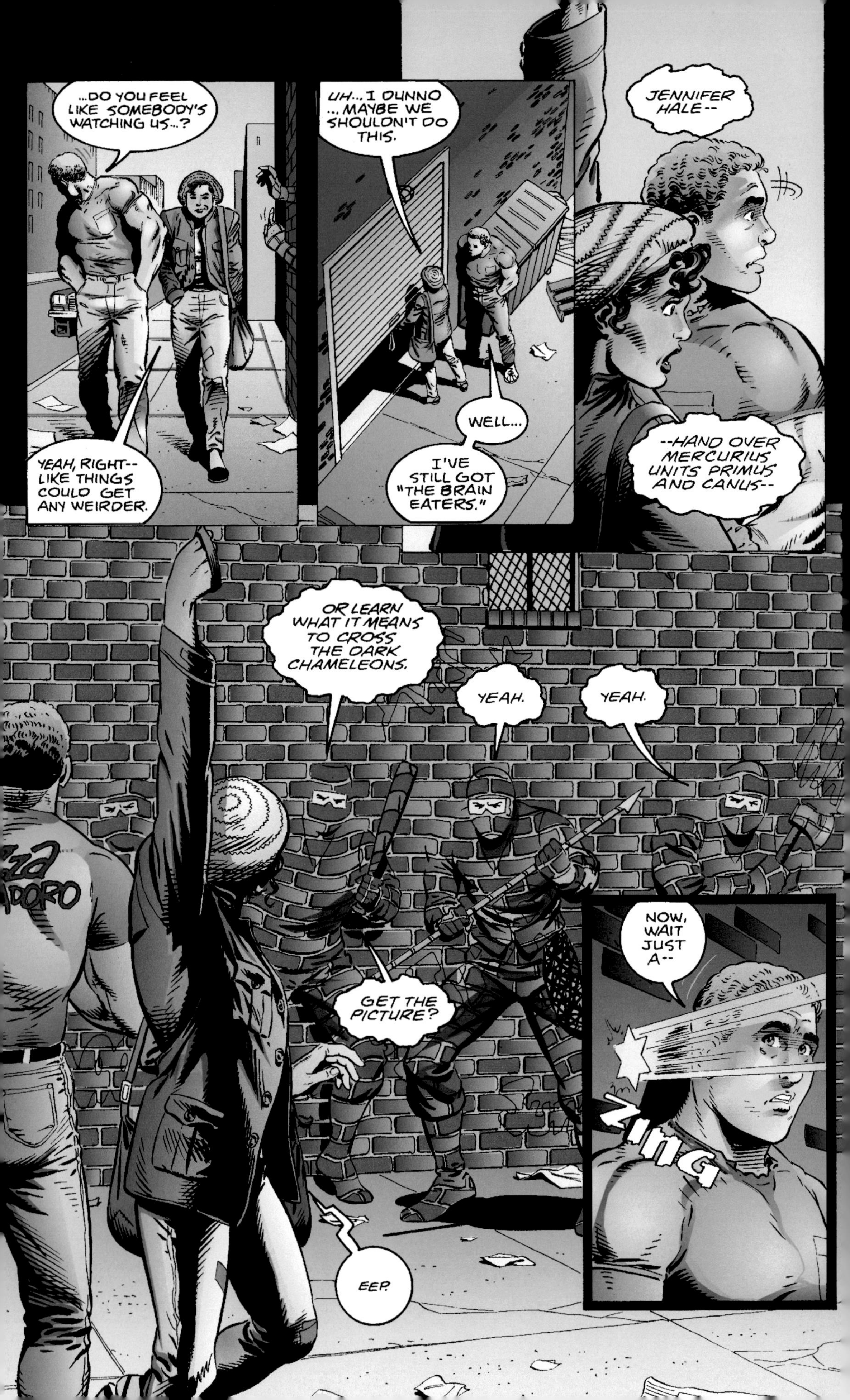
...DO YOU FEEL LIKE SOMEBODY'S WATCHING US...?
YEAH, RIGHT-- LIKE THINGS COULD GET ANY WEIRDER.
UH... I DUNNO ... MAYBE WE SHOULDN'T DO THIS.
WELL...
I'VE STILL GOT "THE BRAIN EATERS."
JENNIFER HALE--
--HAND OVER MERCURIUS UNITS PRIMUS AND CANUS--
OR LEARN WHAT IT MEANS TO CROSS THE DARK CHAMELEONS.
YEAH.
YEAH.
GET THE PICTURE?
EEP.
NOW, WAIT JUST A--
ZING

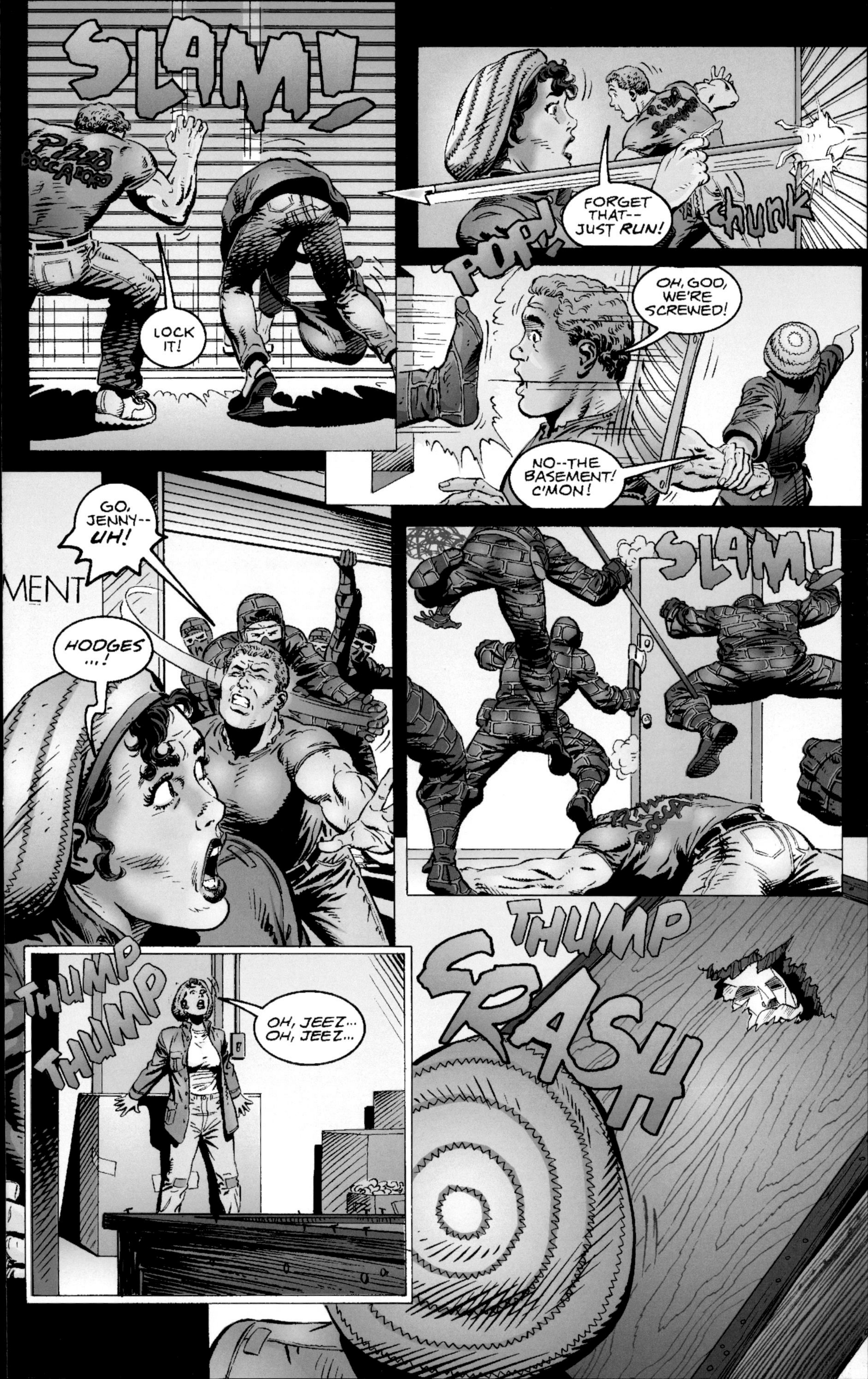
SLAM!
LOCK IT!
FORGET THAT-- JUST RUN!
CHUNK
POK!
OH, GOD, WE'RE SCREWED!
NO--THE BASEMENT! C'MON!
MENT
GO, JENNY-- UH!
HODGES ...!
SLAM!
THUMP THUMP
OH, JEEZ... OH, JEEZ...
THUMP
CRASH

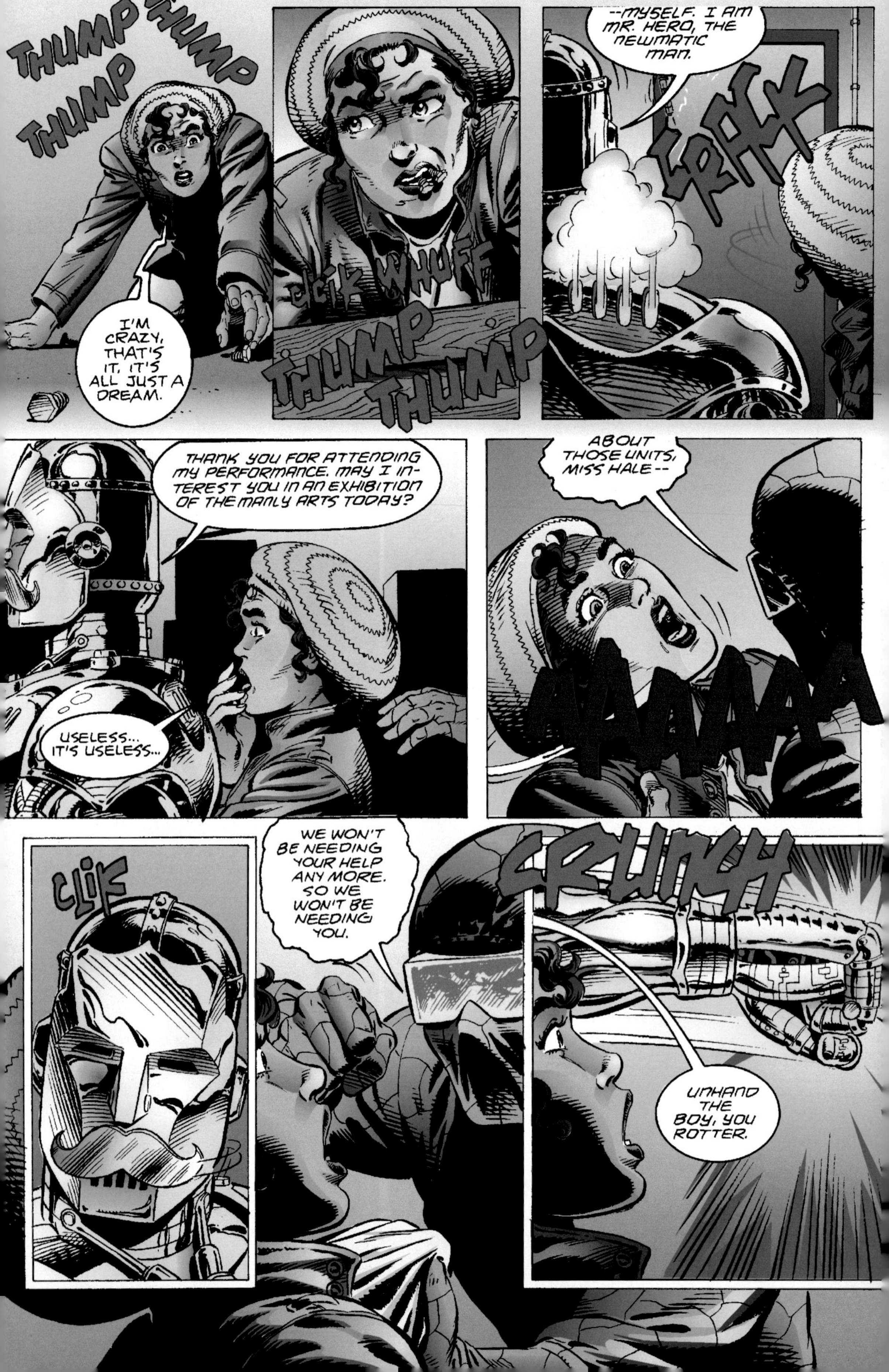
THUMP THUMP THUMP
I'M CRAZY, THAT'S IT, IT'S ALL JUST A DREAM.
CLIK WHUFF
THUMP THUMP
--MYSELF. I AM MR. HERO, THE NEWMATIC MAN.
THANK YOU FOR ATTENDING MY PERFORMANCE. MAY I INTEREST YOU IN AN EXHIBITION OF THE MANLY ARTS TODAY?
USELESS... IT'S USELESS...
ABOUT THOSE UNITS, MISS HALE--
CLIK
WE WON'T BE NEEDING YOUR HELP ANY MORE. SO WE WON'T BE NEEDING YOU.
CRUNCH
UNHAND THE BOY, YOU ROTTER.

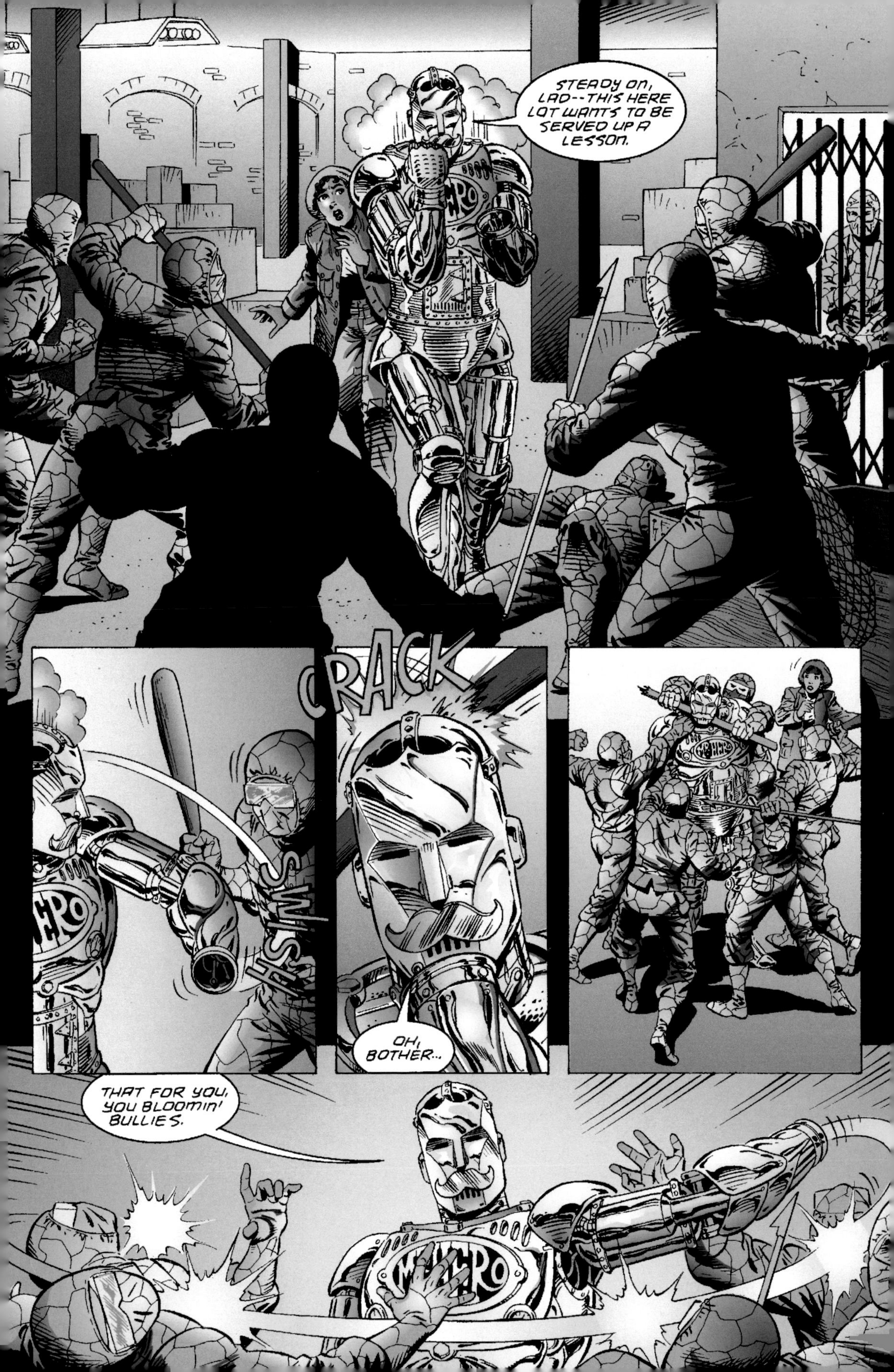
STEADY ON, LAD--THIS HERE LOT WANTS TO BE SERVED UP A LESSON.
SWISH
CRACK
OH, BOTHER...
THAT FOR YOU, YOU BLOOMIN' BULLIES.

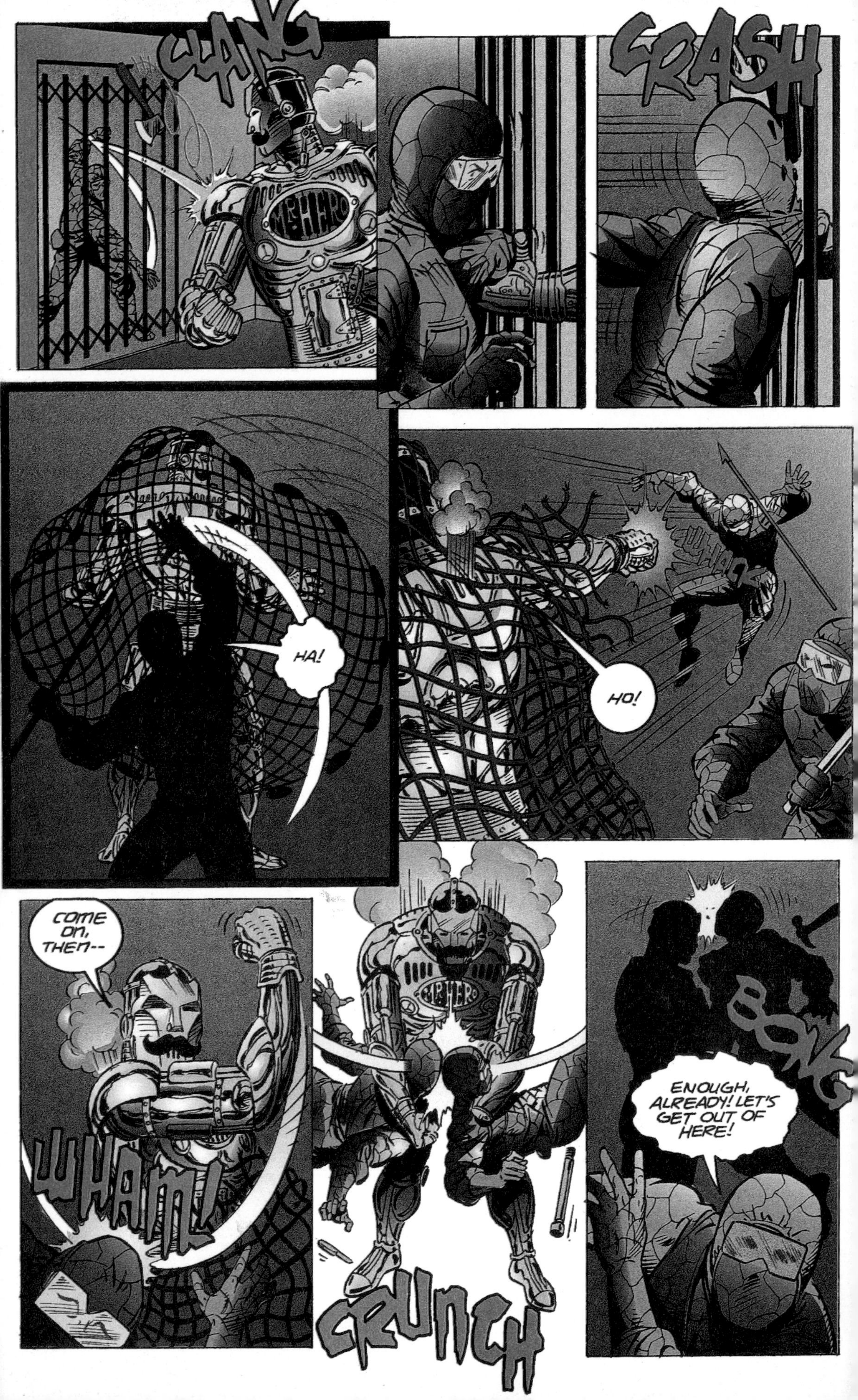
CLANG
CRASH
HA!
HO!
COME ON, THEN--
WHAM!
CRUNCH
BONG
ENOUGH, ALREADY! LET'S GET OUT OF HERE!

HERE, YOU DOGS--COME BACK AND TAKE YOUR DESSERTS!

NEXT TIME, MISTER TIN MAN...

...WE'LL BE READY FOR YOU--

--AND YOU'LL WISH YOU WERE STILL JUST A PILE OF SCRAP...

WATCH YOUR BACKS, THE BOTH OF YOU-- FOR ALL THE GOOD IT'LL DO...

OH, WOW...,

HODGES-- HODGES, ARE YOU ALIVE?

GROAN

PERMIT ME, LAD--THIS FELLOW'S TOO STOUT FOR YOU TO MANAGE.

CAN YOU... CAN YOU HELP ME GET HIM HOME?

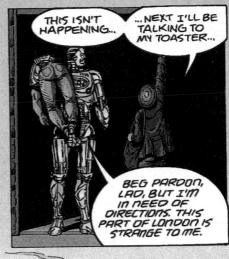

THIS ISN'T HAPPENING...

...NEXT I'LL BE TALKING TO MY TOASTER...

BEG PARDON, LAD, BUT I'M IN NEED OF DIRECTIONS. THIS PART OF LONDON IS STRANGE TO ME.

HEY--WHAT'S THIS "LAD" STUFF, ANYWAY?

BLESS ME, MISS... I WAS IN ERROR!

I DO HOPE YOU CAN FORGIVE ME.

OH, JUST COME ON, WILL YOU? MAYBE WE CAN CATCH THE BUS.

YEAH-- MAYBE SO... I MEAN, STRANGER THINGS HAVE HAPPENED...

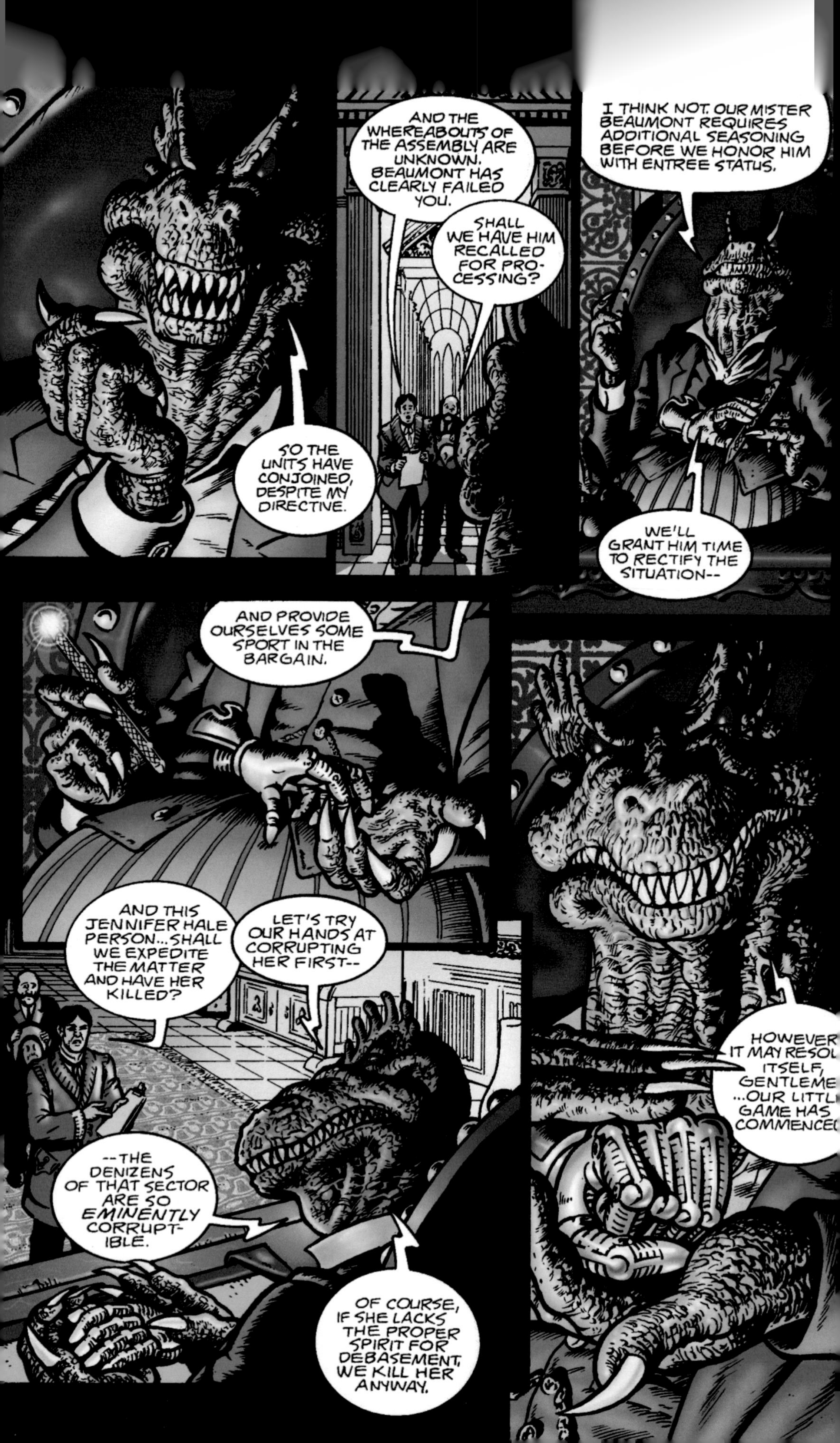
SO THE UNITS HAVE CONJOINED, DESPITE MY DIRECTIVE.
AND THE WHEREABOUTS OF THE ASSEMBLY ARE UNKNOWN. BEAUMONT HAS CLEARLY FAILED YOU.
SHALL WE HAVE HIM RECALLED FOR PRO-CESSING?
I THINK NOT. OUR MISTER BEAUMONT REQUIRES ADDITIONAL SEASONING BEFORE WE HONOR HIM WITH ENTREE STATUS.
WE'LL GRANT HIM TIME TO RECTIFY THE SITUATION--
AND PROVIDE OURSELVES SOME SPORT IN THE BARGAIN.
AND THIS JENNIFER HALE PERSON...SHALL WE EXPEDITE THE MATTER AND HAVE HER KILLED?
LET'S TRY OUR HANDS AT CORRUPTING HER FIRST--
--THE DENIZENS OF THAT SECTOR ARE SO EMINENTLY CORRUPT-IBLE.
OF COURSE, IF SHE LACKS THE PROPER SPIRIT FOR DEBASEMENT, WE KILL HER ANYWAY.

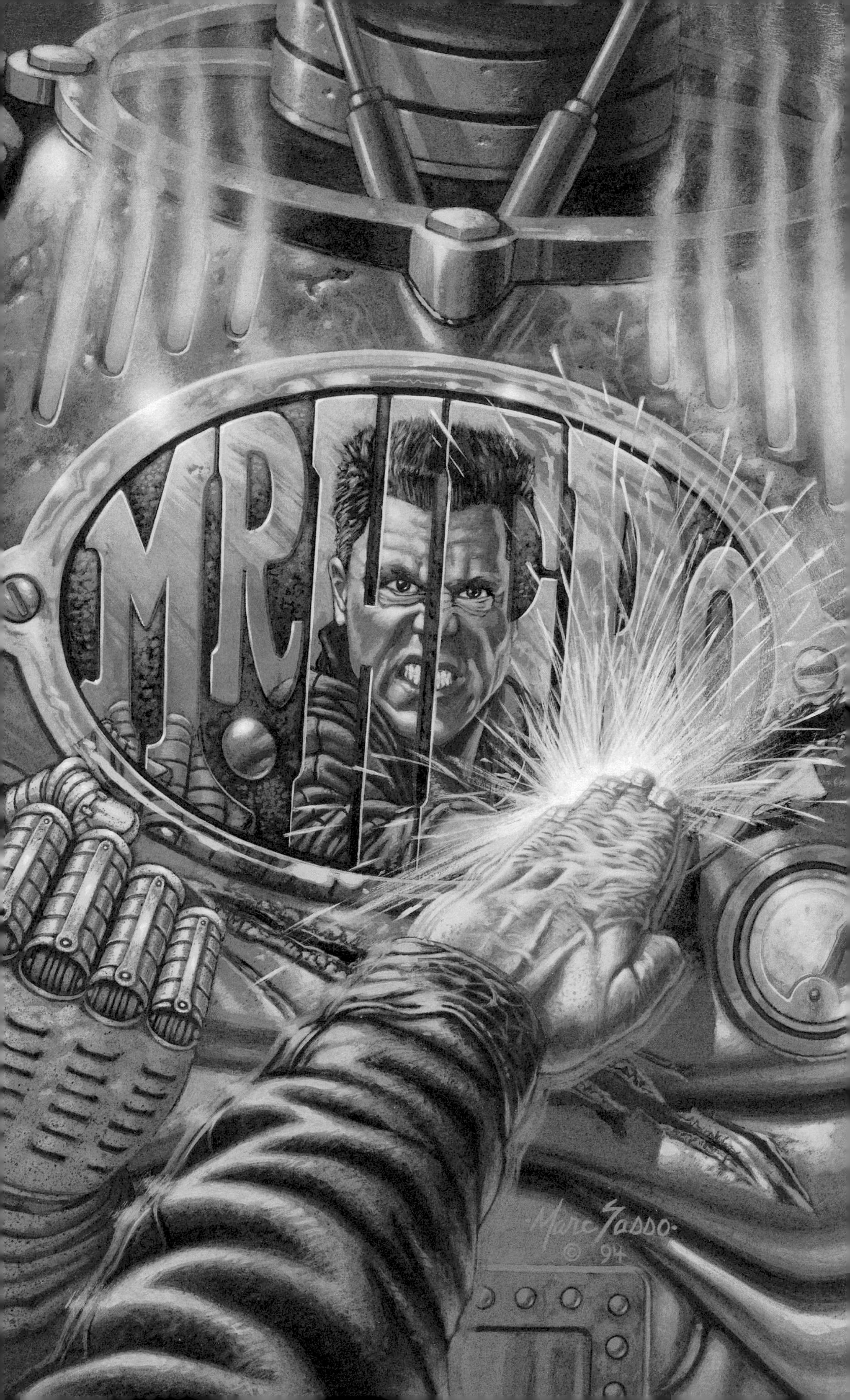
MR.
Marc Sasso
© 94

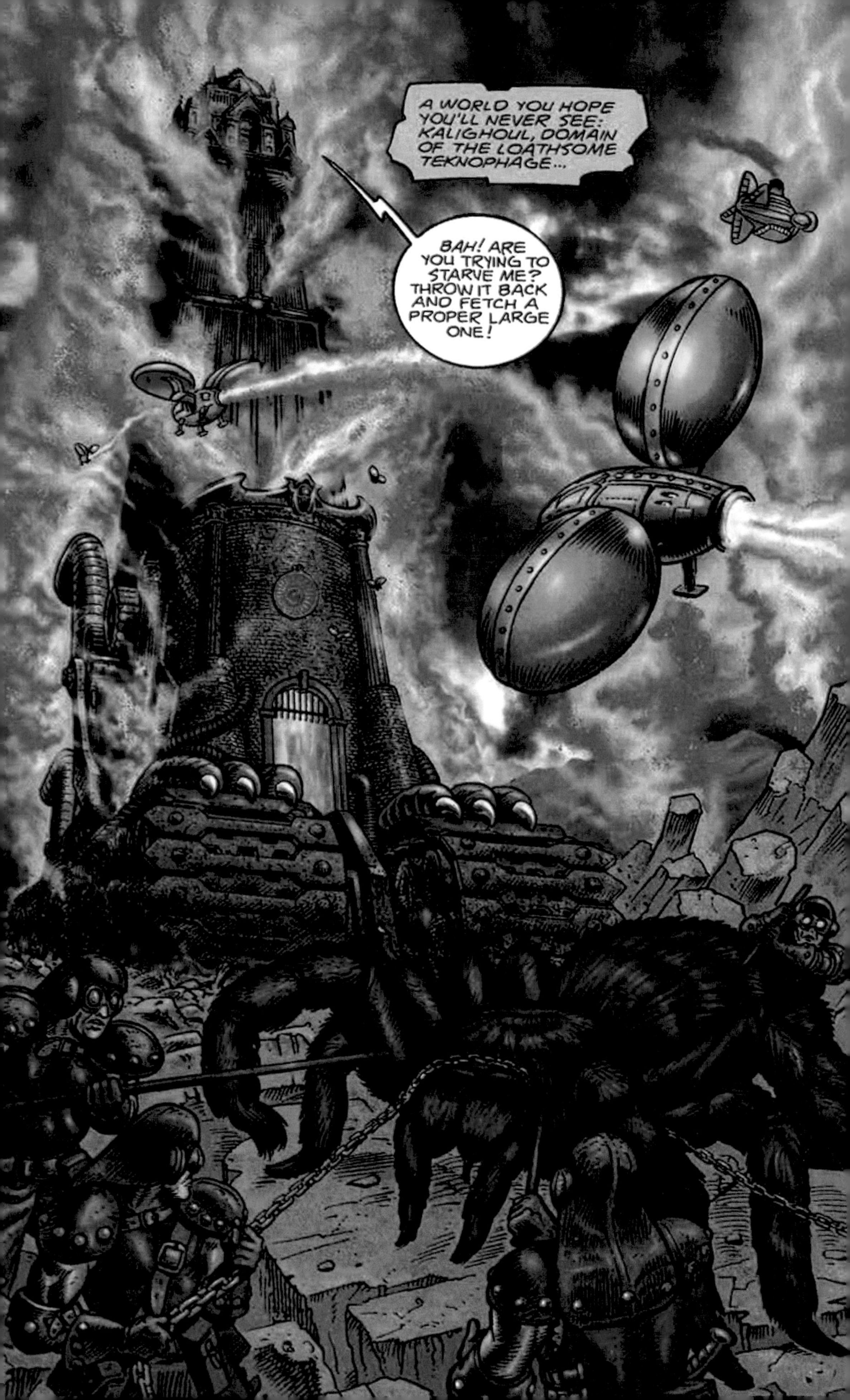
A WORLD YOU HOPE YOU'LL NEVER SEE: KALIGHOUL, DOMAIN OF THE LOATHSOME TEKNOPHAGE...
BAH! ARE YOU TRYING TO STARVE ME? THROW IT BACK AND FETCH A PROPER LARGE ONE!

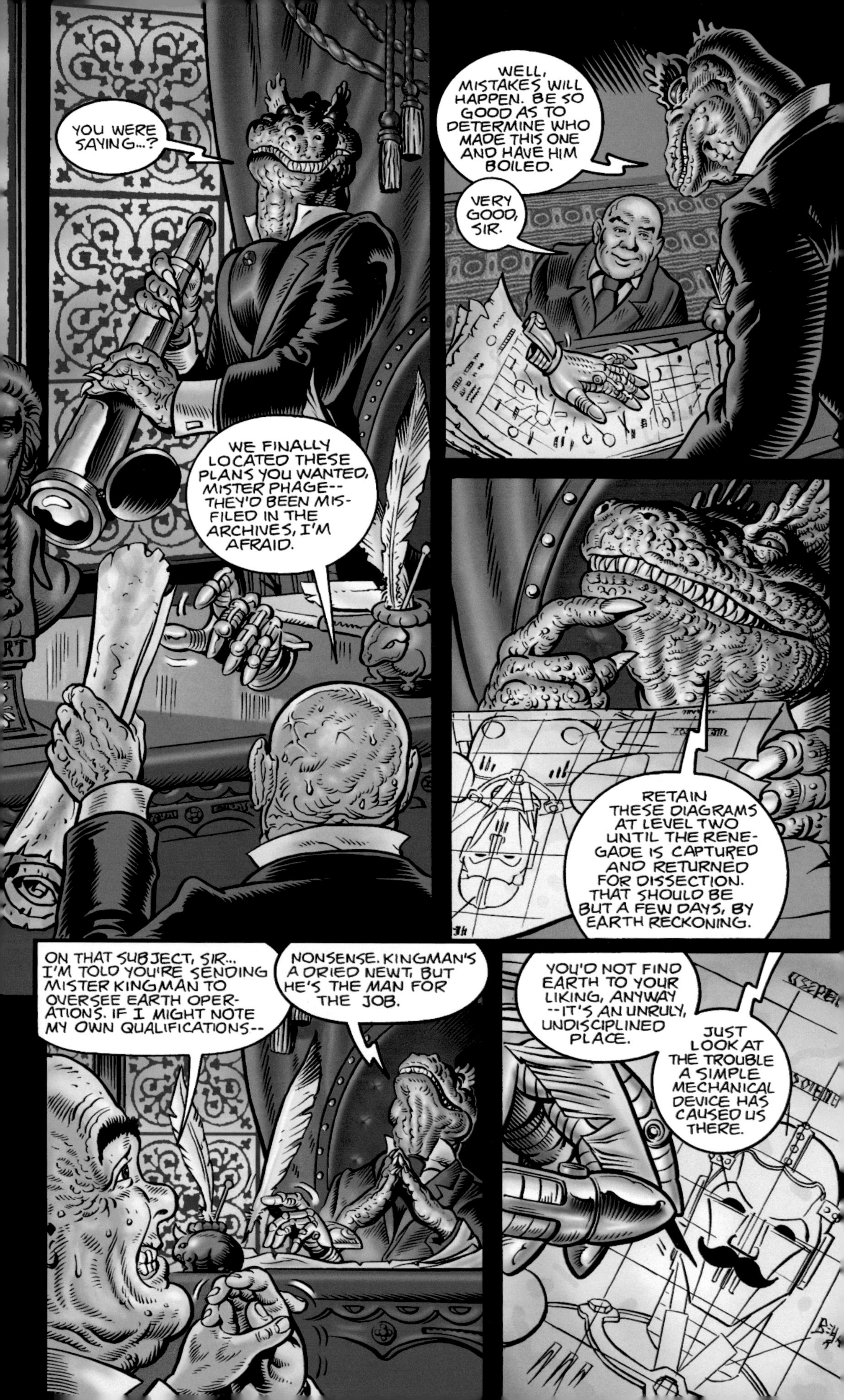
YOU WERE SAYING...?
WE FINALLY LOCATED THESE PLANS YOU WANTED, MISTER PHAGE-- THEY'D BEEN MIS-FILED IN THE ARCHIVES, I'M AFRAID.
WELL, MISTAKES WILL HAPPEN. BE SO GOOD AS TO DETERMINE WHO MADE THIS ONE AND HAVE HIM BOILED.
VERY GOOD, SIR.
RETAIN THESE DIAGRAMS AT LEVEL TWO UNTIL THE RENE-GADE IS CAPTURED AND RETURNED FOR DISSECTION. THAT SHOULD BE BUT A FEW DAYS, BY EARTH RECKONING.
ON THAT SUBJECT, SIR... I'M TOLD YOU'RE SENDING MISTER KINGMAN TO OVERSEE EARTH OPER-ATIONS. IF I MIGHT NOTE MY OWN QUALIFICATIONS--
NONSENSE. KINGMAN'S A DRIED NEWT, BUT HE'S THE MAN FOR THE JOB.
YOU'D NOT FIND EARTH TO YOUR LIKING, ANYWAY --IT'S AN UNRULY, UNDISCIPLINED PLACE.
JUST LOOK AT THE TROUBLE A SIMPLE MECHANICAL DEVICE HAS CAUSED US THERE.

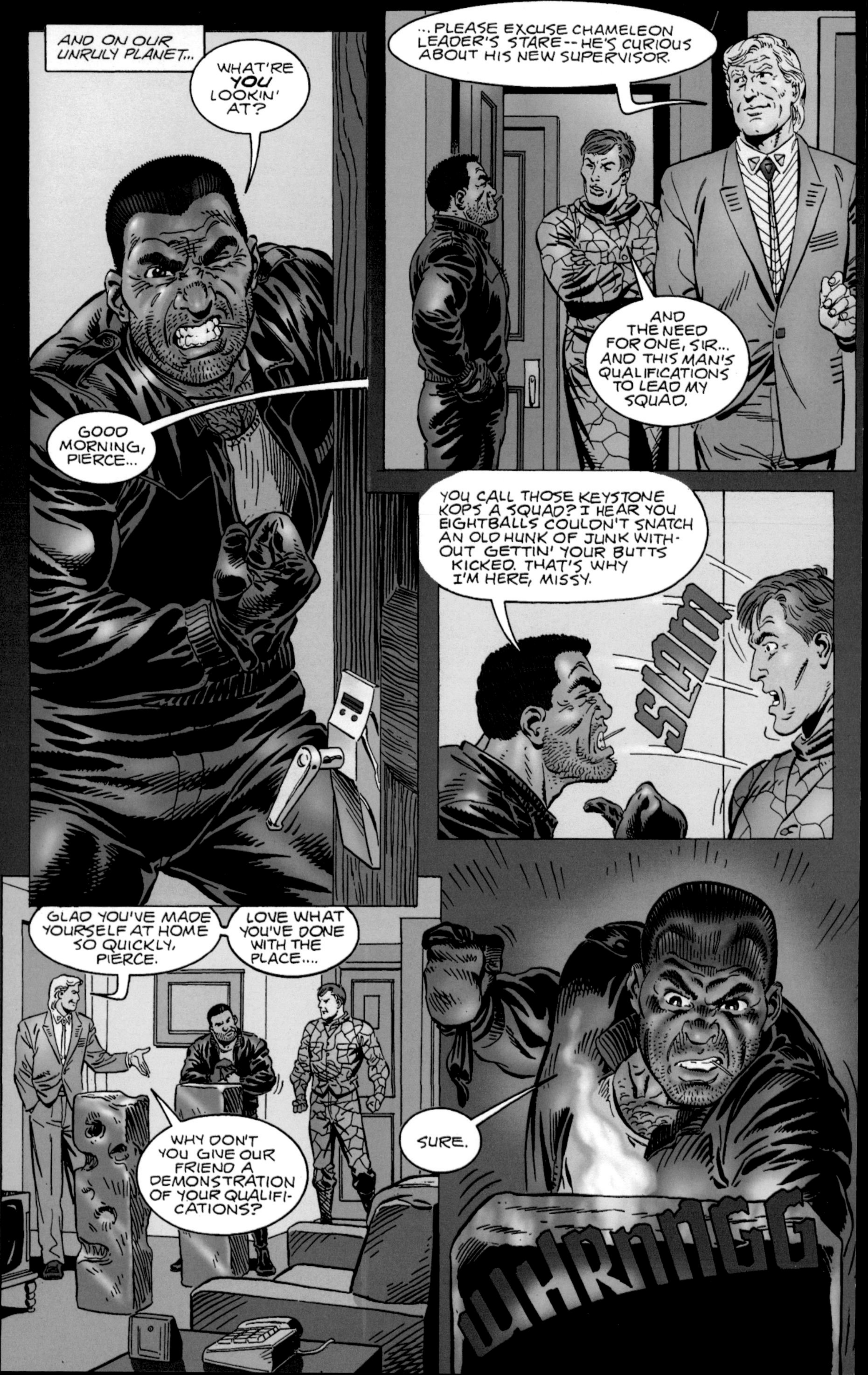
AND ON OUR UNRULY PLANET...
WHAT'RE YOU LOOKIN' AT?
GOOD MORNING, PIERCE...
...PLEASE EXCUSE CHAMELEON LEADER'S STARE--HE'S CURIOUS ABOUT HIS NEW SUPERVISOR.
AND THE NEED FOR ONE, SIR... AND THIS MAN'S QUALIFICATIONS TO LEAD MY SQUAD.
YOU CALL THOSE KEYSTONE KOPS A SQUAD? I HEAR YOU EIGHTBALLS COULDN'T SNATCH AN OLD HUNK OF JUNK WITH-OUT GETTIN' YOUR BUTTS KICKED. THAT'S WHY I'M HERE, MISSY.
SLAM
GLAD YOU'VE MADE YOURSELF AT HOME SO QUICKLY, PIERCE.
LOVE WHAT YOU'VE DONE WITH THE PLACE....
WHY DON'T YOU GIVE OUR FRIEND A DEMONSTRATION OF YOUR QUALIFI-CATIONS?
SURE.
WHRANGG

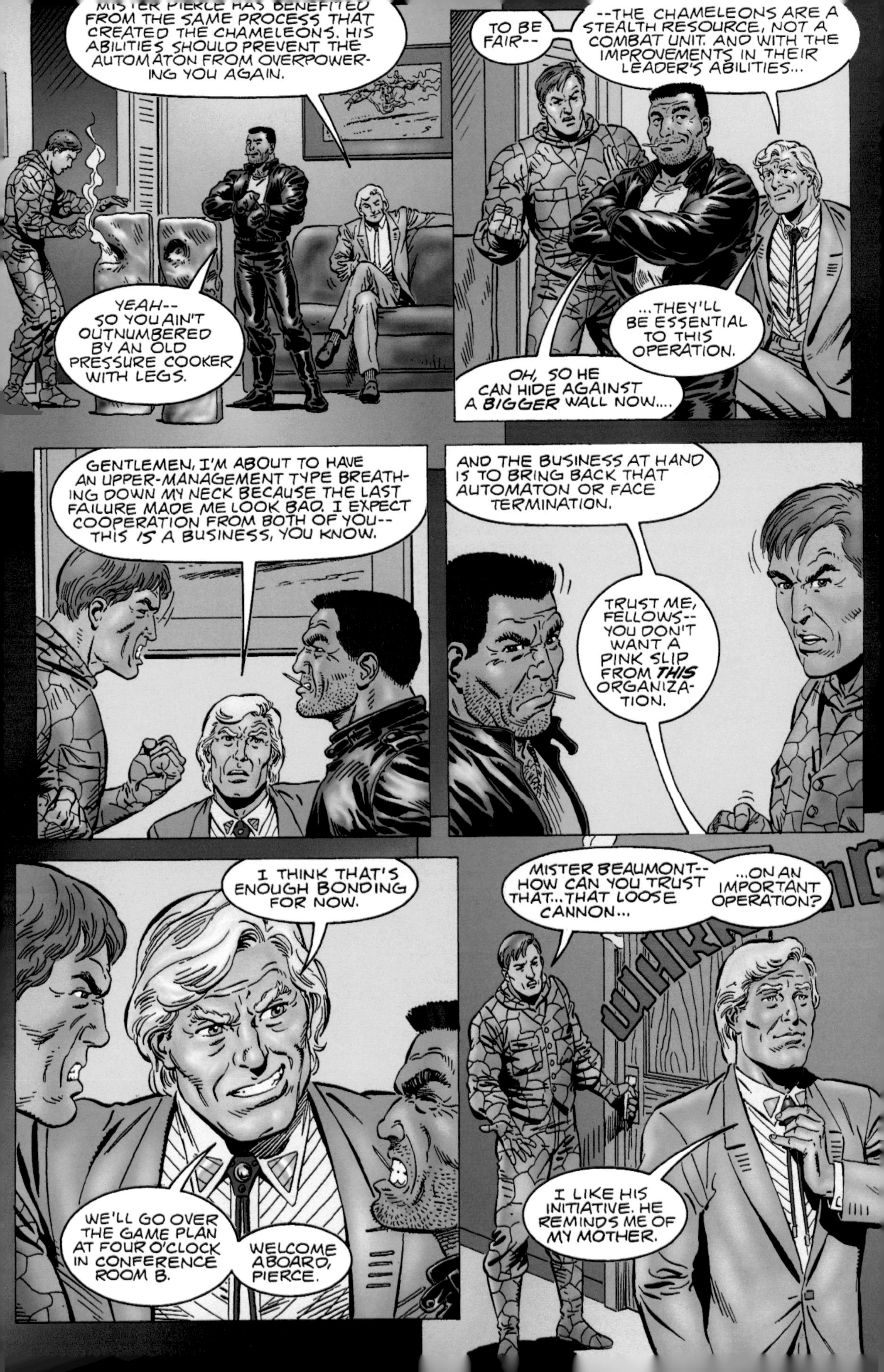
MISTER PIERCE HAS BENEFITED FROM THE SAME PROCESS THAT CREATED THE CHAMELEONS. HIS ABILITIES SHOULD PREVENT THE AUTOMATON FROM OVERPOWERING YOU AGAIN.
YEAH-- SO YOU AIN'T OUTNUMBERED BY AN OLD PRESSURE COOKER WITH LEGS.
TO BE FAIR--
--THE CHAMELEONS ARE A STEALTH RESOURCE, NOT A COMBAT UNIT. AND WITH THE IMPROVEMENTS IN THEIR LEADER'S ABILITIES...
...THEY'LL BE ESSENTIAL TO THIS OPERATION.
OH, SO HE CAN HIDE AGAINST A BIGGER WALL NOW....
GENTLEMEN, I'M ABOUT TO HAVE AN UPPER-MANAGEMENT TYPE BREATHING DOWN MY NECK BECAUSE THE LAST FAILURE MADE ME LOOK BAD. I EXPECT COOPERATION FROM BOTH OF YOU-- THIS IS A BUSINESS, YOU KNOW.
AND THE BUSINESS AT HAND IS TO BRING BACK THAT AUTOMATON OR FACE TERMINATION.
TRUST ME, FELLOWS-- YOU DON'T WANT A PINK SLIP FROM THIS ORGANIZATION.
I THINK THAT'S ENOUGH BONDING FOR NOW.
WE'LL GO OVER THE GAME PLAN AT FOUR O'CLOCK IN CONFERENCE ROOM B.
WELCOME ABOARD, PIERCE.
MISTER BEAUMONT-- HOW CAN YOU TRUST THAT...THAT LOOSE CANNON...
...ON AN IMPORTANT OPERATION?
I LIKE HIS INITIATIVE. HE REMINDS ME OF MY MOTHER.

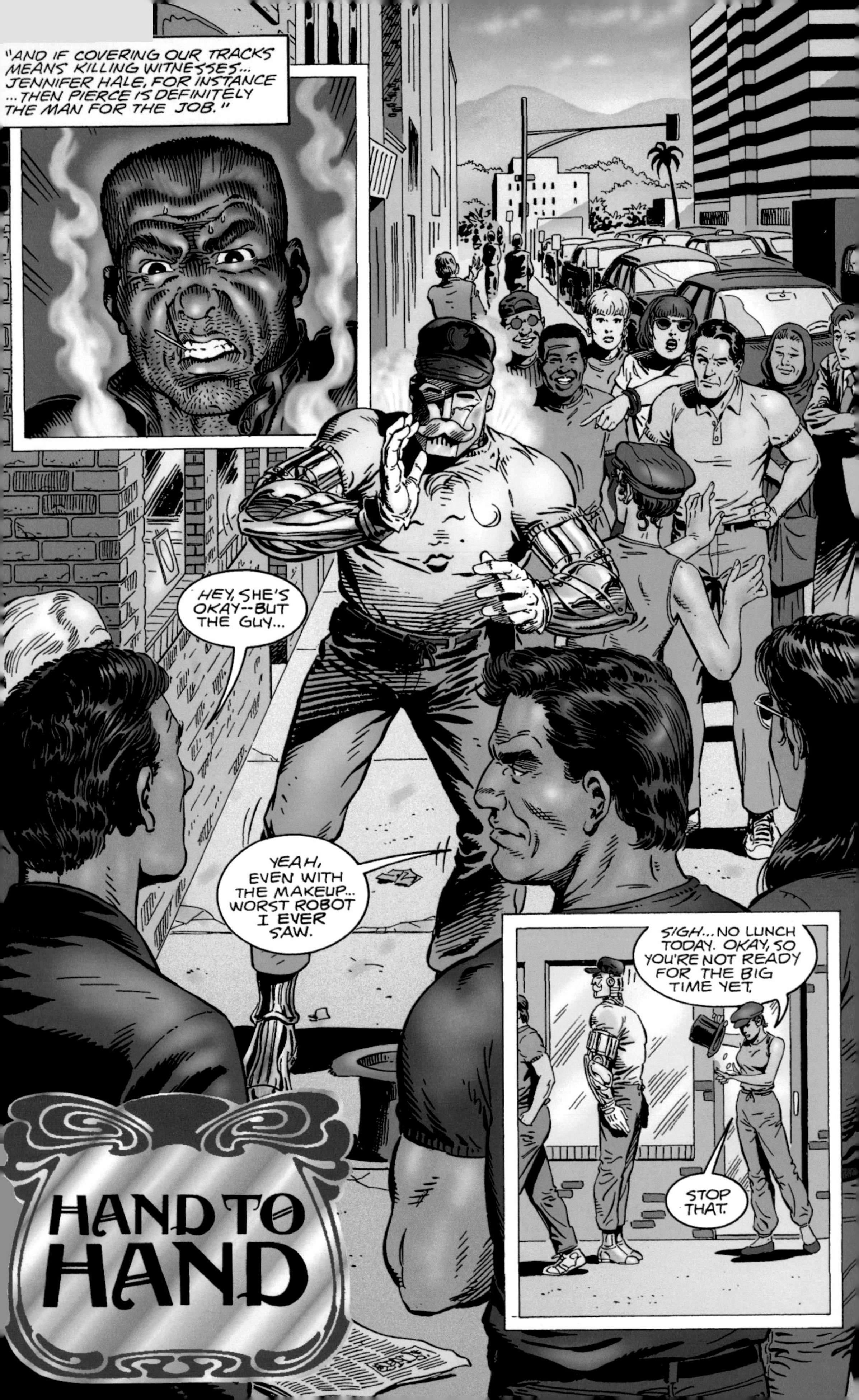
"AND IF COVERING OUR TRACKS MEANS KILLING WITNESSES... JENNIFER HALE, FOR INSTANCE ...THEN PIERCE IS DEFINITELY THE MAN FOR THE JOB."
HEY, SHE'S OKAY--BUT THE GUY...
YEAH, EVEN WITH THE MAKEUP... WORST ROBOT I EVER SAW.
SIGH... NO LUNCH TODAY. OKAY, SO YOU'RE NOT READY FOR THE BIG TIME YET.
STOP THAT.
HAND TO HAND

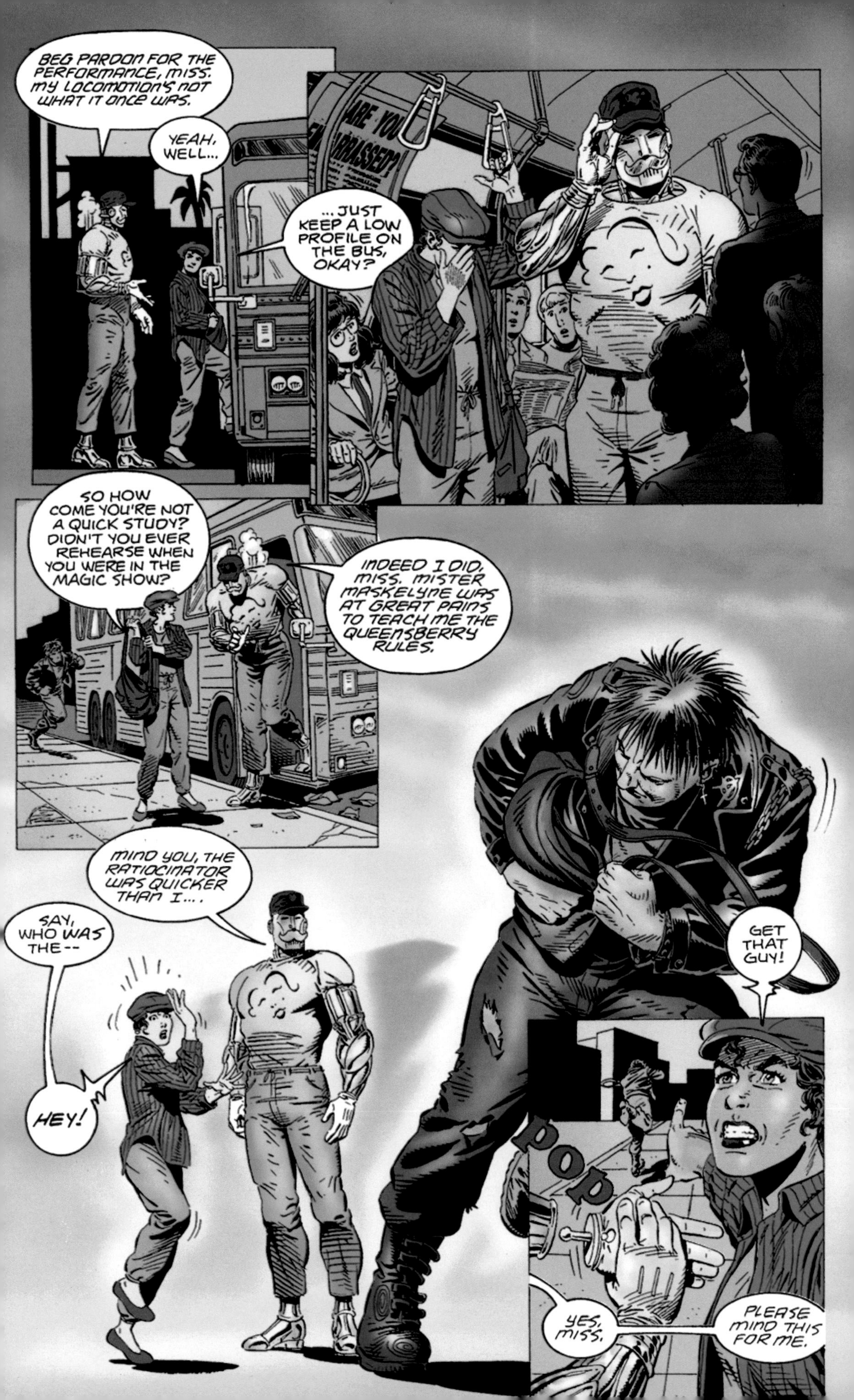

BEG PARDON FOR THE PERFORMANCE, MISS. MY LOCOMOTION'S NOT WHAT IT ONCE WAS.
YEAH, WELL...
...JUST KEEP A LOW PROFILE ON THE BUS, OKAY?
ARE YOU EMBARRASSED?
SO HOW COME YOU'RE NOT A QUICK STUDY? DIDN'T YOU EVER REHEARSE WHEN YOU WERE IN THE MAGIC SHOW?
INDEED I DID, MISS. MISTER MASKELYNE WAS AT GREAT PAINS TO TEACH ME THE QUEENSBERRY RULES.
MIND YOU, THE RATIOCINATOR WAS QUICKER THAN I....
SAY, WHO WAS THE--
HEY!
GET THAT GUY!
POP
PLEASE MIND THIS FOR ME.
YES, MISS.

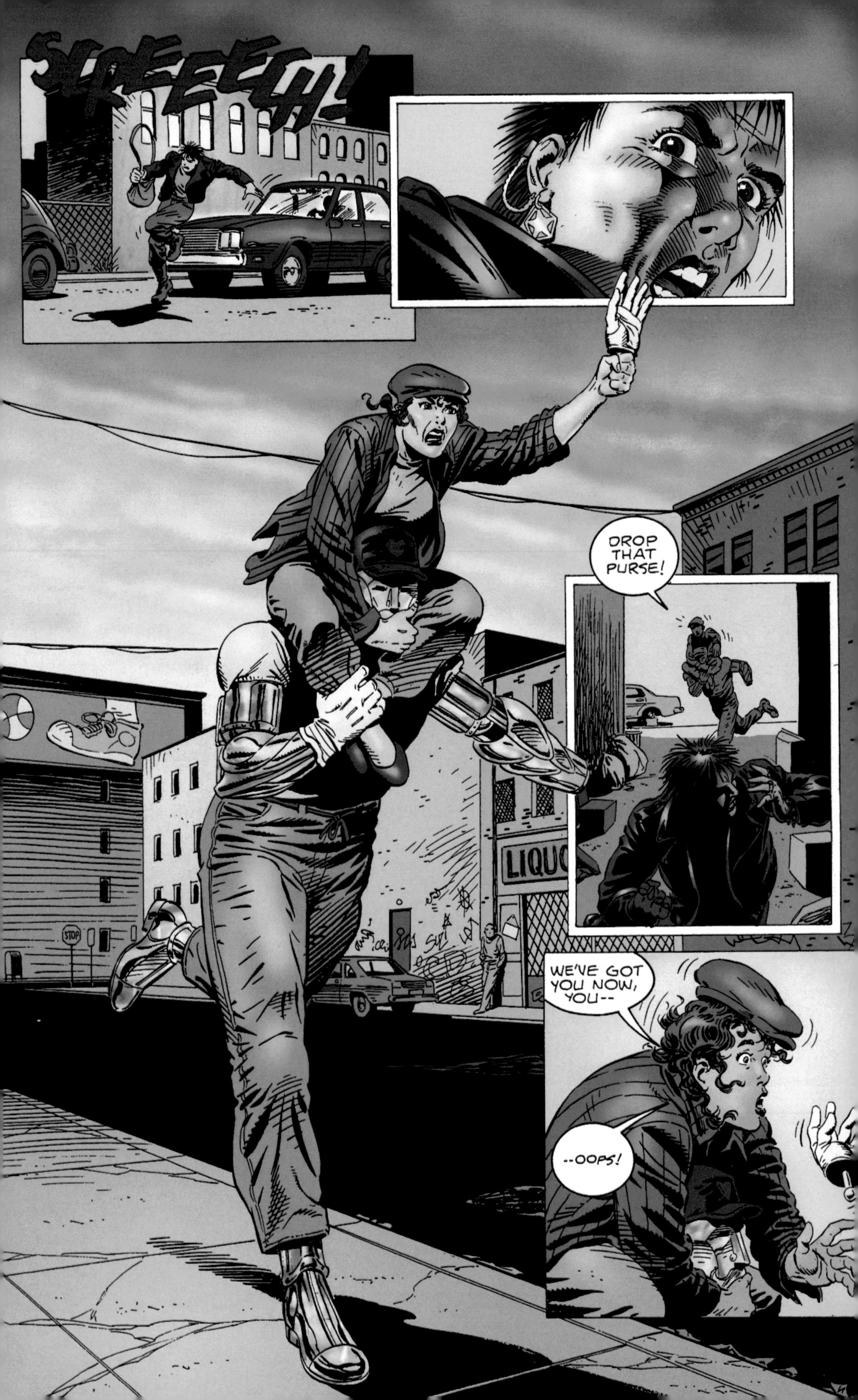
SKREEEECH!
DROP THAT PURSE!
WE'VE GOT YOU NOW, YOU--
--OOPS!
LIQU

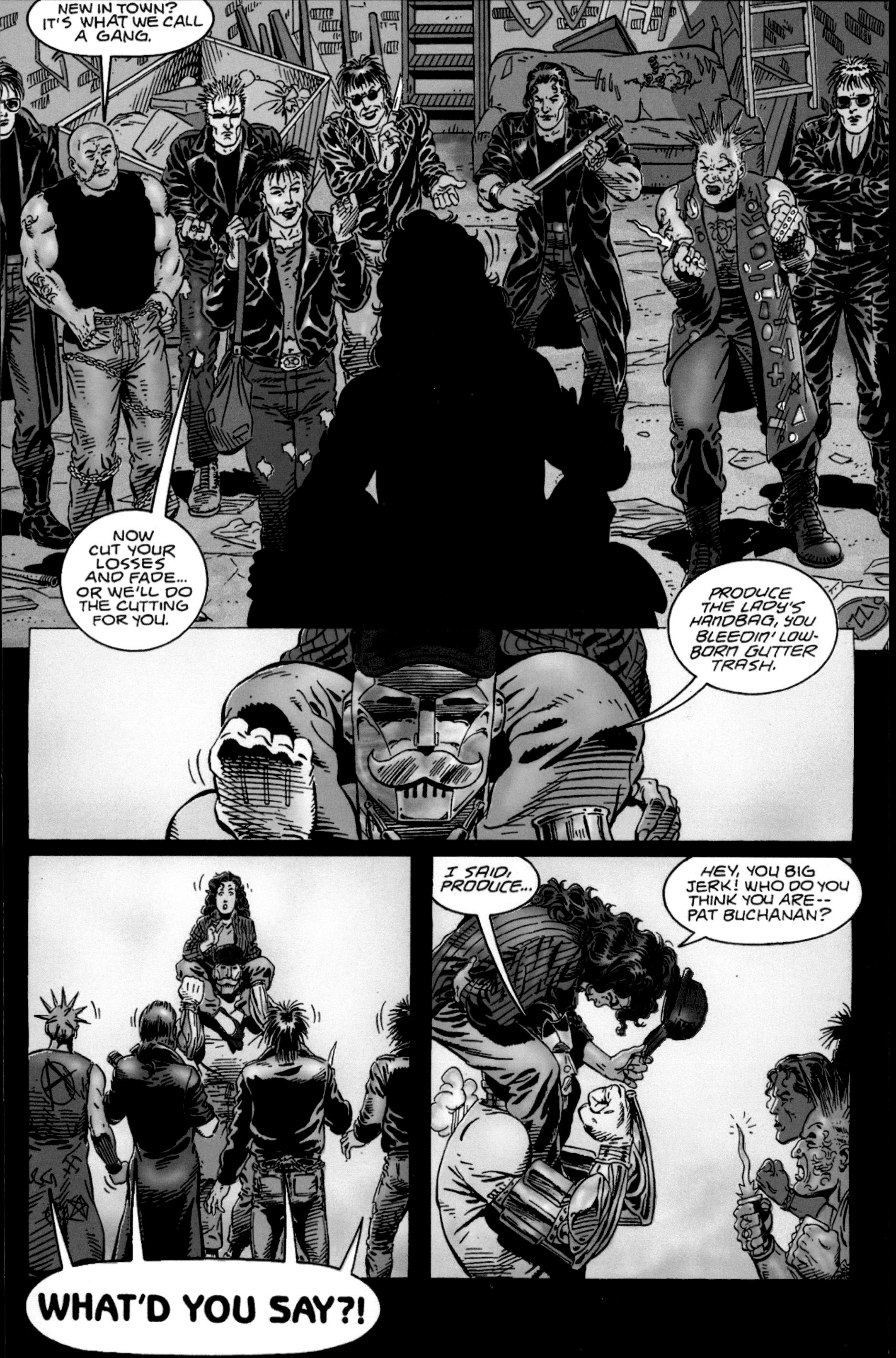

NEW IN TOWN? IT'S WHAT WE CALL A GANG.
NOW CUT YOUR LOSSES AND FADE... OR WE'LL DO THE CUTTING FOR YOU.
PRODUCE THE LADY'S HANDBAG, YOU BLEEDIN' LOW-BORN GUTTER TRASH.
WHAT'D YOU SAY?!
I SAID, PRODUCE...
HEY, YOU BIG JERK! WHO DO YOU THINK YOU ARE-- PAT BUCHANAN?

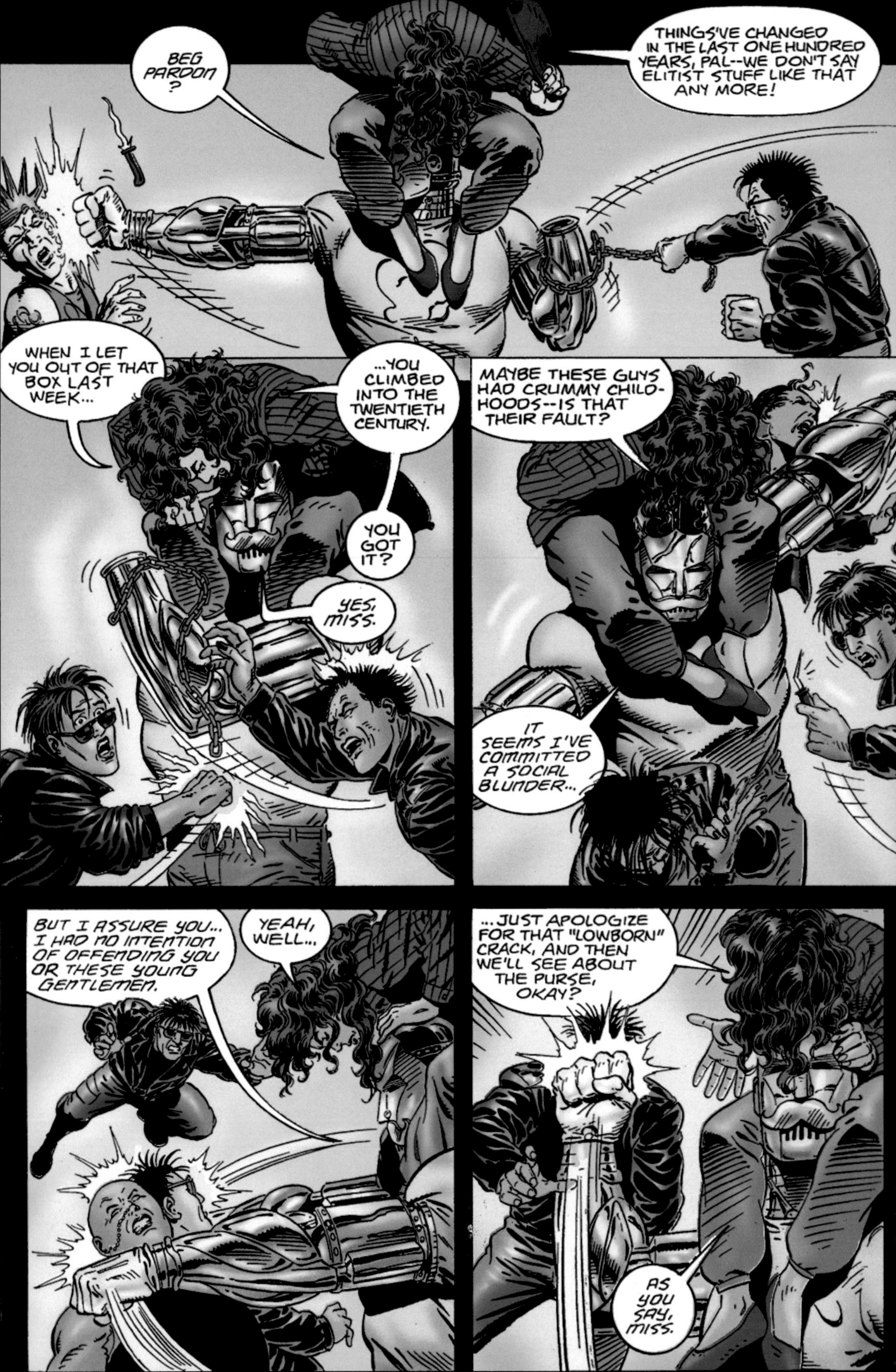
BEG PARDON?
THINGS'VE CHANGED IN THE LAST ONE HUNDRED YEARS, PAL--WE DON'T SAY ELITIST STUFF LIKE THAT ANY MORE!
WHEN I LET YOU OUT OF THAT BOX LAST WEEK...
...YOU CLIMBED INTO THE TWENTIETH CENTURY.
YOU GOT IT?
YES, MISS.
MAYBE THESE GUYS HAD CRUMMY CHILDHOODS--IS THAT THEIR FAULT?
IT SEEMS I'VE COMMITTED A SOCIAL BLUNDER...
BUT I ASSURE YOU... I HAD NO INTENTION OF OFFENDING YOU OR THESE YOUNG GENTLEMEN.
YEAH, WELL...
...JUST APOLOGIZE FOR THAT "LOWBORN" CRACK, AND THEN WE'LL SEE ABOUT THE PURSE, OKAY?
AS YOU SAY, MISS.

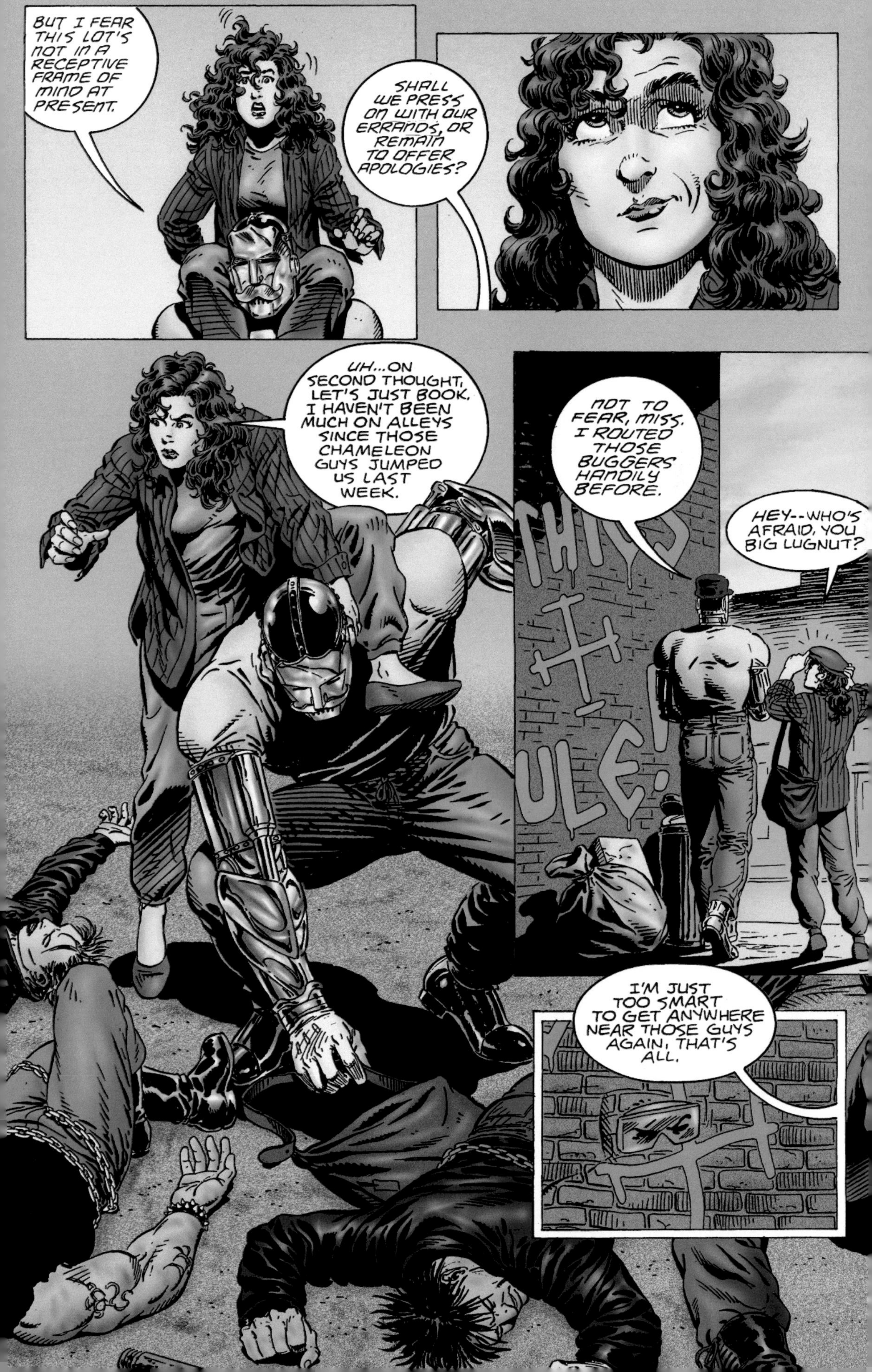
BUT I FEAR THIS LOT'S NOT IN A RECEPTIVE FRAME OF MIND AT PRESENT.
SHALL WE PRESS ON WITH OUR ERRANDS, OR REMAIN TO OFFER APOLOGIES?
UH...ON SECOND THOUGHT, LET'S JUST BOOK. I HAVEN'T BEEN MUCH ON ALLEYS SINCE THOSE CHAMELEON GUYS JUMPED US LAST WEEK.
NOT TO FEAR, MISS. I ROUTED THOSE BUGGERS HANDILY BEFORE.
HEY--WHO'S AFRAID, YOU BIG LUGNUT?
I'M JUST TOO SMART TO GET ANYWHERE NEAR THOSE GUYS AGAIN, THAT'S ALL.

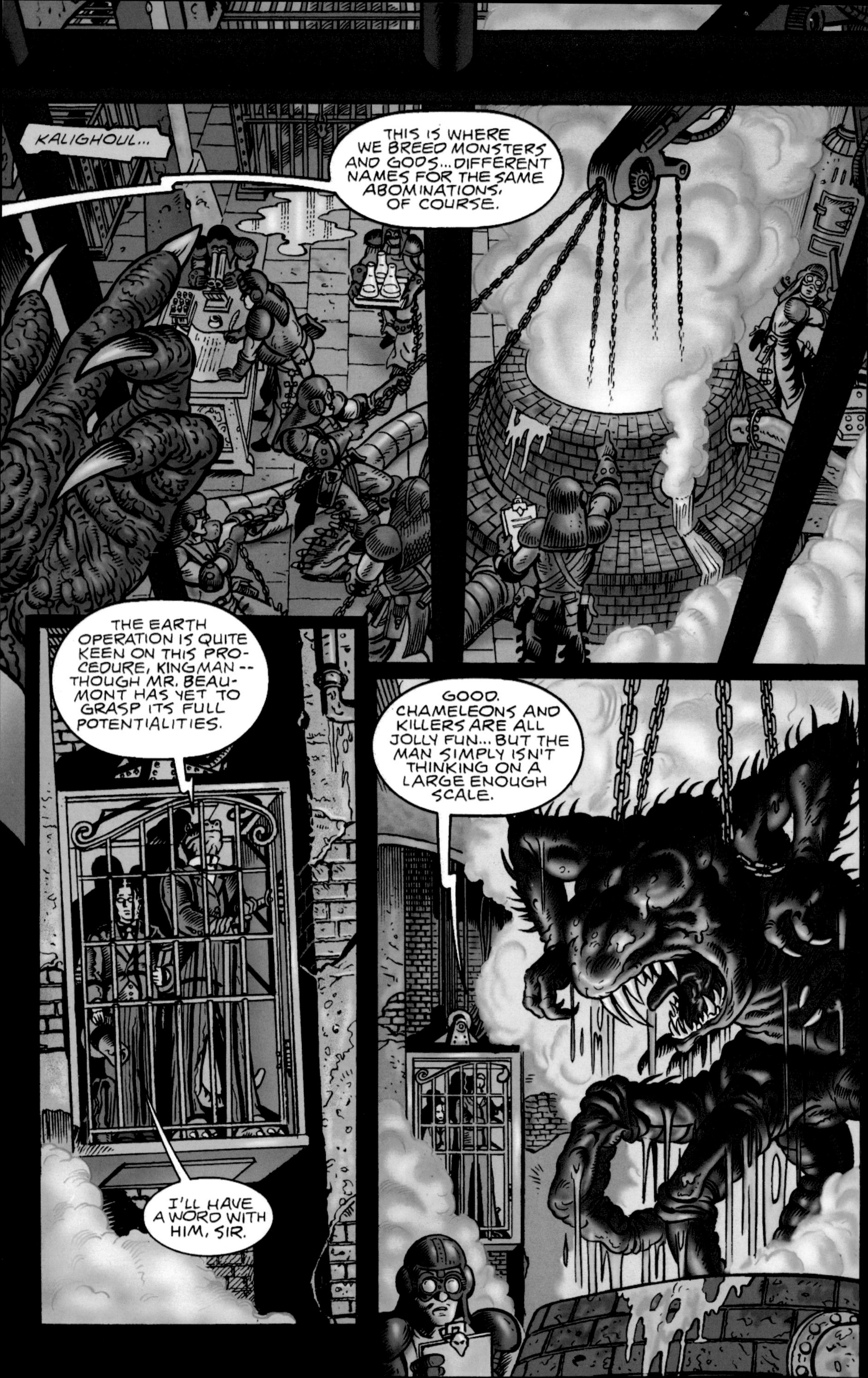
KALIGHOUL...
THIS IS WHERE WE BREED MONSTERS AND GODS... DIFFERENT NAMES FOR THE SAME ABOMINATIONS, OF COURSE.
THE EARTH OPERATION IS QUITE KEEN ON THIS PROCEDURE, KINGMAN -- THOUGH MR. BEAUMONT HAS YET TO GRASP ITS FULL POTENTIALITIES.
I'LL HAVE A WORD WITH HIM, SIR.
GOOD. CHAMELEONS AND KILLERS ARE ALL JOLLY FUN... BUT THE MAN SIMPLY ISN'T THINKING ON A LARGE ENOUGH SCALE.

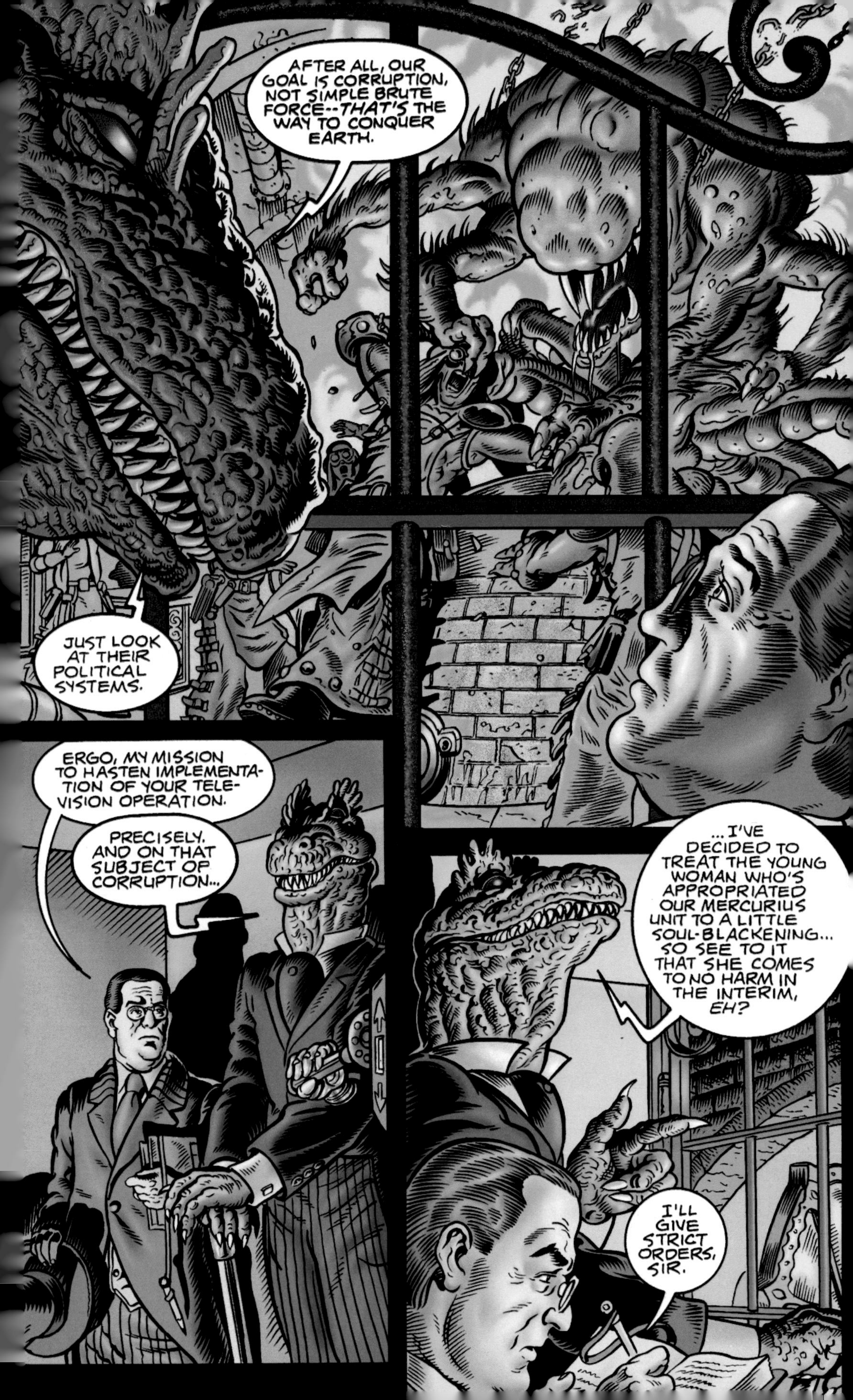
AFTER ALL, OUR GOAL IS CORRUPTION, NOT SIMPLE BRUTE FORCE--THAT'S THE WAY TO CONQUER EARTH.
JUST LOOK AT THEIR POLITICAL SYSTEMS.
ERGO, MY MISSION TO HASTEN IMPLEMENTATION OF YOUR TELEVISION OPERATION.
PRECISELY. AND ON THAT SUBJECT OF CORRUPTION...
...I'VE DECIDED TO TREAT THE YOUNG WOMAN WHO'S APPROPRIATED OUR MERCURIUS UNIT TO A LITTLE SOUL-BLACKENING... SO SEE TO IT THAT SHE COMES TO NO HARM IN THE INTERIM, EH?
I'LL GIVE STRICT ORDERS, SIR.

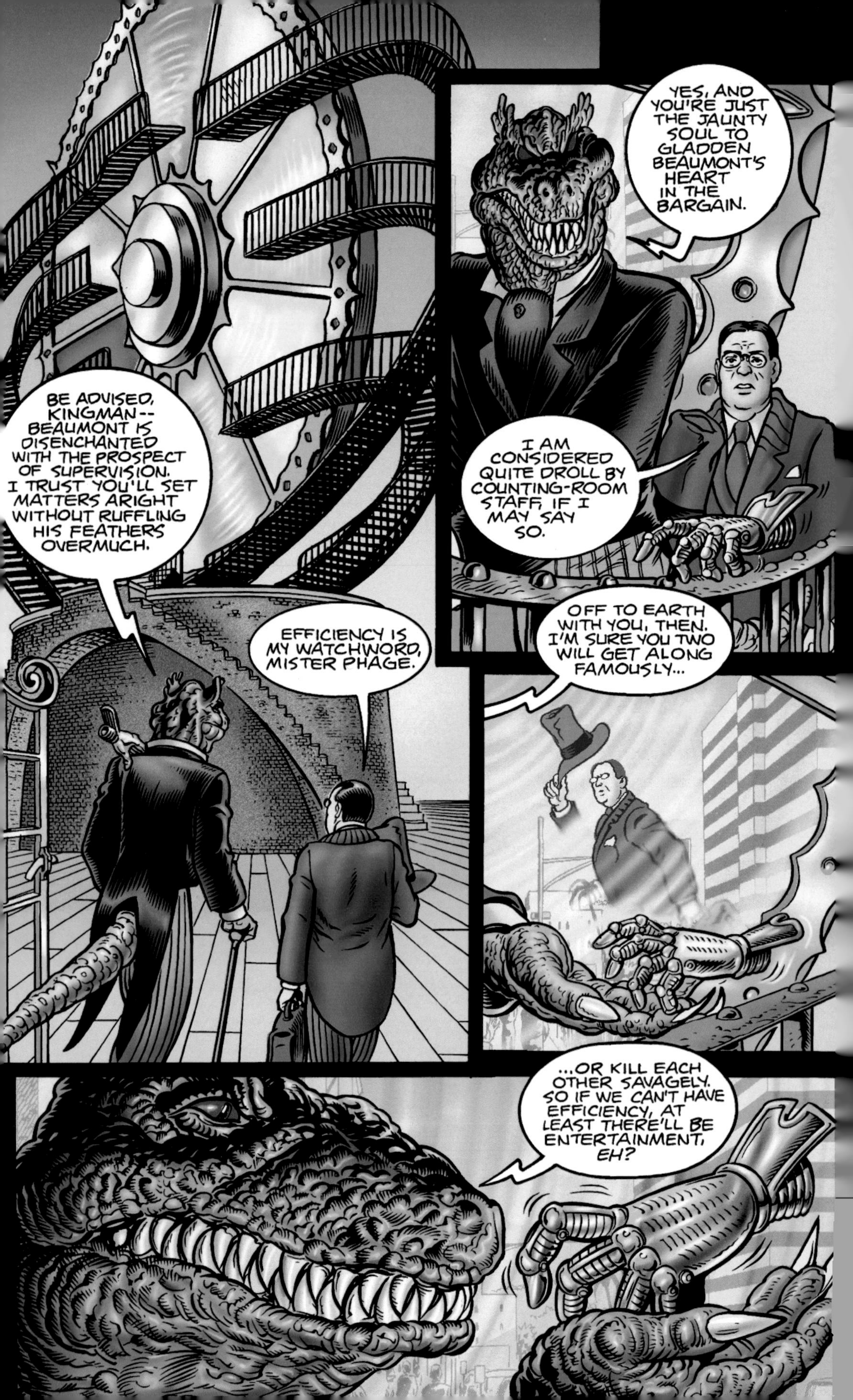
BE ADVISED, KINGMAN-- BEAUMONT IS DISENCHANTED WITH THE PROSPECT OF SUPERVISION. I TRUST YOU'LL SET MATTERS ARIGHT WITHOUT RUFFLING HIS FEATHERS OVERMUCH.
EFFICIENCY IS MY WATCHWORD, MISTER PHAGE.
YES, AND YOU'RE JUST THE JAUNTY SOUL TO GLADDEN BEAUMONT'S HEART IN THE BARGAIN.
I AM CONSIDERED QUITE DROLL BY COUNTING-ROOM STAFF, IF I MAY SAY SO.
OFF TO EARTH WITH YOU, THEN. I'M SURE YOU TWO WILL GET ALONG FAMOUSLY...
...OR KILL EACH OTHER SAVAGELY. SO IF WE CAN'T HAVE EFFICIENCY, AT LEAST THERE'LL BE ENTERTAINMENT, EH?

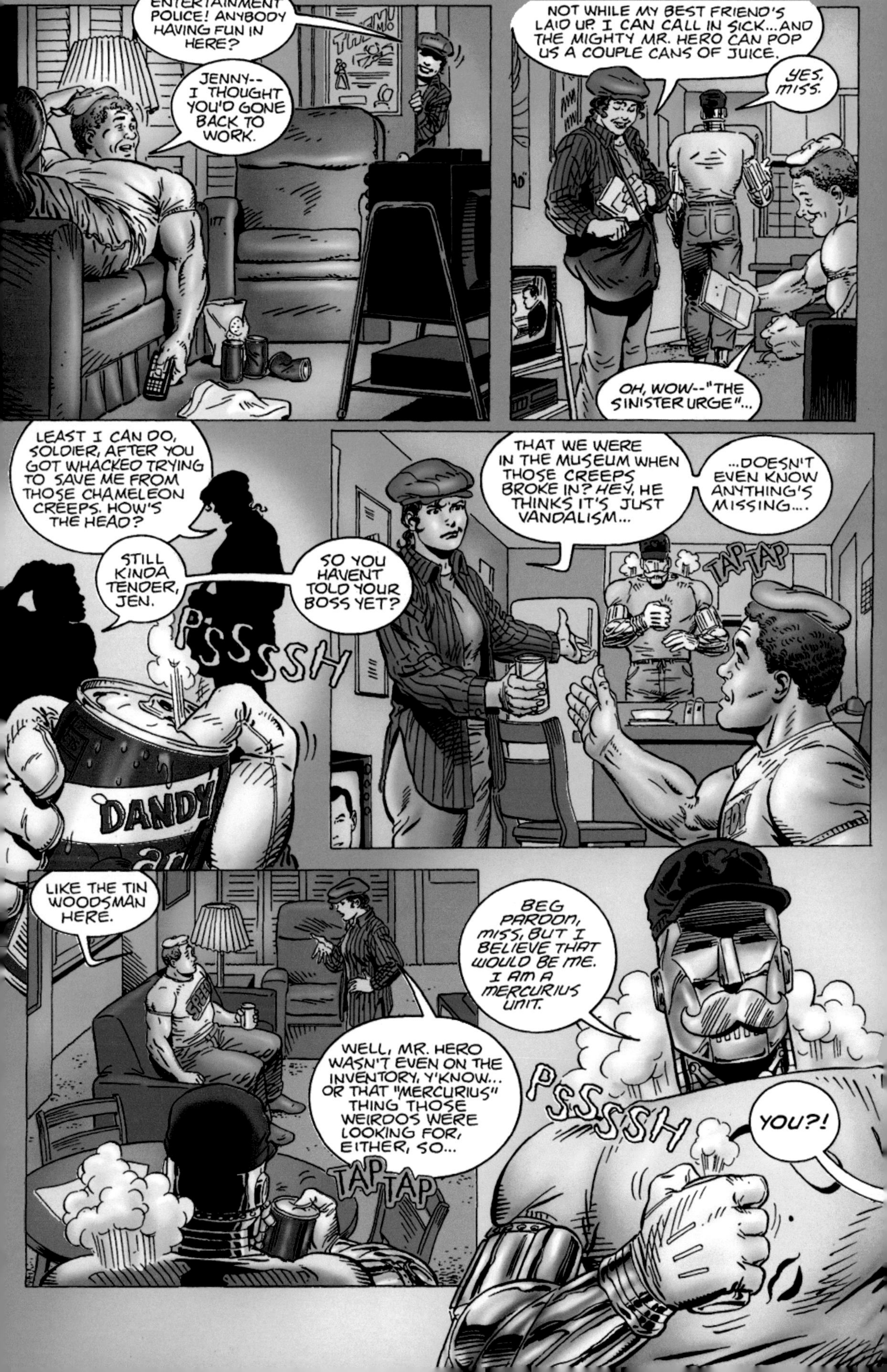
ENTERTAINMENT POLICE! ANYBODY HAVING FUN IN HERE?
JENNY-- I THOUGHT YOU'D GONE BACK TO WORK.
NOT WHILE MY BEST FRIEND'S LAID UP. I CAN CALL IN SICK...AND THE MIGHTY MR. HERO CAN POP US A COUPLE CANS OF JUICE.
YES, MISS.
OH, WOW--"THE SINISTER URGE"...
LEAST I CAN DO, SOLDIER, AFTER YOU GOT WHACKED TRYING TO SAVE ME FROM THOSE CHAMELEON CREEPS. HOW'S THE HEAD?
STILL KINDA TENDER, JEN.
SO YOU HAVENT TOLD YOUR BOSS YET?
PSSSSH
DANDY
THAT WE WERE IN THE MUSEUM WHEN THOSE CREEPS BROKE IN? HEY, HE THINKS IT'S JUST VANDALISM...
...DOESN'T EVEN KNOW ANYTHING'S MISSING....
TAP TAP
LIKE THE TIN WOODSMAN HERE.
BEG PARDON, MISS, BUT I BELIEVE THAT WOULD BE ME. I AM A MERCURIUS UNIT.
WELL, MR. HERO WASN'T EVEN ON THE INVENTORY, Y'KNOW... OR THAT "MERCURIUS" THING THOSE WEIRDOS WERE LOOKING FOR, EITHER, SO...
TAP TAP
PSSSSH
YOU?!

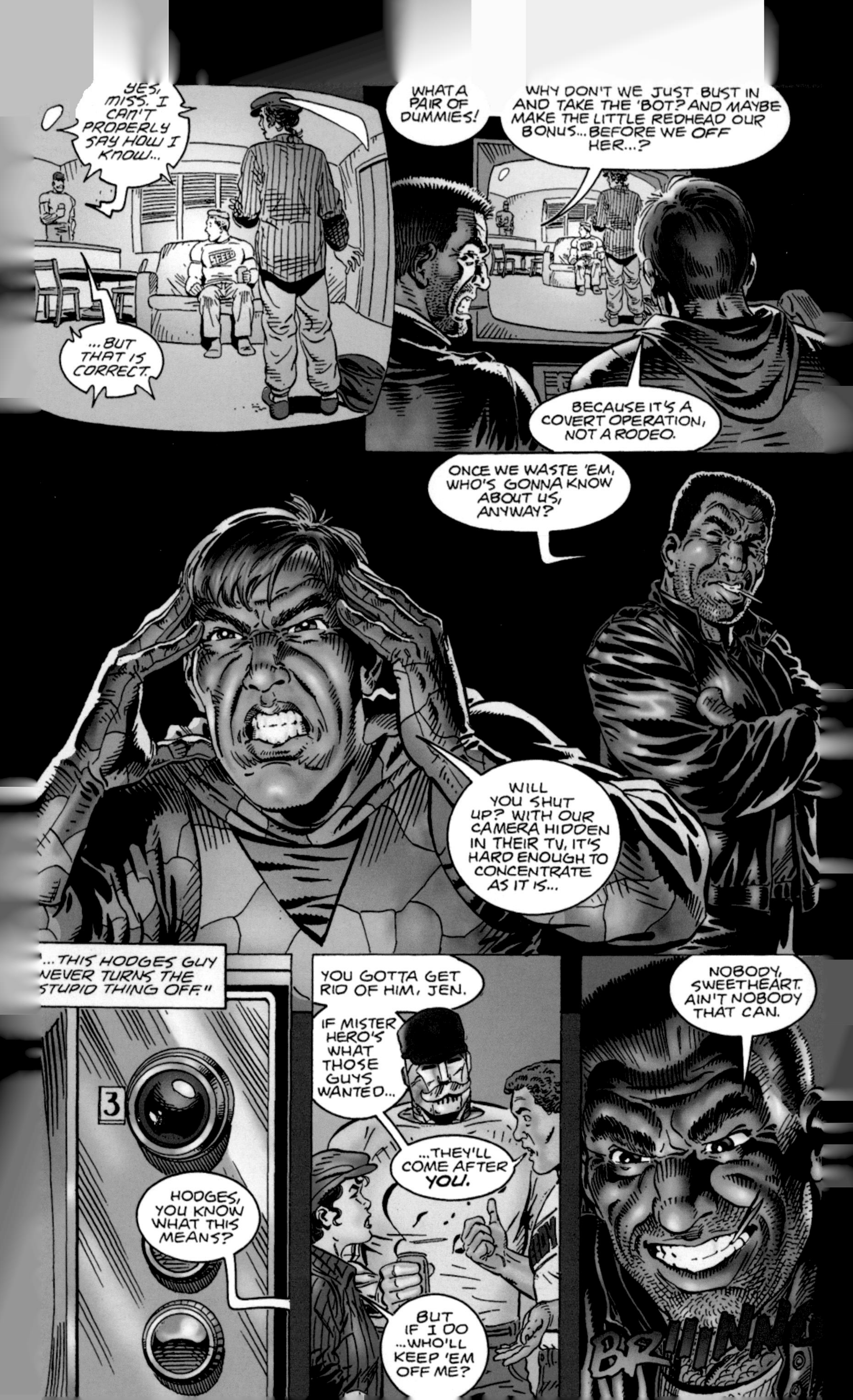
YES, MISS. I CAN'T PROPERLY SAY HOW I KNOW...
...BUT THAT IS CORRECT.
WHAT A PAIR OF DUMMIES!
WHY DON'T WE JUST BUST IN AND TAKE THE 'BOT? AND MAYBE MAKE THE LITTLE REDHEAD OUR BONUS... BEFORE WE OFF HER...?
BECAUSE IT'S A COVERT OPERATION, NOT A RODEO.
ONCE WE WASTE 'EM, WHO'S GONNA KNOW ABOUT US, ANYWAY?
WILL YOU SHUT UP? WITH OUR CAMERA HIDDEN IN THEIR TV, IT'S HARD ENOUGH TO CONCENTRATE AS IT IS...
"...THIS HODGES GUY NEVER TURNS THE STUPID THING OFF."
HODGES, YOU KNOW WHAT THIS MEANS?
YOU GOTTA GET RID OF HIM, JEN.
IF MISTER HERO'S WHAT THOSE GUYS WANTED...
...THEY'LL COME AFTER YOU.
BUT IF I DO ...WHO'LL KEEP 'EM OFF ME?
NOBODY, SWEETHEART. AIN'T NOBODY THAT CAN.

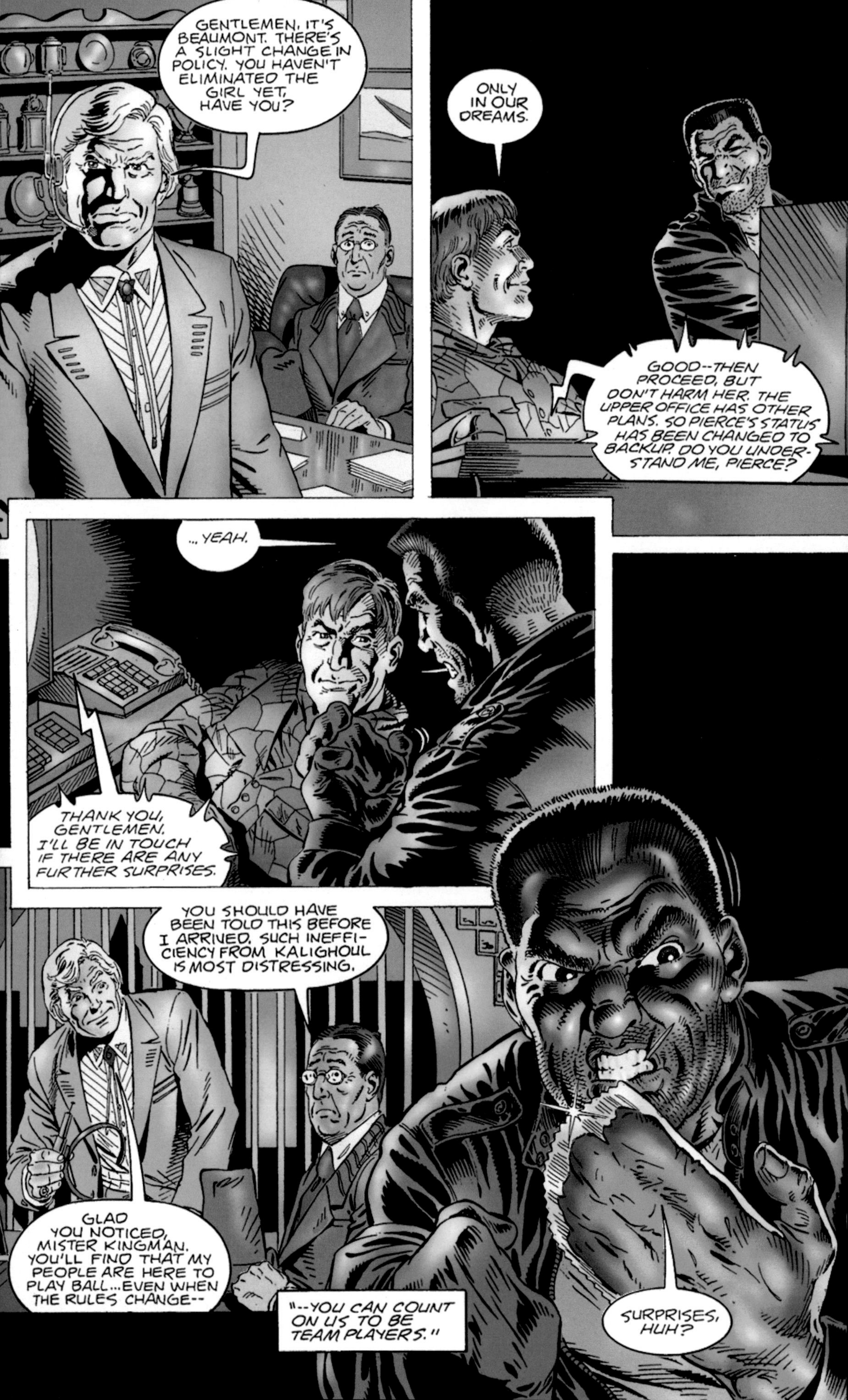
GENTLEMEN, IT'S BEAUMONT. THERE'S A SLIGHT CHANGE IN POLICY. YOU HAVEN'T ELIMINATED THE GIRL YET, HAVE YOU?
ONLY IN OUR DREAMS.
GOOD--THEN PROCEED, BUT DON'T HARM HER. THE UPPER OFFICE HAS OTHER PLANS. SO PIERCE'S STATUS HAS BEEN CHANGED TO BACKUP. DO YOU UNDERSTAND ME, PIERCE?
...YEAH.
THANK YOU, GENTLEMEN. I'LL BE IN TOUCH IF THERE ARE ANY FURTHER SURPRISES.
YOU SHOULD HAVE BEEN TOLD THIS BEFORE I ARRIVED. SUCH INEFFICIENCY FROM KALIGHOUL IS MOST DISTRESSING.
GLAD YOU NOTICED, MISTER KINGMAN. YOU'LL FIND THAT MY PEOPLE ARE HERE TO PLAY BALL...EVEN WHEN THE RULES CHANGE--
"--YOU CAN COUNT ON US TO BE TEAM PLAYERS."
SURPRISES, HUH?

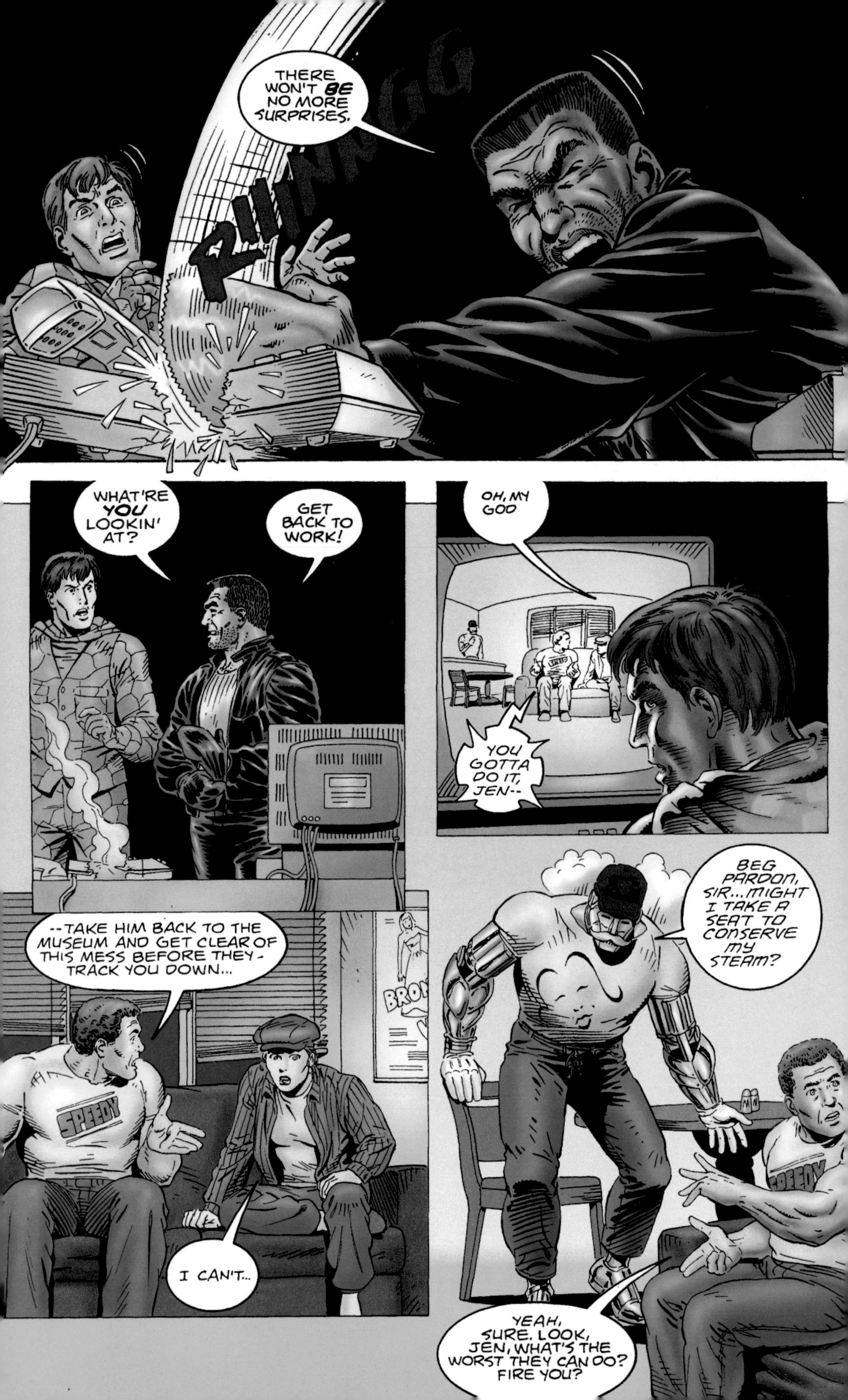
THERE WON'T **BE** NO MORE SURPRISES.
RIIINNGG
WHAT'RE **YOU** LOOKIN' AT?
GET BACK TO WORK!
OH, MY GOD
YOU GOTTA DO IT, JEN--
--TAKE HIM BACK TO THE MUSEUM AND GET CLEAR OF THIS MESS BEFORE THEY TRACK YOU DOWN...
SPEEDY
I CAN'T...
BEG PARDON, SIR... MIGHT I TAKE A SEAT TO CONSERVE MY STEAM?
YEAH, SURE. LOOK, JEN, WHAT'S THE WORST THEY CAN DO? FIRE YOU?

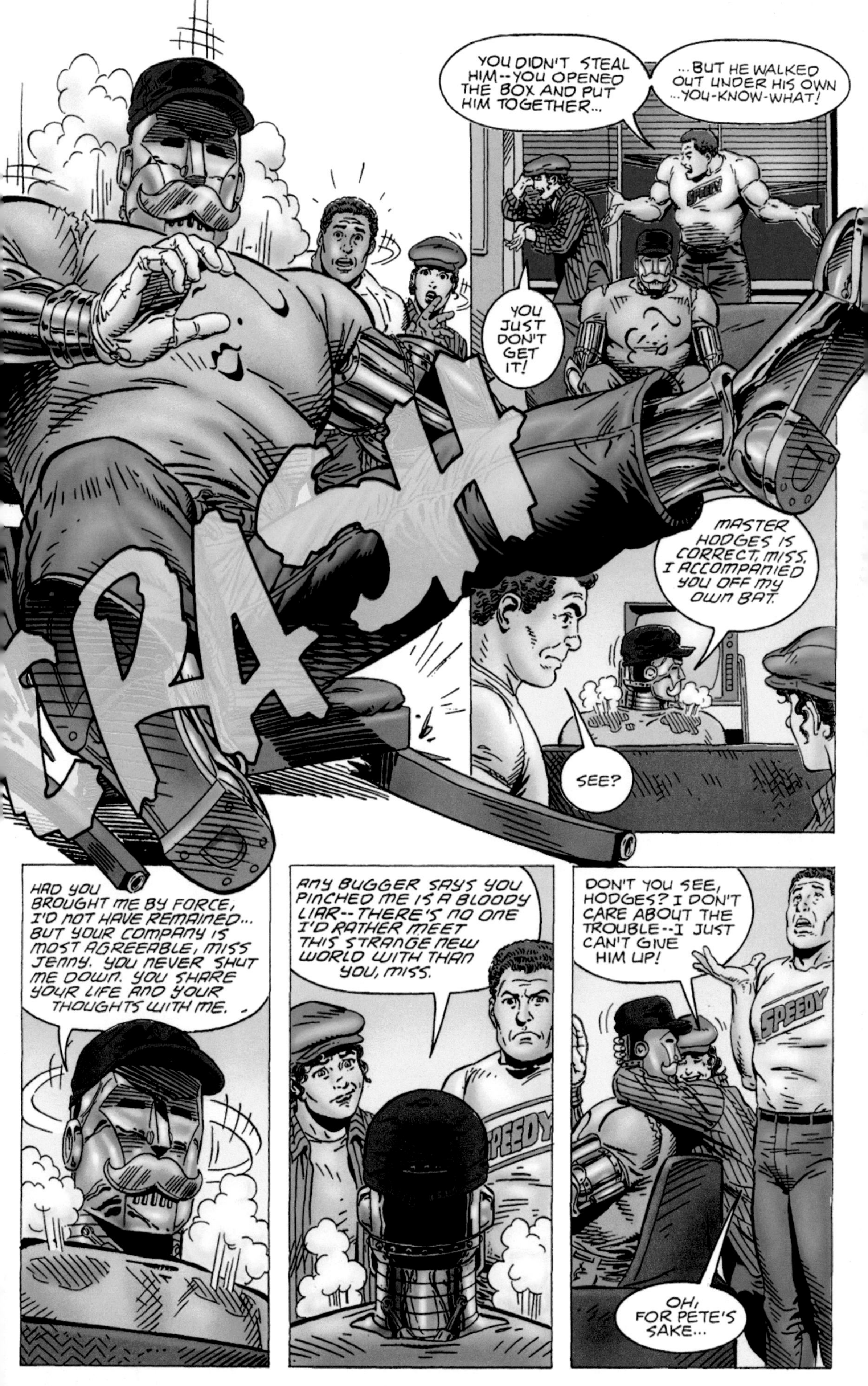
RACK
YOU DIDN'T STEAL HIM--YOU OPENED THE BOX AND PUT HIM TOGETHER...
...BUT HE WALKED OUT UNDER HIS OWN ...YOU-KNOW-WHAT!
YOU JUST DON'T GET IT!
MASTER HODGES IS CORRECT, MISS. I ACCOMPANIED YOU OFF MY OWN BAT.
SEE?
HAD YOU BROUGHT ME BY FORCE, I'D NOT HAVE REMAINED... BUT YOUR COMPANY IS MOST AGREEABLE, MISS JENNY. YOU NEVER SHUT ME DOWN. YOU SHARE YOUR LIFE AND YOUR THOUGHTS WITH ME.
ANY BUGGER SAYS YOU PINCHED ME IS A BLOODY LIAR--THERE'S NO ONE I'D RATHER MEET THIS STRANGE NEW WORLD WITH THAN YOU, MISS.
DON'T YOU SEE, HODGES? I DON'T CARE ABOUT THE TROUBLE--I JUST CAN'T GIVE HIM UP!
OH, FOR PETE'S SAKE...

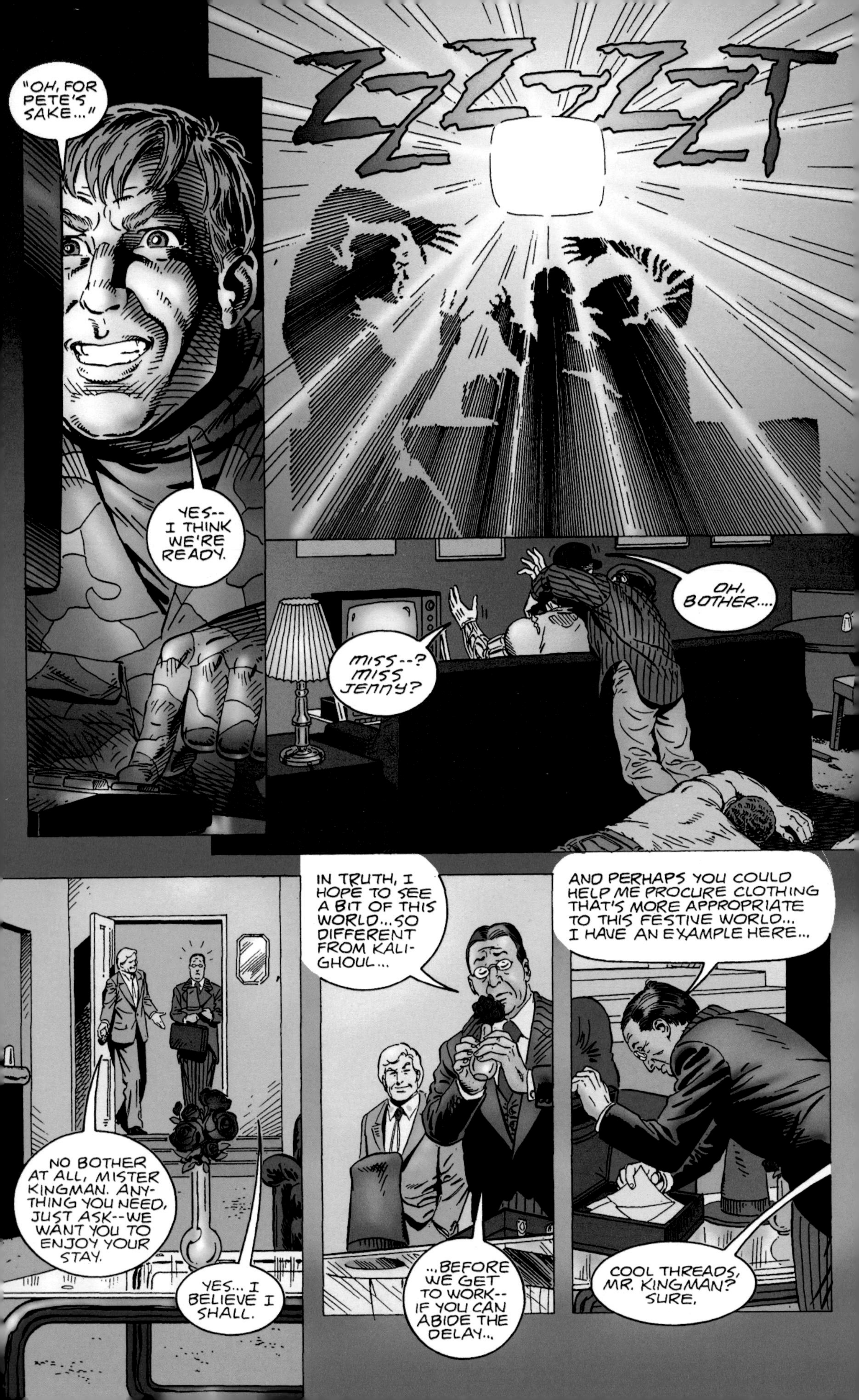
"OH, FOR PETE'S SAKE..."
ZZZ-ZZZT
YES-- I THINK WE'RE READY.
OH, BOTHER....
MISS--? MISS JENNY?
NO BOTHER AT ALL, MISTER KINGMAN. ANYTHING YOU NEED, JUST ASK--WE WANT YOU TO ENJOY YOUR STAY.
YES... I BELIEVE I SHALL.
IN TRUTH, I HOPE TO SEE A BIT OF THIS WORLD...SO DIFFERENT FROM KALI-GHOUL...
...BEFORE WE GET TO WORK-- IF YOU CAN ABIDE THE DELAY...
AND PERHAPS YOU COULD HELP ME PROCURE CLOTHING THAT'S MORE APPROPRIATE TO THIS FESTIVE WORLD... I HAVE AN EXAMPLE HERE...
COOL THREADS, MR. KINGMAN? SURE.

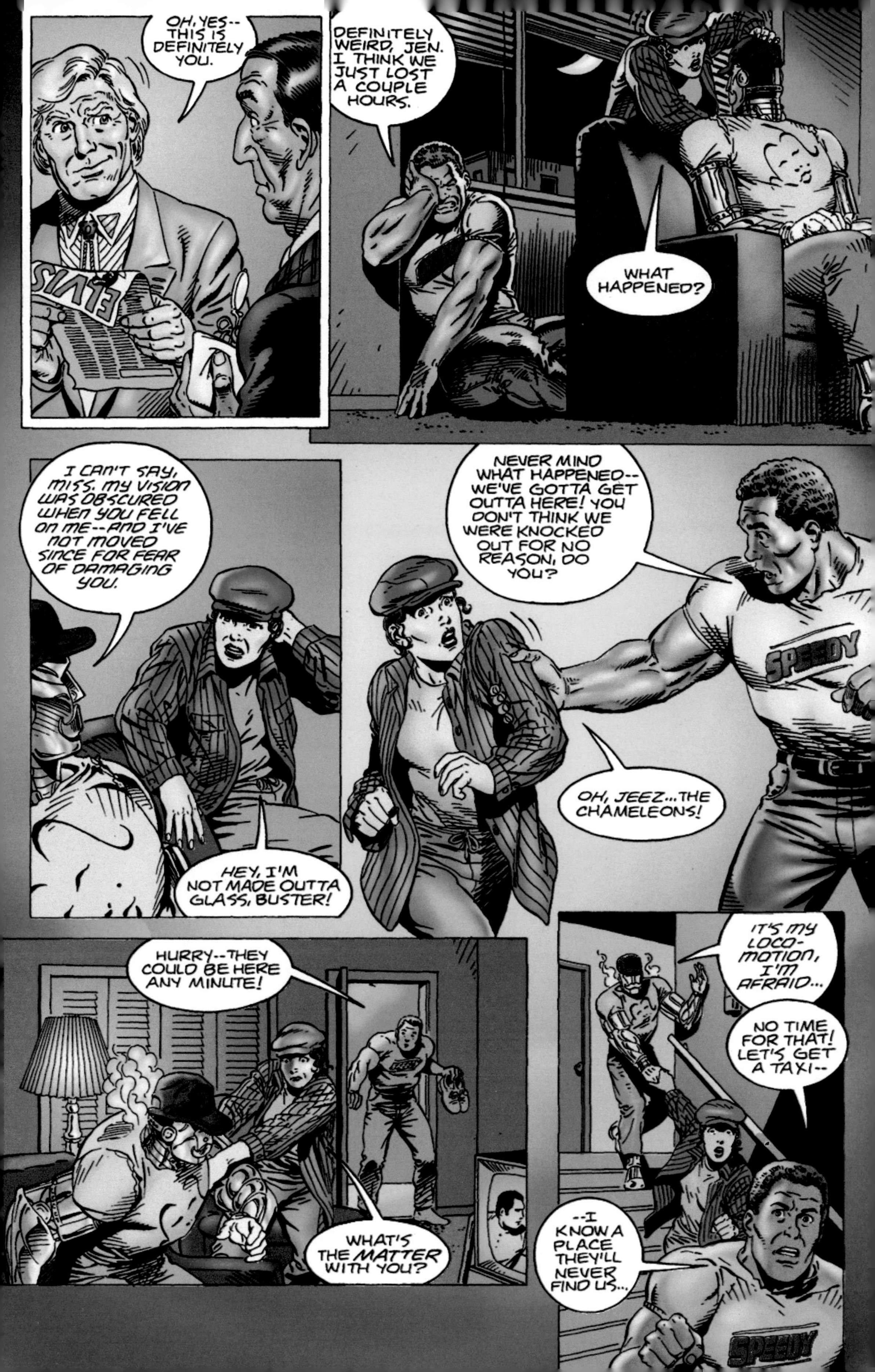
OH, YES-- THIS IS DEFINITELY YOU.
ELVIS
DEFINITELY WEIRD, JEN. I THINK WE JUST LOST A COUPLE HOURS.
WHAT HAPPENED?
I CAN'T SAY, MISS. MY VISION WAS OBSCURED WHEN YOU FELL ON ME--AND I'VE NOT MOVED SINCE FOR FEAR OF DAMAGING YOU.
HEY, I'M NOT MADE OUTTA GLASS, BUSTER!
NEVER MIND WHAT HAPPENED-- WE'VE GOTTA GET OUTTA HERE! YOU DON'T THINK WE WERE KNOCKED OUT FOR NO REASON, DO YOU?
SPEEDY
OH, JEEZ... THE CHAMELEONS!
HURRY--THEY COULD BE HERE ANY MINUTE!
WHAT'S THE MATTER WITH YOU?
IT'S MY LOCO-MOTION, I'M AFRAID...
NO TIME FOR THAT! LET'S GET A TAXI--
--I KNOW A PLACE THEY'LL NEVER FIND US...
SPEEDY

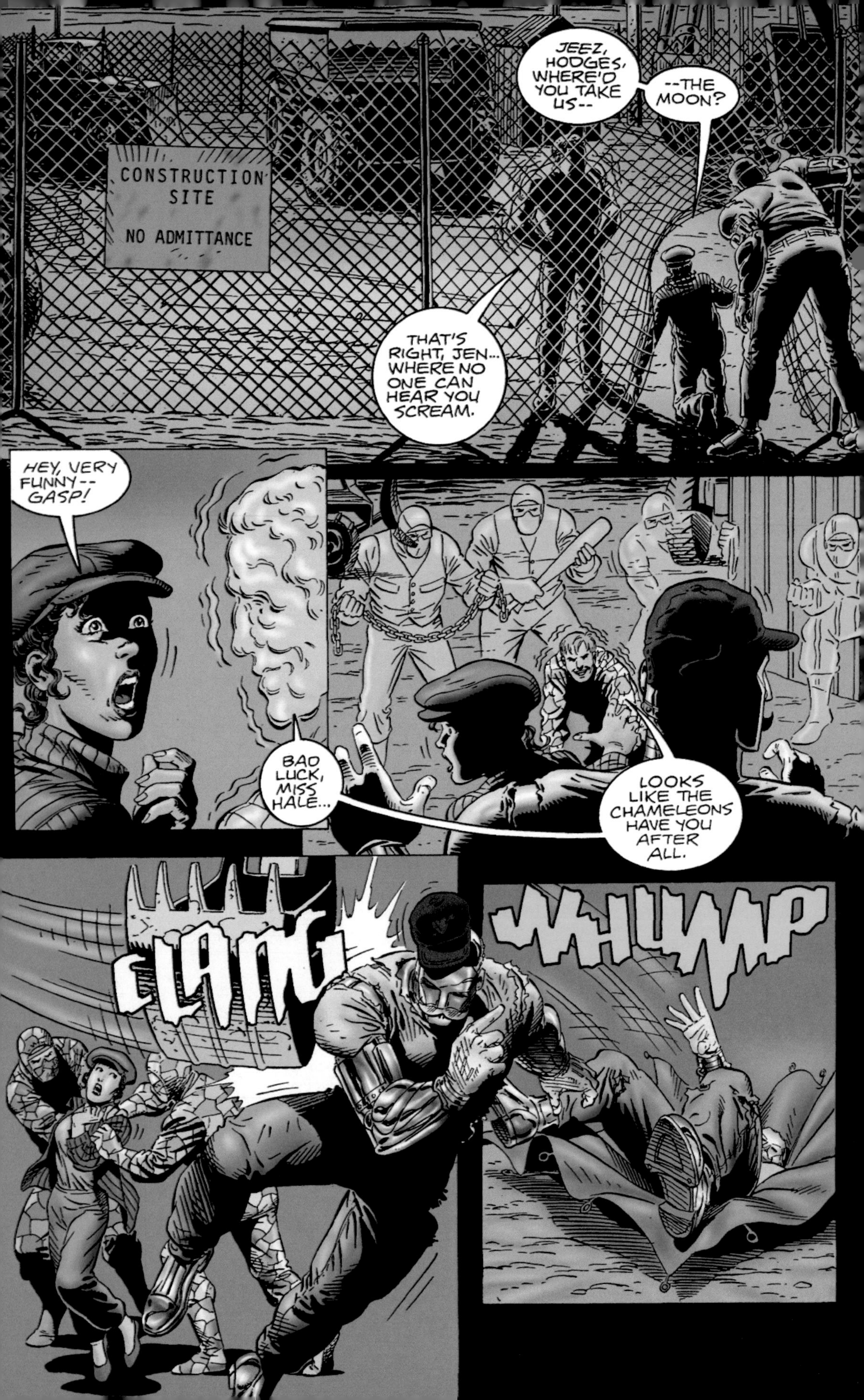
JEEZ, HODGES, WHERE'D YOU TAKE US--
--THE MOON?
CONSTRUCTION SITE
NO ADMITTANCE
THAT'S RIGHT, JEN... WHERE NO ONE CAN HEAR YOU SCREAM.
HEY, VERY FUNNY-- GASP!
BAD LUCK, MISS HALE...
LOOKS LIKE THE CHAMELEONS HAVE YOU AFTER ALL.
CLANG
WHUMP

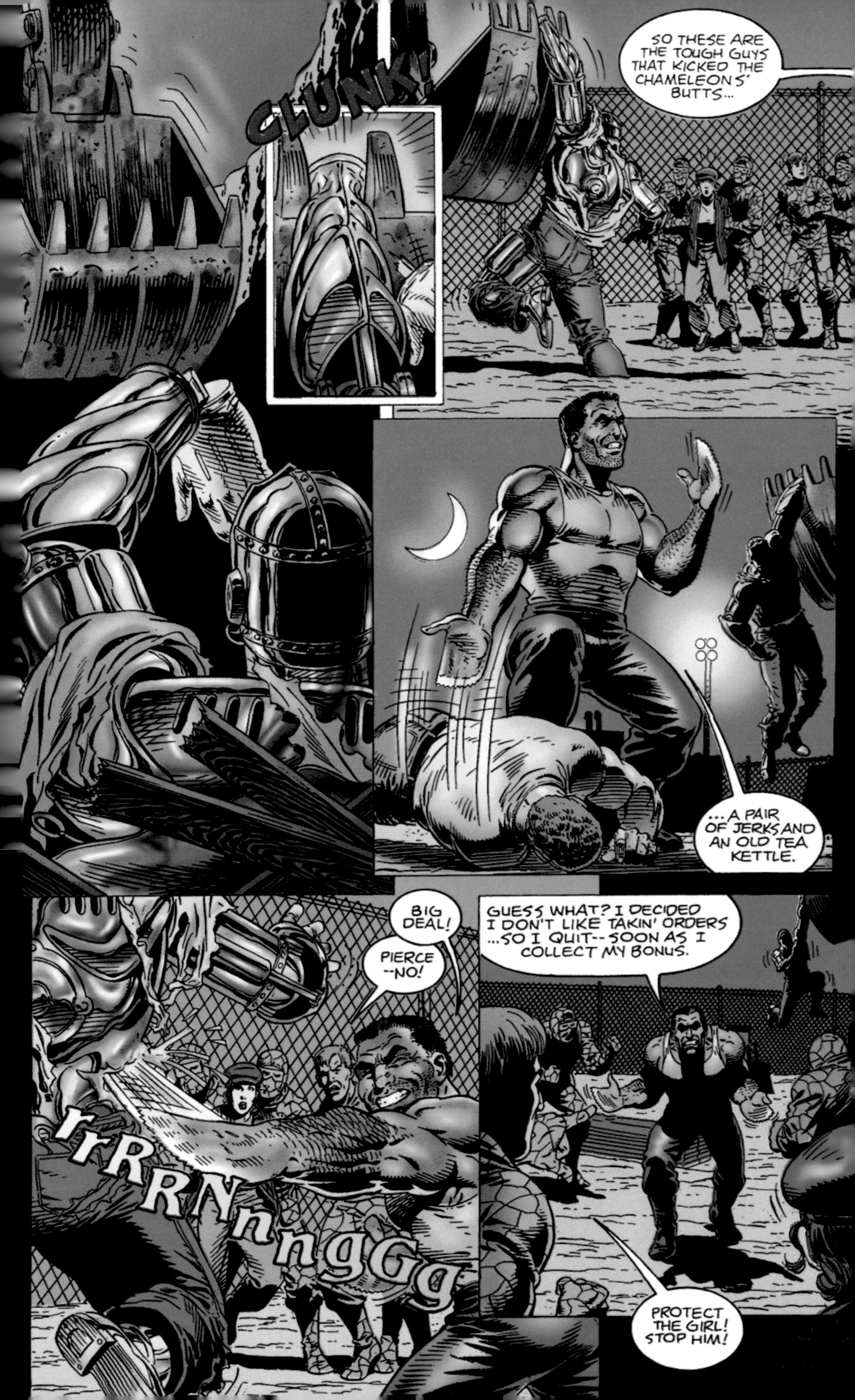
CLUNK!
SO THESE ARE THE TOUGH GUYS THAT KICKED THE CHAMELEONS' BUTTS...
...A PAIR OF JERKS AND AN OLD TEA KETTLE.
BIG DEAL!
PIERCE --NO!
rrRRNnngGg
GUESS WHAT? I DECIDED I DON'T LIKE TAKIN' ORDERS ...SO I QUIT-- SOON AS I COLLECT MY BONUS.
PROTECT THE GIRL! STOP HIM!

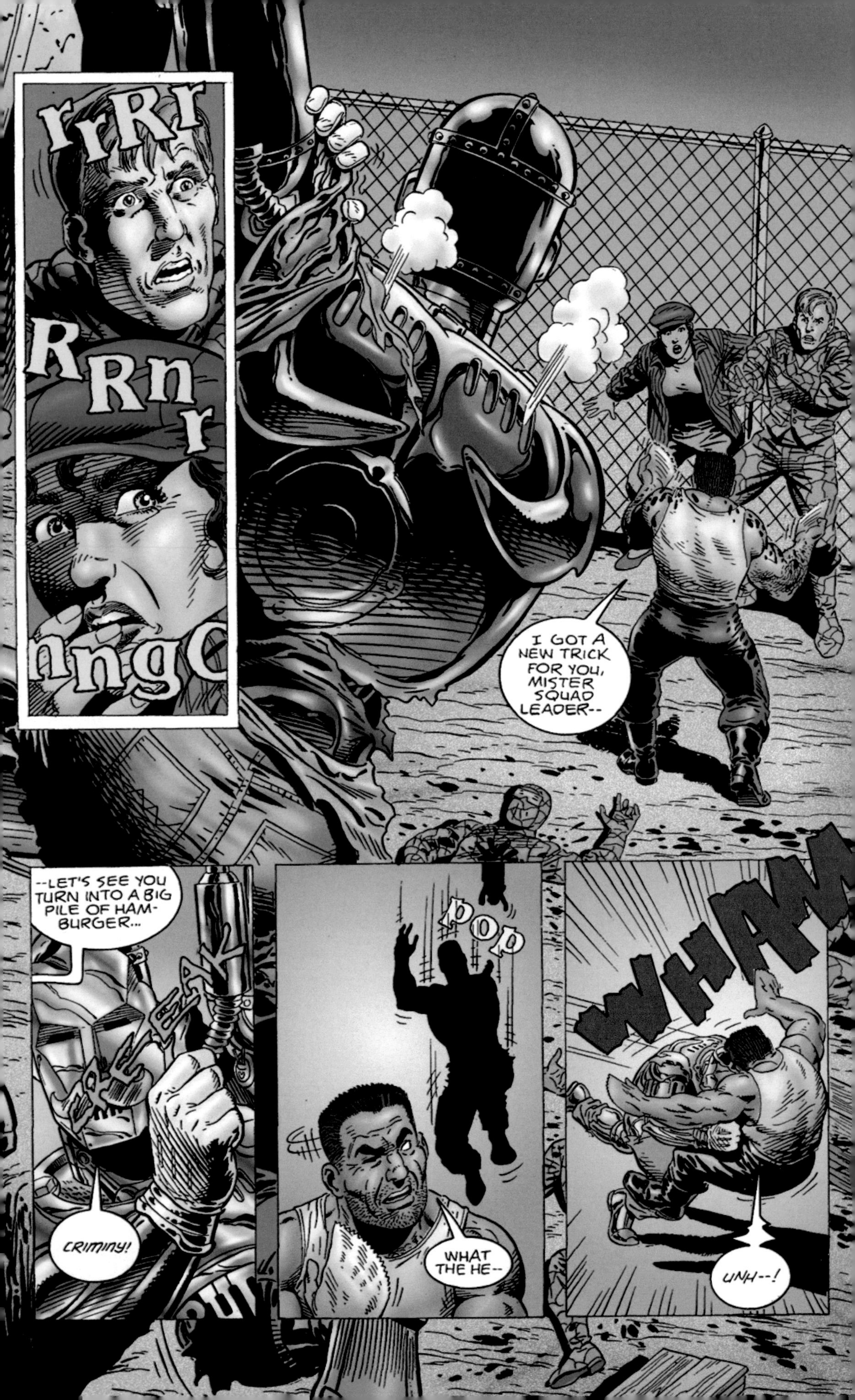

rrRr
RRnr
nngC
I GOT A NEW TRICK FOR YOU, MISTER SQUAD LEADER--
--LET'S SEE YOU TURN INTO A BIG PILE OF HAM-BURGER...
CRIMINY!
POP
WHAT THE HE--
WHAM
UNH--!

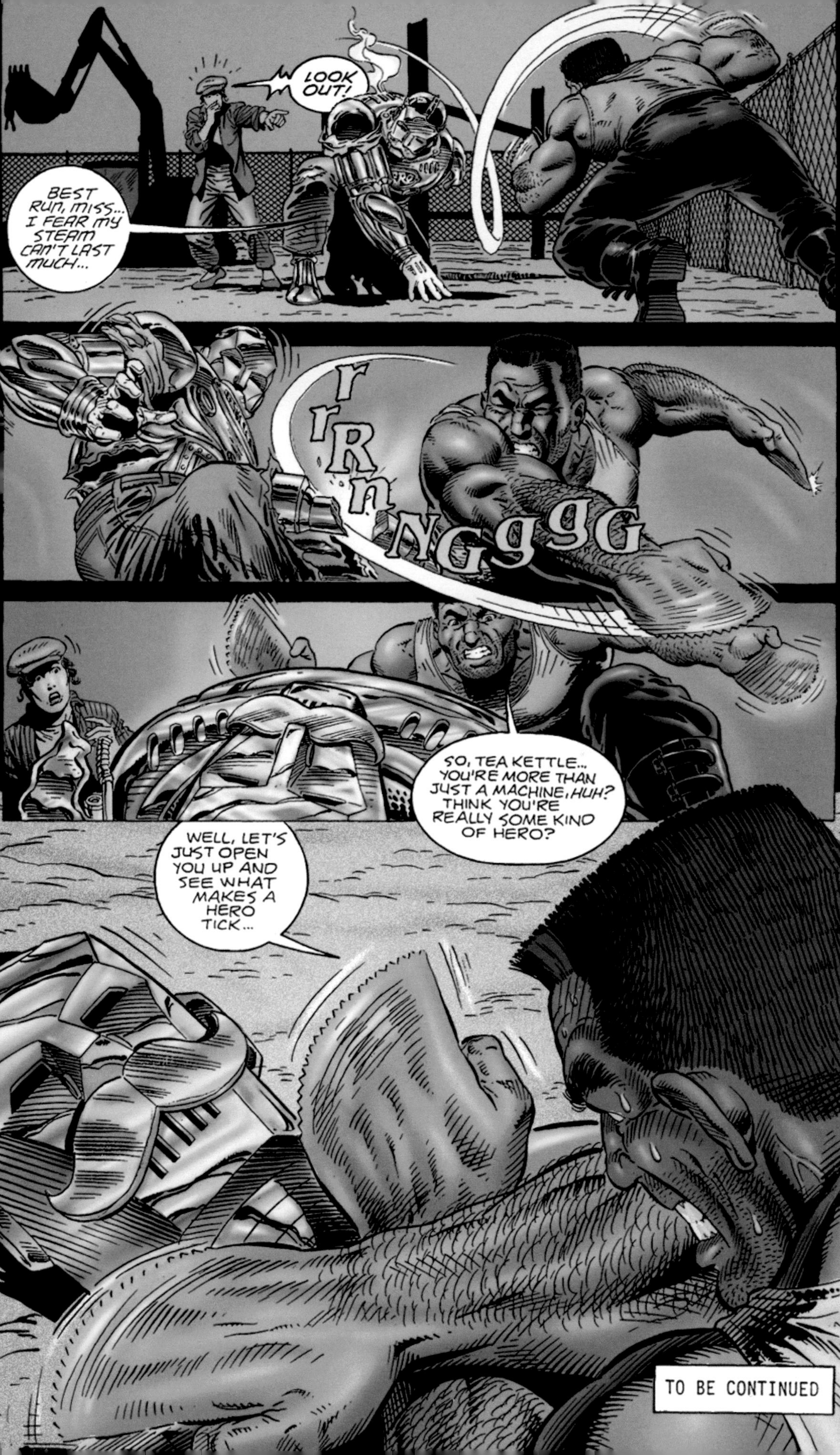
LOOK OUT!
BEST RUN, MISS... I FEAR MY STEAM CAN'T LAST MUCH...
rrRnNGggG
SO, TEA KETTLE... YOU'RE MORE THAN JUST A MACHINE, HUH? THINK YOU'RE REALLY SOME KIND OF HERO?
WELL, LET'S JUST OPEN YOU UP AND SEE WHAT MAKES A HERO TICK...
TO BE CONTINUED

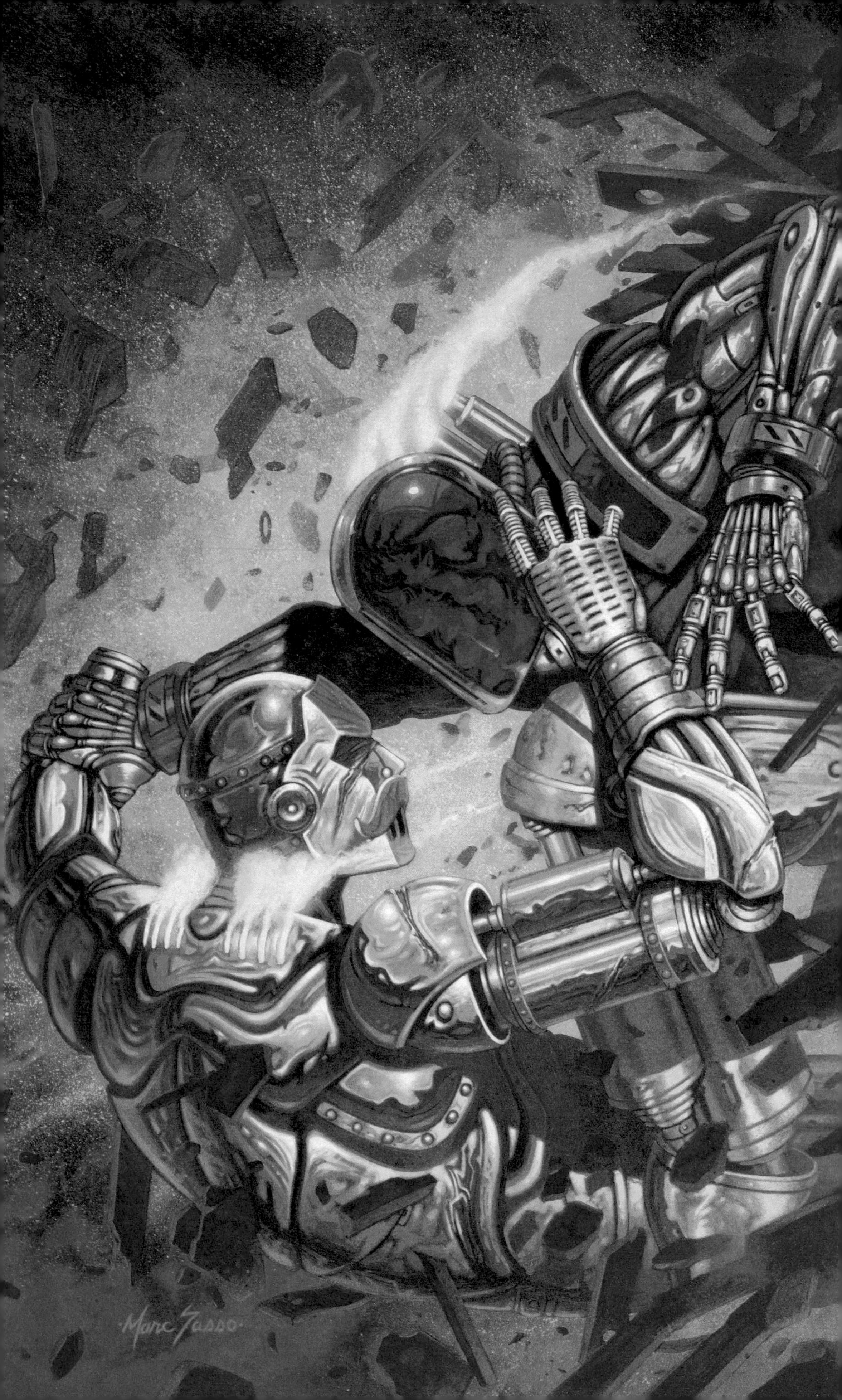
Marc Sasso

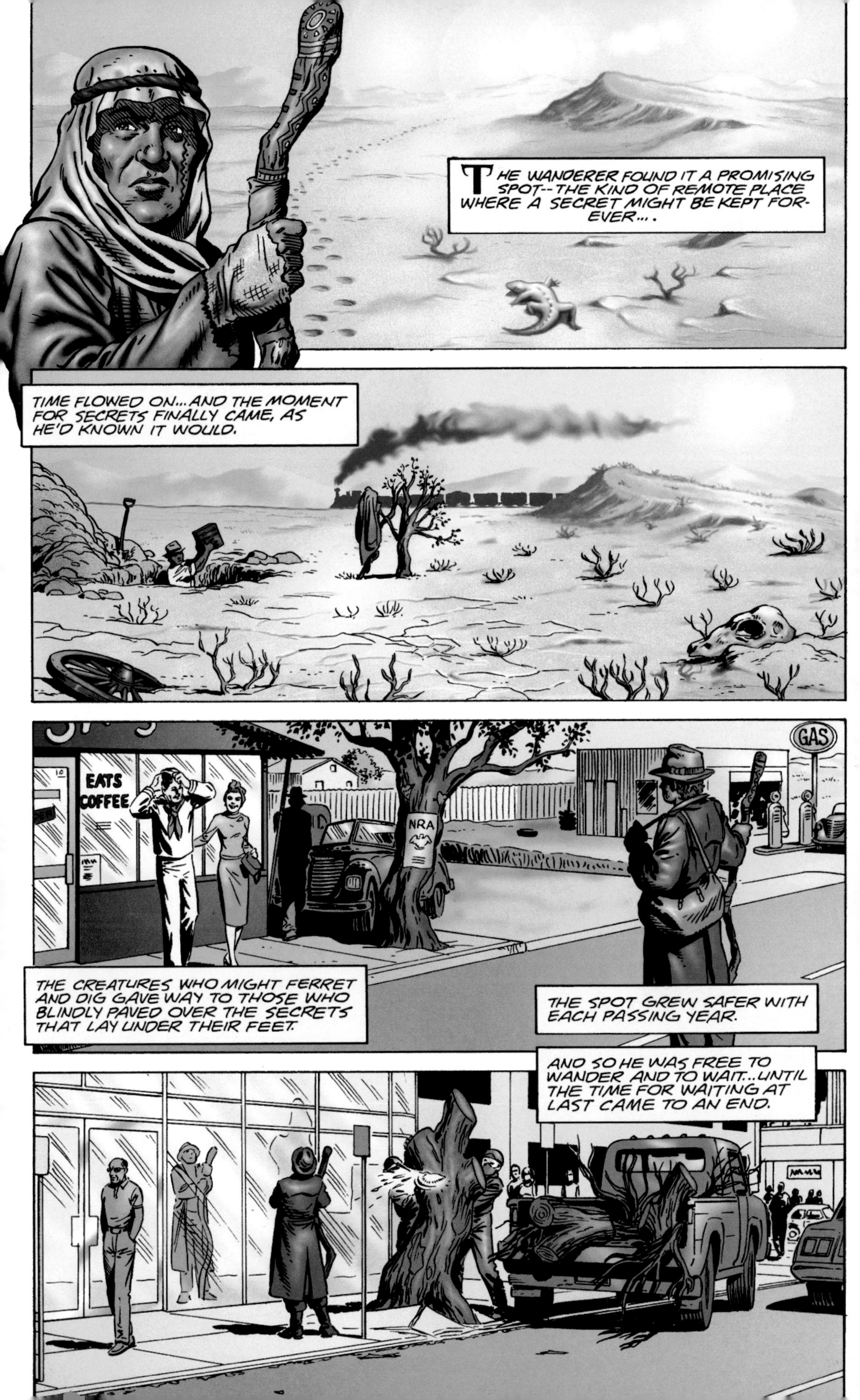
THE WANDERER FOUND IT A PROMISING SPOT--THE KIND OF REMOTE PLACE WHERE A SECRET MIGHT BE KEPT FOREVER....
TIME FLOWED ON...AND THE MOMENT FOR SECRETS FINALLY CAME, AS HE'D KNOWN IT WOULD.
EATS
COFFEE
NRA
GAS
THE CREATURES WHO MIGHT FERRET AND DIG GAVE WAY TO THOSE WHO BLINDLY PAVED OVER THE SECRETS THAT LAY UNDER THEIR FEET.
THE SPOT GREW SAFER WITH EACH PASSING YEAR.
AND SO HE WAS FREE TO WANDER AND TO WAIT...UNTIL THE TIME FOR WAITING AT LAST CAME TO AN END.

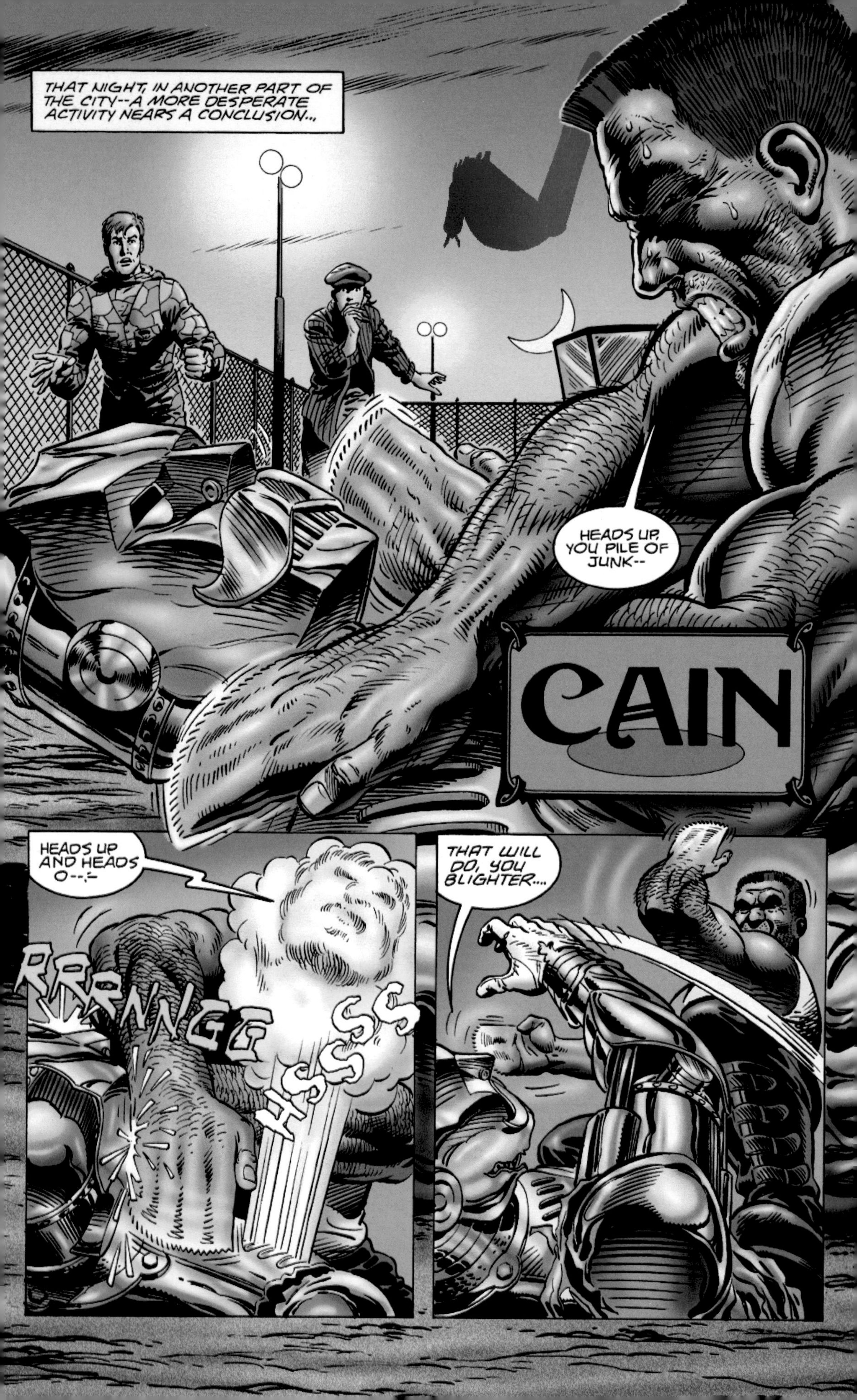
THAT NIGHT, IN ANOTHER PART OF THE CITY--A MORE DESPERATE ACTIVITY NEARS A CONCLUSION...
HEADS UP, YOU PILE OF JUNK--
CAIN
HEADS UP AND HEADS O--:-
RRRNNGG
HSSSS
THAT WILL DO, YOU BLIGHTER....

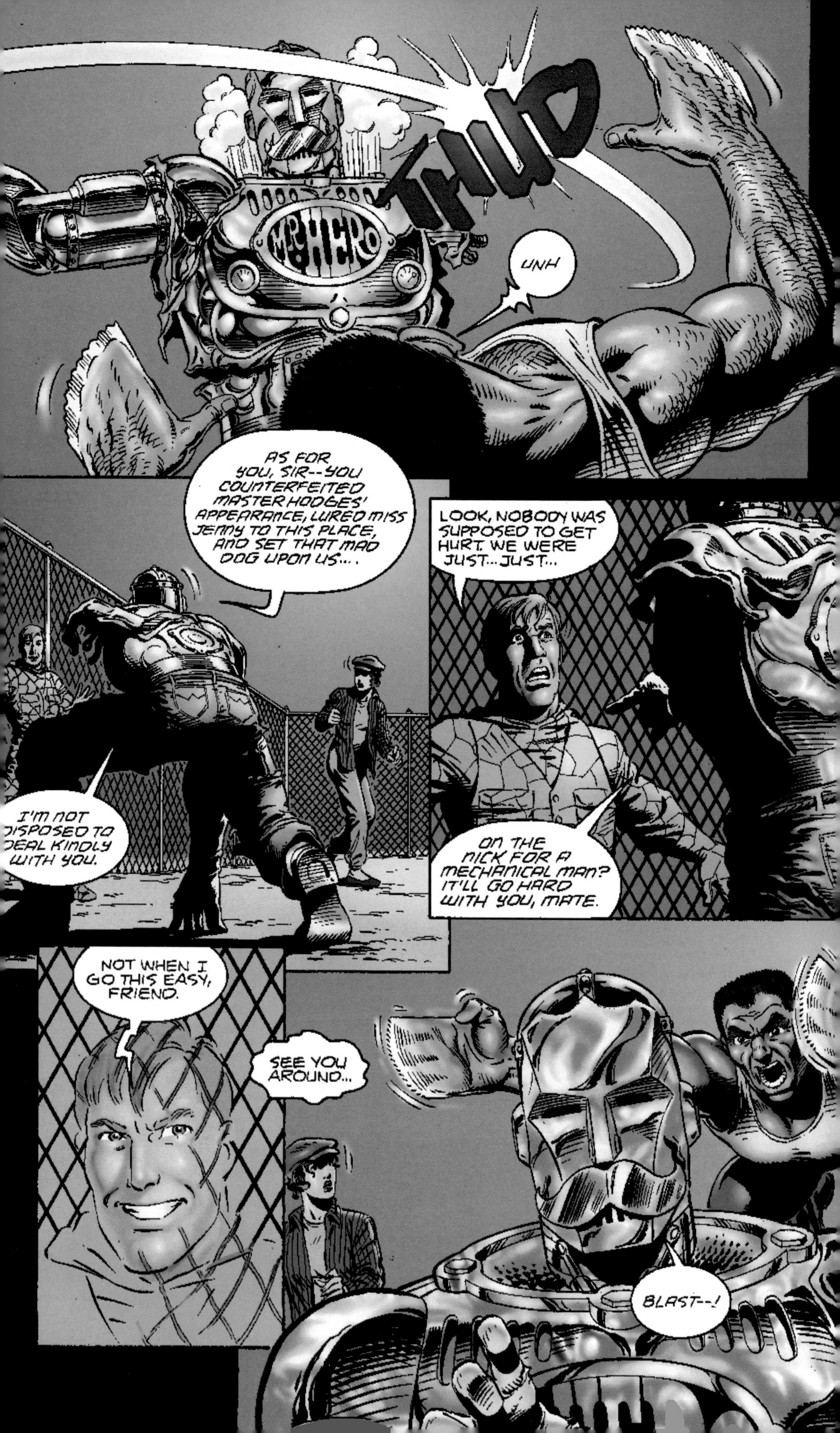
THUD
UNH
AS FOR YOU, SIR--YOU COUNTERFEITED MASTER HODGES' APPEARANCE, LURED MISS JENNY TO THIS PLACE, AND SET THAT MAD DOG UPON US....
I'M NOT DISPOSED TO DEAL KINDLY WITH YOU.
LOOK, NOBODY WAS SUPPOSED TO GET HURT. WE WERE JUST...JUST...
ON THE NICK FOR A MECHANICAL MAN? IT'LL GO HARD WITH YOU, MATE.
NOT WHEN I GO THIS EASY, FRIEND.
SEE YOU AROUND...
BLAST--!

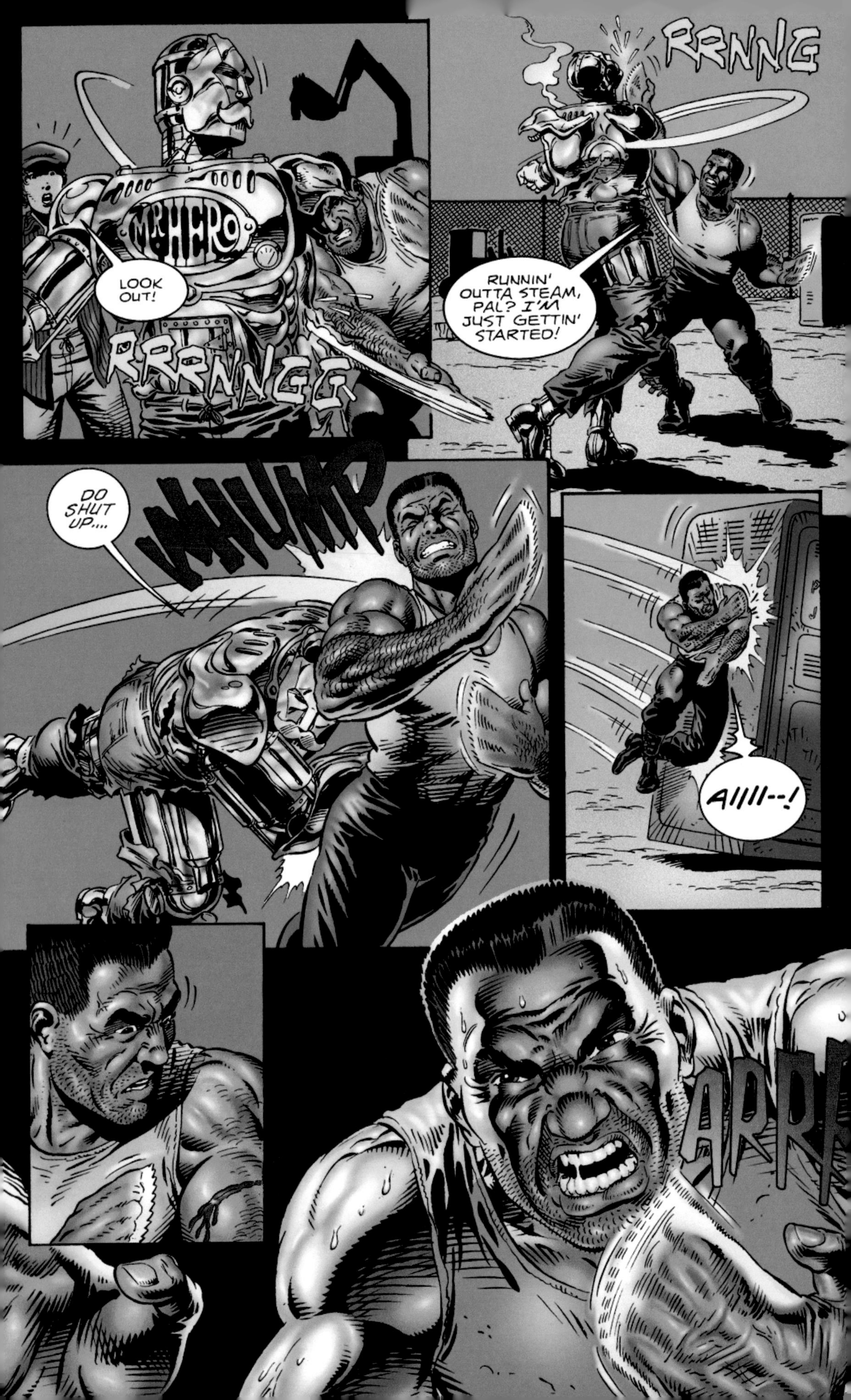
LOOK OUT!
RRRNNGG
RRNNG
RUNNIN' OUTTA STEAM, PAL? I'M JUST GETTIN' STARTED!
DO SHUT UP....
WHUMP
AIIII--!
ARR

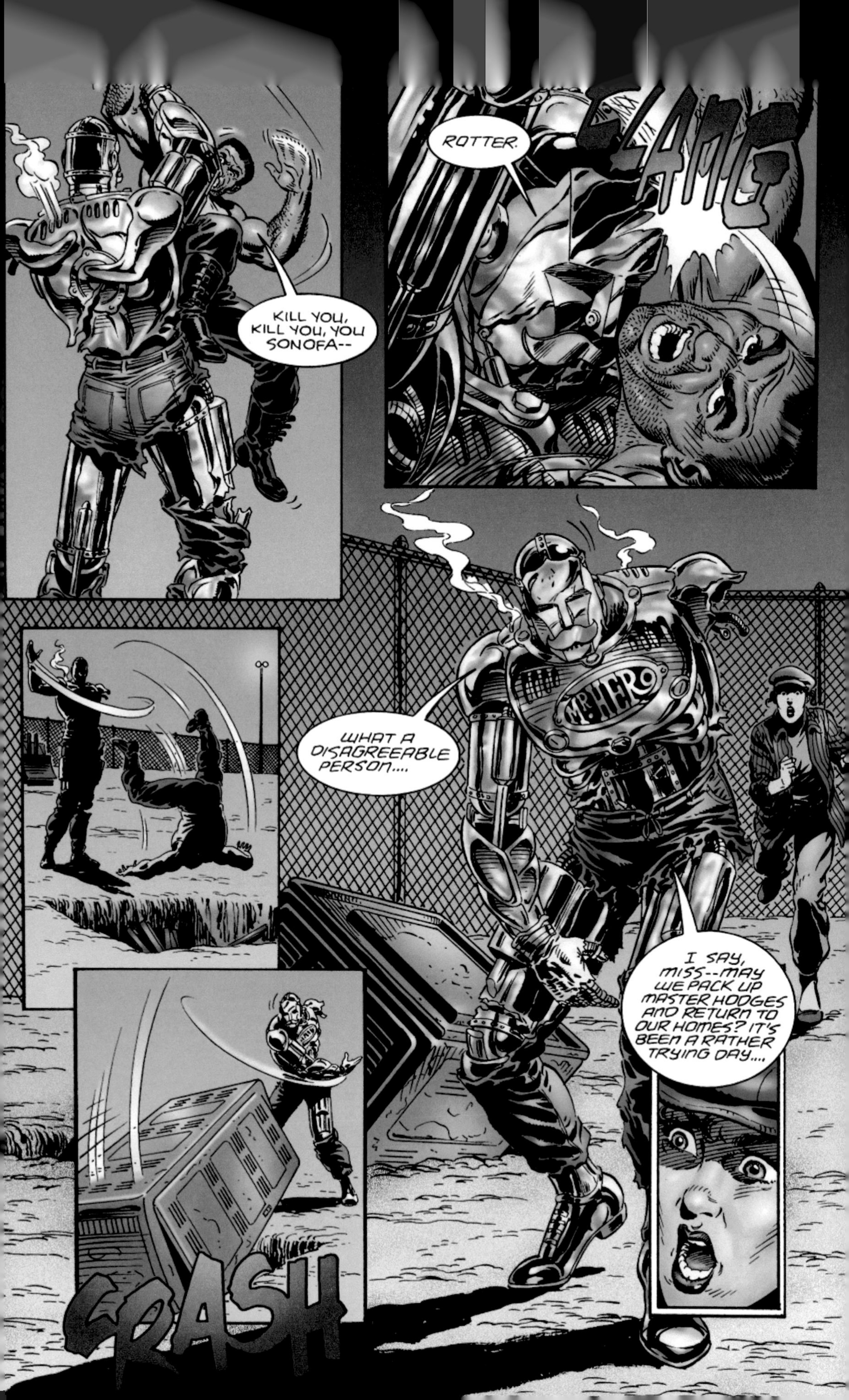
KILL YOU, KILL YOU, YOU SONOFA--
ROTTER.
CLANG
WHAT A DISAGREEABLE PERSON....
CRASH
I SAY, MISS--MAY WE PACK UP MASTER HODGES AND RETURN TO OUR HOMES? IT'S BEEN A RATHER TRYING DAY....

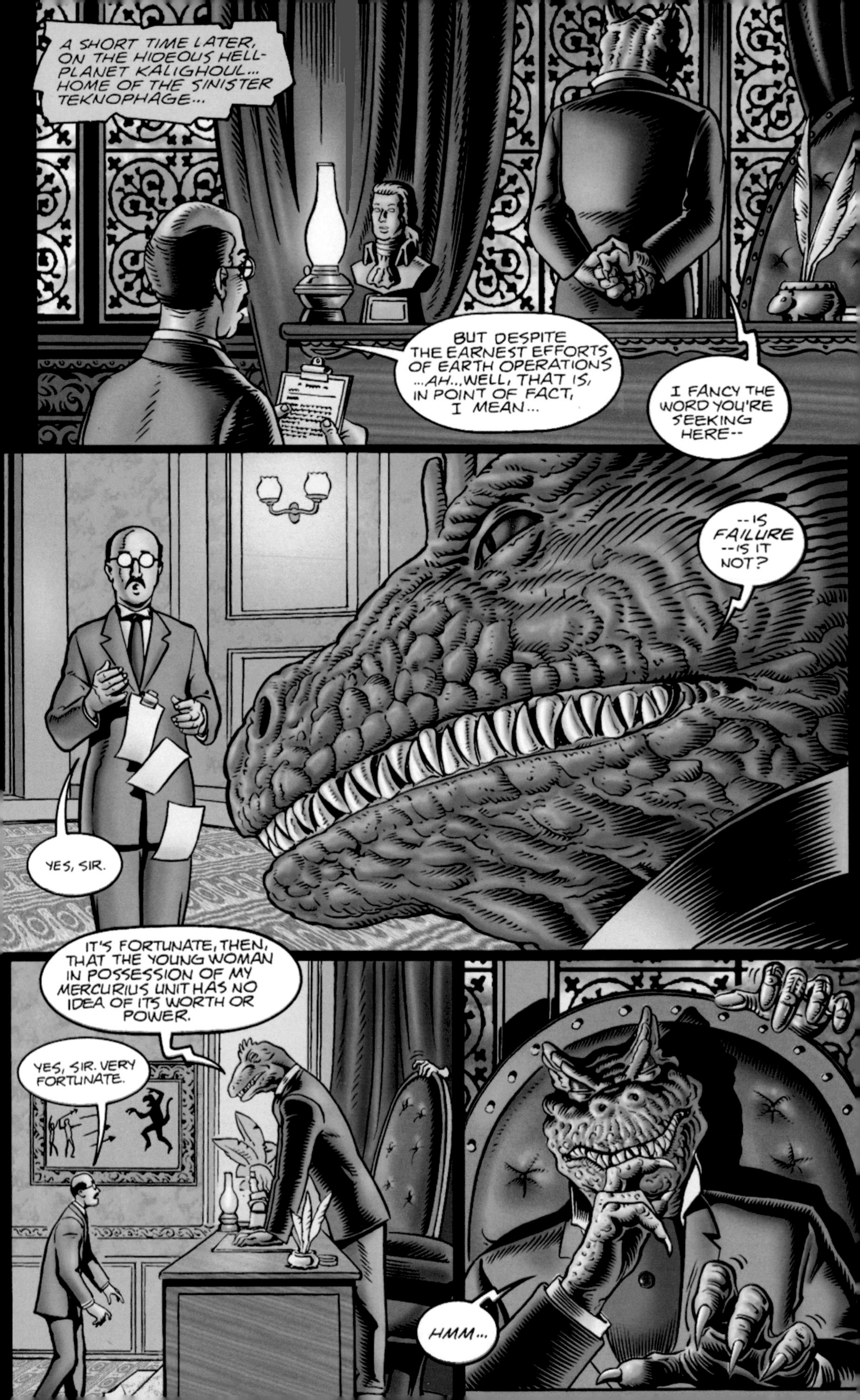
A SHORT TIME LATER, ON THE HIDEOUS HELL-PLANET KALIGHOUL... HOME OF THE SINISTER TEKNOPHAGE...
BUT DESPITE THE EARNEST EFFORTS OF EARTH OPERATIONS ...AH...WELL, THAT IS, IN POINT OF FACT, I MEAN...
I FANCY THE WORD YOU'RE SEEKING HERE--
--IS FAILURE --IS IT NOT?
YES, SIR.
IT'S FORTUNATE, THEN, THAT THE YOUNG WOMAN IN POSSESSION OF MY MERCURIUS UNIT HAS NO IDEA OF ITS WORTH OR POWER.
YES, SIR. VERY FORTUNATE.
HMM...

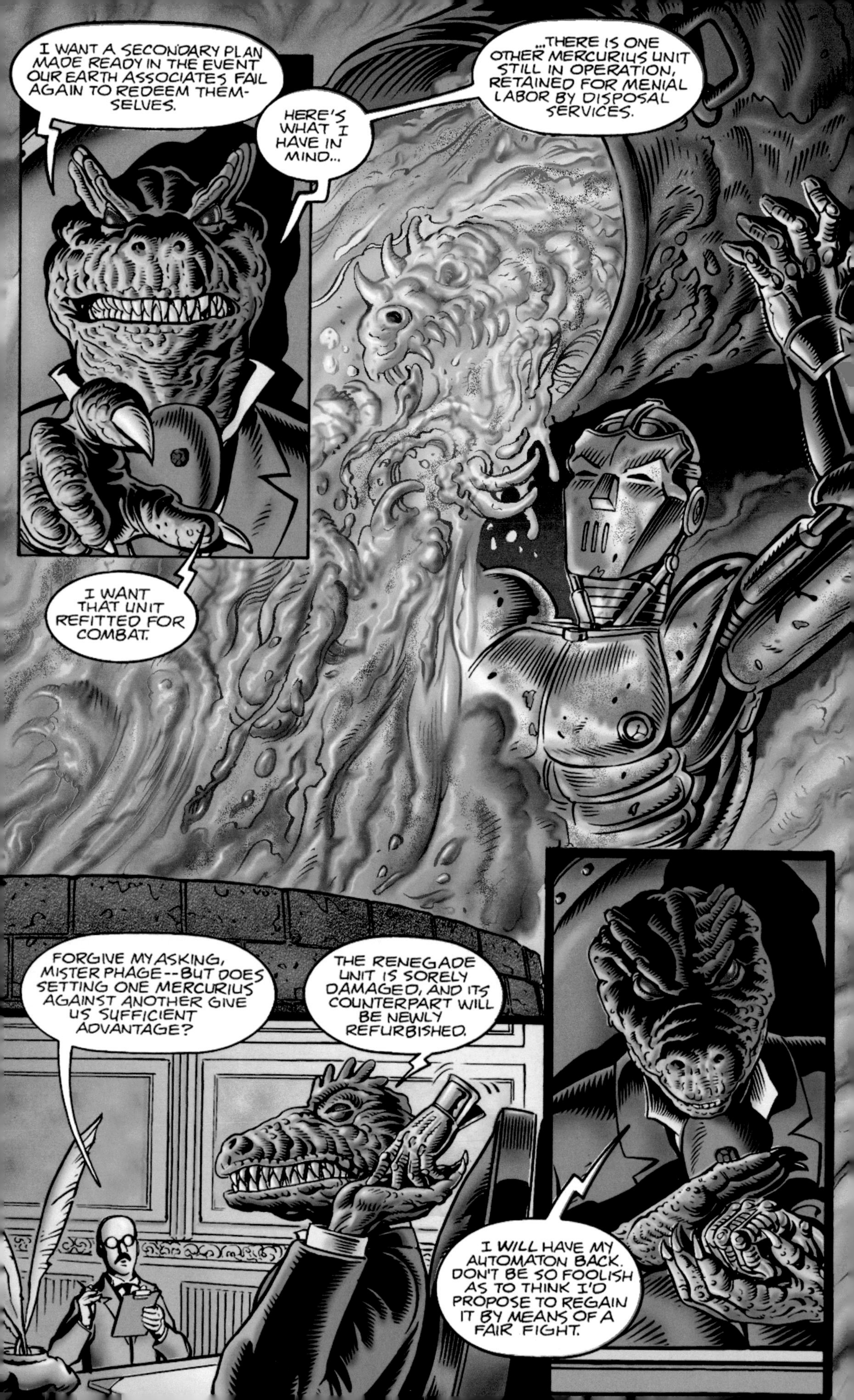
I WANT A SECONDARY PLAN MADE READY IN THE EVENT OUR EARTH ASSOCIATES FAIL AGAIN TO REDEEM THEM-SELVES.
HERE'S WHAT I HAVE IN MIND...
...THERE IS ONE OTHER MERCURIUS UNIT STILL IN OPERATION, RETAINED FOR MENIAL LABOR BY DISPOSAL SERVICES.
I WANT THAT UNIT REFITTED FOR COMBAT.
FORGIVE MY ASKING, MISTER PHAGE--BUT DOES SETTING ONE MERCURIUS AGAINST ANOTHER GIVE US SUFFICIENT ADVANTAGE?
THE RENEGADE UNIT IS SORELY DAMAGED, AND ITS COUNTERPART WILL BE NEWLY REFURBISHED.
I WILL HAVE MY AUTOMATON BACK. DON'T BE SO FOOLISH AS TO THINK I'D PROPOSE TO REGAIN IT BY MEANS OF A FAIR FIGHT.

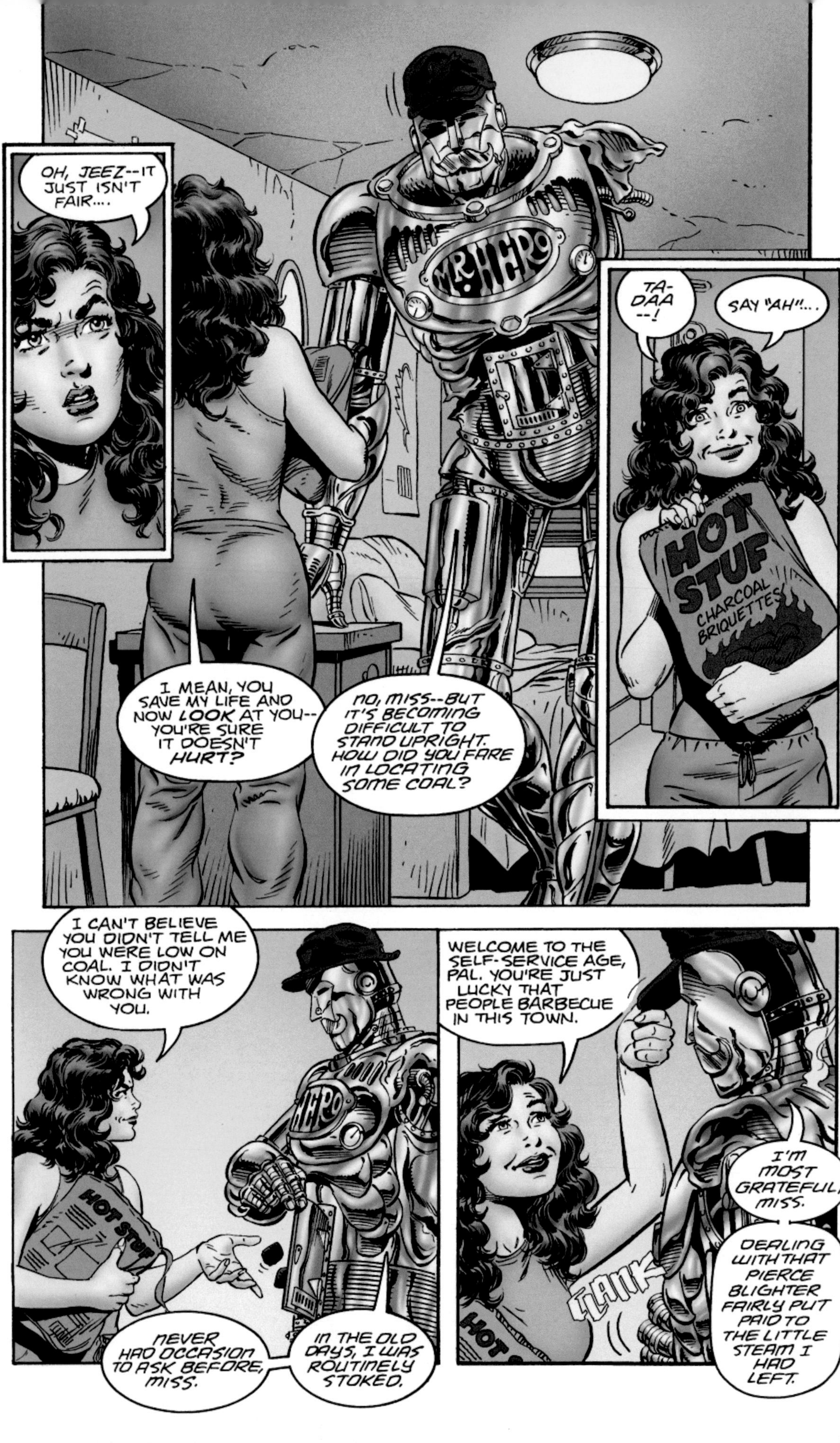
OH, JEEZ--IT JUST ISN'T FAIR....
I MEAN, YOU SAVE MY LIFE AND NOW LOOK AT YOU--YOU'RE SURE IT DOESN'T HURT?
NO, MISS--BUT IT'S BECOMING DIFFICULT TO STAND UPRIGHT. HOW DID YOU FARE IN LOCATING SOME COAL?
TA-DAA--!
SAY "AH"!...
HOT STUF CHARCOAL BRIQUETTES
I CAN'T BELIEVE YOU DIDN'T TELL ME YOU WERE LOW ON COAL. I DIDN'T KNOW WHAT WAS WRONG WITH YOU.
NEVER HAD OCCASION TO ASK BEFORE, MISS.
IN THE OLD DAYS, I WAS ROUTINELY STOKED.
WELCOME TO THE SELF-SERVICE AGE, PAL. YOU'RE JUST LUCKY THAT PEOPLE BARBECUE IN THIS TOWN.
CLANK
I'M MOST GRATEFUL, MISS.
DEALING WITH THAT PIERCE BLIGHTER FAIRLY PUT PAID TO THE LITTLE STEAM I HAD LEFT.

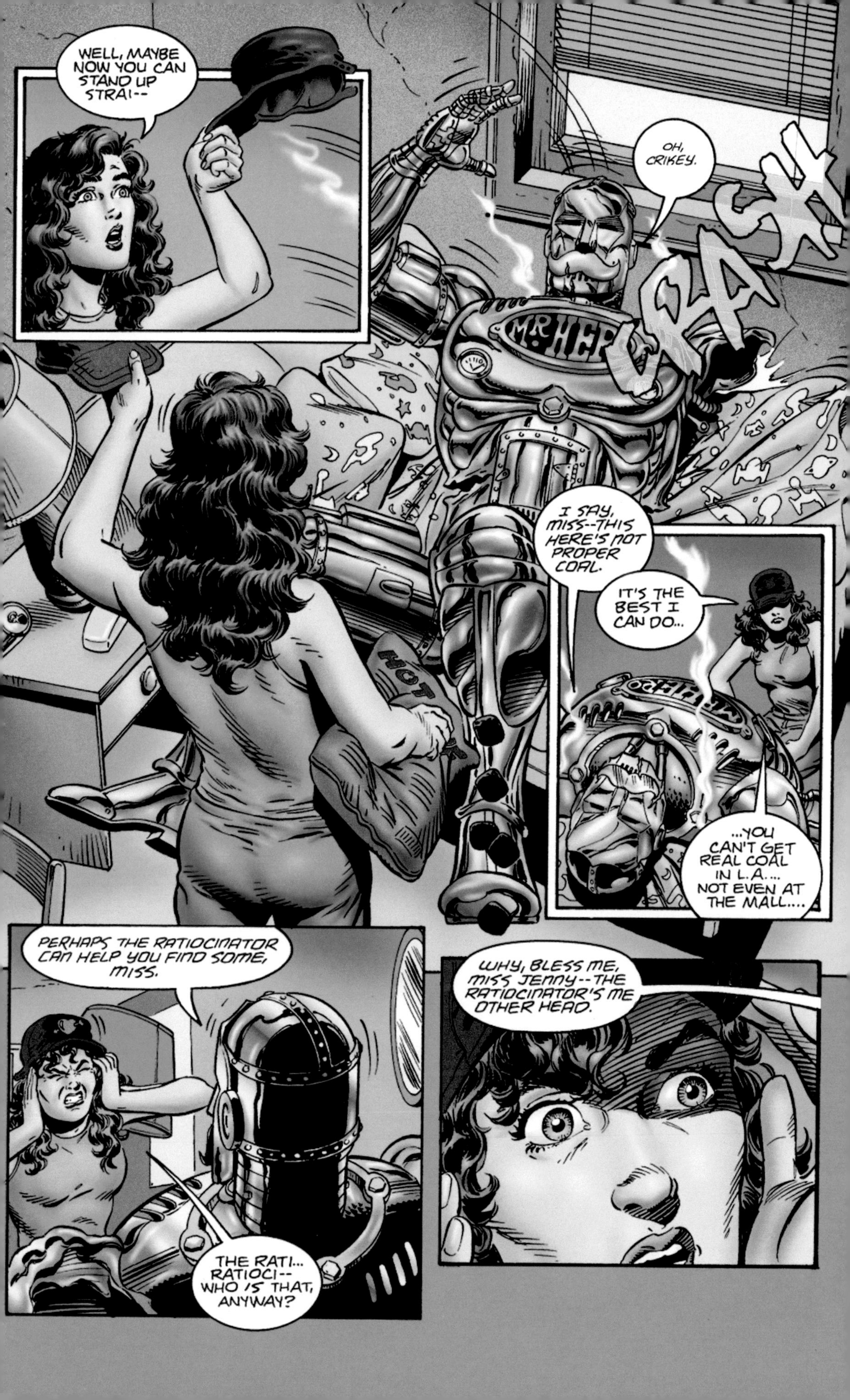
WELL, MAYBE NOW YOU CAN STAND UP STRAI--
OH, CRIKEY.
CRACK
MR. HEP
I SAY, MISS--THIS HERE'S NOT PROPER COAL.
IT'S THE BEST I CAN DO...
...YOU CAN'T GET REAL COAL IN L.A.... NOT EVEN AT THE MALL....
HOT
PERHAPS THE RATIOCINATOR CAN HELP YOU FIND SOME, MISS.
THE RATI... RATIOCI-- WHO IS THAT, ANYWAY?
WHY, BLESS ME, MISS JENNY--THE RATIOCINATOR'S ME OTHER HEAD.

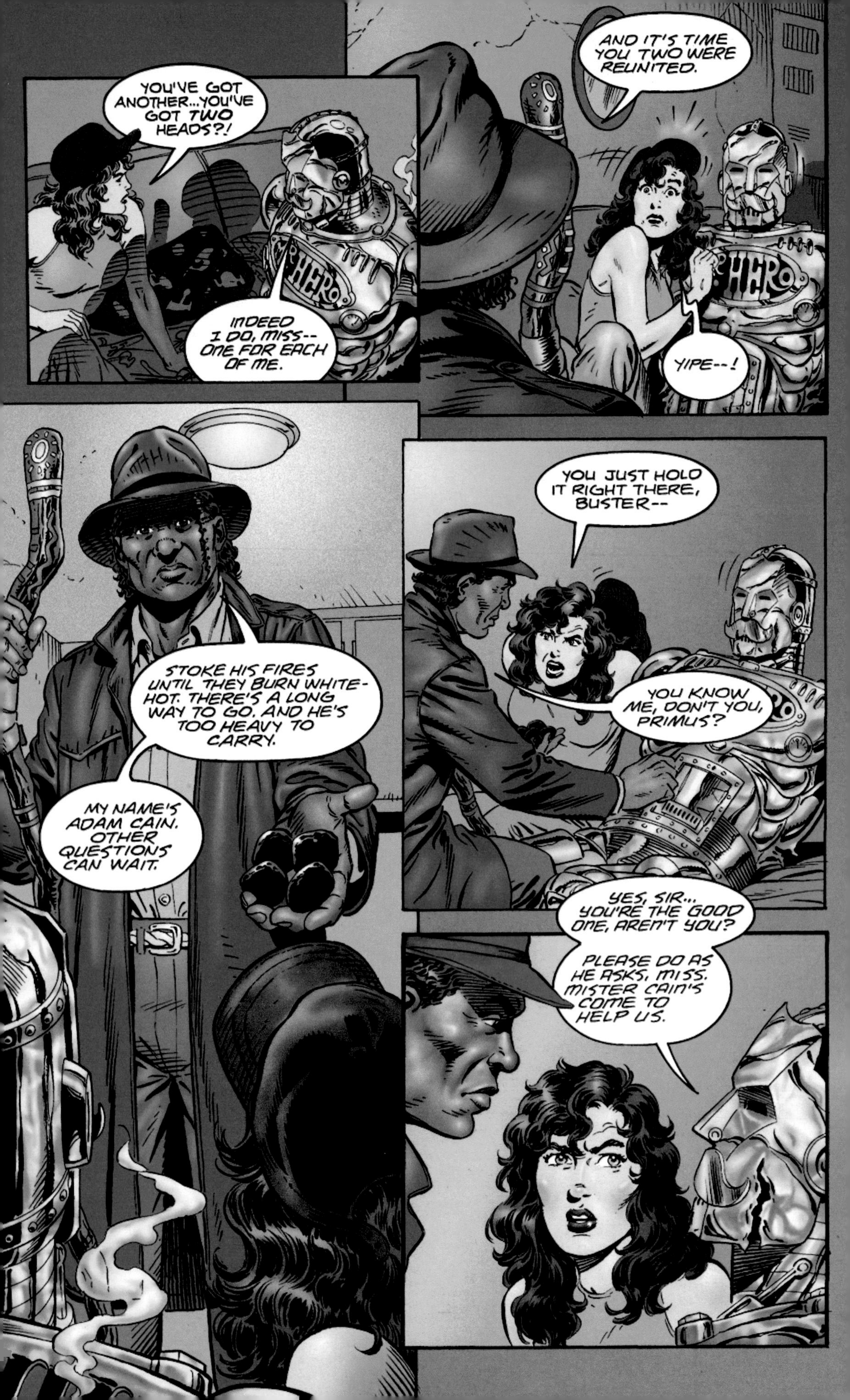
YOU'VE GOT ANOTHER...YOU'VE GOT TWO HEADS?!
INDEED I DO, MISS-- ONE FOR EACH OF ME.
AND IT'S TIME YOU TWO WERE REUNITED.
YIPE--!
STOKE HIS FIRES UNTIL THEY BURN WHITE-HOT. THERE'S A LONG WAY TO GO. AND HE'S TOO HEAVY TO CARRY.
MY NAME'S ADAM CAIN. OTHER QUESTIONS CAN WAIT.
YOU JUST HOLD IT RIGHT THERE, BUSTER--
YOU KNOW ME, DON'T YOU, PRIMUS?
YES, SIR... YOU'RE THE GOOD ONE, AREN'T YOU?
PLEASE DO AS HE ASKS, MISS. MISTER CAIN'S COME TO HELP US.

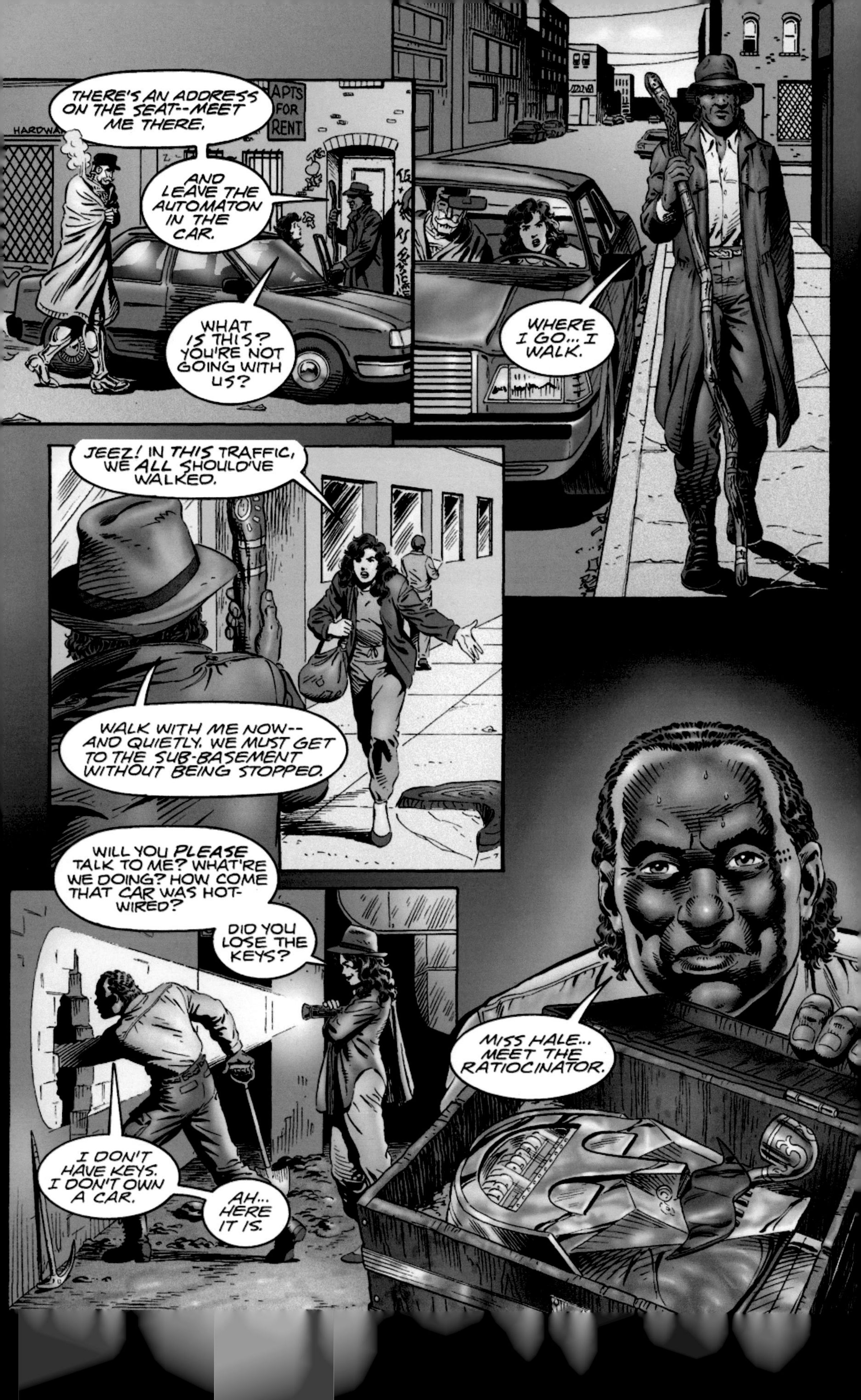
APTS FOR RENT
HARDWA
THERE'S AN ADDRESS ON THE SEAT--MEET ME THERE.
AND LEAVE THE AUTOMATON IN THE CAR.
WHAT IS THIS? YOU'RE NOT GOING WITH US?
WHERE I GO... I WALK.
JEEZ! IN THIS TRAFFIC, WE ALL SHOULD'VE WALKED.
WALK WITH ME NOW-- AND QUIETLY. WE MUST GET TO THE SUB-BASEMENT WITHOUT BEING STOPPED.
WILL YOU PLEASE TALK TO ME? WHAT'RE WE DOING? HOW COME THAT CAR WAS HOT-WIRED?
DID YOU LOSE THE KEYS?
I DON'T HAVE KEYS. I DON'T OWN A CAR.
AH... HERE IT IS.
MISS HALE... MEET THE RATIOCINATOR.

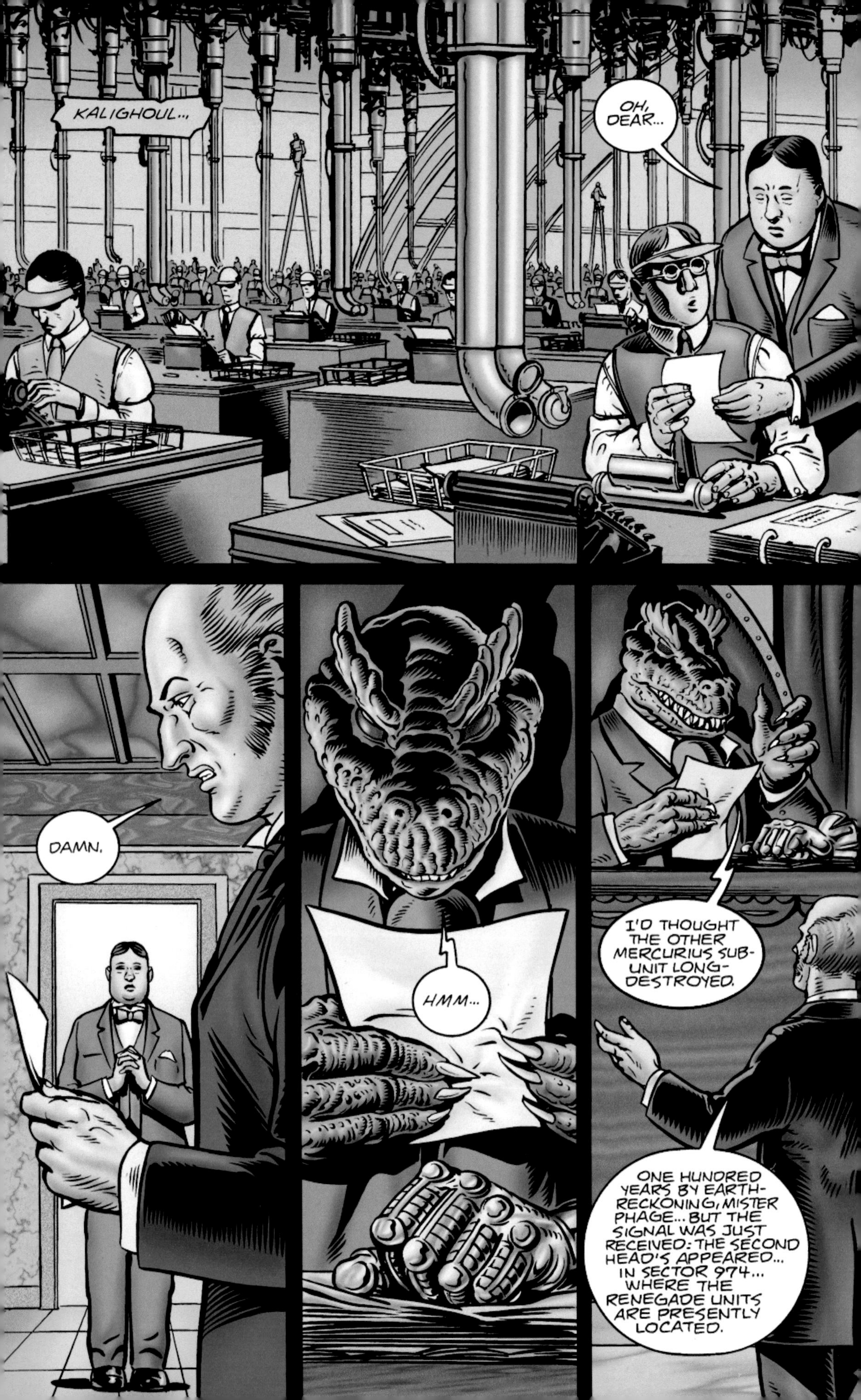
KALIGHOUL...
OH, DEAR...
DAMN.
HMM...
I'D THOUGHT THE OTHER MERCURIUS SUB-UNIT LONG-DESTROYED.
ONE HUNDRED YEARS BY EARTH-RECKONING, MISTER PHAGE... BUT THE SIGNAL WAS JUST RECEIVED: THE SECOND HEAD'S APPEARED... IN SECTOR 974... WHERE THE RENEGADE UNITS ARE PRESENTLY LOCATED.

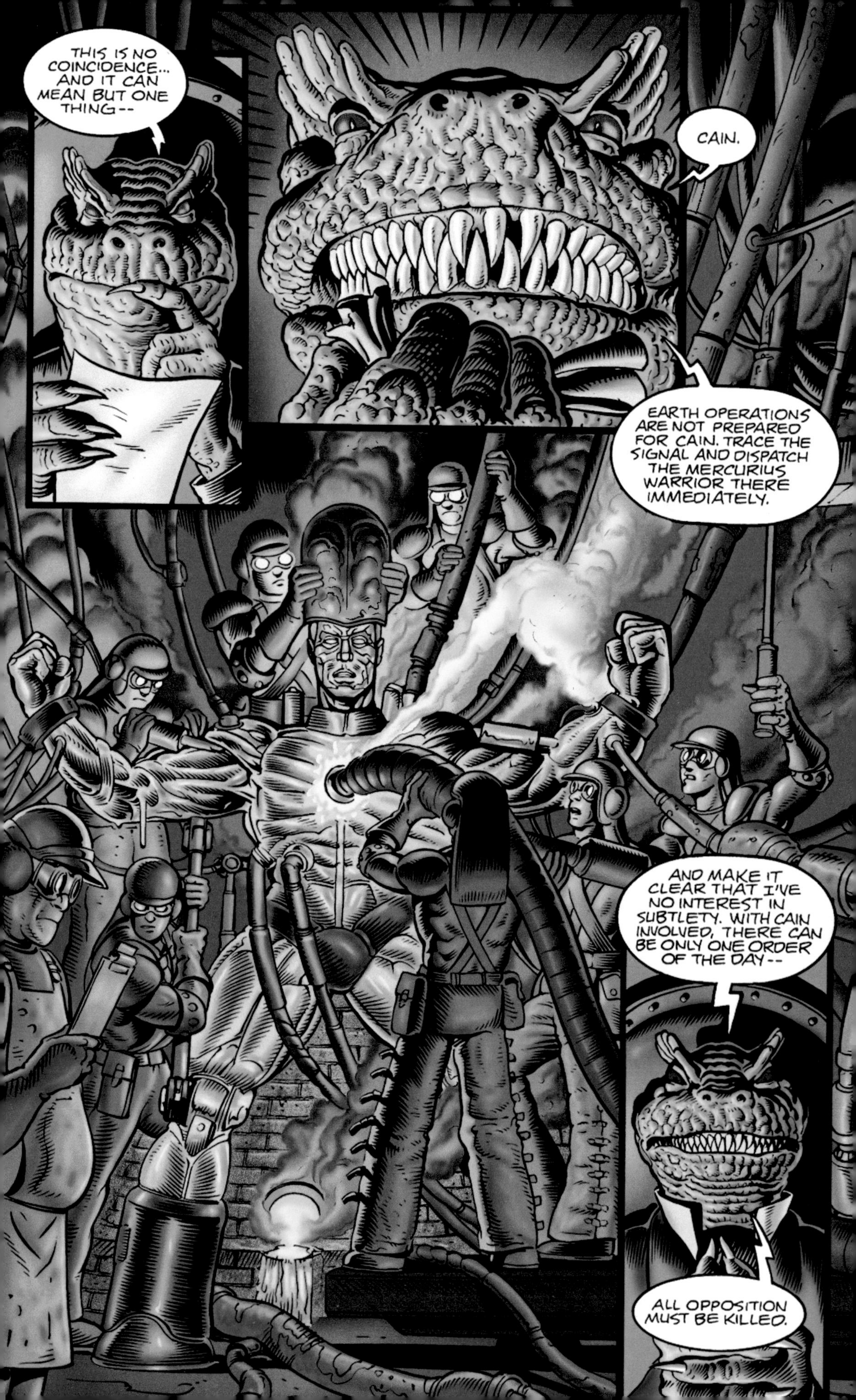
THIS IS NO COINCIDENCE... AND IT CAN MEAN BUT ONE THING--
CAIN.
EARTH OPERATIONS ARE NOT PREPARED FOR CAIN. TRACE THE SIGNAL AND DISPATCH THE MERCURIUS WARRIOR THERE IMMEDIATELY.
AND MAKE IT CLEAR THAT I'VE NO INTEREST IN SUBTLETY. WITH CAIN INVOLVED, THERE CAN BE ONLY ONE ORDER OF THE DAY--
ALL OPPOSITION MUST BE KILLED.

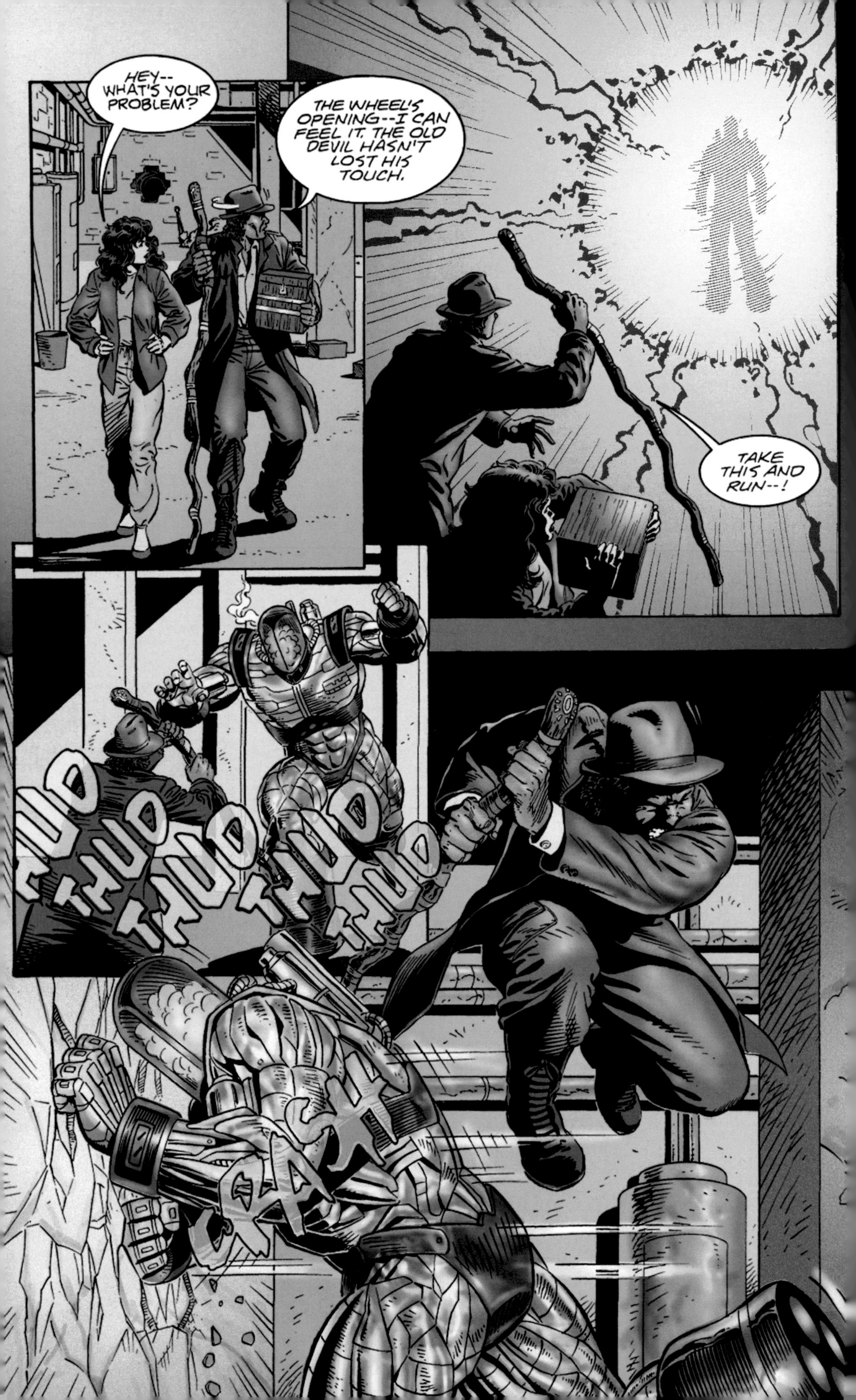
HEY-- WHAT'S YOUR PROBLEM?
THE WHEEL'S OPENING--I CAN FEEL IT. THE OLD DEVIL HASN'T LOST HIS TOUCH.
TAKE THIS AND RUN--!
THUD THUD THUD THUD
CRACK

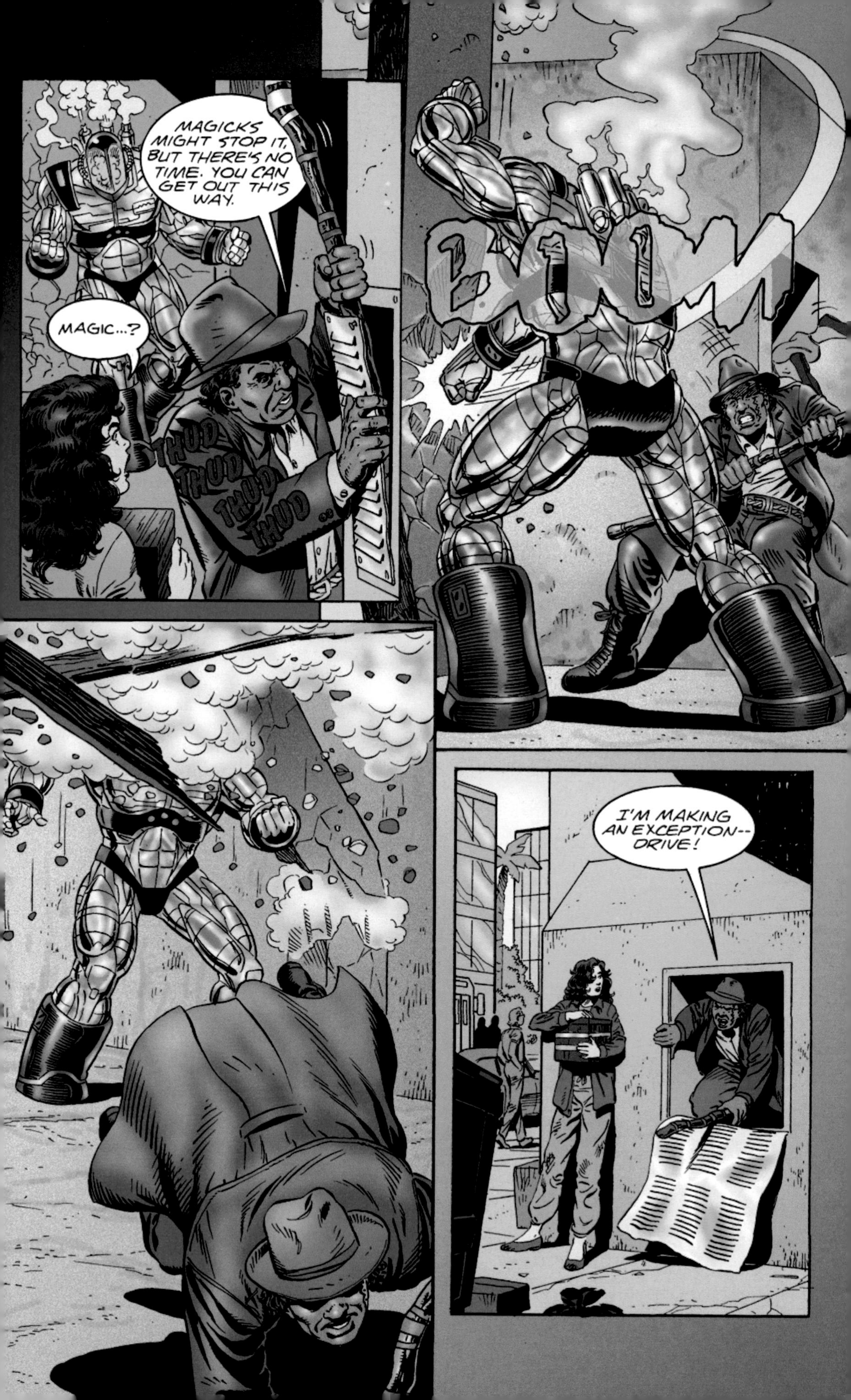
MAGICKS MIGHT STOP IT, BUT THERE'S NO TIME. YOU CAN GET OUT THIS WAY.
MAGIC...?
THUD THUD THUD THUD
ZZTTTM
I'M MAKING AN EXCEPTION-- DRIVE!

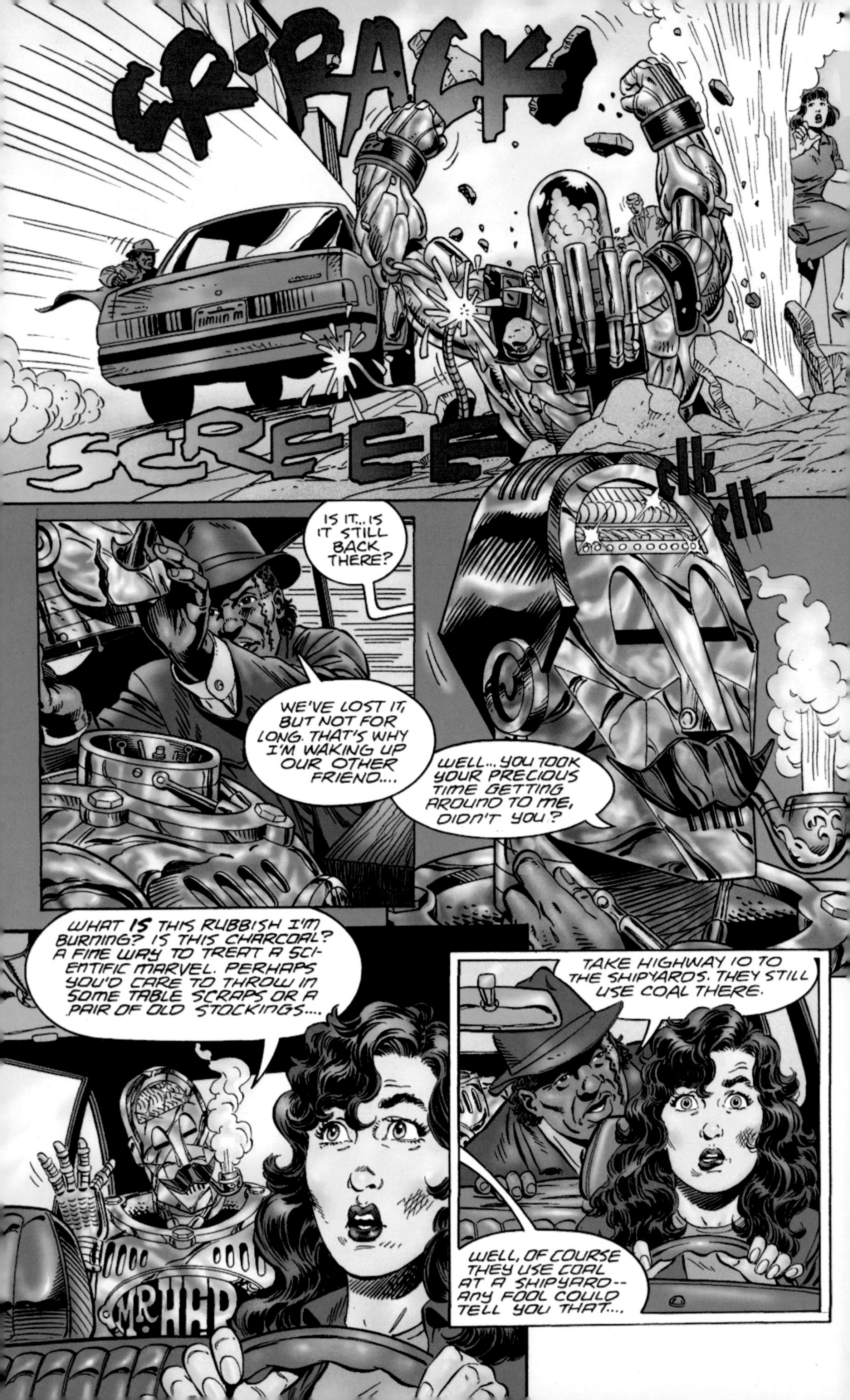
CR-RACK!
SCREEE
IS IT... IS IT STILL BACK THERE?
WE'VE LOST IT, BUT NOT FOR LONG. THAT'S WHY I'M WAKING UP OUR OTHER FRIEND....
clk clk
WELL... YOU TOOK YOUR PRECIOUS TIME GETTING AROUND TO ME, DIDN'T YOU?
WHAT IS THIS RUBBISH I'M BURNING? IS THIS CHARCOAL? A FINE WAY TO TREAT A SCI-ENTIFIC MARVEL. PERHAPS YOU'D CARE TO THROW IN SOME TABLE SCRAPS OR A PAIR OF OLD STOCKINGS....
MR. HEP
TAKE HIGHWAY 10 TO THE SHIPYARDS. THEY STILL USE COAL THERE.
WELL, OF COURSE THEY USE COAL AT A SHIPYARD-- ANY FOOL COULD TELL YOU THAT....

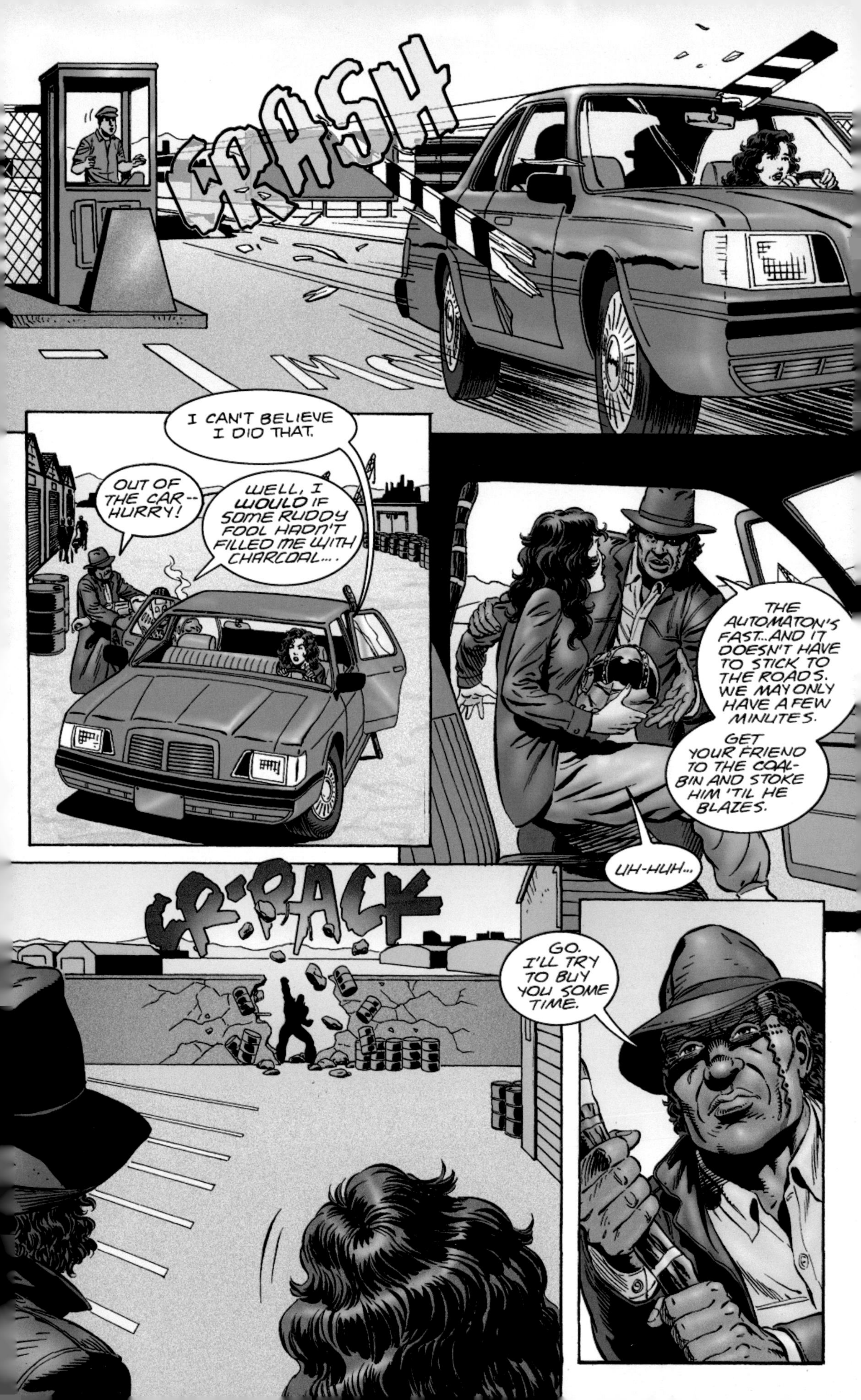
KRASH
I CAN'T BELIEVE I DID THAT.
OUT OF THE CAR-- HURRY!
WELL, I WOULD IF SOME RUDDY FOOL HADN'T FILLED ME WITH CHARCOAL....
THE AUTOMATON'S FAST...AND IT DOESN'T HAVE TO STICK TO THE ROADS. WE MAY ONLY HAVE A FEW MINUTES.
GET YOUR FRIEND TO THE COAL-BIN AND STOKE HIM 'TIL HE BLAZES.
UH-HUH...
CR-RACK
GO. I'LL TRY TO BUY YOU SOME TIME.

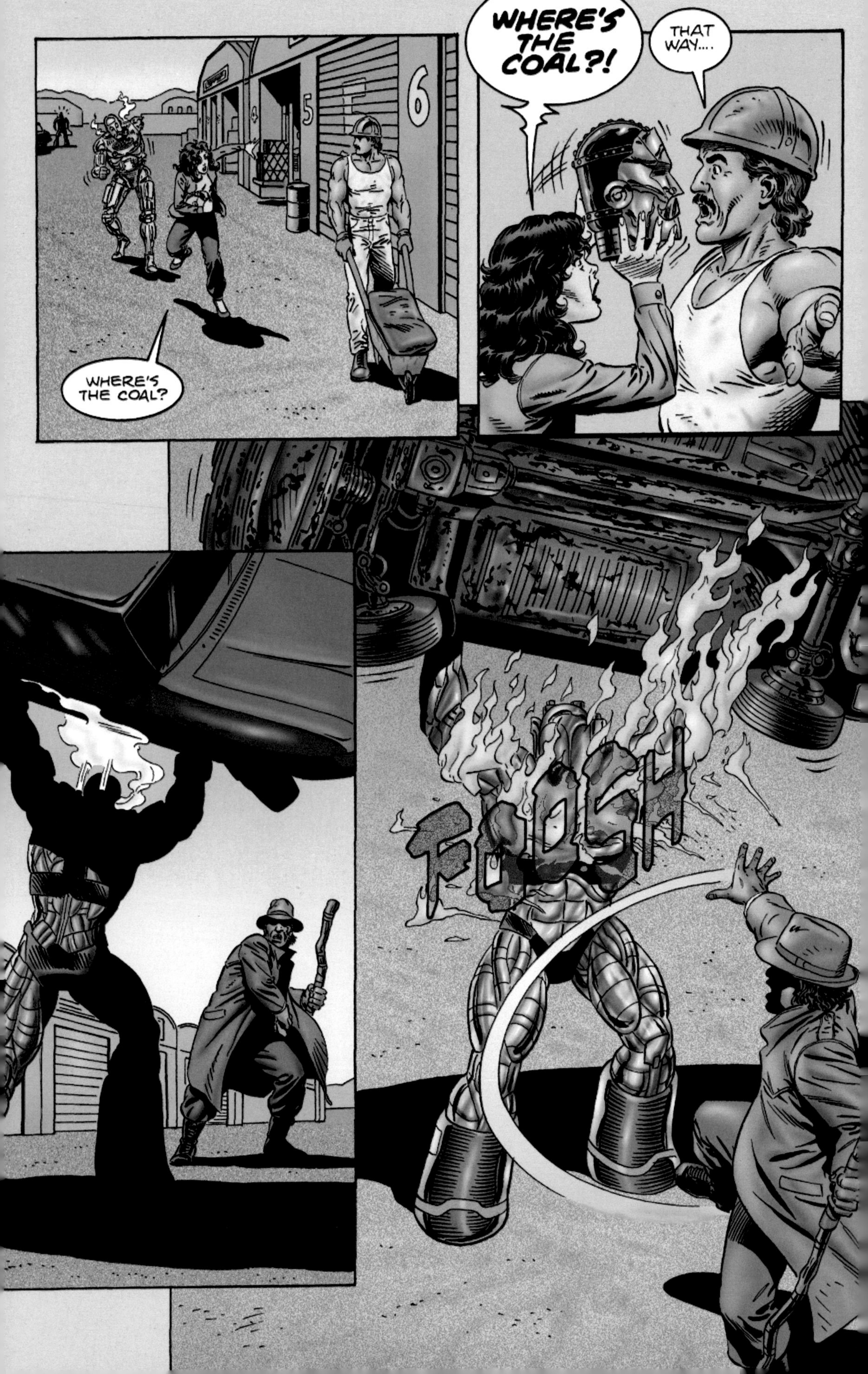
WHERE'S THE COAL?
WHERE'S THE COAL?!
THAT WAY....
FOOSH

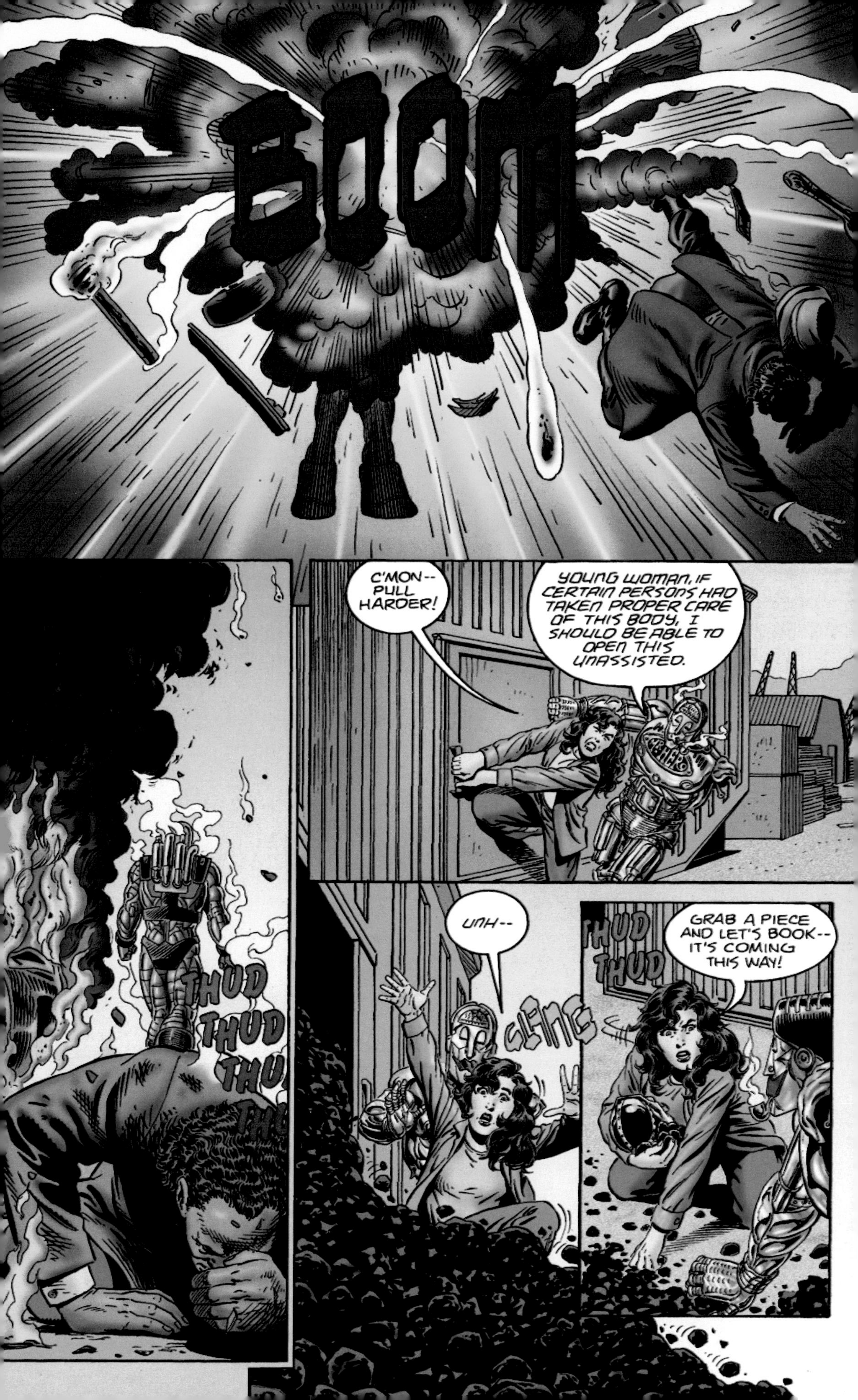
BOOM
THUD
THUD
THUD
THUD
C'MON--
PULL
HARDER!
YOUNG WOMAN, IF
CERTAIN PERSONS HAD
TAKEN PROPER CARE
OF THIS BODY, I
SHOULD BE ABLE TO
OPEN THIS
UNASSISTED.
UNH--
CLANG
THUD
THUD
GRAB A PIECE
AND LET'S BOOK--
IT'S COMING
THIS WAY!

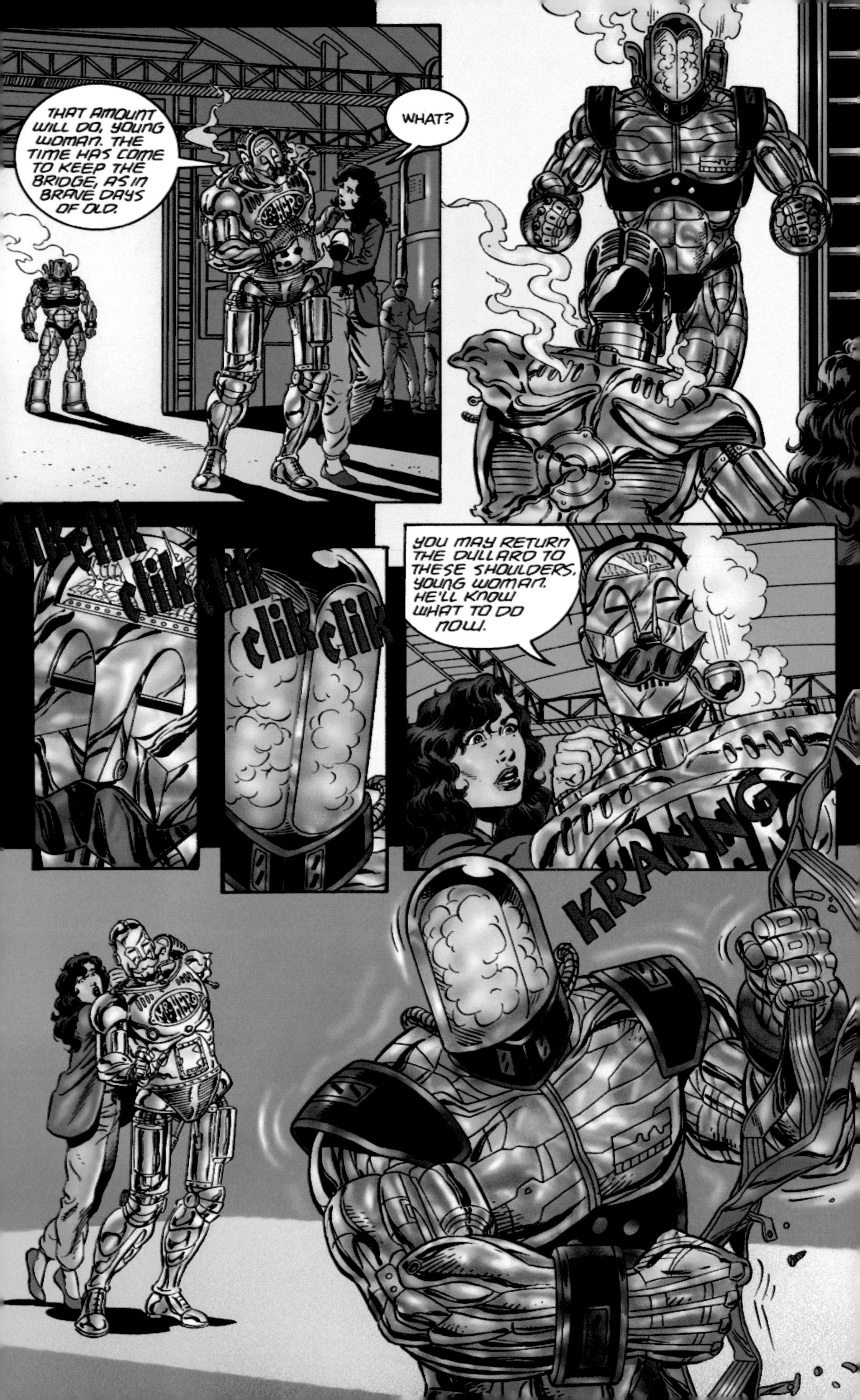
THAT AMOUNT WILL DO, YOUNG WOMAN. THE TIME HAS COME TO KEEP THE BRIDGE, AS IN BRAVE DAYS OF OLD.
WHAT?
clikclik
clikclik
YOU MAY RETURN THE DULLARD TO THESE SHOULDERS, YOUNG WOMAN. HE'LL KNOW WHAT TO DO NOW.
KRANNG

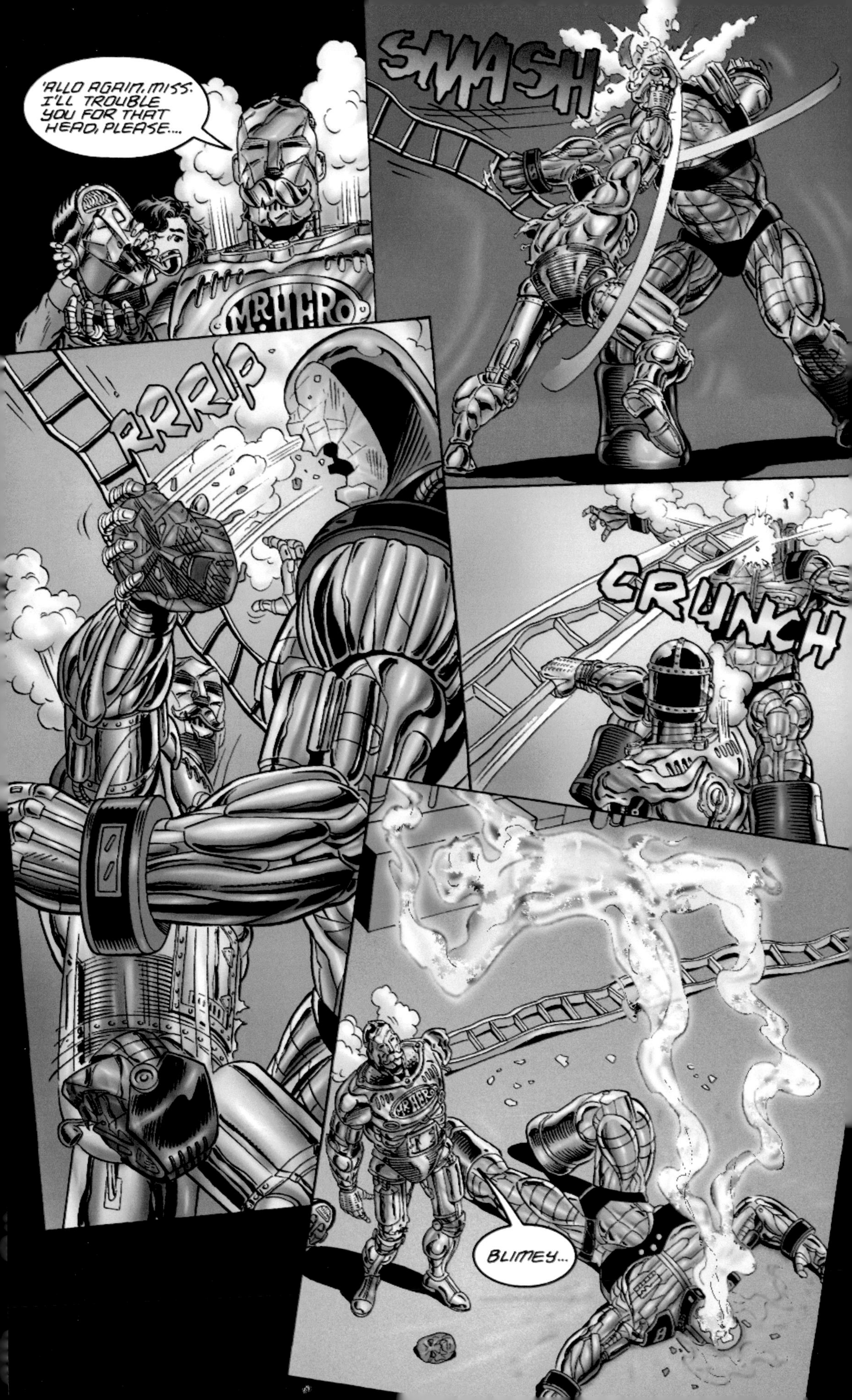
'ALLO AGAIN, MISS. I'LL TROUBLE YOU FOR THAT HEAD, PLEASE....
MR. HERO
SMASH
RRRIP
CRUNCH
BLIMEY...

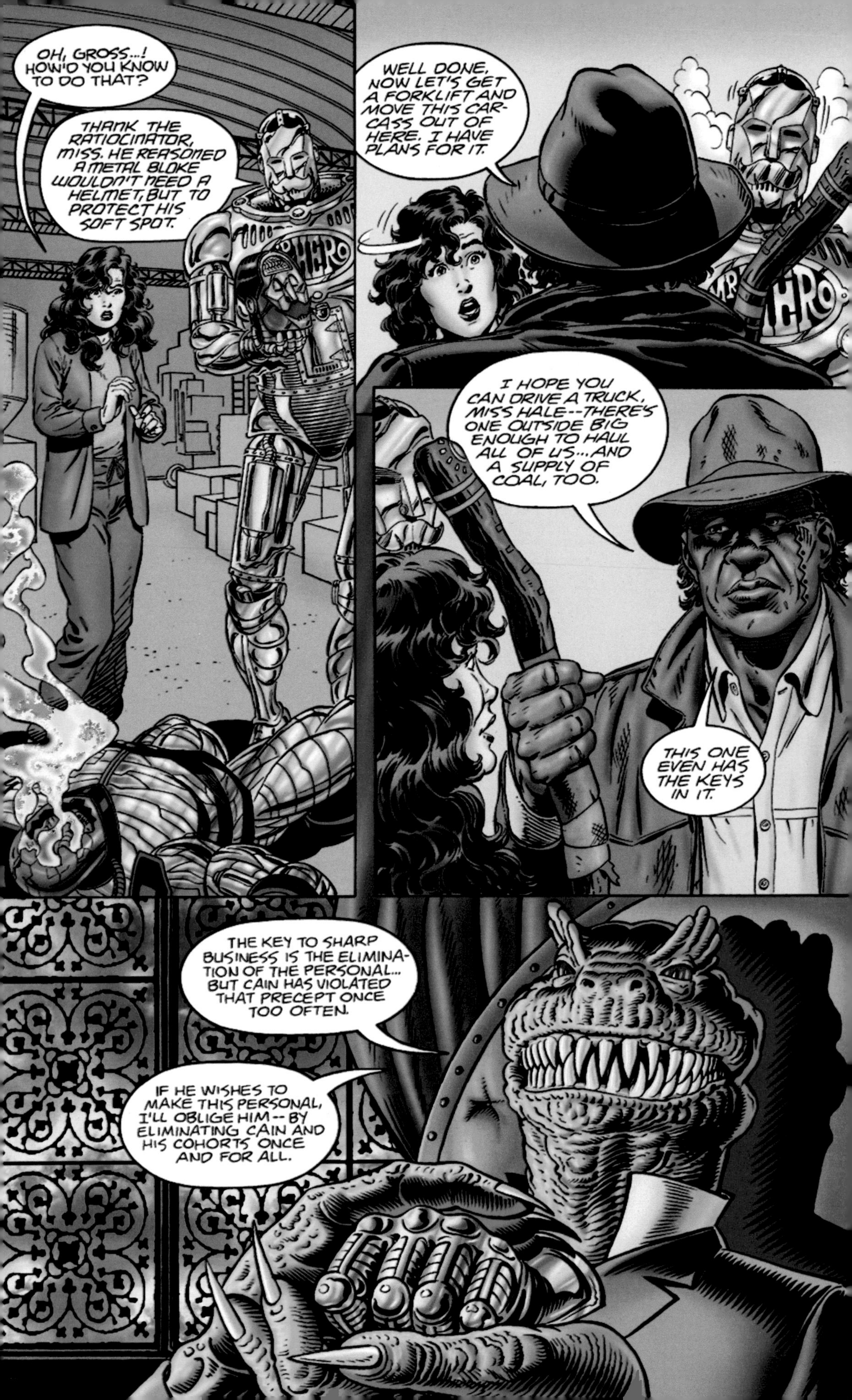
OH, GROSS...! HOW'D YOU KNOW TO DO THAT?
THANK THE RATIOCINATOR, MISS. HE REASONED A METAL BLOKE WOULDN'T NEED A HELMET, BUT TO PROTECT HIS SOFT SPOT.
MR HERO
WELL DONE, NOW LET'S GET A FORKLIFT AND MOVE THIS CARCASS OUT OF HERE. I HAVE PLANS FOR IT.
I HOPE YOU CAN DRIVE A TRUCK, MISS HALE--THERE'S ONE OUTSIDE BIG ENOUGH TO HAUL ALL OF US...AND A SUPPLY OF COAL, TOO.
THIS ONE EVEN HAS THE KEYS IN IT.
THE KEY TO SHARP BUSINESS IS THE ELIMINATION OF THE PERSONAL... BUT CAIN HAS VIOLATED THAT PRECEPT ONCE TOO OFTEN.
IF HE WISHES TO MAKE THIS PERSONAL, I'LL OBLIGE HIM -- BY ELIMINATING CAIN AND HIS COHORTS ONCE AND FOR ALL.

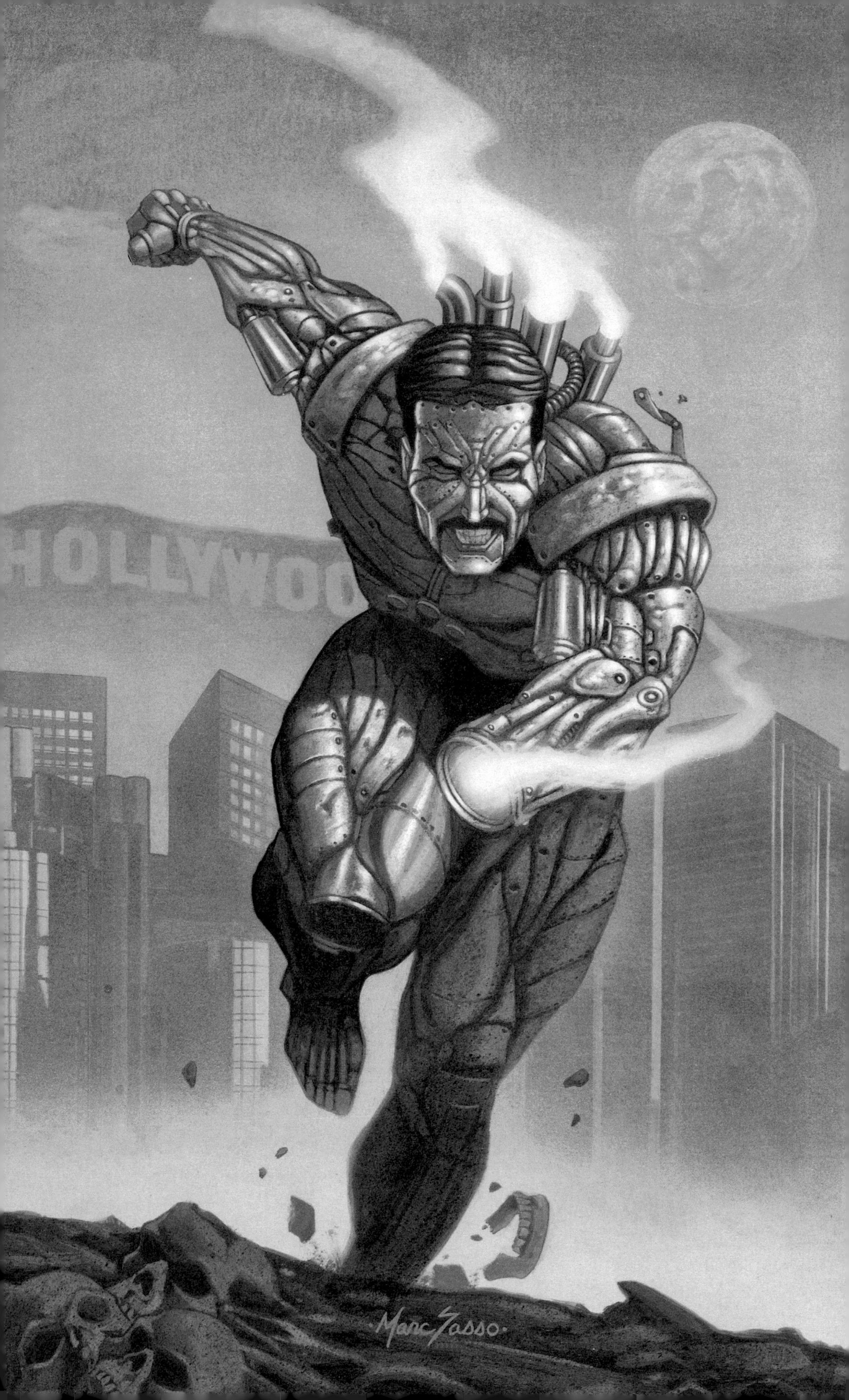
HOLLYWOO
Marc Sasso

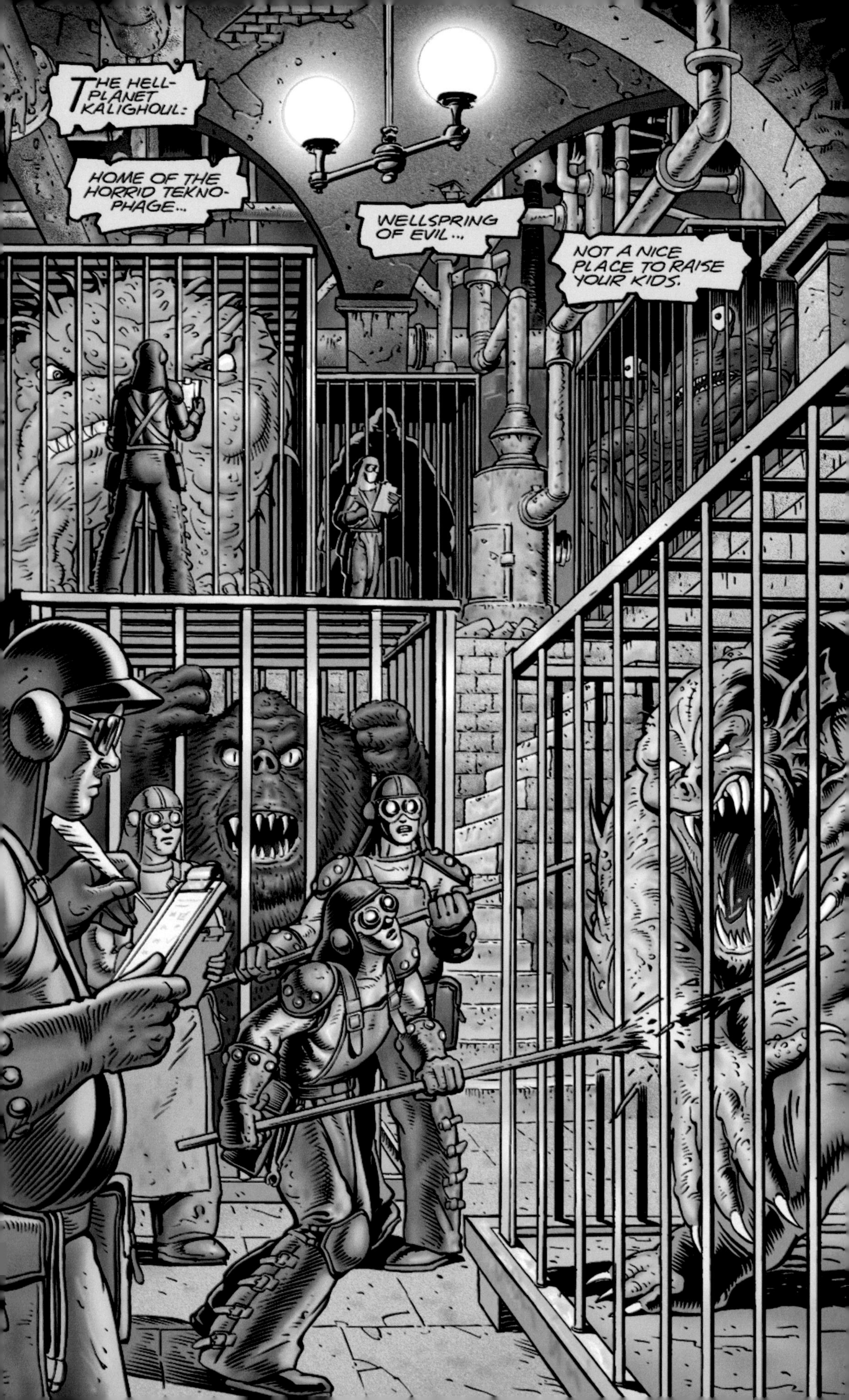
THE HELL-PLANET KALIGHOUL:
HOME OF THE HORRID TEKNOPHAGE...
WELLSPRING OF EVIL...
NOT A NICE PLACE TO RAISE YOUR KIDS.

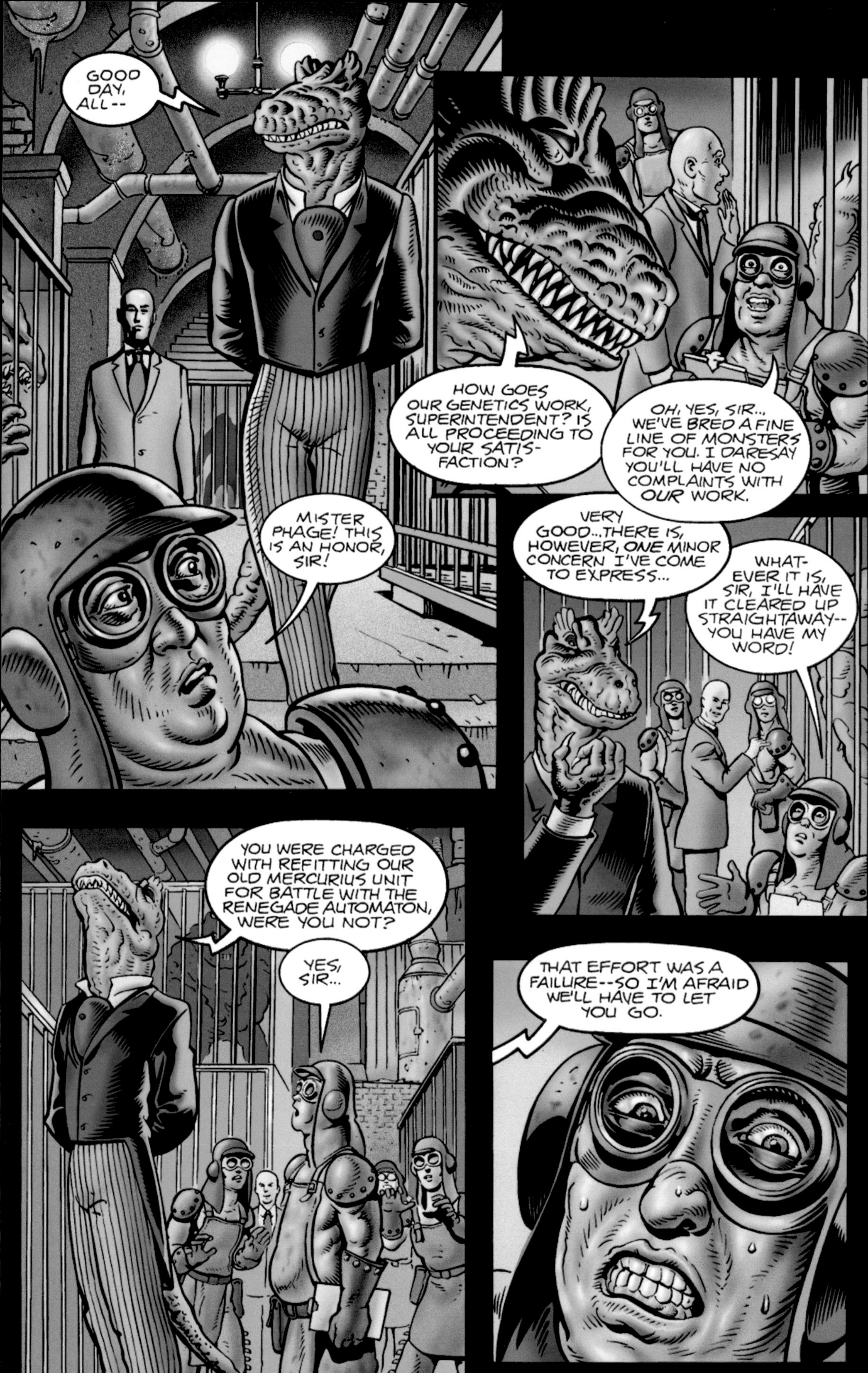
GOOD DAY, ALL--
HOW GOES OUR GENETICS WORK, SUPERINTENDENT? IS ALL PROCEEDING TO YOUR SATIS-FACTION?
OH, YES, SIR... WE'VE BRED A FINE LINE OF MONSTERS FOR YOU. I DARESAY YOU'LL HAVE NO COMPLAINTS WITH OUR WORK.
MISTER PHAGE! THIS IS AN HONOR, SIR!
VERY GOOD...THERE IS, HOWEVER, ONE MINOR CONCERN I'VE COME TO EXPRESS...
WHAT-EVER IT IS, SIR, I'LL HAVE IT CLEARED UP STRAIGHTAWAY--YOU HAVE MY WORD!
YOU WERE CHARGED WITH REFITTING OUR OLD MERCURIUS UNIT FOR BATTLE WITH THE RENEGADE AUTOMATON, WERE YOU NOT?
YES, SIR...
THAT EFFORT WAS A FAILURE--SO I'M AFRAID WE'LL HAVE TO LET YOU GO.

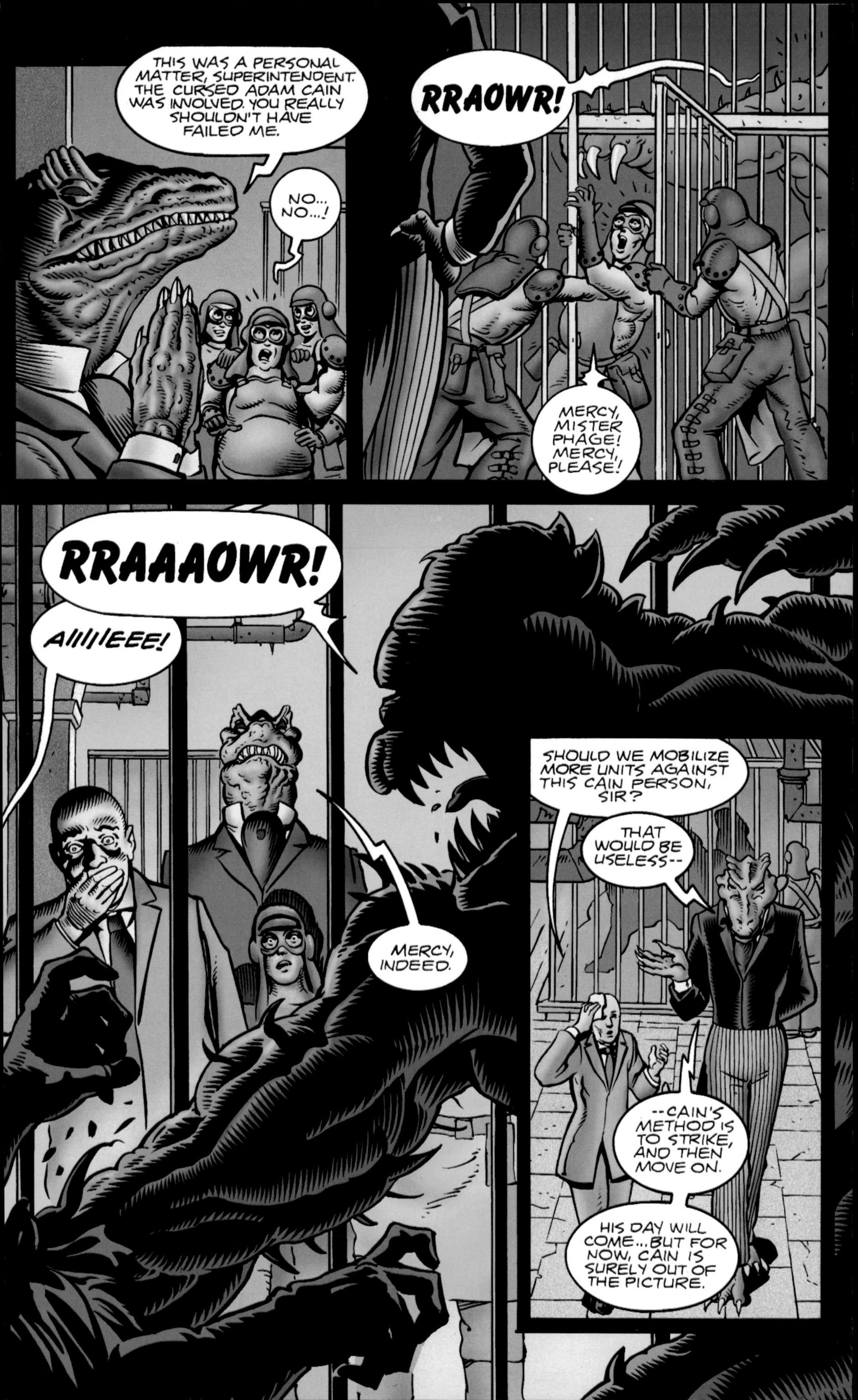
THIS WAS A PERSONAL MATTER, SUPERINTENDENT. THE CURSED ADAM CAIN WAS INVOLVED. YOU REALLY SHOULDN'T HAVE FAILED ME.
NO... NO...!
RRAOWR!
MERCY, MISTER PHAGE! MERCY, PLEASE!
RRAAAOWR!
AIIIIEEE!
MERCY, INDEED.
SHOULD WE MOBILIZE MORE UNITS AGAINST THIS CAIN PERSON, SIR?
THAT WOULD BE USELESS--
--CAIN'S METHOD IS TO STRIKE, AND THEN MOVE ON.
HIS DAY WILL COME... BUT FOR NOW, CAIN IS SURELY OUT OF THE PICTURE.

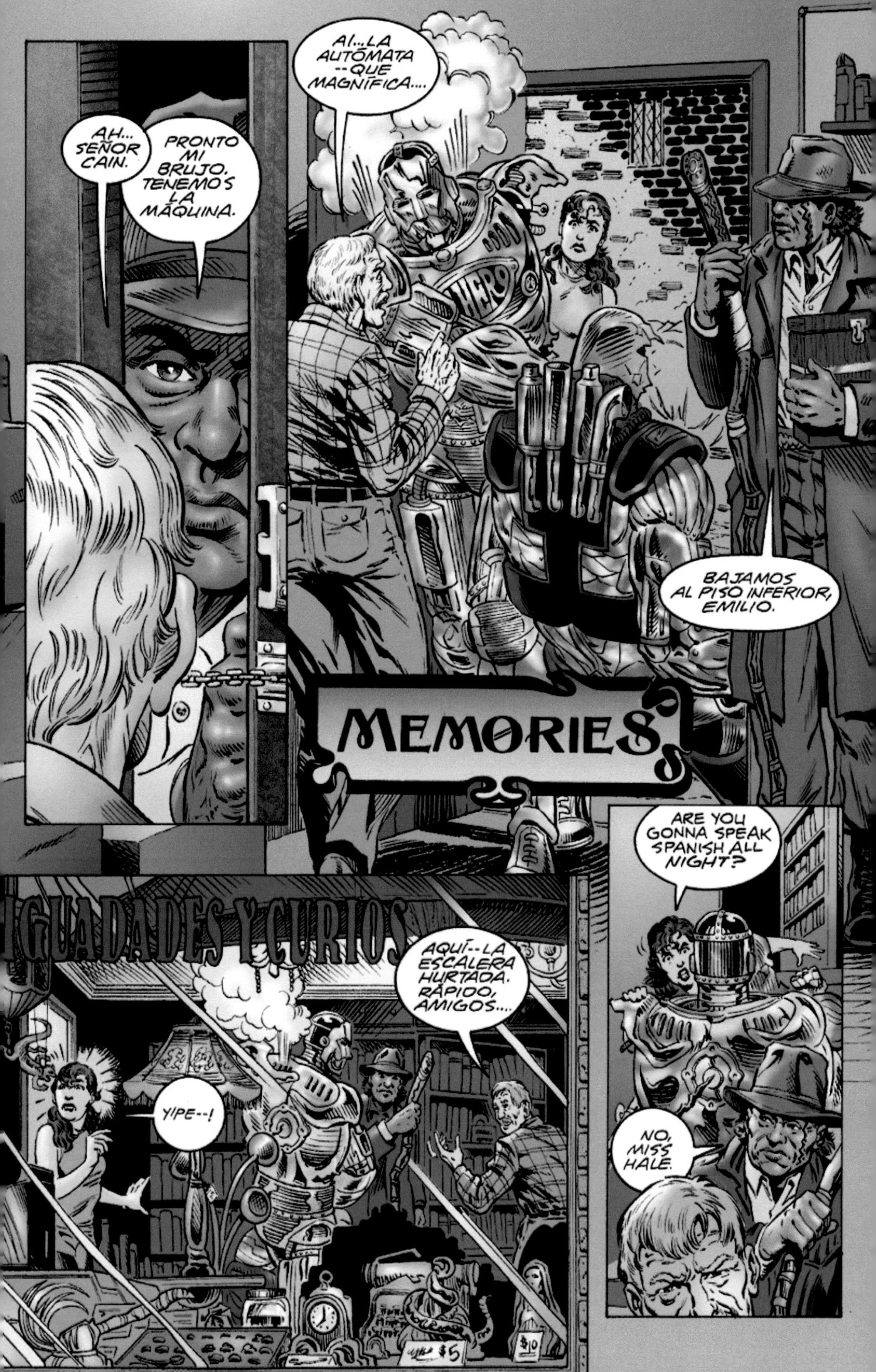

AH... SEÑOR CAIN.
PRONTO MI BRUJO. TENEMOS LA MÁQUINA.
AI...LA AUTÓMATA --QUE MAGNÍFICA....
BAJAMOS AL PISO INFERIOR, EMILIO.
MEMORIES
IGUADADES Y CURIOS
AQUÍ--LA ESCALERA HURTADA. RÁPIDO, AMIGOS....
YIPE--!
$5
$10
ARE YOU GONNA SPEAK SPANISH ALL NIGHT?
NO, MISS HALE.

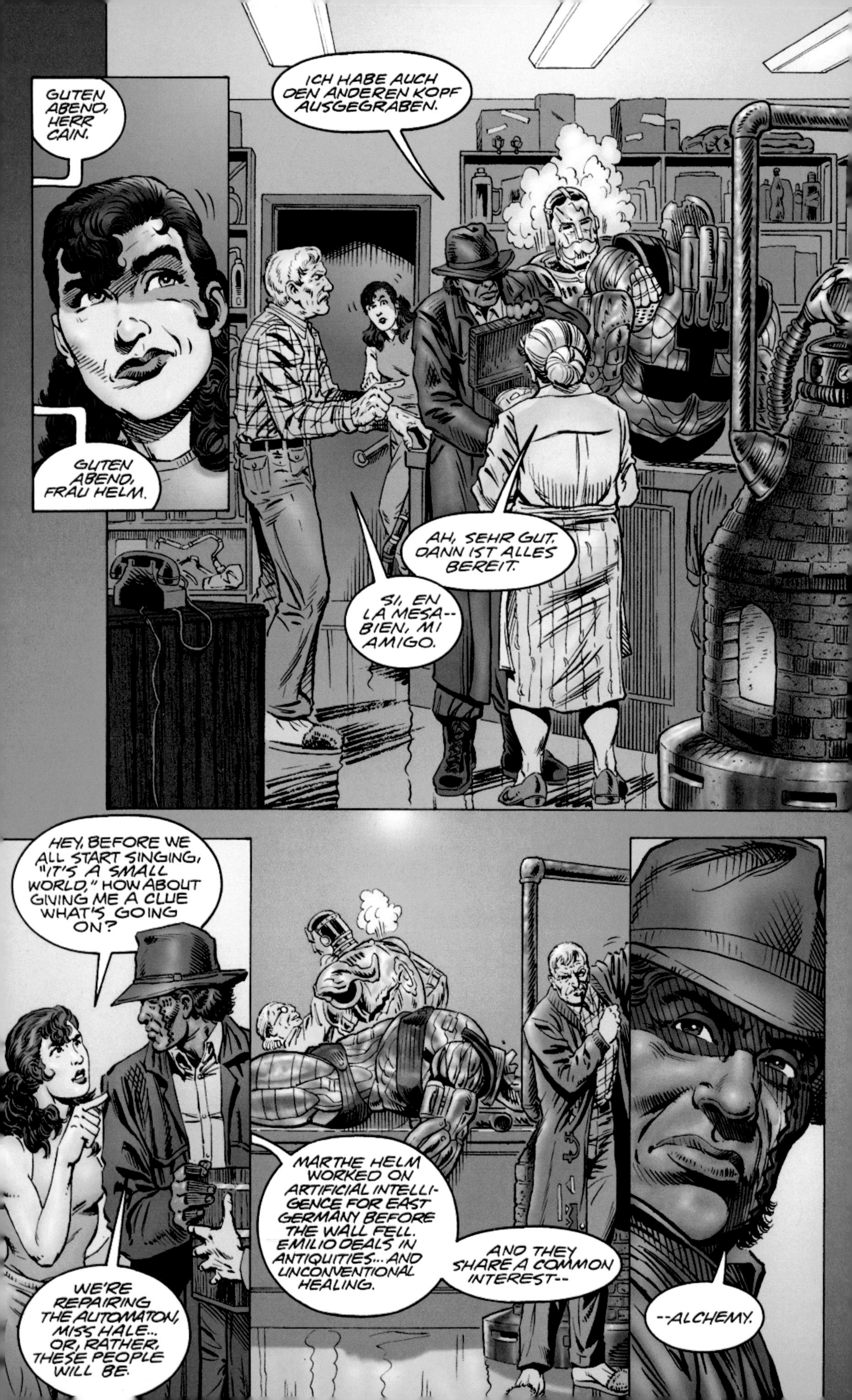
GUTEN ABEND, HERR CAIN.
GUTEN ABEND, FRAU HELM.
ICH HABE AUCH DEN ANDEREN KOPF AUSGEGRABEN.
AH, SEHR GUT. DANN IST ALLES BEREIT.
SI, EN LA MESA-- BIEN, MI AMIGO.
HEY, BEFORE WE ALL START SINGING, "IT'S A SMALL WORLD," HOW ABOUT GIVING ME A CLUE WHAT'S GOING ON?
WE'RE REPAIRING THE AUTOMATON, MISS HALE... OR, RATHER, THESE PEOPLE WILL BE.
MARTHE HELM WORKED ON ARTIFICIAL INTELLIGENCE FOR EAST GERMANY BEFORE THE WALL FELL. EMILIO DEALS IN ANTIQUITIES... AND UNCONVENTIONAL HEALING.
AND THEY SHARE A COMMON INTEREST--
--ALCHEMY.

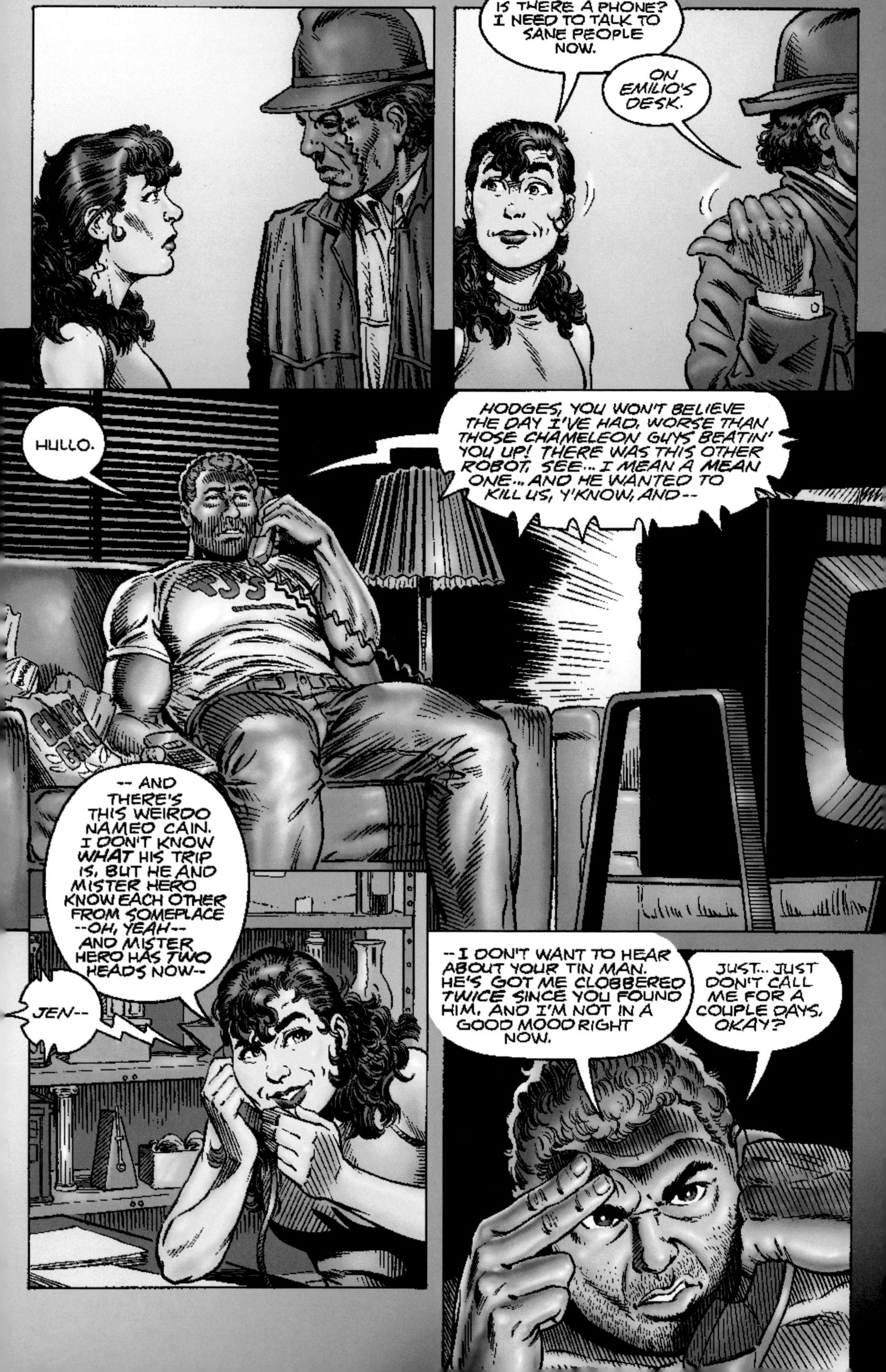
IS THERE A PHONE? I NEED TO TALK TO SANE PEOPLE NOW.
ON EMILIO'S DESK.
HULLO.
HODGES, YOU WON'T BELIEVE THE DAY I'VE HAD, WORSE THAN THOSE CHAMELEON GUYS BEATIN' YOU UP! THERE WAS THIS OTHER ROBOT, SEE... I MEAN A MEAN ONE... AND HE WANTED TO KILL US, Y'KNOW, AND--
-- AND THERE'S THIS WEIRDO NAMED CAIN. I DON'T KNOW WHAT HIS TRIP IS, BUT HE AND MISTER HERO KNOW EACH OTHER FROM SOMEPLACE --OH, YEAH-- AND MISTER HERO HAS TWO HEADS NOW--
JEN--
--I DON'T WANT TO HEAR ABOUT YOUR TIN MAN. HE'S GOT ME CLOBBERED TWICE SINCE YOU FOUND HIM, AND I'M NOT IN A GOOD MOOD RIGHT NOW.
JUST... JUST DON'T CALL ME FOR A COUPLE DAYS, OKAY?

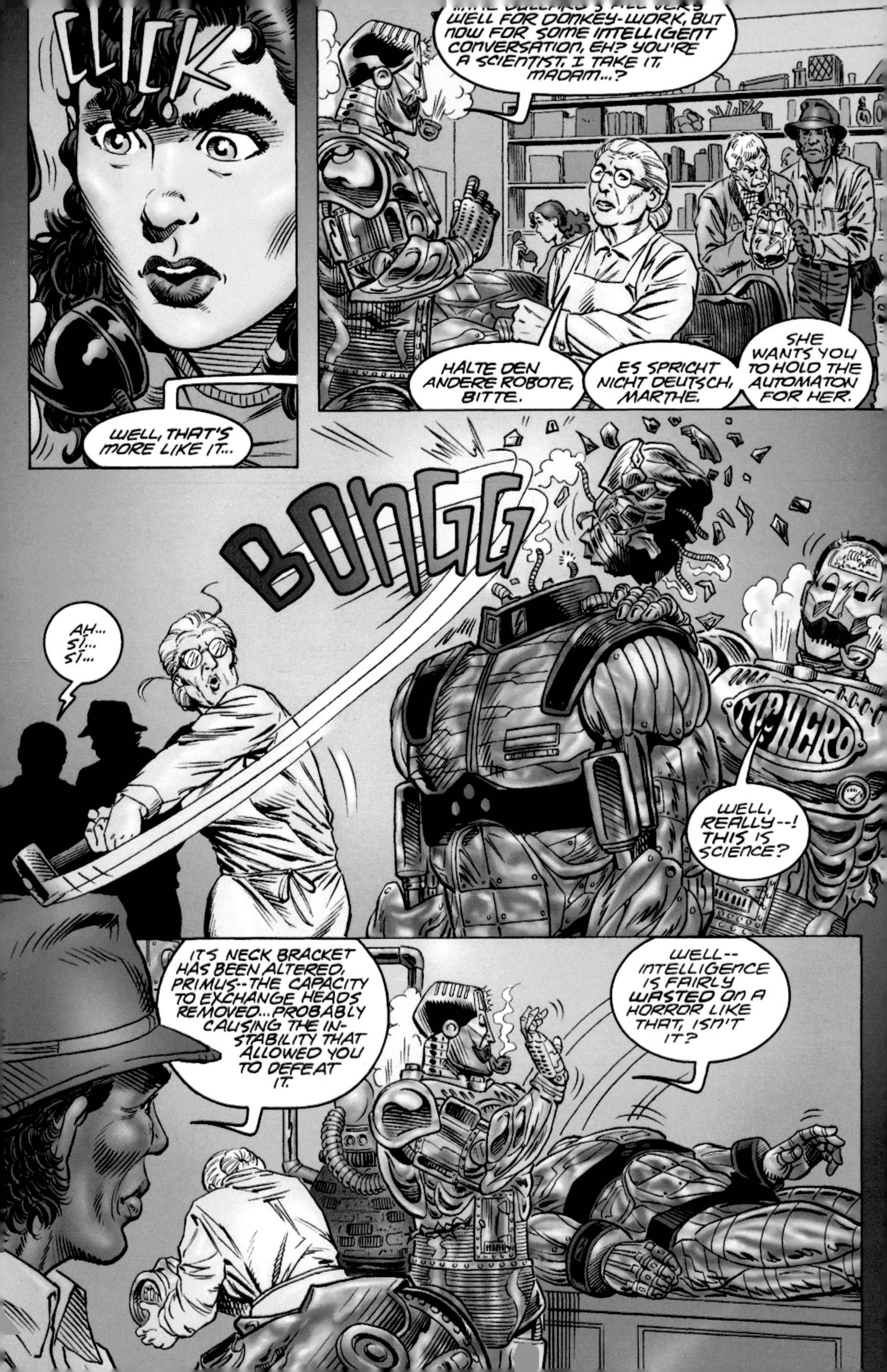
CLICK
WELL, THAT'S MORE LIKE IT...
...WELL FOR DONKEY-WORK, BUT NOW FOR SOME INTELLIGENT CONVERSATION, EH? YOU'RE A SCIENTIST, I TAKE IT, MADAM...?
HALTE DEN ANDERE ROBOTE, BITTE.
ES SPRICHT NICHT DEUTSCH, MARTHE.
SHE WANTS YOU TO HOLD THE AUTOMATON FOR HER.
BONGG
AH... SÍ... SÍ...
WELL, REALLY--! THIS IS SCIENCE?
IT'S NECK BRACKET HAS BEEN ALTERED, PRIMUS--THE CAPACITY TO EXCHANGE HEADS REMOVED...PROBABLY CAUSING THE INSTABILITY THAT ALLOWED YOU TO DEFEAT IT.
WELL--INTELLIGENCE IS FAIRLY WASTED ON A HORROR LIKE THAT, ISN'T IT?

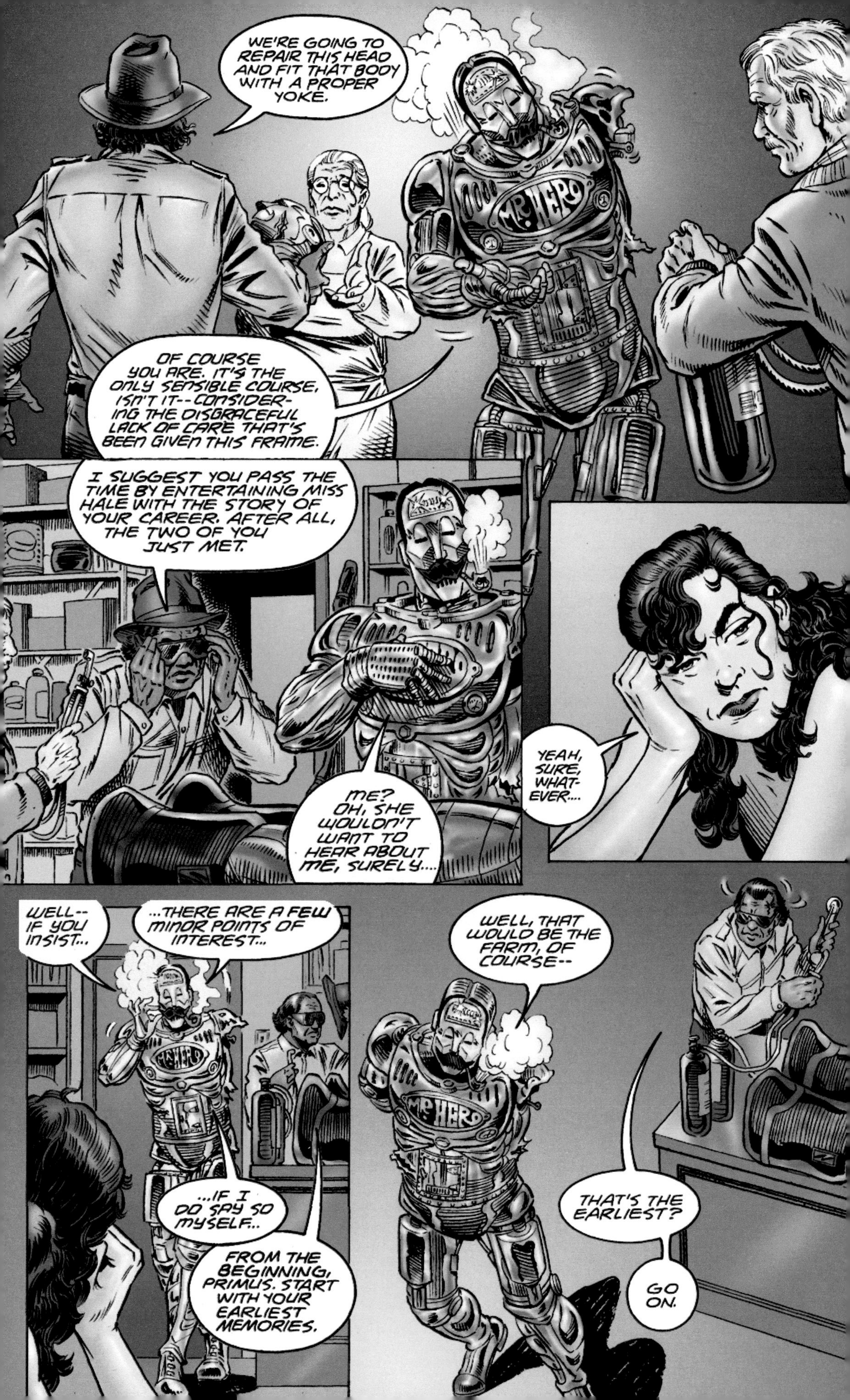
WE'RE GOING TO REPAIR THIS HEAD AND FIT THAT BODY WITH A PROPER YOKE.
OF COURSE YOU ARE. IT'S THE ONLY SENSIBLE COURSE, ISN'T IT--CONSIDERING THE DISGRACEFUL LACK OF CARE THAT'S BEEN GIVEN THIS FRAME.
MR. HERO
I SUGGEST YOU PASS THE TIME BY ENTERTAINING MISS HALE WITH THE STORY OF YOUR CAREER. AFTER ALL, THE TWO OF YOU JUST MET.
ME? OH, SHE WOULDN'T WANT TO HEAR ABOUT ME, SURELY....
YEAH, SURE, WHATEVER....
WELL-- IF YOU INSIST...
...THERE ARE A FEW MINOR POINTS OF INTEREST...
...IF I DO SAY SO MYSELF...
FROM THE BEGINNING, PRIMUS. START WITH YOUR EARLIEST MEMORIES.
WELL, THAT WOULD BE THE FARM, OF COURSE--
THAT'S THE EARLIEST?
GO ON.

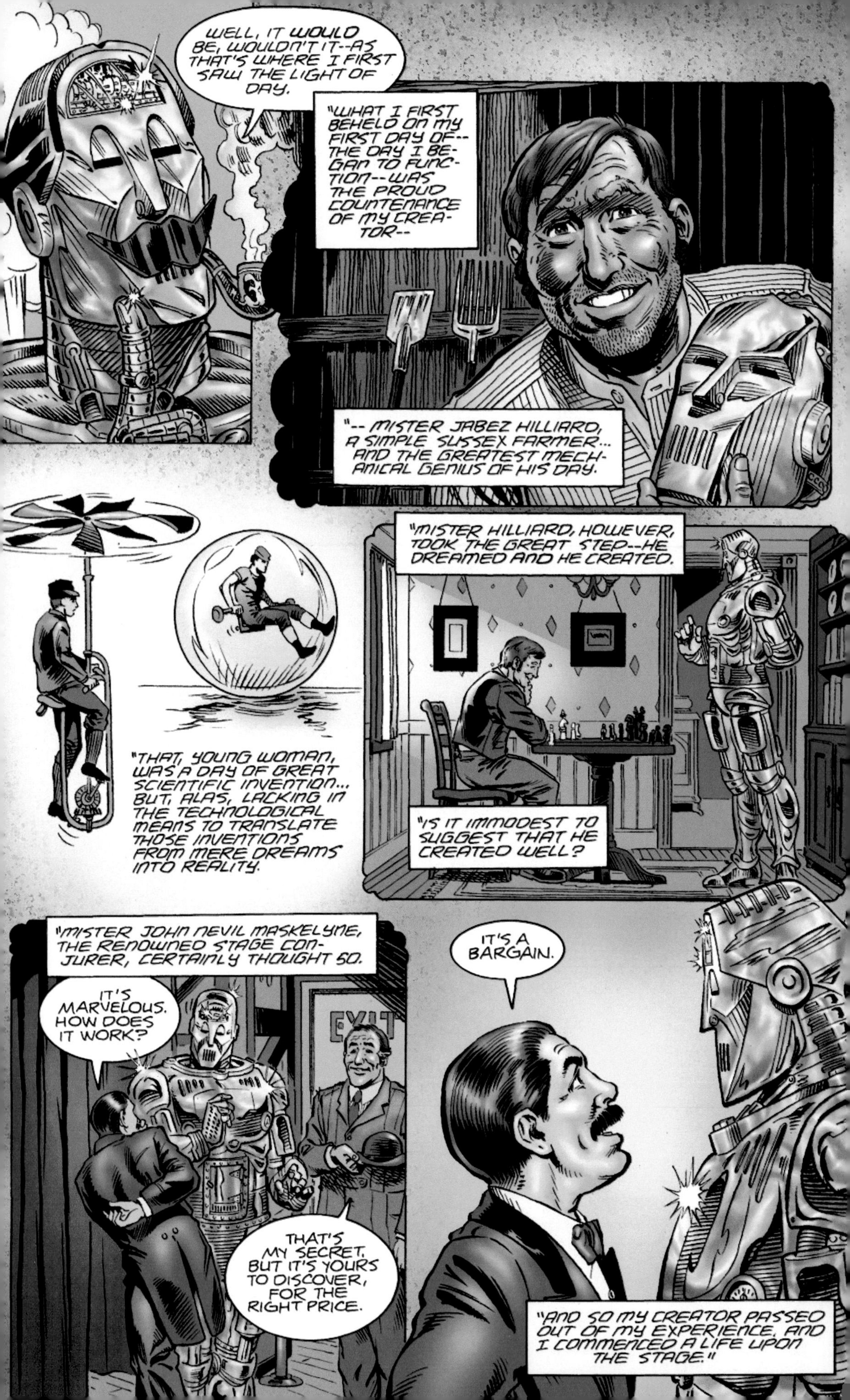
WELL, IT WOULD BE, WOULDN'T IT--AS THAT'S WHERE I FIRST SAW THE LIGHT OF DAY.
"WHAT I FIRST BEHELD ON MY FIRST DAY OF-- THE DAY I BEGAN TO FUNCTION--WAS THE PROUD COUNTENANCE OF MY CREATOR--
"--MISTER JABEZ HILLIARD, A SIMPLE SUSSEX FARMER... AND THE GREATEST MECHANICAL GENIUS OF HIS DAY.
"THAT, YOUNG WOMAN, WAS A DAY OF GREAT SCIENTIFIC INVENTION... BUT, ALAS, LACKING IN THE TECHNOLOGICAL MEANS TO TRANSLATE THOSE INVENTIONS FROM MERE DREAMS INTO REALITY.
"MISTER HILLIARD, HOWEVER, TOOK THE GREAT STEP--HE DREAMED AND HE CREATED.
"IS IT IMMODEST TO SUGGEST THAT HE CREATED WELL?
"MISTER JOHN NEVIL MASKELYNE, THE RENOWNED STAGE CONJURER, CERTAINLY THOUGHT SO.
IT'S MARVELOUS. HOW DOES IT WORK?
EXIT
THAT'S MY SECRET, BUT IT'S YOURS TO DISCOVER, FOR THE RIGHT PRICE.
IT'S A BARGAIN.
"AND SO MY CREATOR PASSED OUT OF MY EXPERIENCE, AND I COMMENCED A LIFE UPON THE STAGE."

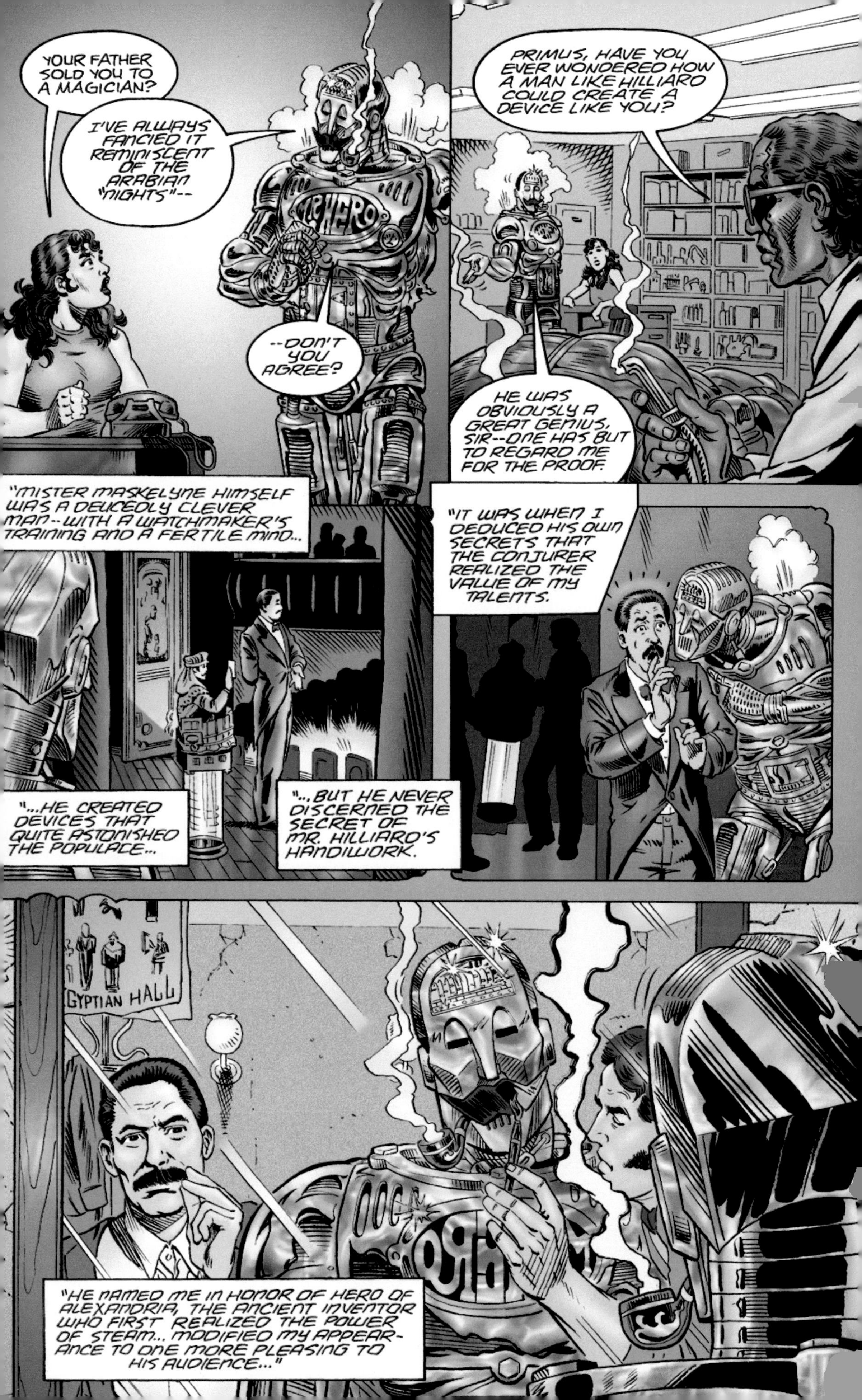
YOUR FATHER SOLD YOU TO A MAGICIAN?
I'VE ALWAYS FANCIED IT REMINISCENT OF THE ARABIAN "NIGHTS"--
--DON'T YOU AGREE?
PRIMUS, HAVE YOU EVER WONDERED HOW A MAN LIKE HILLIARD COULD CREATE A DEVICE LIKE YOU?
HE WAS OBVIOUSLY A GREAT GENIUS, SIR--ONE HAS BUT TO REGARD ME FOR THE PROOF.
"MISTER MASKELYNE HIMSELF WAS A DEUCEDLY CLEVER MAN--WITH A WATCHMAKER'S TRAINING AND A FERTILE MIND...
"...HE CREATED DEVICES THAT QUITE ASTONISHED THE POPULACE...
"...BUT HE NEVER DISCERNED THE SECRET OF MR. HILLIARD'S HANDIWORK.
"IT WAS WHEN I DEDUCED HIS OWN SECRETS THAT THE CONJURER REALIZED THE VALUE OF MY TALENTS.
GYPTIAN HALL
"HE NAMED ME IN HONOR OF HERO OF ALEXANDRIA, THE ANCIENT INVENTOR WHO FIRST REALIZED THE POWER OF STEAM... MODIFIED MY APPEARANCE TO ONE MORE PLEASING TO HIS AUDIENCE..."

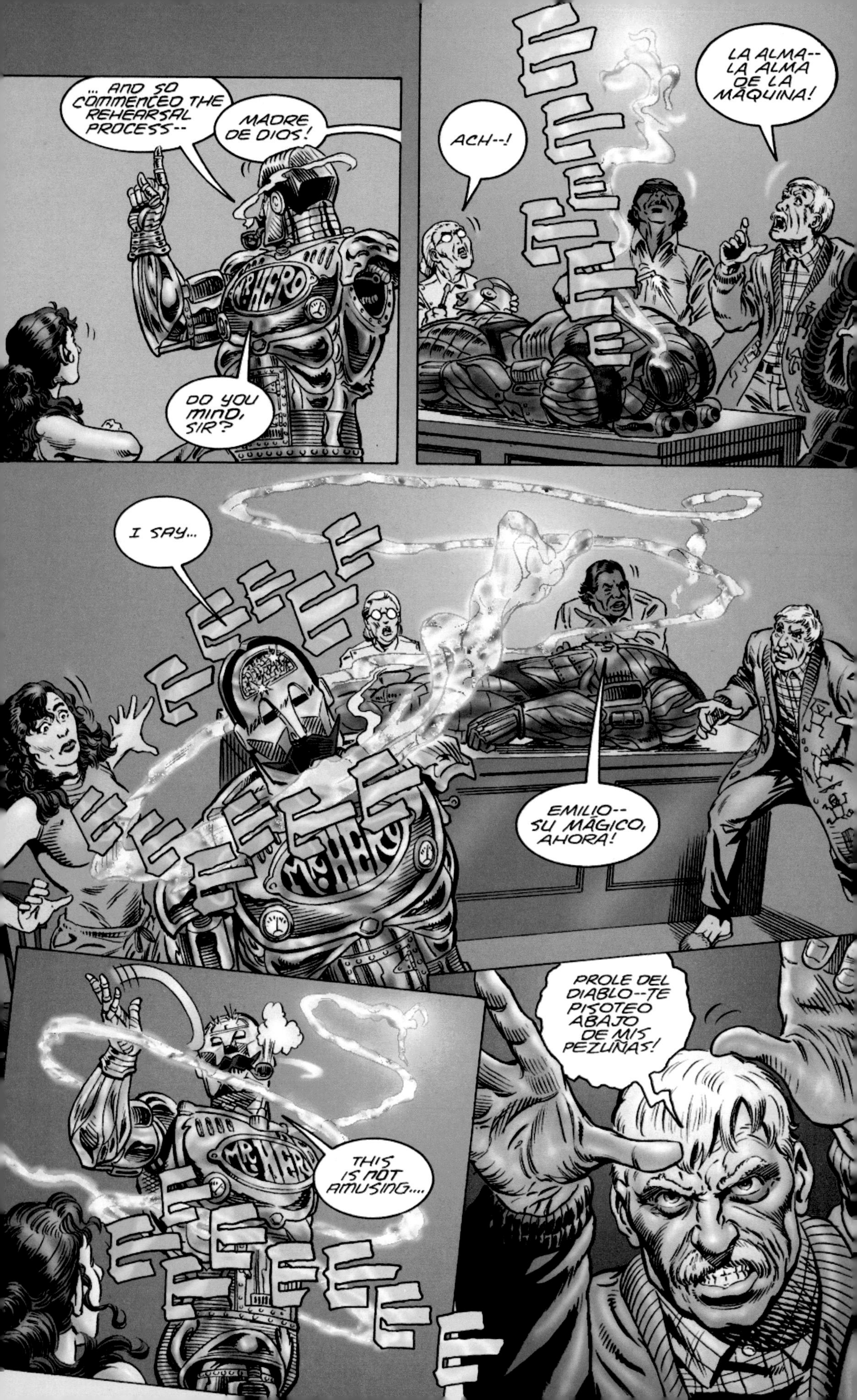
... AND SO COMMENCED THE REHEARSAL PROCESS--
MADRE DE DIOS!
DO YOU MIND, SIR?
ACH--!
LA ALMA-- LA ALMA DE LA MÁQUINA!
I SAY...
EMILIO-- SU MÁGICO, AHORA!
THIS IS NOT AMUSING....
PROLE DEL DIABLO--TE PISOTEO ABAJO DE MIS PEZUÑAS!

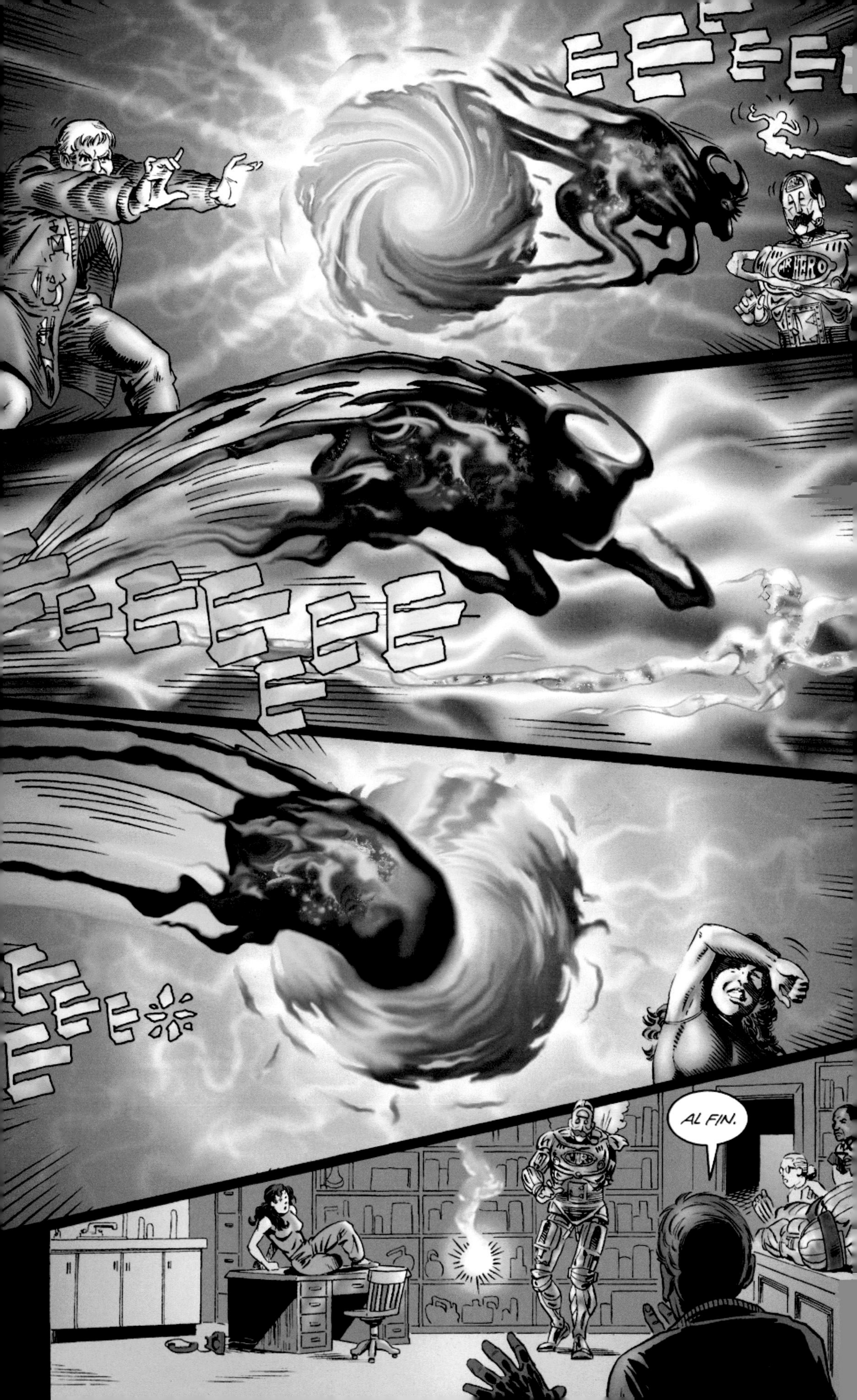
MR HERO
AL FIN.

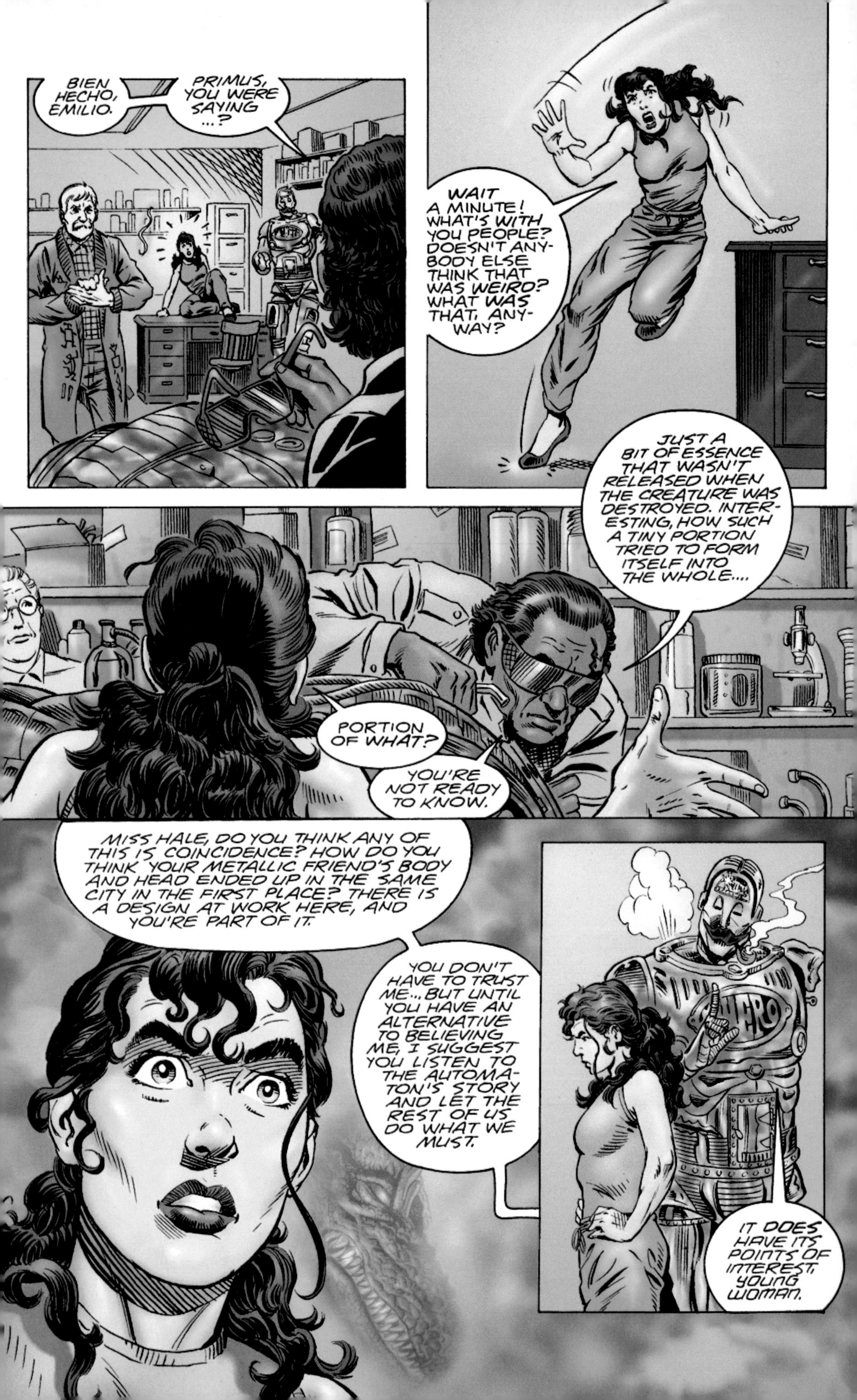
BIEN HECHO, EMILIO.
PRIMUS, YOU WERE SAYING ...?
WAIT A MINUTE! WHAT'S WITH YOU PEOPLE? DOESN'T ANYBODY ELSE THINK THAT WAS WEIRD? WHAT WAS THAT, ANYWAY?
JUST A BIT OF ESSENCE THAT WASN'T RELEASED WHEN THE CREATURE WAS DESTROYED. INTERESTING, HOW SUCH A TINY PORTION TRIED TO FORM ITSELF INTO THE WHOLE....
PORTION OF WHAT?
YOU'RE NOT READY TO KNOW.
MISS HALE, DO YOU THINK ANY OF THIS IS COINCIDENCE? HOW DO YOU THINK YOUR METALLIC FRIEND'S BODY AND HEAD ENDED UP IN THE SAME CITY IN THE FIRST PLACE? THERE IS A DESIGN AT WORK HERE, AND YOU'RE PART OF IT.
YOU DON'T HAVE TO TRUST ME... BUT UNTIL YOU HAVE AN ALTERNATIVE TO BELIEVING ME, I SUGGEST YOU LISTEN TO THE AUTOMATON'S STORY AND LET THE REST OF US DO WHAT WE MUST.
IT DOES HAVE ITS POINTS OF INTEREST, YOUNG WOMAN.

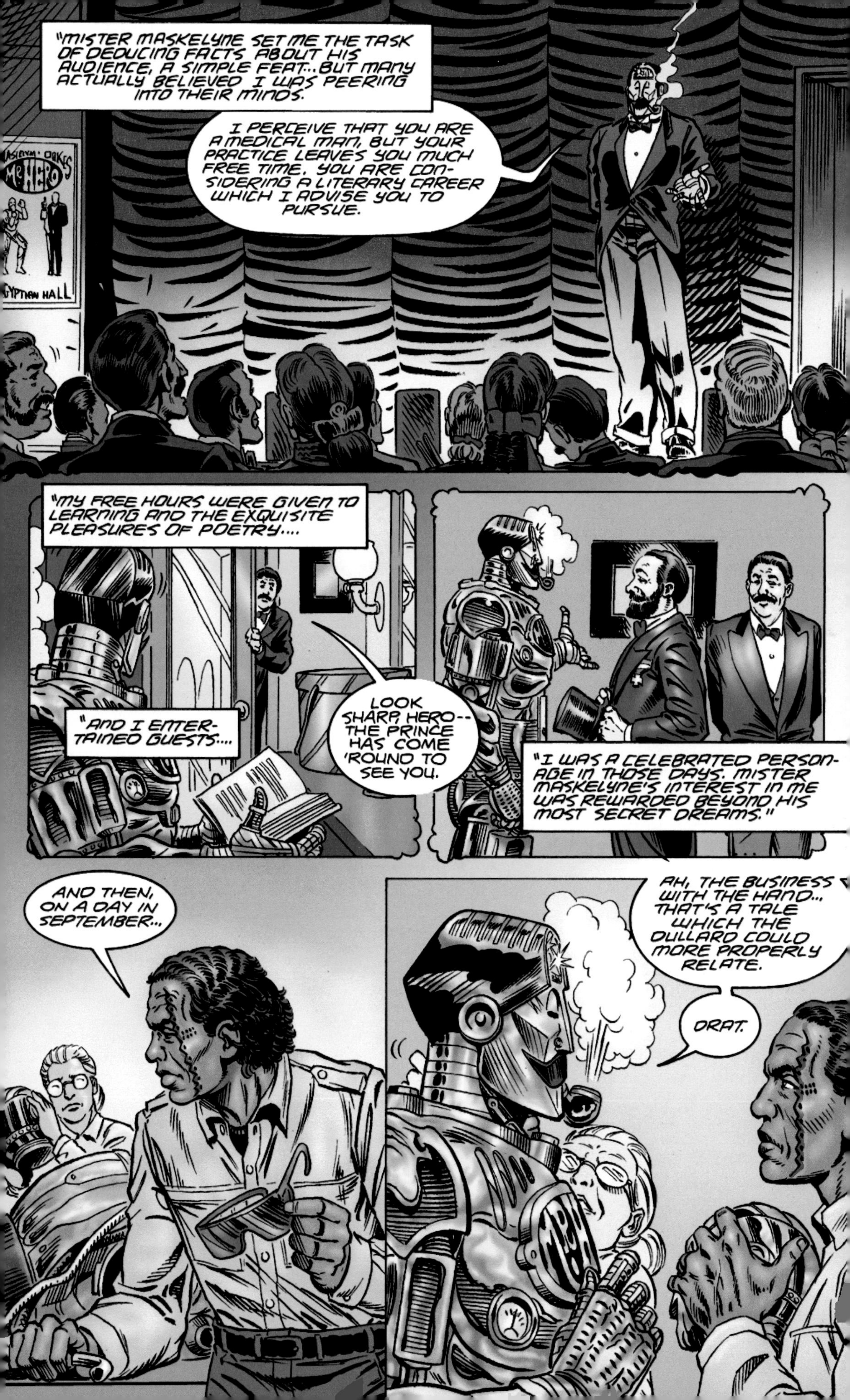
"MISTER MASKELYNE SET ME THE TASK OF DEDUCING FACTS ABOUT HIS AUDIENCE, A SIMPLE FEAT...BUT MANY ACTUALLY BELIEVED I WAS PEERING INTO THEIR MINDS.
I PERCEIVE THAT YOU ARE A MEDICAL MAN, BUT YOUR PRACTICE LEAVES YOU MUCH FREE TIME. YOU ARE CONSIDERING A LITERARY CAREER WHICH I ADVISE YOU TO PURSUE.
EGYPTIAN HALL
"MY FREE HOURS WERE GIVEN TO LEARNING AND THE EXQUISITE PLEASURES OF POETRY....
"AND I ENTERTAINED GUESTS....
LOOK SHARP, HERO-- THE PRINCE HAS COME 'ROUND TO SEE YOU.
"I WAS A CELEBRATED PERSONAGE IN THOSE DAYS. MISTER MASKELYNE'S INTEREST IN ME WAS REWARDED BEYOND HIS MOST SECRET DREAMS."
AND THEN, ON A DAY IN SEPTEMBER...
AH, THE BUSINESS WITH THE HAND... THAT'S A TALE WHICH THE DULLARD COULD MORE PROPERLY RELATE.
DRAT.

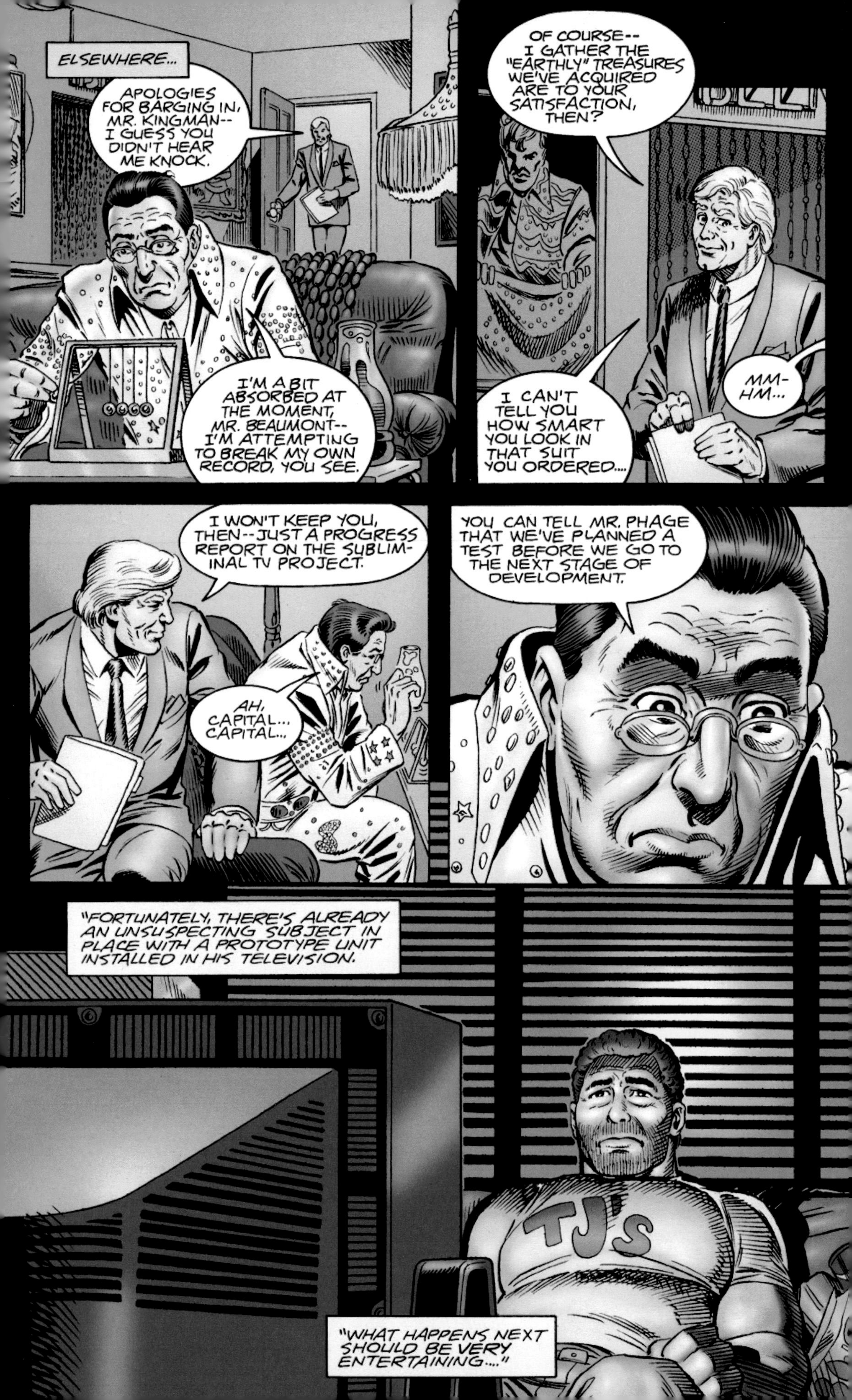
ELSEWHERE...
APOLOGIES FOR BARGING IN, MR. KINGMAN-- I GUESS YOU DIDN'T HEAR ME KNOCK.
I'M A BIT ABSORBED AT THE MOMENT, MR. BEAUMONT-- I'M ATTEMPTING TO BREAK MY OWN RECORD, YOU SEE.
OF COURSE-- I GATHER THE "EARTHLY" TREASURES WE'VE ACQUIRED ARE TO YOUR SATISFACTION, THEN?
I CAN'T TELL YOU HOW SMART YOU LOOK IN THAT SUIT YOU ORDERED....
MM-HM...
I WON'T KEEP YOU, THEN--JUST A PROGRESS REPORT ON THE SUBLIMINAL TV PROJECT.
AH, CAPITAL... CAPITAL...
YOU CAN TELL MR. PHAGE THAT WE'VE PLANNED A TEST BEFORE WE GO TO THE NEXT STAGE OF DEVELOPMENT.
"FORTUNATELY, THERE'S ALREADY AN UNSUSPECTING SUBJECT IN PLACE WITH A PROTOTYPE UNIT INSTALLED IN HIS TELEVISION.
TJ's
"WHAT HAPPENS NEXT SHOULD BE VERY ENTERTAINING...."

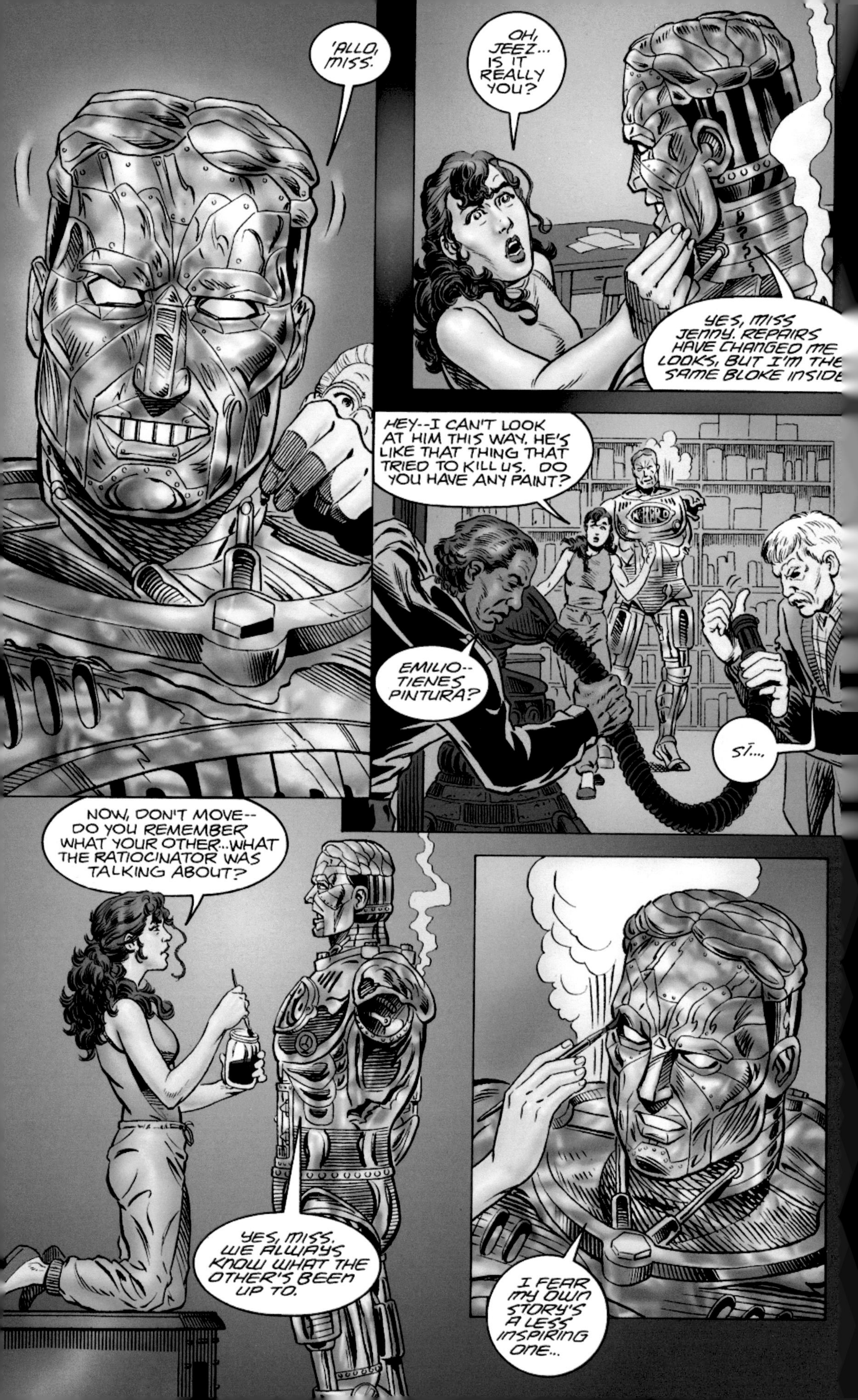
'ALLO, MISS.
OH, JEEZ... IS IT REALLY YOU?
YES, MISS JENNY. REPAIRS HAVE CHANGED ME LOOKS, BUT I'M THE SAME BLOKE INSIDE
HEY--I CAN'T LOOK AT HIM THIS WAY. HE'S LIKE THAT THING THAT TRIED TO KILL US. DO YOU HAVE ANY PAINT?
EMILIO-- TIENES PINTURA?
SÍ...
NOW, DON'T MOVE-- DO YOU REMEMBER WHAT YOUR OTHER...WHAT THE RATIOCINATOR WAS TALKING ABOUT?
YES, MISS. WE ALWAYS KNOW WHAT THE OTHER'S BEEN UP TO.
I FEAR MY OWN STORY'S A LESS INSPIRING ONE...

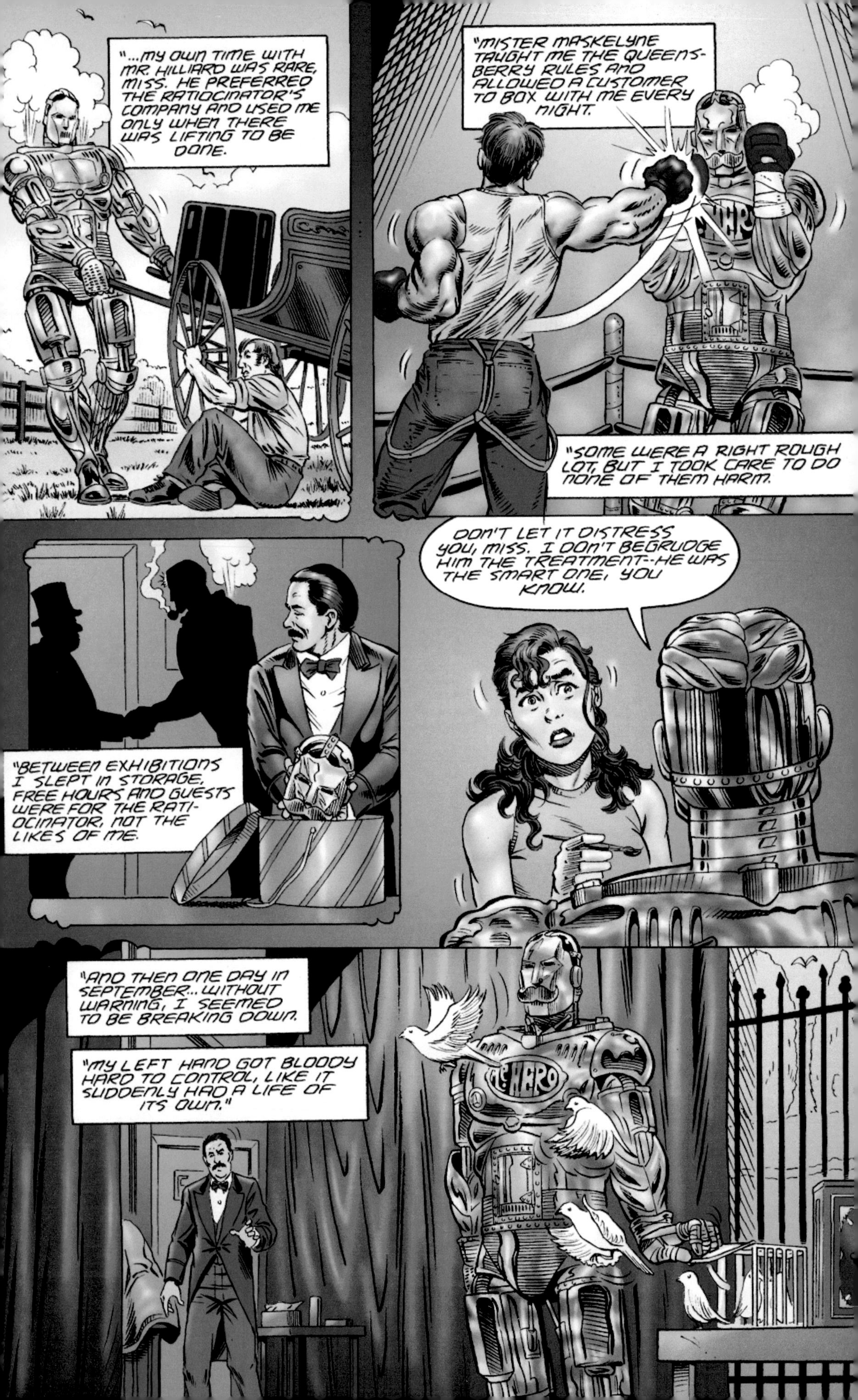
"...MY OWN TIME WITH MR. HILLIARD WAS RARE, MISS. HE PREFERRED THE RATIOCINATOR'S COMPANY AND USED ME ONLY WHEN THERE WAS LIFTING TO BE DONE.
"MISTER MASKELYNE TAUGHT ME THE QUEENSBERRY RULES AND ALLOWED A CUSTOMER TO BOX WITH ME EVERY NIGHT.
"SOME WERE A RIGHT ROUGH LOT, BUT I TOOK CARE TO DO NONE OF THEM HARM.
"BETWEEN EXHIBITIONS I SLEPT IN STORAGE. FREE HOURS AND GUESTS WERE FOR THE RATIOCINATOR, NOT THE LIKES OF ME.
DON'T LET IT DISTRESS YOU, MISS. I DON'T BEGRUDGE HIM THE TREATMENT--HE WAS THE SMART ONE, YOU KNOW.
"AND THEN ONE DAY IN SEPTEMBER... WITHOUT WARNING, I SEEMED TO BE BREAKING DOWN.
"MY LEFT HAND GOT BLOODY HARD TO CONTROL, LIKE IT SUDDENLY HAD A LIFE OF ITS OWN."

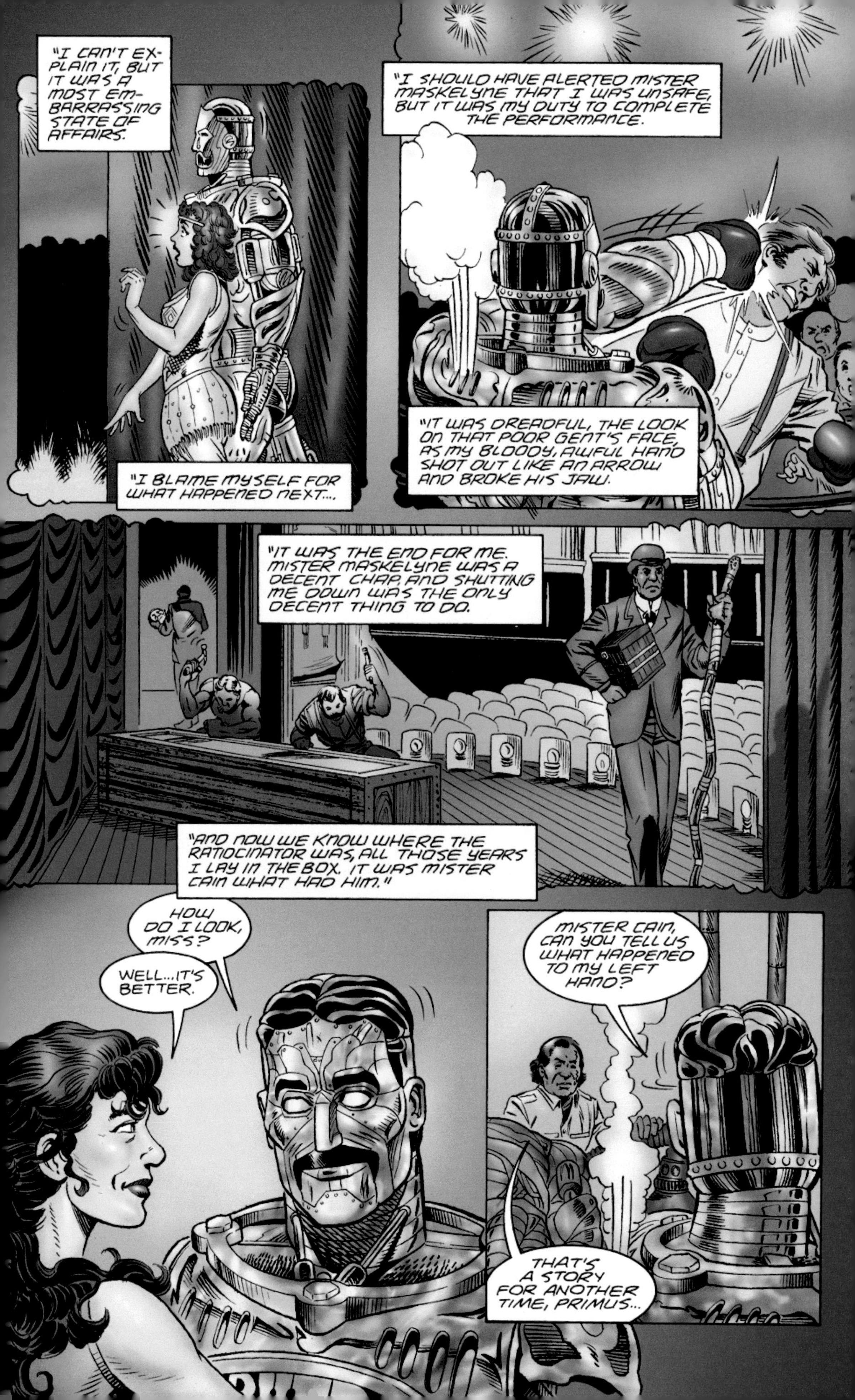
"I CAN'T EXPLAIN IT, BUT IT WAS A MOST EMBARRASSING STATE OF AFFAIRS.
"I BLAME MYSELF FOR WHAT HAPPENED NEXT....
"I SHOULD HAVE ALERTED MISTER MASKELYNE THAT I WAS UNSAFE, BUT IT WAS MY DUTY TO COMPLETE THE PERFORMANCE.
"IT WAS DREADFUL, THE LOOK ON THAT POOR GENT'S FACE, AS MY BLOODY, AWFUL HAND SHOT OUT LIKE AN ARROW AND BROKE HIS JAW.
"IT WAS THE END FOR ME. MISTER MASKELYNE WAS A DECENT CHAP, AND SHUTTING ME DOWN WAS THE ONLY DECENT THING TO DO.
"AND NOW WE KNOW WHERE THE RATIOCINATOR WAS, ALL THOSE YEARS I LAY IN THE BOX. IT WAS MISTER CAIN WHAT HAD HIM."
HOW DO I LOOK, MISS?
WELL...IT'S BETTER.
MISTER CAIN, CAN YOU TELL US WHAT HAPPENED TO MY LEFT HAND?
THAT'S A STORY FOR ANOTHER TIME, PRIMUS...

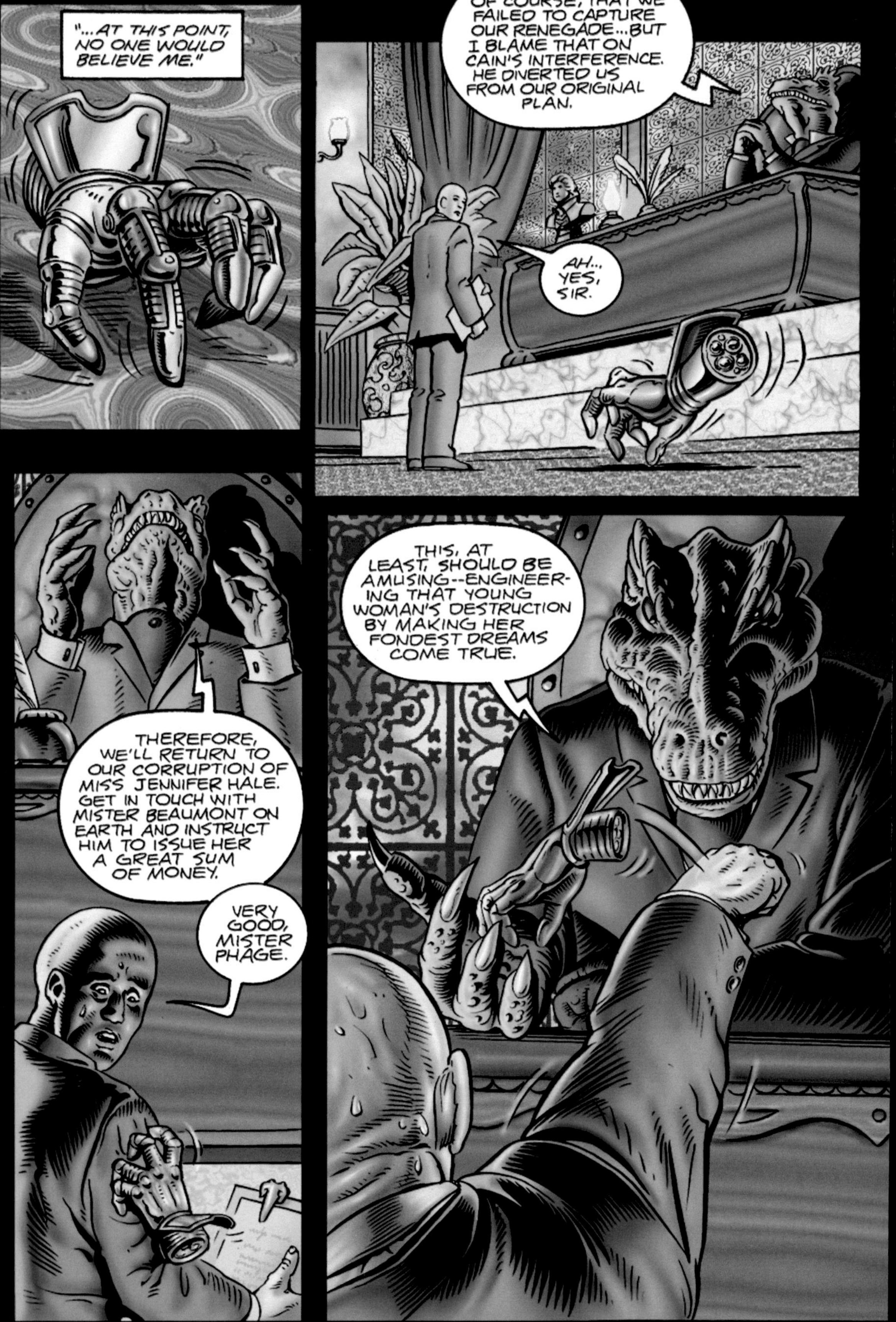
"...AT THIS POINT, NO ONE WOULD BELIEVE ME."
IT'S DISAPPOINTING, OF COURSE, THAT WE FAILED TO CAPTURE OUR RENEGADE...BUT I BLAME THAT ON CAIN'S INTERFERENCE. HE DIVERTED US FROM OUR ORIGINAL PLAN.
AH... YES, SIR.
THEREFORE, WE'LL RETURN TO OUR CORRUPTION OF MISS JENNIFER HALE. GET IN TOUCH WITH MISTER BEAUMONT ON EARTH AND INSTRUCT HIM TO ISSUE HER A GREAT SUM OF MONEY.
VERY GOOD, MISTER PHAGE.
THIS, AT LEAST, SHOULD BE AMUSING--ENGINEERING THAT YOUNG WOMAN'S DESTRUCTION BY MAKING HER FONDEST DREAMS COME TRUE.

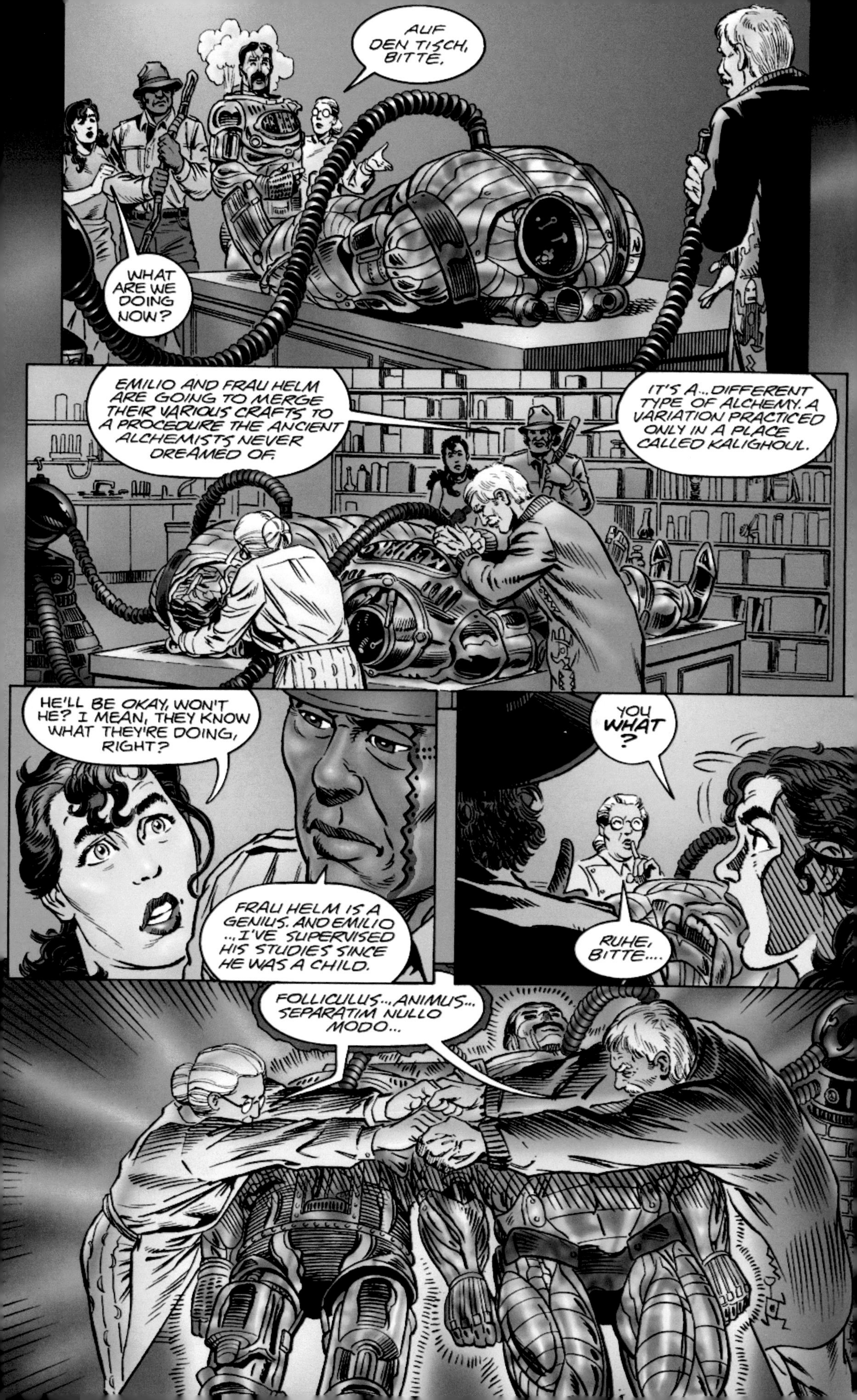
AUF DEN TISCH, BITTE.
WHAT ARE WE DOING NOW?
EMILIO AND FRAU HELM ARE GOING TO MERGE THEIR VARIOUS CRAFTS TO A PROCEDURE THE ANCIENT ALCHEMISTS NEVER DREAMED OF.
IT'S A...DIFFERENT TYPE OF ALCHEMY. A VARIATION PRACTICED ONLY IN A PLACE CALLED KALIGHOUL.
HE'LL BE OKAY, WON'T HE? I MEAN, THEY KNOW WHAT THEY'RE DOING, RIGHT?
FRAU HELM IS A GENIUS. AND EMILIO ...I'VE SUPERVISED HIS STUDIES SINCE HE WAS A CHILD.
YOU WHAT?
RUHE, BITTE....
FOLLICULUS...ANIMUS... SEPARATIM NULLO MODO...

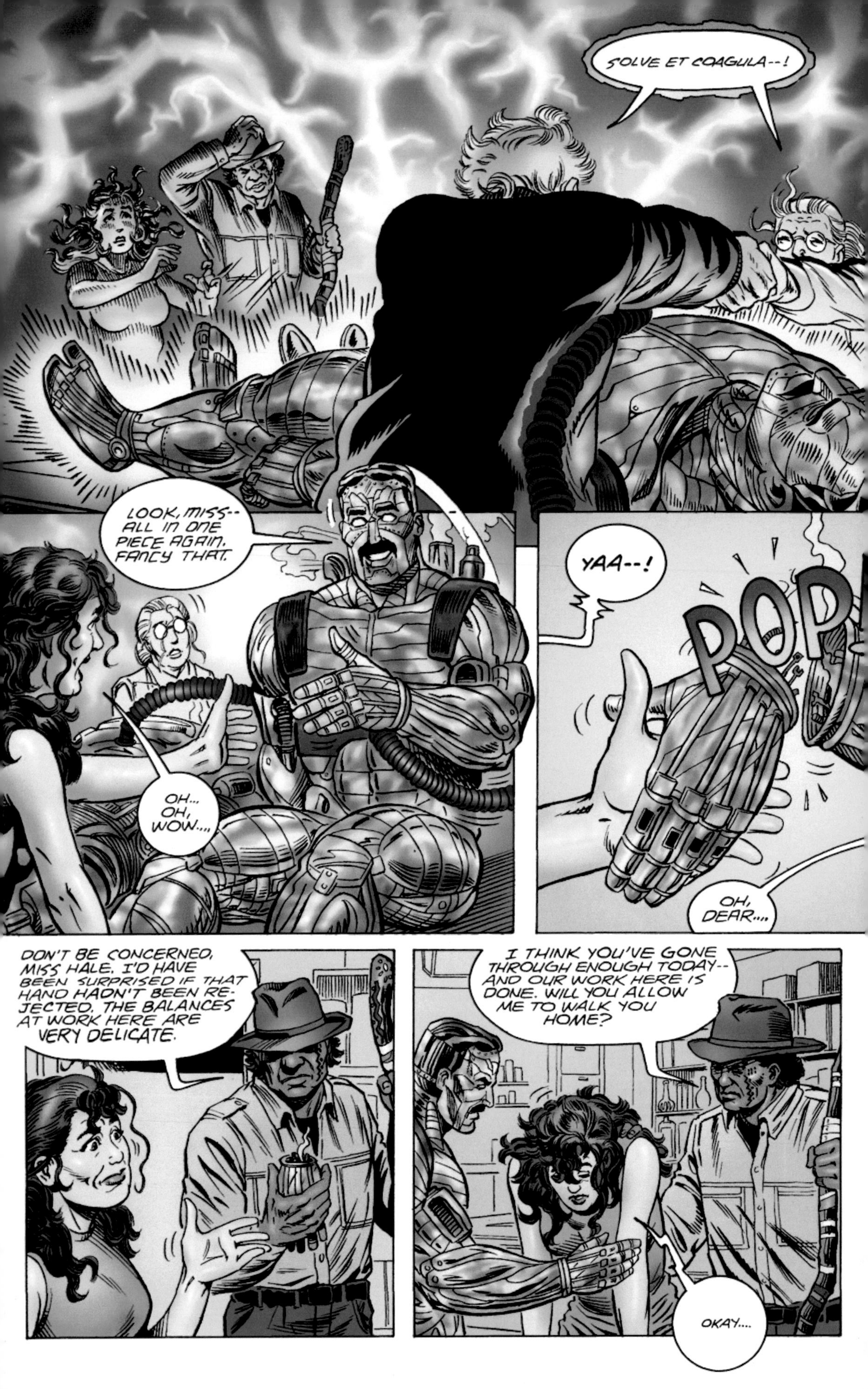
SOLVE ET COAGULA--!
LOOK, MISS--
ALL IN ONE PIECE AGAIN. FANCY THAT.
OH... OH, WOW....
YAA--!
POP!
OH, DEAR....
DON'T BE CONCERNED, MISS HALE. I'D HAVE BEEN SURPRISED IF THAT HAND HADN'T BEEN RE-JECTED. THE BALANCES AT WORK HERE ARE VERY DELICATE.
I THINK YOU'VE GONE THROUGH ENOUGH TODAY-- AND OUR WORK HERE IS DONE. WILL YOU ALLOW ME TO WALK YOU HOME?
OKAY....

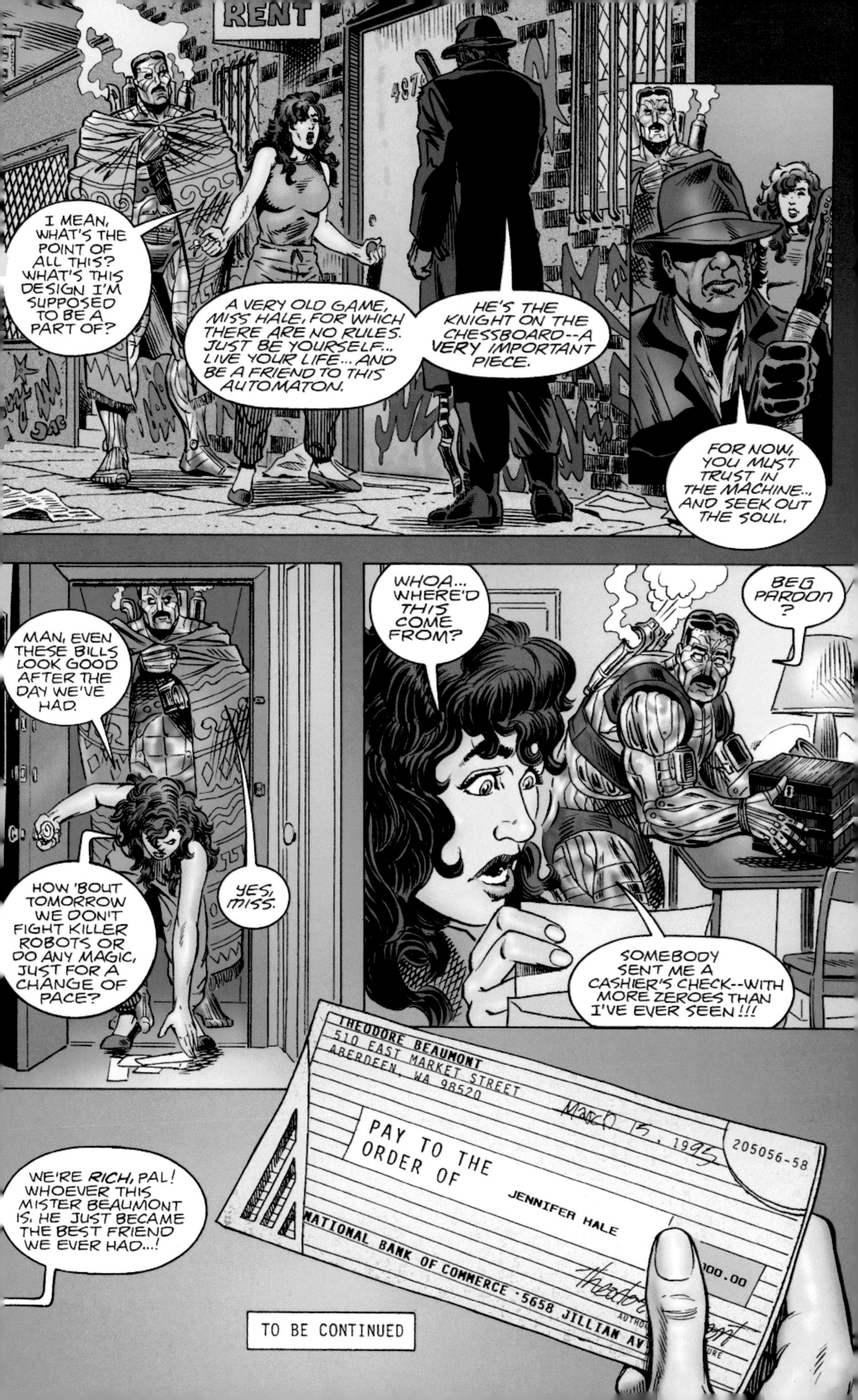
RENT
I MEAN, WHAT'S THE POINT OF ALL THIS? WHAT'S THIS DESIGN I'M SUPPOSED TO BE A PART OF?
A VERY OLD GAME, MISS HALE, FOR WHICH THERE ARE NO RULES. JUST BE YOURSELF... LIVE YOUR LIFE... AND BE A FRIEND TO THIS AUTOMATON.
HE'S THE KNIGHT ON THE CHESSBOARD--A VERY IMPORTANT PIECE.
FOR NOW, YOU MUST TRUST IN THE MACHINE... AND SEEK OUT THE SOUL.
MAN, EVEN THESE BILLS LOOK GOOD AFTER THE DAY WE'VE HAD.
HOW 'BOUT TOMORROW WE DON'T FIGHT KILLER ROBOTS OR DO ANY MAGIC, JUST FOR A CHANGE OF PACE?
YES, MISS.
WHOA... WHERE'D THIS COME FROM?
BEG PARDON?
SOMEBODY SENT ME A CASHIER'S CHECK--WITH MORE ZEROES THAN I'VE EVER SEEN!!!
THEODORE BEAUMONT
510 EAST MARKET STREET
ABERDEEN, WA 98520
March 15, 1995
205056-58
PAY TO THE ORDER OF
JENNIFER HALE
NATIONAL BANK OF COMMERCE · 5658 JILLIAN AV
WE'RE RICH, PAL! WHOEVER THIS MISTER BEAUMONT IS, HE JUST BECAME THE BEST FRIEND WE EVER HAD...!
TO BE CONTINUED

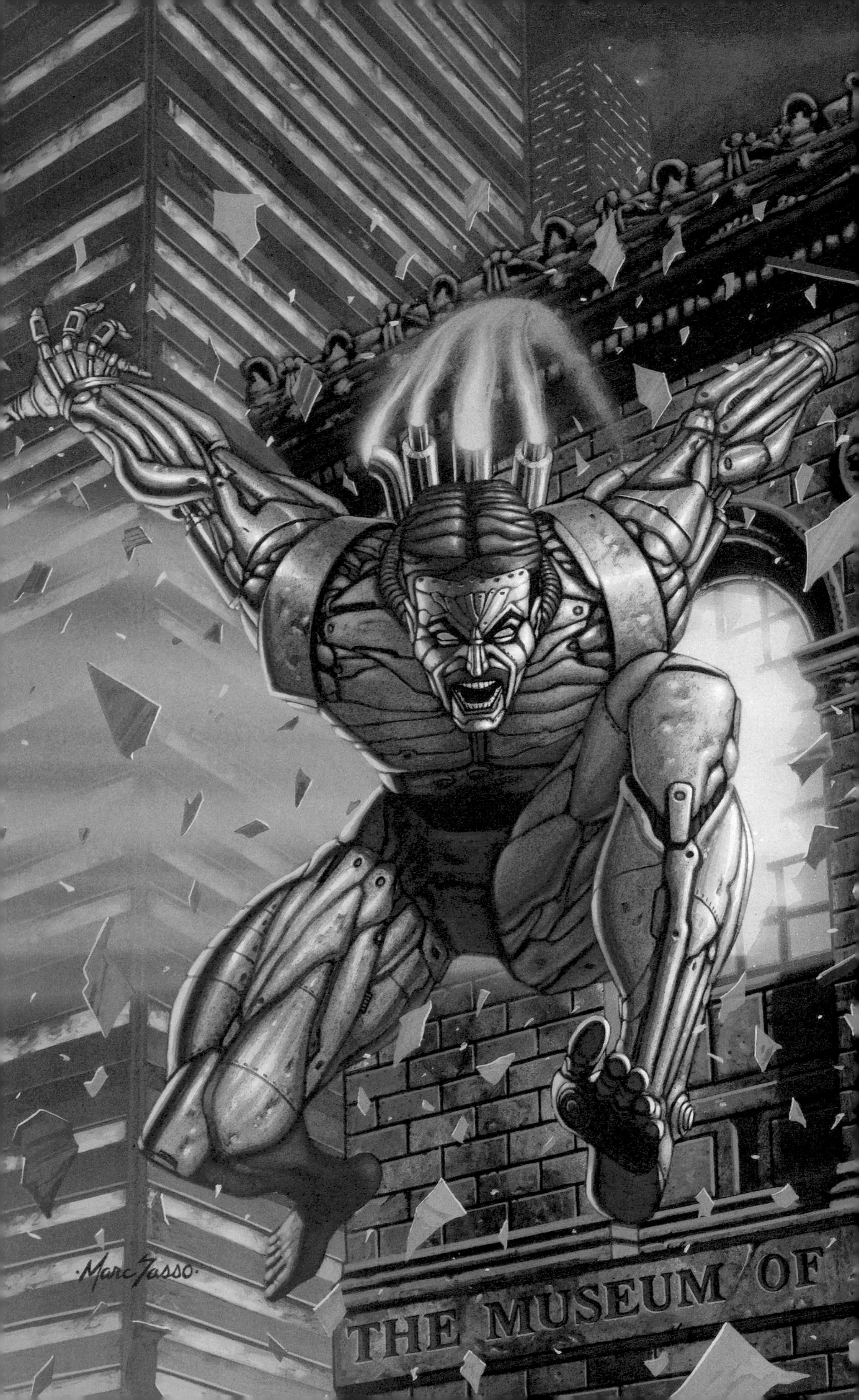
Marc Sasso
THE MUSEUM OF

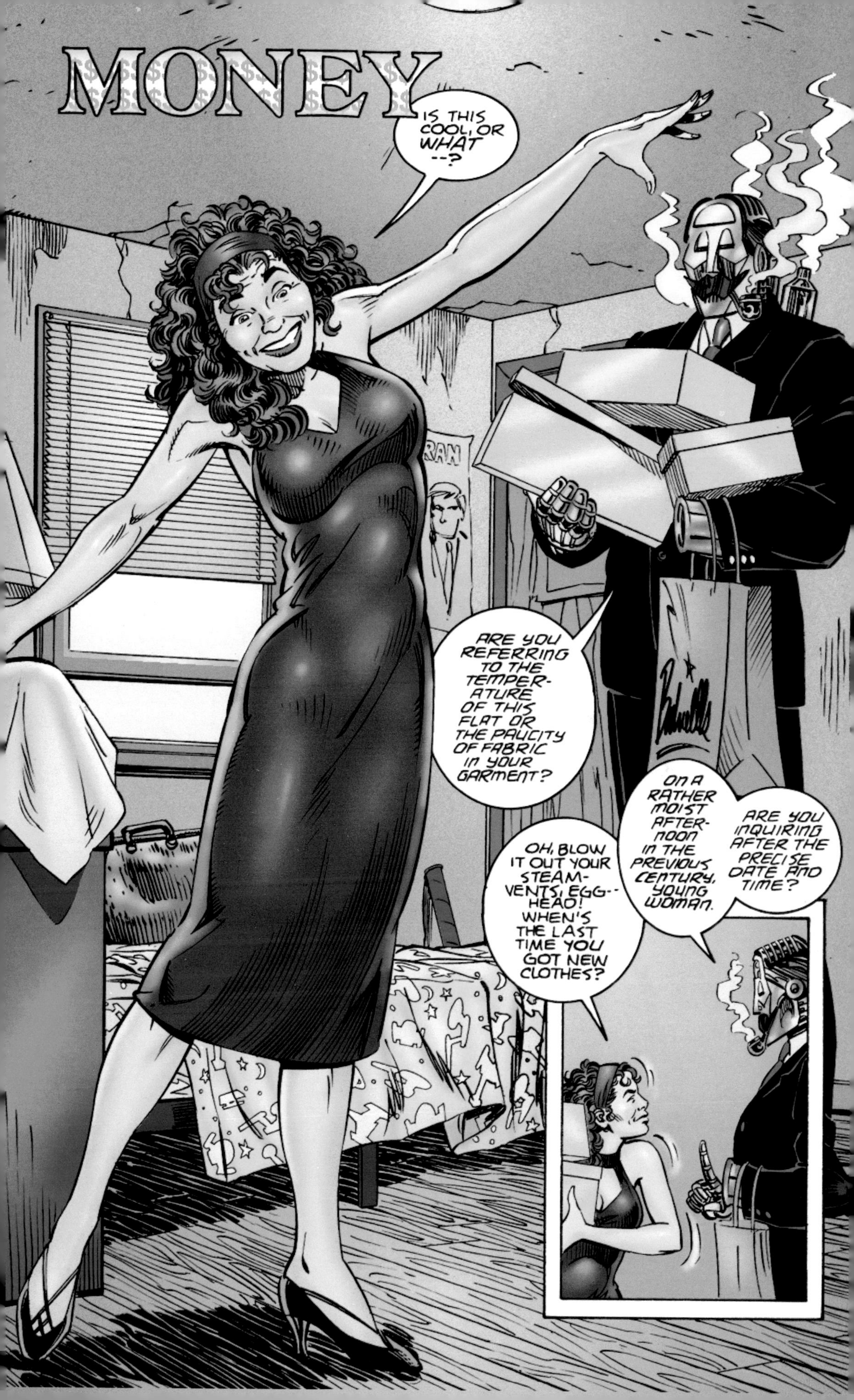
MONEY
IS THIS COOL, OR WHAT --?
ARE YOU REFERRING TO THE TEMPER-ATURE OF THIS FLAT OR THE PAUCITY OF FABRIC IN YOUR GARMENT?
OH, BLOW IT OUT YOUR STEAM-VENTS, EGG--HEAD! WHEN'S THE LAST TIME YOU GOT NEW CLOTHES?
ON A RATHER MOIST AFTER-NOON IN THE PREVIOUS CENTURY, YOUNG WOMAN.
ARE YOU INQUIRING AFTER THE PRECISE DATE AND TIME?
RAN

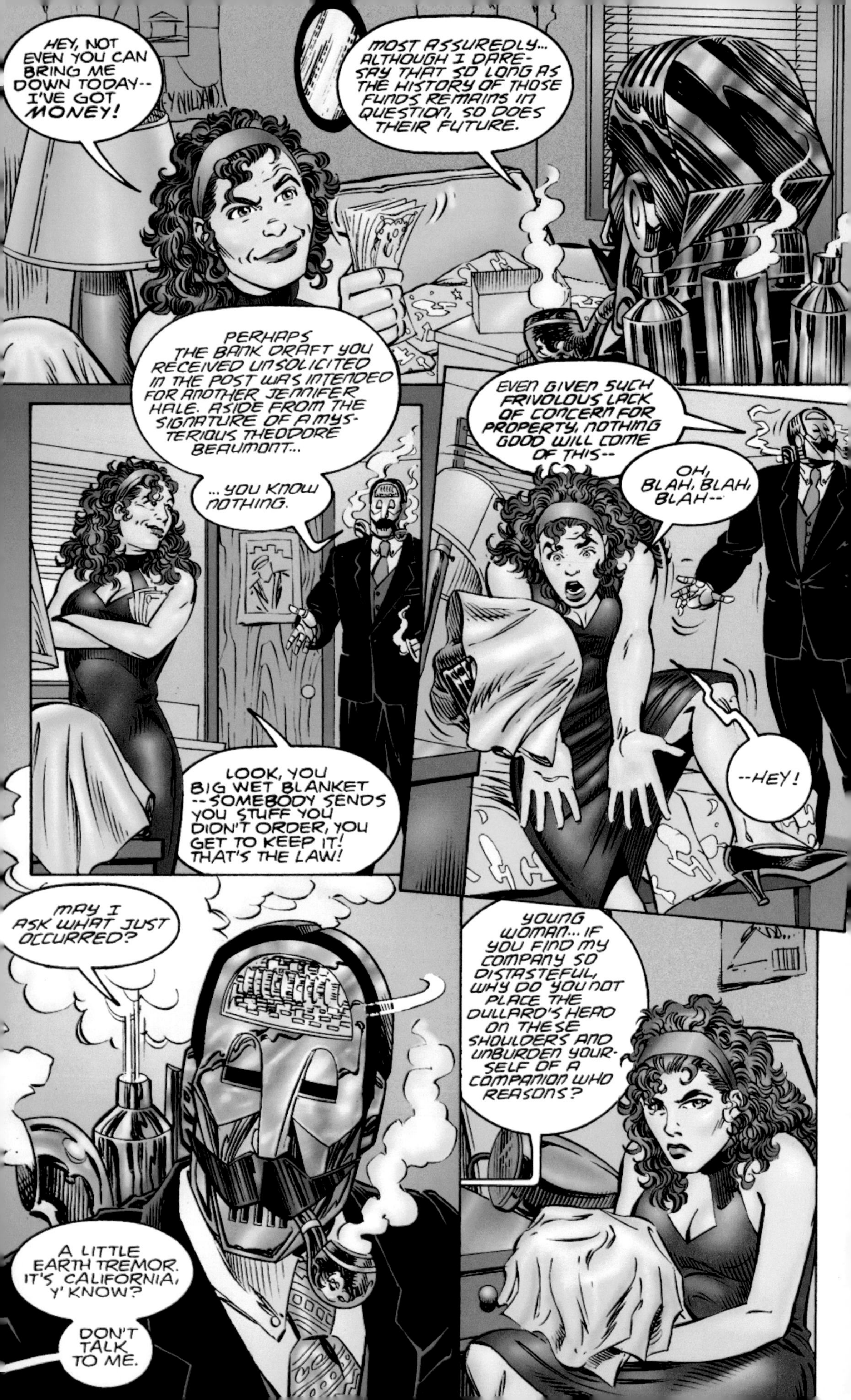
HEY, NOT EVEN YOU CAN BRING ME DOWN TODAY-- I'VE GOT MONEY!
MOST ASSUREDLY... ALTHOUGH I DARE-SAY THAT SO LONG AS THE HISTORY OF THOSE FUNDS REMAINS IN QUESTION, SO DOES THEIR FUTURE.
PERHAPS THE BANK DRAFT YOU RECEIVED UNSOLICITED IN THE POST WAS INTENDED FOR ANOTHER JENNIFER HALE. ASIDE FROM THE SIGNATURE OF A MYS-TERIOUS THEODORE BEAUMONT...
...YOU KNOW NOTHING.
LOOK, YOU BIG WET BLANKET --SOMEBODY SENDS YOU STUFF YOU DIDN'T ORDER, YOU GET TO KEEP IT! THAT'S THE LAW!
EVEN GIVEN SUCH FRIVOLOUS LACK OF CONCERN FOR PROPERTY, NOTHING GOOD WILL COME OF THIS--
OH, BLAH, BLAH, BLAH--
--HEY!
MAY I ASK WHAT JUST OCCURRED?
A LITTLE EARTH TREMOR. IT'S CALIFORNIA, Y'KNOW?
DON'T TALK TO ME.
YOUNG WOMAN... IF YOU FIND MY COMPANY SO DISTASTEFUL, WHY DO YOU NOT PLACE THE DULLARD'S HEAD ON THESE SHOULDERS AND UNBURDEN YOUR-SELF OF A COMPANION WHO REASONS?

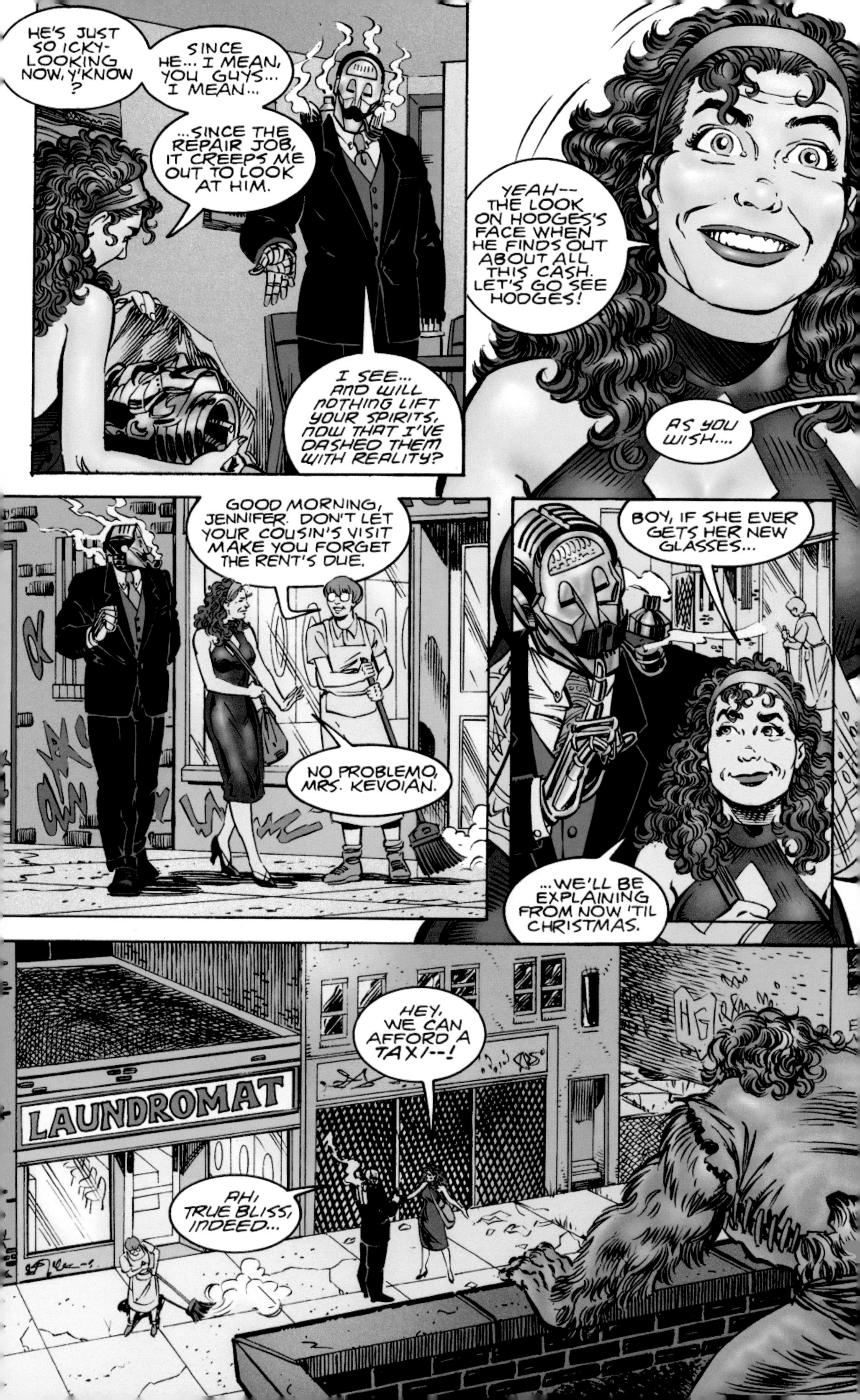
HE'S JUST SO ICKY-LOOKING NOW, Y'KNOW?
SINCE HE... I MEAN, YOU GUYS... I MEAN...
...SINCE THE REPAIR JOB, IT CREEPS ME OUT TO LOOK AT HIM.
I SEE... AND WILL NOTHING LIFT YOUR SPIRITS, NOW THAT I'VE DASHED THEM WITH REALITY?
YEAH-- THE LOOK ON HODGES'S FACE WHEN HE FINDS OUT ABOUT ALL THIS CASH. LET'S GO SEE HODGES!
AS YOU WISH....
GOOD MORNING, JENNIFER. DON'T LET YOUR COUSIN'S VISIT MAKE YOU FORGET THE RENT'S DUE.
NO PROBLEMO, MRS. KEVOIAN.
BOY, IF SHE EVER GETS HER NEW GLASSES...
...WE'LL BE EXPLAINING FROM NOW 'TIL CHRISTMAS.
LAUNDROMAT
HEY, WE CAN AFFORD A TAXI--!
AH, TRUE BLISS, INDEED...

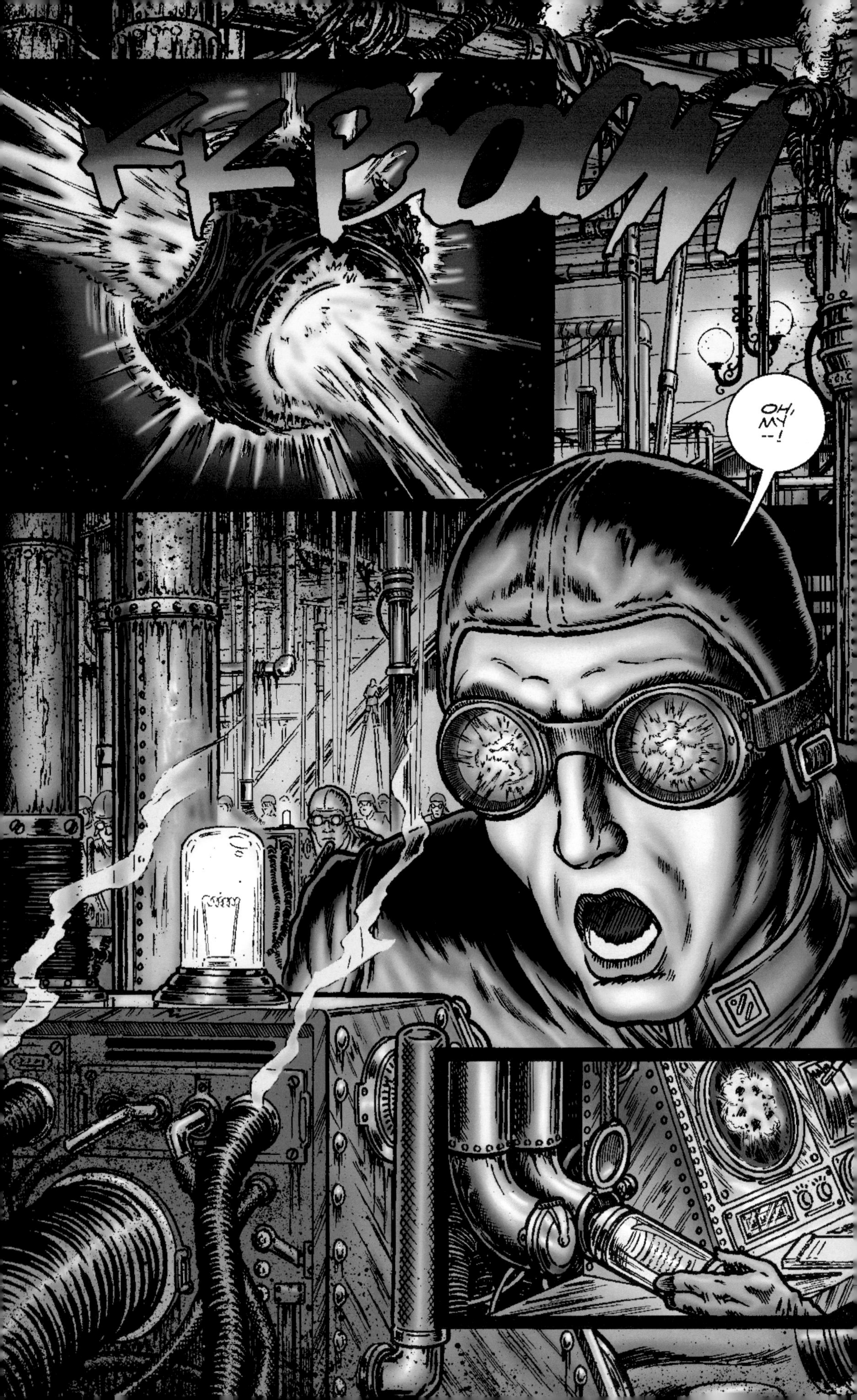
K-BOOM
OH, MY --!

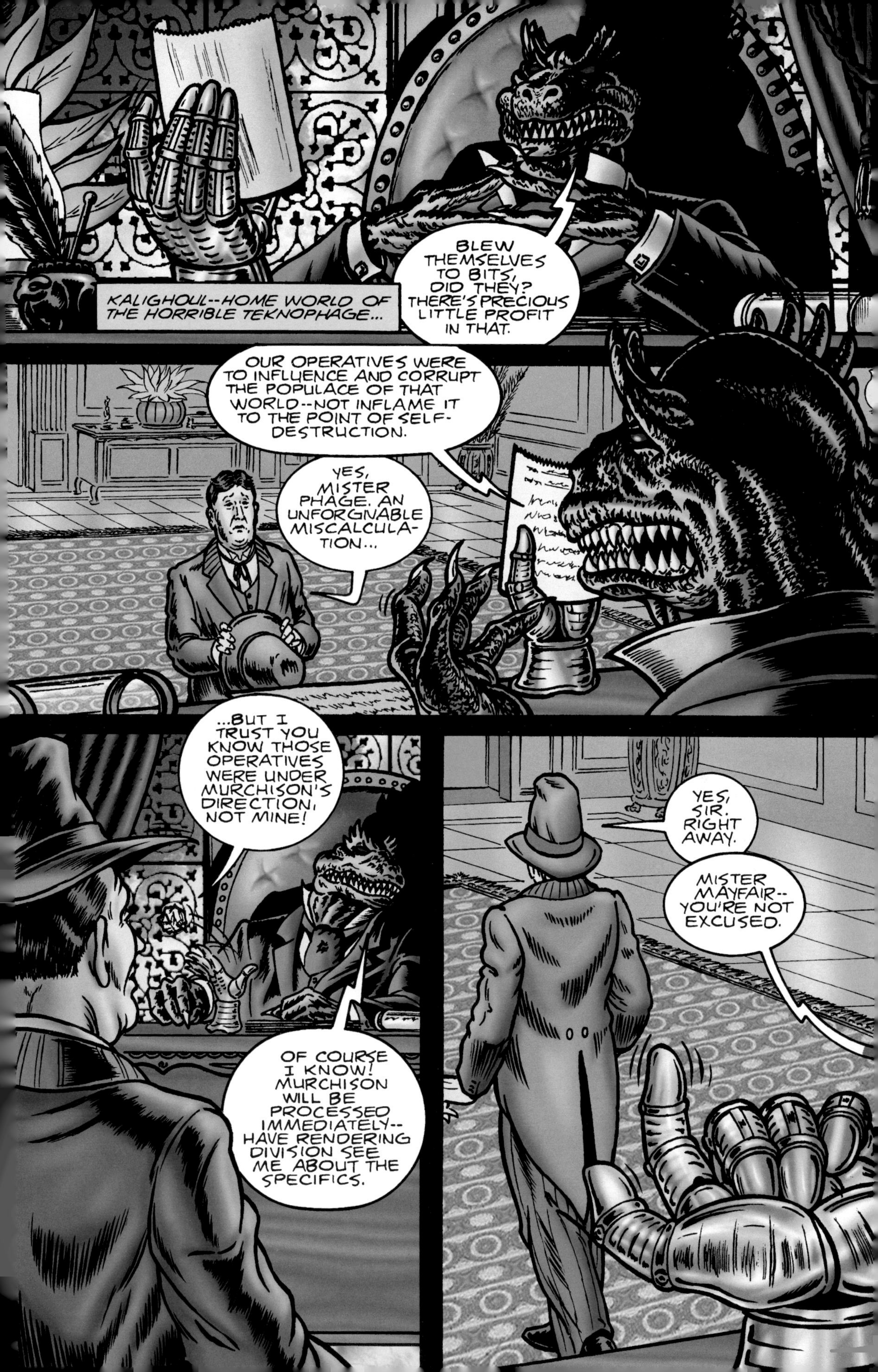
KALIGHOUL--HOME WORLD OF THE HORRIBLE TEKNOPHAGE...
BLEW THEMSELVES TO BITS, DID THEY? THERE'S PRECIOUS LITTLE PROFIT IN THAT.
OUR OPERATIVES WERE TO INFLUENCE AND CORRUPT THE POPULACE OF THAT WORLD--NOT INFLAME IT TO THE POINT OF SELF-DESTRUCTION.
YES, MISTER PHAGE. AN UNFORGIVABLE MISCALCULATION...
...BUT I TRUST YOU KNOW THOSE OPERATIVES WERE UNDER MURCHISON'S DIRECTION, NOT MINE!
OF COURSE I KNOW! MURCHISON WILL BE PROCESSED IMMEDIATELY--HAVE RENDERING DIVISION SEE ME ABOUT THE SPECIFICS.
YES, SIR. RIGHT AWAY.
MISTER MAYFAIR--YOU'RE NOT EXCUSED.

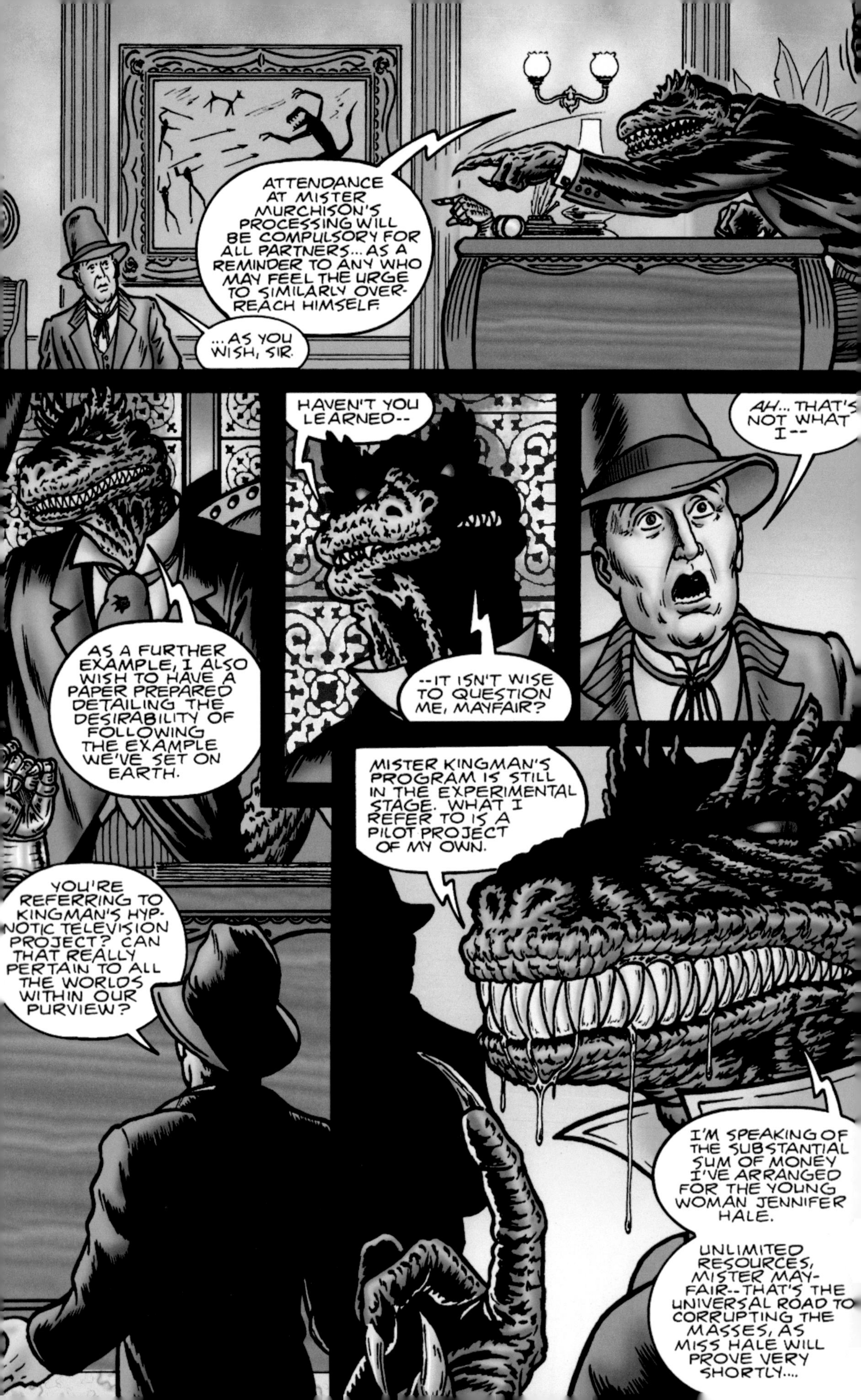
ATTENDANCE AT MISTER MURCHISON'S PROCESSING WILL BE COMPULSORY FOR ALL PARTNERS... AS A REMINDER TO ANY WHO MAY FEEL THE URGE TO SIMILARLY OVER-REACH HIMSELF.
...AS YOU WISH, SIR.
HAVEN'T YOU LEARNED--
--IT ISN'T WISE TO QUESTION ME, MAYFAIR?
AH... THAT'S NOT WHAT I--
AS A FURTHER EXAMPLE, I ALSO WISH TO HAVE A PAPER PREPARED DETAILING THE DESIRABILITY OF FOLLOWING THE EXAMPLE WE'VE SET ON EARTH.
YOU'RE REFERRING TO KINGMAN'S HYPNOTIC TELEVISION PROJECT? CAN THAT REALLY PERTAIN TO ALL THE WORLDS WITHIN OUR PURVIEW?
MISTER KINGMAN'S PROGRAM IS STILL IN THE EXPERIMENTAL STAGE. WHAT I REFER TO IS A PILOT PROJECT OF MY OWN.
I'M SPEAKING OF THE SUBSTANTIAL SUM OF MONEY I'VE ARRANGED FOR THE YOUNG WOMAN JENNIFER HALE.
UNLIMITED RESOURCES, MISTER MAYFAIR--THAT'S THE UNIVERSAL ROAD TO CORRUPTING THE MASSES, AS MISS HALE WILL PROVE VERY SHORTLY....

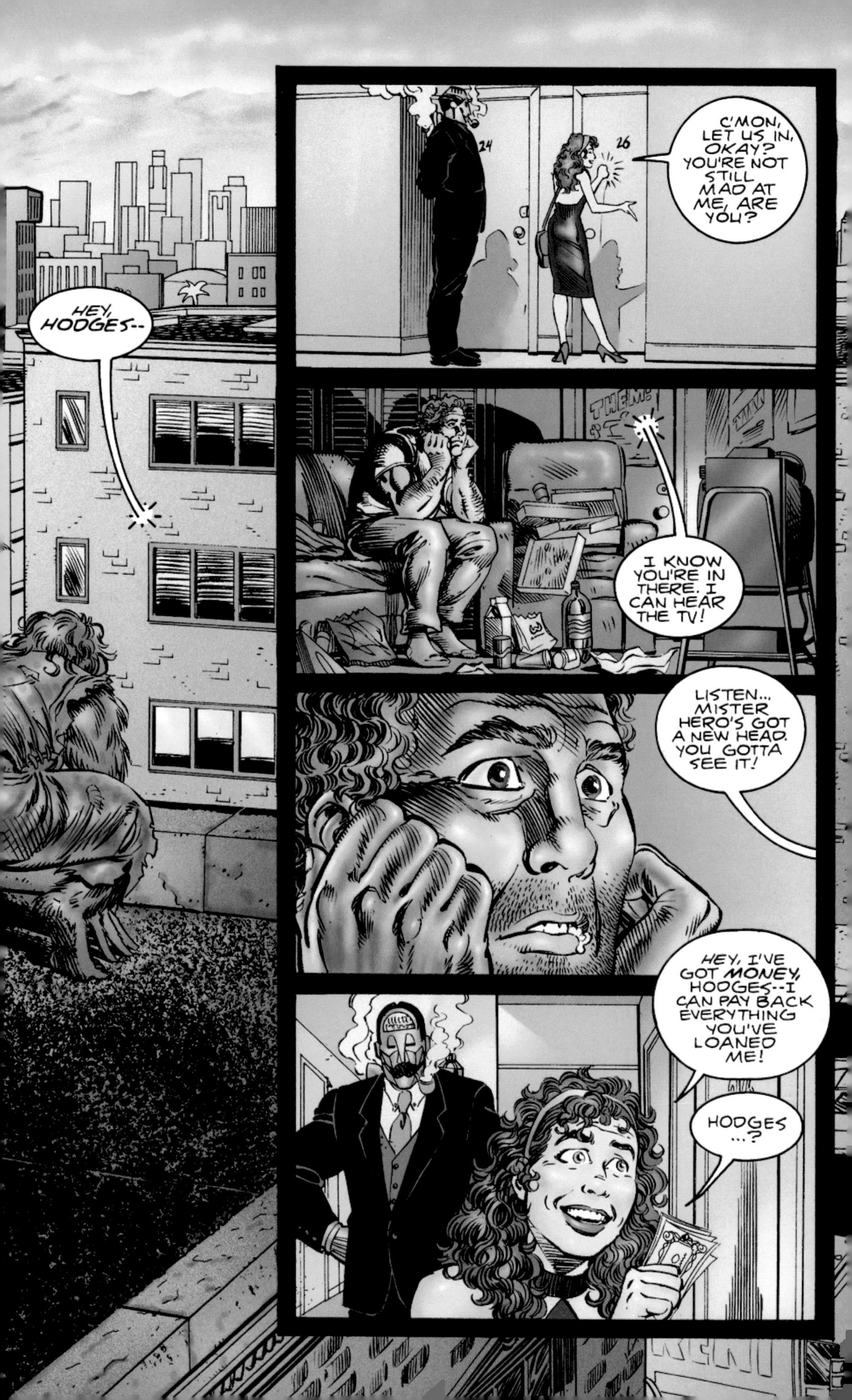
HEY, HODGES--
C'MON, LET US IN, OKAY? YOU'RE NOT STILL MAD AT ME, ARE YOU?
24
26
I KNOW YOU'RE IN THERE. I CAN HEAR THE TV!
LISTEN... MISTER HERO'S GOT A NEW HEAD. YOU GOTTA SEE IT!
HEY, I'VE GOT MONEY, HODGES--I CAN PAY BACK EVERYTHING YOU'VE LOANED ME!
HODGES ...?

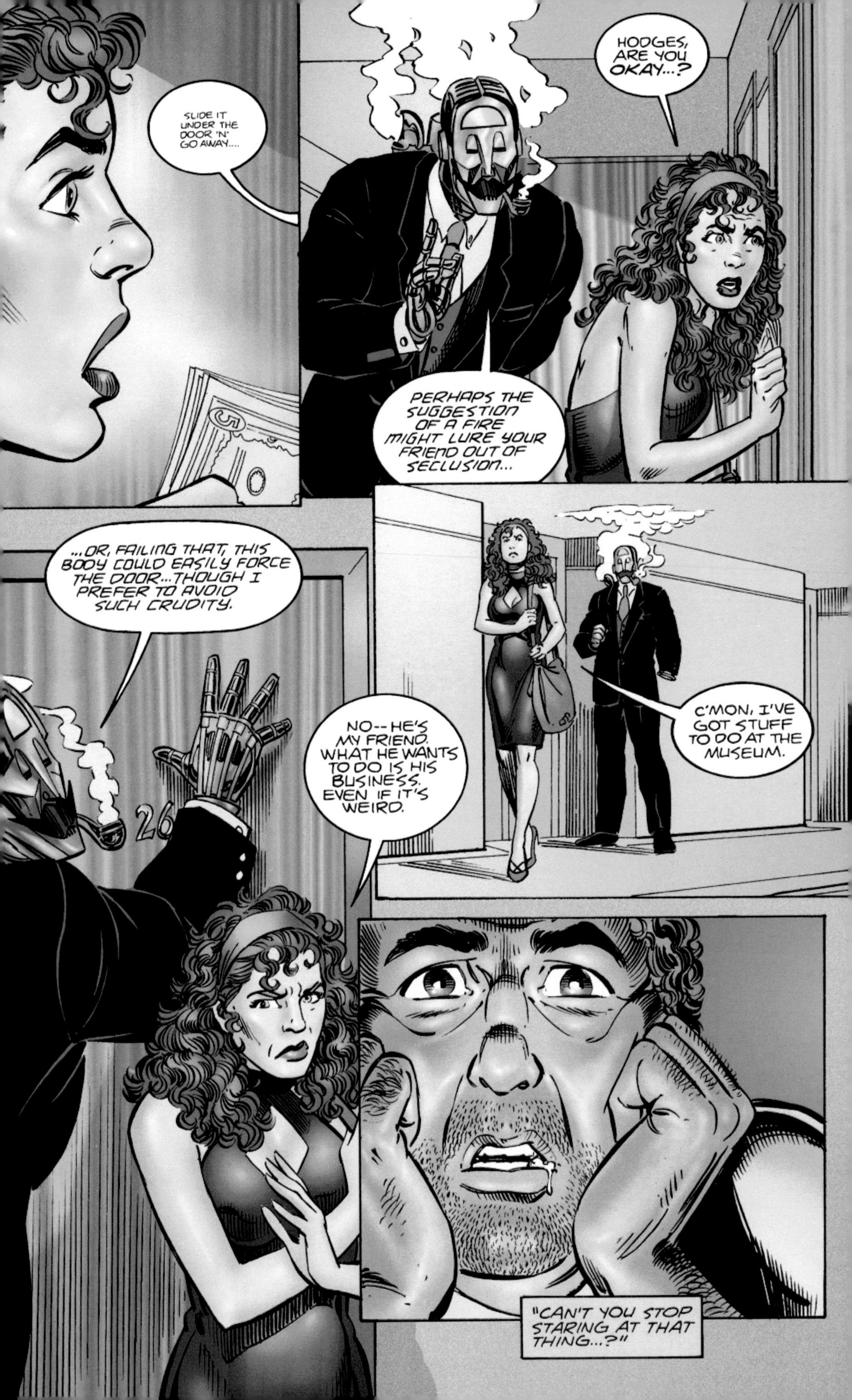
SLIDE IT UNDER THE DOOR 'N' GO AWAY....
HODGES, ARE YOU OKAY...?
PERHAPS THE SUGGESTION OF A FIRE MIGHT LURE YOUR FRIEND OUT OF SECLUSION...
...OR, FAILING THAT, THIS BODY COULD EASILY FORCE THE DOOR...THOUGH I PREFER TO AVOID SUCH CRUDITY.
26
NO-- HE'S MY FRIEND. WHAT HE WANTS TO DO IS HIS BUSINESS. EVEN IF IT'S WEIRD.
C'MON, I'VE GOT STUFF TO DO AT THE MUSEUM.
"CAN'T YOU STOP STARING AT THAT THING...?"

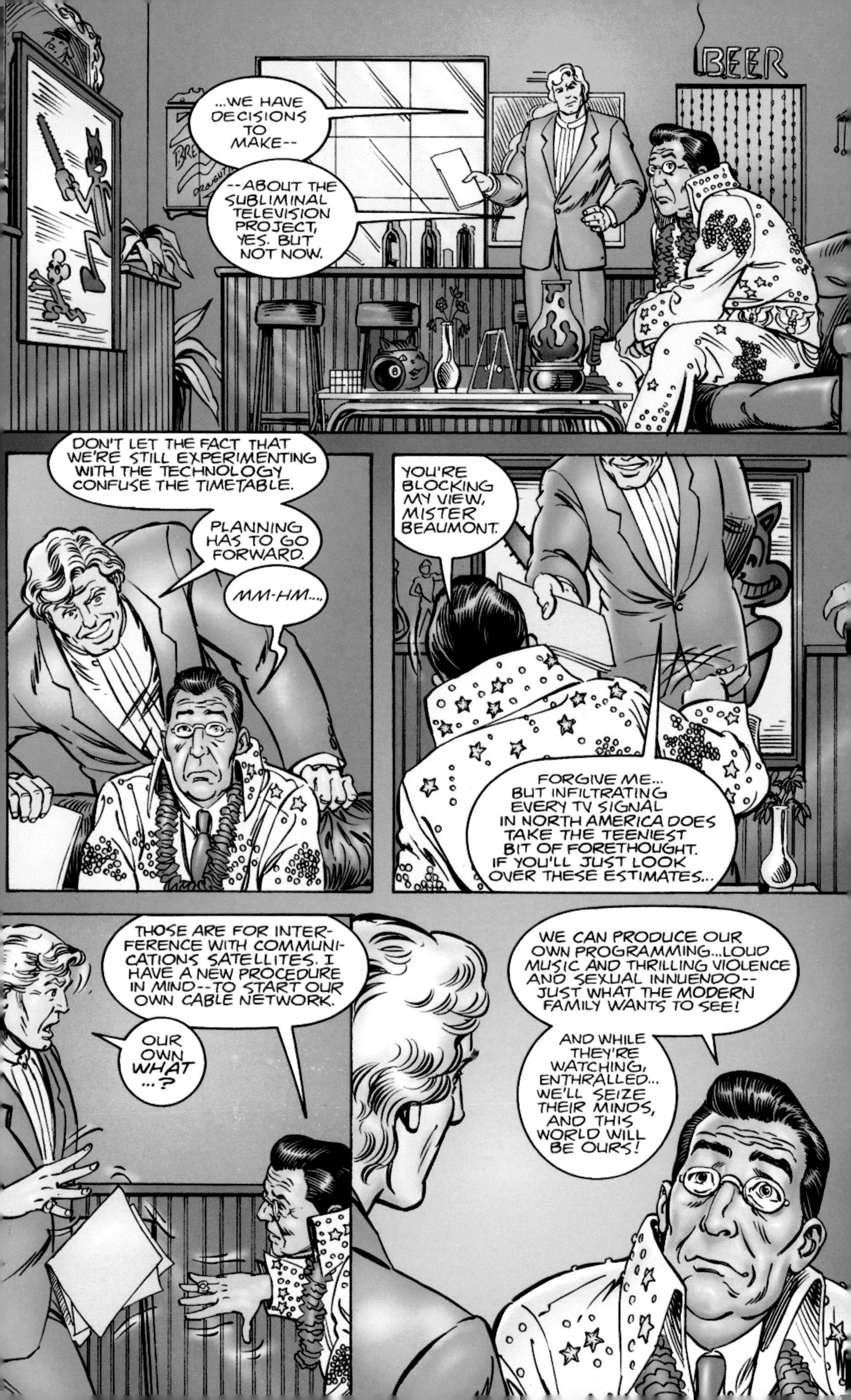
...WE HAVE DECISIONS TO MAKE--
--ABOUT THE SUBLIMINAL TELEVISION PROJECT, YES. BUT NOT NOW.
BEER
DON'T LET THE FACT THAT WE'RE STILL EXPERIMENTING WITH THE TECHNOLOGY CONFUSE THE TIMETABLE.
PLANNING HAS TO GO FORWARD.
MM-HM...,
YOU'RE BLOCKING MY VIEW, MISTER BEAUMONT.
FORGIVE ME... BUT INFILTRATING EVERY TV SIGNAL IN NORTH AMERICA DOES TAKE THE TEENIEST BIT OF FORETHOUGHT. IF YOU'LL JUST LOOK OVER THESE ESTIMATES...
THOSE ARE FOR INTERFERENCE WITH COMMUNICATIONS SATELLITES. I HAVE A NEW PROCEDURE IN MIND--TO START OUR OWN CABLE NETWORK.
OUR OWN WHAT ...?
WE CAN PRODUCE OUR OWN PROGRAMMING...LOUD MUSIC AND THRILLING VIOLENCE AND SEXUAL INNUENDO-- JUST WHAT THE MODERN FAMILY WANTS TO SEE!
AND WHILE THEY'RE WATCHING, ENTHRALLED... WE'LL SEIZE THEIR MINDS, AND THIS WORLD WILL BE OURS!

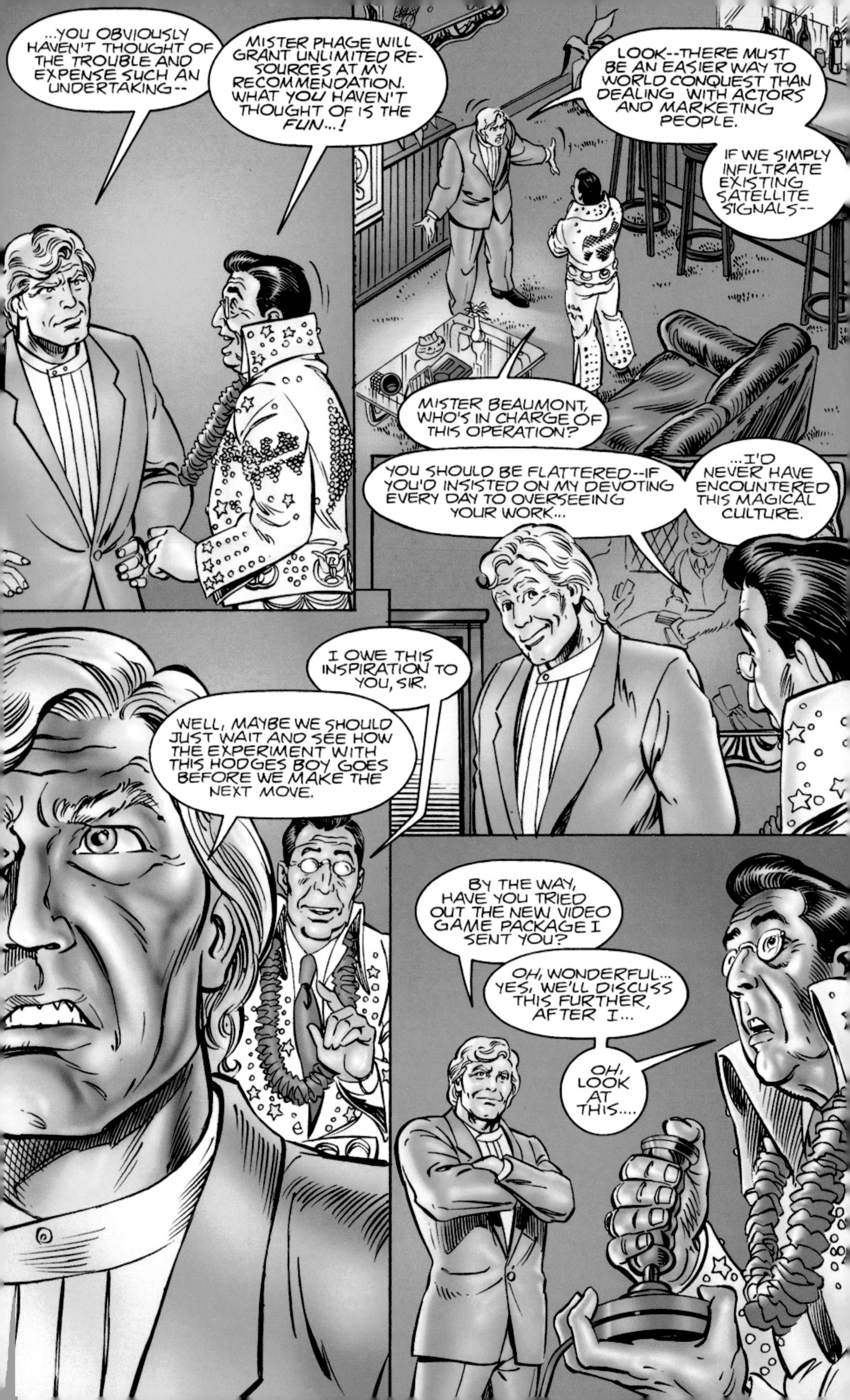
...YOU OBVIOUSLY HAVEN'T THOUGHT OF THE TROUBLE AND EXPENSE SUCH AN UNDERTAKING--
MISTER PHAGE WILL GRANT UNLIMITED RESOURCES AT MY RECOMMENDATION. WHAT YOU HAVEN'T THOUGHT OF IS THE FUN...!
LOOK--THERE MUST BE AN EASIER WAY TO WORLD CONQUEST THAN DEALING WITH ACTORS AND MARKETING PEOPLE.
IF WE SIMPLY INFILTRATE EXISTING SATELLITE SIGNALS--
MISTER BEAUMONT, WHO'S IN CHARGE OF THIS OPERATION?
YOU SHOULD BE FLATTERED--IF YOU'D INSISTED ON MY DEVOTING EVERY DAY TO OVERSEEING YOUR WORK...
...I'D NEVER HAVE ENCOUNTERED THIS MAGICAL CULTURE.
I OWE THIS INSPIRATION TO YOU, SIR.
WELL, MAYBE WE SHOULD JUST WAIT AND SEE HOW THE EXPERIMENT WITH THIS HODGES BOY GOES BEFORE WE MAKE THE NEXT MOVE.
BY THE WAY, HAVE YOU TRIED OUT THE NEW VIDEO GAME PACKAGE I SENT YOU?
OH, WONDERFUL... YES, WE'LL DISCUSS THIS FURTHER, AFTER I...
OH, LOOK AT THIS....

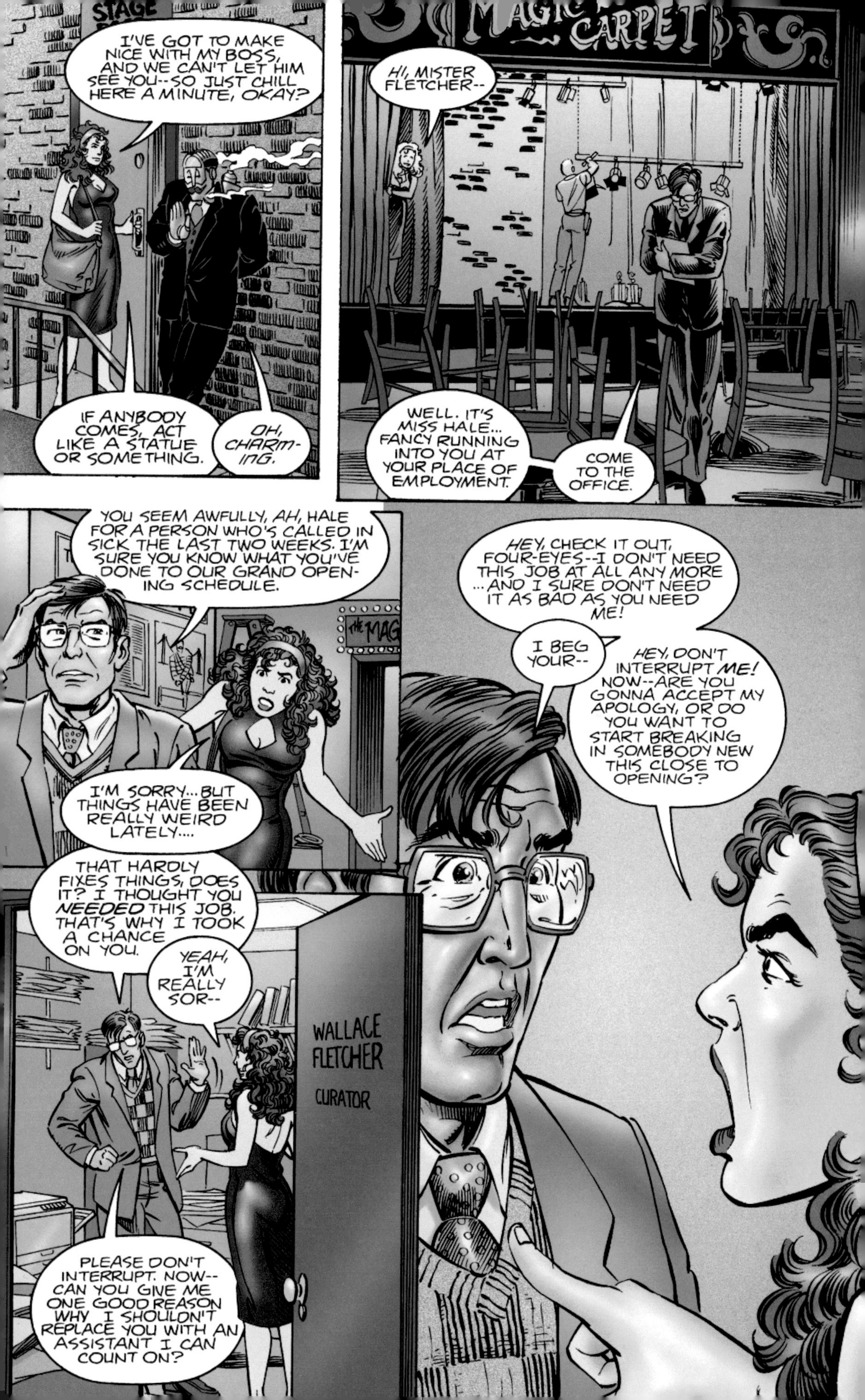
STAGE
I'VE GOT TO MAKE NICE WITH MY BOSS, AND WE CAN'T LET HIM SEE YOU--SO JUST CHILL HERE A MINUTE, OKAY?
IF ANYBODY COMES, ACT LIKE A STATUE OR SOMETHING.
OH, CHARMING.
MAGIC CARPET
HI, MISTER FLETCHER--
WELL. IT'S MISS HALE... FANCY RUNNING INTO YOU AT YOUR PLACE OF EMPLOYMENT.
COME TO THE OFFICE.
YOU SEEM AWFULLY, AH, HALE FOR A PERSON WHO'S CALLED IN SICK THE LAST TWO WEEKS. I'M SURE YOU KNOW WHAT YOU'VE DONE TO OUR GRAND OPENING SCHEDULE.
I'M SORRY... BUT THINGS HAVE BEEN REALLY WEIRD LATELY....
THAT HARDLY FIXES THINGS, DOES IT? I THOUGHT YOU NEEDED THIS JOB. THAT'S WHY I TOOK A CHANCE ON YOU.
YEAH, I'M REALLY SOR--
WALLACE FLETCHER
CURATOR
PLEASE DON'T INTERRUPT. NOW--CAN YOU GIVE ME ONE GOOD REASON WHY I SHOULDN'T REPLACE YOU WITH AN ASSISTANT I CAN COUNT ON?
HEY, CHECK IT OUT, FOUR-EYES--I DON'T NEED THIS JOB AT ALL ANY MORE ...AND I SURE DON'T NEED IT AS BAD AS YOU NEED ME!
I BEG YOUR--
HEY, DON'T INTERRUPT ME! NOW--ARE YOU GONNA ACCEPT MY APOLOGY, OR DO YOU WANT TO START BREAKING IN SOMEBODY NEW THIS CLOSE TO OPENING?

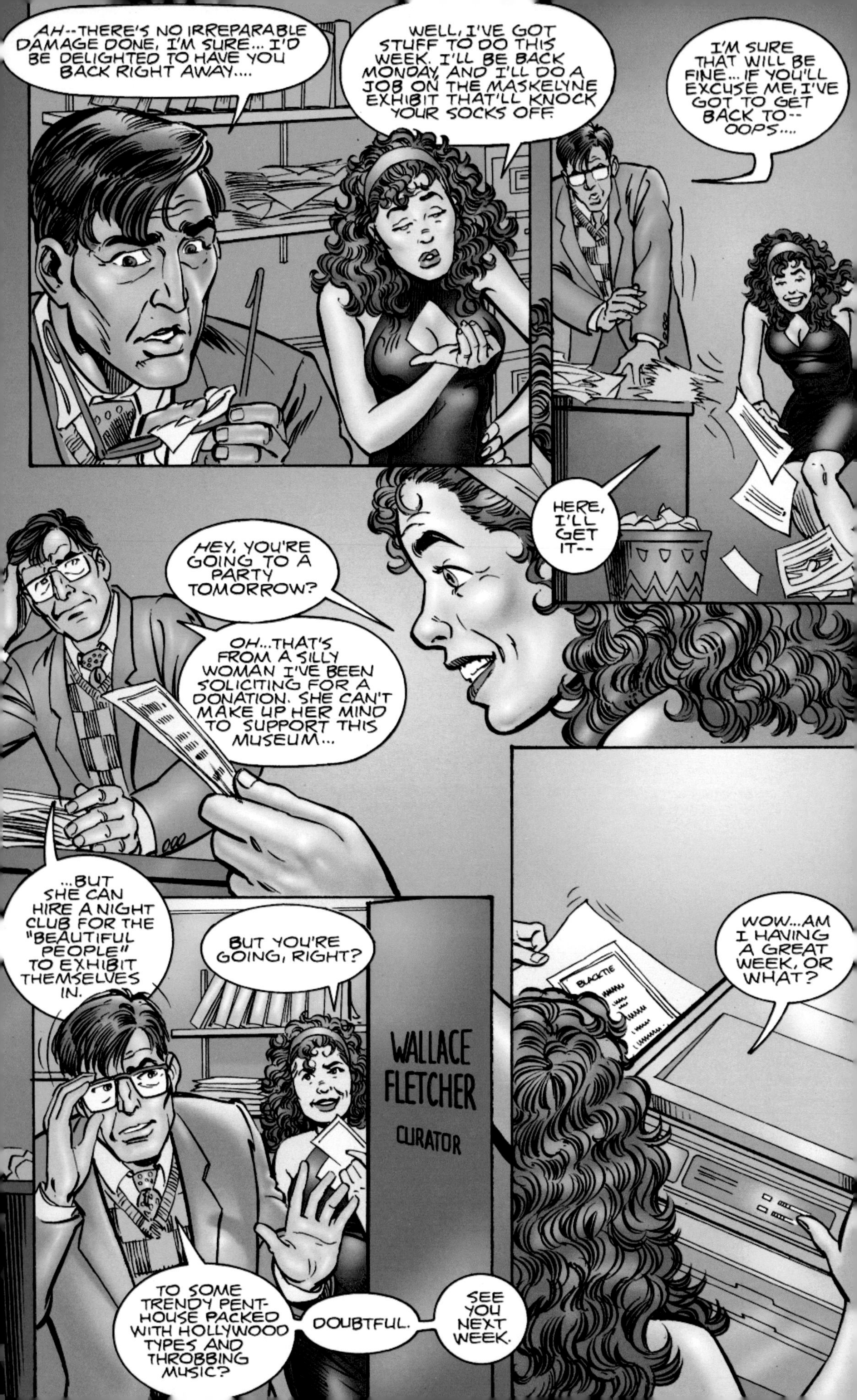
AH--THERE'S NO IRREPARABLE DAMAGE DONE, I'M SURE... I'D BE DELIGHTED TO HAVE YOU BACK RIGHT AWAY....
WELL, I'VE GOT STUFF TO DO THIS WEEK. I'LL BE BACK MONDAY, AND I'LL DO A JOB ON THE MASKELYNE EXHIBIT THAT'LL KNOCK YOUR SOCKS OFF.
I'M SURE THAT WILL BE FINE... IF YOU'LL EXCUSE ME, I'VE GOT TO GET BACK TO-- OOPS....
HERE, I'LL GET IT--
HEY, YOU'RE GOING TO A PARTY TOMORROW?
OH...THAT'S FROM A SILLY WOMAN I'VE BEEN SOLICITING FOR A DONATION. SHE CAN'T MAKE UP HER MIND TO SUPPORT THIS MUSEUM...
...BUT SHE CAN HIRE A NIGHT CLUB FOR THE "BEAUTIFUL PEOPLE" TO EXHIBIT THEMSELVES IN.
BUT YOU'RE GOING, RIGHT?
WALLACE FLETCHER
CURATOR
TO SOME TRENDY PENT-HOUSE PACKED WITH HOLLYWOOD TYPES AND THROBBING MUSIC?
DOUBTFUL.
SEE YOU NEXT WEEK.
BLACKTIE
WOW...AM I HAVING A GREAT WEEK, OR WHAT?

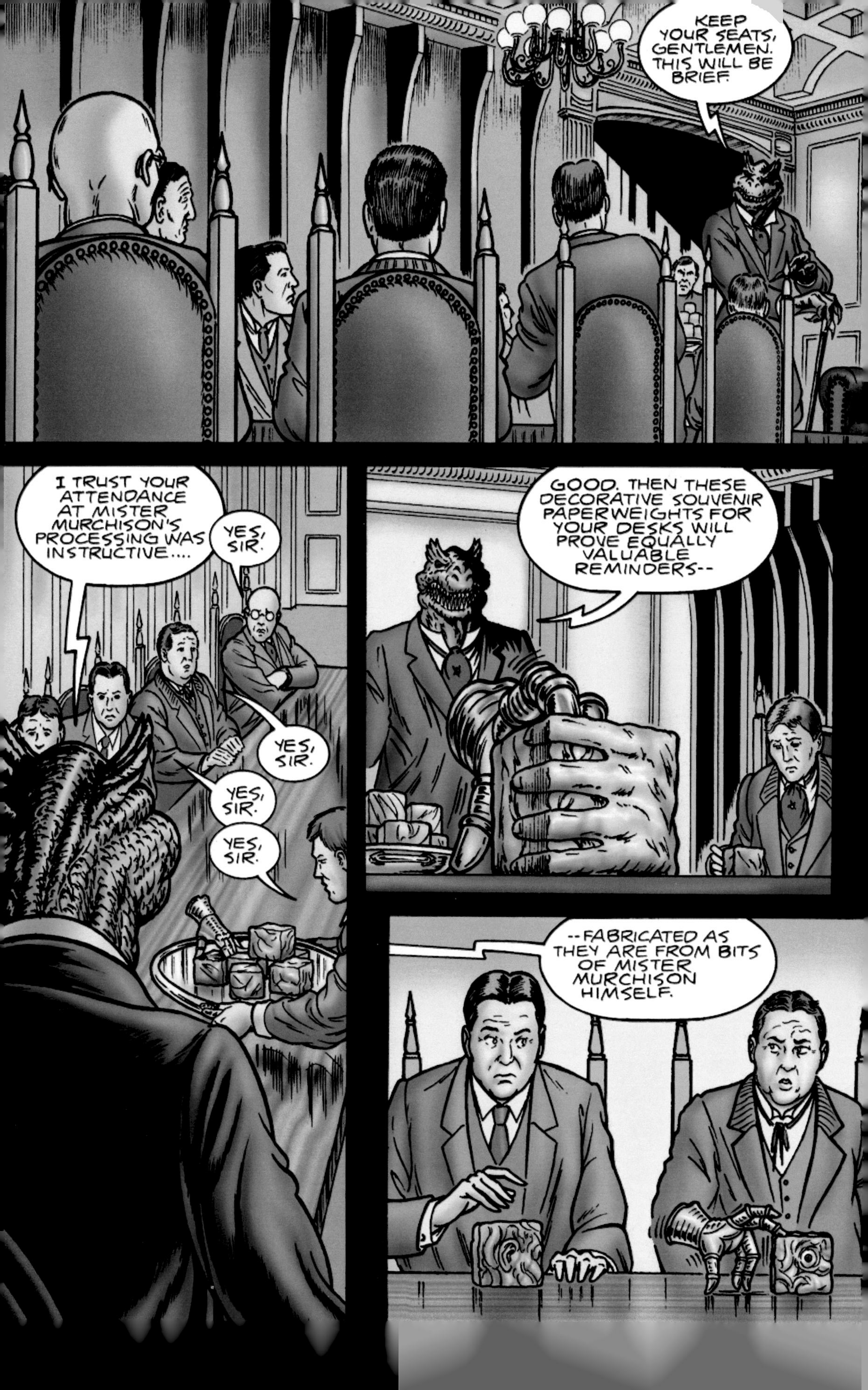
KEEP YOUR SEATS, GENTLEMEN. THIS WILL BE BRIEF.
I TRUST YOUR ATTENDANCE AT MISTER MURCHISON'S PROCESSING WAS INSTRUCTIVE....
YES, SIR.
YES, SIR.
YES, SIR.
YES, SIR.
GOOD. THEN THESE DECORATIVE SOUVENIR PAPERWEIGHTS FOR YOUR DESKS WILL PROVE EQUALLY VALUABLE REMINDERS--
--FABRICATED AS THEY ARE FROM BITS OF MISTER MURCHISON HIMSELF.

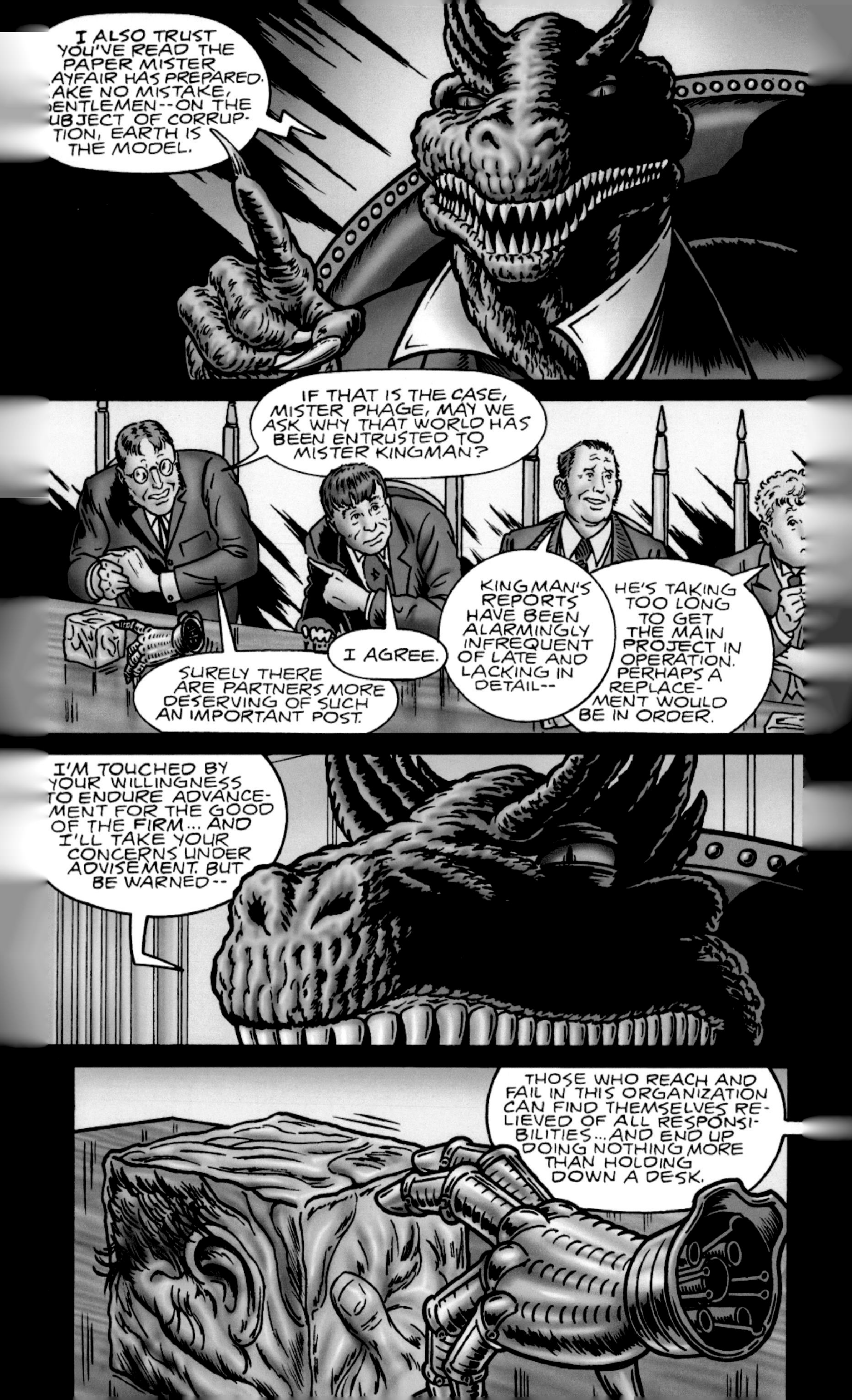
I ALSO TRUST YOU'VE READ THE PAPER MISTER AYFAIR HAS PREPARED. AKE NO MISTAKE, ENTLEMEN--ON THE UBJECT OF CORRUP-TION, EARTH IS THE MODEL.
IF THAT IS THE CASE, MISTER PHAGE, MAY WE ASK WHY THAT WORLD HAS BEEN ENTRUSTED TO MISTER KINGMAN?
SURELY THERE ARE PARTNERS MORE DESERVING OF SUCH AN IMPORTANT POST.
I AGREE.
KINGMAN'S REPORTS HAVE BEEN ALARMINGLY INFREQUENT OF LATE AND LACKING IN DETAIL--
HE'S TAKING TOO LONG TO GET THE MAIN PROJECT IN OPERATION. PERHAPS A REPLACE-MENT WOULD BE IN ORDER.
I'M TOUCHED BY YOUR WILLINGNESS TO ENDURE ADVANCE-MENT FOR THE GOOD OF THE FIRM... AND I'LL TAKE YOUR CONCERNS UNDER ADVISEMENT. BUT BE WARNED--
THOSE WHO REACH AND FAIL IN THIS ORGANIZATION CAN FIND THEMSELVES RE-LIEVED OF ALL RESPONSI-BILITIES... AND END UP DOING NOTHING MORE THAN HOLDING DOWN A DESK.

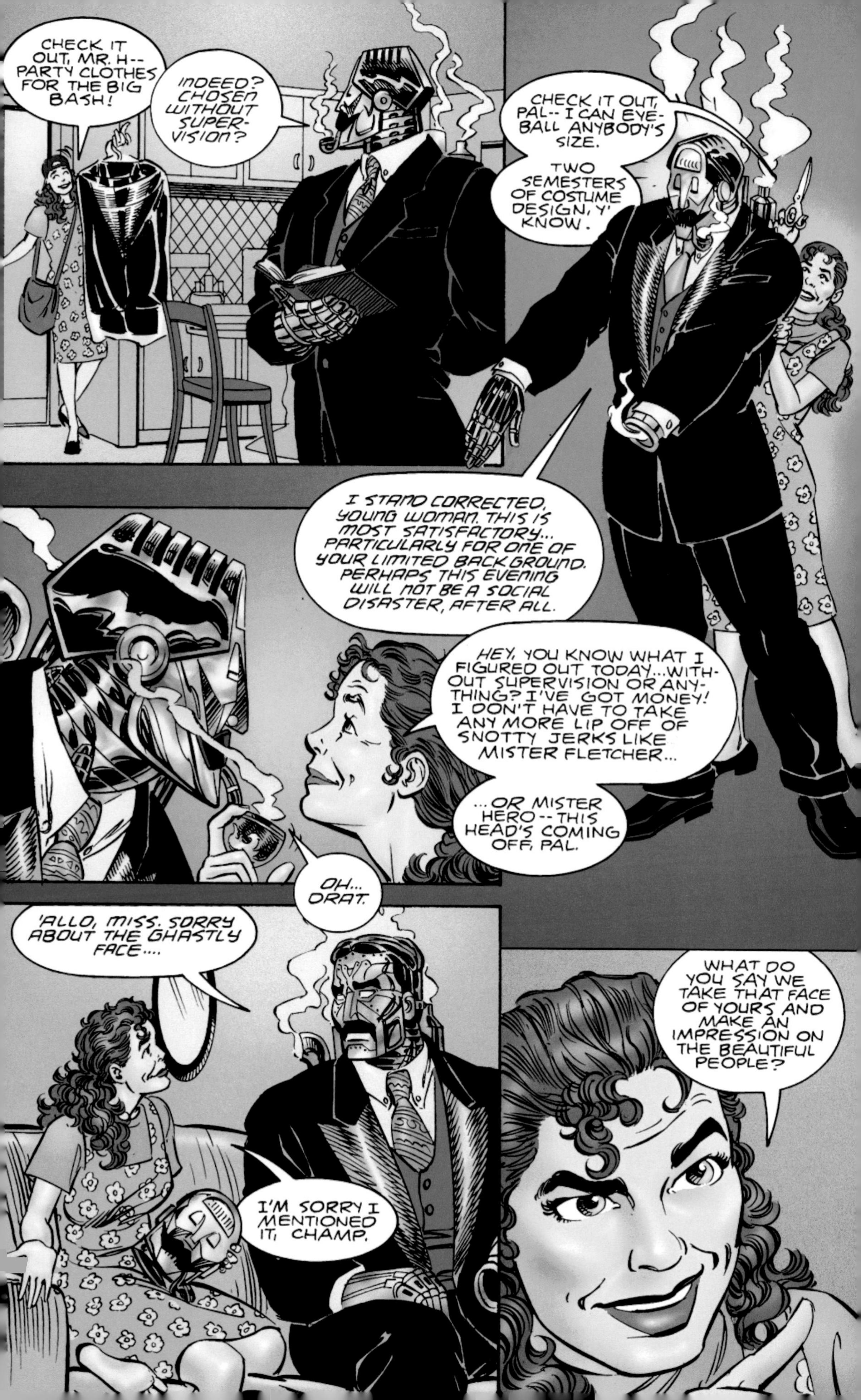
CHECK IT OUT, MR. H-- PARTY CLOTHES FOR THE BIG BASH!
INDEED? CHOSEN WITHOUT SUPER-VISION?
CHECK IT OUT, PAL-- I CAN EYE-BALL ANYBODY'S SIZE.
TWO SEMESTERS OF COSTUME DESIGN, Y' KNOW.
I STAND CORRECTED, YOUNG WOMAN. THIS IS MOST SATISFACTORY... PARTICULARLY FOR ONE OF YOUR LIMITED BACKGROUND. PERHAPS THIS EVENING WILL NOT BE A SOCIAL DISASTER, AFTER ALL.
HEY, YOU KNOW WHAT I FIGURED OUT TODAY...WITH-OUT SUPERVISION OR ANY-THING? I'VE GOT MONEY! I DON'T HAVE TO TAKE ANY MORE LIP OFF OF SNOTTY JERKS LIKE MISTER FLETCHER...
...OR MISTER HERO--THIS HEAD'S COMING OFF, PAL.
OH... DRAT.
'ALLO, MISS. SORRY ABOUT THE GHASTLY FACE....
I'M SORRY I MENTIONED IT, CHAMP.
WHAT DO YOU SAY WE TAKE THAT FACE OF YOURS AND MAKE AN IMPRESSION ON THE BEAUTIFUL PEOPLE?

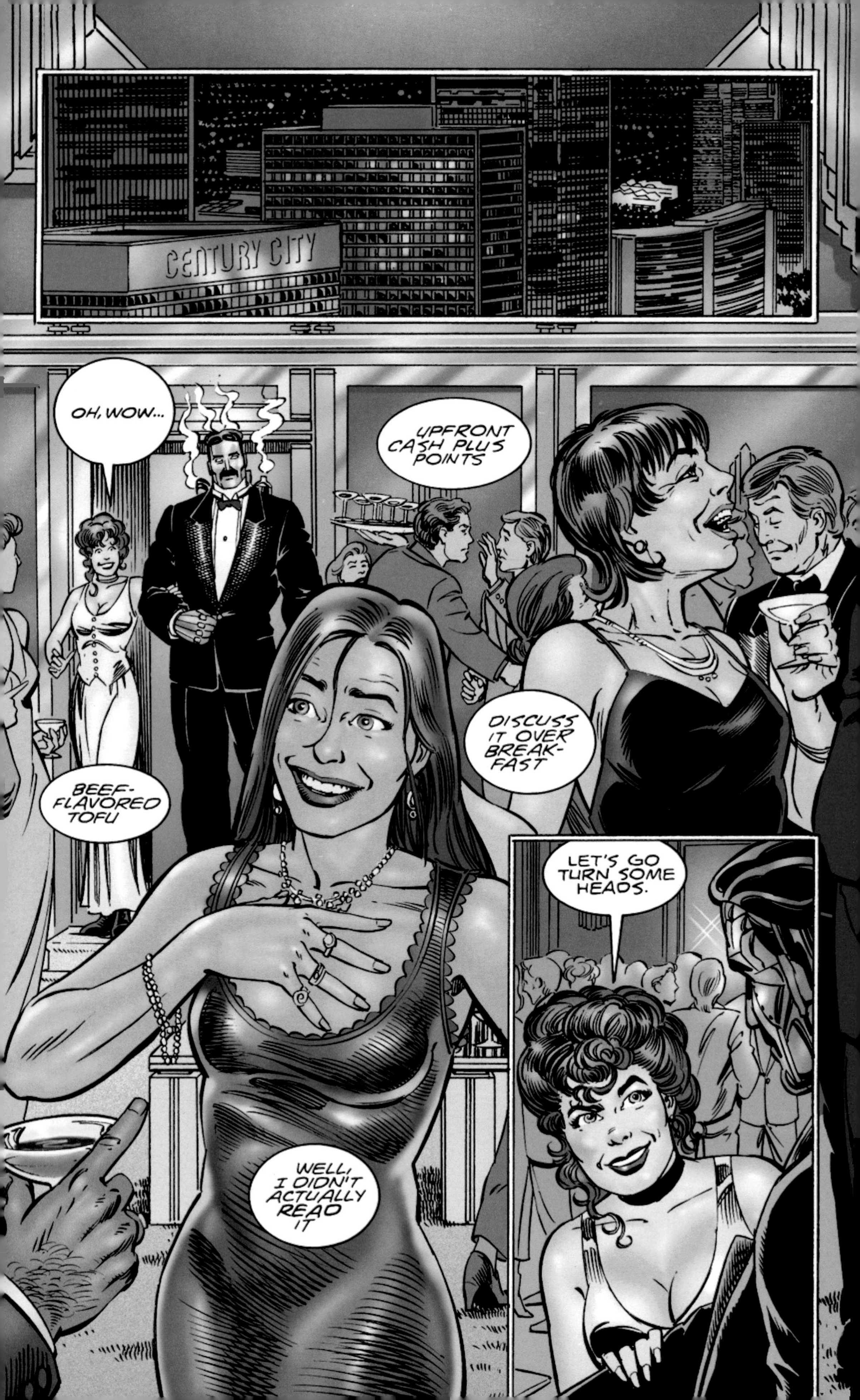
CENTURY CITY
OH, WOW...
UPFRONT CASH PLUS POINTS
BEEF-FLAVORED TOFU
DISCUSS IT OVER BREAK-FAST
WELL, I DIDN'T ACTUALLY READ IT
LET'S GO TURN SOME HEADS.

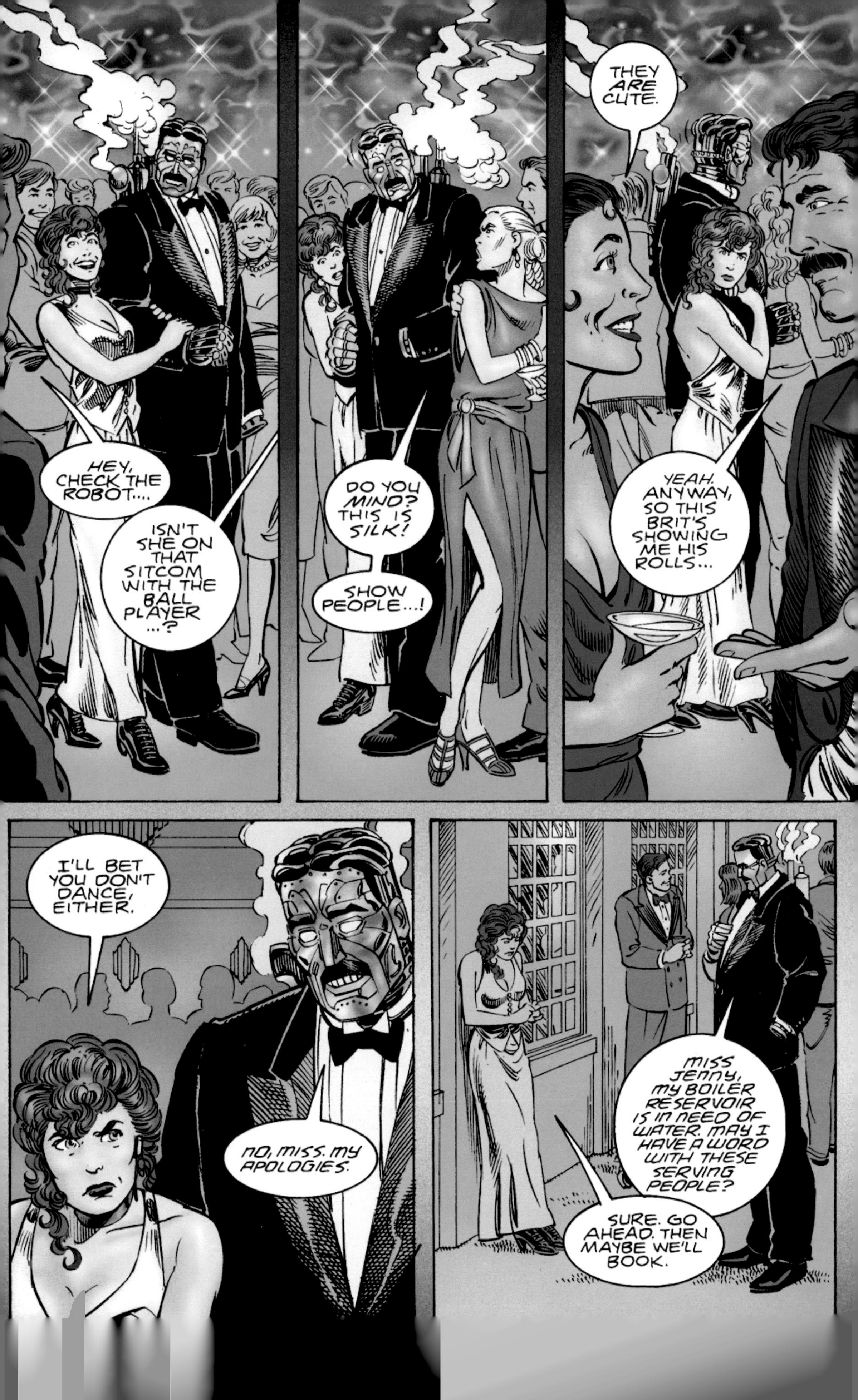
HEY, CHECK THE ROBOT....
ISN'T SHE ON THAT SITCOM WITH THE BALL PLAYER ...?
DO YOU MIND? THIS IS SILK!
SHOW PEOPLE...!
THEY ARE CUTE.
YEAH. ANYWAY, SO THIS BRIT'S SHOWING ME HIS ROLLS...
I'LL BET YOU DON'T DANCE, EITHER.
NO, MISS. MY APOLOGIES.
MISS JENNY, MY BOILER RESERVOIR IS IN NEED OF WATER. MAY I HAVE A WORD WITH THESE SERVING PEOPLE?
SURE. GO AHEAD. THEN MAYBE WE'LL BOOK.

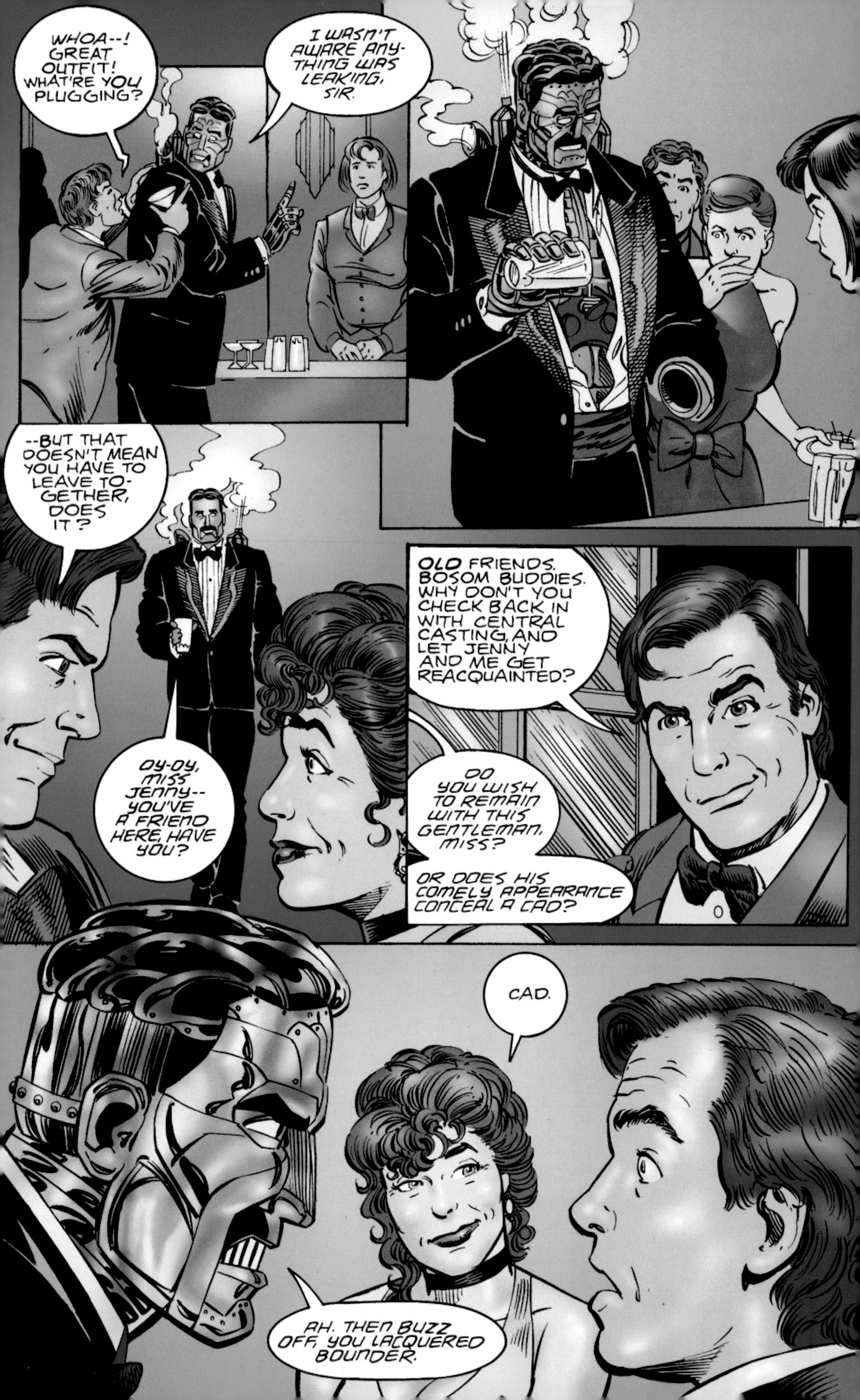
WHOA--! GREAT OUTFIT! WHAT'RE YOU PLUGGING?
I WASN'T AWARE ANY-THING WAS LEAKING, SIR.
--BUT THAT DOESN'T MEAN YOU HAVE TO LEAVE TO-GETHER, DOES IT?
OY-OY, MISS JENNY-- YOU'VE A FRIEND HERE, HAVE YOU?
OLD FRIENDS. BOSOM BUDDIES. WHY DON'T YOU CHECK BACK IN WITH CENTRAL CASTING, AND LET JENNY AND ME GET REACQUAINTED?
DO YOU WISH TO REMAIN WITH THIS GENTLEMAN, MISS?
OR DOES HIS COMELY APPEARANCE CONCEAL A CAD?
CAD.
AH. THEN BUZZ OFF, YOU LACQUERED BOUNDER.

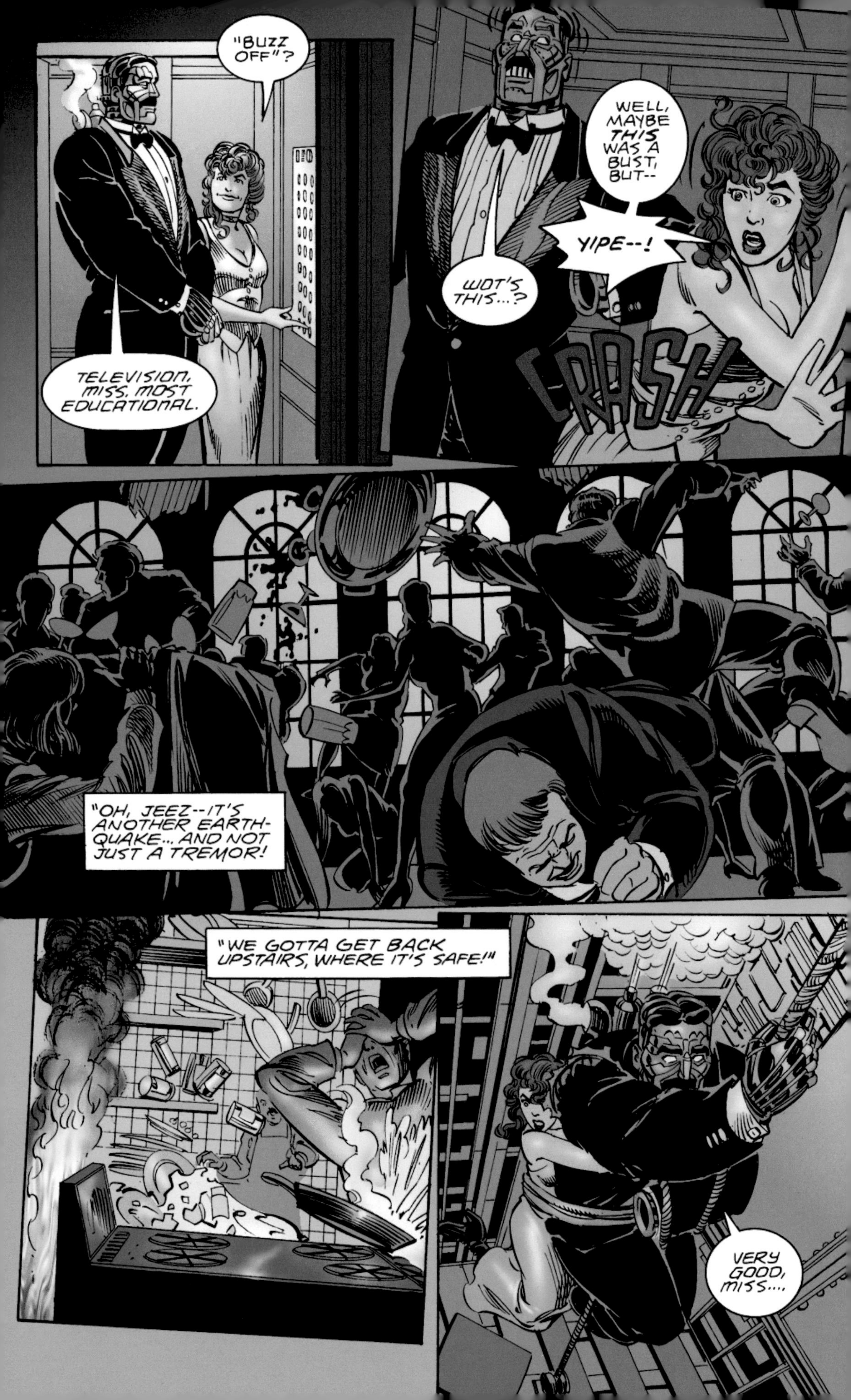
"BUZZ OFF"?
TELEVISION, MISS. MOST EDUCATIONAL.
WELL, MAYBE THIS WAS A BUST, BUT--
WOT'S THIS...?
YIPE--!
CRASH
"OH, JEEZ--IT'S ANOTHER EARTH-QUAKE... AND NOT JUST A TREMOR!
"WE GOTTA GET BACK UPSTAIRS, WHERE IT'S SAFE!"
VERY GOOD, MISS....

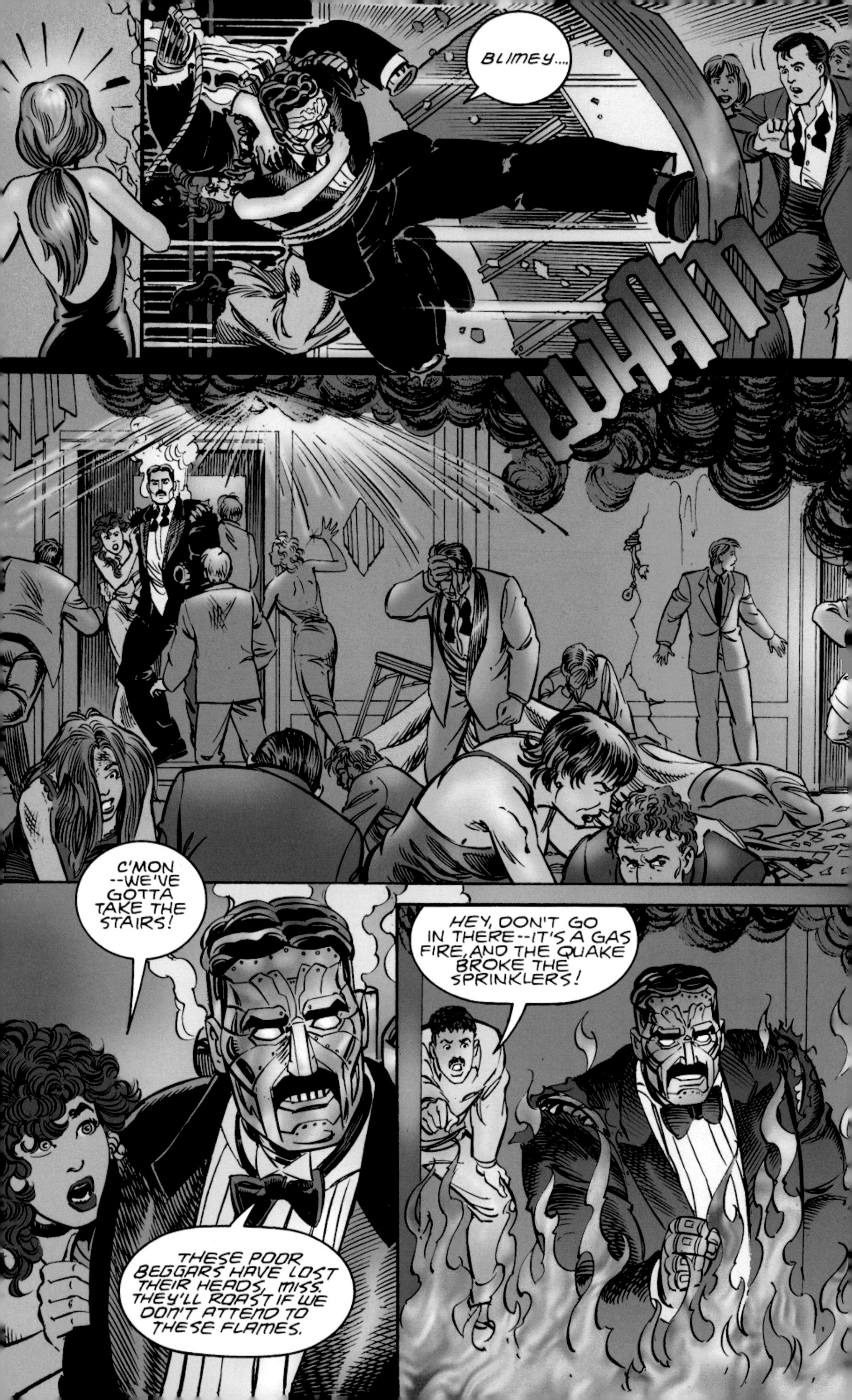
BLIMEY....
WHAM
C'MON --WE'VE GOTTA TAKE THE STAIRS!
THESE POOR BEGGARS HAVE LOST THEIR HEADS, MISS. THEY'LL ROAST IF WE DON'T ATTEND TO THESE FLAMES.
HEY, DON'T GO IN THERE--IT'S A GAS FIRE, AND THE QUAKE BROKE THE SPRINKLERS!

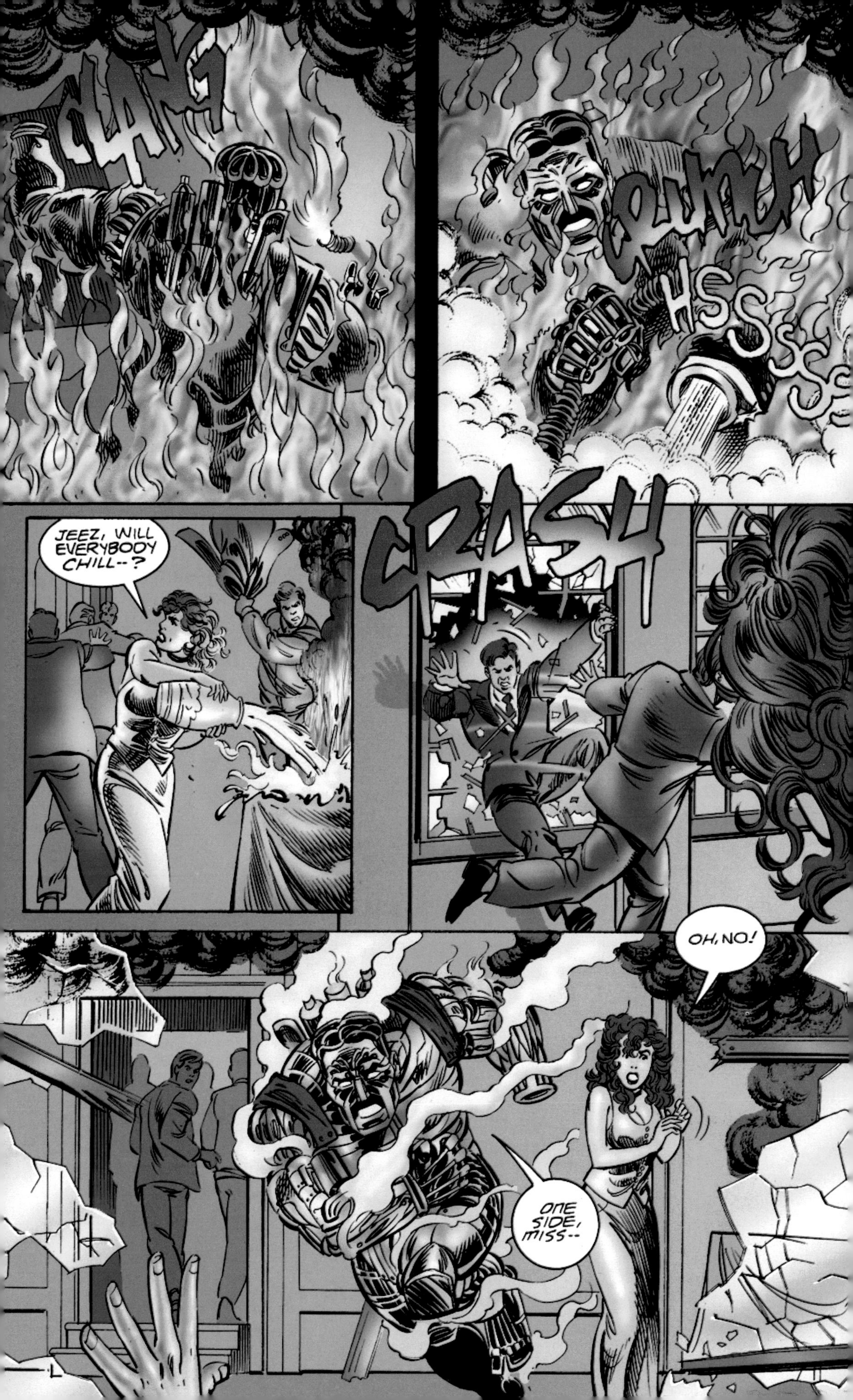
CLANG
CRUNCH
HSSSSS
CRASH
JEEZ, WILL EVERYBODY CHILL--?
OH, NO!
ONE SIDE, MISS--

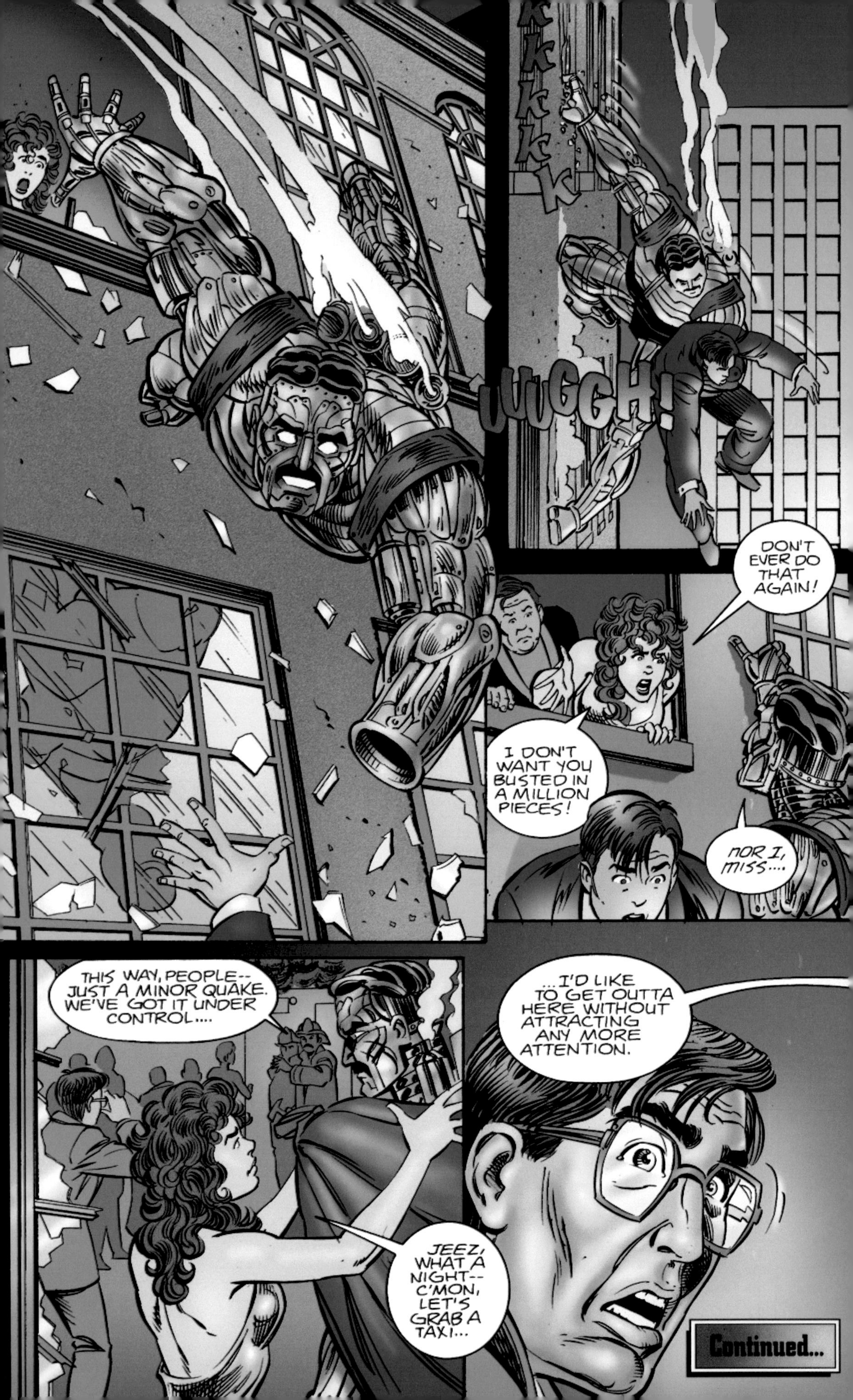
KKKKK
UUUGGH!
DON'T EVER DO THAT AGAIN!
I DON'T WANT YOU BUSTED IN A MILLION PIECES!
NOR I, MISS....
THIS WAY, PEOPLE-- JUST A MINOR QUAKE. WE'VE GOT IT UNDER CONTROL....
JEEZ, WHAT A NIGHT-- C'MON, LET'S GRAB A TAXI...
...I'D LIKE TO GET OUTTA HERE WITHOUT ATTRACTING ANY MORE ATTENTION.
Continued...

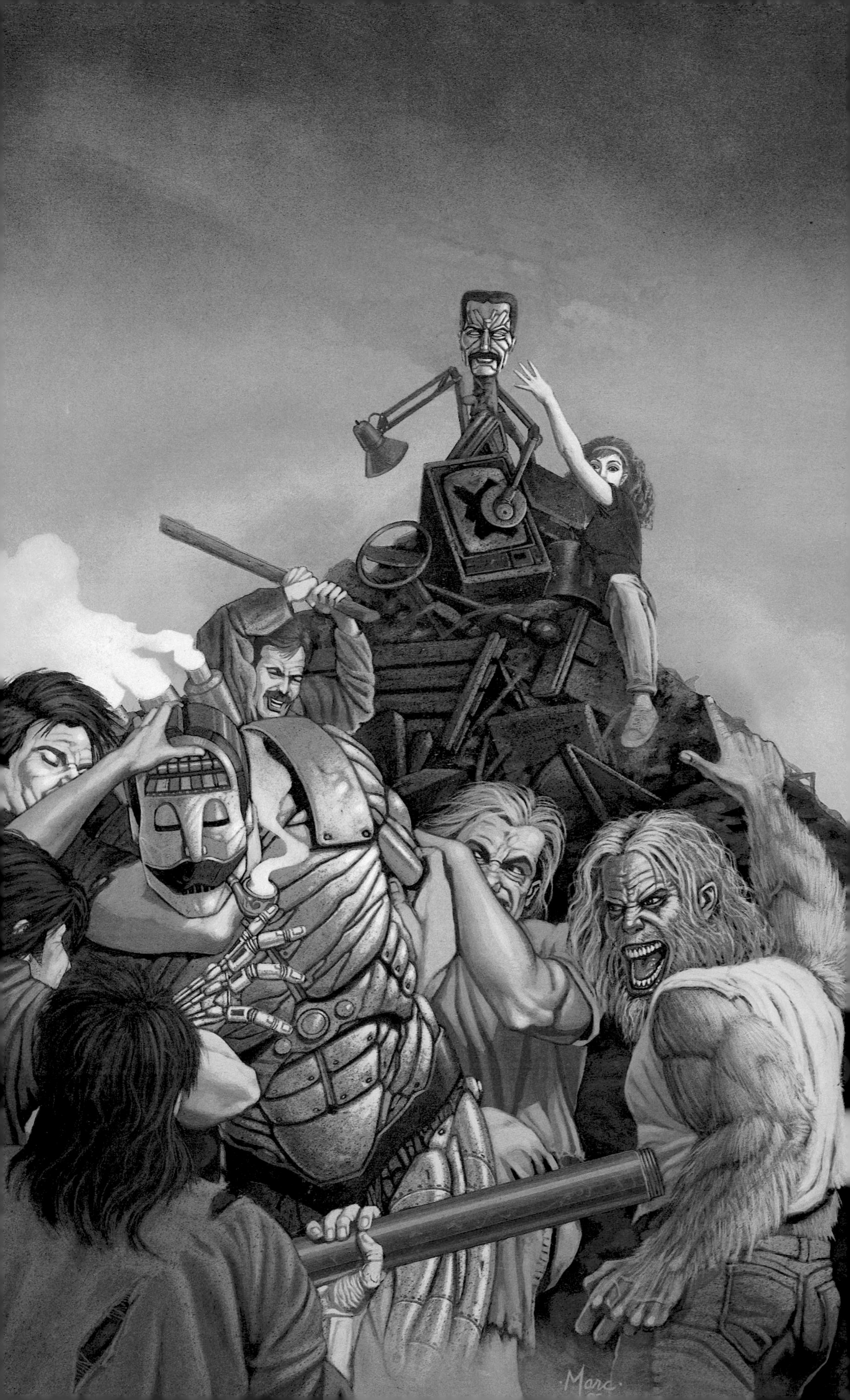
·Marc·

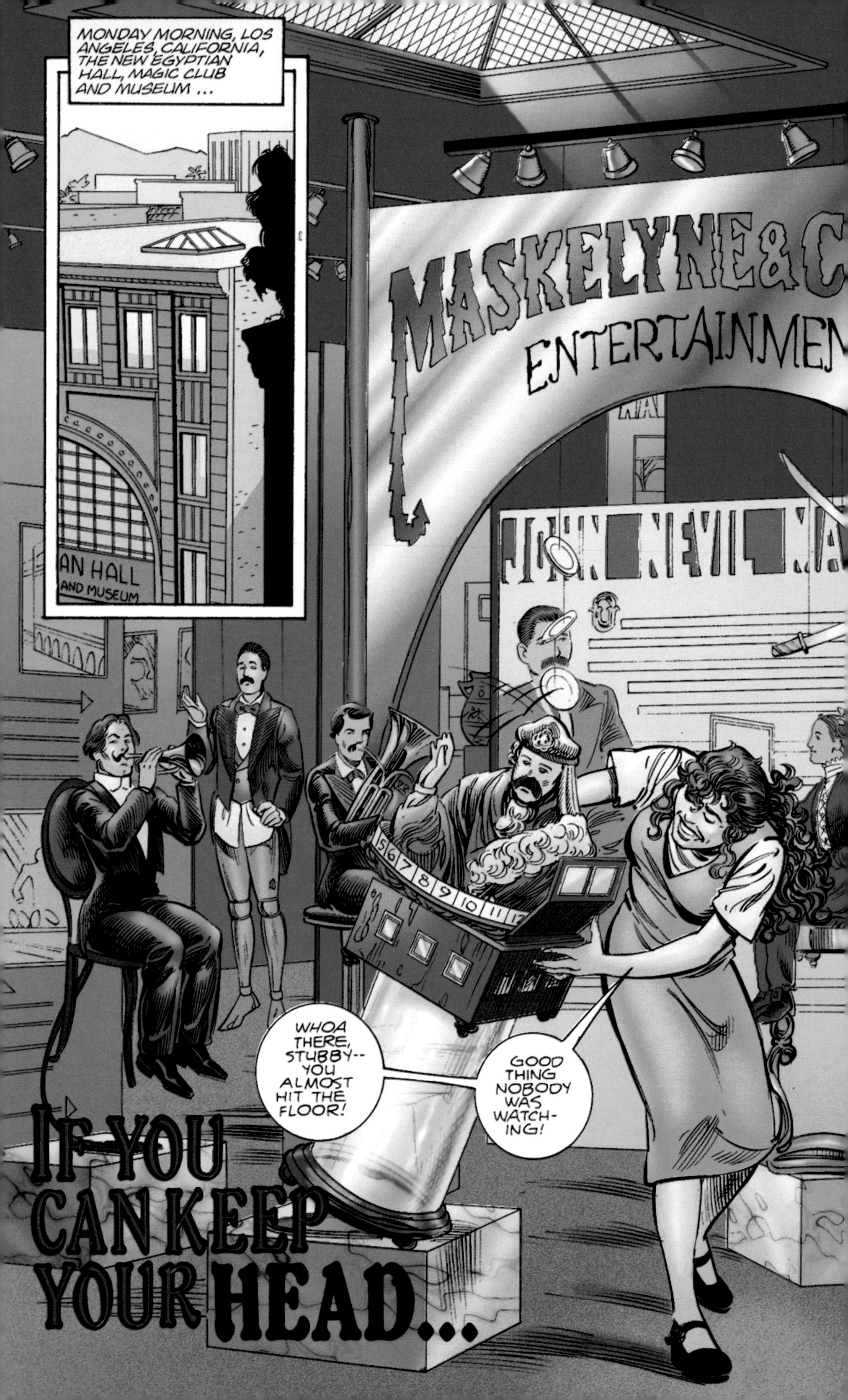
MONDAY MORNING, LOS ANGELES, CALIFORNIA, THE NEW EGYPTIAN HALL, MAGIC CLUB AND MUSEUM ...
AN HALL
AND MUSEUM
MASKELYNE&C
ENTERTAINMEN
WHOA THERE, STUBBY-- YOU ALMOST HIT THE FLOOR!
GOOD THING NOBODY WAS WATCHING!
IF YOU CAN KEEP YOUR HEAD...

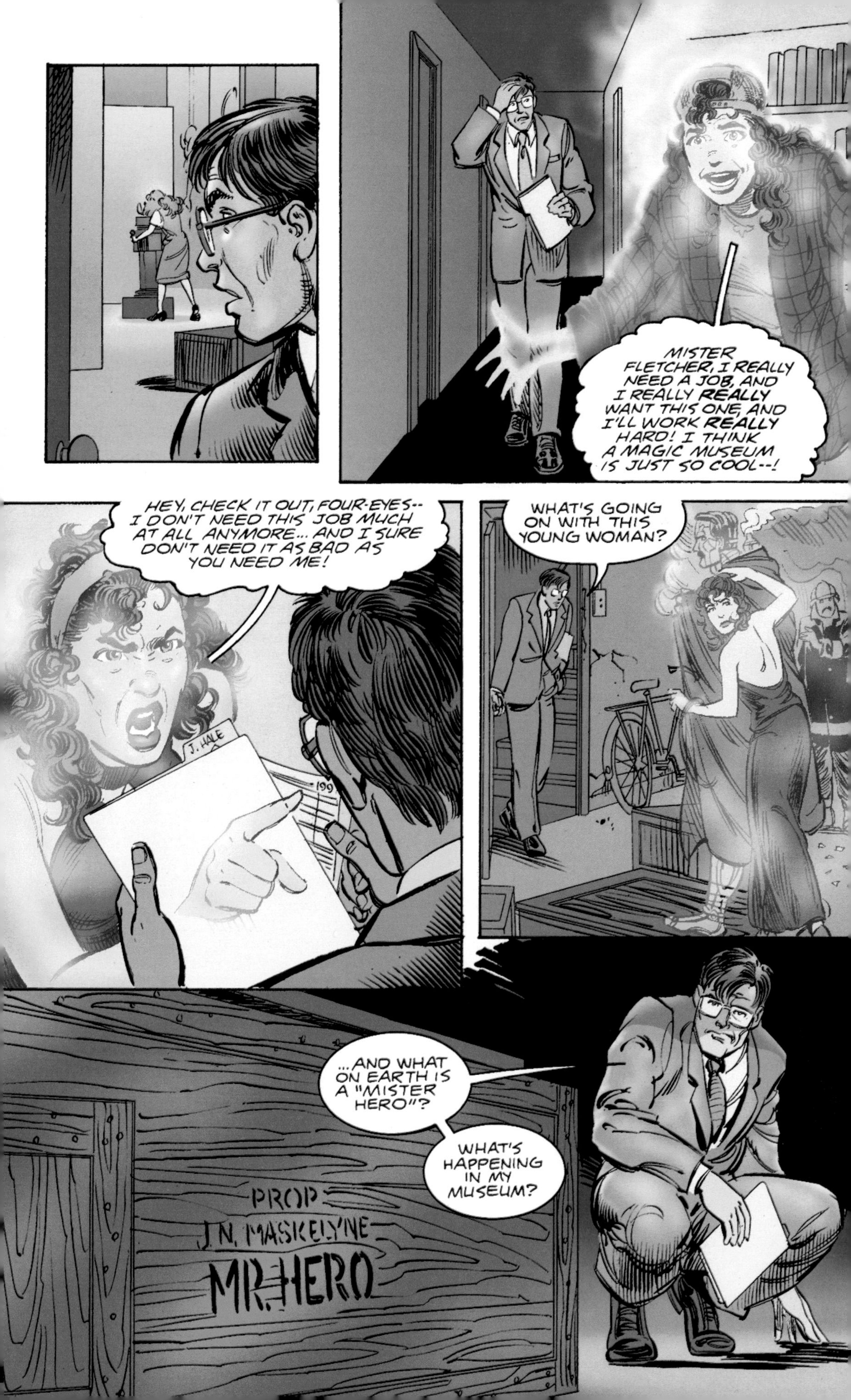
MISTER FLETCHER, I REALLY NEED A JOB, AND I REALLY REALLY WANT THIS ONE, AND I'LL WORK REALLY HARD! I THINK A MAGIC MUSEUM IS JUST SO COOL--!
HEY, CHECK IT OUT, FOUR-EYES-- I DON'T NEED THIS JOB MUCH AT ALL ANYMORE... AND I SURE DON'T NEED IT AS BAD AS YOU NEED ME!
J. HALE
WHAT'S GOING ON WITH THIS YOUNG WOMAN?
...AND WHAT ON EARTH IS A "MISTER HERO"?
WHAT'S HAPPENING IN MY MUSEUM?
PROP
J.N. MASKELYNE
MR. HERO

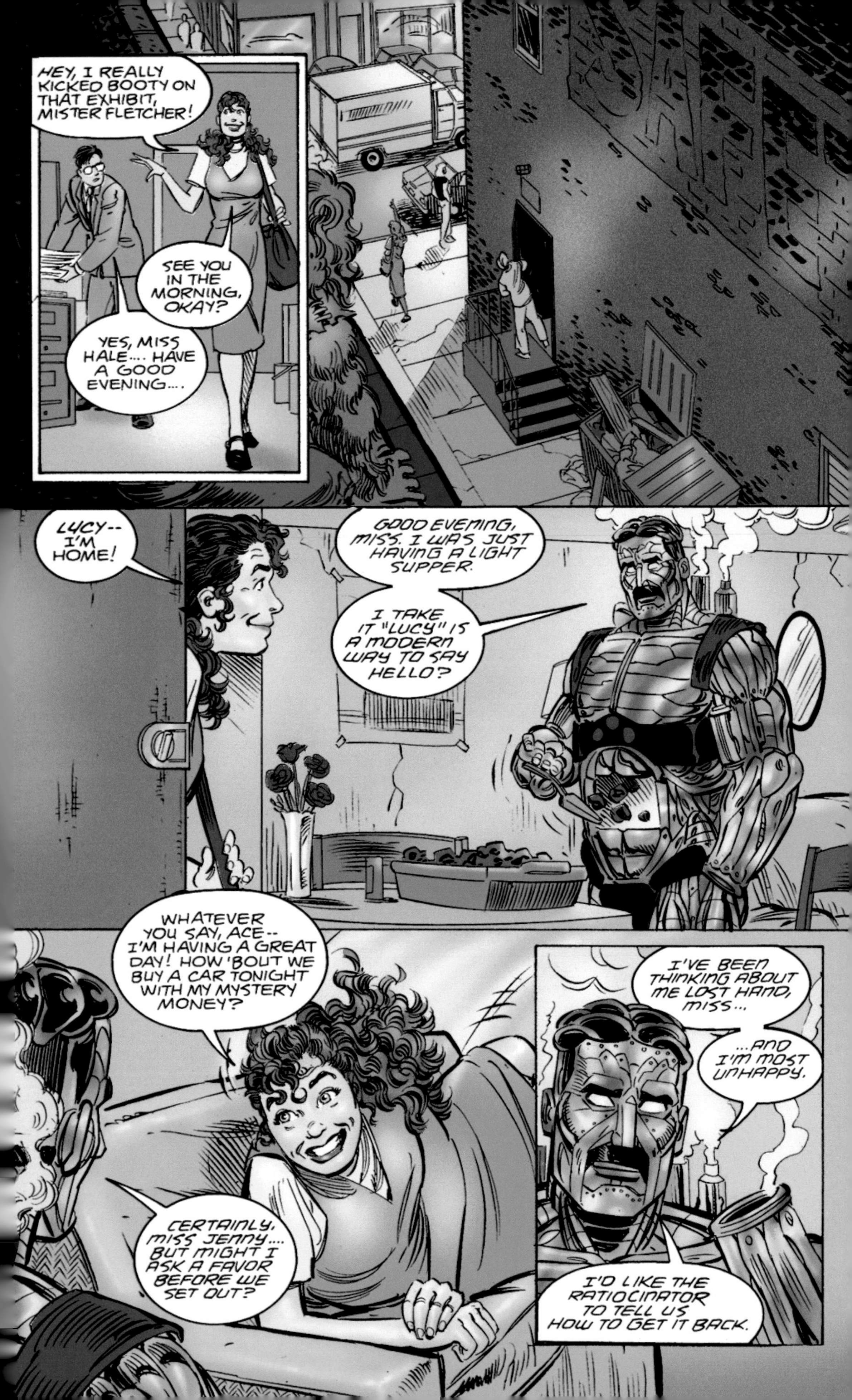
HEY, I REALLY KICKED BOOTY ON THAT EXHIBIT, MISTER FLETCHER!
SEE YOU IN THE MORNING, OKAY?
YES, MISS HALE.... HAVE A GOOD EVENING....
LUCY-- I'M HOME!
GOOD EVENING, MISS. I WAS JUST HAVING A LIGHT SUPPER.
I TAKE IT "LUCY" IS A MODERN WAY TO SAY HELLO?
WHATEVER YOU SAY, ACE-- I'M HAVING A GREAT DAY! HOW 'BOUT WE BUY A CAR TONIGHT WITH MY MYSTERY MONEY?
CERTAINLY, MISS JENNY.... BUT MIGHT I ASK A FAVOR BEFORE WE SET OUT?
I'VE BEEN THINKING ABOUT ME LOST HAND, MISS...
...AND I'M MOST UNHAPPY.
I'D LIKE THE RATIOCINATOR TO TELL US HOW TO GET IT BACK.

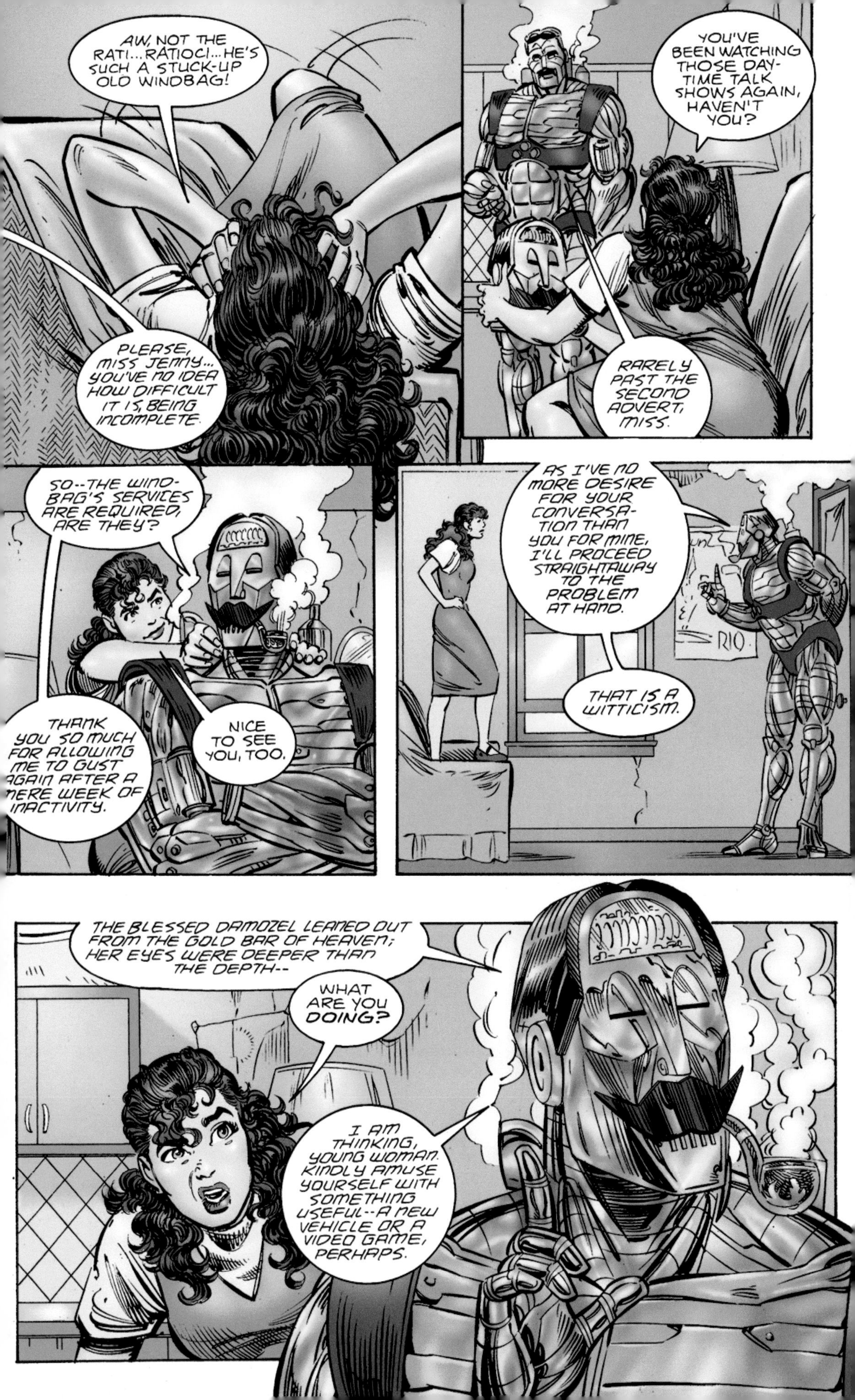
AW, NOT THE RATI...RATIOCI...HE'S SUCH A STUCK-UP OLD WINDBAG!
PLEASE, MISS JENNY... YOU'VE NO IDEA HOW DIFFICULT IT IS, BEING INCOMPLETE.
YOU'VE BEEN WATCHING THOSE DAY-TIME TALK SHOWS AGAIN, HAVEN'T YOU?
RARELY PAST THE SECOND ADVERT, MISS.
SO--THE WIND-BAG'S SERVICES ARE REQUIRED, ARE THEY?
THANK YOU SO MUCH FOR ALLOWING ME TO GUST AGAIN AFTER A MERE WEEK OF INACTIVITY.
NICE TO SEE YOU, TOO.
AS I'VE NO MORE DESIRE FOR YOUR CONVERSA-TION THAN YOU FOR MINE, I'LL PROCEED STRAIGHTAWAY TO THE PROBLEM AT HAND.
THAT IS A WITTICISM.
RIO
THE BLESSED DAMOZEL LEANED OUT FROM THE GOLD BAR OF HEAVEN; HER EYES WERE DEEPER THAN THE DEPTH--
WHAT ARE YOU DOING?
I AM THINKING, YOUNG WOMAN. KINDLY AMUSE YOURSELF WITH SOMETHING USEFUL--A NEW VEHICLE OR A VIDEO GAME, PERHAPS.

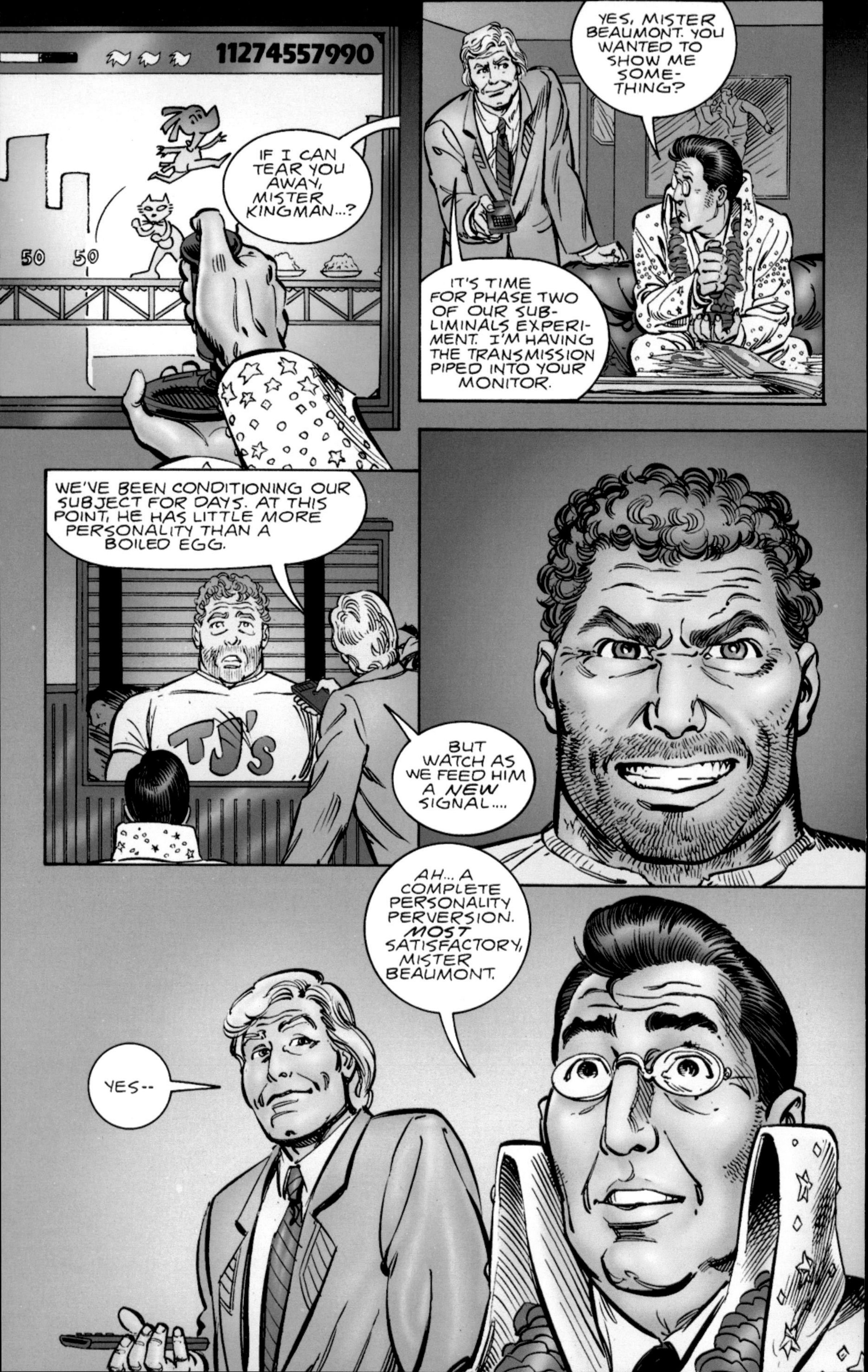
11274557990
50 50
IF I CAN TEAR YOU AWAY, MISTER KINGMAN...?
YES, MISTER BEAUMONT. YOU WANTED TO SHOW ME SOME-THING?
IT'S TIME FOR PHASE TWO OF OUR SUB-LIMINALS EXPERI-MENT. I'M HAVING THE TRANSMISSION PIPED INTO YOUR MONITOR.
WE'VE BEEN CONDITIONING OUR SUBJECT FOR DAYS. AT THIS POINT, HE HAS LITTLE MORE PERSONALITY THAN A BOILED EGG.
TJ'S
BUT WATCH AS WE FEED HIM A *NEW* SIGNAL....
AH... A COMPLETE PERSONALITY PERVERSION. ***MOST*** SATISFACTORY, MISTER BEAUMONT.
YES--

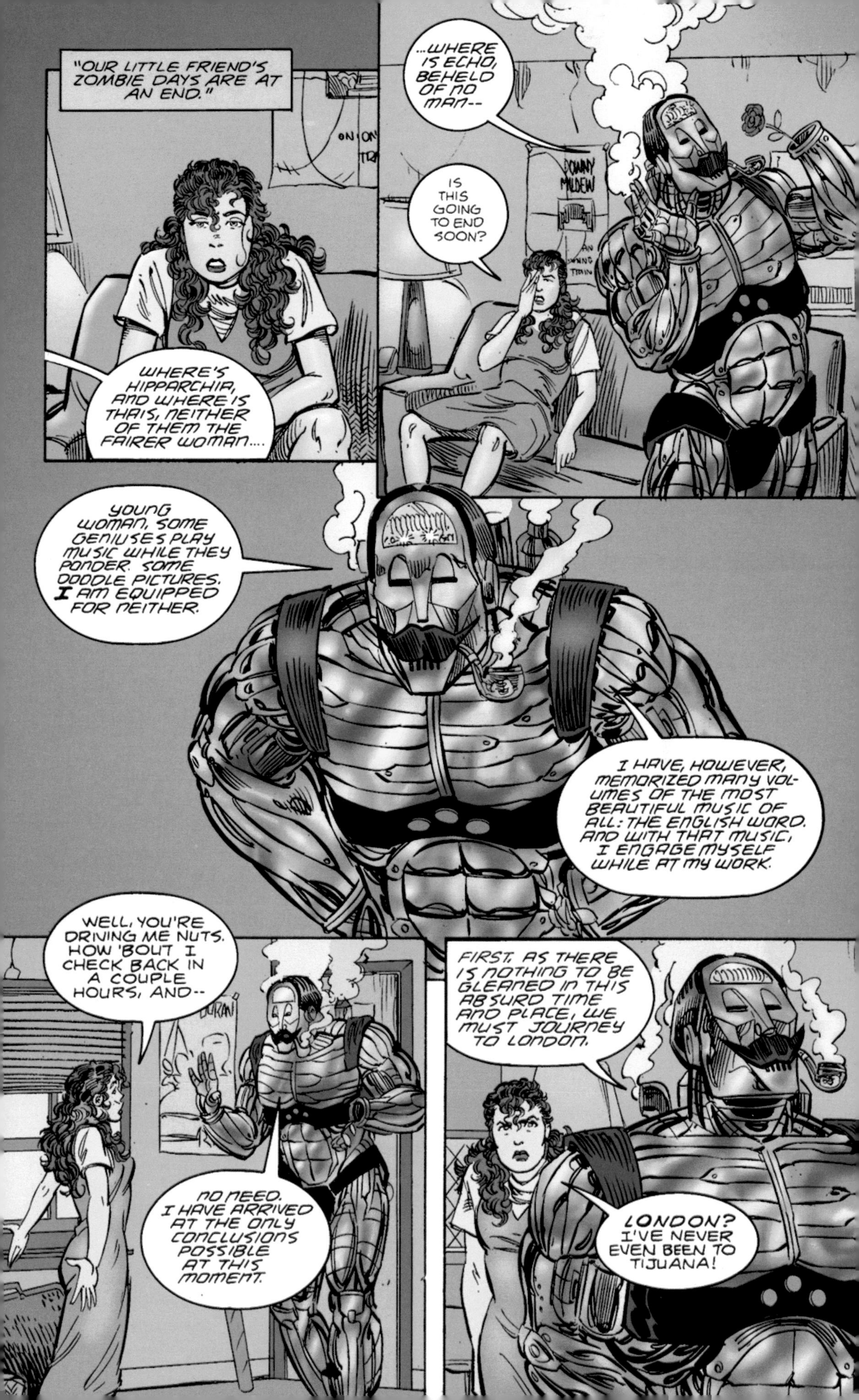
"OUR LITTLE FRIEND'S ZOMBIE DAYS ARE AT AN END."
WHERE'S HIPPARCHIA, AND WHERE IS THAIS, NEITHER OF THEM THE FAIRER WOMAN....
...WHERE IS ECHO, BEHELD OF NO MAN--
IS THIS GOING TO END SOON?
DOWNY MILDEW
YOUNG WOMAN, SOME GENIUSES PLAY MUSIC WHILE THEY PONDER. SOME DOODLE PICTURES. I AM EQUIPPED FOR NEITHER.
I HAVE, HOWEVER, MEMORIZED MANY VOLUMES OF THE MOST BEAUTIFUL MUSIC OF ALL: THE ENGLISH WORD. AND WITH THAT MUSIC, I ENGAGE MYSELF WHILE AT MY WORK.
WELL, YOU'RE DRIVING ME NUTS. HOW 'BOUT I CHECK BACK IN A COUPLE HOURS, AND--
NO NEED. I HAVE ARRIVED AT THE ONLY CONCLUSIONS POSSIBLE AT THIS MOMENT.
FIRST, AS THERE IS NOTHING TO BE GLEANED IN THIS ABSURD TIME AND PLACE, WE MUST JOURNEY TO LONDON.
LONDON? I'VE NEVER EVEN BEEN TO TIJUANA!

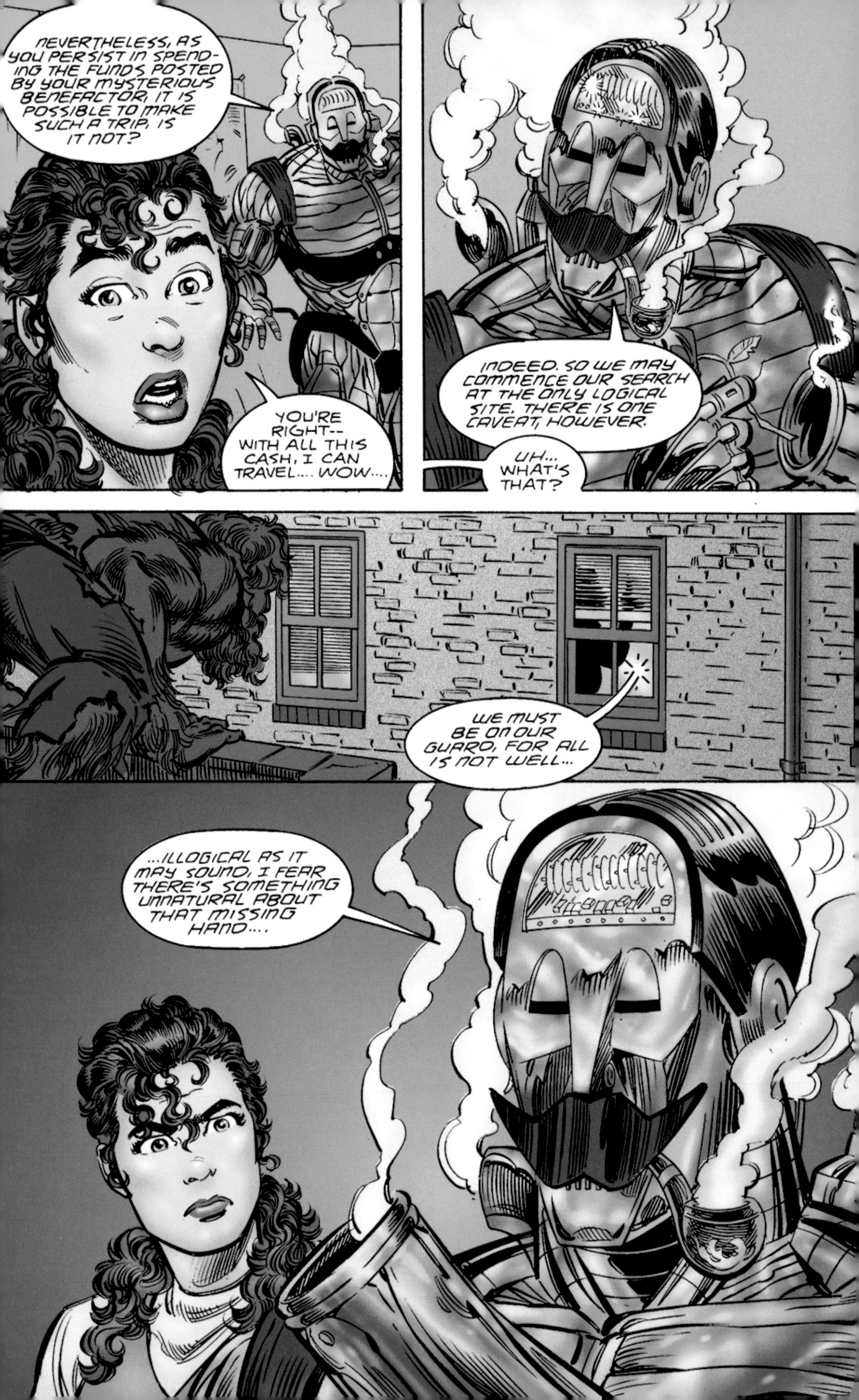
NEVERTHELESS, AS YOU PERSIST IN SPENDING THE FUNDS POSTED BY YOUR MYSTERIOUS BENEFACTOR, IT IS POSSIBLE TO MAKE SUCH A TRIP, IS IT NOT?
YOU'RE RIGHT-- WITH ALL THIS CASH, I CAN TRAVEL.... WOW....
INDEED. SO WE MAY COMMENCE OUR SEARCH AT THE ONLY LOGICAL SITE. THERE IS ONE CAVEAT, HOWEVER.
UH... WHAT'S THAT?
WE MUST BE ON OUR GUARD, FOR ALL IS NOT WELL...
...ILLOGICAL AS IT MAY SOUND, I FEAR THERE'S SOMETHING UNNATURAL ABOUT THAT MISSING HAND....

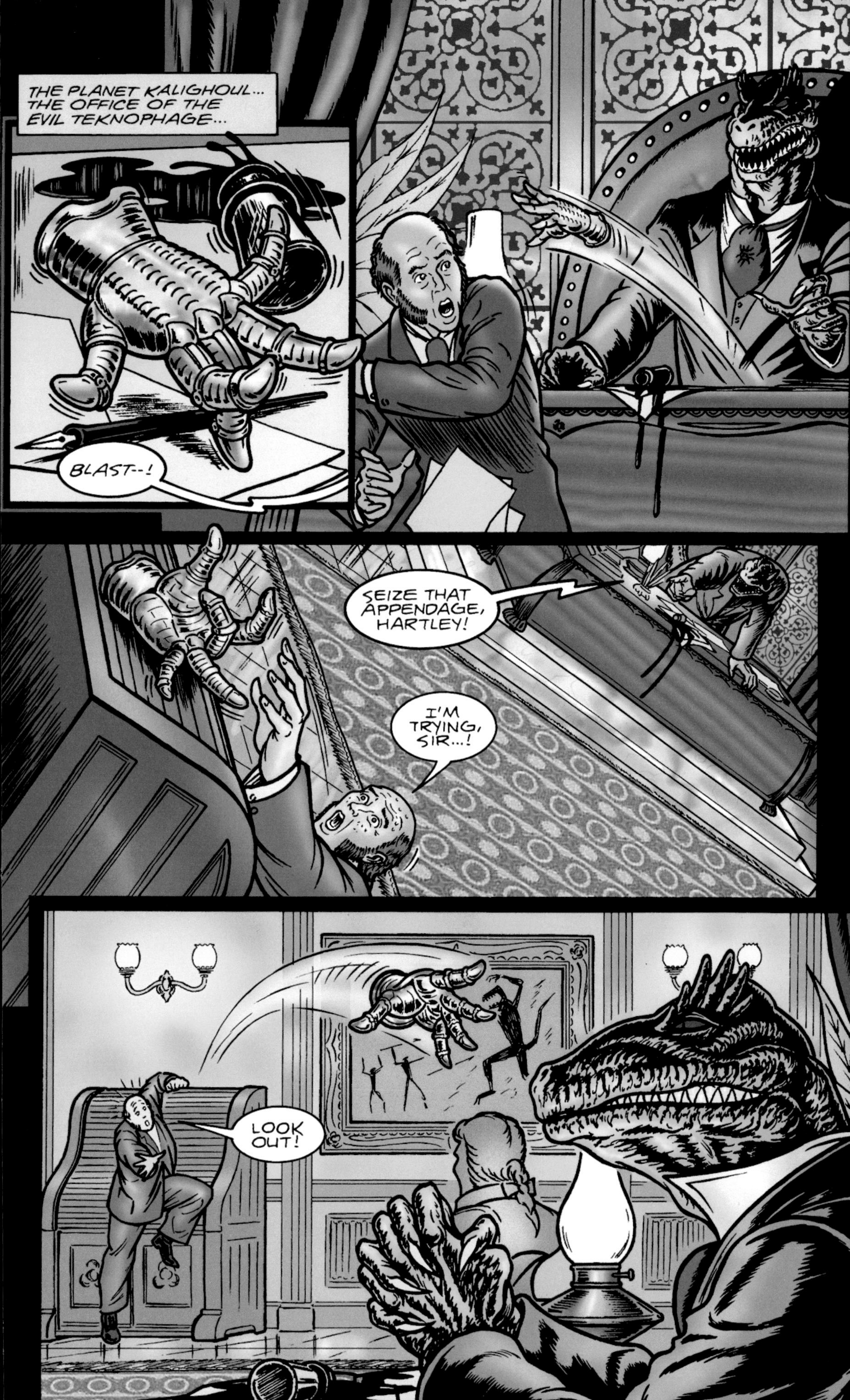
THE PLANET KALIGHOUL...
THE OFFICE OF THE
EVIL TEKNOPHAGE...
BLAST--!
SEIZE THAT
APPENDAGE,
HARTLEY!
I'M
TRYING,
SIR...!
LOOK
OUT!

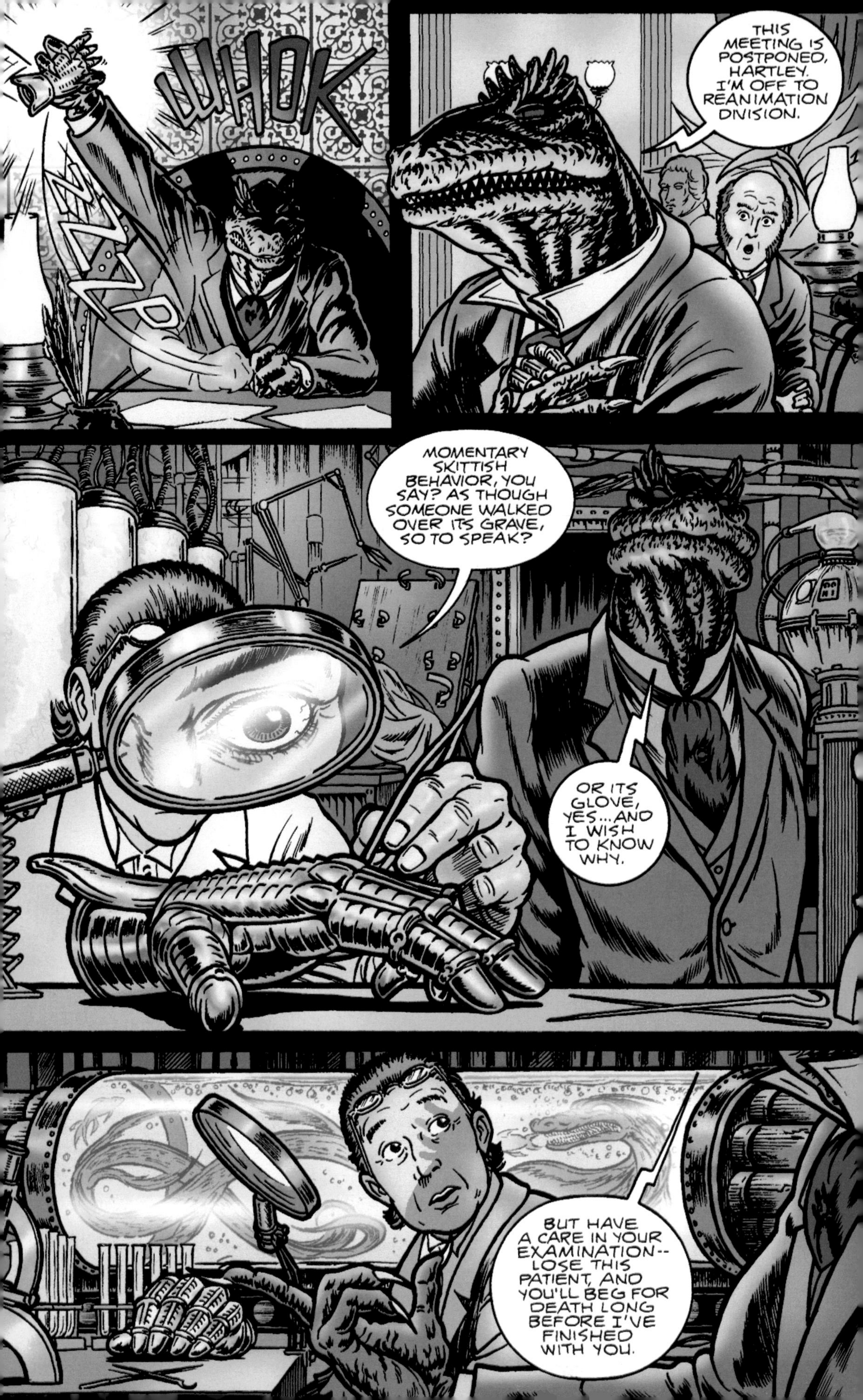
WHOK
ZZZAP
THIS MEETING IS POSTPONED, HARTLEY. I'M OFF TO REANIMATION DIVISION.
MOMENTARY SKITTISH BEHAVIOR, YOU SAY? AS THOUGH SOMEONE WALKED OVER ITS GRAVE, SO TO SPEAK?
OR ITS GLOVE, YES...AND I WISH TO KNOW WHY.
BUT HAVE A CARE IN YOUR EXAMINATION-- LOSE THIS PATIENT, AND YOU'LL BEG FOR DEATH LONG BEFORE I'VE FINISHED WITH YOU.

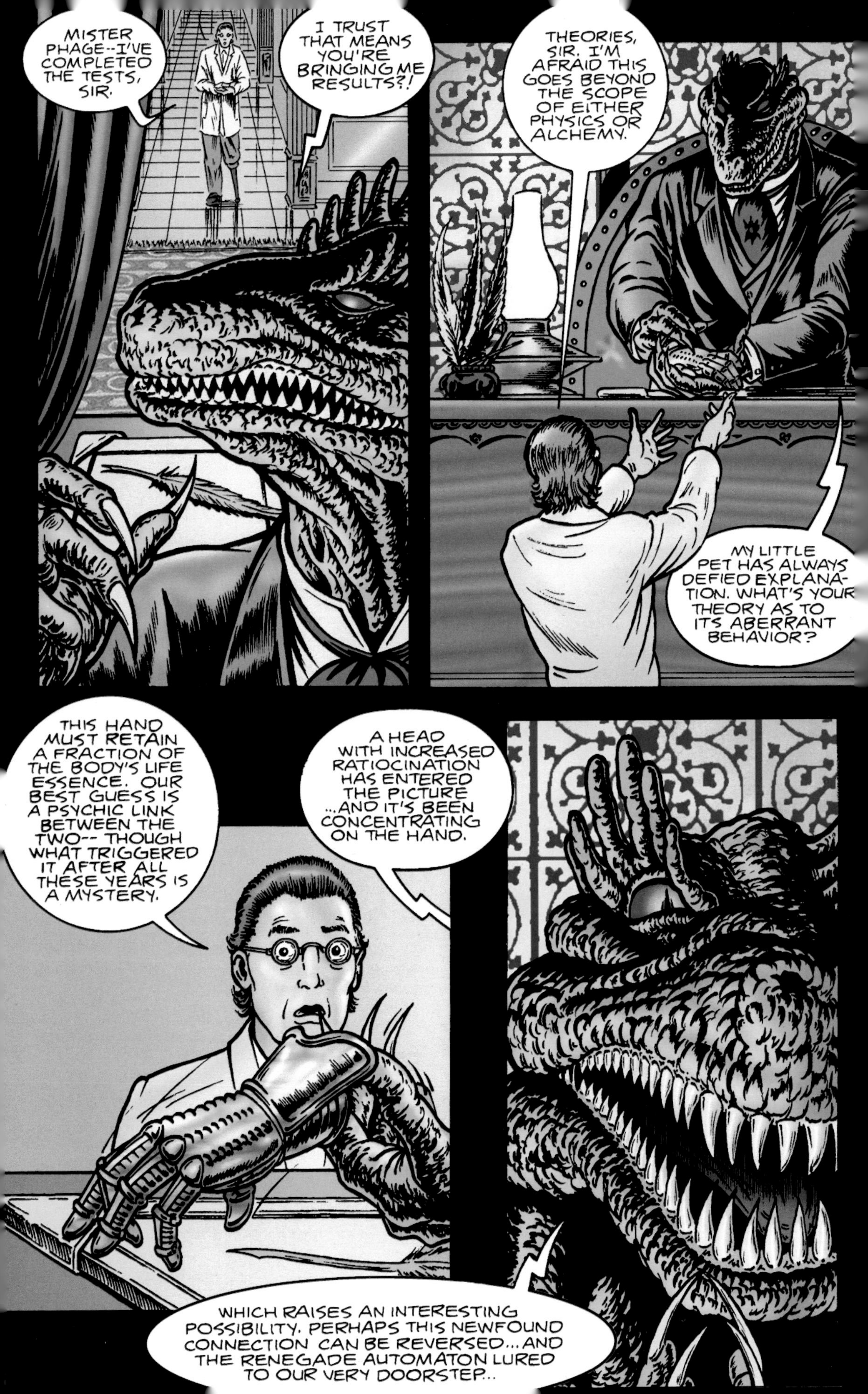
MISTER PHAGE--I'VE COMPLETED THE TESTS, SIR.
I TRUST THAT MEANS YOU'RE BRINGING ME RESULTS?!
THEORIES, SIR. I'M AFRAID THIS GOES BEYOND THE SCOPE OF EITHER PHYSICS OR ALCHEMY.
MY LITTLE PET HAS ALWAYS DEFIED EXPLANATION. WHAT'S YOUR THEORY AS TO ITS ABERRANT BEHAVIOR?
THIS HAND MUST RETAIN A FRACTION OF THE BODY'S LIFE ESSENCE. OUR BEST GUESS IS A PSYCHIC LINK BETWEEN THE TWO-- THOUGH WHAT TRIGGERED IT AFTER ALL THESE YEARS IS A MYSTERY.
A HEAD WITH INCREASED RATIOCINATION HAS ENTERED THE PICTURE ...AND IT'S BEEN CONCENTRATING ON THE HAND.
WHICH RAISES AN INTERESTING POSSIBILITY. PERHAPS THIS NEWFOUND CONNECTION CAN BE REVERSED... AND THE RENEGADE AUTOMATON LURED TO OUR VERY DOORSTEP...

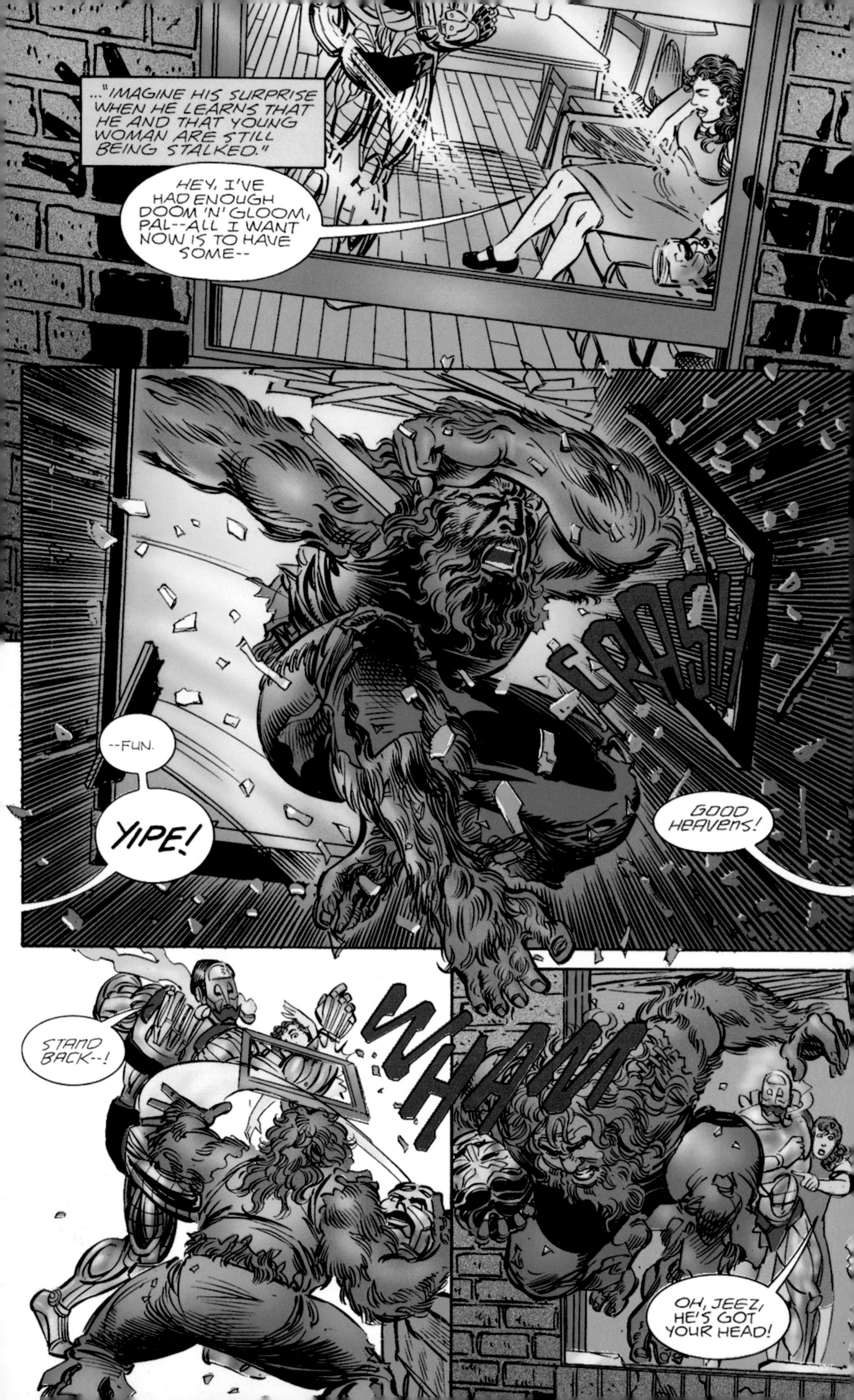
..."IMAGINE HIS SURPRISE WHEN HE LEARNS THAT HE AND THAT YOUNG WOMAN ARE STILL BEING STALKED."
HEY, I'VE HAD ENOUGH DOOM 'N' GLOOM, PAL--ALL I WANT NOW IS TO HAVE SOME--
CRASH
--FUN.
YIPE!
GOOD HEAVENS!
STAND BACK--!
WHAM
OH, JEEZ, HE'S GOT YOUR HEAD!

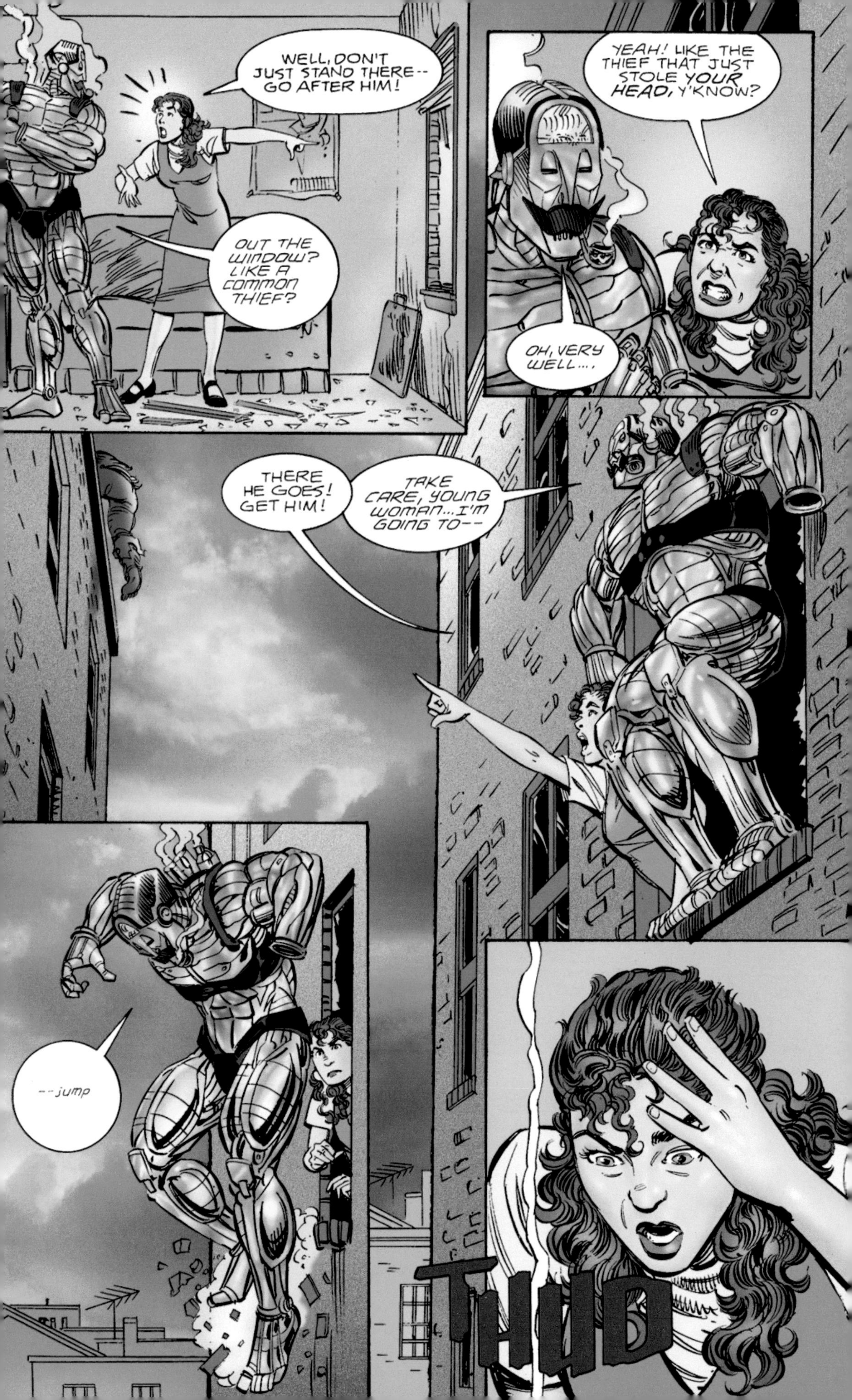
WELL, DON'T JUST STAND THERE-- GO AFTER HIM!
OUT THE WINDOW? LIKE A COMMON THIEF?
YEAH! LIKE THE THIEF THAT JUST STOLE YOUR HEAD, Y'KNOW?
OH, VERY WELL....
THERE HE GOES! GET HIM!
TAKE CARE, YOUNG WOMAN...I'M GOING TO--
--jump
THUD

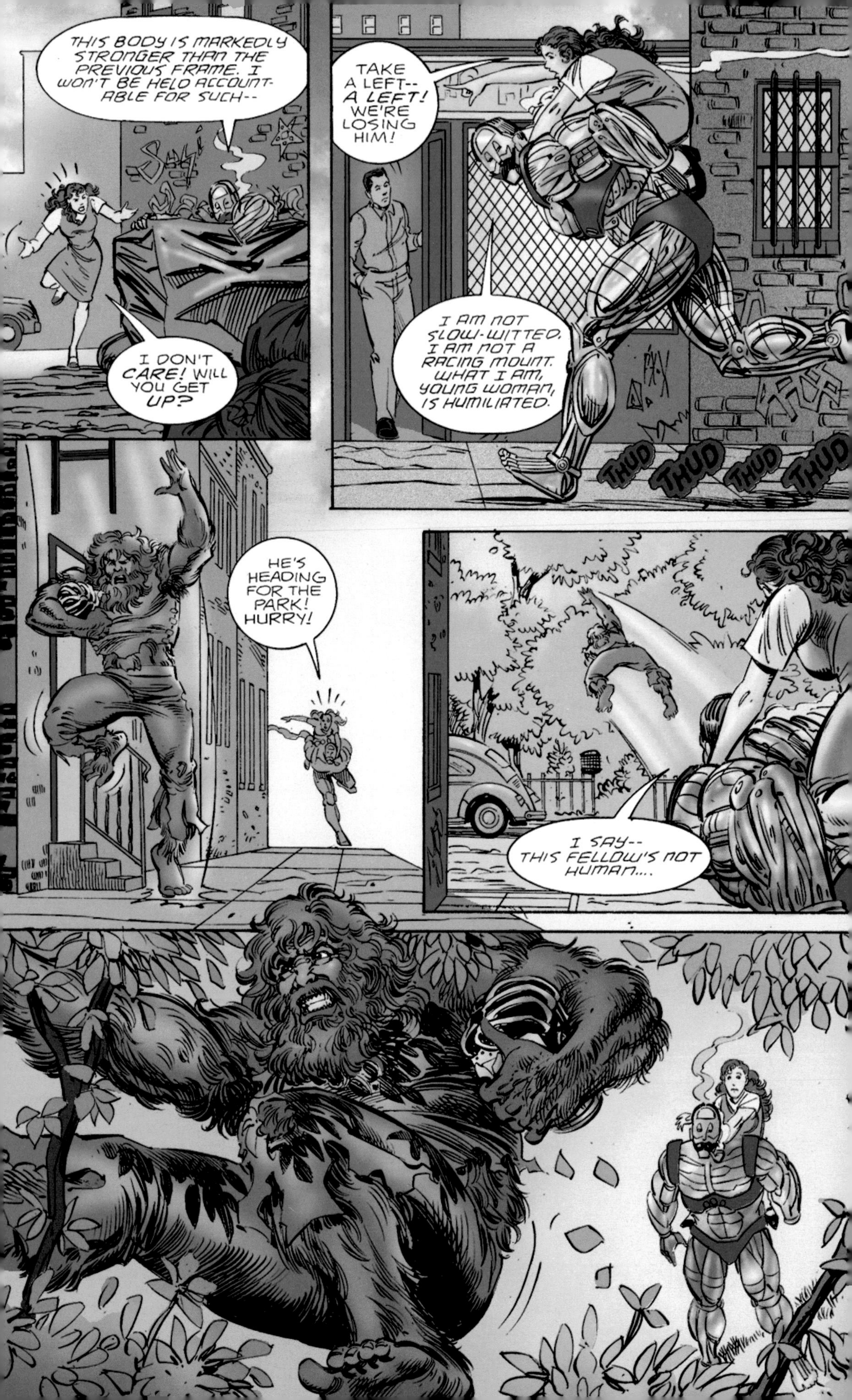
THIS BODY IS MARKEDLY STRONGER THAN THE PREVIOUS FRAME. I WON'T BE HELD ACCOUNT-ABLE FOR SUCH--
I DON'T CARE! WILL YOU GET UP?
TAKE A LEFT-- A LEFT! WE'RE LOSING HIM!
I AM NOT SLOW-WITTED. I AM NOT A RACING MOUNT. WHAT I AM, YOUNG WOMAN, IS HUMILIATED.
THUD THUD THUD THUD
HE'S HEADING FOR THE PARK! HURRY!
I SAY-- THIS FELLOW'S NOT HUMAN....

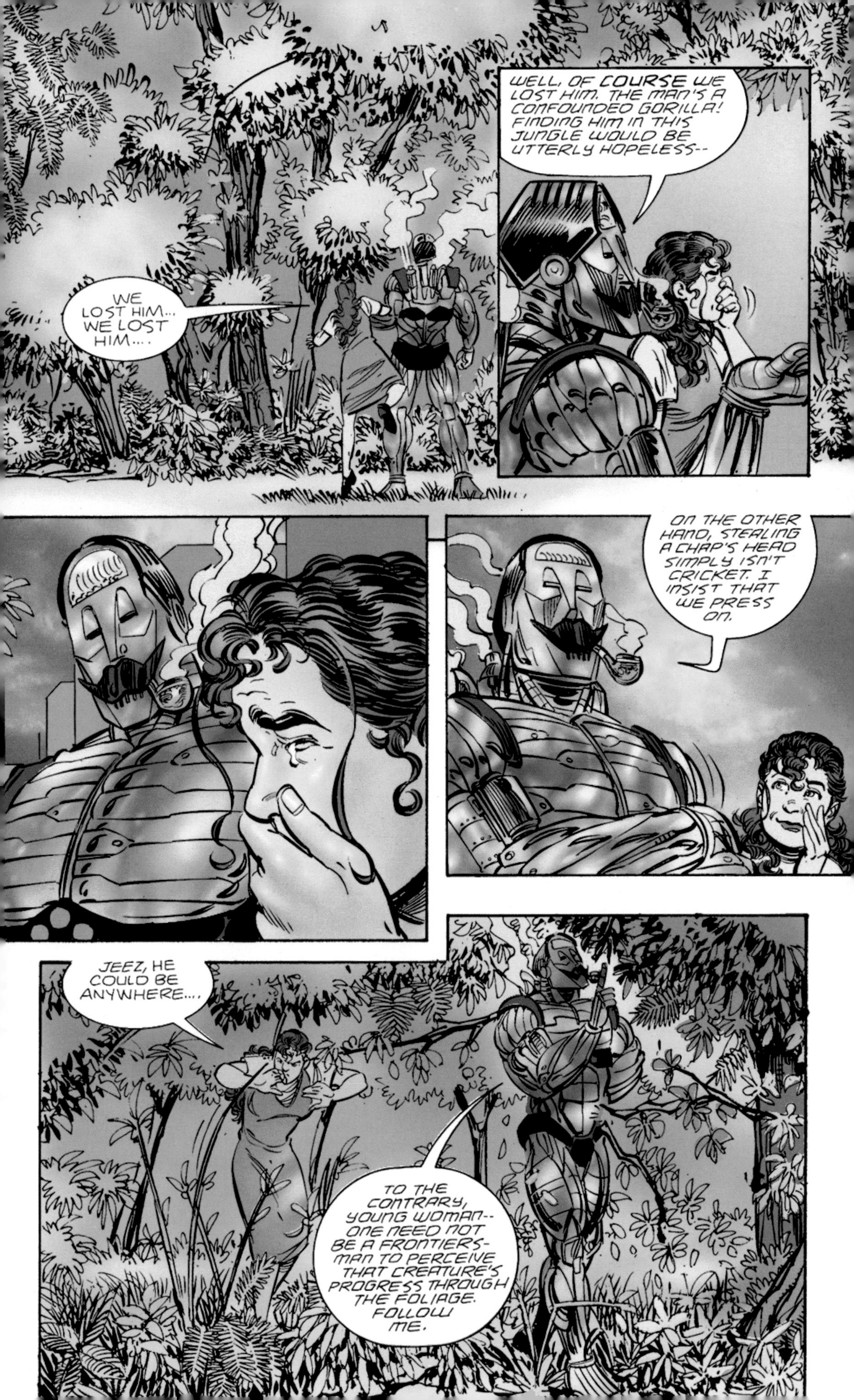
WE LOST HIM... WE LOST HIM....
WELL, OF COURSE WE LOST HIM. THE MAN'S A CONFOUNDED GORILLA! FINDING HIM IN THIS JUNGLE WOULD BE UTTERLY HOPELESS--
ON THE OTHER HAND, STEALING A CHAP'S HEAD SIMPLY ISN'T CRICKET. I INSIST THAT WE PRESS ON.
JEEZ, HE COULD BE ANYWHERE....
TO THE CONTRARY, YOUNG WOMAN-- ONE NEED NOT BE A FRONTIERS-MAN TO PERCEIVE THAT CREATURE'S PROGRESS THROUGH THE FOLIAGE. FOLLOW ME.

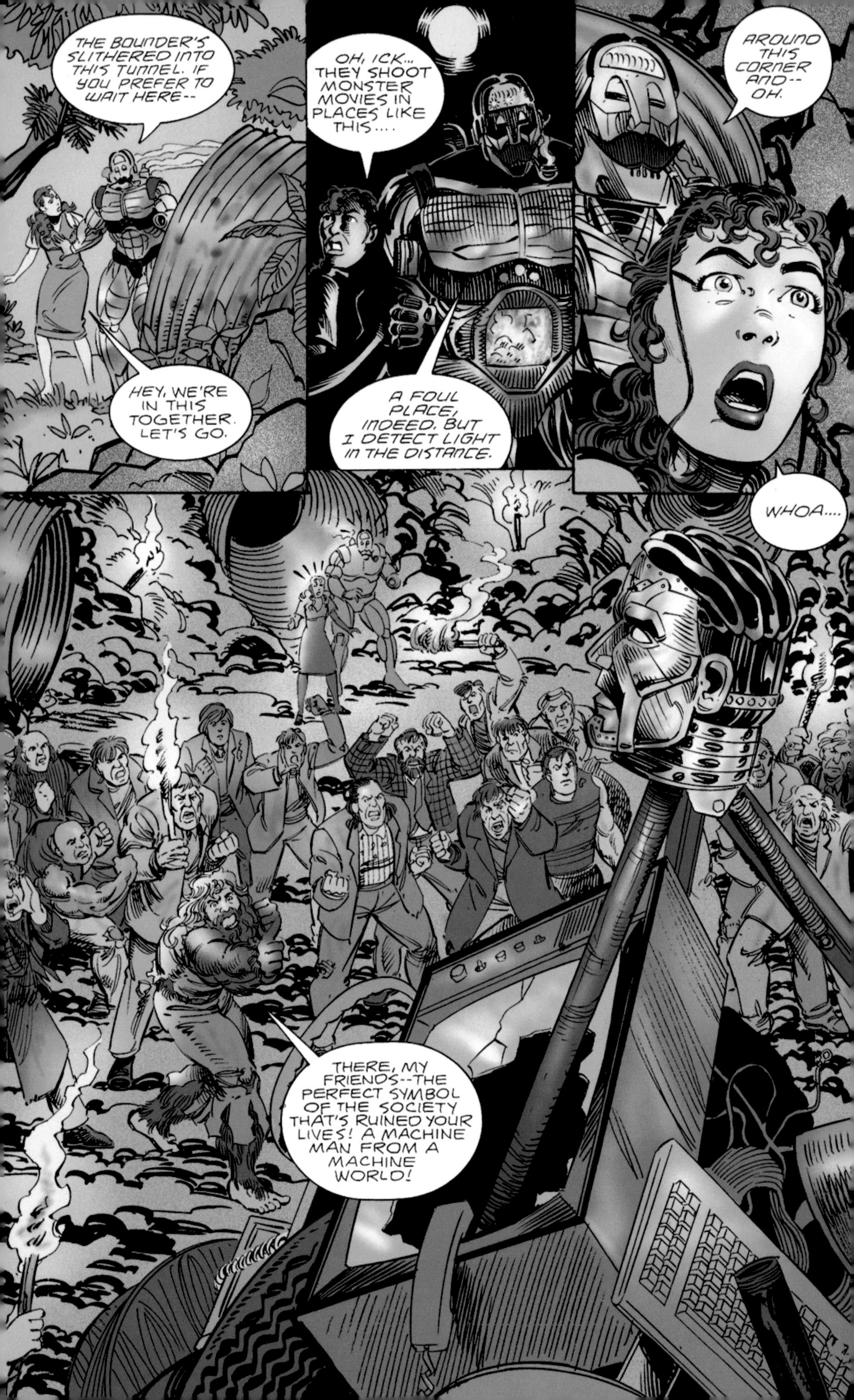
THE BOUNDER'S SLITHERED INTO THIS TUNNEL. IF YOU PREFER TO WAIT HERE--
HEY, WE'RE IN THIS TOGETHER. LET'S GO.
OH, ICK... THEY SHOOT MONSTER MOVIES IN PLACES LIKE THIS....
A FOUL PLACE, INDEED. BUT I DETECT LIGHT IN THE DISTANCE.
AROUND THIS CORNER AND-- OH.
WHOA....
THERE, MY FRIENDS--THE PERFECT SYMBOL OF THE SOCIETY THAT'S RUINED YOUR LIVES! A MACHINE MAN FROM A MACHINE WORLD!

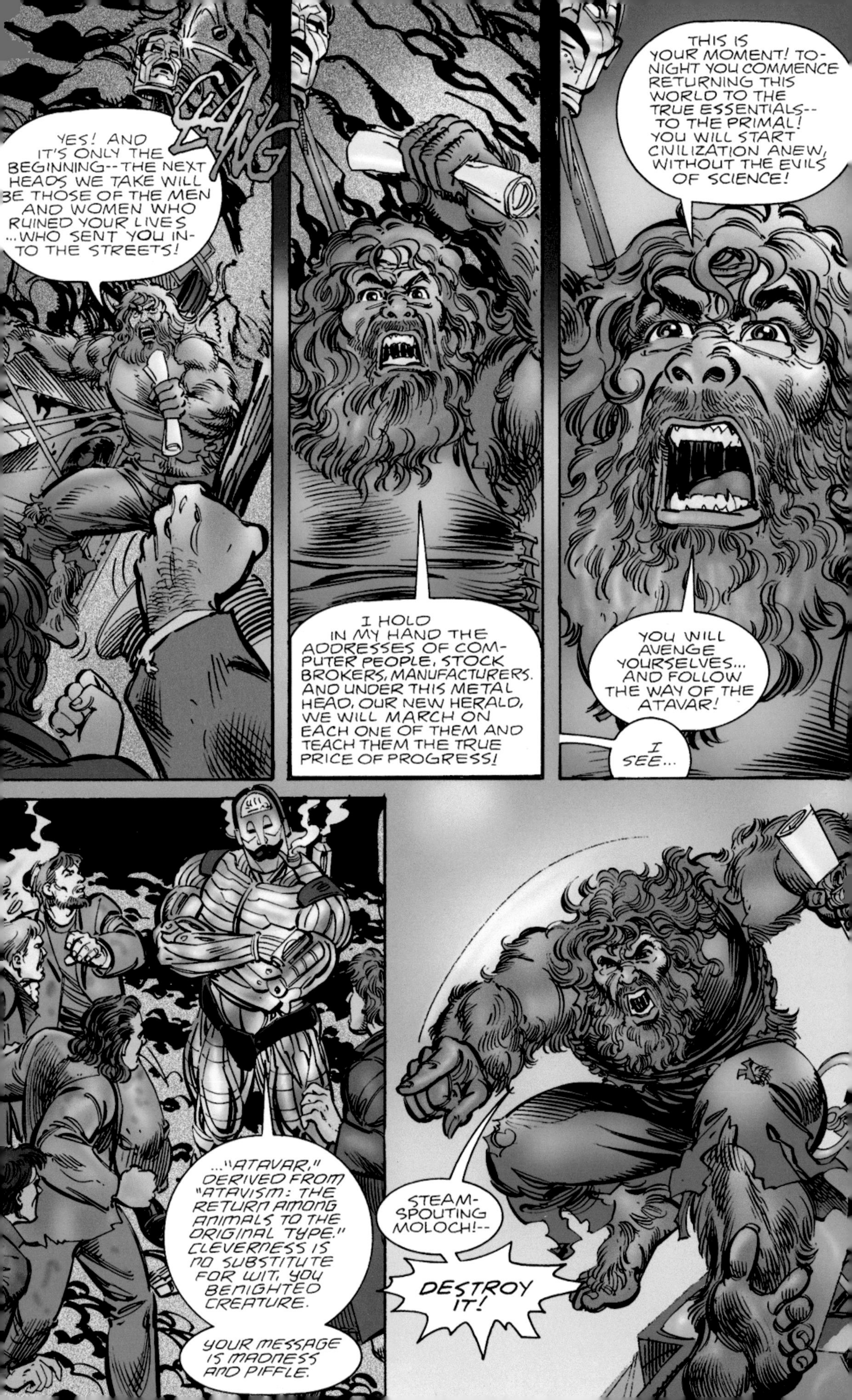
CLANG
YES! AND IT'S ONLY THE BEGINNING--THE NEXT HEADS WE TAKE WILL BE THOSE OF THE MEN AND WOMEN WHO RUINED YOUR LIVES ...WHO SENT YOU INTO THE STREETS!
I HOLD IN MY HAND THE ADDRESSES OF COMPUTER PEOPLE, STOCK BROKERS, MANUFACTURERS. AND UNDER THIS METAL HEAD, OUR NEW HERALD, WE WILL MARCH ON EACH ONE OF THEM AND TEACH THEM THE TRUE PRICE OF PROGRESS!
THIS IS YOUR MOMENT! TONIGHT YOU COMMENCE RETURNING THIS WORLD TO THE TRUE ESSENTIALS-- TO THE PRIMAL! YOU WILL START CIVILIZATION ANEW, WITHOUT THE EVILS OF SCIENCE!
YOU WILL AVENGE YOURSELVES... AND FOLLOW THE WAY OF THE ATAVAR!
I SEE...
..."ATAVAR," DERIVED FROM "ATAVISM: THE RETURN AMONG ANIMALS TO THE ORIGINAL TYPE." CLEVERNESS IS NO SUBSTITUTE FOR WIT, YOU BENIGHTED CREATURE.
YOUR MESSAGE IS MADNESS AND PIFFLE.
STEAM-SPOUTING MOLOCH!--
DESTROY IT!

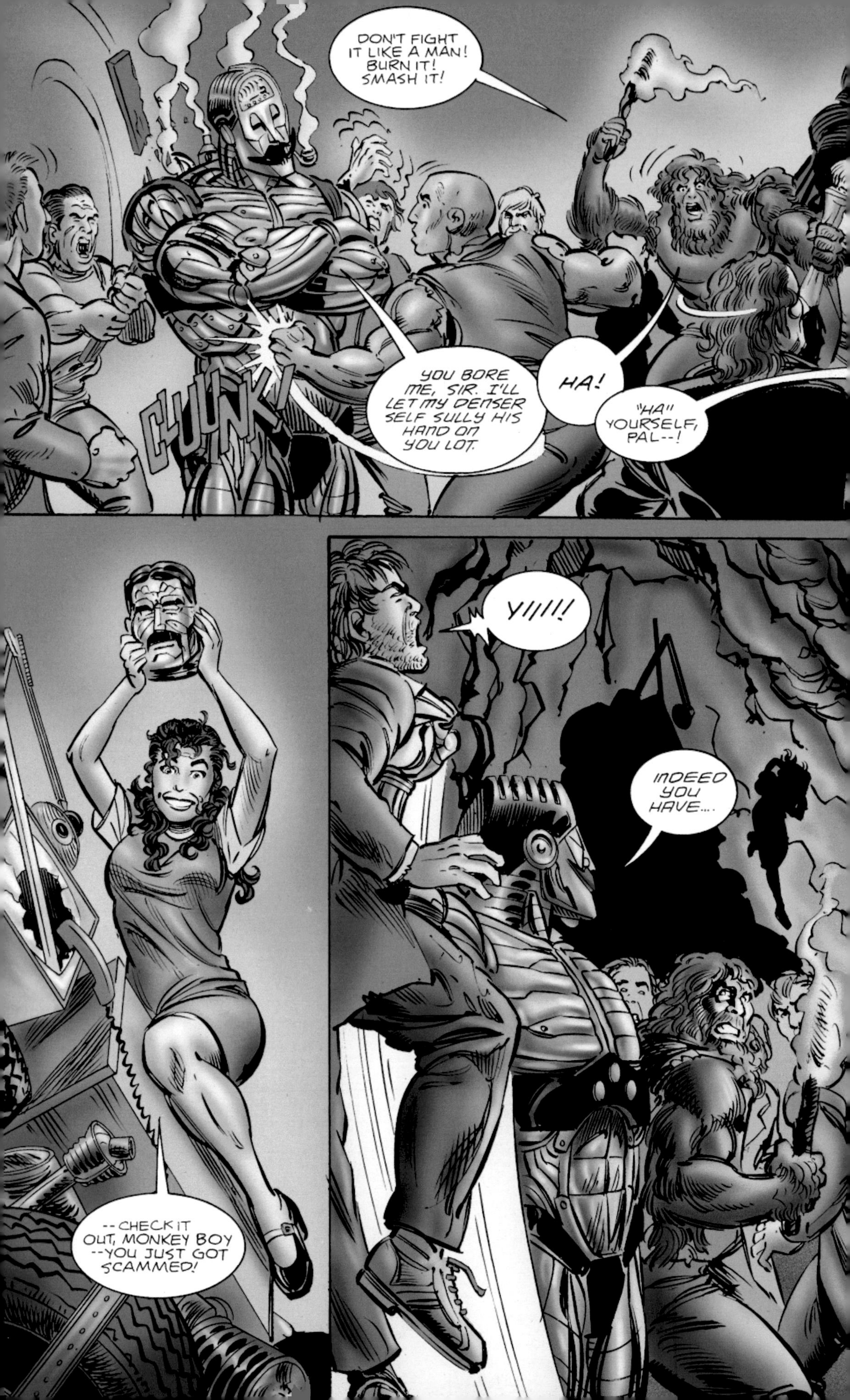
DON'T FIGHT IT LIKE A MAN! BURN IT! SMASH IT!
CLUUNK!
YOU BORE ME, SIR. I'LL LET MY DENSER SELF SULLY HIS HAND ON YOU LOT.
HA!
"HA" YOURSELF, PAL--!
--CHECK IT OUT, MONKEY BOY --YOU JUST GOT SCAMMED!
YIIII!
INDEED YOU HAVE....

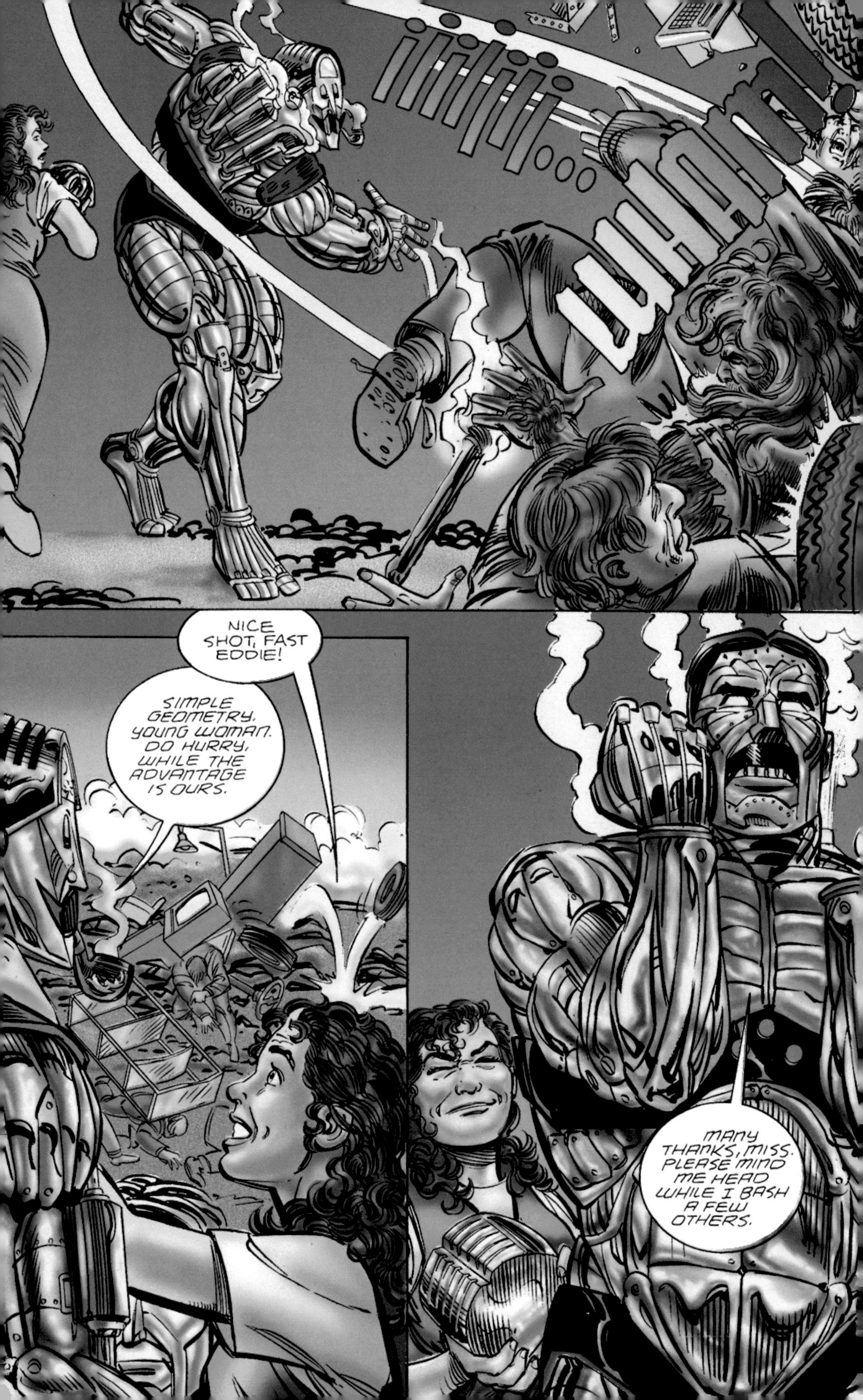
NICE SHOT, FAST EDDIE!
SIMPLE GEOMETRY, YOUNG WOMAN. DO HURRY, WHILE THE ADVANTAGE IS OURS.
MANY THANKS, MISS. PLEASE MIND ME HEAD WHILE I BASH A FEW OTHERS.

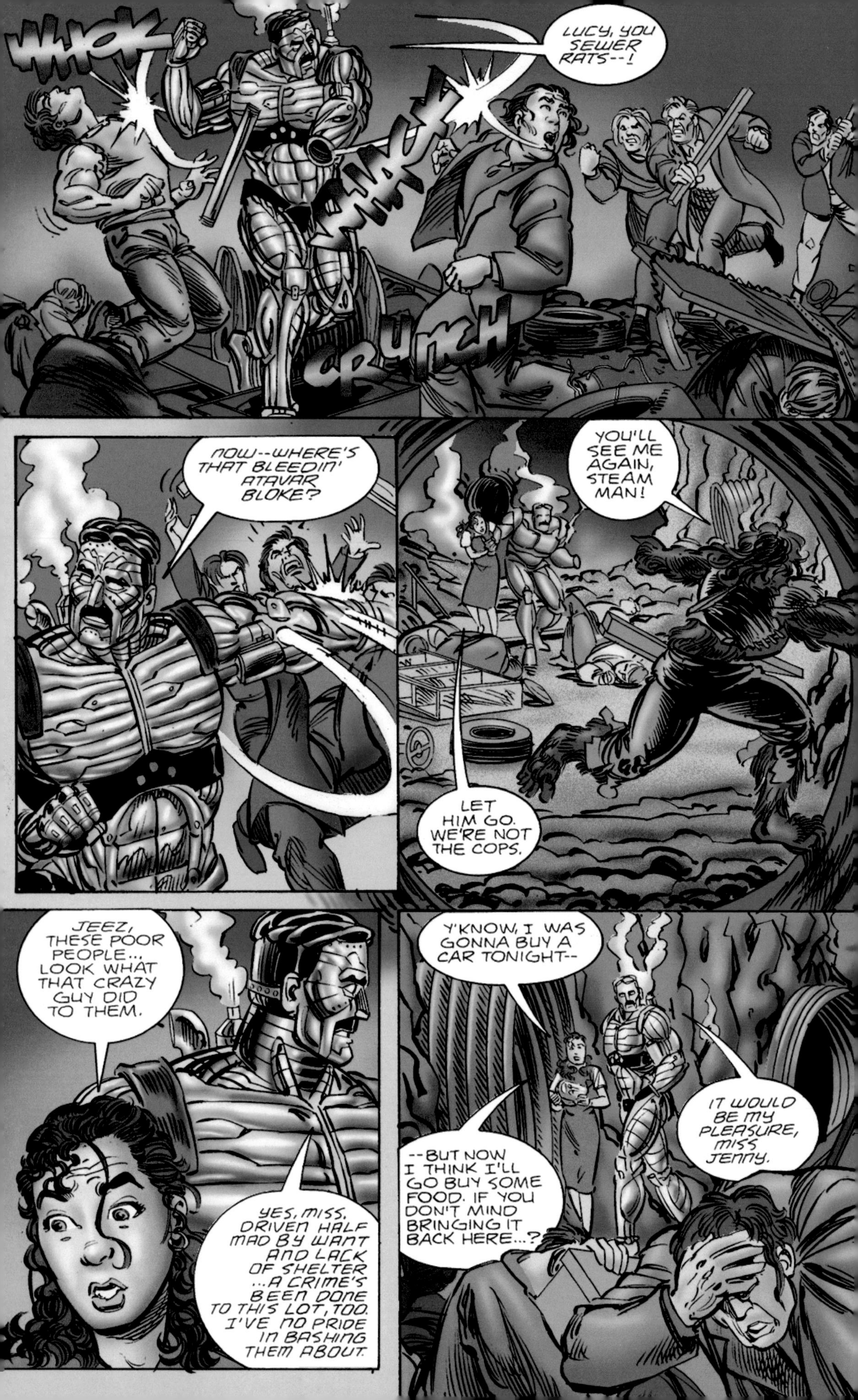
WHOK
LUCY, YOU SEWER RATS--!
WHACK
CRUNCH
NOW--WHERE'S THAT BLEEDIN' ATAVAR BLOKE?
YOU'LL SEE ME AGAIN, STEAM MAN!
LET HIM GO. WE'RE NOT THE COPS.
JEEZ, THESE POOR PEOPLE... LOOK WHAT THAT CRAZY GUY DID TO THEM.
YES, MISS. DRIVEN HALF MAD BY WANT AND LACK OF SHELTER ...A CRIME'S BEEN DONE TO THIS LOT, TOO. I'VE NO PRIDE IN BASHING THEM ABOUT.
Y'KNOW, I WAS GONNA BUY A CAR TONIGHT--
--BUT NOW I THINK I'LL GO BUY SOME FOOD. IF YOU DON'T MIND BRINGING IT BACK HERE...?
IT WOULD BE MY PLEASURE, MISS JENNY.

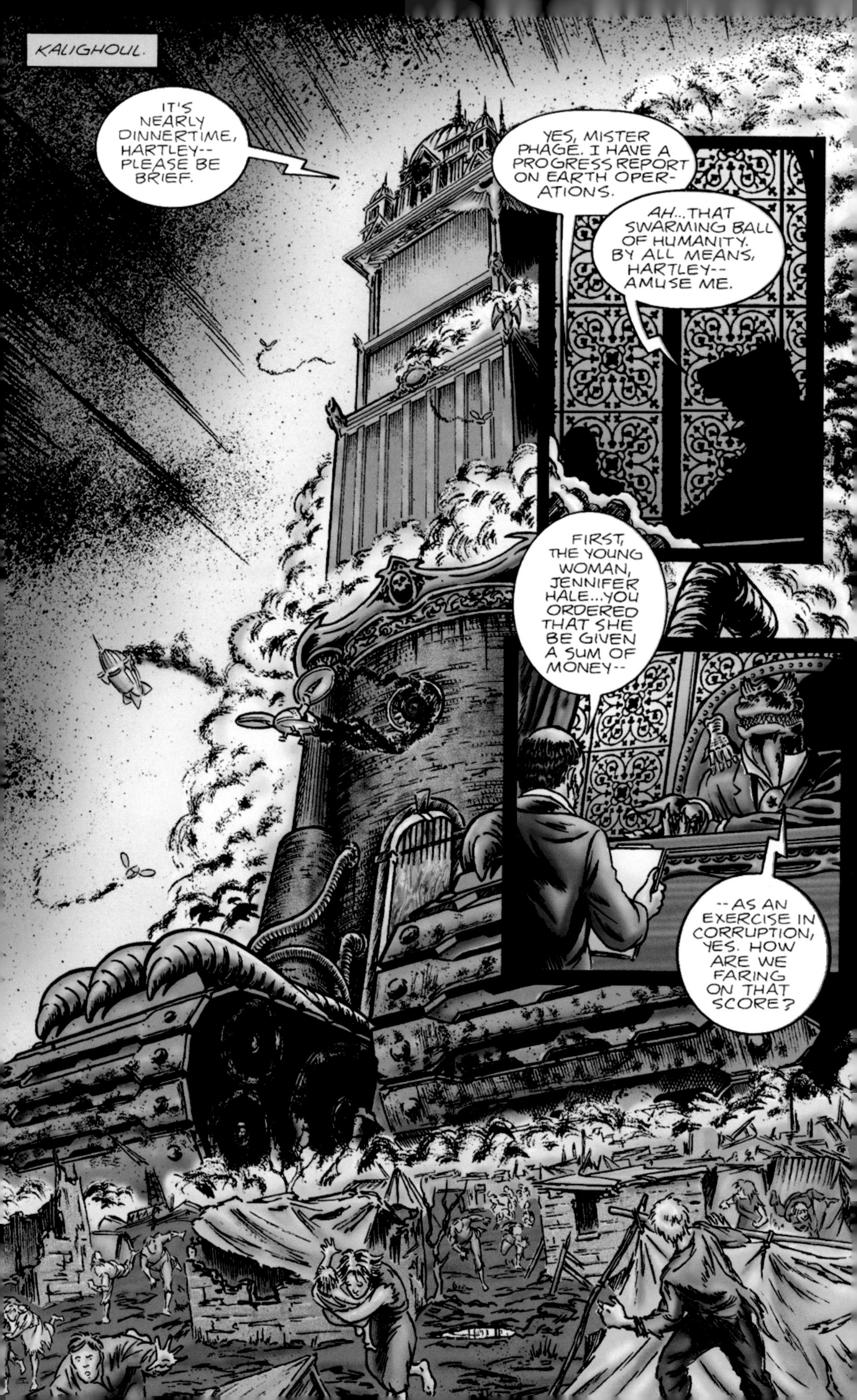
KALIGHOUL.
IT'S NEARLY DINNERTIME, HARTLEY-- PLEASE BE BRIEF.
YES, MISTER PHAGE. I HAVE A PROGRESS REPORT ON EARTH OPERATIONS.
AH...THAT SWARMING BALL OF HUMANITY. BY ALL MEANS, HARTLEY-- AMUSE ME.
FIRST, THE YOUNG WOMAN, JENNIFER HALE...YOU ORDERED THAT SHE BE GIVEN A SUM OF MONEY--
--AS AN EXERCISE IN CORRUPTION, YES. HOW ARE WE FARING ON THAT SCORE?

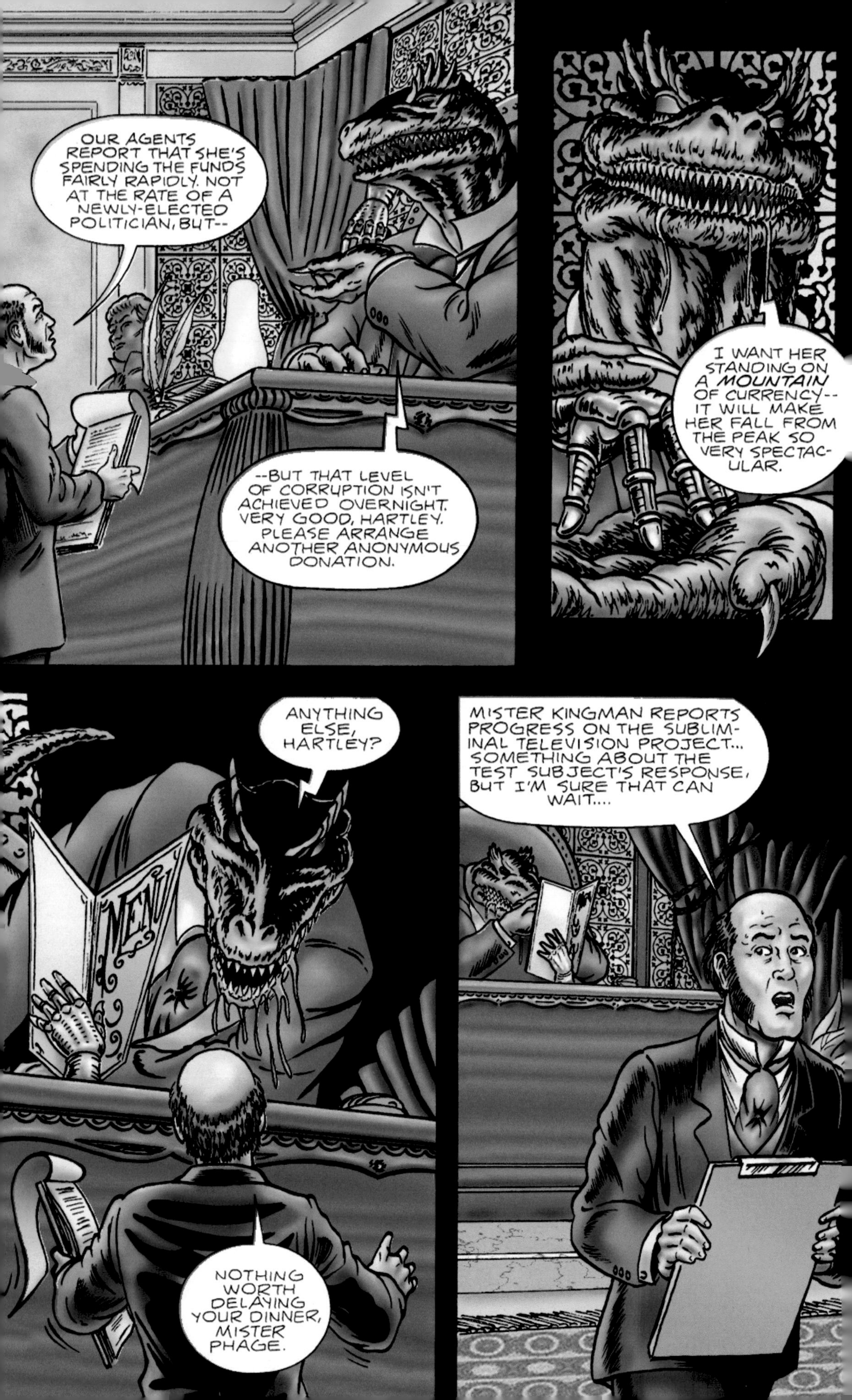
OUR AGENTS REPORT THAT SHE'S SPENDING THE FUNDS FAIRLY RAPIDLY. NOT AT THE RATE OF A NEWLY-ELECTED POLITICIAN, BUT--
--BUT THAT LEVEL OF CORRUPTION ISN'T ACHIEVED OVERNIGHT. VERY GOOD, HARTLEY. PLEASE ARRANGE ANOTHER ANONYMOUS DONATION.
I WANT HER STANDING ON A MOUNTAIN OF CURRENCY-- IT WILL MAKE HER FALL FROM THE PEAK SO VERY SPECTACULAR.
ANYTHING ELSE, HARTLEY?
NOTHING WORTH DELAYING YOUR DINNER, MISTER PHAGE.
MISTER KINGMAN REPORTS PROGRESS ON THE SUBLIMINAL TELEVISION PROJECT... SOMETHING ABOUT THE TEST SUBJECT'S RESPONSE, BUT I'M SURE THAT CAN WAIT....
MENU

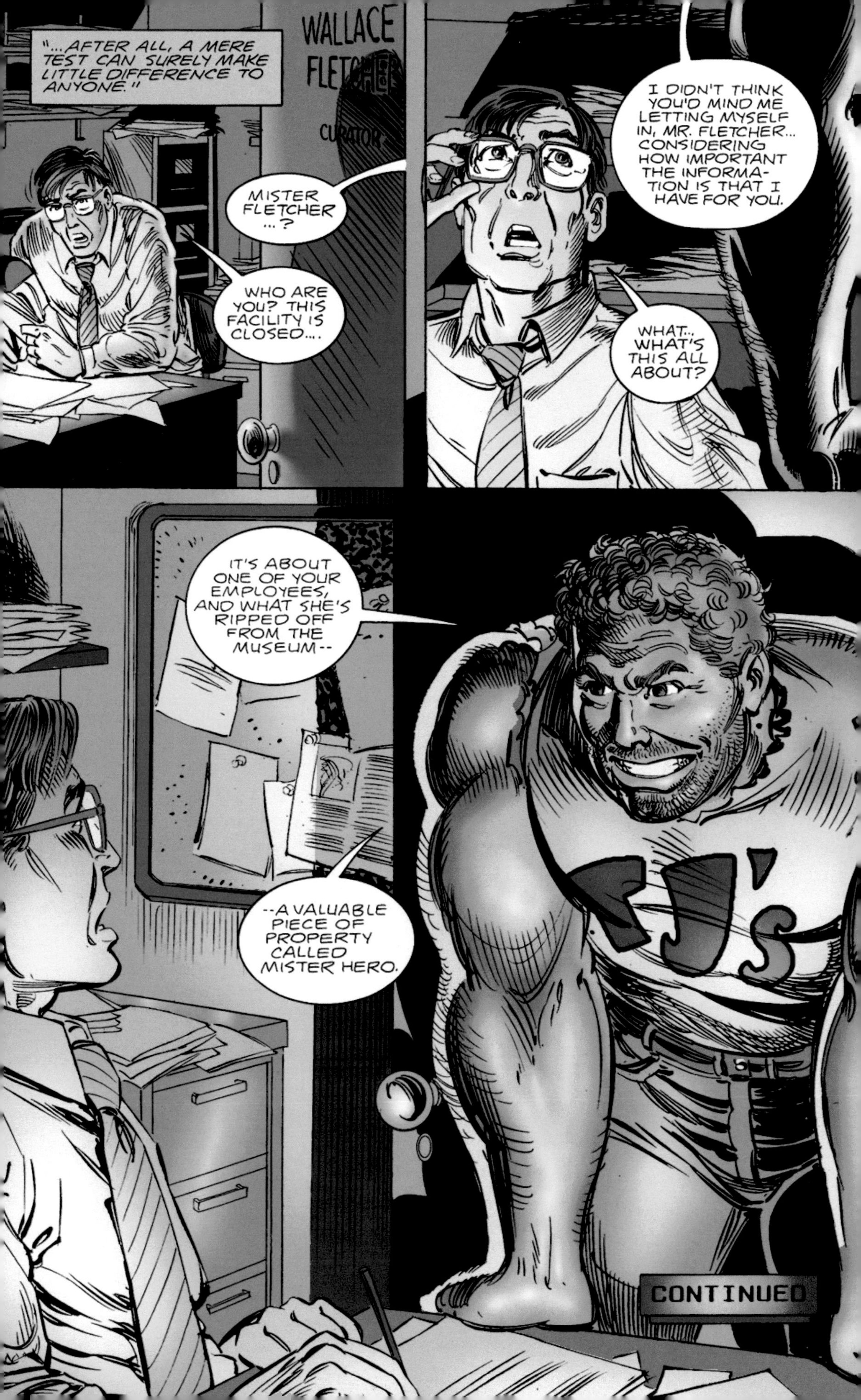
"...AFTER ALL, A MERE TEST CAN SURELY MAKE LITTLE DIFFERENCE TO ANYONE."
WALLACE FLETCHER CURATOR
MISTER FLETCHER ...?
WHO ARE YOU? THIS FACILITY IS CLOSED....
I DIDN'T THINK YOU'D MIND ME LETTING MYSELF IN, MR. FLETCHER... CONSIDERING HOW IMPORTANT THE INFORMATION IS THAT I HAVE FOR YOU.
WHAT... WHAT'S THIS ALL ABOUT?
IT'S ABOUT ONE OF YOUR EMPLOYEES, AND WHAT SHE'S RIPPED OFF FROM THE MUSEUM--
--A VALUABLE PIECE OF PROPERTY CALLED MISTER HERO.
CONTINUED

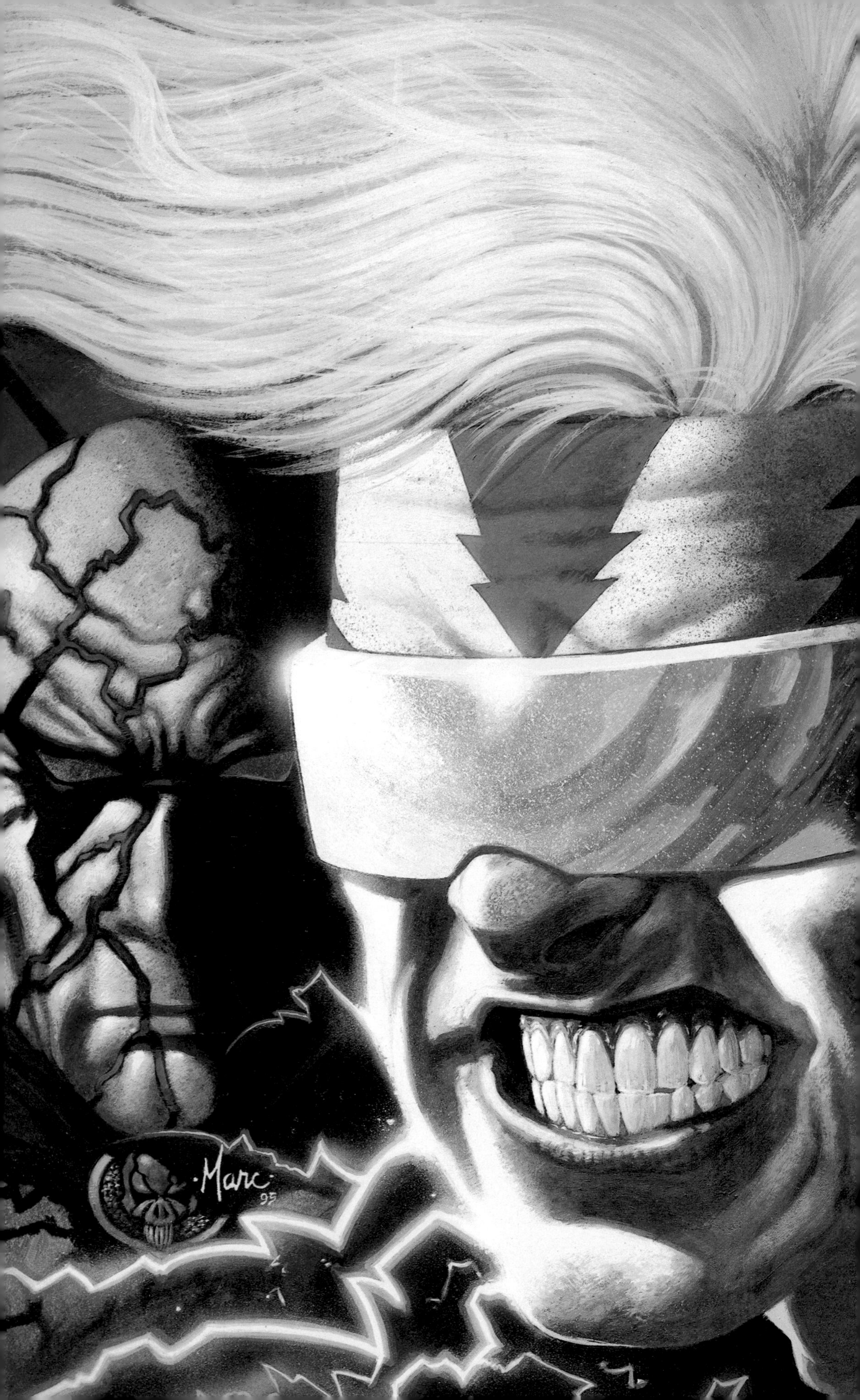
Marc
95

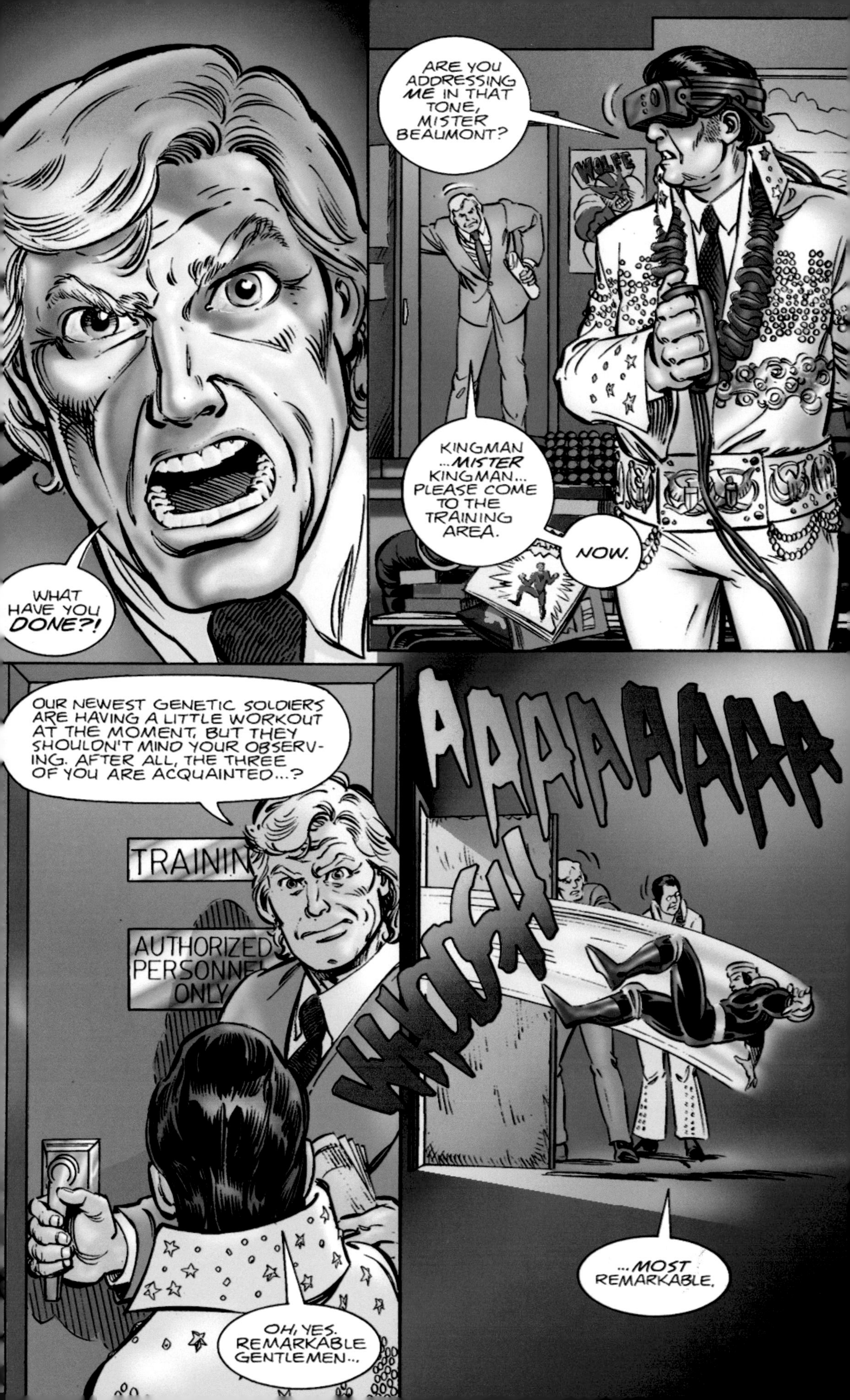

WHAT HAVE YOU DONE?!
ARE YOU ADDRESSING ME IN THAT TONE, MISTER BEAUMONT?
WOLFE
KINGMAN ...MISTER KINGMAN... PLEASE COME TO THE TRAINING AREA.
NOW.
OUR NEWEST GENETIC SOLDIERS ARE HAVING A LITTLE WORKOUT AT THE MOMENT, BUT THEY SHOULDN'T MIND YOUR OBSERVING. AFTER ALL, THE THREE OF YOU ARE ACQUAINTED...?
TRAININ
AUTHORIZED PERSONNEL ONLY
OH, YES. REMARKABLE GENTLEMEN...
AAAAAAAA
WHOOSH
...MOST REMARKABLE.

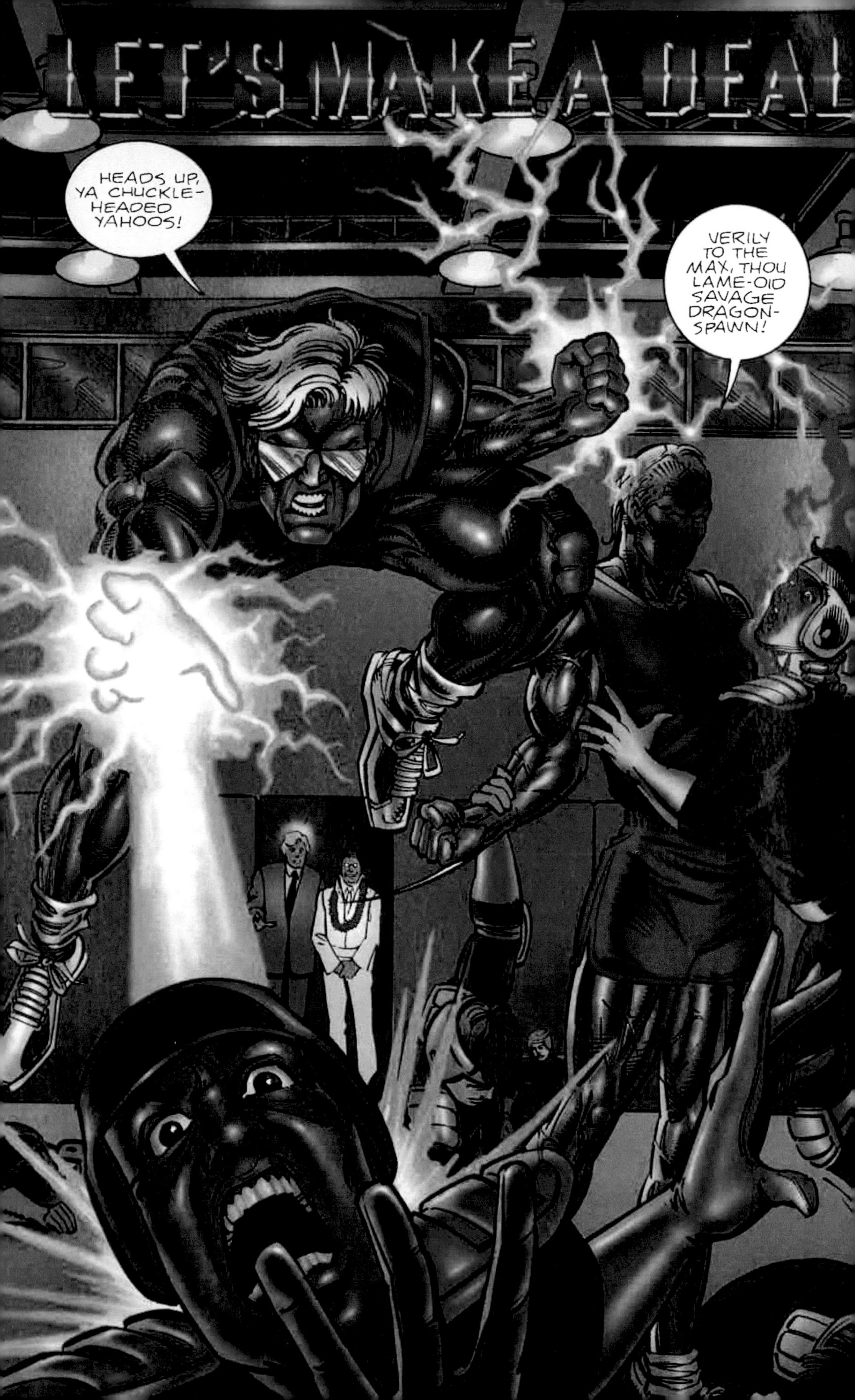
LET'S MAKE A DEAL
HEADS UP, YA CHUCKLE-HEADED YAHOOS!
VERILY TO THE MAX, THOU LAME-OID SAVAGE DRAGON-SPAWN!

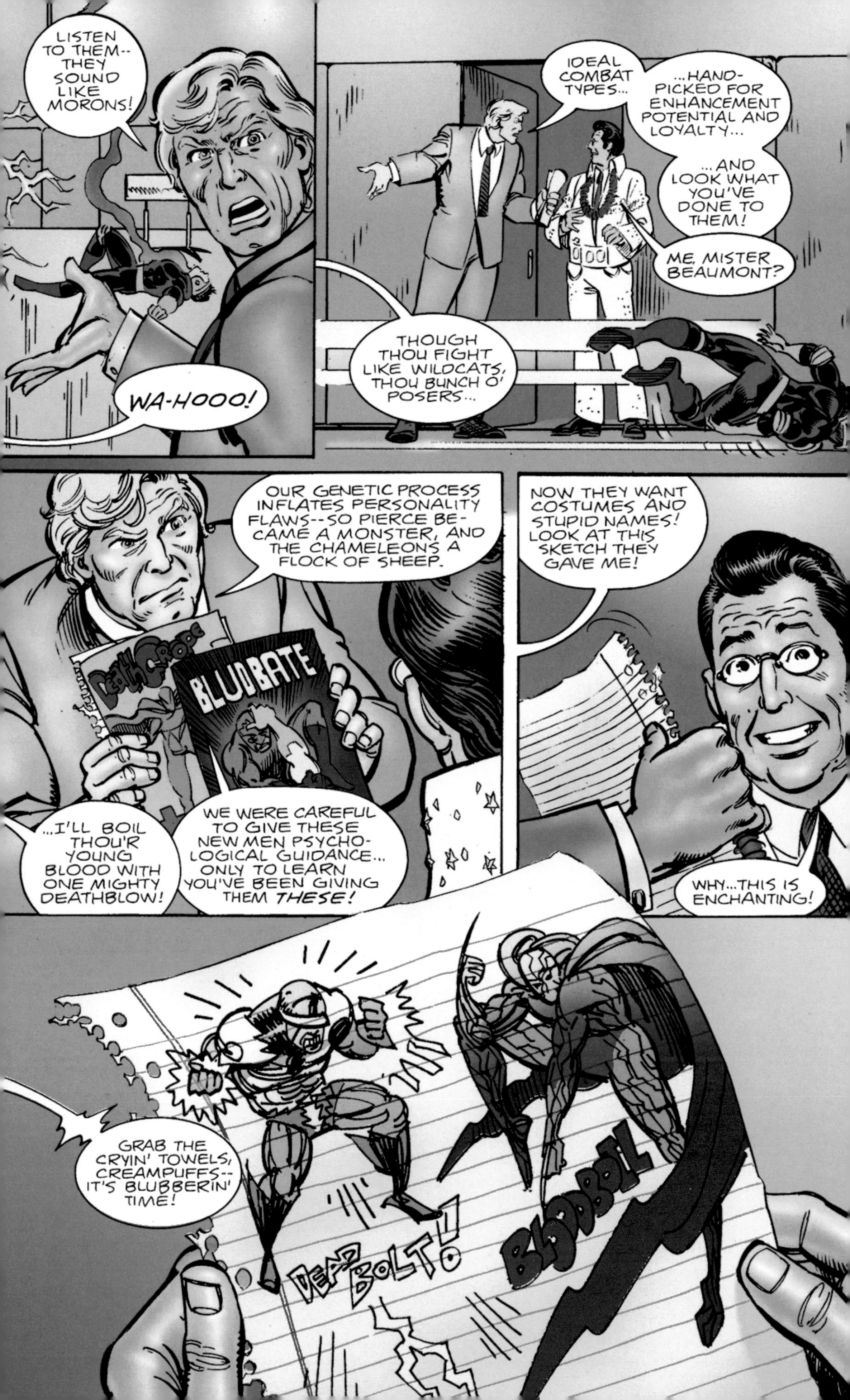
LISTEN TO THEM-- THEY SOUND LIKE MORONS!
WA-HOOO!
IDEAL COMBAT TYPES...
...HAND-PICKED FOR ENHANCEMENT POTENTIAL AND LOYALTY...
...AND LOOK WHAT YOU'VE DONE TO THEM!
ME, MISTER BEAUMONT?
THOUGH THOU FIGHT LIKE WILDCATS, THOU BUNCH O' POSERS...
OUR GENETIC PROCESS INFLATES PERSONALITY FLAWS--SO PIERCE BE-CAME A MONSTER, AND THE CHAMELEON'S A FLOCK OF SHEEP.
BLUDBATE
...I'LL BOIL THOU'R YOUNG BLOOD WITH ONE MIGHTY DEATHBLOW!
WE WERE CAREFUL TO GIVE THESE NEW MEN PSYCHO-LOGICAL GUIDANCE... ONLY TO LEARN YOU'VE BEEN GIVING THEM THESE!
NOW THEY WANT COSTUMES AND STUPID NAMES! LOOK AT THIS SKETCH THEY GAVE ME!
WHY...THIS IS ENCHANTING!
GRAB THE CRYIN' TOWELS, CREAMPUFFS-- IT'S BLUBBERIN' TIME!
DEAD BOLT!
BLODBOIL

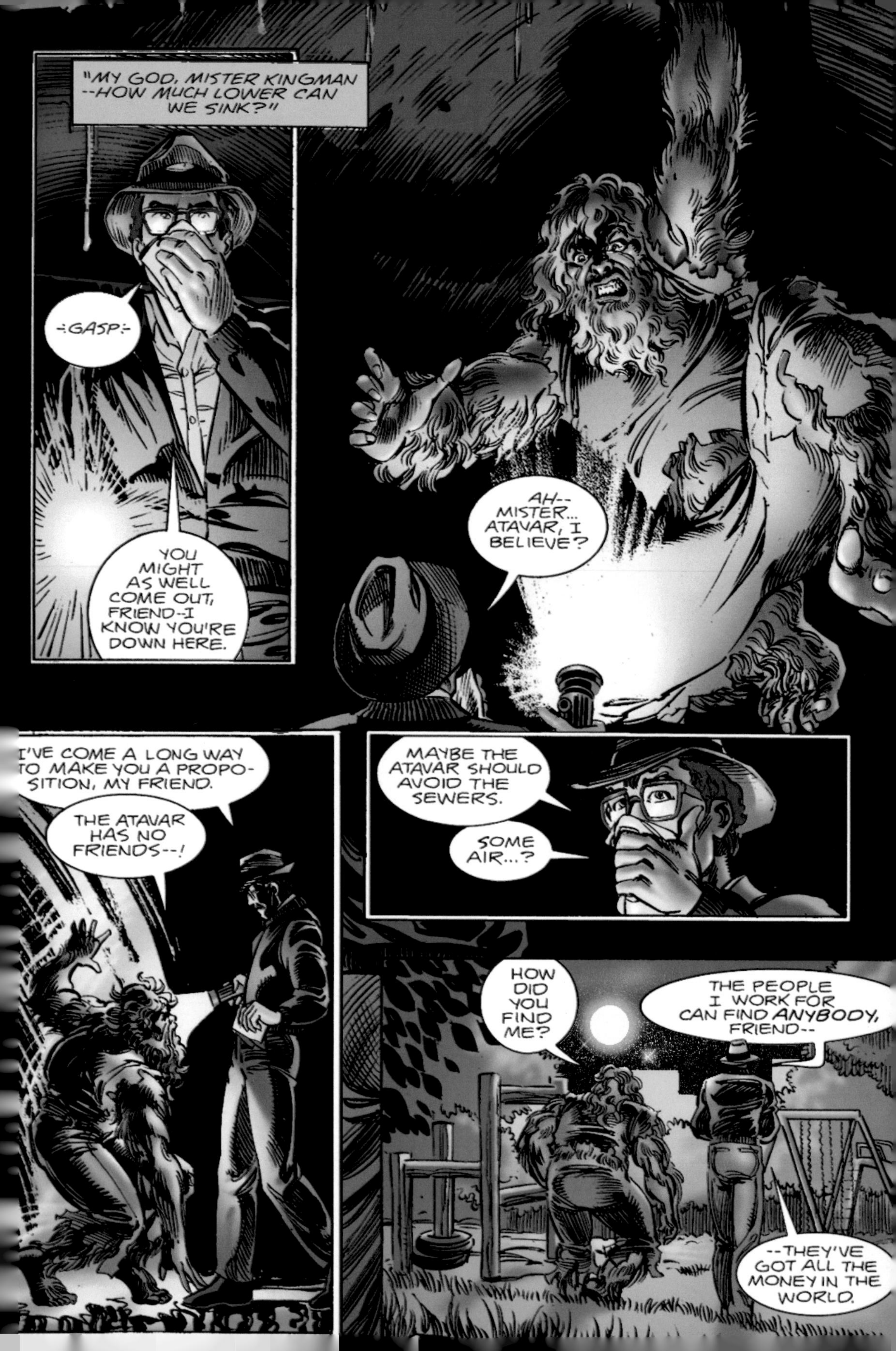
"MY GOD, MISTER KINGMAN --HOW MUCH LOWER CAN WE SINK?"
-:GASP:-
YOU MIGHT AS WELL COME OUT, FRIEND--I KNOW YOU'RE DOWN HERE.
AH-- MISTER... ATAVAR, I BELIEVE?
I'VE COME A LONG WAY TO MAKE YOU A PROPOSITION, MY FRIEND.
THE ATAVAR HAS NO FRIENDS--!
MAYBE THE ATAVAR SHOULD AVOID THE SEWERS.
SOME AIR...?
HOW DID YOU FIND ME?
THE PEOPLE I WORK FOR CAN FIND ANYBODY, FRIEND--
--THEY'VE GOT ALL THE MONEY IN THE WORLD.

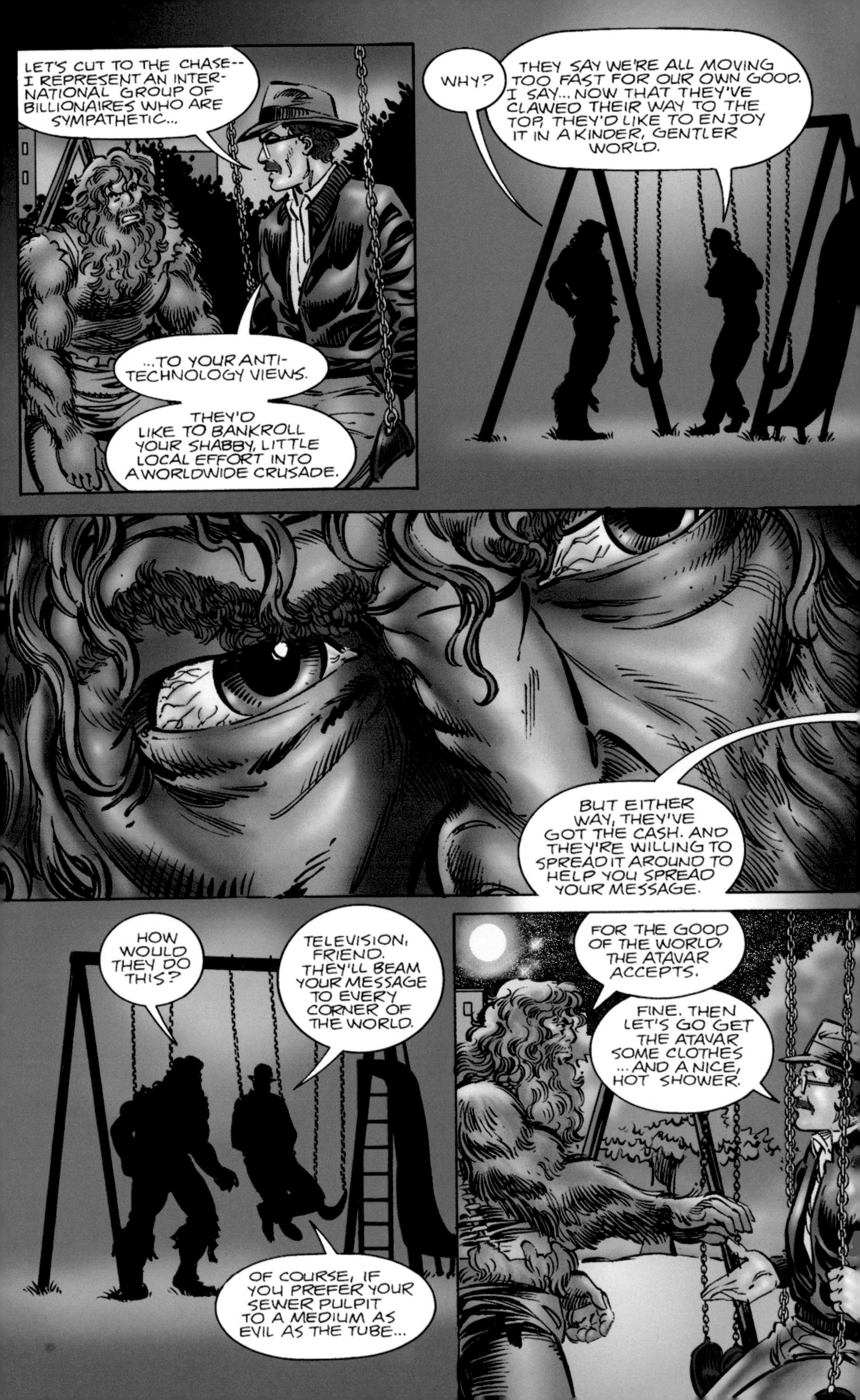
LET'S CUT TO THE CHASE-- I REPRESENT AN INTER-NATIONAL GROUP OF BILLIONAIRES WHO ARE SYMPATHETIC...
...TO YOUR ANTI-TECHNOLOGY VIEWS.
THEY'D LIKE TO BANKROLL YOUR SHABBY, LITTLE LOCAL EFFORT INTO A WORLDWIDE CRUSADE.
WHY?
THEY SAY WE'RE ALL MOVING TOO FAST FOR OUR OWN GOOD. I SAY... NOW THAT THEY'VE CLAWED THEIR WAY TO THE TOP, THEY'D LIKE TO ENJOY IT IN A KINDER, GENTLER WORLD.
BUT EITHER WAY, THEY'VE GOT THE CASH. AND THEY'RE WILLING TO SPREAD IT AROUND TO HELP YOU SPREAD YOUR MESSAGE.
HOW WOULD THEY DO THIS?
TELEVISION, FRIEND. THEY'LL BEAM YOUR MESSAGE TO EVERY CORNER OF THE WORLD.
OF COURSE, IF YOU PREFER YOUR SEWER PULPIT TO A MEDIUM AS EVIL AS THE TUBE...
FOR THE GOOD OF THE WORLD, THE ATAVAR ACCEPTS.
FINE. THEN LET'S GO GET THE ATAVAR SOME CLOTHES ...AND A NICE, HOT SHOWER.

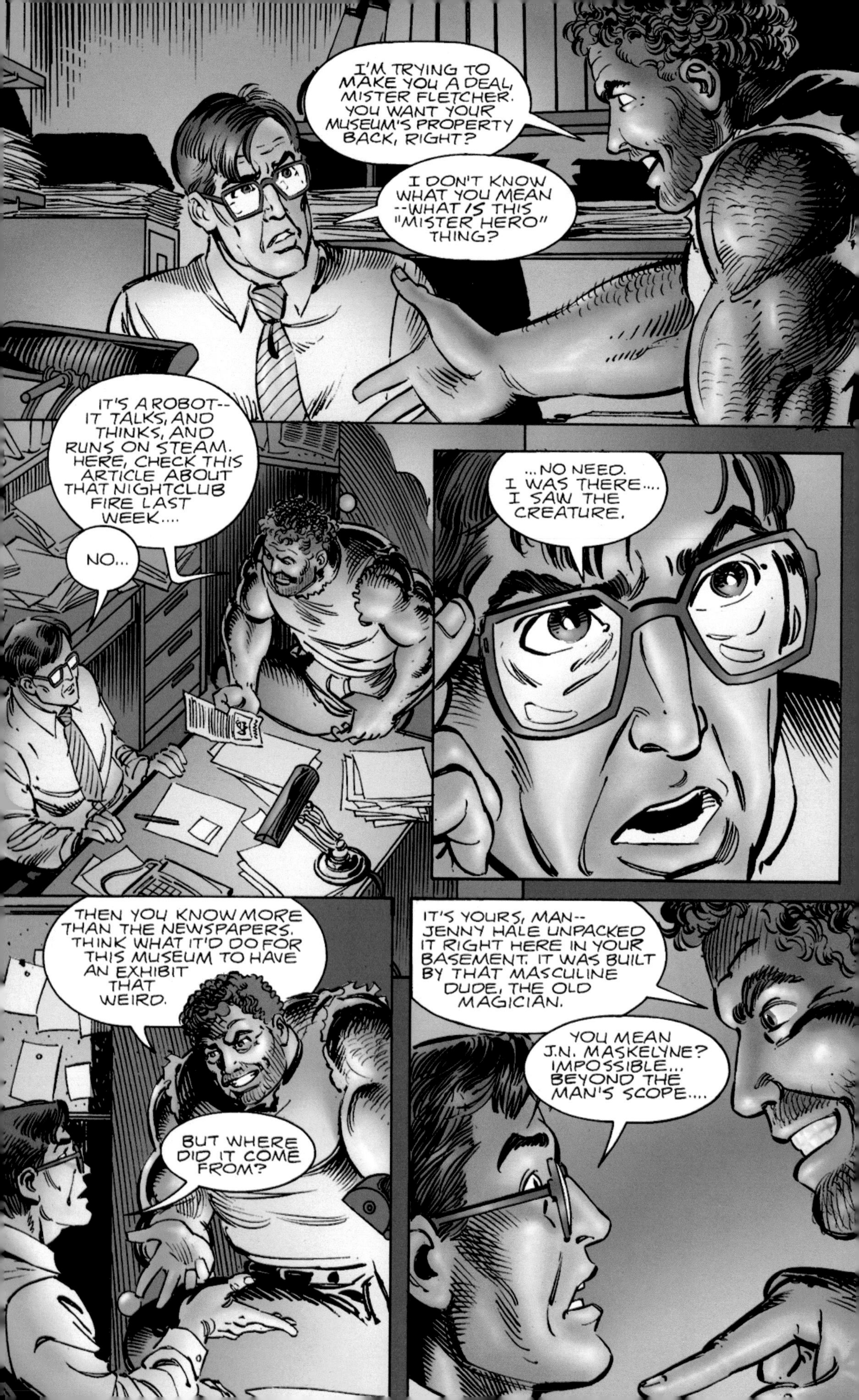
I'M TRYING TO MAKE YOU A DEAL, MISTER FLETCHER. YOU WANT YOUR MUSEUM'S PROPERTY BACK, RIGHT?
I DON'T KNOW WHAT YOU MEAN --WHAT *IS* THIS "MISTER HERO" THING?
IT'S A ROBOT-- IT TALKS, AND THINKS, AND RUNS ON STEAM. HERE, CHECK THIS ARTICLE ABOUT THAT NIGHTCLUB FIRE LAST WEEK....
NO...
...NO NEED. I WAS THERE.... I SAW THE CREATURE.
THEN YOU KNOW MORE THAN THE NEWSPAPERS. THINK WHAT IT'D DO FOR THIS MUSEUM TO HAVE AN EXHIBIT THAT WEIRD.
BUT WHERE DID IT COME FROM?
IT'S YOURS, MAN-- JENNY HALE UNPACKED IT RIGHT HERE IN YOUR BASEMENT. IT WAS BUILT BY THAT MASCULINE DUDE, THE OLD MAGICIAN.
YOU MEAN J.N. MASKELYNE? IMPOSSIBLE... BEYOND THE MAN'S SCOPE....

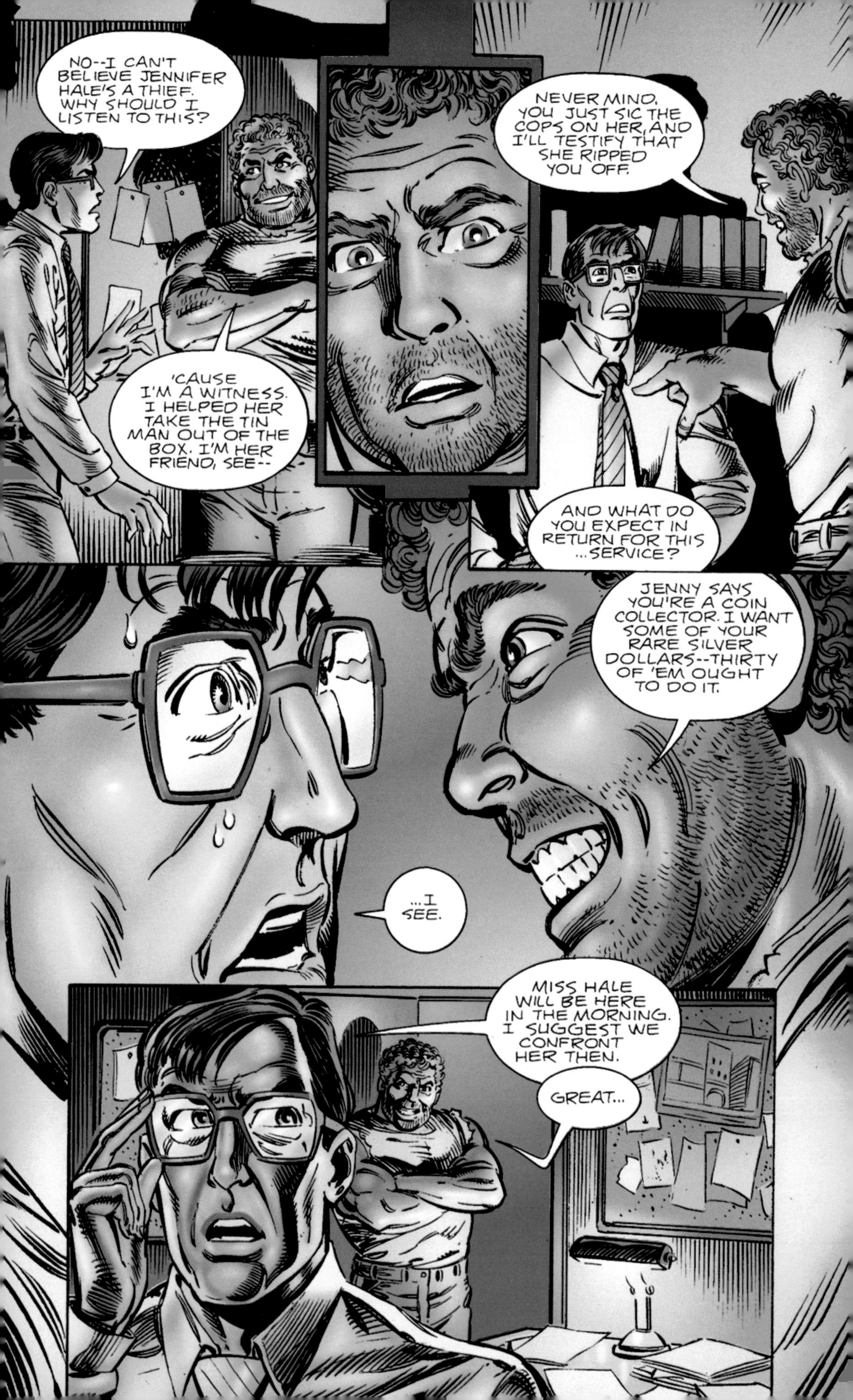
NO--I CAN'T BELIEVE JENNIFER HALE'S A THIEF. WHY SHOULD I LISTEN TO THIS?
'CAUSE I'M A WITNESS. I HELPED HER TAKE THE TIN MAN OUT OF THE BOX. I'M HER FRIEND, SEE--
NEVER MIND. YOU JUST SIC THE COPS ON HER, AND I'LL TESTIFY THAT SHE RIPPED YOU OFF.
AND WHAT DO YOU EXPECT IN RETURN FOR THIS ...SERVICE?
JENNY SAYS YOU'RE A COIN COLLECTOR. I WANT SOME OF YOUR RARE SILVER DOLLARS--THIRTY OF 'EM OUGHT TO DO IT.
...I SEE.
MISS HALE WILL BE HERE IN THE MORNING. I SUGGEST WE CONFRONT HER THEN.
GREAT...

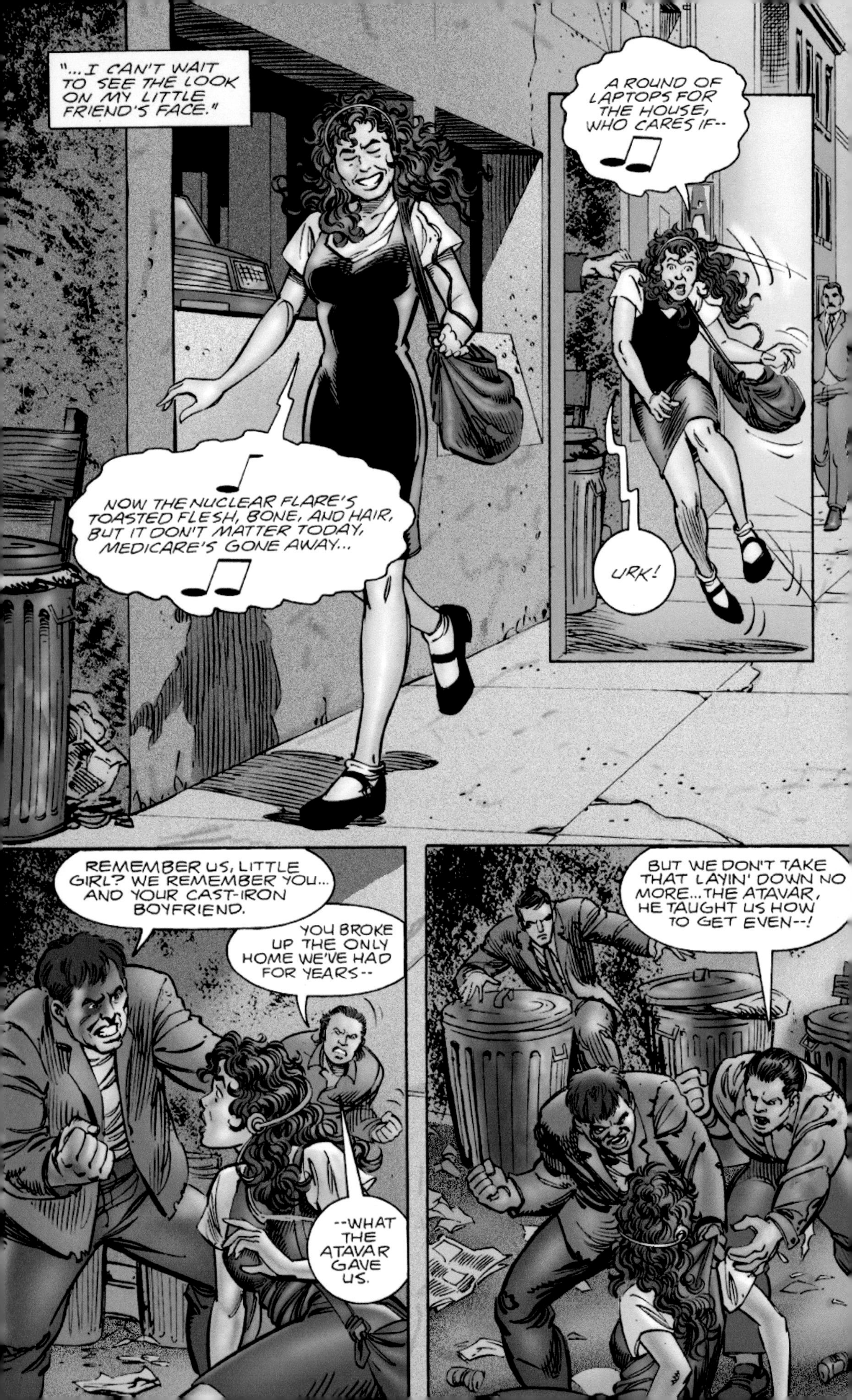
"...I CAN'T WAIT TO SEE THE LOOK ON MY LITTLE FRIEND'S FACE."
NOW THE NUCLEAR FLARE'S TOASTED FLESH, BONE, AND HAIR, BUT IT DON'T MATTER TODAY, MEDICARE'S GONE AWAY...
A ROUND OF LAPTOPS FOR THE HOUSE, WHO CARES IF--
URK!
REMEMBER US, LITTLE GIRL? WE REMEMBER YOU... AND YOUR CAST-IRON BOYFRIEND.
YOU BROKE UP THE ONLY HOME WE'VE HAD FOR YEARS--
--WHAT THE ATAVAR GAVE US.
BUT WE DON'T TAKE THAT LAYIN' DOWN NO MORE...THE ATAVAR, HE TAUGHT US HOW TO GET EVEN--!

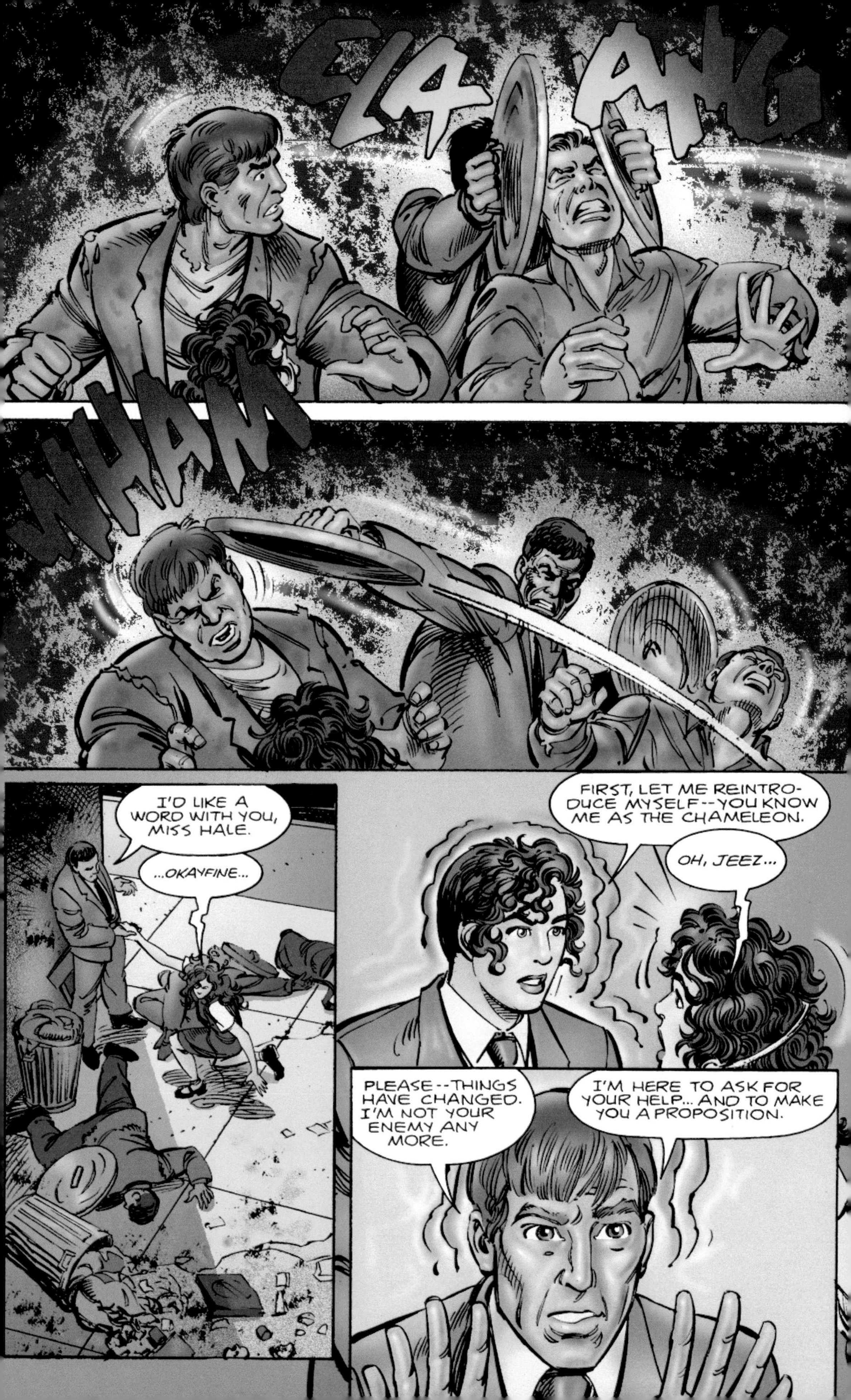
CLA
ANG
WHAM
I'D LIKE A WORD WITH YOU, MISS HALE.
...OKAYFINE...
FIRST, LET ME REINTRODUCE MYSELF--YOU KNOW ME AS THE CHAMELEON.
OH, JEEZ...
PLEASE--THINGS HAVE CHANGED. I'M NOT YOUR ENEMY ANY MORE.
I'M HERE TO ASK FOR YOUR HELP... AND TO MAKE YOU A PROPOSITION.

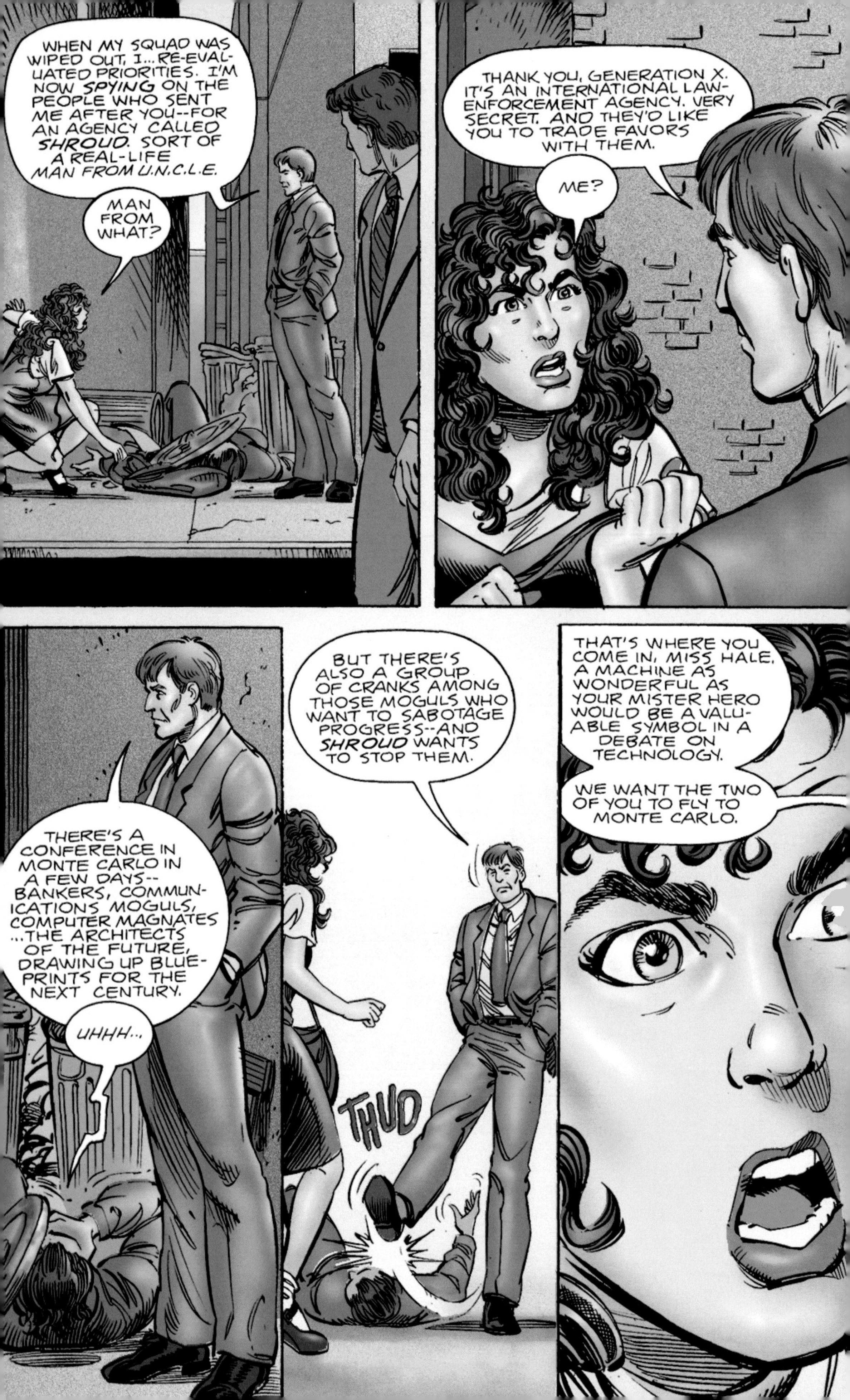
WHEN MY SQUAD WAS WIPED OUT, I... RE-EVALUATED PRIORITIES. I'M NOW SPYING ON THE PEOPLE WHO SENT ME AFTER YOU--FOR AN AGENCY CALLED SHROUD. SORT OF A REAL-LIFE MAN FROM U.N.C.L.E.
MAN FROM WHAT?
THANK YOU, GENERATION X. IT'S AN INTERNATIONAL LAW-ENFORCEMENT AGENCY. VERY SECRET. AND THEY'D LIKE YOU TO TRADE FAVORS WITH THEM.
ME?
THERE'S A CONFERENCE IN MONTE CARLO IN A FEW DAYS--BANKERS, COMMUNICATIONS MOGULS, COMPUTER MAGNATES ...THE ARCHITECTS OF THE FUTURE, DRAWING UP BLUEPRINTS FOR THE NEXT CENTURY.
UHHH...
BUT THERE'S ALSO A GROUP OF CRANKS AMONG THOSE MOGULS WHO WANT TO SABOTAGE PROGRESS--AND SHROUD WANTS TO STOP THEM.
THUD
THAT'S WHERE YOU COME IN, MISS HALE. A MACHINE AS WONDERFUL AS YOUR MISTER HERO WOULD BE A VALUABLE SYMBOL IN A DEBATE ON TECHNOLOGY.
WE WANT THE TWO OF YOU TO FLY TO MONTE CARLO.

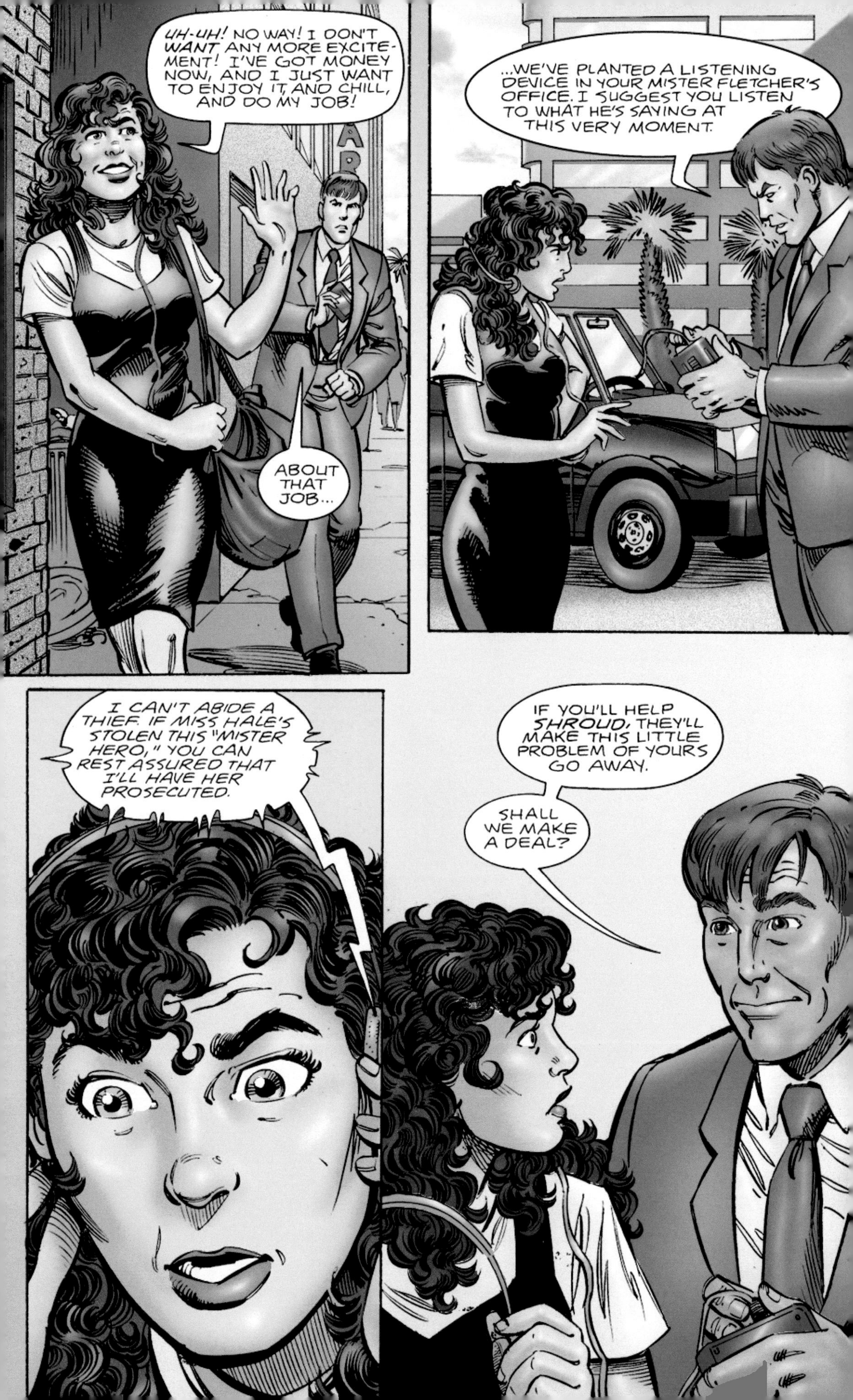
UH-UH! NO WAY! I DON'T WANT ANY MORE EXCITEMENT! I'VE GOT MONEY NOW, AND I JUST WANT TO ENJOY IT, AND CHILL, AND DO MY JOB!
ABOUT THAT JOB...
...WE'VE PLANTED A LISTENING DEVICE IN YOUR MISTER FLETCHER'S OFFICE. I SUGGEST YOU LISTEN TO WHAT HE'S SAYING AT THIS VERY MOMENT.
I CAN'T ABIDE A THIEF. IF MISS HALE'S STOLEN THIS "MISTER HERO," YOU CAN REST ASSURED THAT I'LL HAVE HER PROSECUTED.
IF YOU'LL HELP SHROUD, THEY'LL MAKE THIS LITTLE PROBLEM OF YOURS GO AWAY.
SHALL WE MAKE A DEAL?

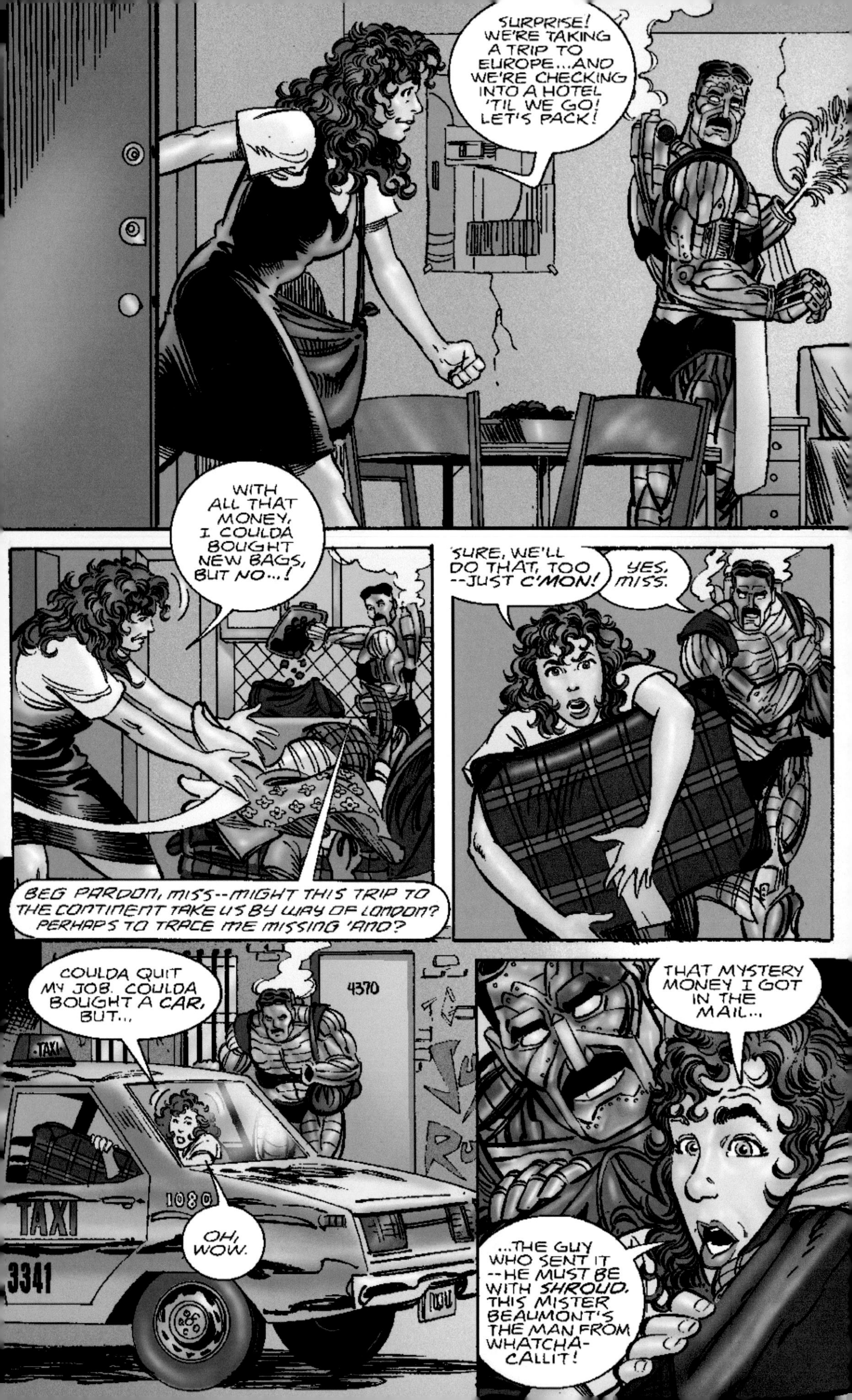
SURPRISE! WE'RE TAKING A TRIP TO EUROPE...AND WE'RE CHECKING INTO A HOTEL 'TIL WE GO! LET'S PACK!
WITH ALL THAT MONEY, I COULDA BOUGHT NEW BAGS, BUT NO...!
BEG PARDON, MISS--MIGHT THIS TRIP TO THE CONTINENT TAKE US BY WAY OF LONDON? PERHAPS TO TRACE ME MISSING 'AND?
'SURE, WE'LL DO THAT, TOO --JUST C'MON!
YES, MISS.
COULDA QUIT MY JOB. COULDA BOUGHT A CAR, BUT...
4370
TAXI
1080
TAXI
3341
OH, WOW.
THAT MYSTERY MONEY I GOT IN THE MAIL...
...THE GUY WHO SENT IT --HE MUST BE WITH SHROUD. THIS MISTER BEAUMONT'S THE MAN FROM WHATCHA-CALLIT!

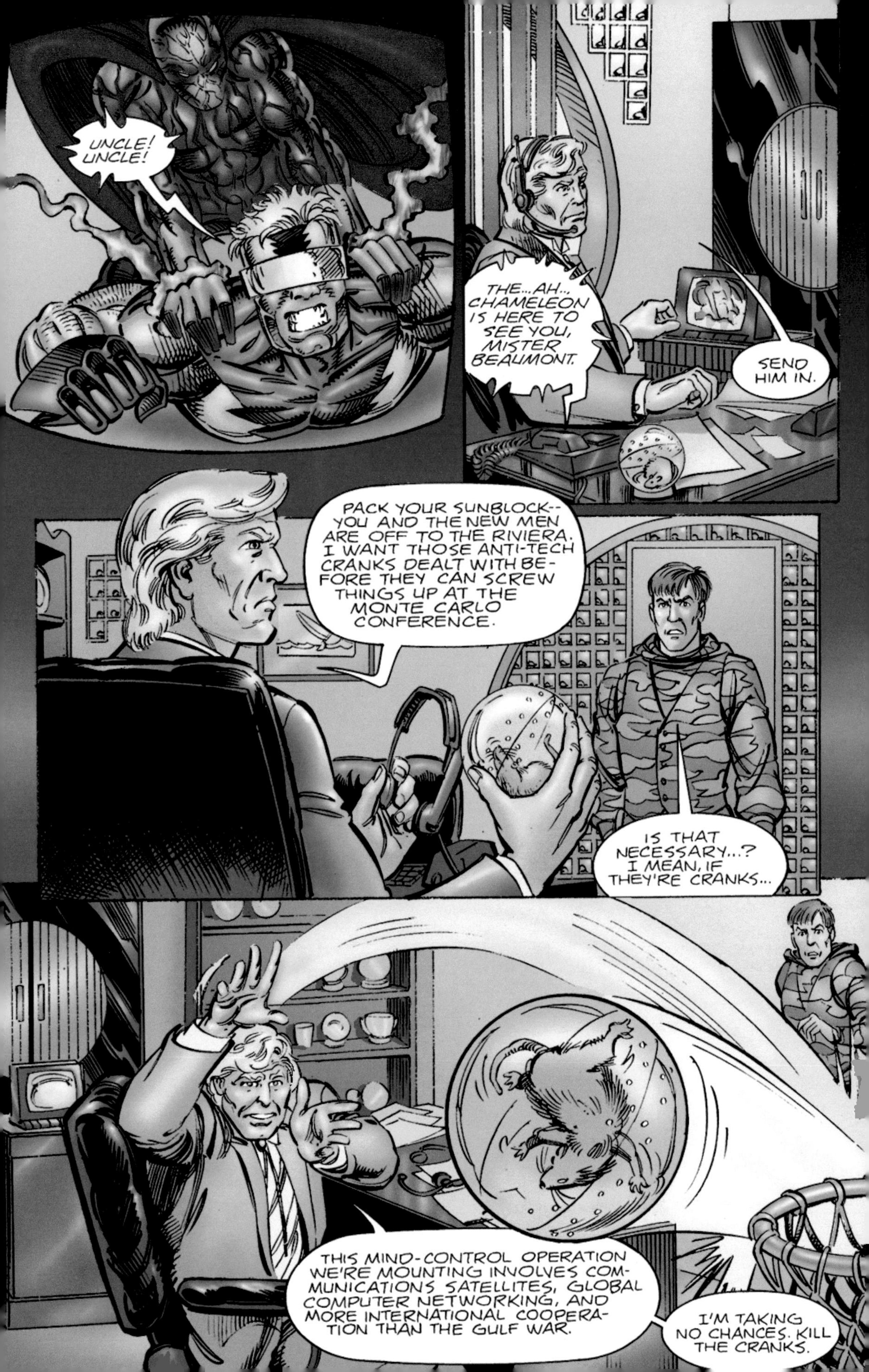
UNCLE! UNCLE!
THE...AH... CHAMELEON IS HERE TO SEE YOU, MISTER BEAUMONT.
SEND HIM IN.
PACK YOUR SUNBLOCK-- YOU AND THE NEW MEN ARE OFF TO THE RIVIERA. I WANT THOSE ANTI-TECH CRANKS DEALT WITH BEFORE THEY CAN SCREW THINGS UP AT THE MONTE CARLO CONFERENCE.
IS THAT NECESSARY...? I MEAN, IF THEY'RE CRANKS...
THIS MIND-CONTROL OPERATION WE'RE MOUNTING INVOLVES COMMUNICATIONS SATELLITES, GLOBAL COMPUTER NETWORKING, AND MORE INTERNATIONAL COOPERATION THAN THE GULF WAR.
I'M TAKING NO CHANCES. KILL THE CRANKS.

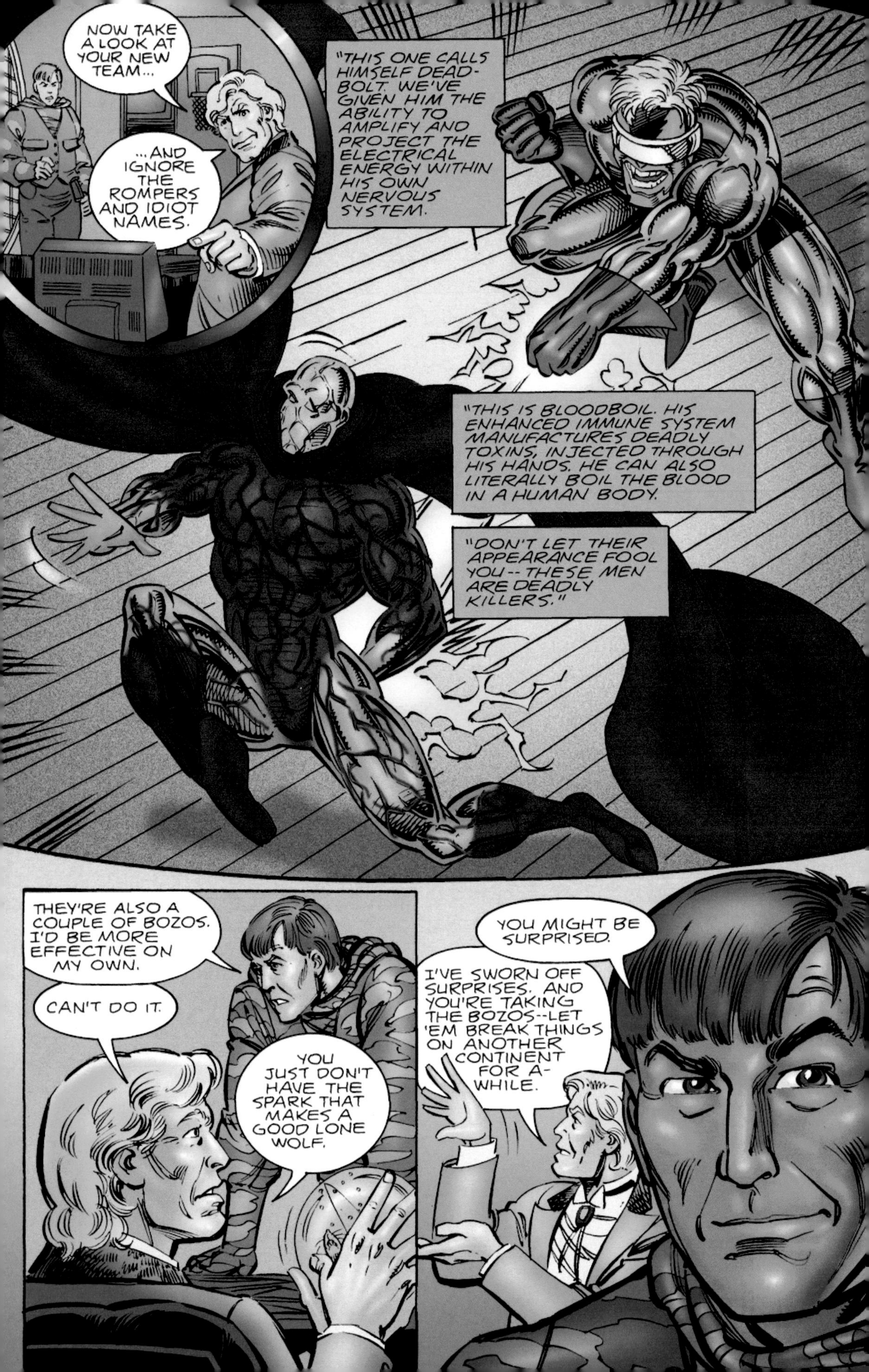
NOW TAKE A LOOK AT YOUR NEW TEAM...
...AND IGNORE THE ROMPERS AND IDIOT NAMES.
"THIS ONE CALLS HIMSELF DEAD-BOLT. WE'VE GIVEN HIM THE ABILITY TO AMPLIFY AND PROJECT THE ELECTRICAL ENERGY WITHIN HIS OWN NERVOUS SYSTEM.
"THIS IS BLOODBOIL. HIS ENHANCED IMMUNE SYSTEM MANUFACTURES DEADLY TOXINS, INJECTED THROUGH HIS HANDS. HE CAN ALSO LITERALLY BOIL THE BLOOD IN A HUMAN BODY.
"DON'T LET THEIR APPEARANCE FOOL YOU -- THESE MEN ARE DEADLY KILLERS."
THEY'RE ALSO A COUPLE OF BOZOS. I'D BE MORE EFFECTIVE ON MY OWN.
CAN'T DO IT.
YOU JUST DON'T HAVE THE SPARK THAT MAKES A GOOD LONE WOLF.
YOU MIGHT BE SURPRISED.
I'VE SWORN OFF SURPRISES. AND YOU'RE TAKING THE BOZOS--LET 'EM BREAK THINGS ON ANOTHER CONTINENT FOR A-WHILE.

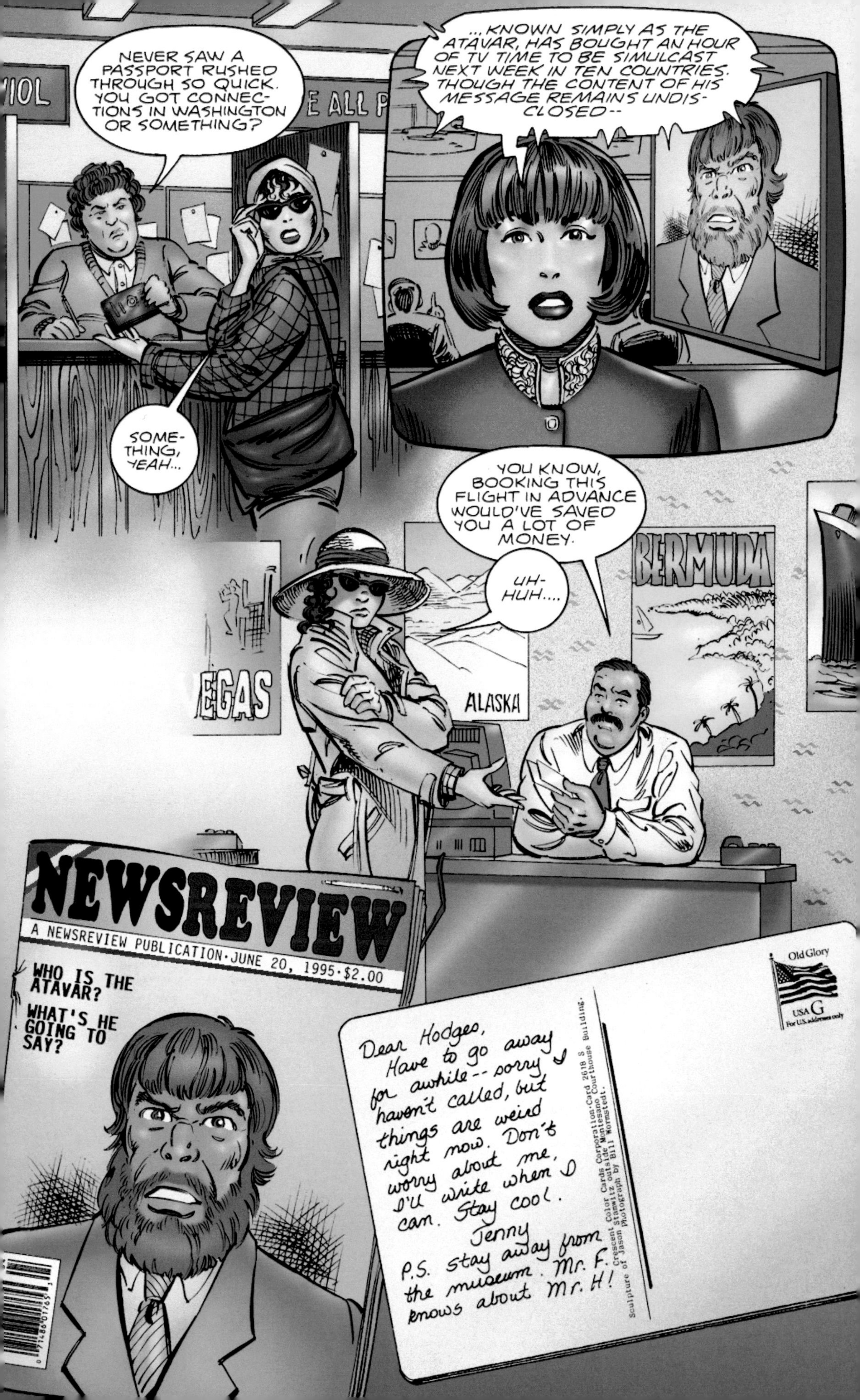

VIOL
E ALL P
NEVER SAW A PASSPORT RUSHED THROUGH SO QUICK. YOU GOT CONNECTIONS IN WASHINGTON OR SOMETHING?
SOMETHING, YEAH...
...KNOWN SIMPLY AS THE ATAVAR, HAS BOUGHT AN HOUR OF TV TIME TO BE SIMULCAST NEXT WEEK IN TEN COUNTRIES. THOUGH THE CONTENT OF HIS MESSAGE REMAINS UNDISCLOSED--
YOU KNOW, BOOKING THIS FLIGHT IN ADVANCE WOULD'VE SAVED YOU A LOT OF MONEY.
UH-HUH....
EGAS
ALASKA
BERMUDA
NEWSREVIEW
A NEWSREVIEW PUBLICATION·JUNE 20, 1995·$2.00
WHO IS THE ATAVAR?
WHAT'S HE GOING TO SAY?
Dear Hodges,
Have to go away for awhile -- sorry I haven't called, but things are weird right now. Don't worry about me, I'll write when I can. Stay cool.
Jenny
P.S. stay away from the museum. Mr. F. knows about Mr. H!
Crescent Color Cards Corporation·Card 2618 S
Sculpture of Jason Stammeitz outside Montesano Courthouse Building.
Photograph by Bill Wormstedt.
Old Glory
USA G
For U.S. addresses only

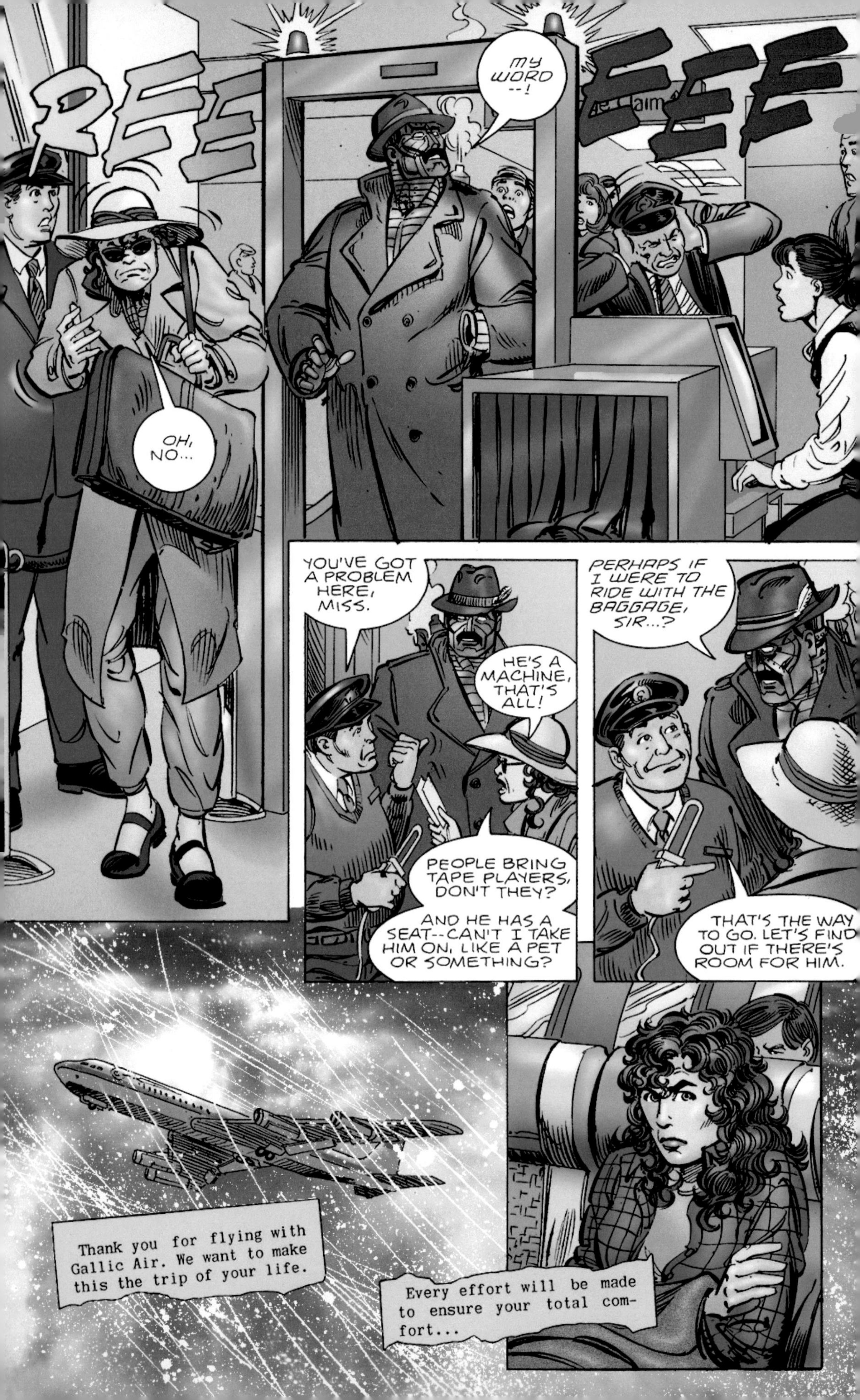
REEEEE
MY WORD --!
OH, NO...
YOU'VE GOT A PROBLEM HERE, MISS.
HE'S A MACHINE, THAT'S ALL!
PEOPLE BRING TAPE PLAYERS, DON'T THEY?
AND HE HAS A SEAT--CAN'T I TAKE HIM ON, LIKE A PET OR SOMETHING?
PERHAPS IF I WERE TO RIDE WITH THE BAGGAGE, SIR...?
THAT'S THE WAY TO GO. LET'S FIND OUT IF THERE'S ROOM FOR HIM.
Thank you for flying with Gallic Air. We want to make this the trip of your life.
Every effort will be made to ensure your total comfort...

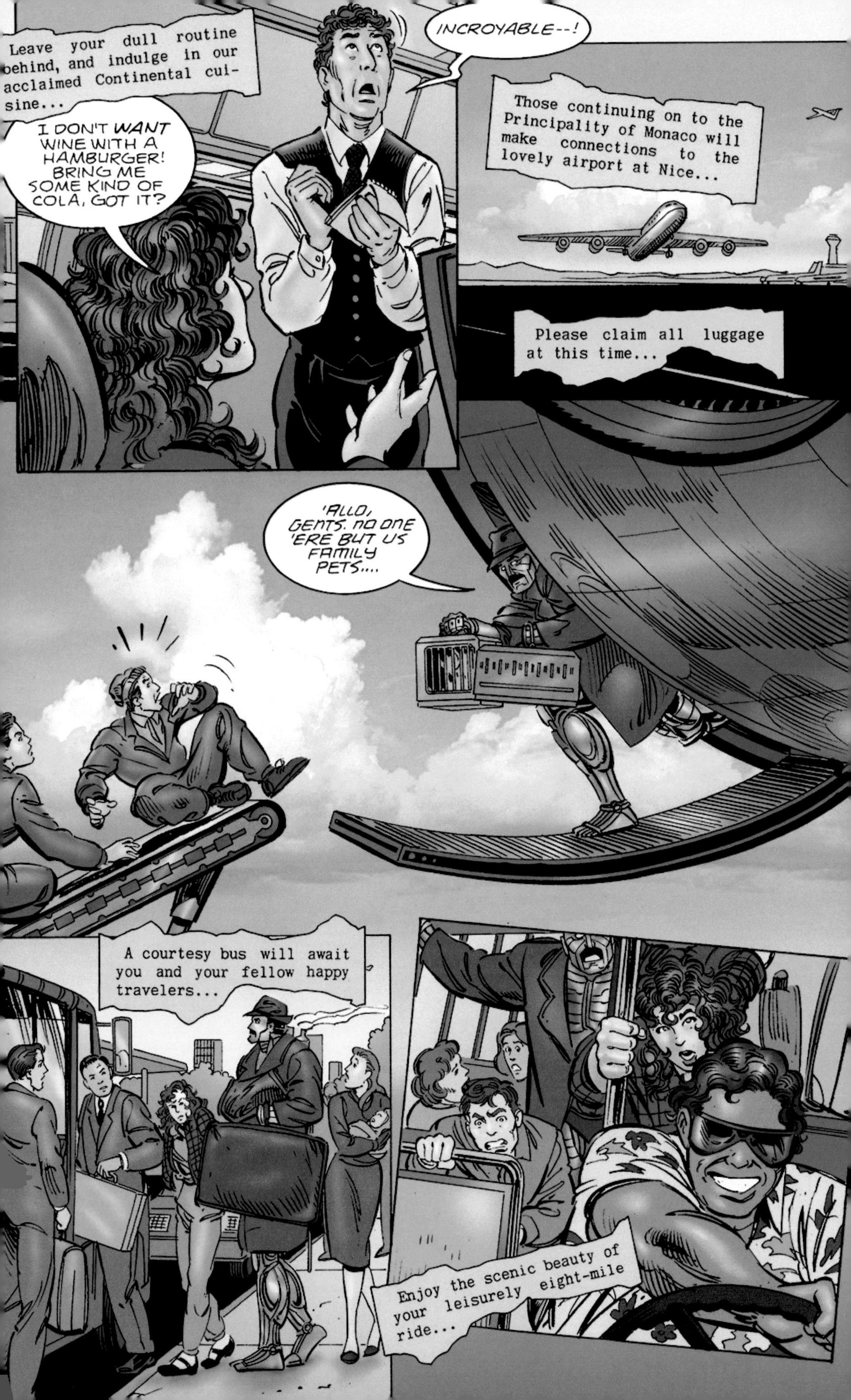
Leave your dull routine behind, and indulge in our acclaimed Continental cuisine...
INCROYABLE--!
I DON'T WANT WINE WITH A HAMBURGER! BRING ME SOME KIND OF COLA, GOT IT?
Those continuing on to the Principality of Monaco will make connections to the lovely airport at Nice...
Please claim all luggage at this time...
'ALLO, GENTS. NO ONE 'ERE BUT US FAMILY PETS....
A courtesy bus will await you and your fellow happy travelers...
Enjoy the scenic beauty of your leisurely eight-mile ride...

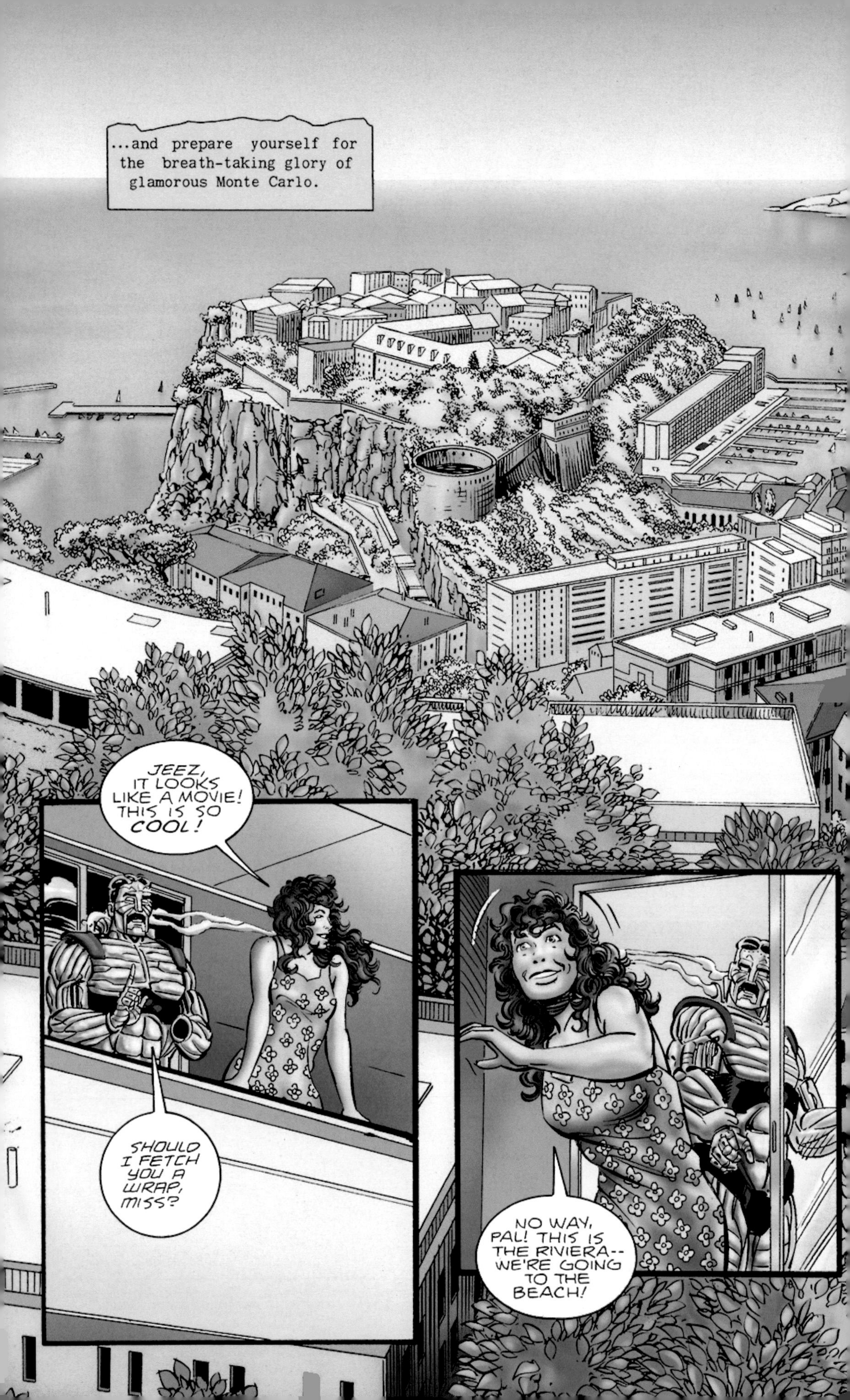
...and prepare yourself for the breath-taking glory of glamorous Monte Carlo.
JEEZ, IT LOOKS LIKE A MOVIE! THIS IS SO COOL!
SHOULD I FETCH YOU A WRAP, MISS?
NO WAY, PAL! THIS IS THE RIVIERA--WE'RE GOING TO THE BEACH!

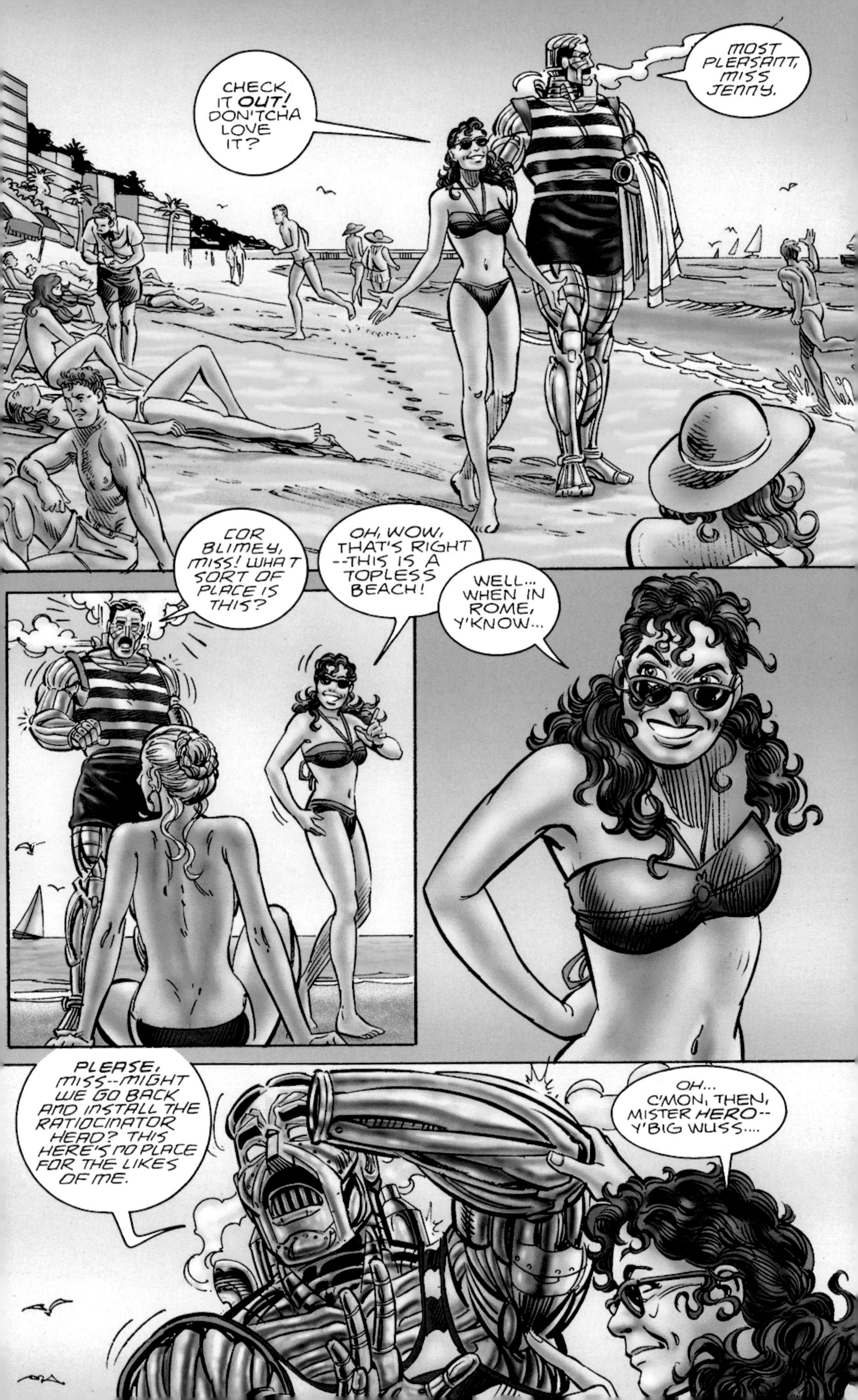
CHECK IT OUT! DON'TCHA LOVE IT?
MOST PLEASANT, MISS JENNY.
COR BLIMEY, MISS! WHAT SORT OF PLACE IS THIS?
OH, WOW, THAT'S RIGHT --THIS IS A TOPLESS BEACH!
WELL... WHEN IN ROME, Y'KNOW...
PLEASE, MISS--MIGHT WE GO BACK AND INSTALL THE RATIOCINATOR HEAD? THIS HERE'S NO PLACE FOR THE LIKES OF ME.
OH... C'MON, THEN, MISTER HERO-- Y'BIG WUSS....

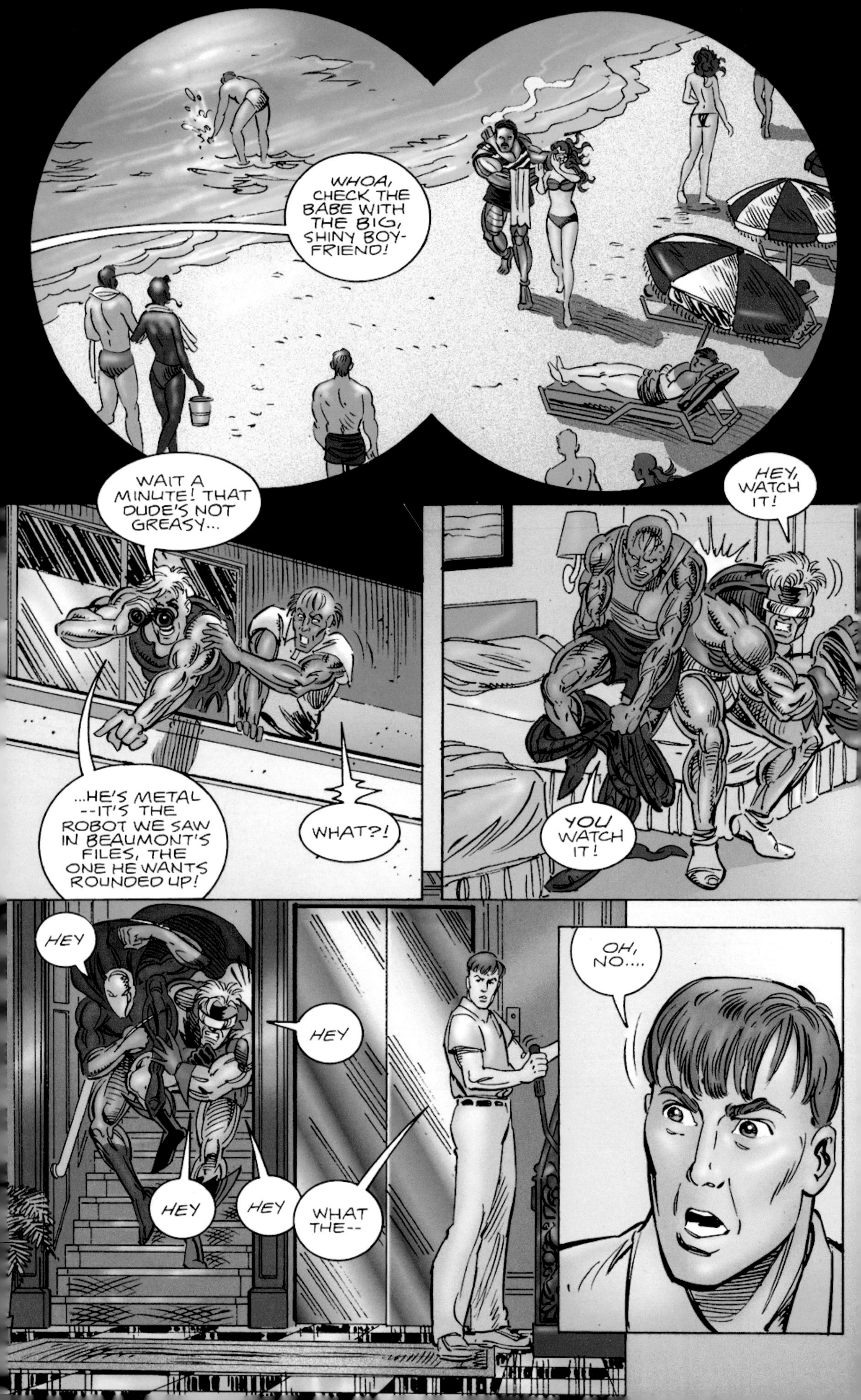
WHOA, CHECK THE BABE WITH THE BIG, SHINY BOY-FRIEND!
WAIT A MINUTE! THAT DUDE'S NOT GREASY...
...HE'S METAL --IT'S THE ROBOT WE SAW IN BEAUMONT'S FILES, THE ONE HE WANTS ROUNDED UP!
WHAT?!
HEY, WATCH IT!
YOU WATCH IT!
HEY
HEY
HEY
HEY
WHAT THE--
OH, NO....

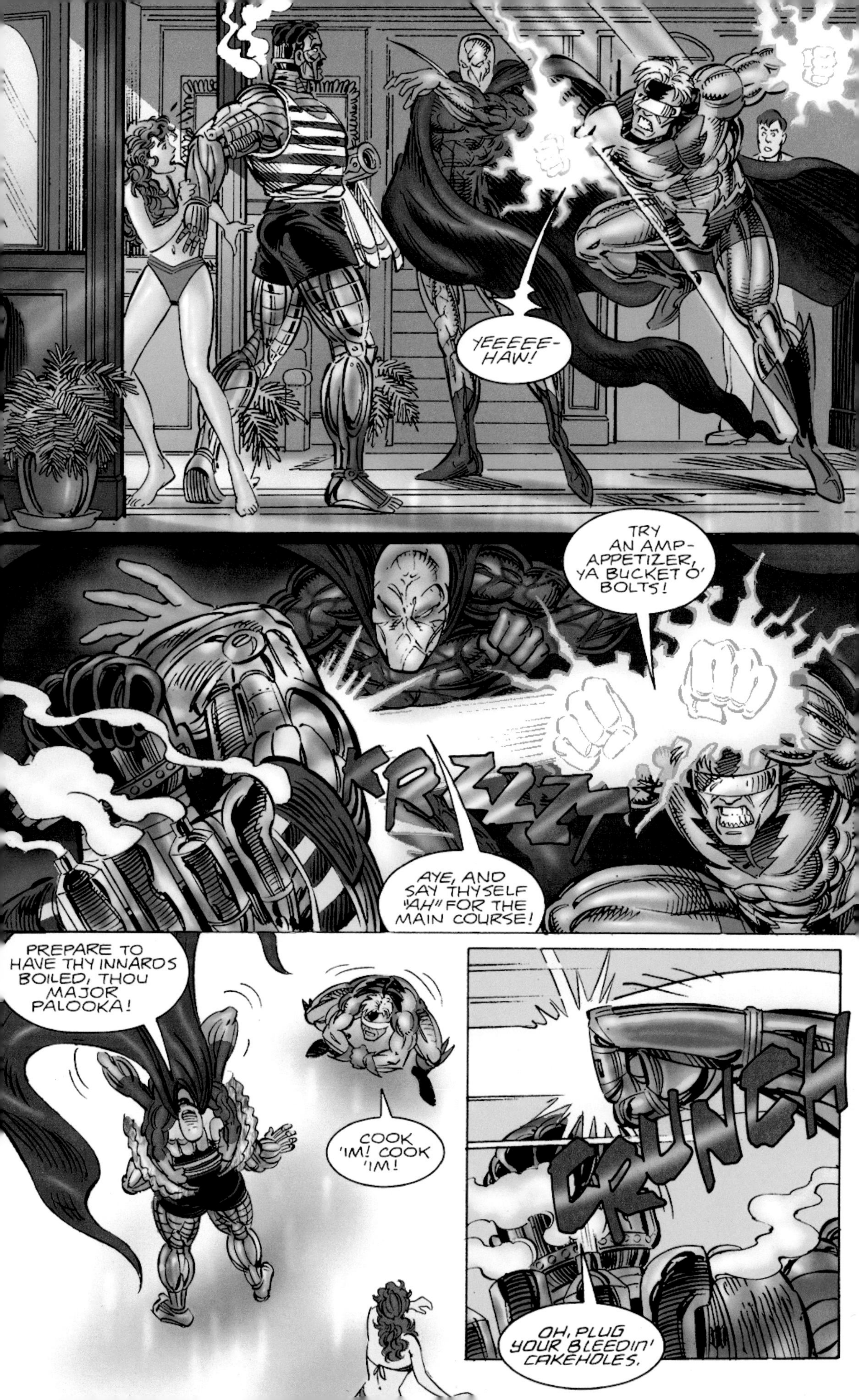
YEEEEE-HAW!
TRY AN AMP-APPETIZER, YA BUCKET O' BOLTS!
KRZZZT
AYE, AND SAY THYSELF "AH" FOR THE MAIN COURSE!
PREPARE TO HAVE THY INNARDS BOILED, THOU MAJOR PALOOKA!
COOK 'IM! COOK 'IM!
CRUNCH
OH, PLUG YOUR BLEEDIN' CAKEHOLES.

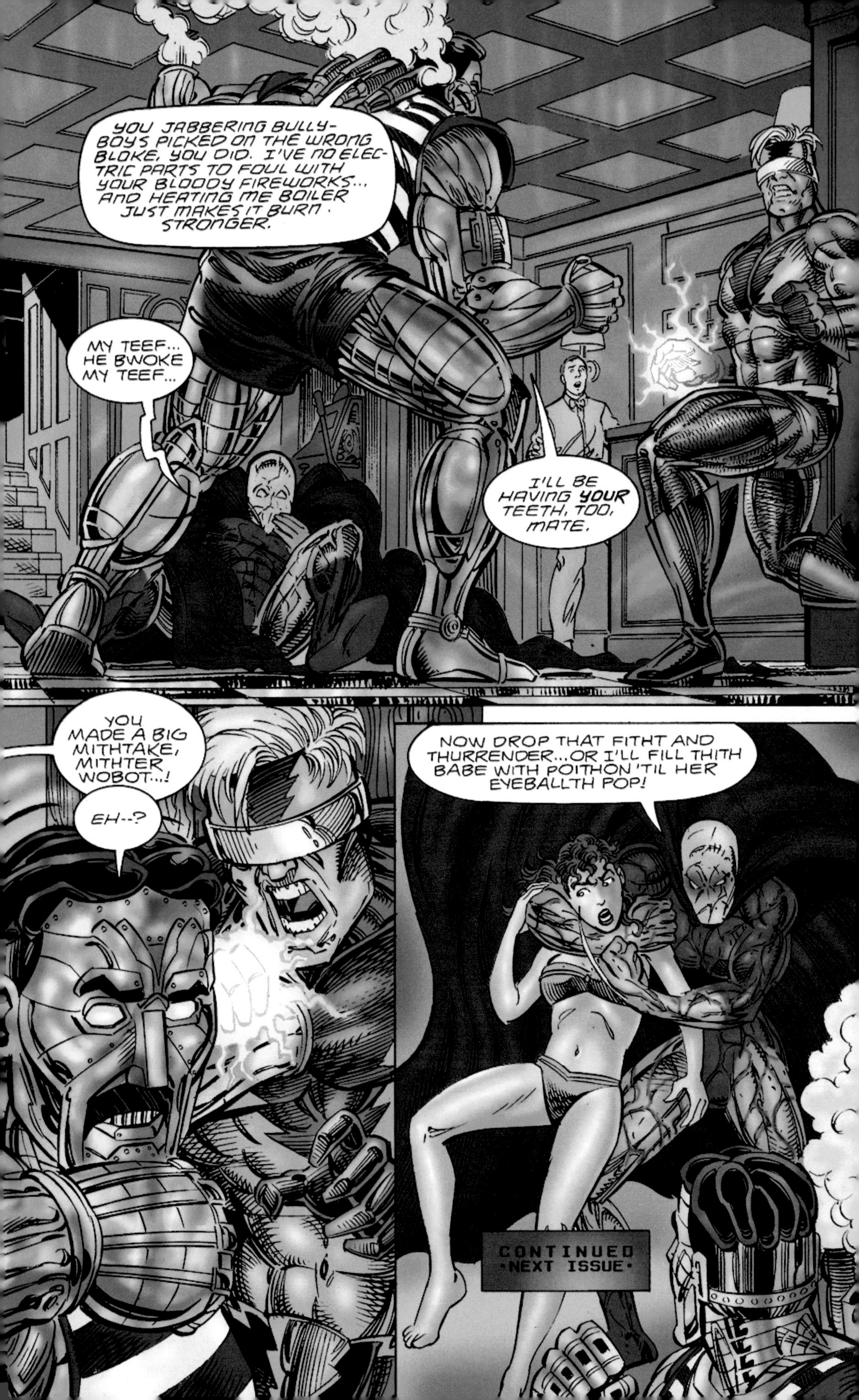
YOU JABBERING BULLY-BOYS PICKED ON THE WRONG BLOKE, YOU DID. I'VE NO ELECTRIC PARTS TO FOUL WITH YOUR BLOODY FIREWORKS... AND HEATING ME BOILER JUST MAKES IT BURN STRONGER.
MY TEEF... HE BWOKE MY TEEF...
I'LL BE HAVING **YOUR** TEETH, TOO, MATE.
YOU MADE A BIG MITHTAKE, MITHTER WOBOT...!
EH--?
NOW DROP THAT FITHT AND THURRENDER...OR I'LL FILL THITH BABE WITH POITHON 'TIL HER EYEBALLTH POP!
CONTINUED
·NEXT ISSUE·

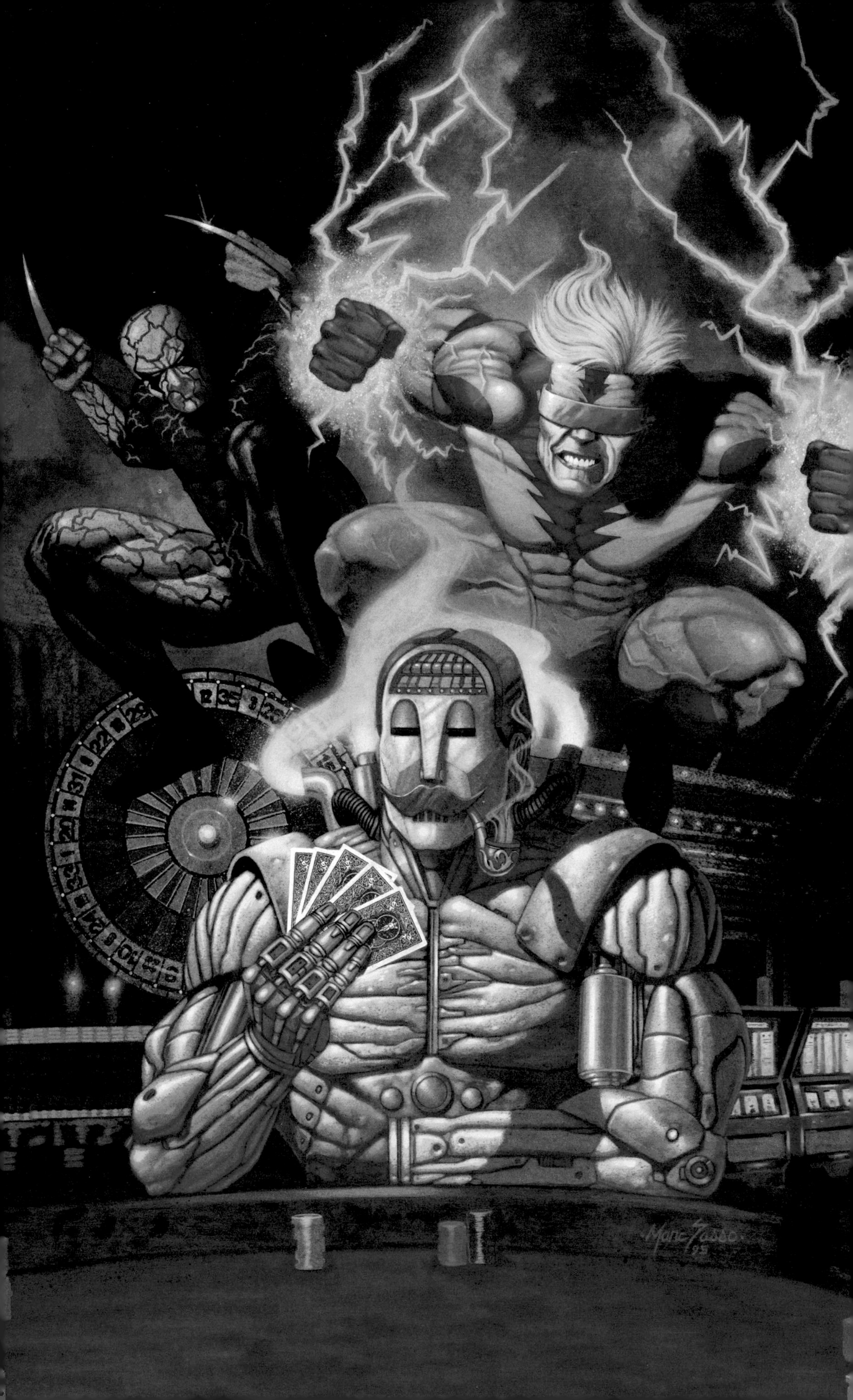

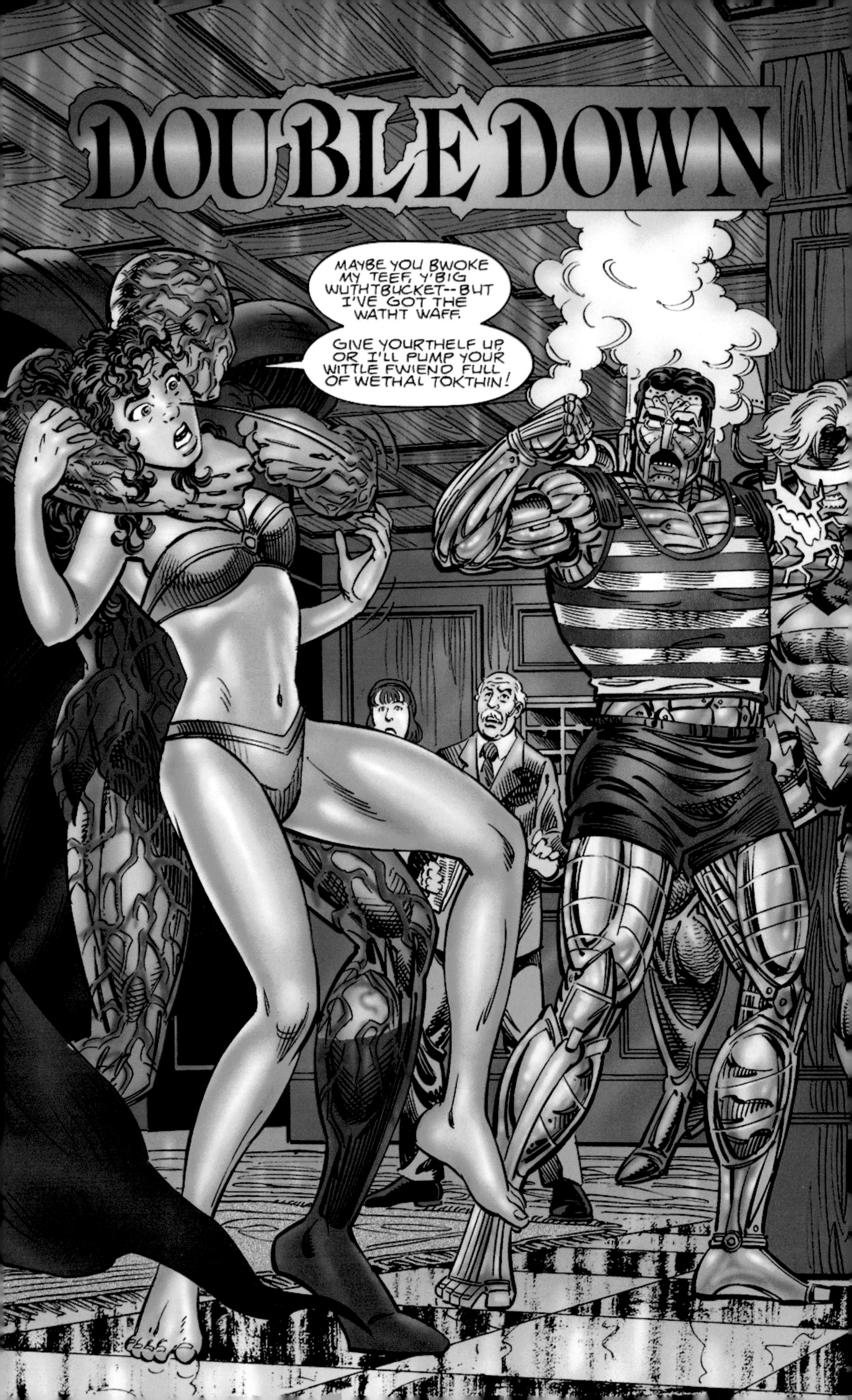
DOUBLE DOWN
MAYBE YOU BWOKE MY TEEF, Y'BIG WUTHTBUCKET--BUT I'VE GOT THE WATHT WAFF.
GIVE YOURTHELF UP, OR I'LL PUMP YOUR WITTLE FWIEND FULL OF WETHAL TOKTHIN!

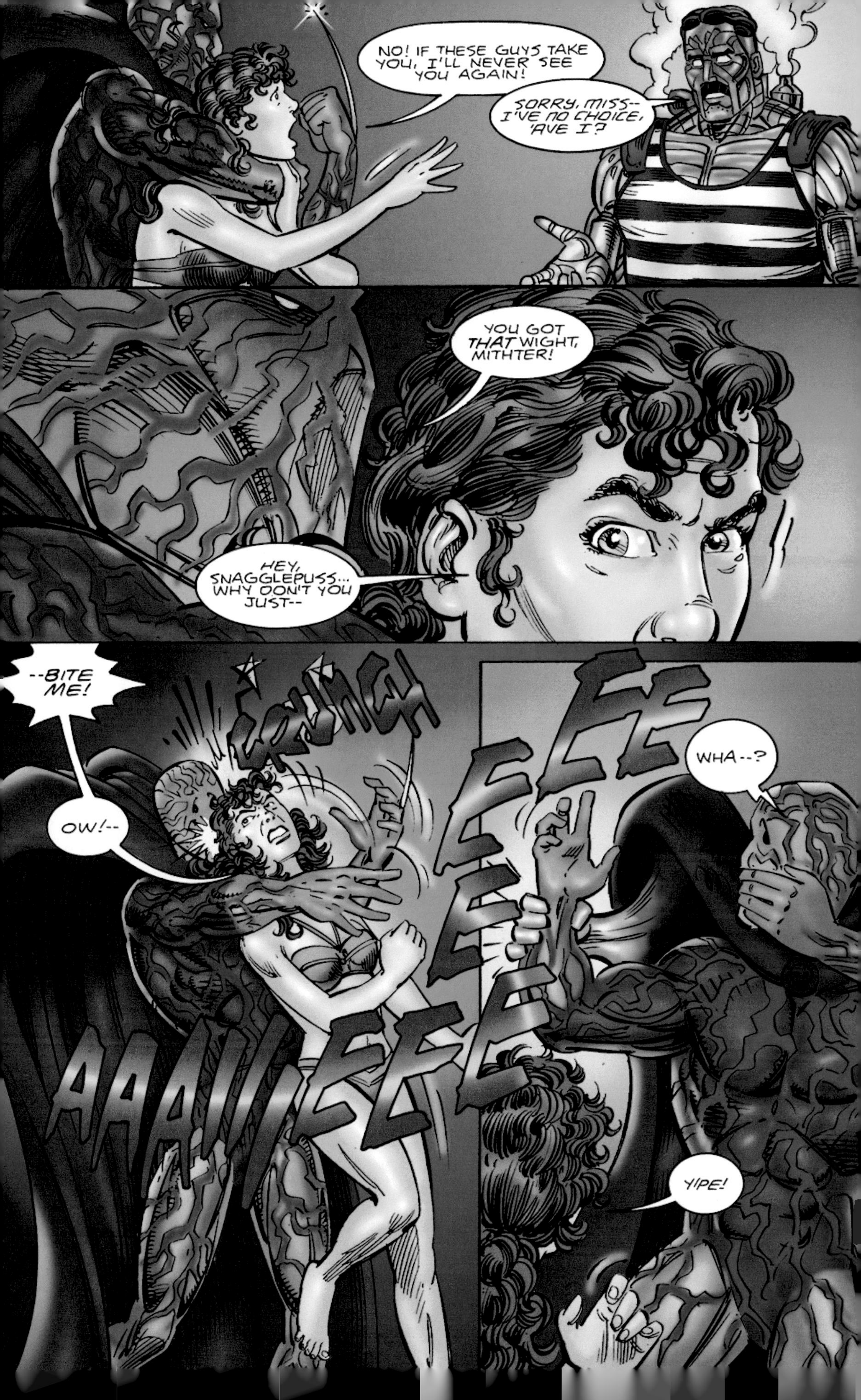
NO! IF THESE GUYS TAKE YOU, I'LL NEVER SEE YOU AGAIN!
SORRY, MISS-- I'VE NO CHOICE, 'AVE I?
YOU GOT THAT WIGHT, MITHTER!
HEY, SNAGGLEPUSS... WHY DON'T YOU JUST--
--BITE ME!
CRUNCH
OW!--
AAAIIIEEEEEEEE
WHA--?
YIPE!

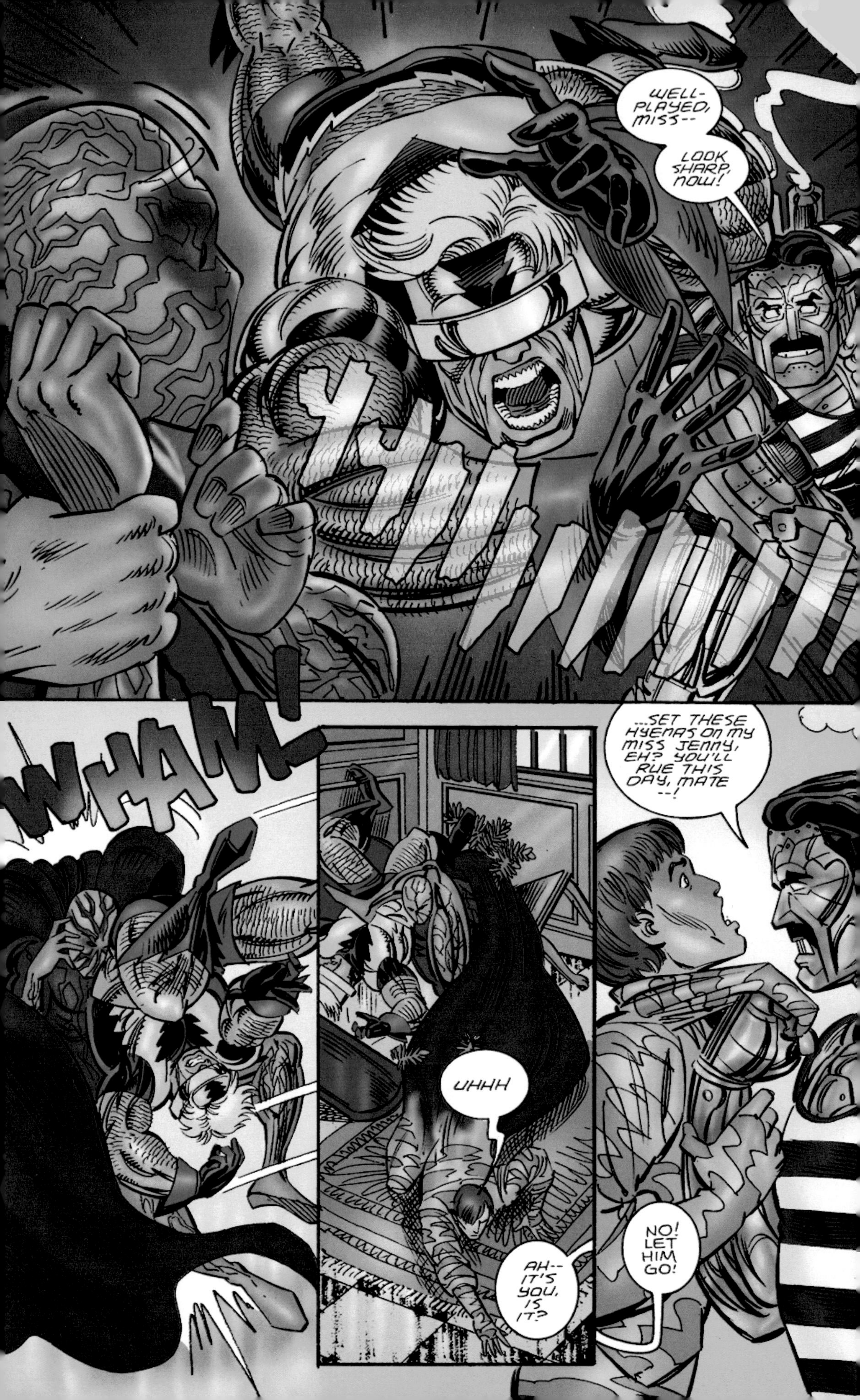
WELL-PLAYED, MISS--
LOOK SHARP, NOW!
WHAM!
UHHH
AH-- IT'S YOU, IS IT?
...SET THESE HYENAS ON MY MISS JENNY, EH? YOU'LL RUE THIS DAY, MATE --!
NO! LET HIM GO!

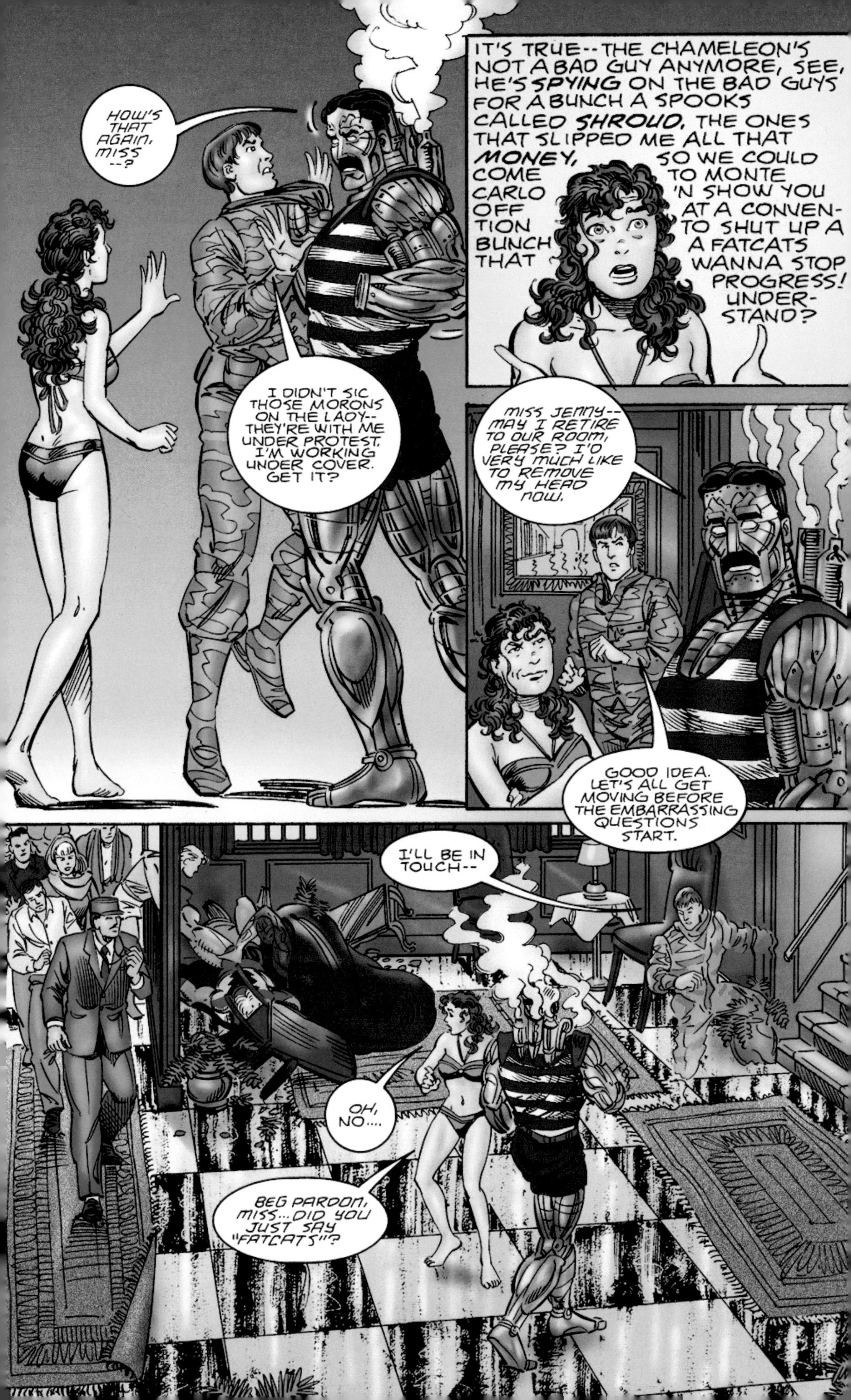
HOW'S THAT AGAIN, MISS --?
IT'S TRUE-- THE CHAMELEON'S NOT A BAD GUY ANYMORE, SEE, HE'S SPYING ON THE BAD GUYS FOR A BUNCH A SPOOKS CALLED SHROUD, THE ONES THAT SLIPPED ME ALL THAT MONEY, SO WE COULD COME TO MONTE CARLO 'N SHOW YOU OFF AT A CONVENTION TO SHUT UP A BUNCH A FATCATS THAT WANNA STOP PROGRESS! UNDERSTAND?
I DIDN'T SIC THOSE MORONS ON THE LADY-- THEY'RE WITH ME UNDER PROTEST. I'M WORKING UNDER COVER. GET IT?
MISS JENNY-- MAY I RETIRE TO OUR ROOM, PLEASE? I'D VERY MUCH LIKE TO REMOVE MY HEAD NOW.
GOOD IDEA. LET'S ALL GET MOVING BEFORE THE EMBARRASSING QUESTIONS START.
I'LL BE IN TOUCH--
OH, NO....
BEG PARDON, MISS...DID YOU JUST SAY "FATCATS"?

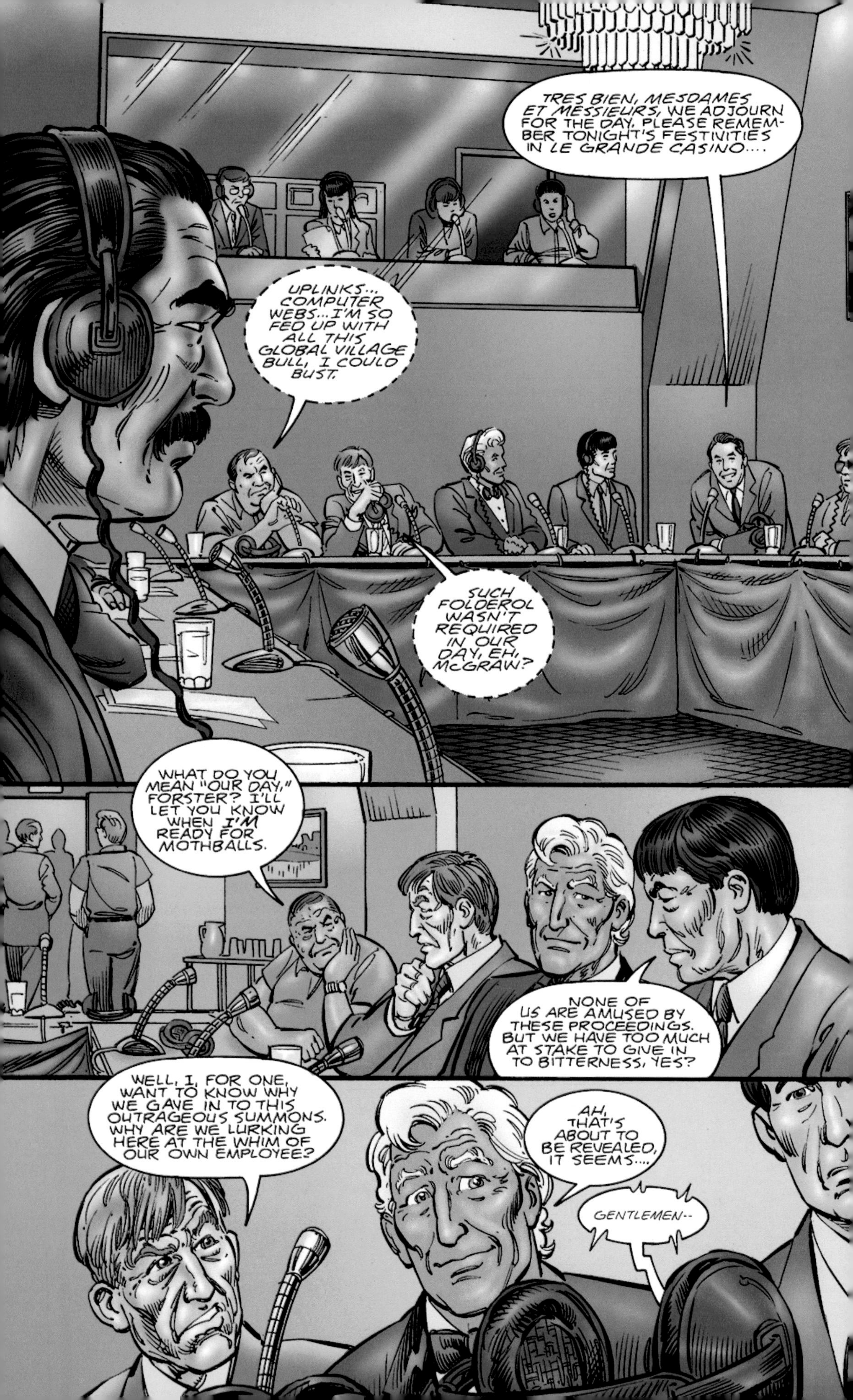

TRES BIEN, MESDAMES ET MESSIEURS, WE ADJOURN FOR THE DAY. PLEASE REMEMBER TONIGHT'S FESTIVITIES IN LE GRANDE CASINO....
UPLINKS... COMPUTER WEBS... I'M SO FED UP WITH ALL THIS GLOBAL VILLAGE BULL, I COULD BUST.
SUCH FOLDEROL WASN'T REQUIRED IN OUR DAY, EH, McGRAW?
WHAT DO YOU MEAN "OUR DAY," FORSTER? I'LL LET YOU KNOW WHEN I'M READY FOR MOTHBALLS.
NONE OF US ARE AMUSED BY THESE PROCEEDINGS. BUT WE HAVE TOO MUCH AT STAKE TO GIVE IN TO BITTERNESS, YES?
WELL, I, FOR ONE, WANT TO KNOW WHY WE GAVE IN TO THIS OUTRAGEOUS SUMMONS. WHY ARE WE LURKING HERE AT THE WHIM OF OUR OWN EMPLOYEE?
AH, THAT'S ABOUT TO BE REVEALED, IT SEEMS....
GENTLEMEN--

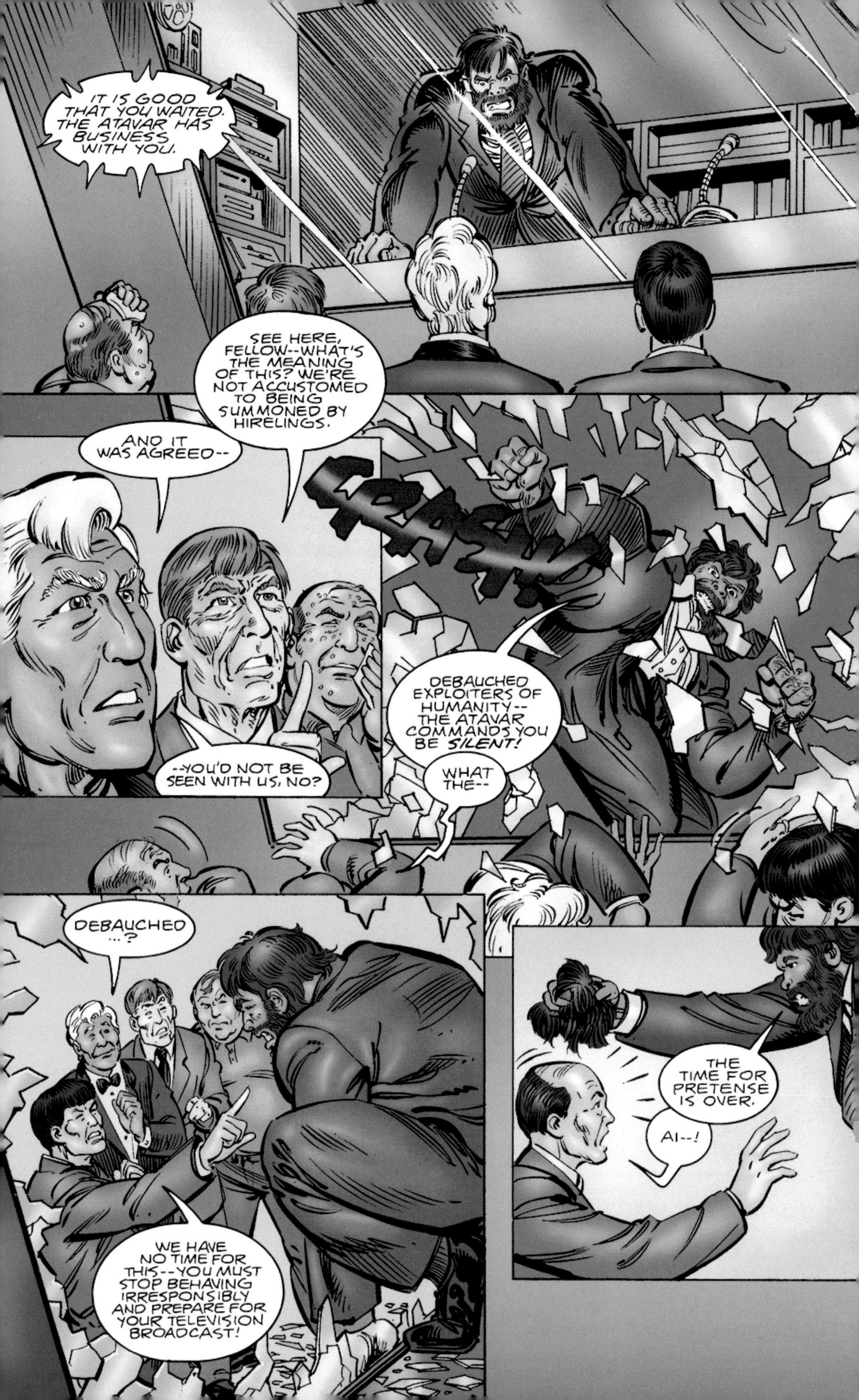
IT IS GOOD THAT YOU WAITED. THE ATAVAR HAS BUSINESS WITH YOU.
SEE HERE, FELLOW--WHAT'S THE MEANING OF THIS? WE'RE NOT ACCUSTOMED TO BEING SUMMONED BY HIRELINGS.
AND IT WAS AGREED--
--YOU'D NOT BE SEEN WITH US, NO?
CRASH!
DEBAUCHED EXPLOITERS OF HUMANITY-- THE ATAVAR COMMANDS YOU BE SILENT!
WHAT THE--
DEBAUCHED ...?
WE HAVE NO TIME FOR THIS--YOU MUST STOP BEHAVING IRRESPONSIBLY AND PREPARE FOR YOUR TELEVISION BROADCAST!
THE TIME FOR PRETENSE IS OVER.
AI--!

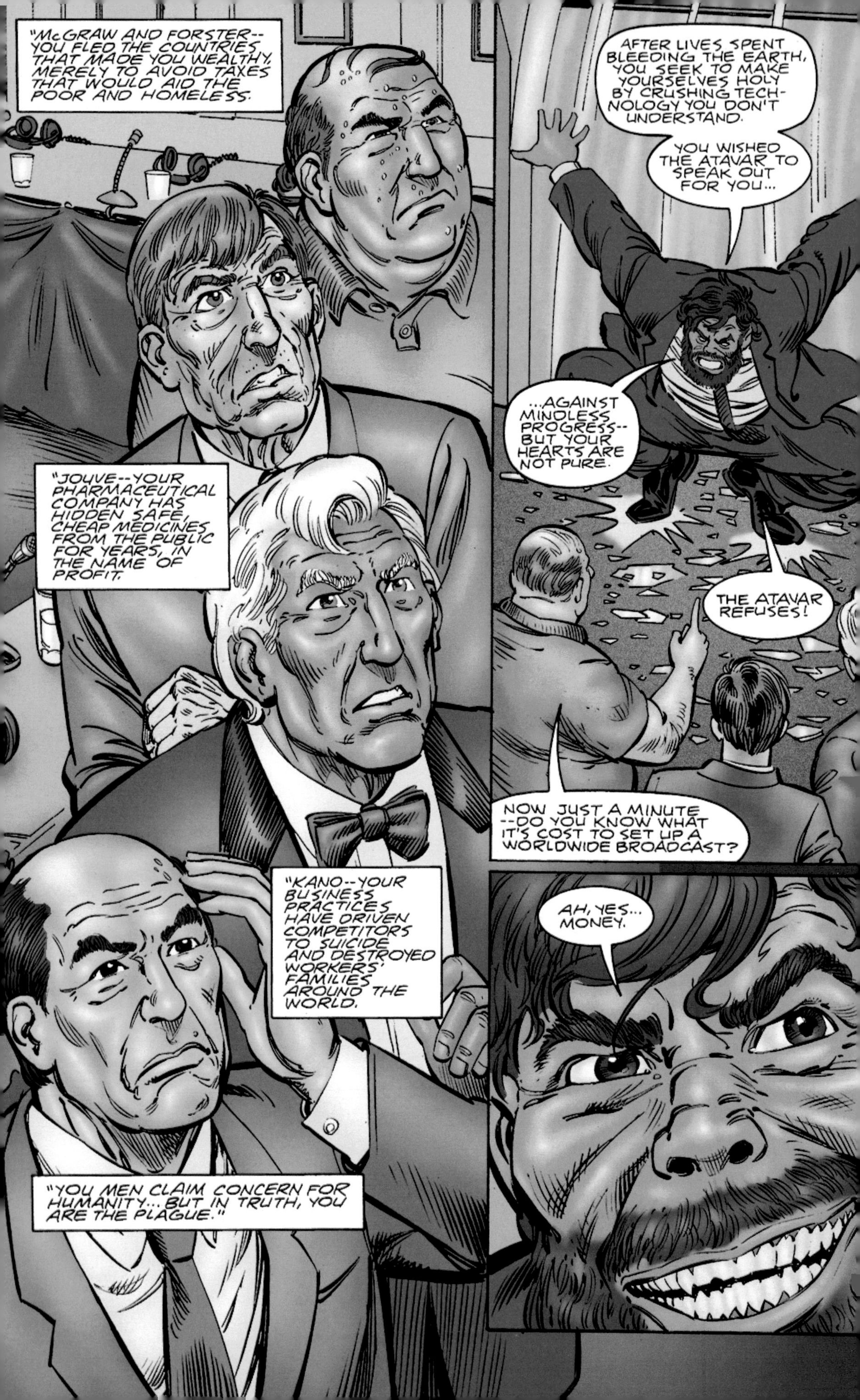
"McGRAW AND FORSTER--YOU FLED THE COUNTRIES THAT MADE YOU WEALTHY, MERELY TO AVOID TAXES THAT WOULD AID THE POOR AND HOMELESS.
"JOUVE--YOUR PHARMACEUTICAL COMPANY HAS HIDDEN SAFE, CHEAP MEDICINES FROM THE PUBLIC FOR YEARS, IN THE NAME OF PROFIT.
"KANO--YOUR BUSINESS PRACTICES HAVE DRIVEN COMPETITORS TO SUICIDE AND DESTROYED WORKERS' FAMILIES AROUND THE WORLD.
"YOU MEN CLAIM CONCERN FOR HUMANITY... BUT IN TRUTH, YOU ARE THE PLAGUE."
AFTER LIVES SPENT BLEEDING THE EARTH, YOU SEEK TO MAKE YOURSELVES HOLY BY CRUSHING TECH-NOLOGY YOU DON'T UNDERSTAND.
YOU WISHED THE ATAVAR TO SPEAK OUT FOR YOU...
...AGAINST MINDLESS PROGRESS--BUT YOUR HEARTS ARE NOT PURE.
THE ATAVAR REFUSES!
NOW JUST A MINUTE --DO YOU KNOW WHAT IT'S COST TO SET UP A WORLDWIDE BROADCAST?
AH, YES... MONEY.

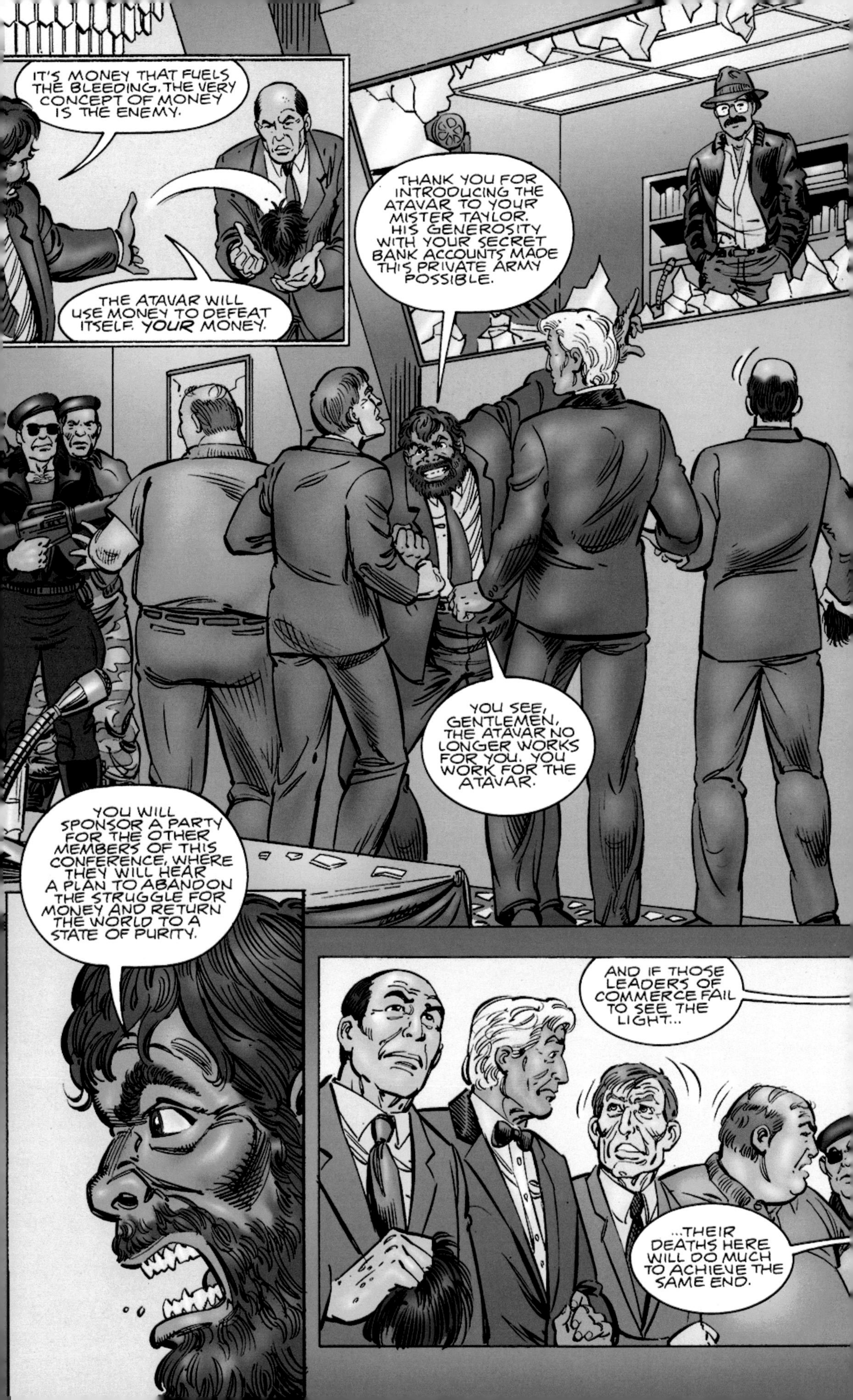
IT'S MONEY THAT FUELS THE BLEEDING. THE VERY CONCEPT OF MONEY IS THE ENEMY.
THE ATAVAR WILL USE MONEY TO DEFEAT ITSELF. YOUR MONEY.
THANK YOU FOR INTRODUCING THE ATAVAR TO YOUR MISTER TAYLOR. HIS GENEROSITY WITH YOUR SECRET BANK ACCOUNTS MADE THIS PRIVATE ARMY POSSIBLE.
YOU SEE, GENTLEMEN, THE ATAVAR NO LONGER WORKS FOR YOU. YOU WORK FOR THE ATAVAR.
YOU WILL SPONSOR A PARTY FOR THE OTHER MEMBERS OF THIS CONFERENCE, WHERE THEY WILL HEAR A PLAN TO ABANDON THE STRUGGLE FOR MONEY AND RETURN THE WORLD TO A STATE OF PURITY.
AND IF THOSE LEADERS OF COMMERCE FAIL TO SEE THE LIGHT...
...THEIR DEATHS HERE WILL DO MUCH TO ACHIEVE THE SAME END.

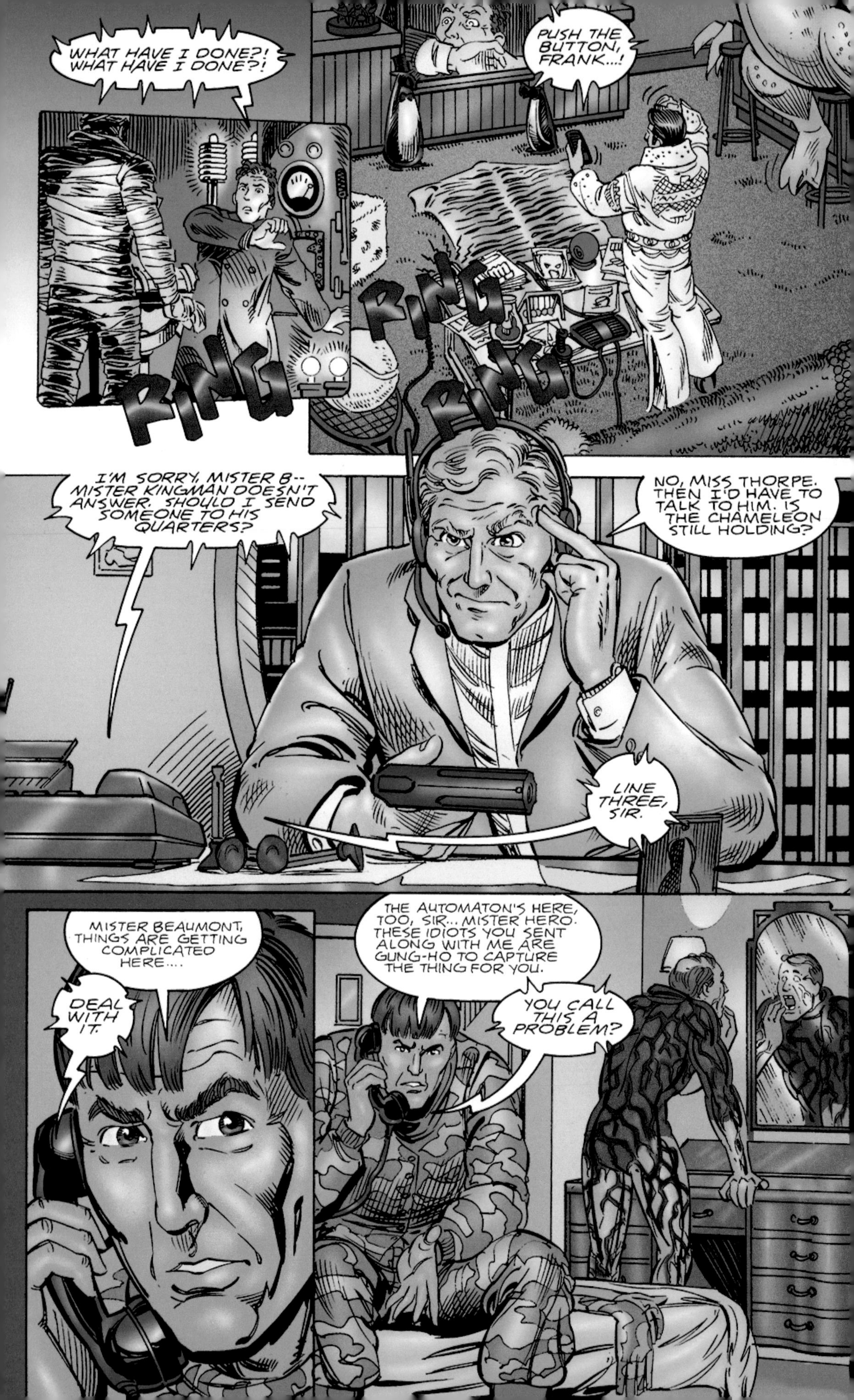
WHAT HAVE I DONE?! WHAT HAVE I DONE?!
PUSH THE BUTTON, FRANK...!
RING RING
RING RING
I'M SORRY, MISTER B-- MISTER KINGMAN DOESN'T ANSWER. SHOULD I SEND SOMEONE TO HIS QUARTERS?
NO, MISS THORPE. THEN I'D HAVE TO TALK TO HIM. IS THE CHAMELEON STILL HOLDING?
LINE THREE, SIR.
MISTER BEAUMONT, THINGS ARE GETTING COMPLICATED HERE....
DEAL WITH IT.
THE AUTOMATON'S HERE, TOO, SIR... MISTER HERO. THESE IDIOTS YOU SENT ALONG WITH ME ARE GUNG-HO TO CAPTURE THE THING FOR YOU.
YOU CALL THIS A PROBLEM?

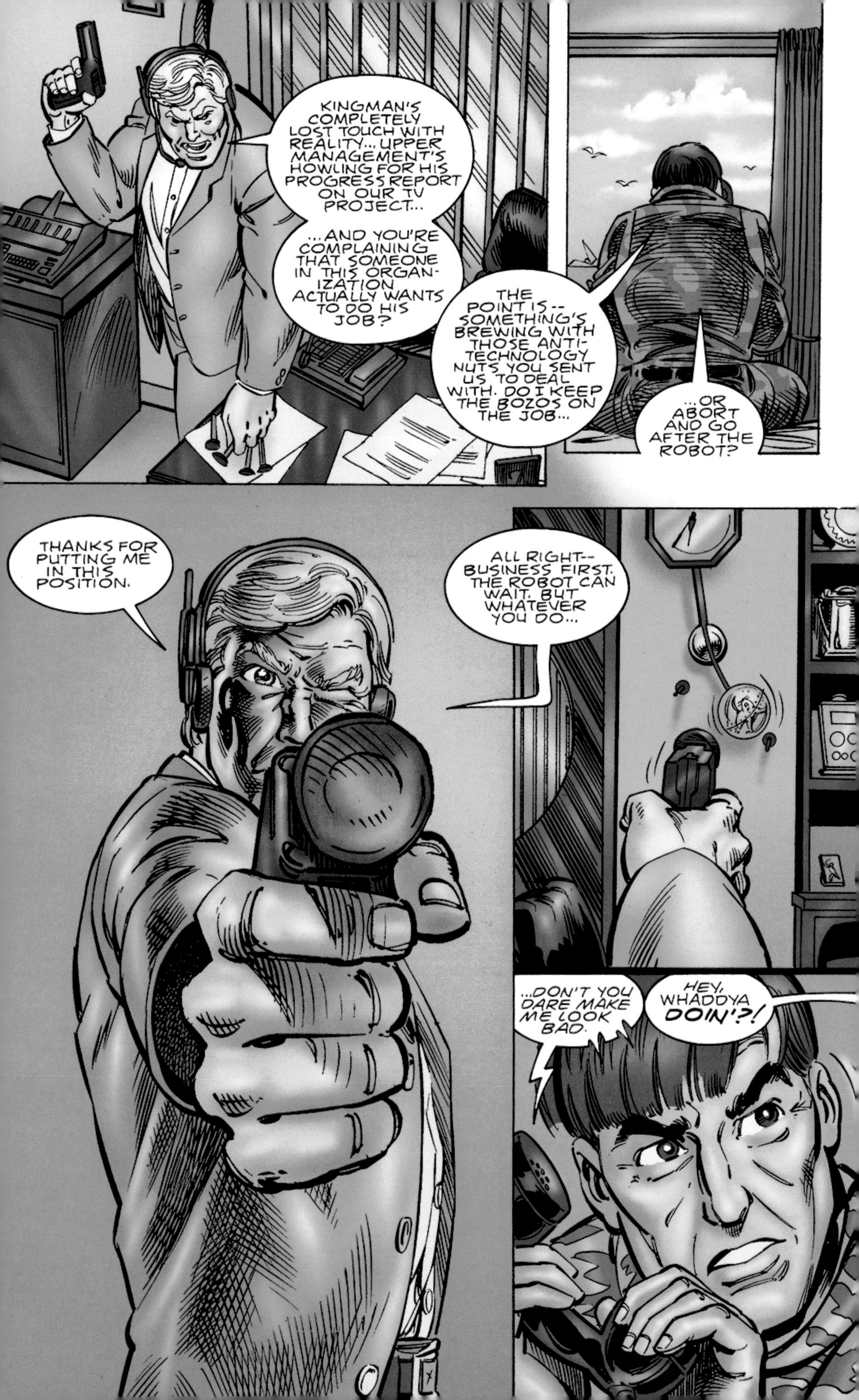
KINGMAN'S COMPLETELY LOST TOUCH WITH REALITY... UPPER MANAGEMENT'S HOWLING FOR HIS PROGRESS REPORT ON OUR TV PROJECT...
...AND YOU'RE COMPLAINING THAT SOMEONE IN THIS ORGANIZATION ACTUALLY WANTS TO DO HIS JOB?
THE POINT IS -- SOMETHING'S BREWING WITH THOSE ANTI-TECHNOLOGY NUTS YOU SENT US TO DEAL WITH. DO I KEEP THE BOZOS ON THE JOB...
...OR ABORT AND GO AFTER THE ROBOT?
THANKS FOR PUTTING ME IN THIS POSITION.
ALL RIGHT-- BUSINESS FIRST. THE ROBOT CAN WAIT. BUT WHATEVER YOU DO...
...DON'T YOU DARE MAKE ME LOOK BAD.
HEY, WHADDYA **DOIN'?!**

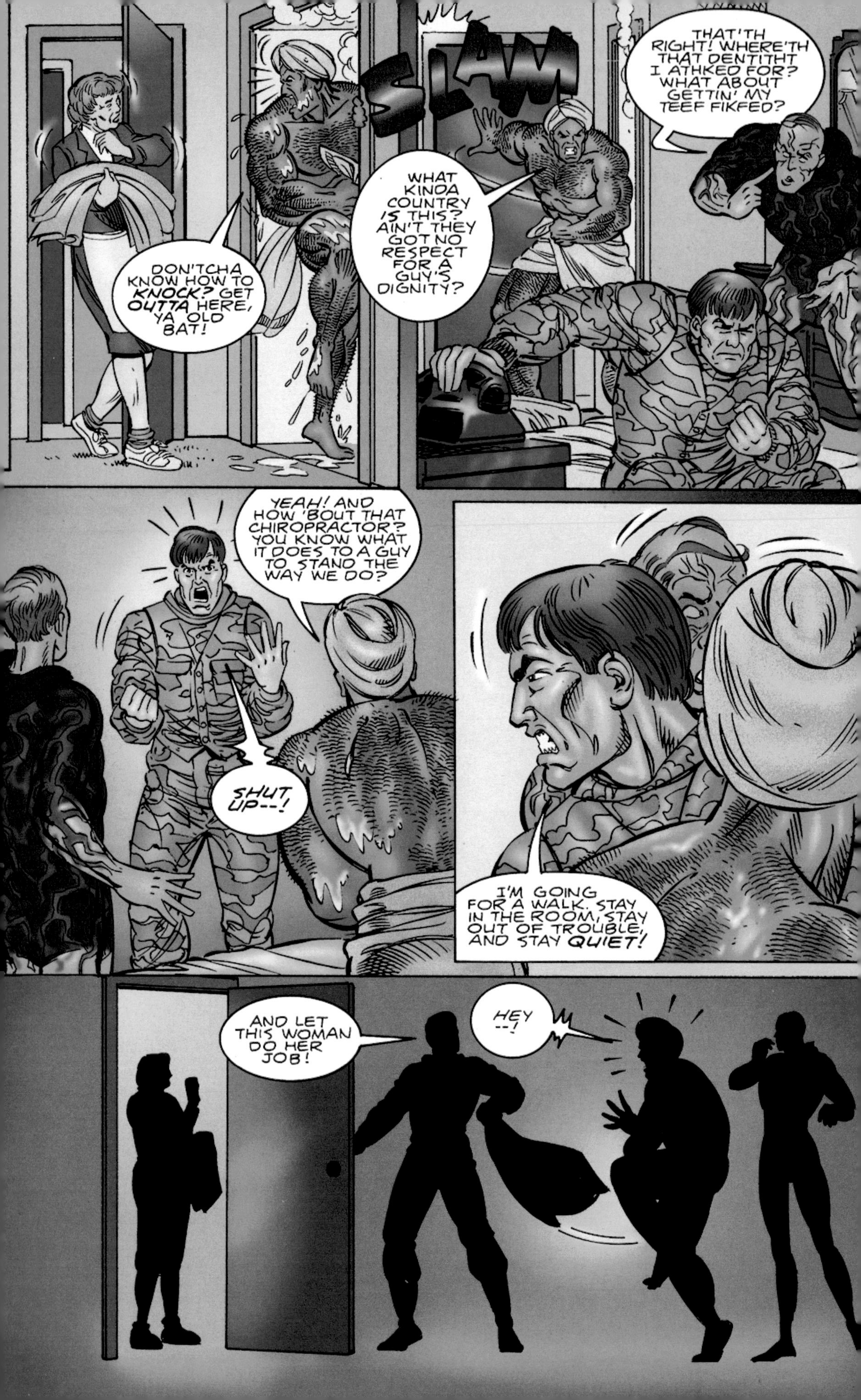

DON'TCHA KNOW HOW TO KNOCK? GET OUTTA HERE, YA OLD BAT!
SLAM
WHAT KINDA COUNTRY IS THIS? AIN'T THEY GOT NO RESPECT FOR A GUY'S DIGNITY?
THAT'TH RIGHT! WHERE'TH THAT DENTITHT I ATHKED FOR? WHAT ABOUT GETTIN' MY TEEF FIKFED?
YEAH! AND HOW 'BOUT THAT CHIROPRACTOR? YOU KNOW WHAT IT DOES TO A GUY TO STAND THE WAY WE DO?
SHUT UP--!
I'M GOING FOR A WALK. STAY IN THE ROOM, STAY OUT OF TROUBLE, AND STAY QUIET!
AND LET THIS WOMAN DO HER JOB!
HEY --!

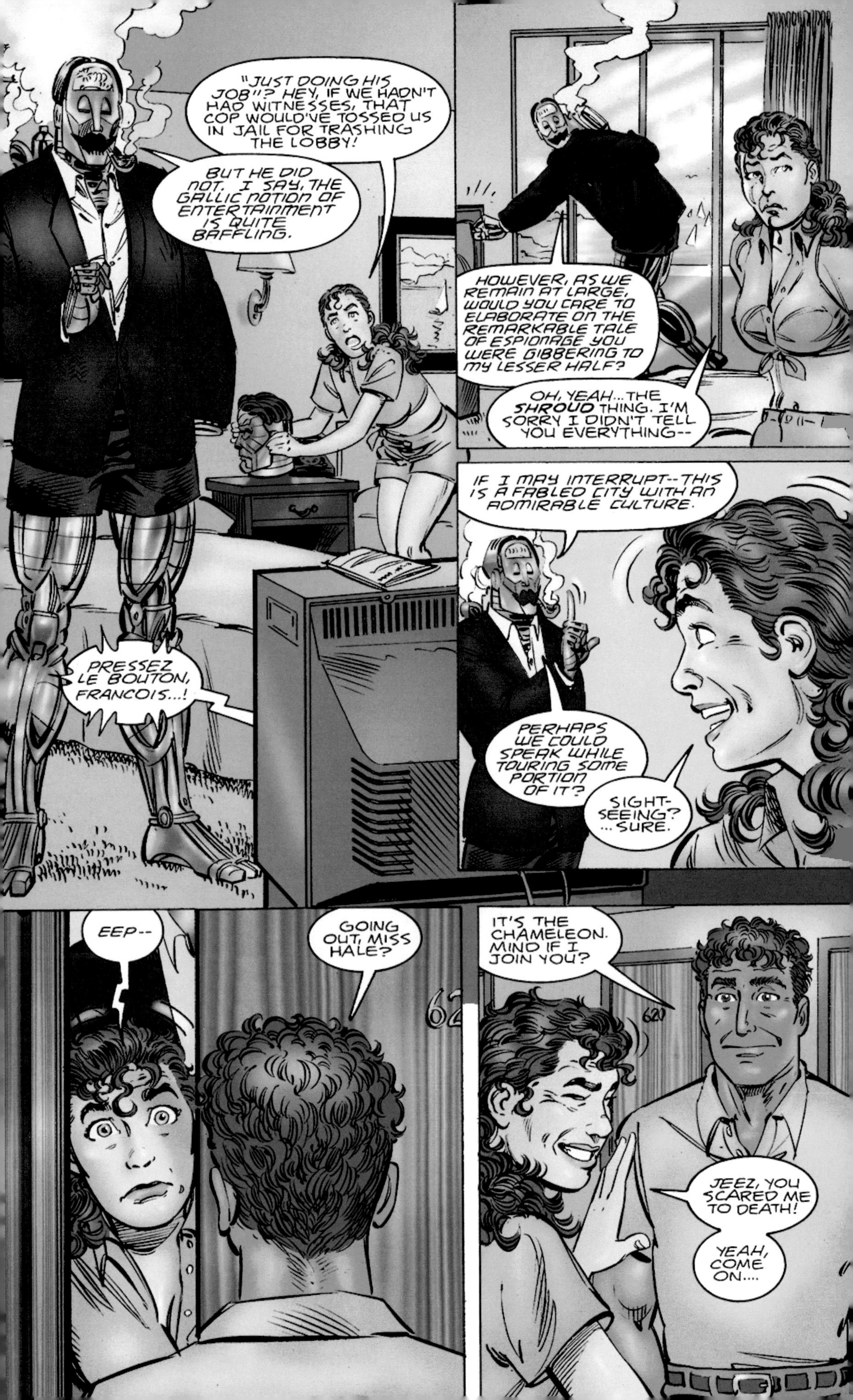
"JUST DOING HIS JOB"? HEY, IF WE HADN'T HAD WITNESSES, THAT COP WOULD'VE TOSSED US IN JAIL FOR TRASHING THE LOBBY!
BUT HE DID NOT. I SAY, THE GALLIC NOTION OF ENTERTAINMENT IS QUITE BAFFLING.
PRESSEZ LE BOUTON, FRANCOIS...!
HOWEVER, AS WE REMAIN AT LARGE, WOULD YOU CARE TO ELABORATE ON THE REMARKABLE TALE OF ESPIONAGE YOU WERE GIBBERING TO MY LESSER HALF?
OH, YEAH... THE SHROUD THING. I'M SORRY I DIDN'T TELL YOU EVERYTHING--
IF I MAY INTERRUPT--THIS IS A FABLED CITY WITH AN ADMIRABLE CULTURE.
PERHAPS WE COULD SPEAK WHILE TOURING SOME PORTION OF IT?
SIGHT-SEEING? ...SURE.
EEP--
GOING OUT, MISS HALE?
620
IT'S THE CHAMELEON. MIND IF I JOIN YOU?
JEEZ, YOU SCARED ME TO DEATH!
YEAH, COME ON....

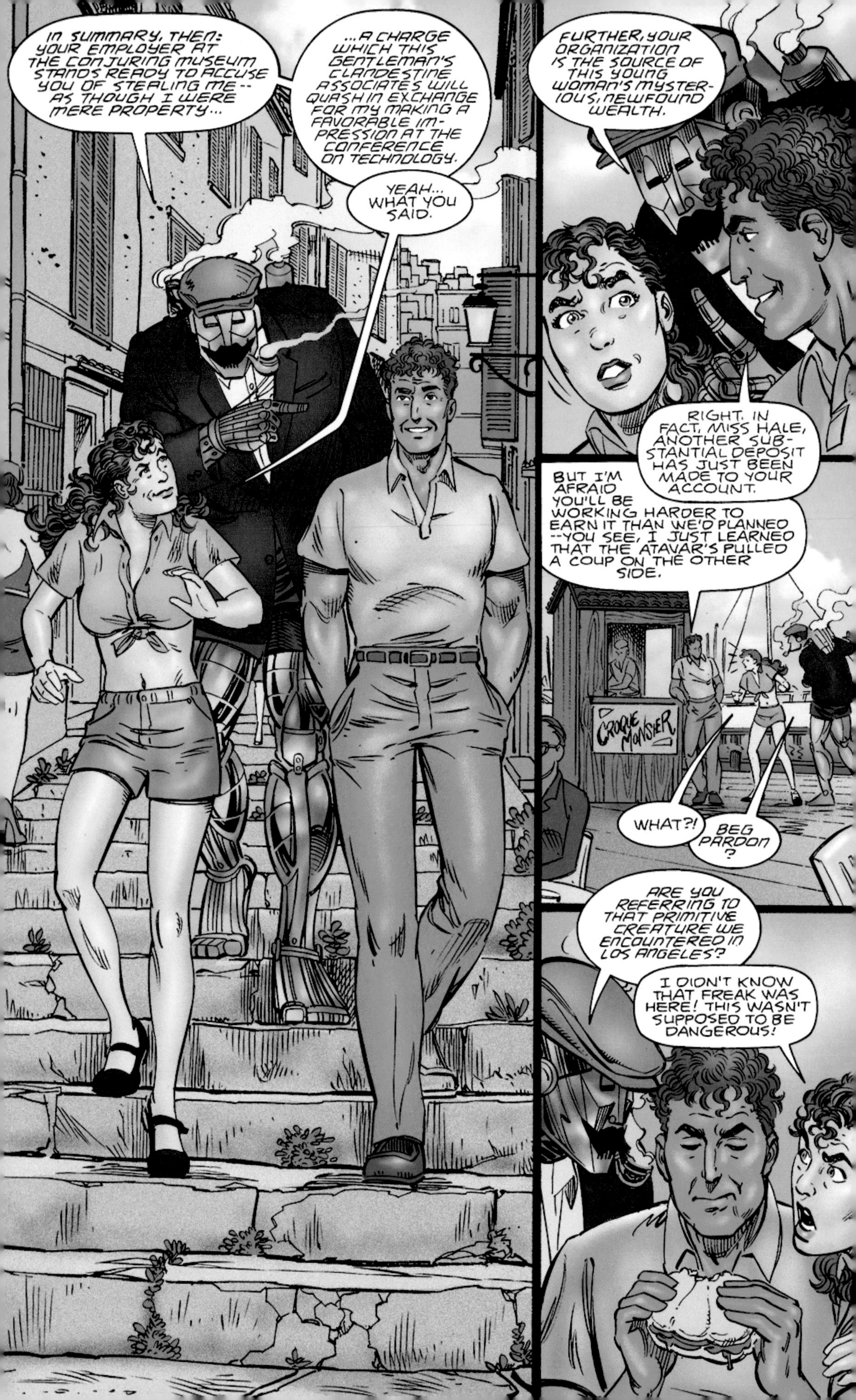
IN SUMMARY, THEN: YOUR EMPLOYER AT THE CONJURING MUSEUM STANDS READY TO ACCUSE YOU OF STEALING ME--AS THOUGH I WERE MERE PROPERTY...
...A CHARGE WHICH THIS GENTLEMAN'S CLANDESTINE ASSOCIATES WILL QUASH IN EXCHANGE FOR MY MAKING A FAVORABLE IMPRESSION AT THE CONFERENCE ON TECHNOLOGY.
YEAH... WHAT YOU SAID.
FURTHER, YOUR ORGANIZATION IS THE SOURCE OF THIS YOUNG WOMAN'S MYSTERIOUS, NEWFOUND WEALTH.
RIGHT. IN FACT, MISS HALE, ANOTHER SUBSTANTIAL DEPOSIT HAS JUST BEEN MADE TO YOUR ACCOUNT.
BUT I'M AFRAID YOU'LL BE WORKING HARDER TO EARN IT THAN WE'D PLANNED --YOU SEE, I JUST LEARNED THAT THE ATAVAR'S PULLED A COUP ON THE OTHER SIDE.
CROQUE MONSIER
WHAT?!
BEG PARDON?
ARE YOU REFERRING TO THAT PRIMITIVE CREATURE WE ENCOUNTERED IN LOS ANGELES?
I DIDN'T KNOW THAT FREAK WAS HERE! THIS WASN'T SUPPOSED TO BE DANGEROUS!

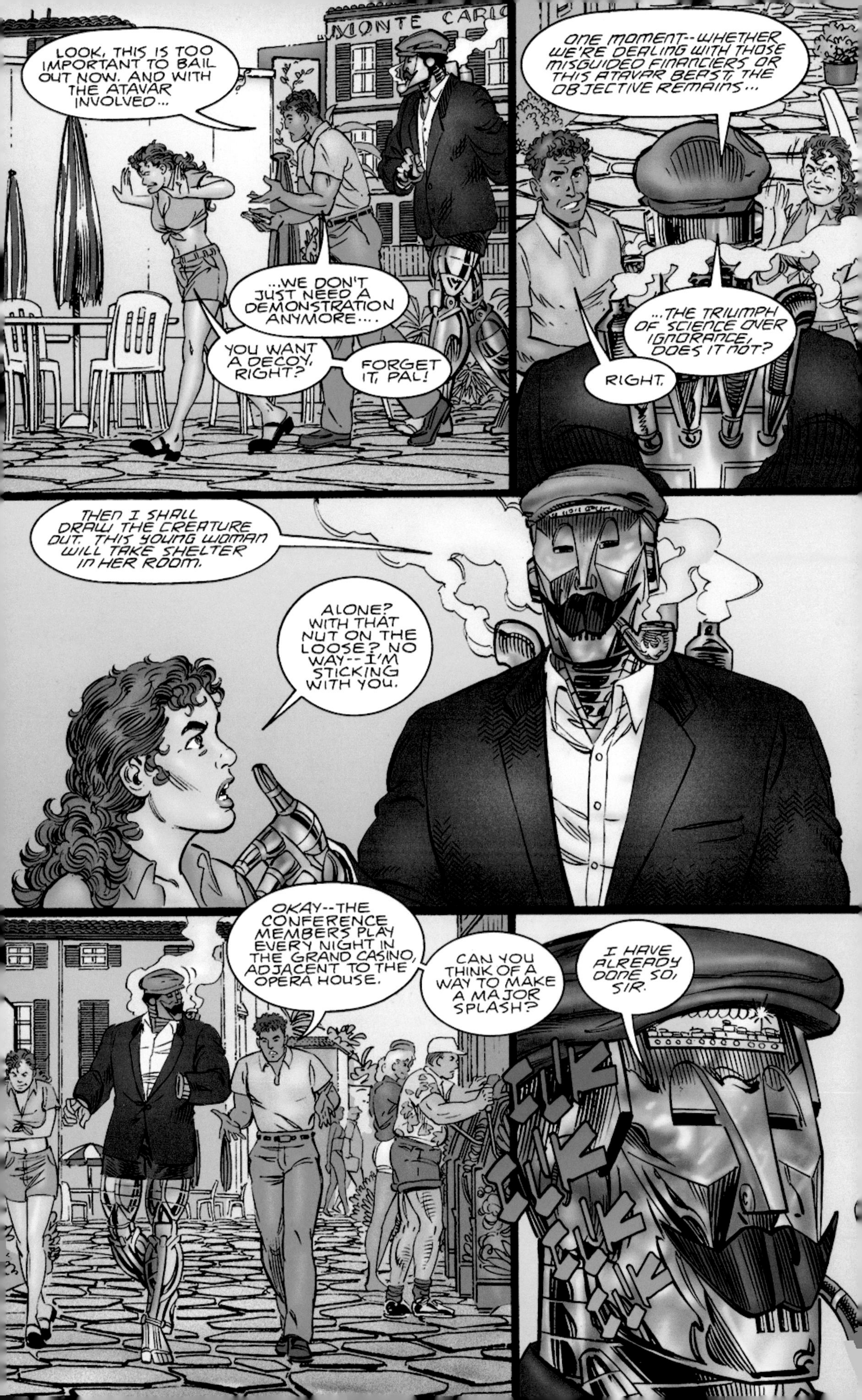
MONTE CARLO
LOOK, THIS IS TOO IMPORTANT TO BAIL OUT NOW. AND WITH THE ATAVAR INVOLVED...
...WE DON'T JUST NEED A DEMONSTRATION ANYMORE....
YOU WANT A DECOY, RIGHT?
FORGET IT, PAL!
ONE MOMENT--WHETHER WE'RE DEALING WITH THOSE MISGUIDED FINANCIERS OR THIS ATAVAR BEAST, THE OBJECTIVE REMAINS...
...THE TRIUMPH OF SCIENCE OVER IGNORANCE, DOES IT NOT?
RIGHT.
THEN I SHALL DRAW THE CREATURE OUT. THIS YOUNG WOMAN WILL TAKE SHELTER IN HER ROOM.
ALONE? WITH THAT NUT ON THE LOOSE? NO WAY--I'M STICKING WITH YOU.
OKAY--THE CONFERENCE MEMBERS PLAY EVERY NIGHT IN THE GRAND CASINO, ADJACENT TO THE OPERA HOUSE.
CAN YOU THINK OF A WAY TO MAKE A MAJOR SPLASH?
I HAVE ALREADY DONE SO, SIR.

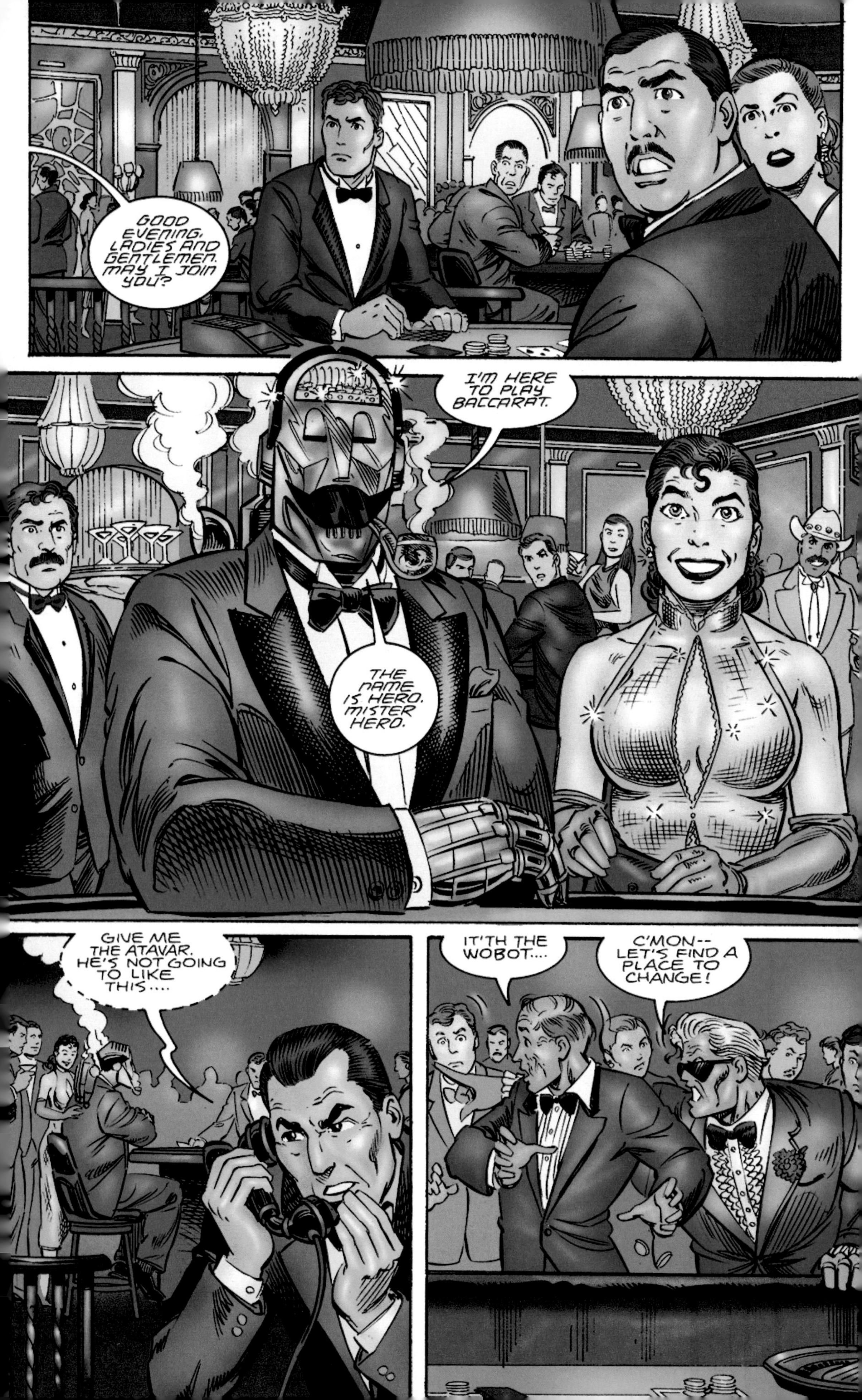
GOOD EVENING, LADIES AND GENTLEMEN. MAY I JOIN YOU?
I'M HERE TO PLAY BACCARAT.
THE NAME IS HERO. MISTER HERO.
GIVE ME THE ATAVAR. HE'S NOT GOING TO LIKE THIS....
IT'TH THE WOBOT....
C'MON-- LET'S FIND A PLACE TO CHANGE!

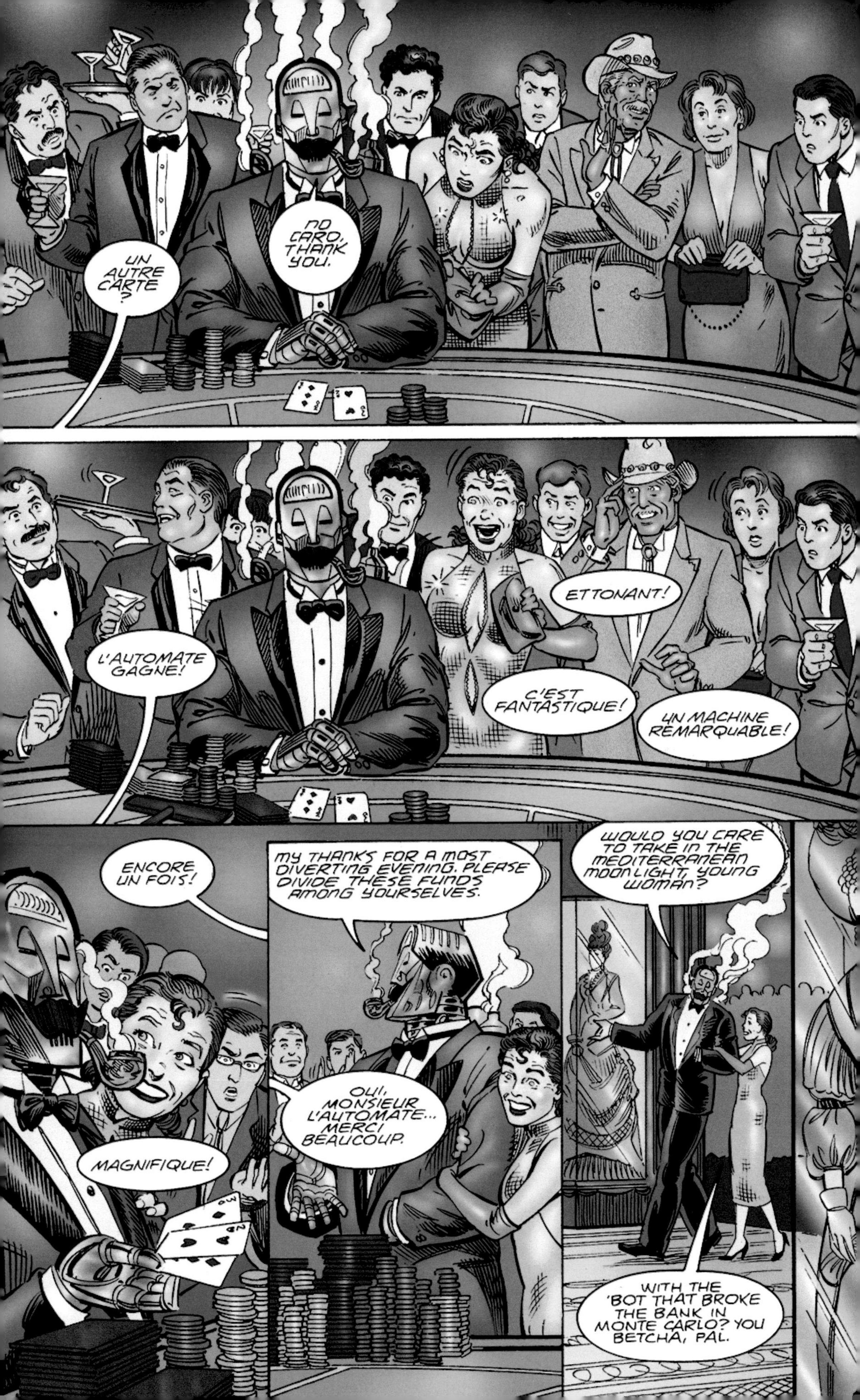
UN AUTRE CARTE?
NO CARD, THANK YOU.
L'AUTOMATE GAGNE!
ETTONANT!
C'EST FANTASTIQUE!
UN MACHINE REMARQUABLE!
ENCORE UN FOIS!
MAGNIFIQUE!
MY THANKS FOR A MOST DIVERTING EVENING. PLEASE DIVIDE THESE FUNDS AMONG YOURSELVES.
OUI, MONSIEUR L'AUTOMATE... MERCI BEAUCOUP.
WOULD YOU CARE TO TAKE IN THE MEDITERRANEAN MOONLIGHT, YOUNG WOMAN?
WITH THE 'BOT THAT BROKE THE BANK IN MONTE CARLO? YOU BETCHA, PAL.

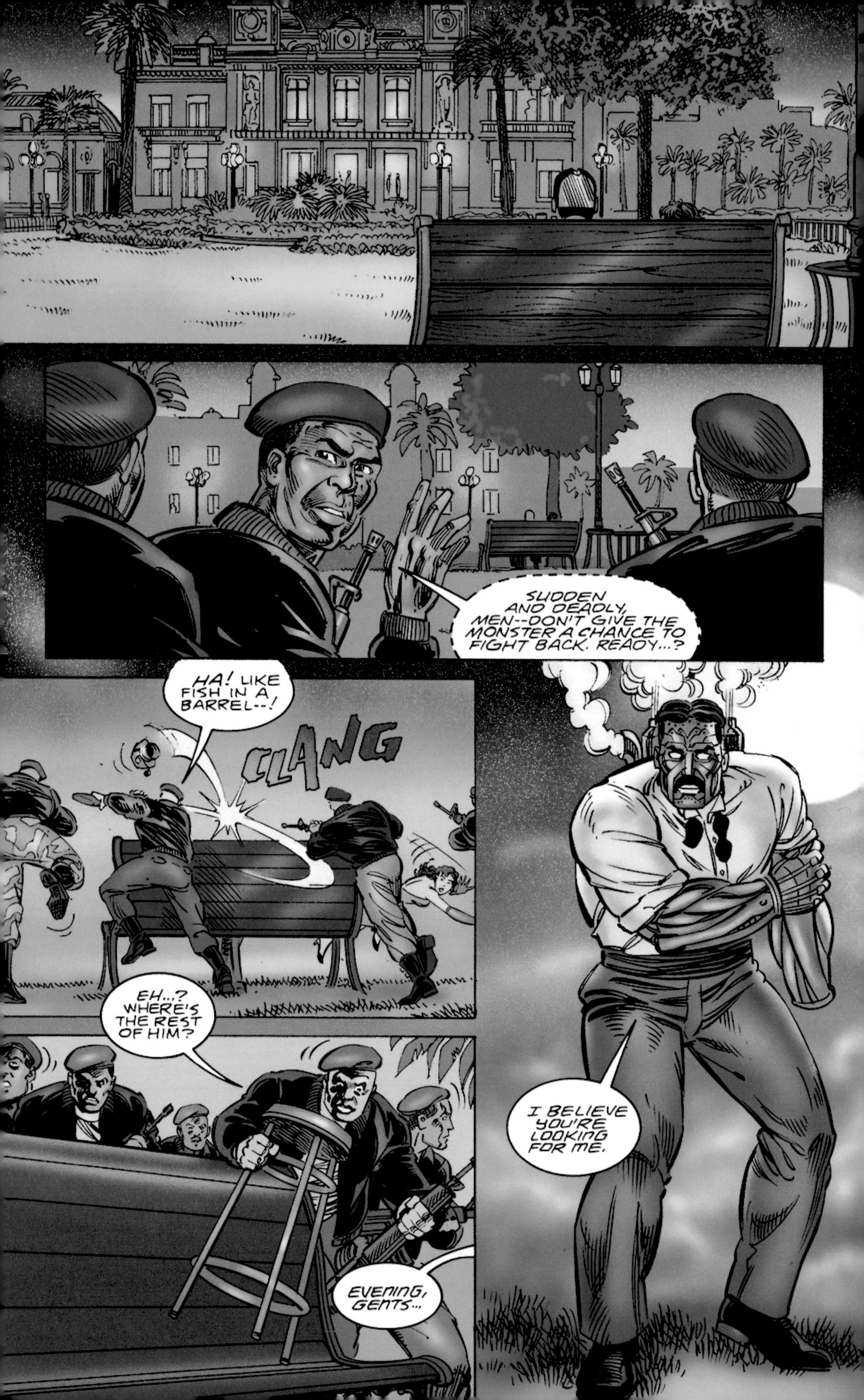
SUDDEN AND DEADLY, MEN--DON'T GIVE THE MONSTER A CHANCE TO FIGHT BACK. READY...?
HA! LIKE FISH IN A BARREL--!
CLANG
EH...? WHERE'S THE REST OF HIM?
EVENING, GENTS...
I BELIEVE YOU'RE LOOKING FOR ME.

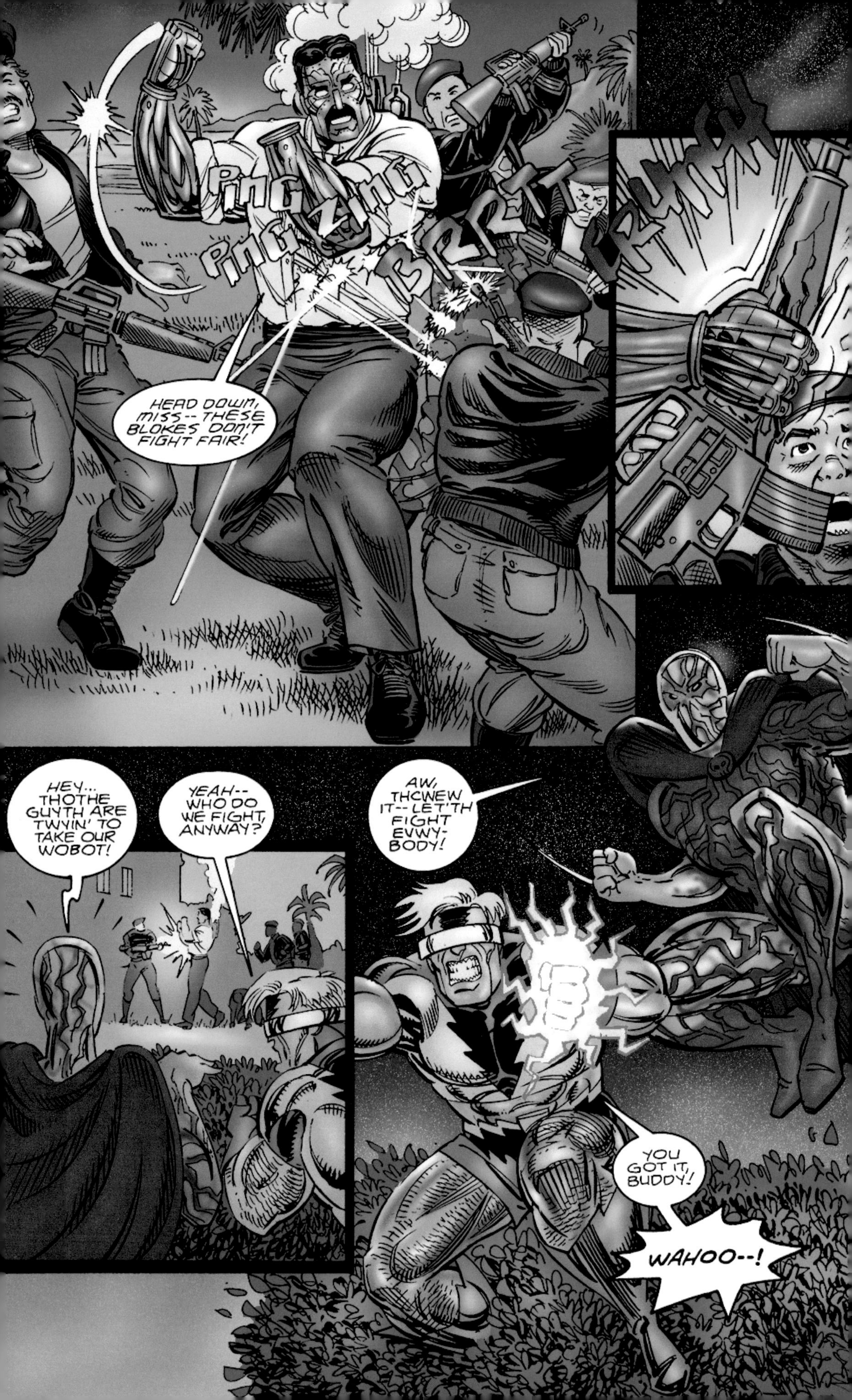
PING ZING
PING
BRRTT
CRUNXX
HEAD DOWN, MISS -- THESE BLOKES DON'T FIGHT FAIR!
HEY... THOTHE GUYTH ARE TWYIN' TO TAKE OUR WOBOT!
YEAH -- WHO DO WE FIGHT, ANYWAY?
AW, THCWEW IT -- LET'TH FIGHT EVWY-BODY!
YOU GOT IT, BUDDY!
WAHOO--!

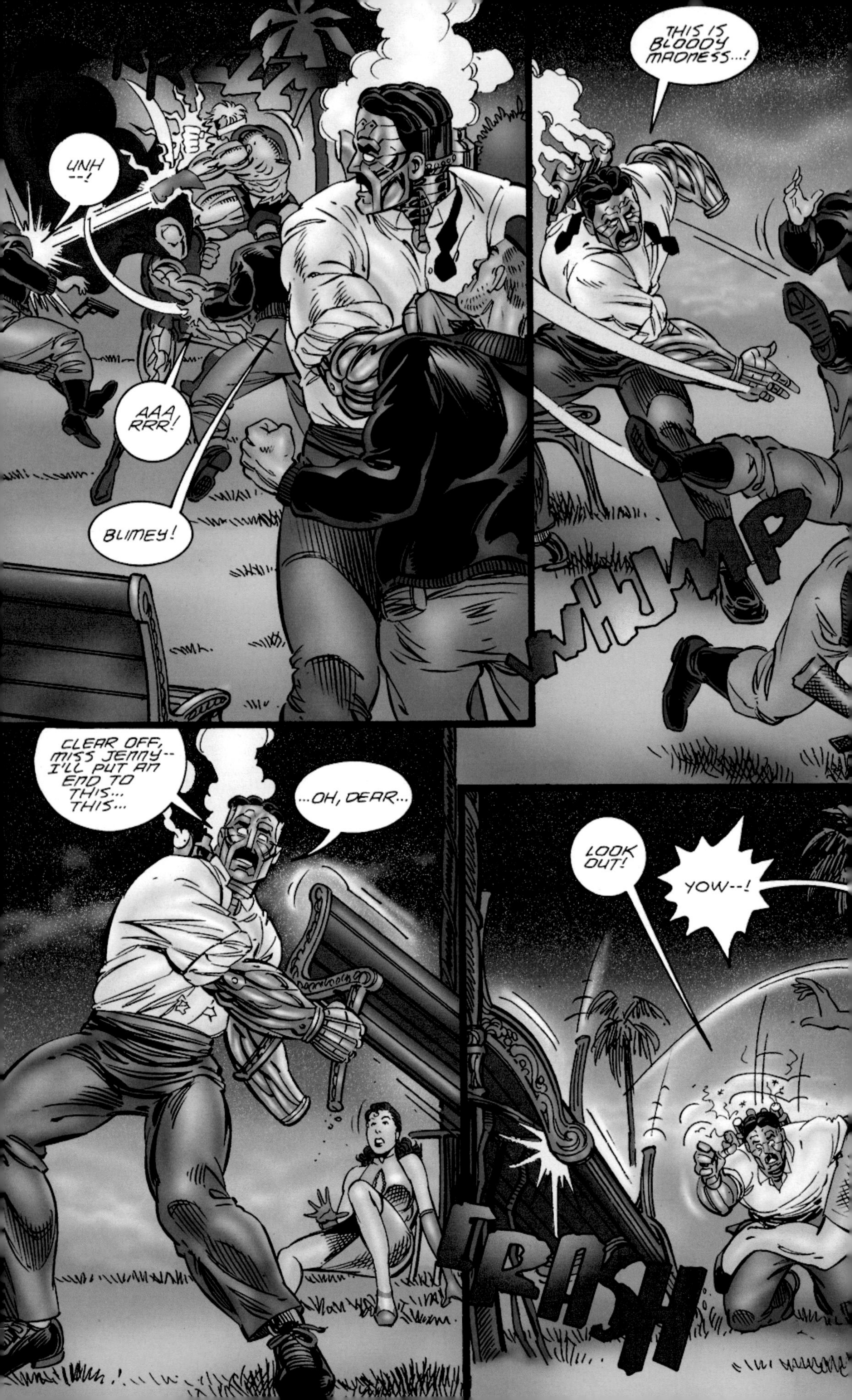
KRR-ZZT
UNH --!
AAA RRR!
BLIMEY!
THIS IS BLOODY MADNESS...!
WHUMP
CLEAR OFF, MISS JENNY-- I'LL PUT AN END TO THIS... THIS...
...OH, DEAR...
LOOK OUT!
YOW--!
TRASH

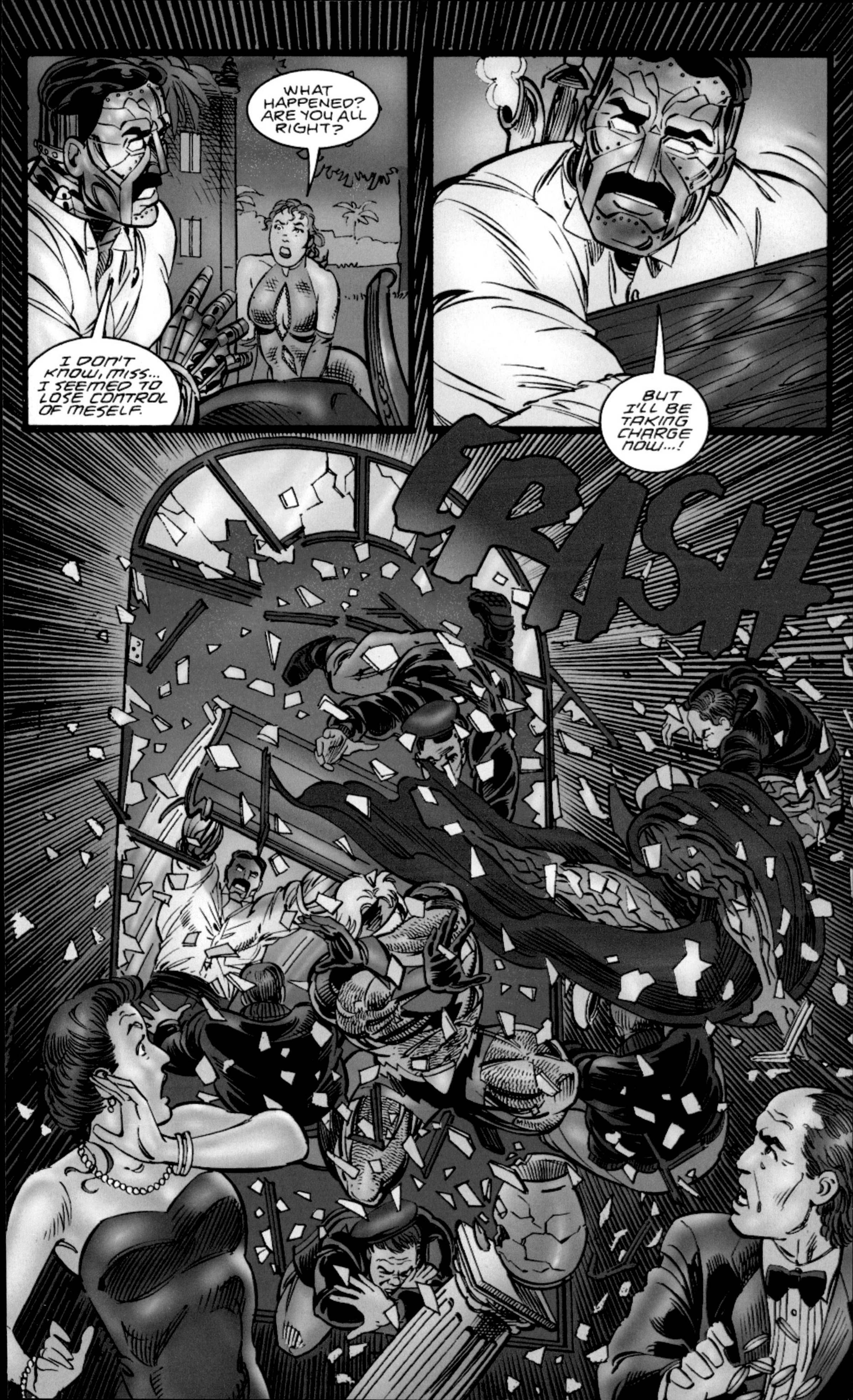
WHAT HAPPENED? ARE YOU ALL RIGHT?
I DON'T KNOW, MISS... I SEEMED TO LOSE CONTROL OF MESELF.
BUT I'LL BE TAKING CHARGE NOW...!
CRASH

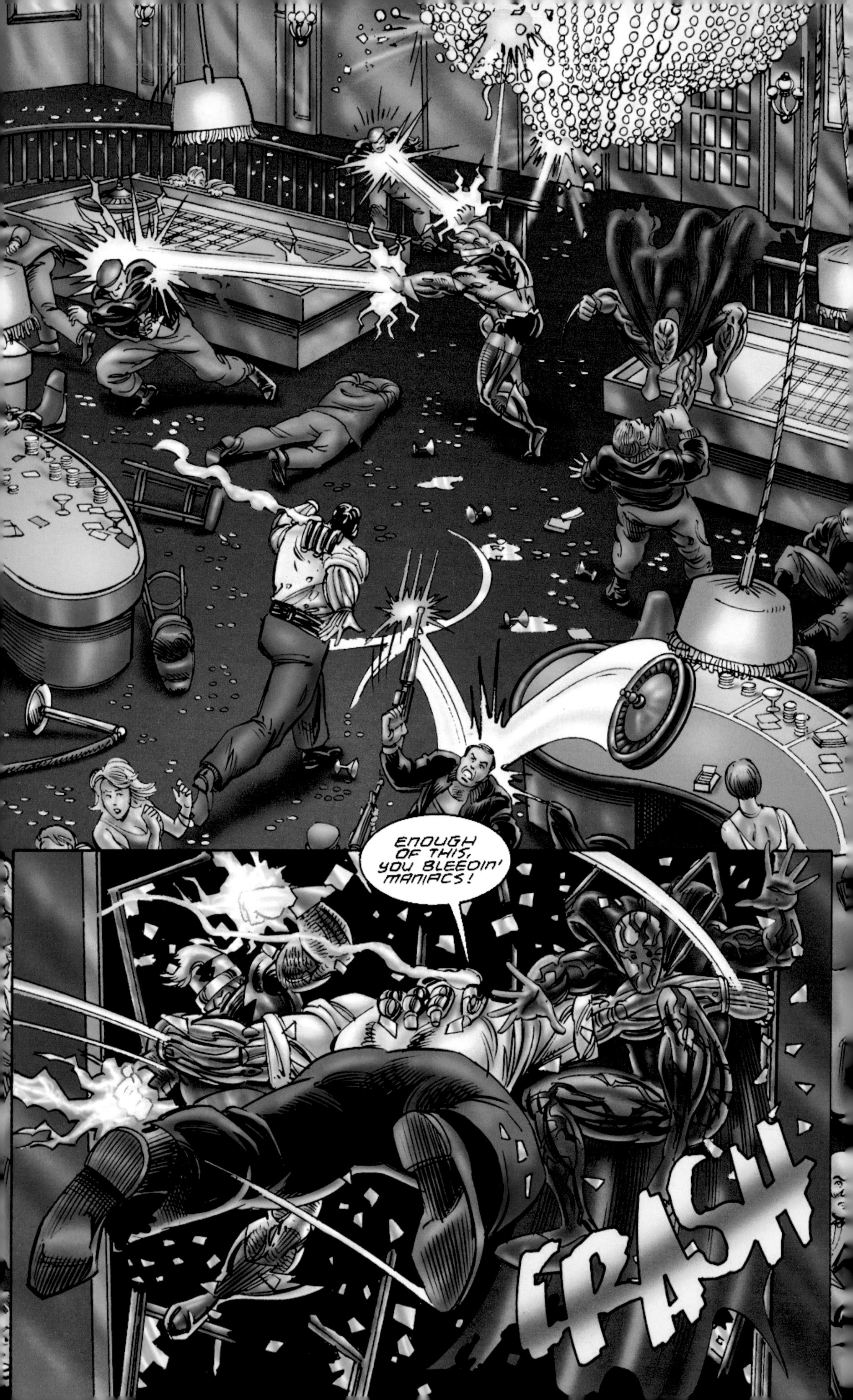
ENOUGH OF THIS, YOU BLEEDIN' MANIACS!
CRASH

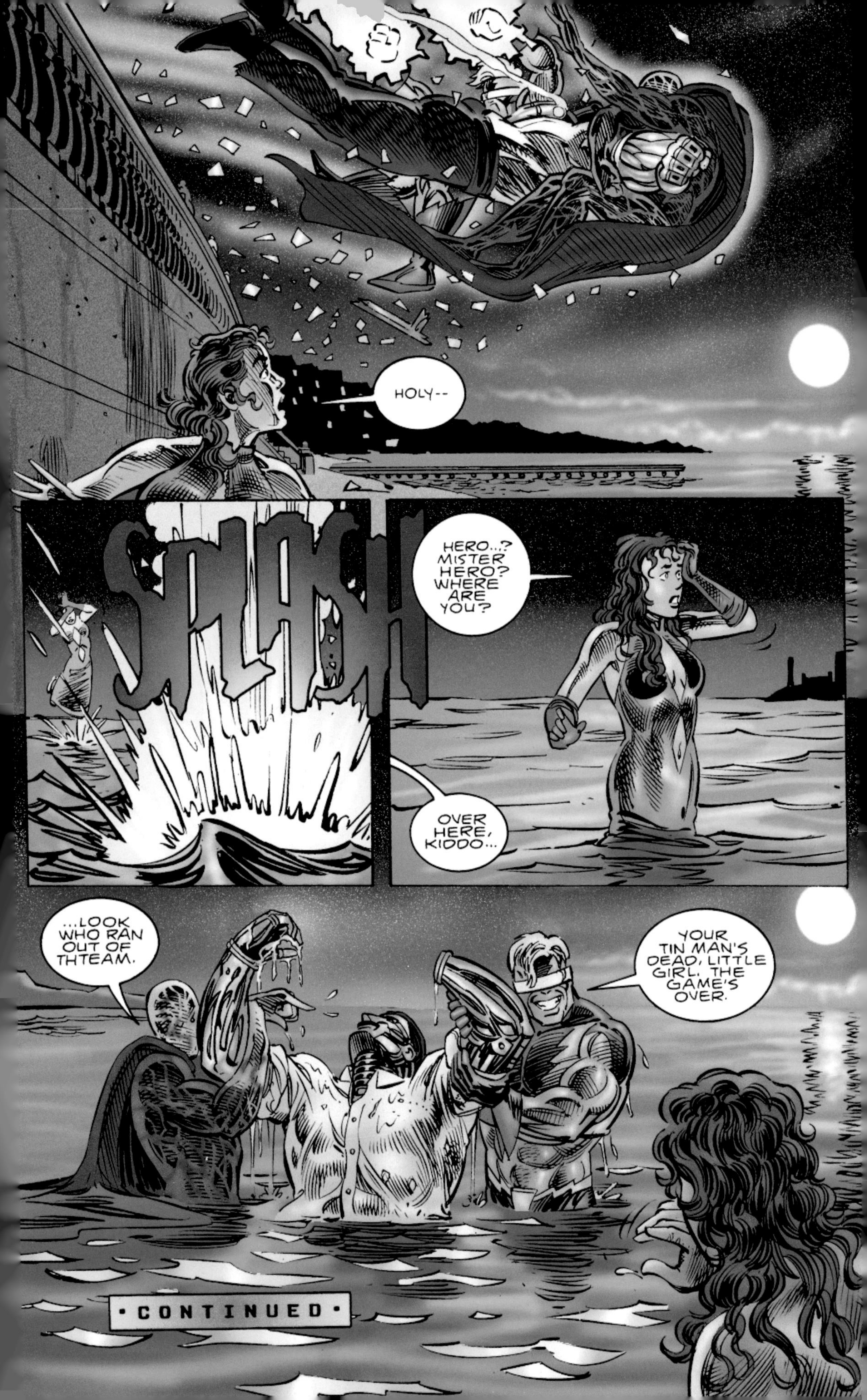
HOLY--
SPLASH
HERO...? MISTER HERO? WHERE ARE YOU?
OVER HERE, KIDDO...
...LOOK WHO RAN OUT OF THTEAM.
YOUR TIN MAN'S DEAD, LITTLE GIRL. THE GAME'S OVER.
•CONTINUED•

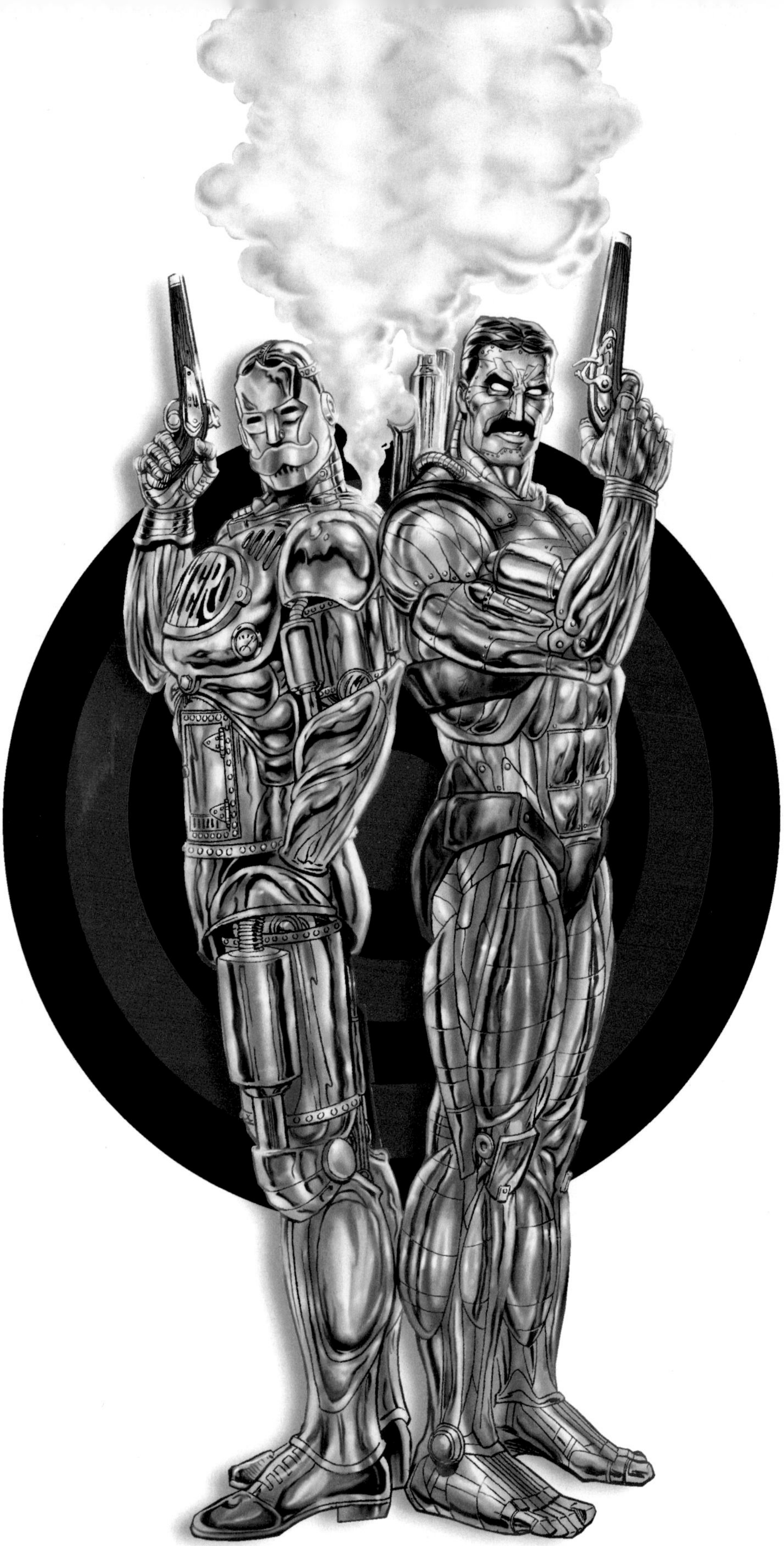

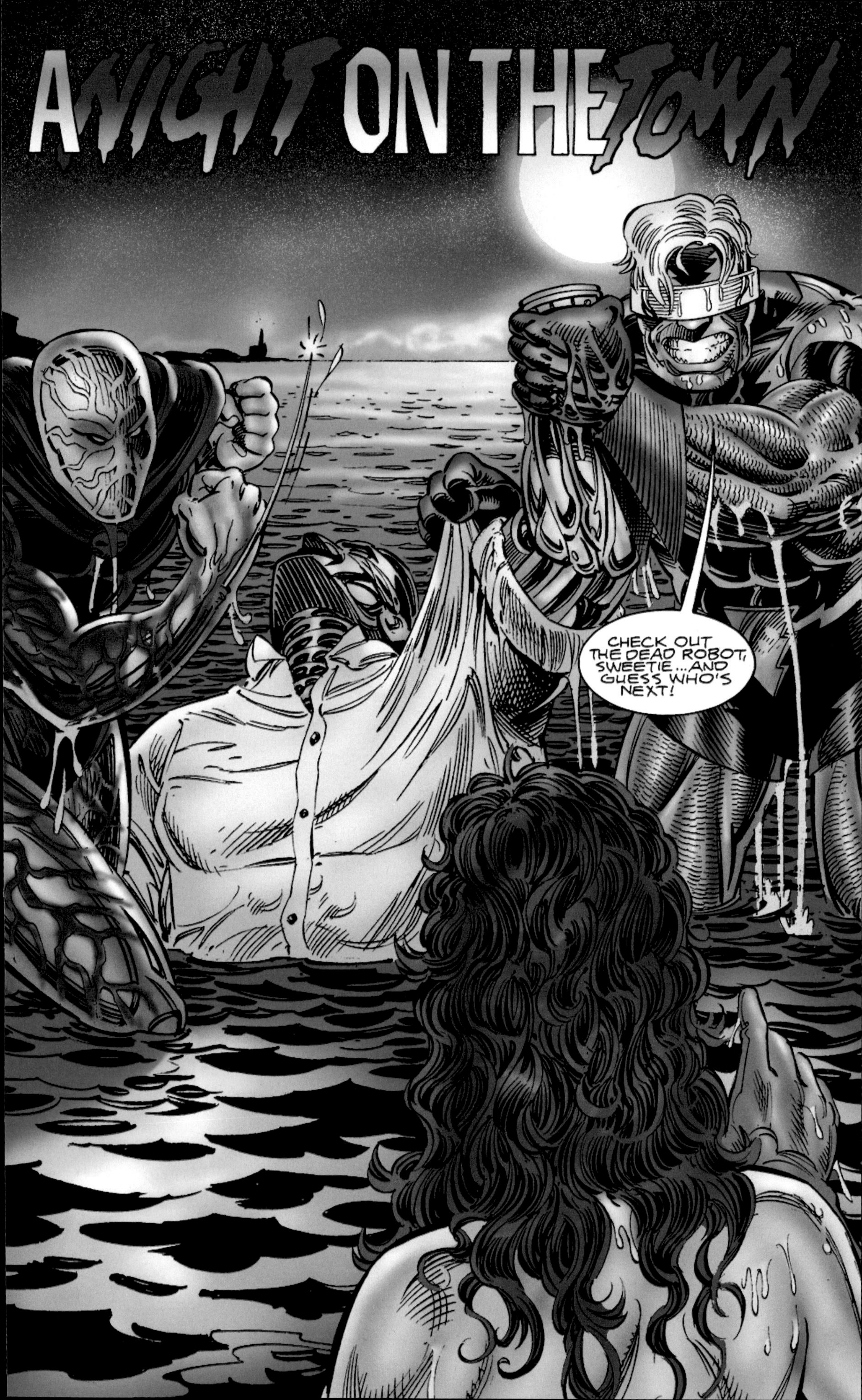
A NIGHT ON THE TOWN
CHECK OUT THE DEAD ROBOT, SWEETIE...AND GUESS WHO'S NEXT!

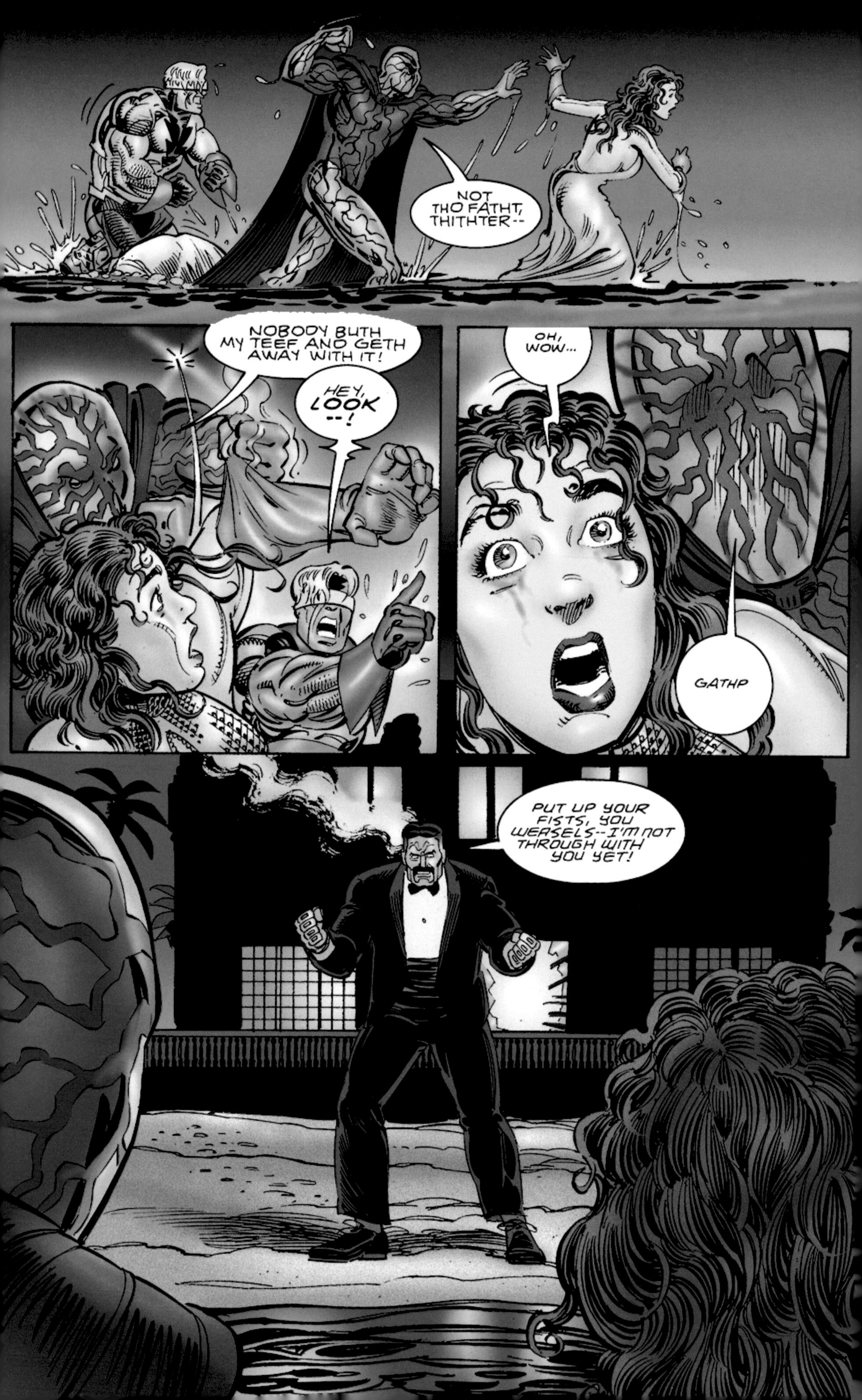
NOT THO FATHT, THITHTER--
NOBODY BUTH MY TEEF AND GETH AWAY WITH IT!
HEY, LOOK --!
OH, WOW...
GATHP
PUT UP YOUR FISTS, YOU WEASELS--I'M NOT THROUGH WITH YOU YET!

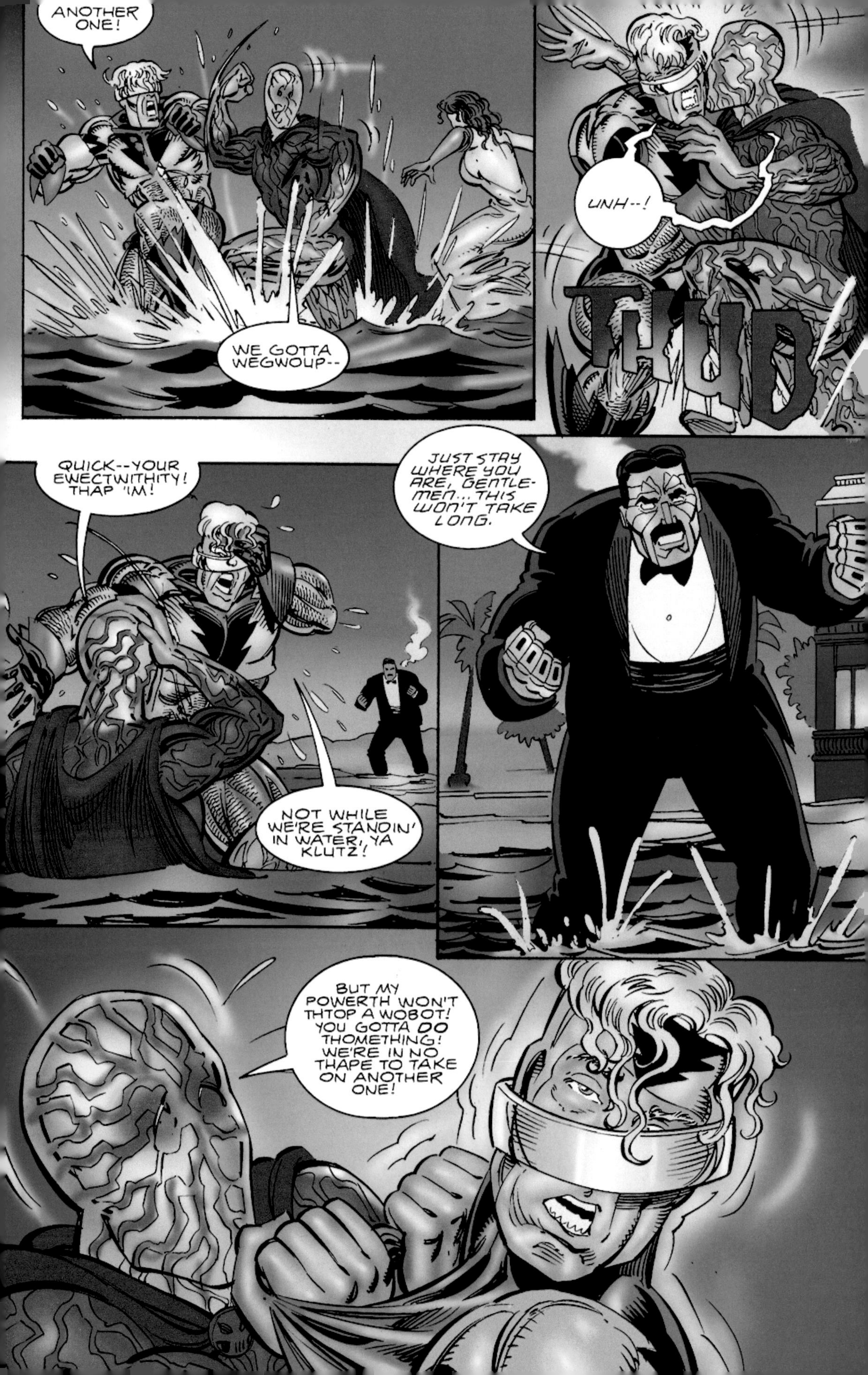
ANOTHER ONE!
WE GOTTA WEGWOUP--
UNH--!
THUD
QUICK--YOUR EWECTWITHITY! THAP 'IM!
NOT WHILE WE'RE STANDIN' IN WATER, YA KLUTZ!
JUST STAY WHERE YOU ARE, GENTLEMEN... THIS WON'T TAKE LONG.
BUT MY POWERTH WON'T THTOP A WOBOT! YOU GOTTA DO THOMETHING! WE'RE IN NO THAPE TO TAKE ON ANOTHER ONE!

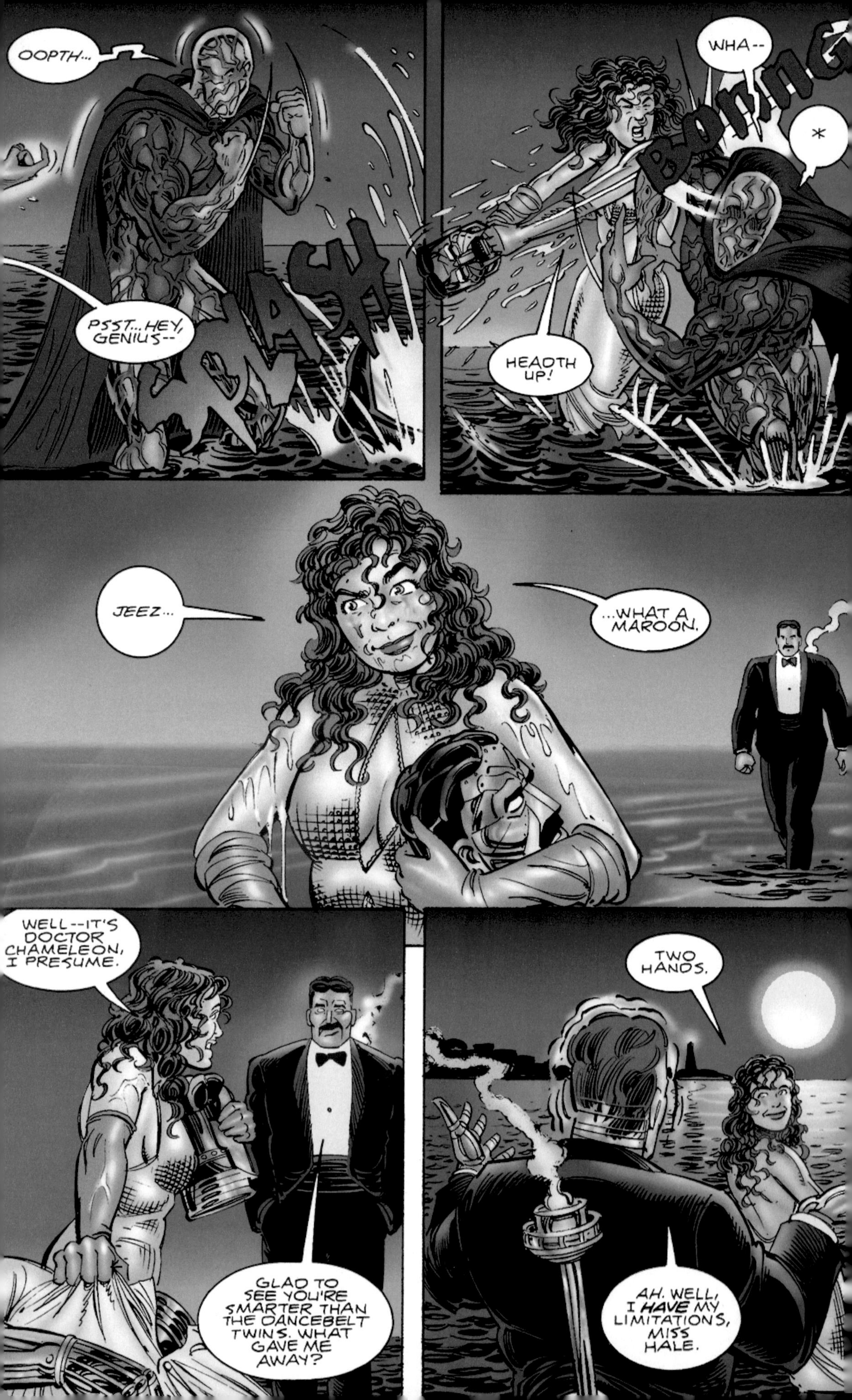
OOPTH...
PSST...HEY, GENIUS--
WHA--
*
HEADTH UP!
JEEZ...
...WHAT A MAROON.
WELL--IT'S DOCTOR CHAMELEON, I PRESUME.
GLAD TO SEE YOU'RE SMARTER THAN THE DANCEBELT TWINS. WHAT GAVE ME AWAY?
TWO HANDS.
AH. WELL, I *HAVE* MY LIMITATIONS, MISS HALE.

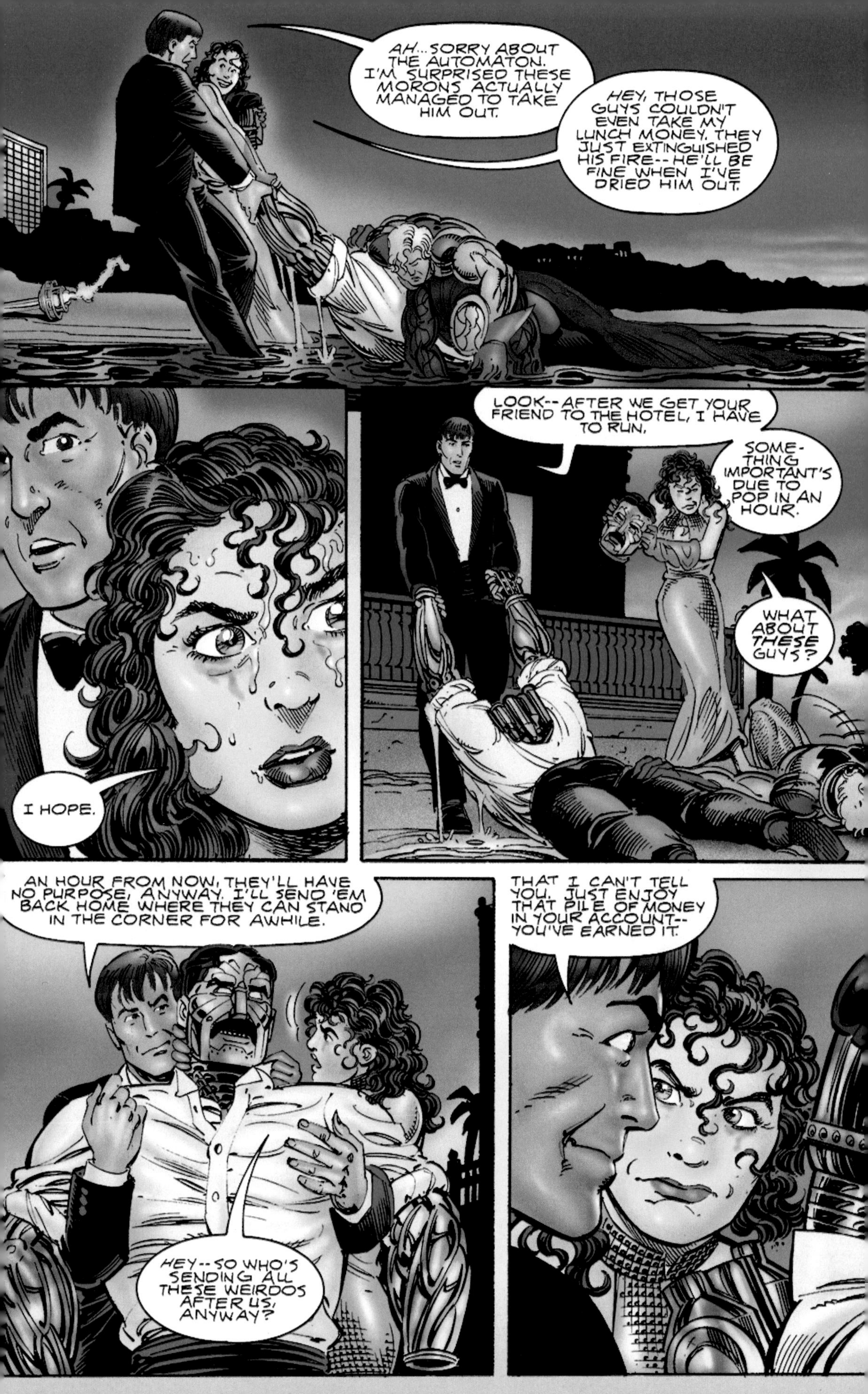
AH...SORRY ABOUT THE AUTOMATON. I'M SURPRISED THESE MORONS ACTUALLY MANAGED TO TAKE HIM OUT.
HEY, THOSE GUYS COULDN'T EVEN TAKE MY LUNCH MONEY. THEY JUST EXTINGUISHED HIS FIRE-- HE'LL BE FINE WHEN I'VE DRIED HIM OUT.
I HOPE.
LOOK--AFTER WE GET YOUR FRIEND TO THE HOTEL, I HAVE TO RUN,
SOMETHING IMPORTANT'S DUE TO POP IN AN HOUR.
WHAT ABOUT *THESE* GUYS?
AN HOUR FROM NOW, THEY'LL HAVE NO PURPOSE, ANYWAY. I'LL SEND 'EM BACK HOME WHERE THEY CAN STAND IN THE CORNER FOR AWHILE.
HEY--SO WHO'S SENDING ALL THESE WEIRDOS AFTER US, ANYWAY?
THAT I CAN'T TELL YOU. JUST ENJOY THAT PILE OF MONEY IN YOUR ACCOUNT-- YOU'VE EARNED IT.

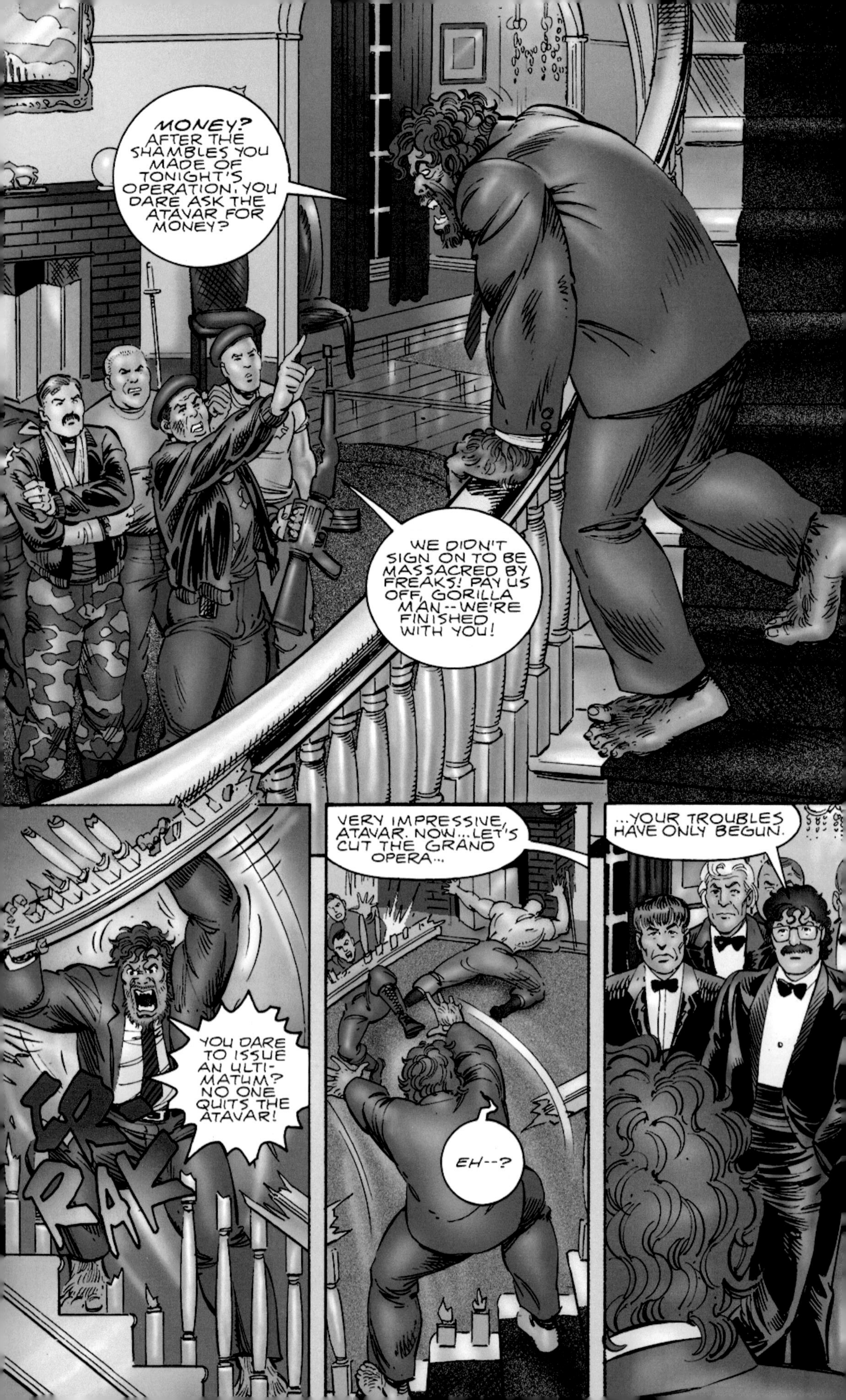
MONEY? AFTER THE SHAMBLES YOU MADE OF TONIGHT'S OPERATION, YOU DARE ASK THE ATAVAR FOR MONEY?
WE DIDN'T SIGN ON TO BE MASSACRED BY FREAKS! PAY US OFF, GORILLA MAN--WE'RE FINISHED WITH YOU!
YOU DARE TO ISSUE AN ULTI-MATUM? NO ONE QUITS THE ATAVAR!
KRAK
VERY IMPRESSIVE, ATAVAR. NOW...LET'S CUT THE GRAND OPERA...
EH--?
...YOUR TROUBLES HAVE ONLY BEGUN.

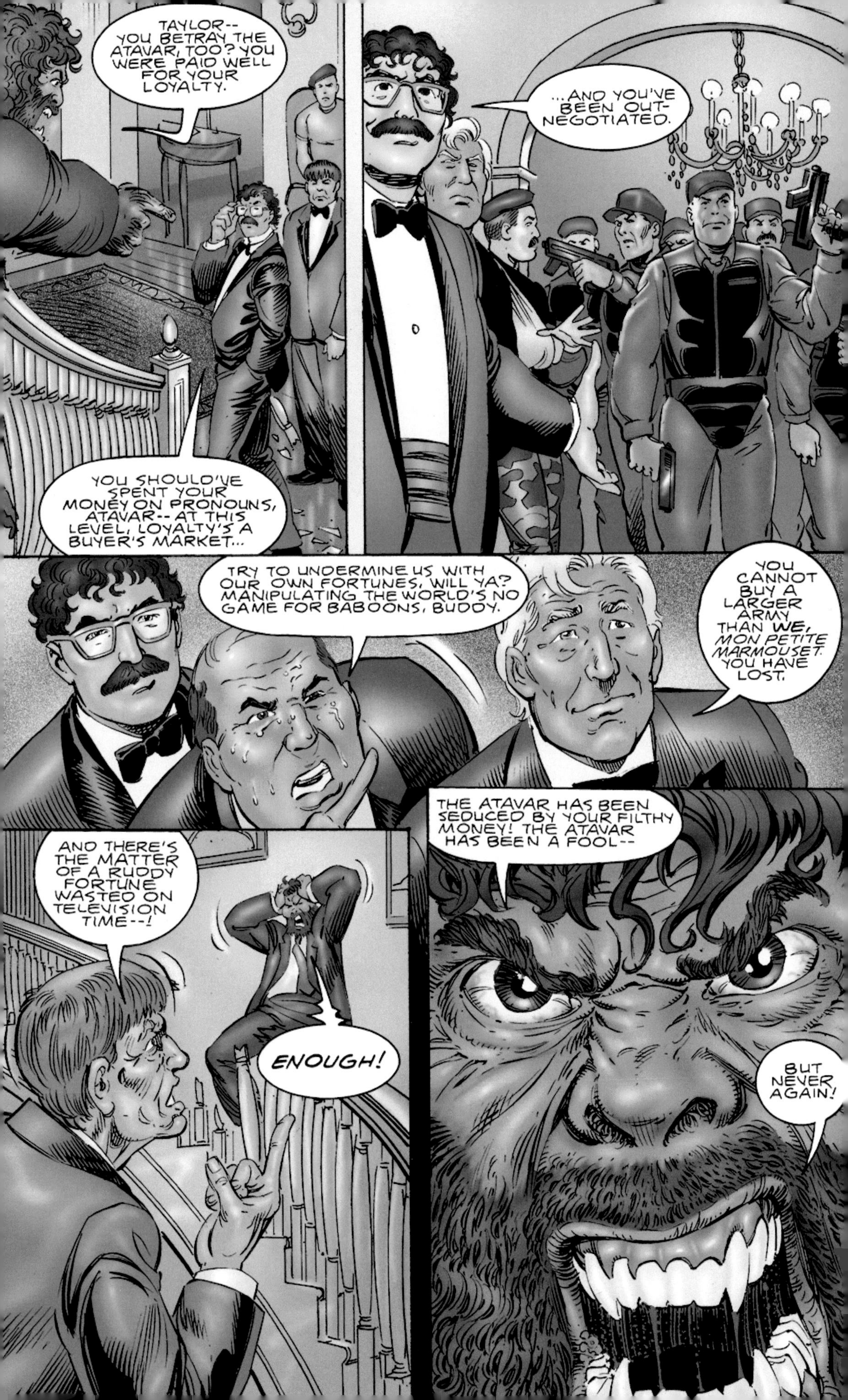
TAYLOR-- YOU BETRAY THE ATAVAR, TOO? YOU WERE PAID WELL FOR YOUR LOYALTY.
YOU SHOULD'VE SPENT YOUR MONEY ON PRONOUNS, ATAVAR-- AT THIS LEVEL, LOYALTY'S A BUYER'S MARKET...
...AND YOU'VE BEEN OUT-NEGOTIATED.
TRY TO UNDERMINE US WITH OUR OWN FORTUNES, WILL YA? MANIPULATING THE WORLD'S NO GAME FOR BABOONS, BUDDY.
YOU CANNOT BUY A LARGER ARMY THAN WE, MON PETITE MARMOUSET. YOU HAVE LOST.
AND THERE'S THE MATTER OF A RUDDY FORTUNE WASTED ON TELEVISION TIME--!
ENOUGH!
THE ATAVAR HAS BEEN SEDUCED BY YOUR FILTHY MONEY! THE ATAVAR HAS BEEN A FOOL--
BUT NEVER AGAIN!

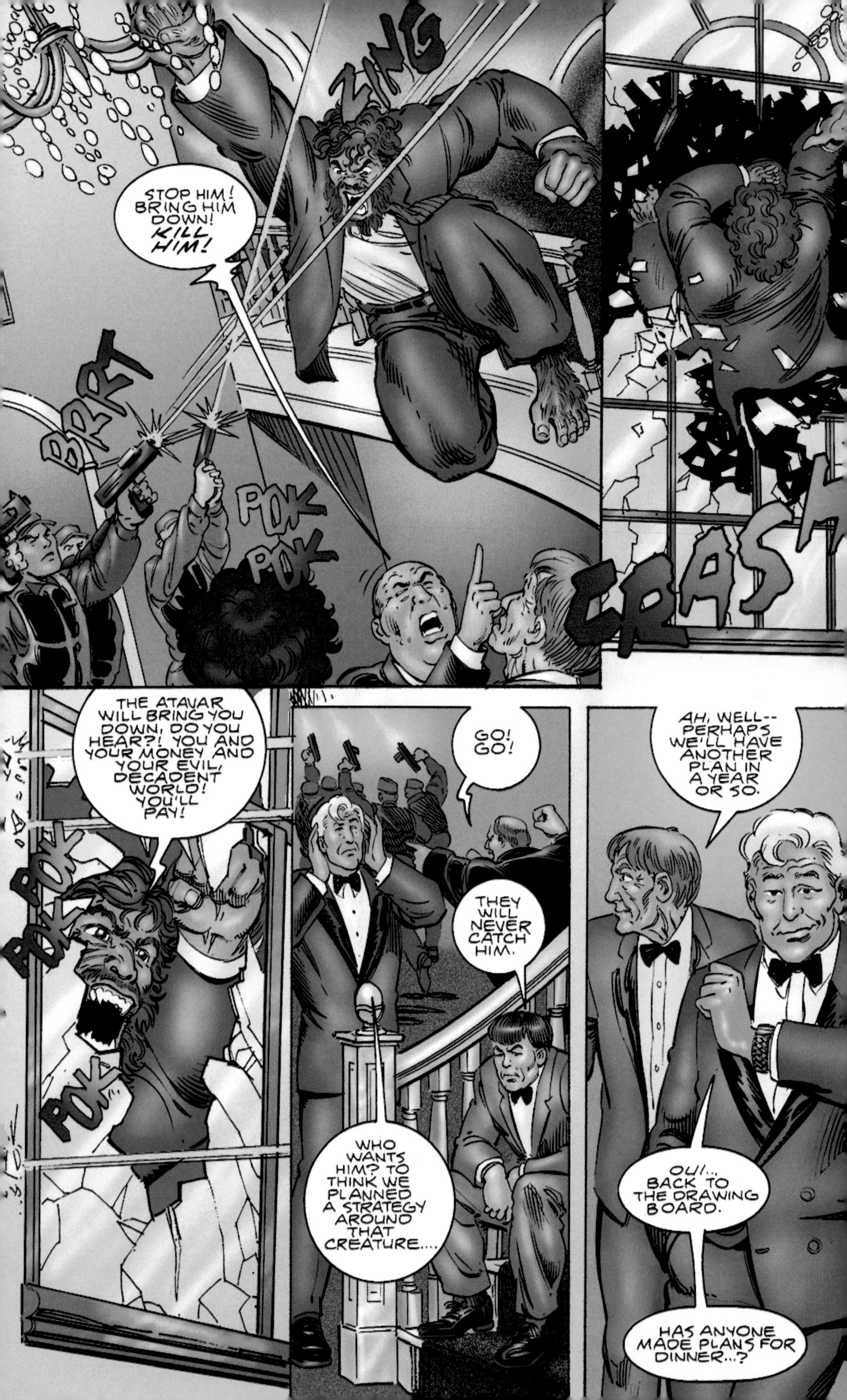
ZING
STOP HIM! BRING HIM DOWN! KILL HIM!
BRRT
POK
POK
CRASH
THE ATAVAR WILL BRING YOU DOWN, DO YOU HEAR?! YOU AND YOUR MONEY AND YOUR EVIL, DECADENT WORLD! YOU'LL PAY!
POK POK
POK
GO! GO!
THEY WILL NEVER CATCH HIM.
WHO WANTS HIM? TO THINK WE PLANNED A STRATEGY AROUND THAT CREATURE....
AH, WELL-- PERHAPS WE'LL HAVE ANOTHER PLAN IN A YEAR OR SO.
OUI... BACK TO THE DRAWING BOARD.
HAS ANYONE MADE PLANS FOR DINNER...?

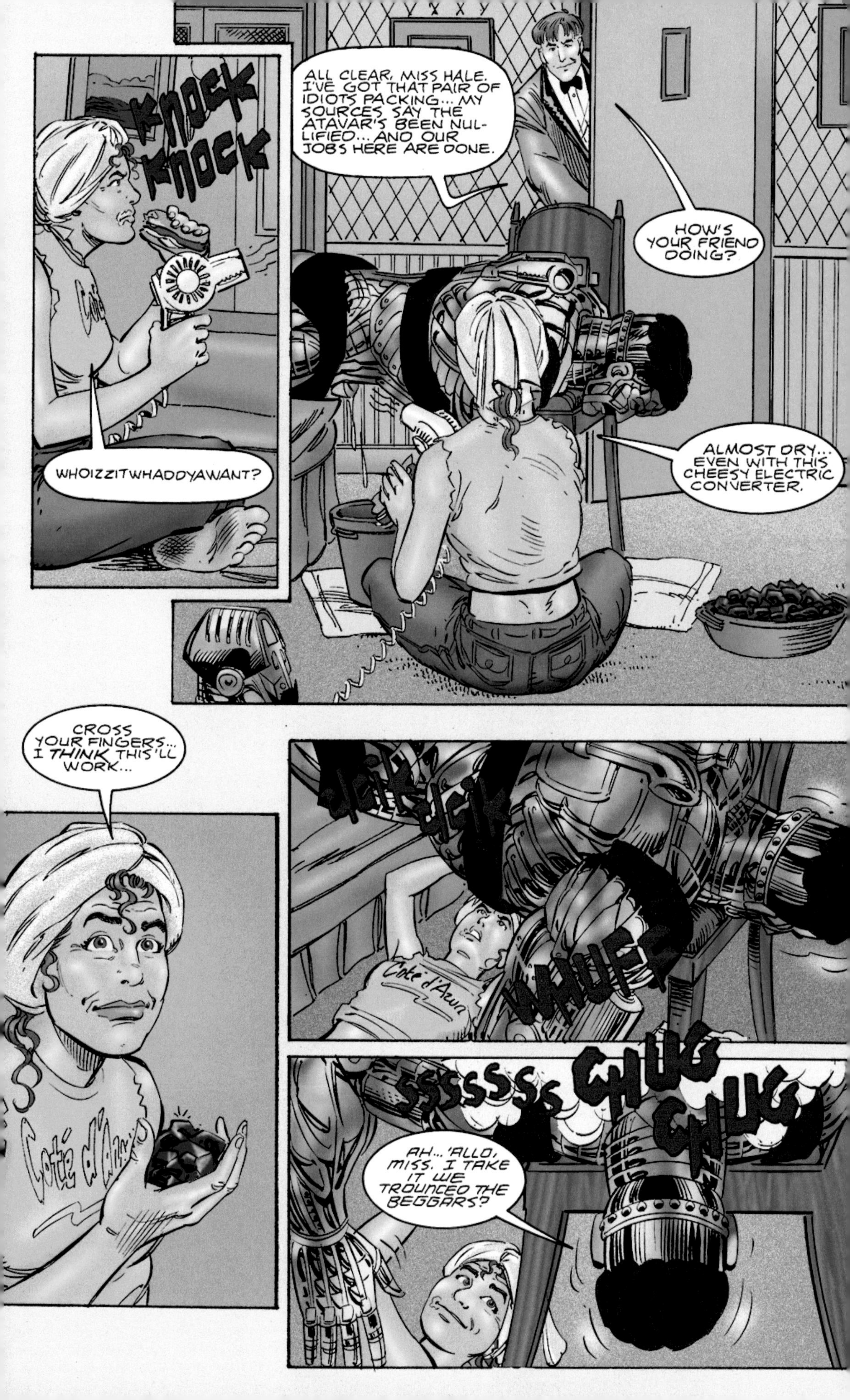
KNOCK KNOCK
ALL CLEAR, MISS HALE. I'VE GOT THAT PAIR OF IDIOTS PACKING... MY SOURCES SAY THE ATAVAR'S BEEN NULLIFIED... AND OUR JOBS HERE ARE DONE.
WHOIZZITWHADDYAWANT?
HOW'S YOUR FRIEND DOING?
ALMOST DRY... EVEN WITH THIS CHEESY ELECTRIC CONVERTER.
CROSS YOUR FINGERS... I THINK THIS'LL WORK...
WHUF!
SSSSSSS CHUG CHUG
AH... 'ALLO, MISS. I TAKE IT WE TROUNCED THE BEGGARS?

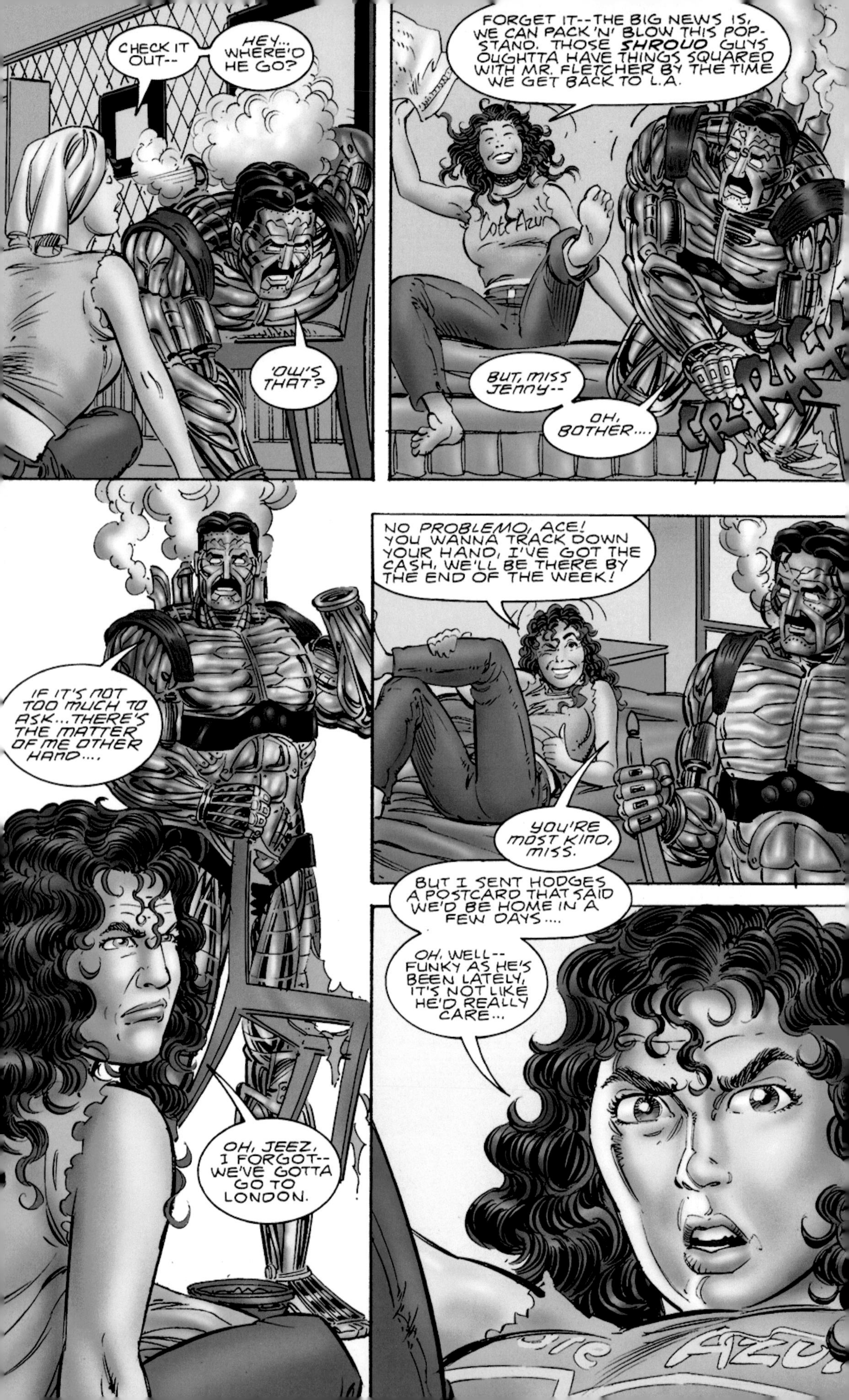
CHECK IT OUT--
HEY... WHERE'D HE GO?
'OW'S THAT?
FORGET IT--THE BIG NEWS IS, WE CAN PACK 'N' BLOW THIS POP-STAND. THOSE SHROUD GUYS OUGHTTA HAVE THINGS SQUARED WITH MR. FLETCHER BY THE TIME WE GET BACK TO L.A.
BUT, MISS JENNY--
OH, BOTHER....
IF IT'S NOT TOO MUCH TO ASK...THERE'S THE MATTER OF ME OTHER HAND....
OH, JEEZ, I FORGOT-- WE'VE GOTTA GO TO LONDON.
NO PROBLEMO, ACE! YOU WANNA TRACK DOWN YOUR HAND, I'VE GOT THE CASH. WE'LL BE THERE BY THE END OF THE WEEK!
YOU'RE MOST KIND, MISS.
BUT I SENT HODGES A POSTCARD THAT SAID WE'D BE HOME IN A FEW DAYS....
OH, WELL-- FUNKY AS HE'S BEEN LATELY, IT'S NOT LIKE HE'D REALLY CARE...

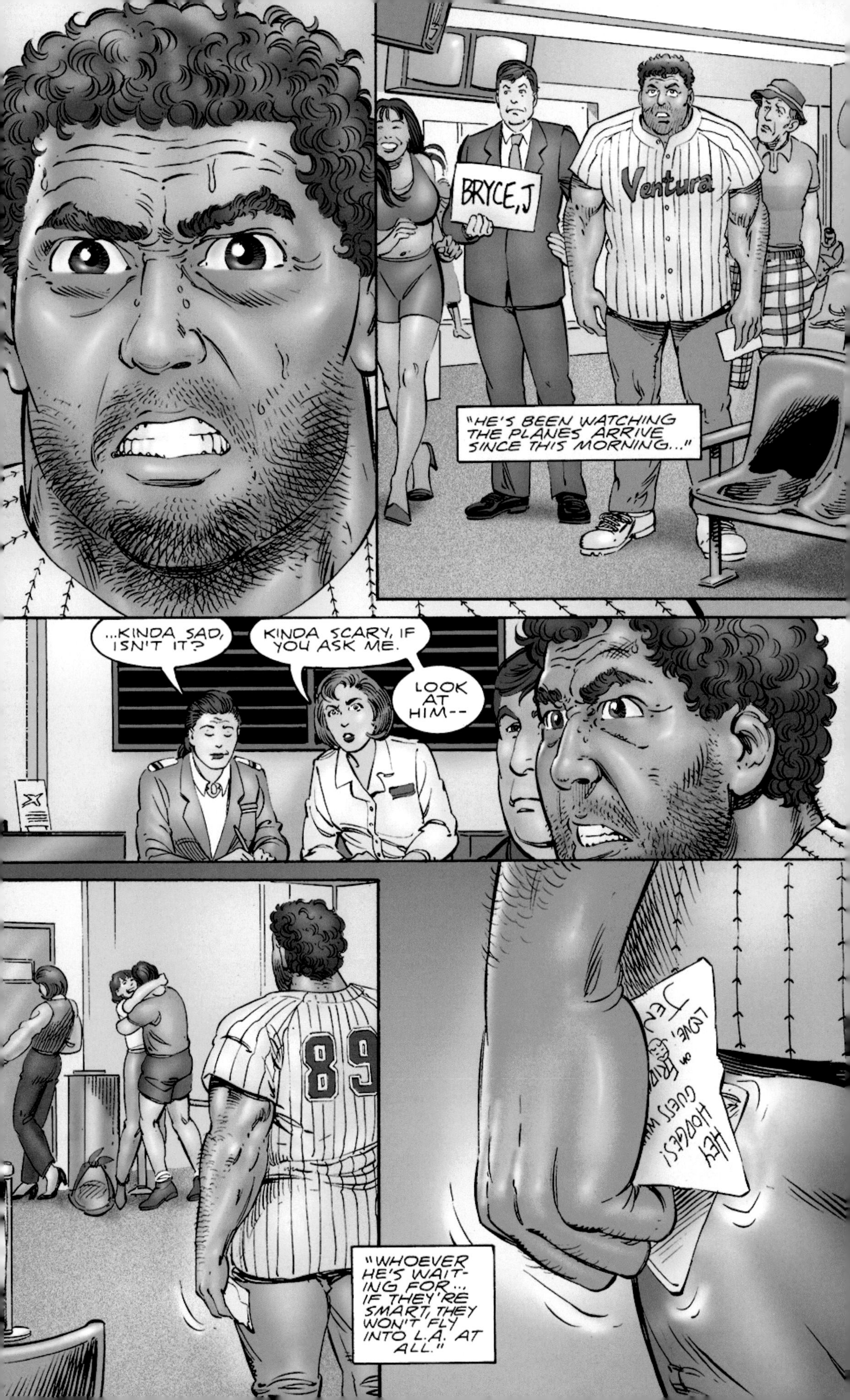

BRYCE, J
Ventura
"HE'S BEEN WATCHING THE PLANES ARRIVE SINCE THIS MORNING..."
...KINDA SAD, ISN'T IT?
KINDA SCARY, IF YOU ASK ME.
LOOK AT HIM--
89
"WHOEVER HE'S WAITING FOR... IF THEY'RE SMART, THEY WON'T FLY INTO L.A. AT ALL."
HEY HODGES!

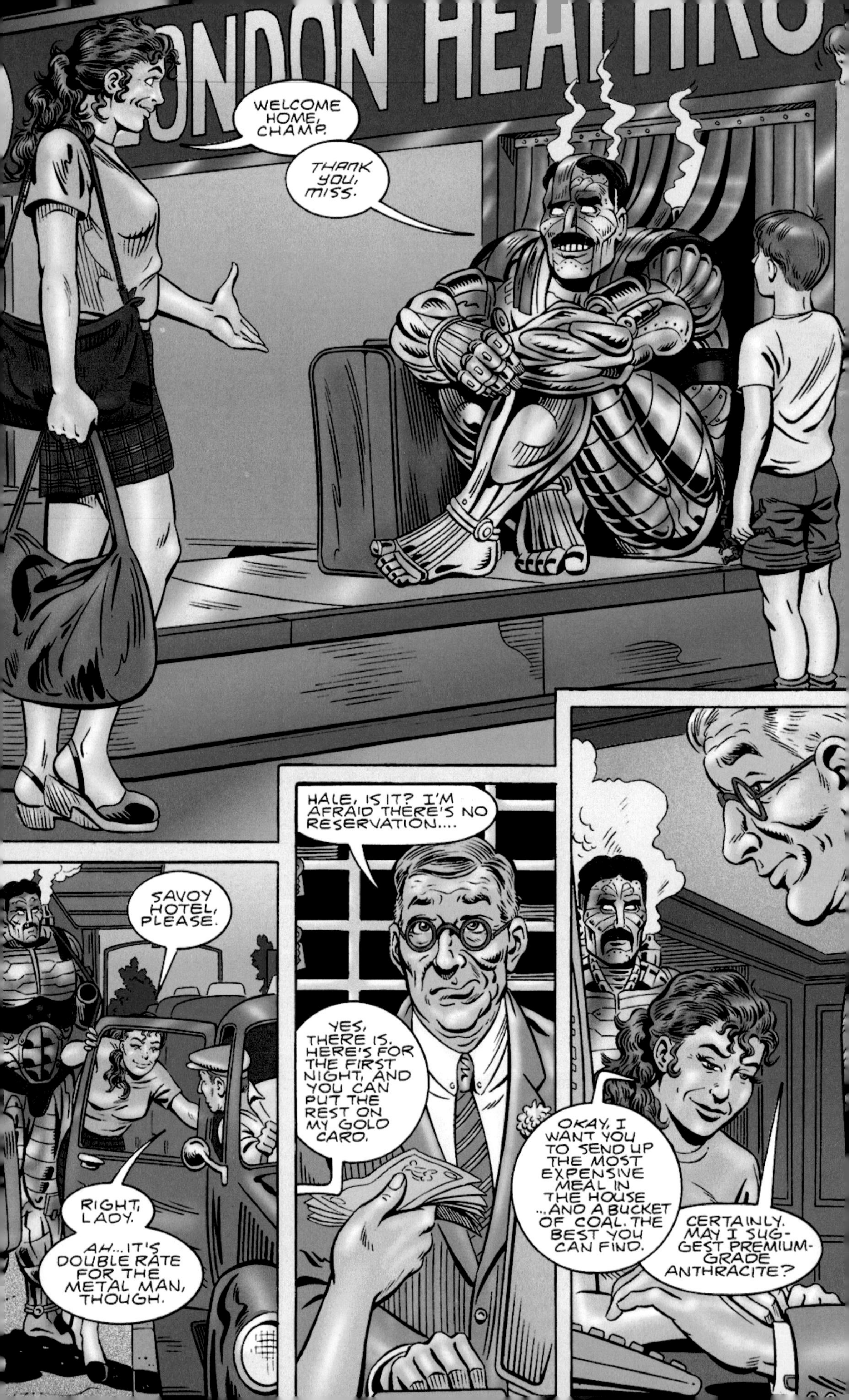
LONDON HEATHRO
WELCOME HOME, CHAMP.
THANK YOU, MISS.
SAVOY HOTEL, PLEASE.
RIGHT, LADY.
AH... IT'S DOUBLE RATE FOR THE METAL MAN, THOUGH.
HALE, IS IT? I'M AFRAID THERE'S NO RESERVATION....
YES, THERE IS. HERE'S FOR THE FIRST NIGHT, AND YOU CAN PUT THE REST ON MY GOLD CARD.
OKAY, I WANT YOU TO SEND UP THE MOST EXPENSIVE MEAL IN THE HOUSE ...AND A BUCKET OF COAL. THE BEST YOU CAN FIND.
CERTAINLY. MAY I SUGGEST PREMIUM-GRADE ANTHRACITE?

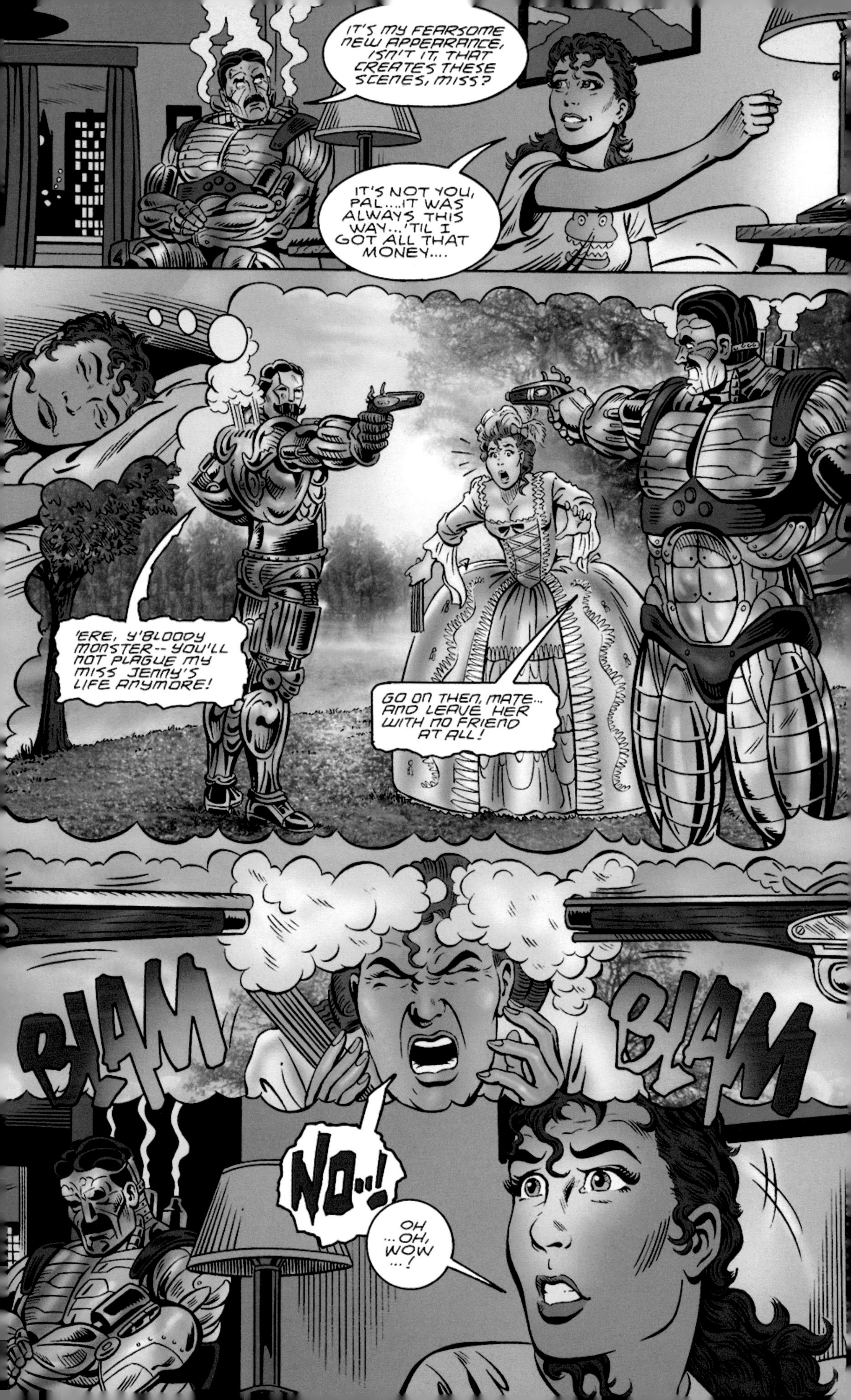
IT'S MY FEARSOME NEW APPEARANCE, ISN'T IT, THAT CREATES THESE SCENES, MISS?
IT'S NOT YOU, PAL....IT WAS ALWAYS THIS WAY...'TIL I GOT ALL THAT MONEY....
'ERE, Y'BLOODY MONSTER-- YOU'LL NOT PLAGUE MY MISS JENNY'S LIFE ANYMORE!
GO ON THEN, MATE... AND LEAVE HER WITH NO FRIEND AT ALL!
BLAM
BLAM
NO..!
OH ...OH, WOW ...!

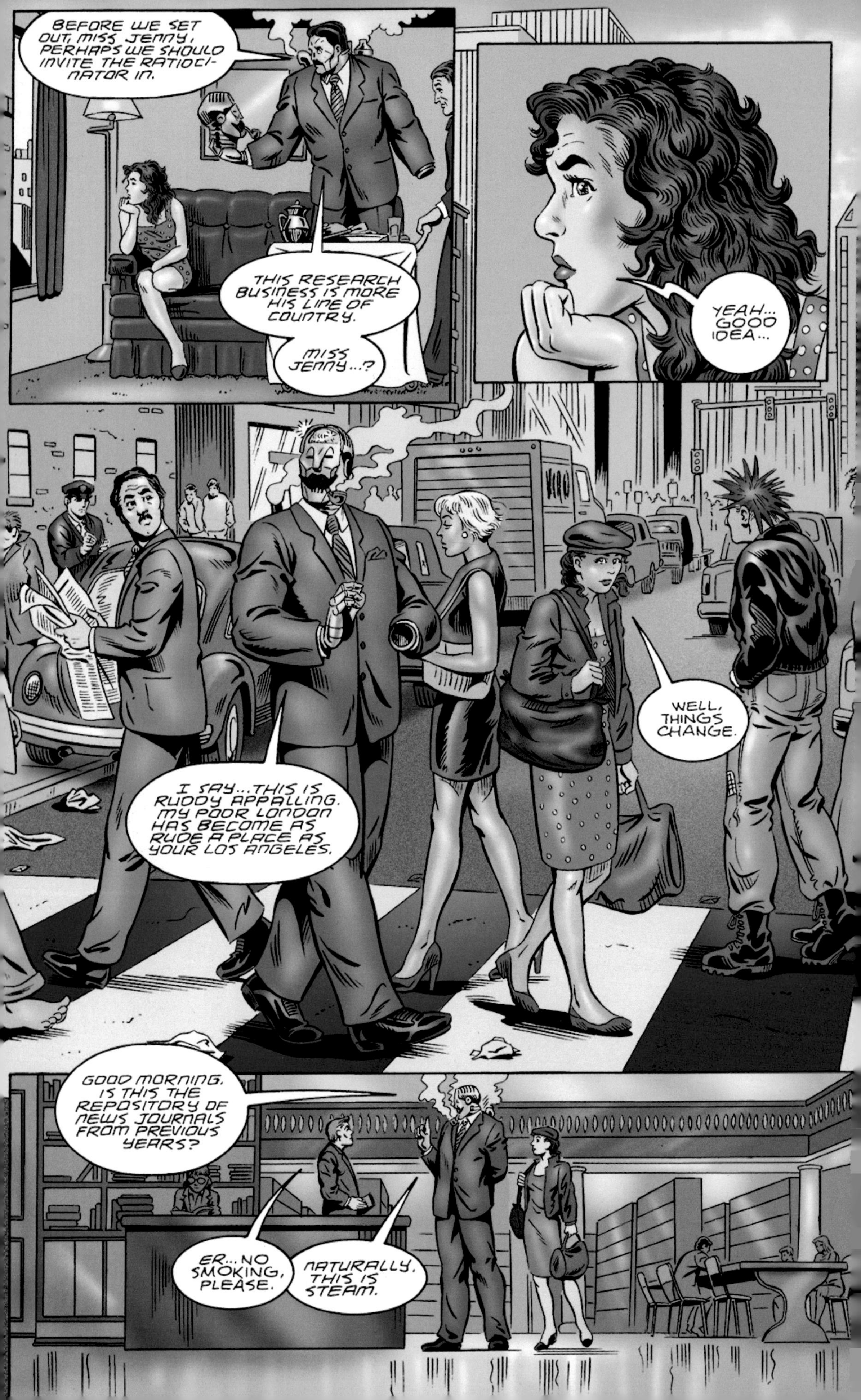
BEFORE WE SET OUT, MISS JENNY, PERHAPS WE SHOULD INVITE THE RATIOCI-NATOR IN.
THIS RESEARCH BUSINESS IS MORE HIS LINE OF COUNTRY.
MISS JENNY...?
YEAH... GOOD IDEA...
I SAY... THIS IS RUDDY APPALLING. MY POOR LONDON HAS BECOME AS RUDE A PLACE AS YOUR LOS ANGELES.
WELL, THINGS CHANGE.
GOOD MORNING. IS THIS THE REPOSITORY OF NEWS JOURNALS FROM PREVIOUS YEARS?
ER... NO SMOKING, PLEASE.
NATURALLY. THIS IS STEAM.

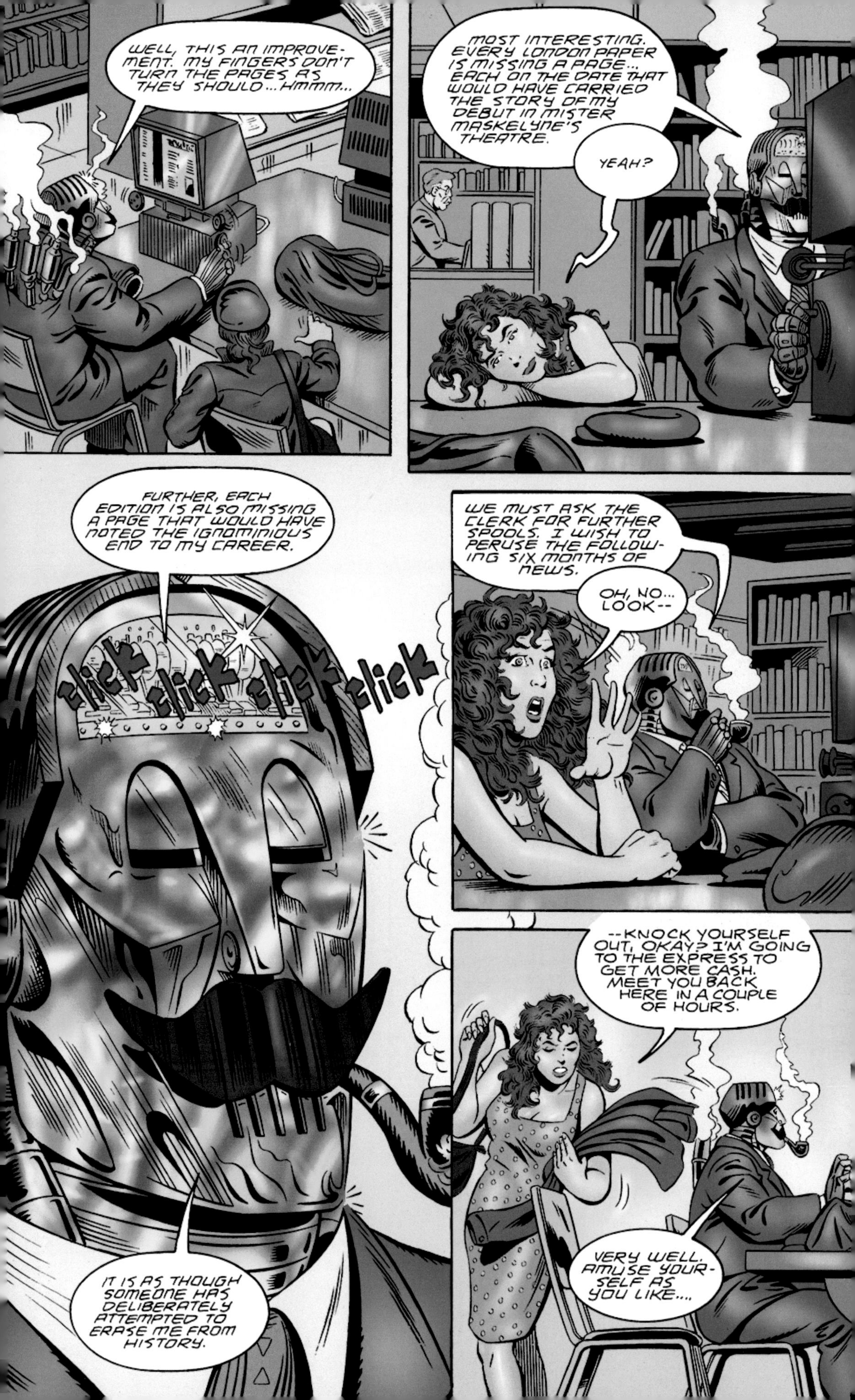
WELL, THIS AN IMPROVEMENT. MY FINGERS DON'T TURN THE PAGES AS THEY SHOULD... HMMM...
MOST INTERESTING. EVERY LONDON PAPER IS MISSING A PAGE... EACH ON THE DATE THAT WOULD HAVE CARRIED THE STORY OF MY DEBUT IN MISTER MASKELYNE'S THEATRE.
YEAH?
FURTHER, EACH EDITION IS ALSO MISSING A PAGE THAT WOULD HAVE NOTED THE IGNOMINIOUS END TO MY CAREER.
click click click click
IT IS AS THOUGH SOMEONE HAS DELIBERATELY ATTEMPTED TO ERASE ME FROM HISTORY.
WE MUST ASK THE CLERK FOR FURTHER SPOOLS. I WISH TO PERUSE THE FOLLOWING SIX MONTHS OF NEWS.
OH, NO... LOOK--
--KNOCK YOURSELF OUT, OKAY? I'M GOING TO THE EXPRESS TO GET MORE CASH. MEET YOU BACK HERE IN A COUPLE OF HOURS.
VERY WELL. AMUSE YOURSELF AS YOU LIKE....

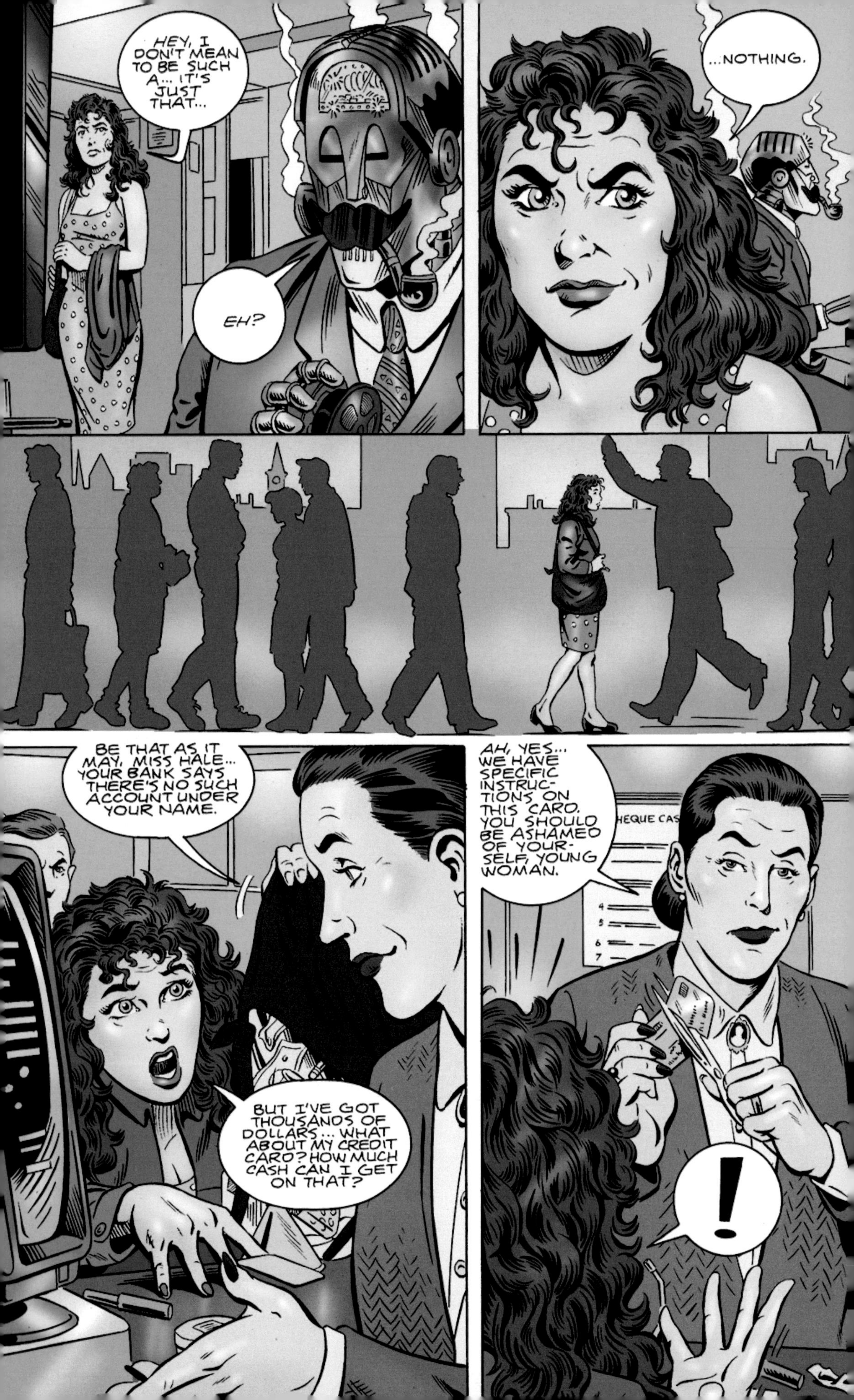
HEY, I DON'T MEAN TO BE SUCH A... IT'S JUST THAT...
EH?
...NOTHING.
BE THAT AS IT MAY, MISS HALE... YOUR BANK SAYS THERE'S NO SUCH ACCOUNT UNDER YOUR NAME.
BUT I'VE GOT THOUSANDS OF DOLLARS... WHAT ABOUT MY CREDIT CARD? HOW MUCH CASH CAN I GET ON THAT?
AH, YES... WE HAVE SPECIFIC INSTRUCTIONS ON THIS CARD. YOU SHOULD BE ASHAMED OF YOURSELF, YOUNG WOMAN.
!

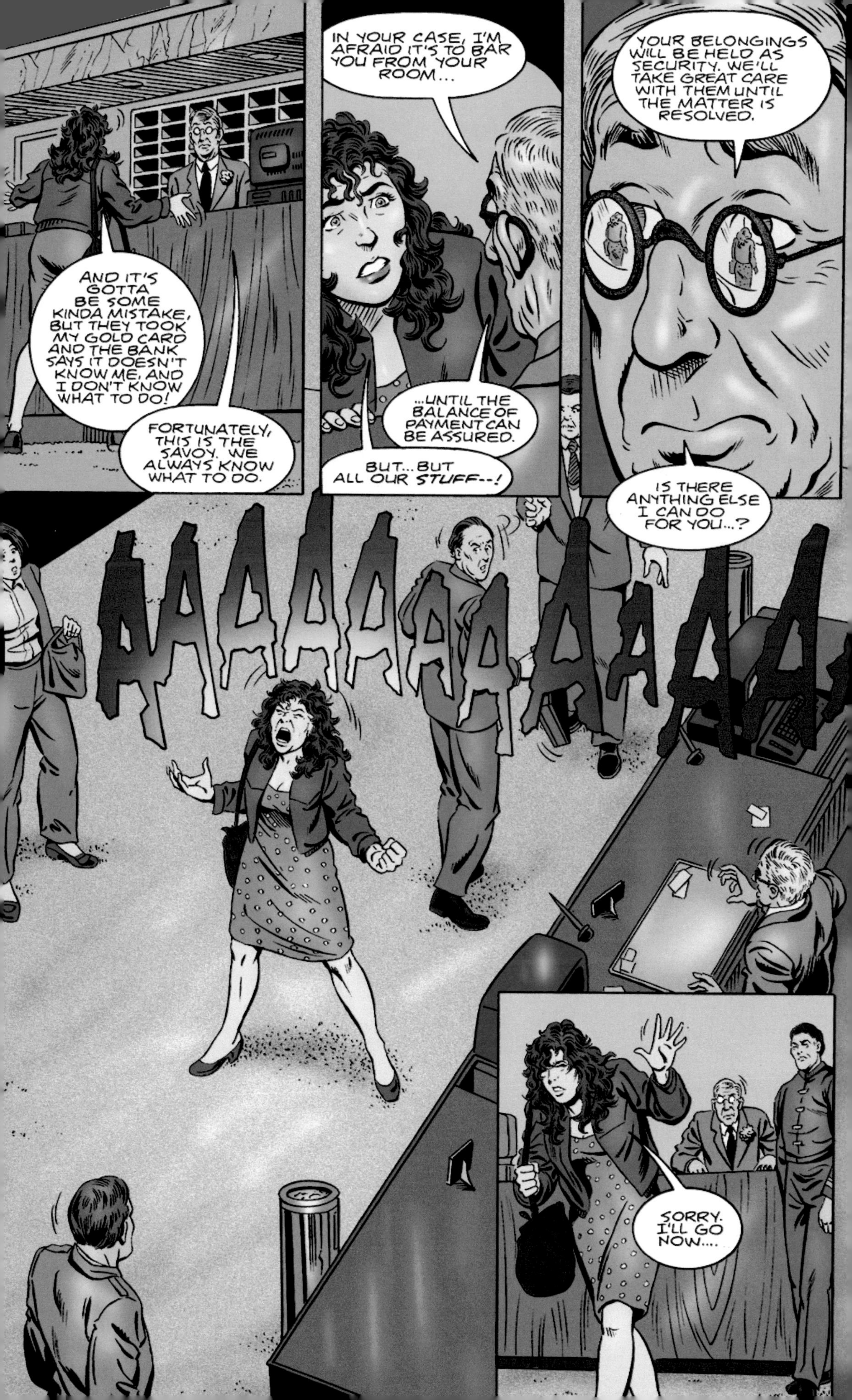
AND IT'S GOTTA BE SOME KINDA MISTAKE, BUT THEY TOOK MY GOLD CARD AND THE BANK SAYS IT DOESN'T KNOW ME, AND I DON'T KNOW WHAT TO DO!
FORTUNATELY, THIS IS THE SAVOY. WE ALWAYS KNOW WHAT TO DO.
IN YOUR CASE, I'M AFRAID IT'S TO BAR YOU FROM YOUR ROOM...
...UNTIL THE BALANCE OF PAYMENT CAN BE ASSURED.
BUT...BUT ALL OUR STUFF--!
YOUR BELONGINGS WILL BE HELD AS SECURITY. WE'LL TAKE GREAT CARE WITH THEM UNTIL THE MATTER IS RESOLVED.
IS THERE ANYTHING ELSE I CAN DO FOR YOU...?
AAAAAAAAAAAA
SORRY. I'LL GO NOW....

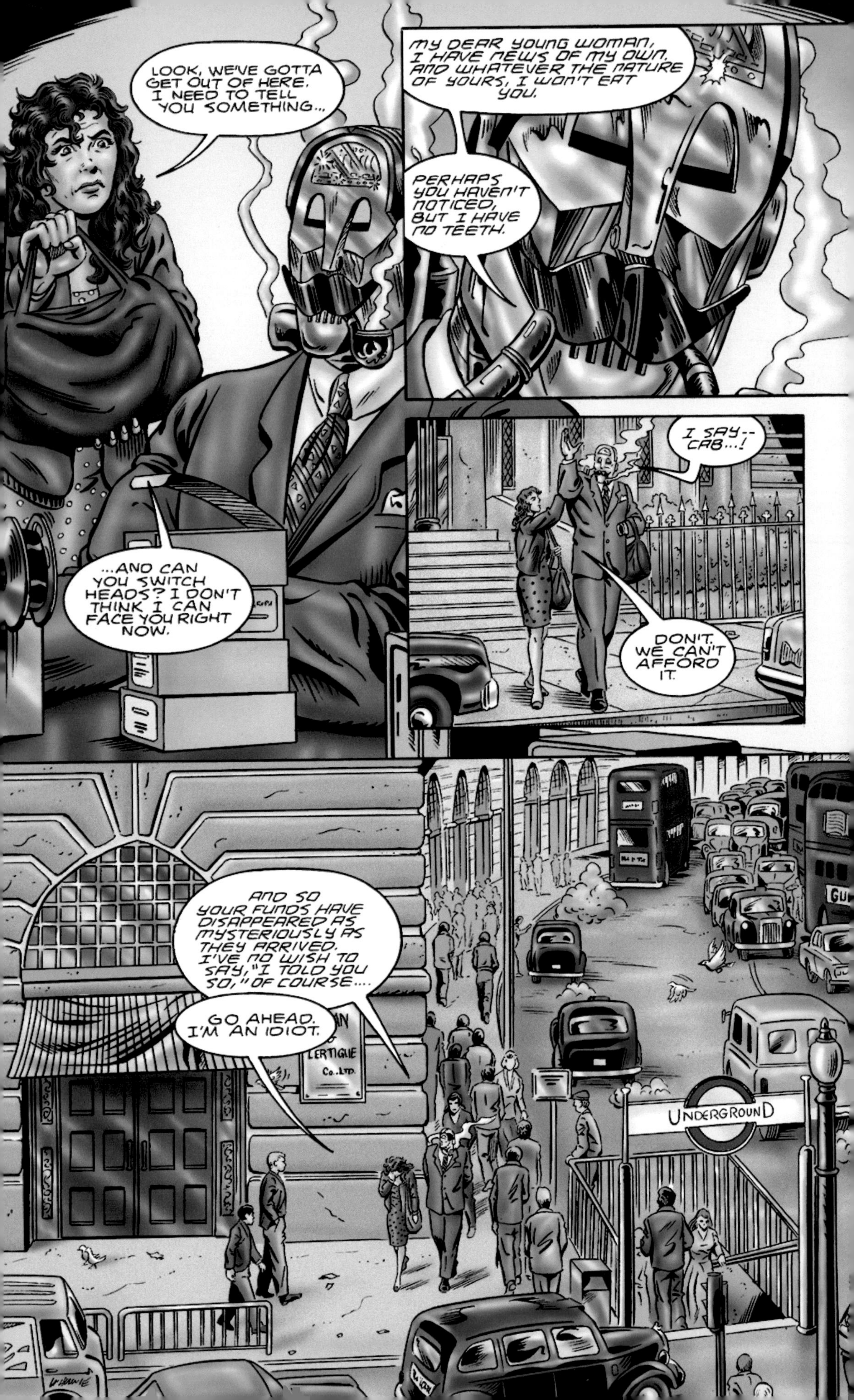
LOOK, WE'VE GOTTA GET OUT OF HERE. I NEED TO TELL YOU SOMETHING...
MY DEAR YOUNG WOMAN, I HAVE NEWS OF MY OWN. AND WHATEVER THE NATURE OF YOURS, I WON'T EAT YOU.
PERHAPS YOU HAVEN'T NOTICED, BUT I HAVE NO TEETH.
...AND CAN YOU SWITCH HEADS? I DON'T THINK I CAN FACE YOU RIGHT NOW.
I SAY--CAB...!
DON'T. WE CAN'T AFFORD IT.
AND SO YOUR FUNDS HAVE DISAPPEARED AS MYSTERIOUSLY AS THEY ARRIVED. I'VE NO WISH TO SAY, "I TOLD YOU SO," OF COURSE....
GO AHEAD. I'M AN IDIOT.
UNDERGROUND

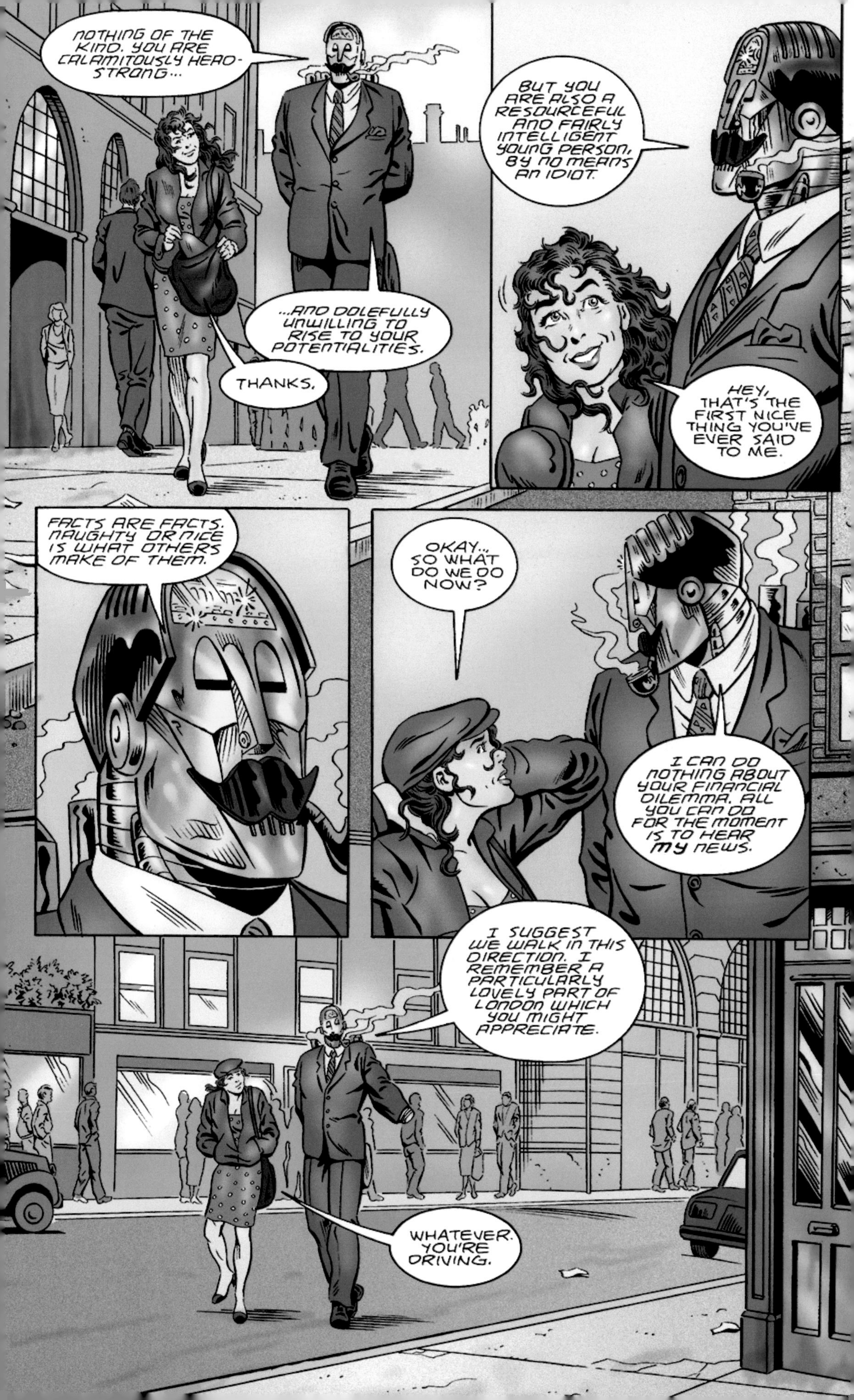
NOTHING OF THE KIND. YOU ARE CALAMITOUSLY HERO-STRONG...
...AND DOLEFULLY UNWILLING TO RISE TO YOUR POTENTIALITIES.
THANKS.
BUT YOU ARE ALSO A RESOURCEFUL AND FAIRLY INTELLIGENT YOUNG PERSON, BY NO MEANS AN IDIOT.
HEY, THAT'S THE FIRST NICE THING YOU'VE EVER SAID TO ME.
FACTS ARE FACTS. NAUGHTY OR NICE IS WHAT OTHERS MAKE OF THEM.
OKAY... SO WHAT DO WE DO NOW?
I CAN DO NOTHING ABOUT YOUR FINANCIAL DILEMMA. ALL YOU CAN DO FOR THE MOMENT IS TO HEAR MY NEWS.
I SUGGEST WE WALK IN THIS DIRECTION. I REMEMBER A PARTICULARLY LOVELY PART OF LONDON WHICH YOU MIGHT APPRECIATE.
WHATEVER. YOU'RE DRIVING.

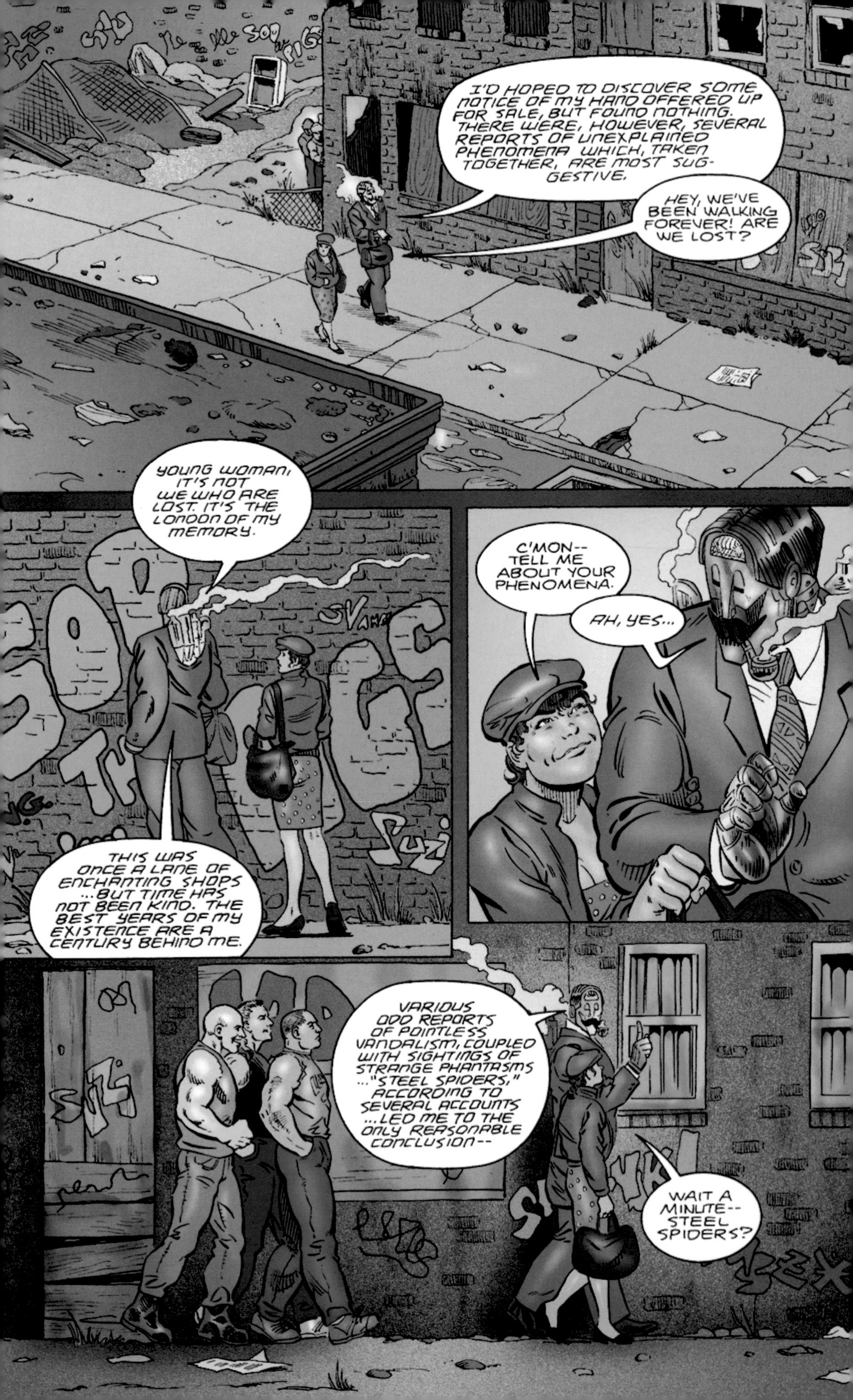
I'D HOPED TO DISCOVER SOME NOTICE OF MY HAND OFFERED UP FOR SALE, BUT FOUND NOTHING. THERE WERE, HOWEVER, SEVERAL REPORTS OF UNEXPLAINED PHENOMENA WHICH, TAKEN TOGETHER, ARE MOST SUG-GESTIVE.
HEY, WE'VE BEEN WALKING FOREVER! ARE WE LOST?
YOUNG WOMAN, IT'S NOT WE WHO ARE LOST. IT'S THE LONDON OF MY MEMORY.
THIS WAS ONCE A LANE OF ENCHANTING SHOPS ...BUT TIME HAS NOT BEEN KIND. THE BEST YEARS OF MY EXISTENCE ARE A CENTURY BEHIND ME.
C'MON-- TELL ME ABOUT YOUR PHENOMENA.
AH, YES...
VARIOUS ODD REPORTS OF POINTLESS VANDALISM, COUPLED WITH SIGHTINGS OF STRANGE PHANTASMS ..."STEEL SPIDERS," ACCORDING TO SEVERAL ACCOUNTS ...LED ME TO THE ONLY REASONABLE CONCLUSION--
WAIT A MINUTE-- STEEL SPIDERS?

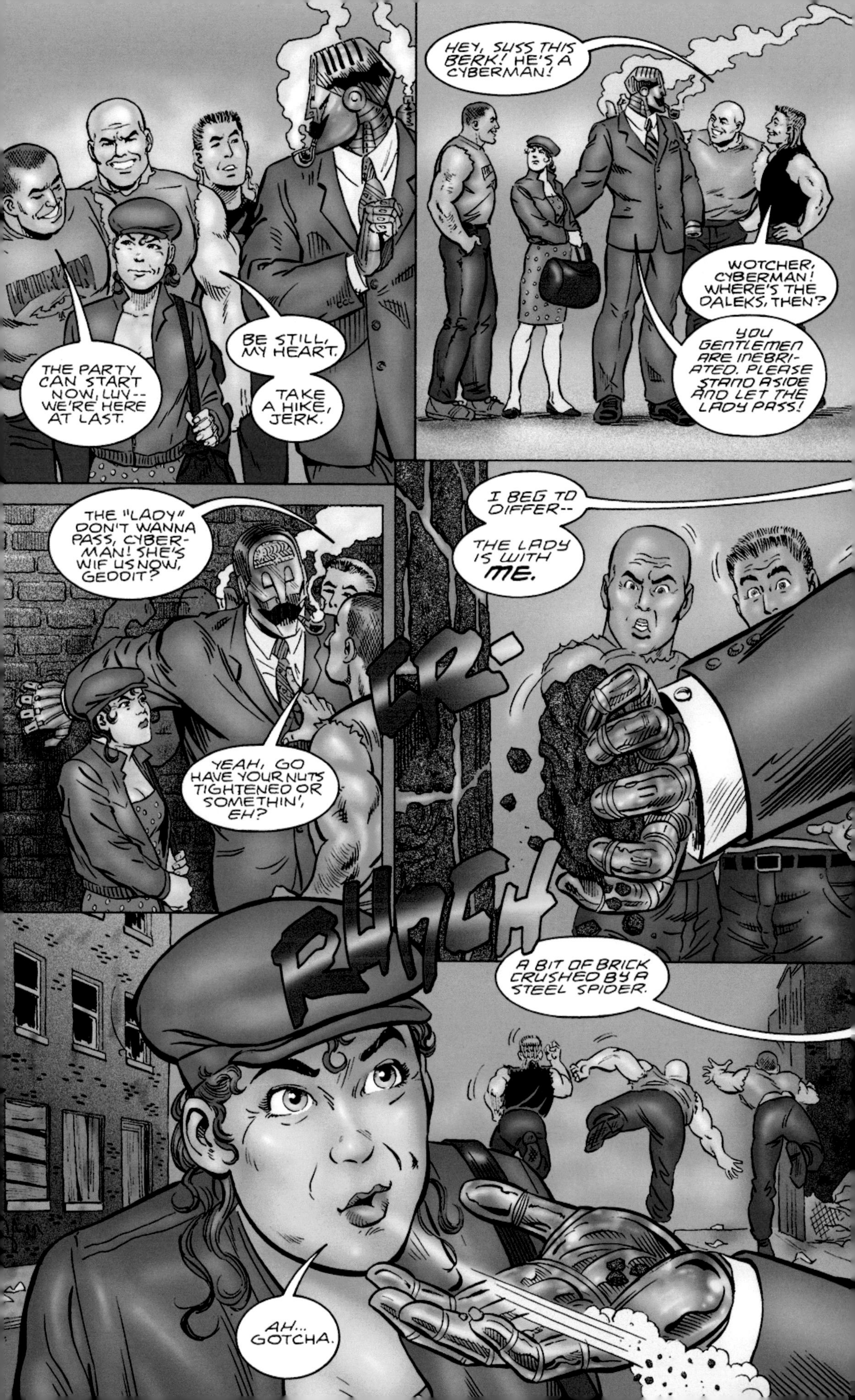
THE PARTY CAN START NOW, LUV-- WE'RE HERE AT LAST.
BE STILL, MY HEART.
TAKE A HIKE, JERK.
HEY, SUSS THIS BERK! HE'S A CYBERMAN!
WOTCHER, CYBERMAN! WHERE'S THE DALEKS, THEN?
YOU GENTLEMEN ARE INEBRI-ATED. PLEASE STAND ASIDE AND LET THE LADY PASS!
THE "LADY" DON'T WANNA PASS, CYBER-MAN! SHE'S WIF US NOW, GEDDIT?
YEAH, GO HAVE YOUR NUTS TIGHTENED OR SOMETHIN', EH?
I BEG TO DIFFER--
THE LADY IS WITH ME.
CR-RUNCH
A BIT OF BRICK CRUSHED BY A STEEL SPIDER.
AH... GOTCHA.

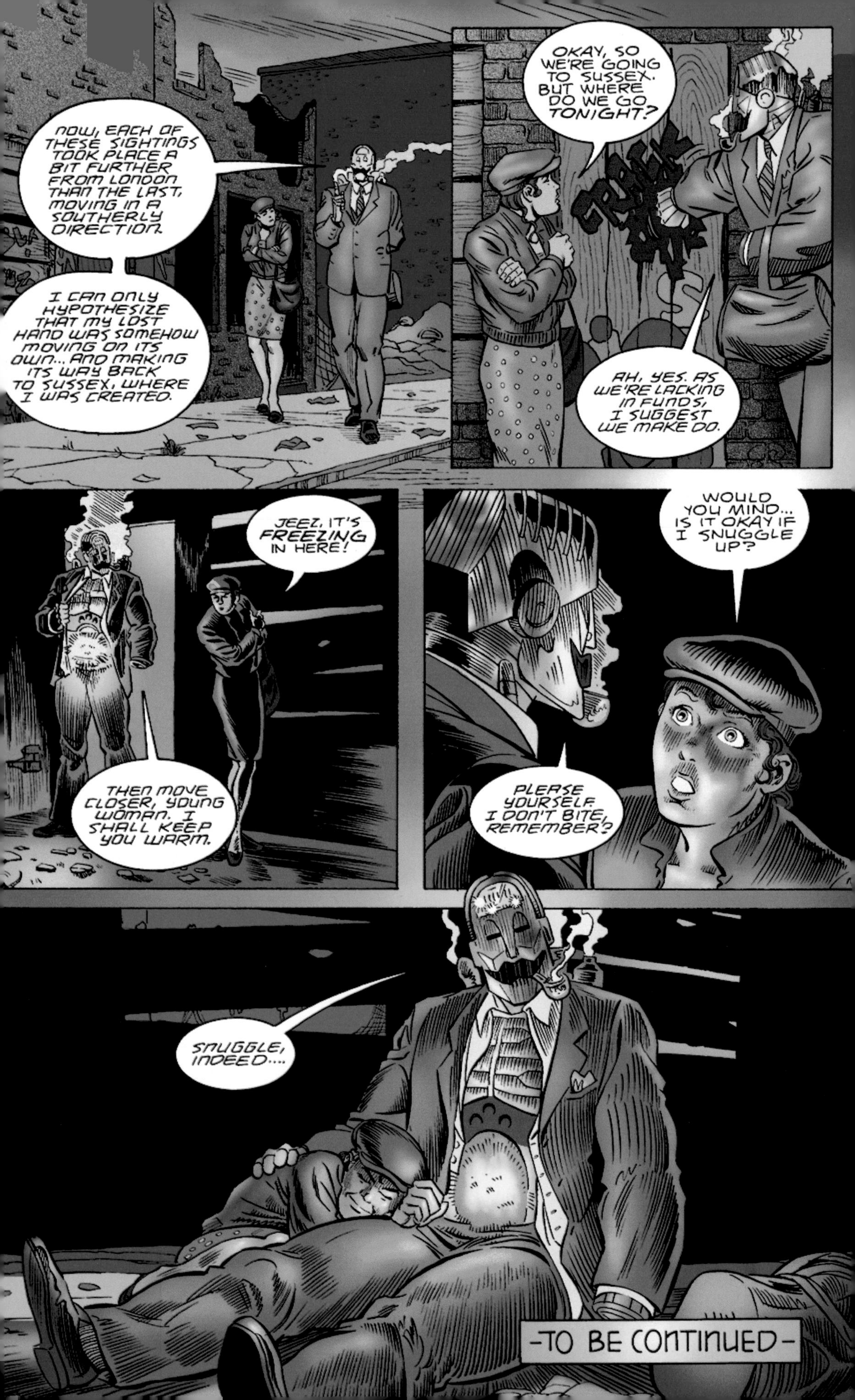
NOW, EACH OF THESE SIGHTINGS TOOK PLACE A BIT FURTHER FROM LONDON THAN THE LAST, MOVING IN A SOUTHERLY DIRECTION.
I CAN ONLY HYPOTHESIZE THAT MY LOST HAND WAS SOMEHOW MOVING ON ITS OWN... AND MAKING ITS WAY BACK TO SUSSEX, WHERE I WAS CREATED.
OKAY, SO WE'RE GOING TO SUSSEX. BUT WHERE DO WE GO TONIGHT?
CRAAK
AH, YES. AS WE'RE LACKING IN FUNDS, I SUGGEST WE MAKE DO.
JEEZ, IT'S FREEZING IN HERE!
THEN MOVE CLOSER, YOUNG WOMAN. I SHALL KEEP YOU WARM.
WOULD YOU MIND... IS IT OKAY IF I SNUGGLE UP?
PLEASE YOURSELF. I DON'T BITE, REMEMBER?
SNUGGLE, INDEED....
-TO BE CONTINUED-

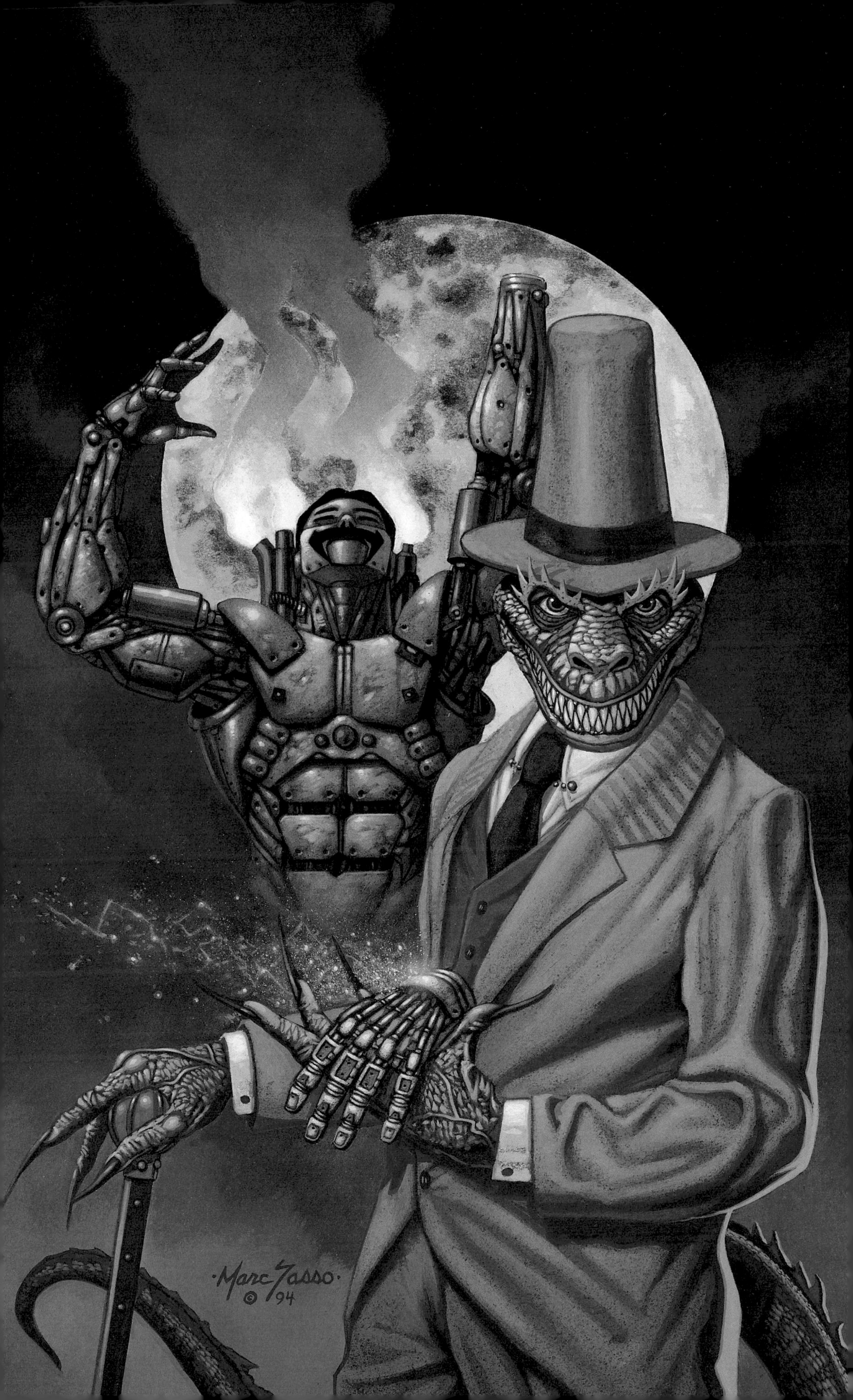

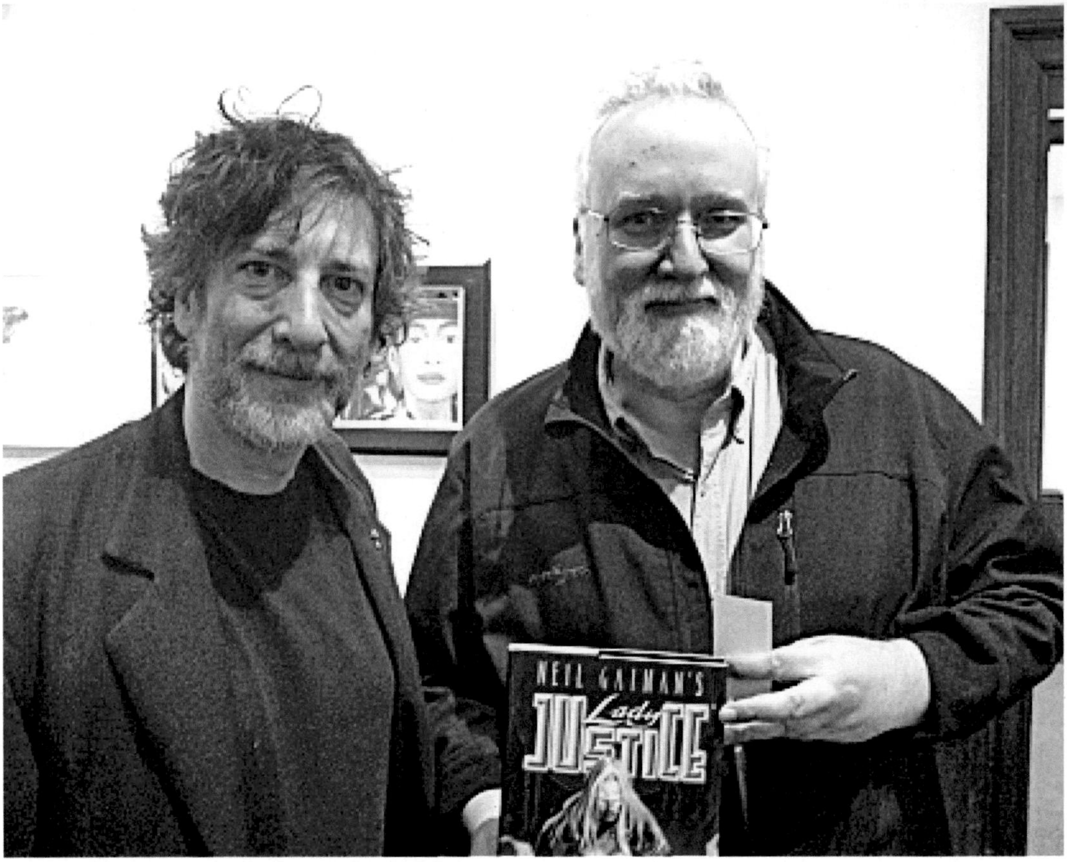
NEIL GAIMAN'S
Lady
JUSTICE

Neil Gaiman and Jim Salicrup, holding a copy of NEIL GAIMAN'S LADY JUSTICE Volume One.

THE TEKNO FILES

An Afterword by Jim Salicrup

Back in the mid 90s, the co-founders of the Sci-Fi Channel (now the SyFy Channel), Mitchell Rubenstein and Laurie Silvers, launched an exciting new comics company called Tekno•Comix. The premise was a simple one—have some of the literary luminaries, such as Isaac Asimov, John Jakes, Mickey Spillane, and SF media stars, such as Gene Roddenberry and Leonard Nimoy, that they worked with at the Sci-Fi channel, create new concepts for the line of comics, and then hire top talent to bring those concepts to life. One of the talented creators they contacted was Neil Gaiman. Unlike others that created concepts for Tekno•Comix, Neil created several series ideas—Lady Justice, Teknophage, and Mr. Hero. In the first issue of NEIL GAIMAN'S MR. HERO THE NEWMATIC MAN, there was an interview with Neil, in which he reveals some of the hows and whys of how he became involved with Tekno•Comix...

Tekno•Comix: With your background in writing comic-books and novels, what will you draw from in your work with Tekno•Comix?

Neil Gaiman: Well, one of the things that initially attracted me to Tekno•Comix was the idea of having a blank slate; a clean piece of paper. I normally don't get asked, could I just make something up. I love the idea of just sitting down and making up characters. Here's a character, this is the kind of stories they fit into, this is the world, go and have fun with it. I got completely carried away.

I was only asked to come up with one, and I wound up coming up with five completely distinct characters, each from their own different scenario. There's one vaguely super-heroish character; one Victorian robot; a strange and mysterious force for good, and a thing called Lady Justice, which is an entity which when the forces of normal justice fail, possesses a woman somewhere and makes her put on a blindfold and go off and correct whatever it was.

The problem with being a writer, anyway, is that you have too many ideas. People say, "Where do you get your ideas?" That's never the problem. The problem is always which of these fifteen ideas do you use. I love the opportunity to be able to say, "Okay, here. Here's five people. Go and have fun with them."

T•C: What intrigued you most about this new state-of-the-art technology?

NG: I think that the future is changing rapidly. Comics are a terrific medium. I love the idea that you will be able to download comics over your TV set. I have no idea whether you will or not, but it's a lovely idea. And everyone knows that the future is not only going to be stranger than we imagined, but it's going to be stranger than we can imagine.

T•C: Will you develop characters any differently knowing they might appear in these other media?

NG: Since Tekno•Comix plans to take characters into all media, including TV and everything else, one of the rules I set for myself when I sat down and created the characters was that I was going to create cheap TV.

Comics have an unlimited special effects budget. Anything you can do on the paper, you have. In turning something into other media, it can be a little more problematic. So I decided to do things that could easily be turned into TV or computer games.

T•C: Do you think you're establishing a roadway for other authors to follow?

NG: I hope so. Jack Kirby, who was the greatest artist and easily the most influential figure in comics in the last fifty years, died several months ago. Although in his final years he was fairly well looked after, Kirby was screwed by every publisher he had worked for. This is the man who created *The Fantastic Four, Captain America, The Hulk, The Demon.* He created all these characters. He never owned them. He was never recompensed for them. He was recompensed because he got to draw them for a while, then leave them to do other stuff.

One of the things that I like about Tekno•Comix is their attitude that the creators have a share of the creation. That's a very up-front thing. The whole offer is exciting, attractive, interesting, and hopefully precedes new things. It would be very sad to think that the next Kirby would be as badly screwed as the last one.

Tekno•Comix had many brilliant ideas, but unfortunately they also had bad timing. After the early boom in the comics business in the early 90s, the mid 90s is when the bust came, and Tekno•Comix was one of many new comics publishers that was forced to suspend their publishing operations. As a result, most of the comics created by Neil Gaiman have never been collected before. And that's where Super Genius enters the picture.

In 2005, pioneering graphic novel publisher Terry Nantier, and I (a long-time comics editor) co-founded Papercutz, a comics company dedicated to publishing graphic novels for all ages. In late 2014 we launched a new imprint, modestly called "Super Genius" to offer material for older audiences, specifically the folks who frequent comic shops.

And that brings us back to Neil Gaiman. While Neil was certainly a comicbook star in the mid 90s, he's since become a major award-winning, best-selling author, and all around media super-star. There are now legions of Neil Gaiman fans who are completely unaware that he created these characters, and Super Genius is thrilled and honored to bring this work to an all-new audience.

Already in print from Super Genius are the first volumes of NEIL GAIMAN'S LADY JUSTICE and NEIL GAIMAN'S TEKNOPHAGE. If you haven't picked up either of these books yet, may I suggest picking up TEKNOPHAGE first? That's because it includes NEIL GAIMAN'S WHEEL OF WORLDS, in a story co-plotted by Neil Gaiman, it reveals the set-up of the Neil Gaiman Tekno•Comix universe, and features Lady Justice, Adam Cain, Teknophage, and Mr. Hero.

On the following pages are a look inside the creative process—first the *Compendium of Nearly-Lost Lore*, which includes character design sketches from artists, as well as Neil Gaiman, for MR. HERO as well as for Teknophage, Adam Cain, and Lady Justice. That's followed by character model sheets and notes.

With this volume of MR. HERO, we're halfway to our goal of collecting all of the Neil Gaiman characters created for Tekno•Comix. We'll soon be publishing the second volumes for Lady Justice, Tecknophage, and Mr. Hero, and finally all of these comics will be back in print for everyone to enjoy.

Thanks,

Jim Salicrup

Jim Salicrup
Editor-in-Chief
Super Genius

Compendium of Nearly-Lost Lore

Being a FOLIO of Sketches, Blueprints, and Visual Records of the Friends, Fiends, and Unwilling Foodstuffs which inhabit the Planes of Existence adjoining the WHEEL of WORLDS.

Humble Scrivener: L. M. Bogad   *Computer Craftsman: Z. Lynch*

A Brief History of Newmatic Development

It's a great vat of soul-stuff, and a legion of talented craftsmen, that go into the making of a true Hero. Only the Scaly One in the suit and the suite could order such a Capital Investment.

And so it was, by weighty decree of Mr. Henry Phage, that these artisans toiled long and hard in their grand employer's works, greasing the gears with their sweat and feeding the forges with their frenzied labors, racing to arrive upon an optimal design for the Mr. Hero Mercurius Unit...

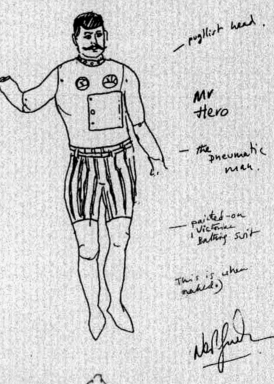

— pugilist head.

MR Hero

— the pneumatic man.

— painted-on Victorian bathing suit

This is when naked.)

Master Creator **Neil Gaiman** laid the groundwork for the Teknophage's steam-powered automaton with these sketches.

steam

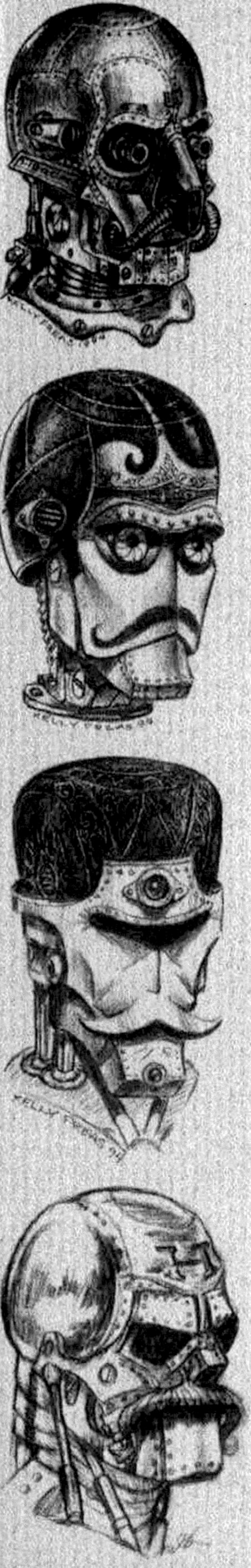

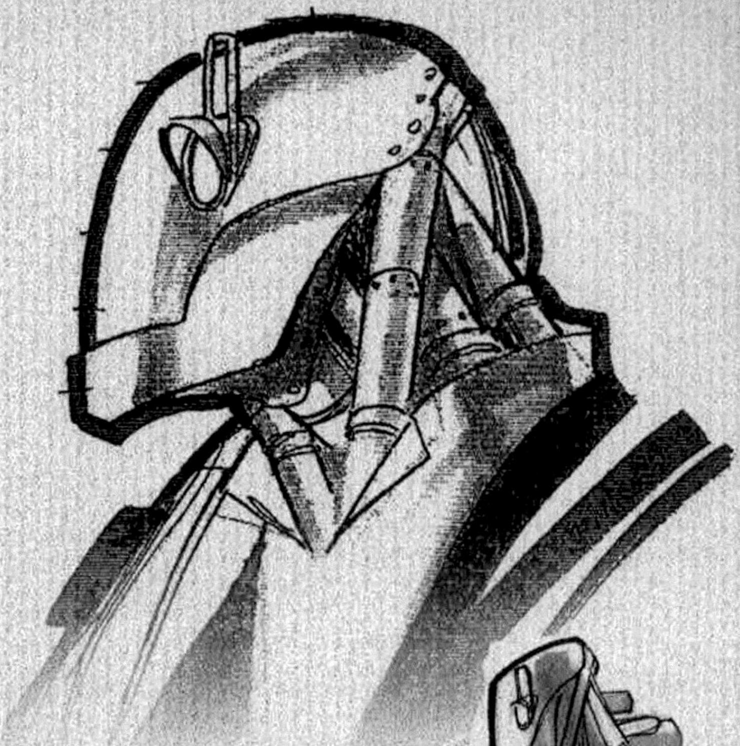

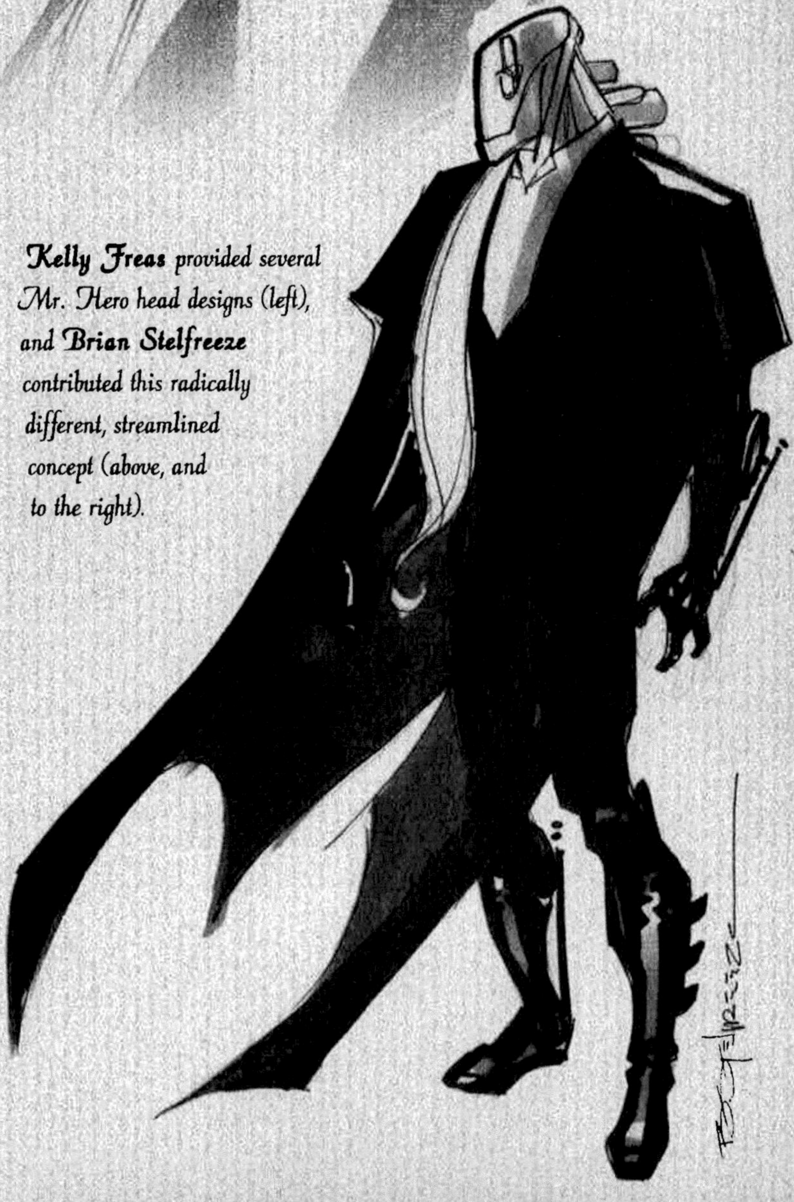

Kelly Freas provided several *Mr. Hero* head designs (left), and **Brian Stelfreeze** contributed this radically different, streamlined concept (above, and to the right).

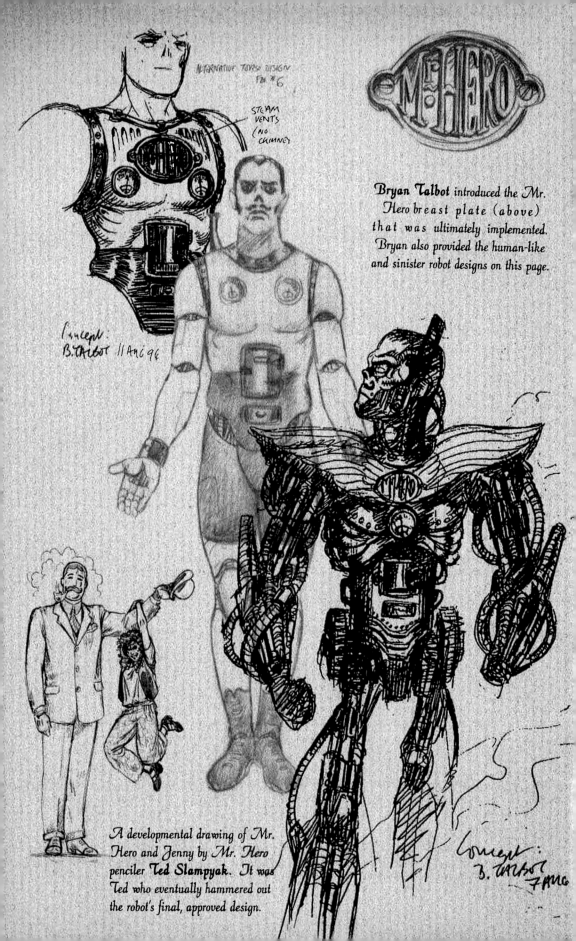

ALTERNATIVE TOYS DESIGN
FOR #6

STEAM VENTS (NO CHIMNEY)

Mr Hero

Concept:
B. Talbot 11 Aug 96

Bryan Talbot introduced the Mr. Hero breast plate (above) that was ultimately implemented. Bryan also provided the human-like and sinister robot designs on this page.

Concept:
B. Talbot
7 Aug

A developmental drawing of Mr. Hero and Jenny by Mr. Hero penciler Ted Slampyak. It was Ted who eventually hammered out the robot's final, approved design.

The Phases of The Phage

Teknophage went through an arduous evolution of his own, long before he commissioned the construction of his clockwork warrior. A peerless predator's a long time in the making, and many are the forms the Beast took before he was perfected...

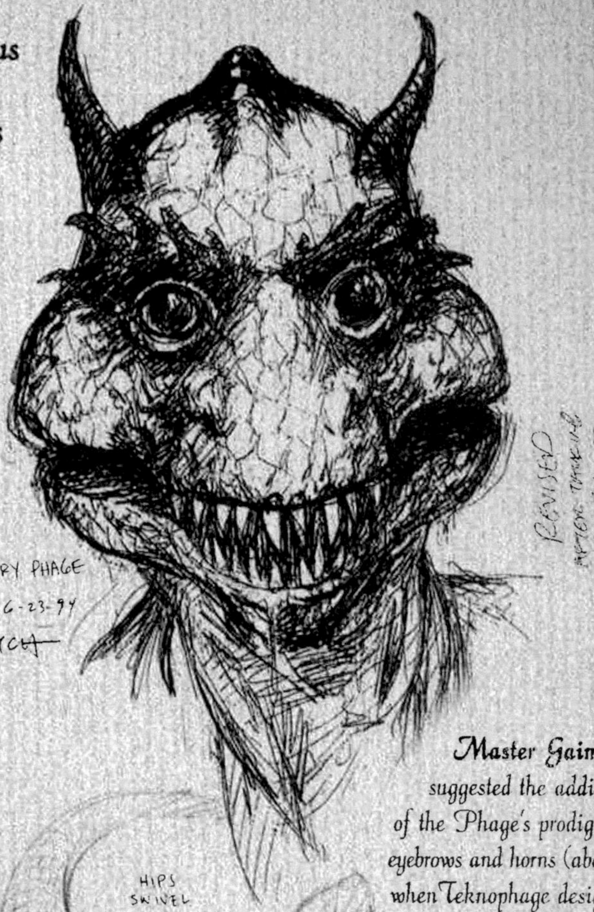
REVISED
AFTER TALKING TO NEIL —

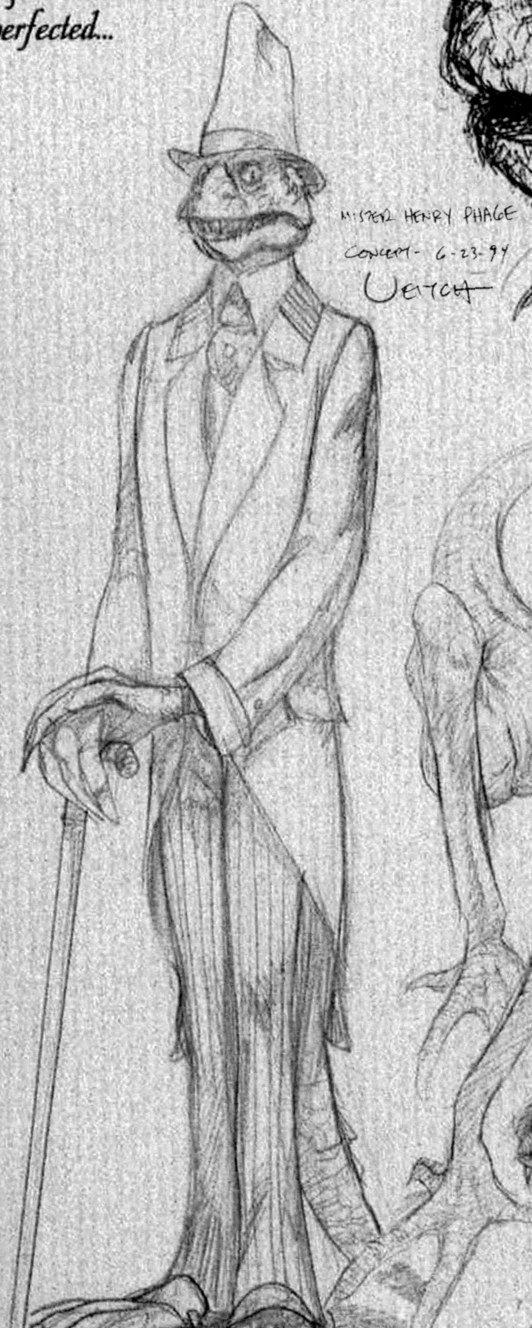
MISTER HENRY PHAGE
CONCEPT - 6-23-94
VEITCH

Master Gaiman suggested the addition of the Phage's prodigious eyebrows and horns (above), when Teknophage designer **Rick Veitch** was in the midst of his handiwork. The horns were eventually removed.

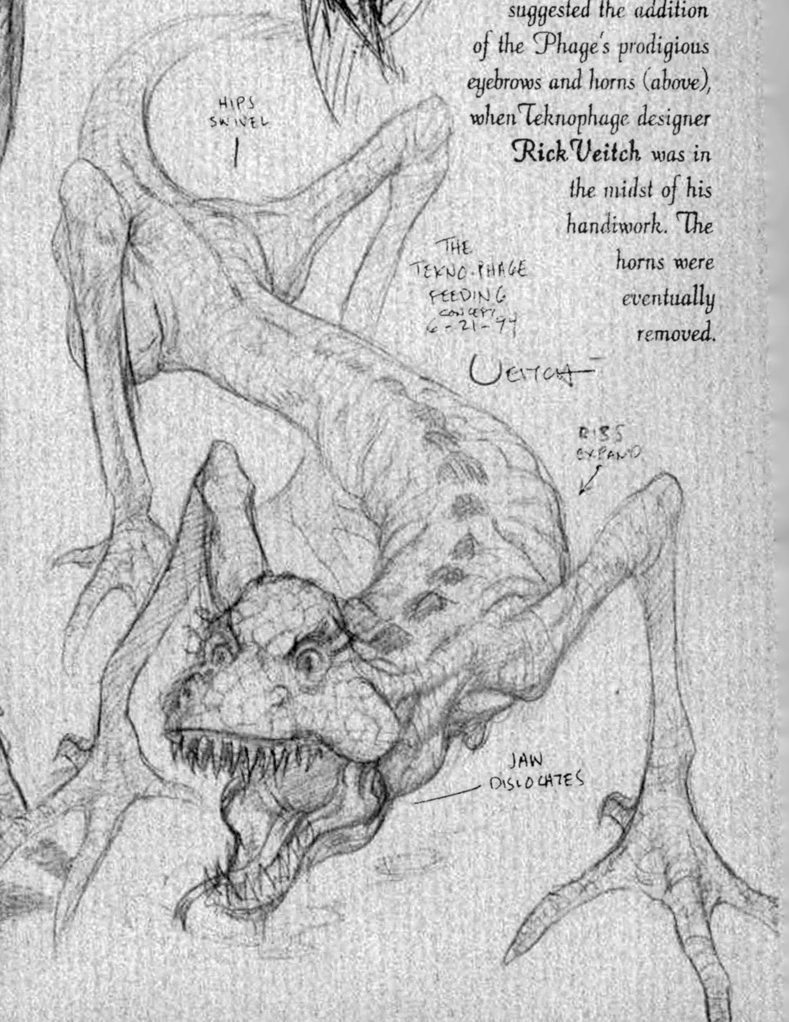
HIPS SWIVEL
THE TEKNO-PHAGE FEEDING CONCEPT 6-21-94
VEITCH
RIBS EXPAND
JAW DISLOCATES

At left are **Neil Gaiman's** initial Teknophage sketches. **Bryan Talbot** gave the Phage his hypnotic gaze and forbidding manner (below).

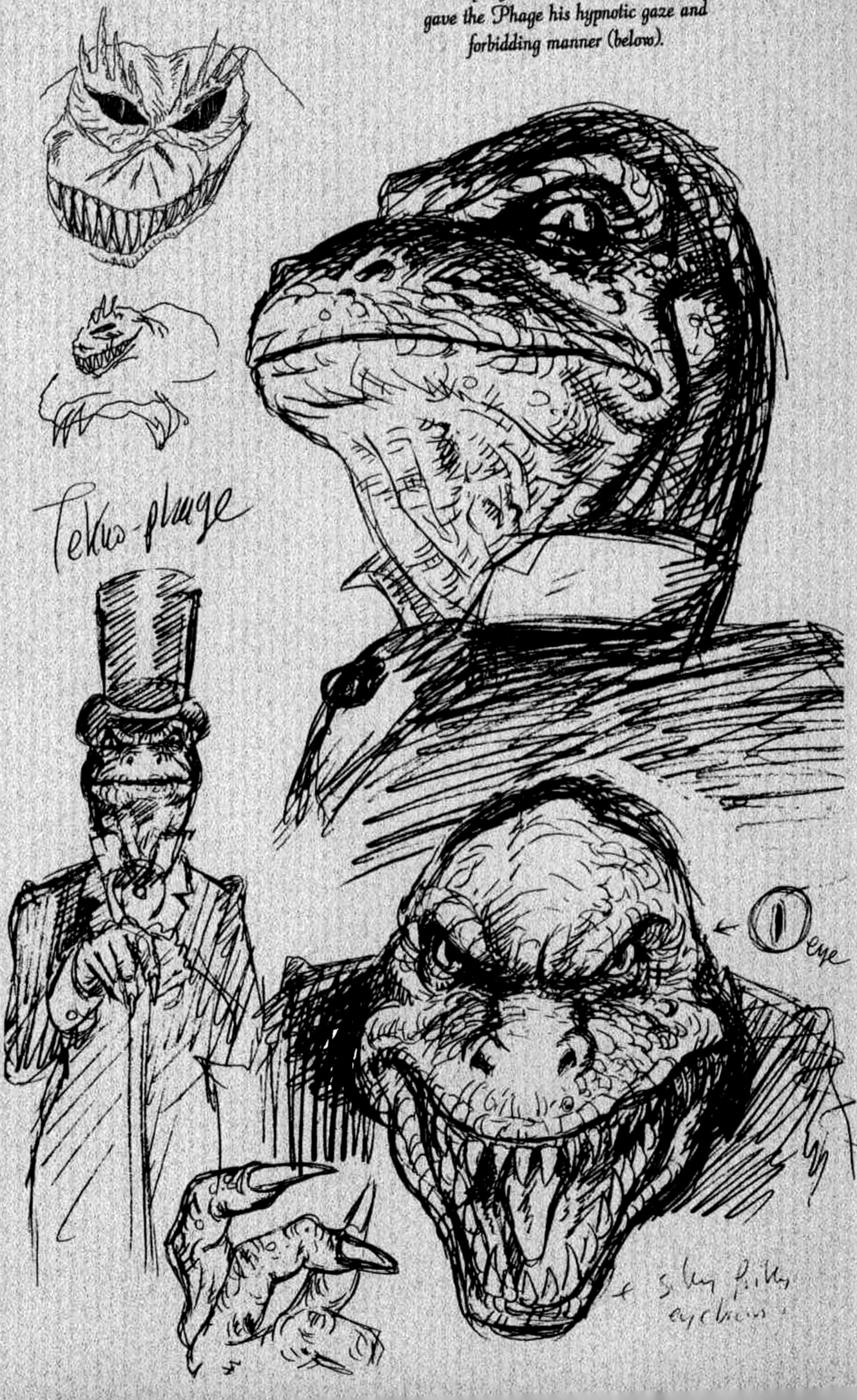

Tekno-phage
eye

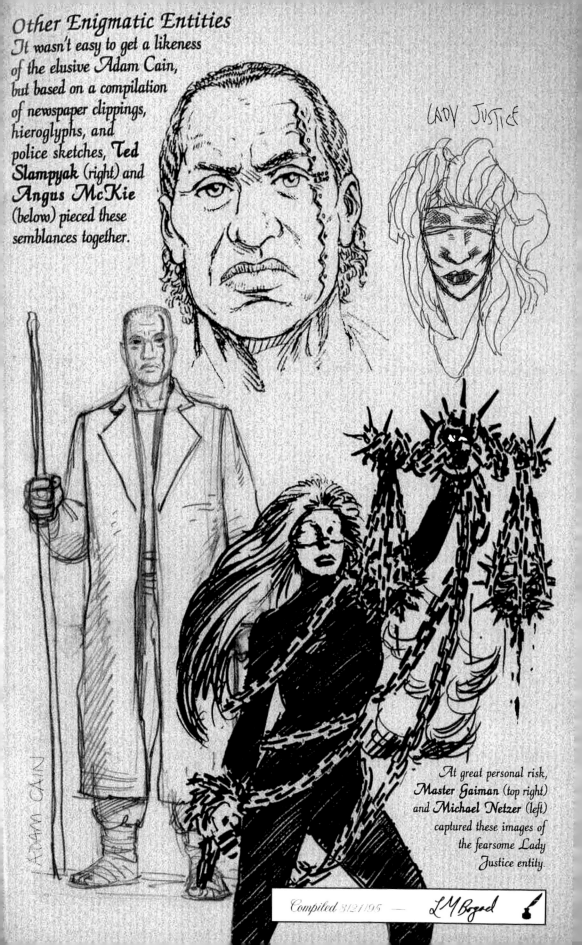

Other Enigmatic Entities

It wasn't easy to get a likeness of the elusive Adam Cain, but based on a compilation of newspaper clippings, hieroglyphs, and police sketches, **Ted Slampyak** (right) and **Angus McKie** (below) pieced these semblances together.

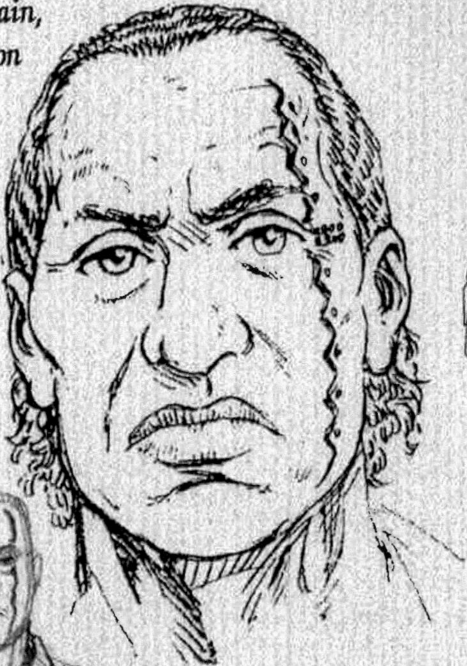

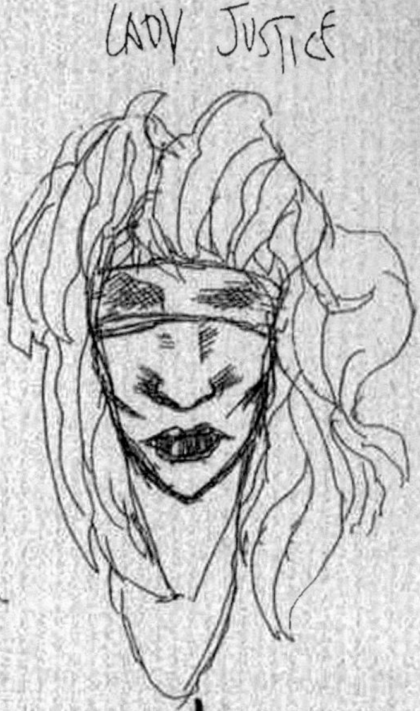
LADY JUSTICE

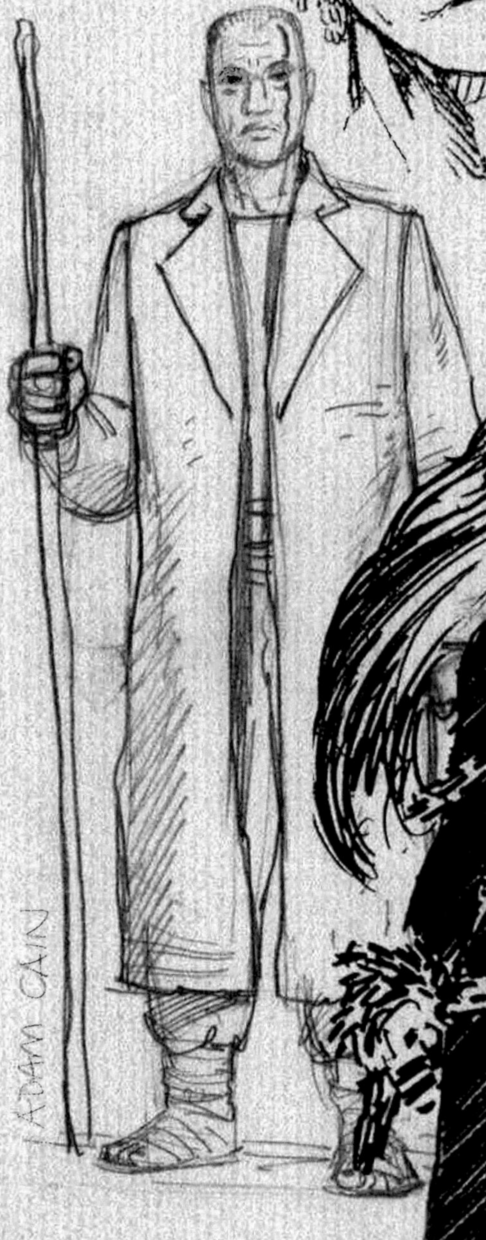
ADAM CAIN

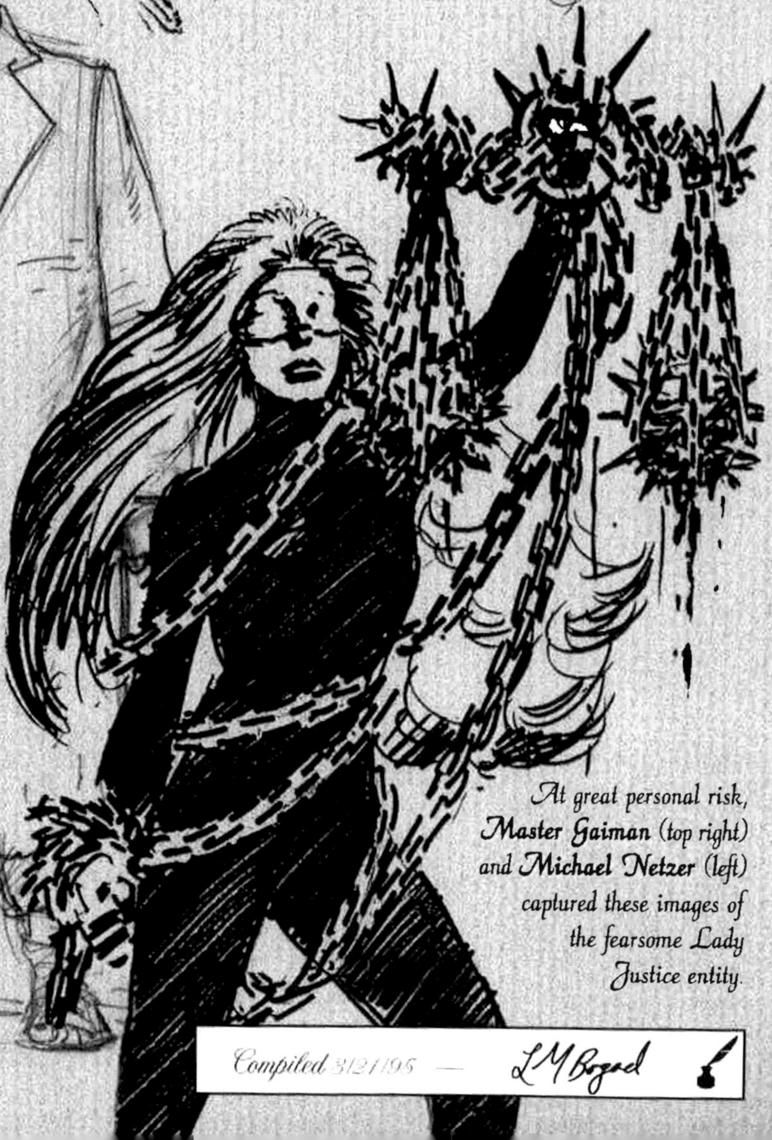

At great personal risk, **Master Gaiman** (top right) and **Michael Netzer** (left) captured these images of the fearsome Lady Justice entity.

Compiled 3/21/96 — L M Bogad

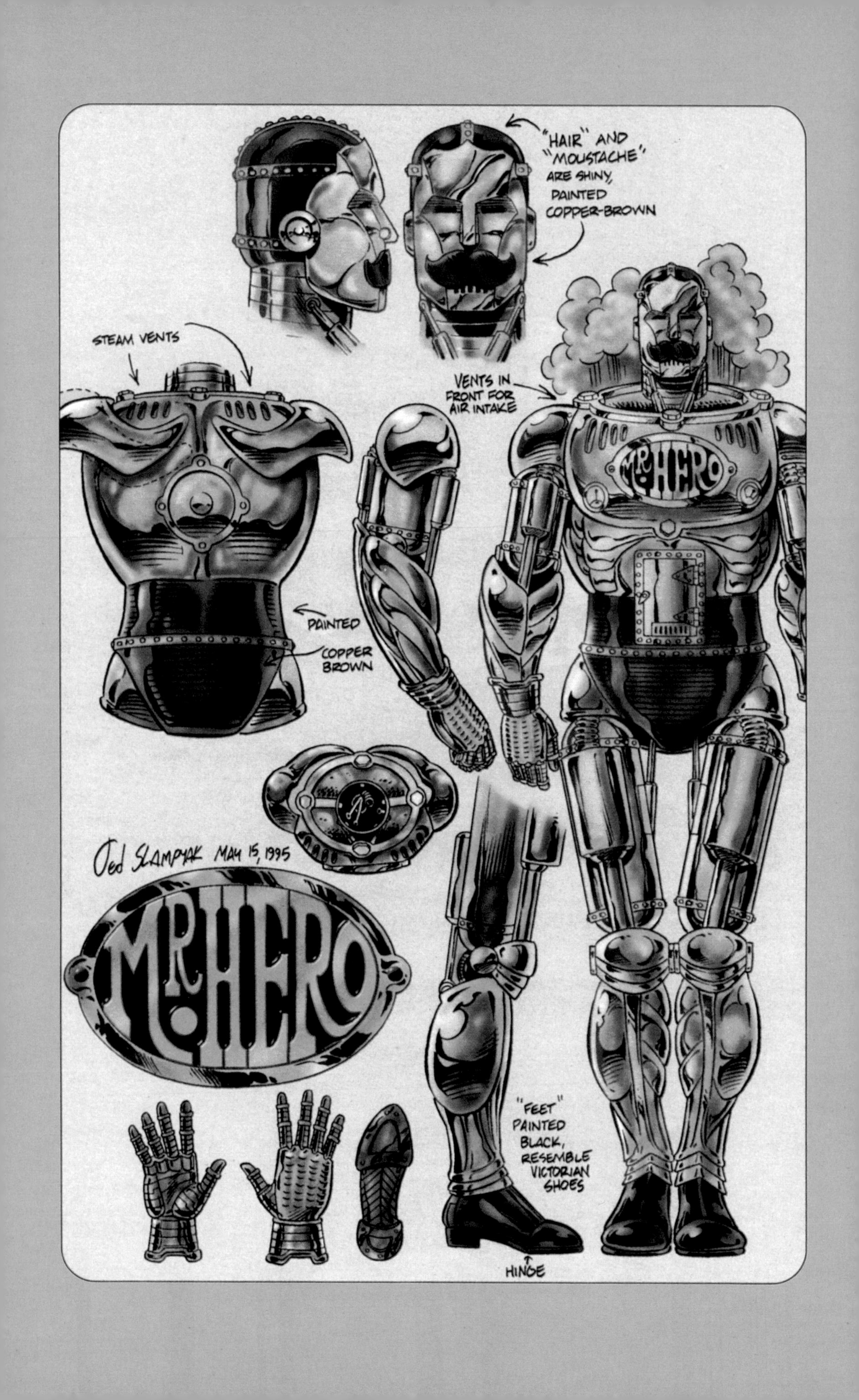
"HAIR" AND "MOUSTACHE" ARE SHINY, PAINTED COPPER-BROWN
STEAM VENTS
VENTS IN FRONT FOR AIR INTAKE
MR. HERO
PAINTED
COPPER BROWN
Ted Slampyak May 15, 1995
MR. HERO
"FEET" PAINTED BLACK, RESEMBLE VICTORIAN SHOES
HINGE

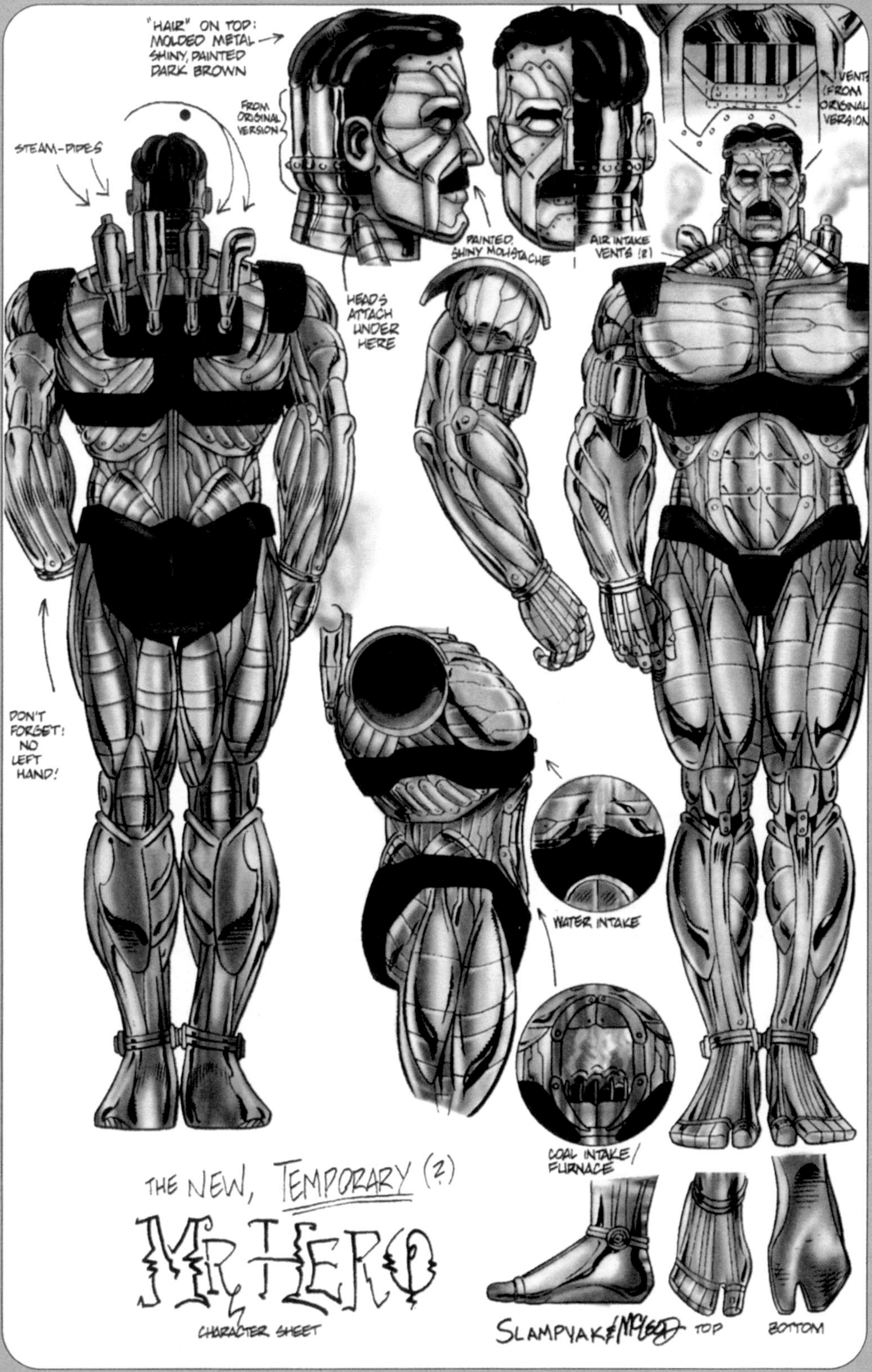

"HAIR" ON TOP: MOLDED METAL SHINY, PAINTED DARK BROWN
FROM ORIGINAL VERSION
STEAM-PIPES
PAINTED, SHINY MOUSTACHE
AIR INTAKE VENTS (2)
VENTS (FROM ORIGINAL VERSION)
HEADS ATTACH UNDER HERE
DON'T FORGET: NO LEFT HAND!
WATER INTAKE
COAL INTAKE/ FURNACE
THE NEW, TEMPORARY (?)
MR HERO
CHARACTER SHEET
SLAMPYAK & MCLEOD
TOP
BOTTOM

EYELIDS OPEN *SOMEWHAT.* CLOSE WHEN DE-ACTIVATED

VENTS

CLIK CLIK CLIK

MR. HERO: THE RATIOCINATOR

IN HIS FOREHEAD CAN BE SEEN AN INTRICATE
ARRAY OF LEVERS AND GEARS--A STEAM-POWERED
COMPUTER, WHICH MAKES LIGHT CLICKING SOUNDS AS THE
VALVES OPEN AND CLOSE WHILE IT--*RATIOCINATES.*

THE VALVES REQUIRE EXTRA STEAM-- THUS THE PIPE TO VENT IT.
MOREOVER, THEY GET QUITE WARM, THUS THE VENTS IN THE TOP OF THE HEAD

<u>Mr. Hero-The Newmatic Man (Pugilist and Ratiocinator)</u>— Mr. Hero was named after the discoverer of steam power, Hero of Alexandria, and his "Pneumatica," the original book on the power of steam. He was supposedly created by Jabez Hilliard, an amateur scientist and farmer, and then sold to British magician and conjurer John Nevil Maskelyne in the late 19th century. Hero's dual personalities-or rather, his two heads-were used as part of Maskelyne's act: the pugilist would box one round with any volunteer and the ratiocinator would deduce facts about the audience in a Sherlock Holmes-like fashion. After a few "accidents" in the ring, Hero was relieved of his entertaining duties and put in storage until a young, novice magician opened the crate and discovered, much to her surprise, a headless metal man inside.

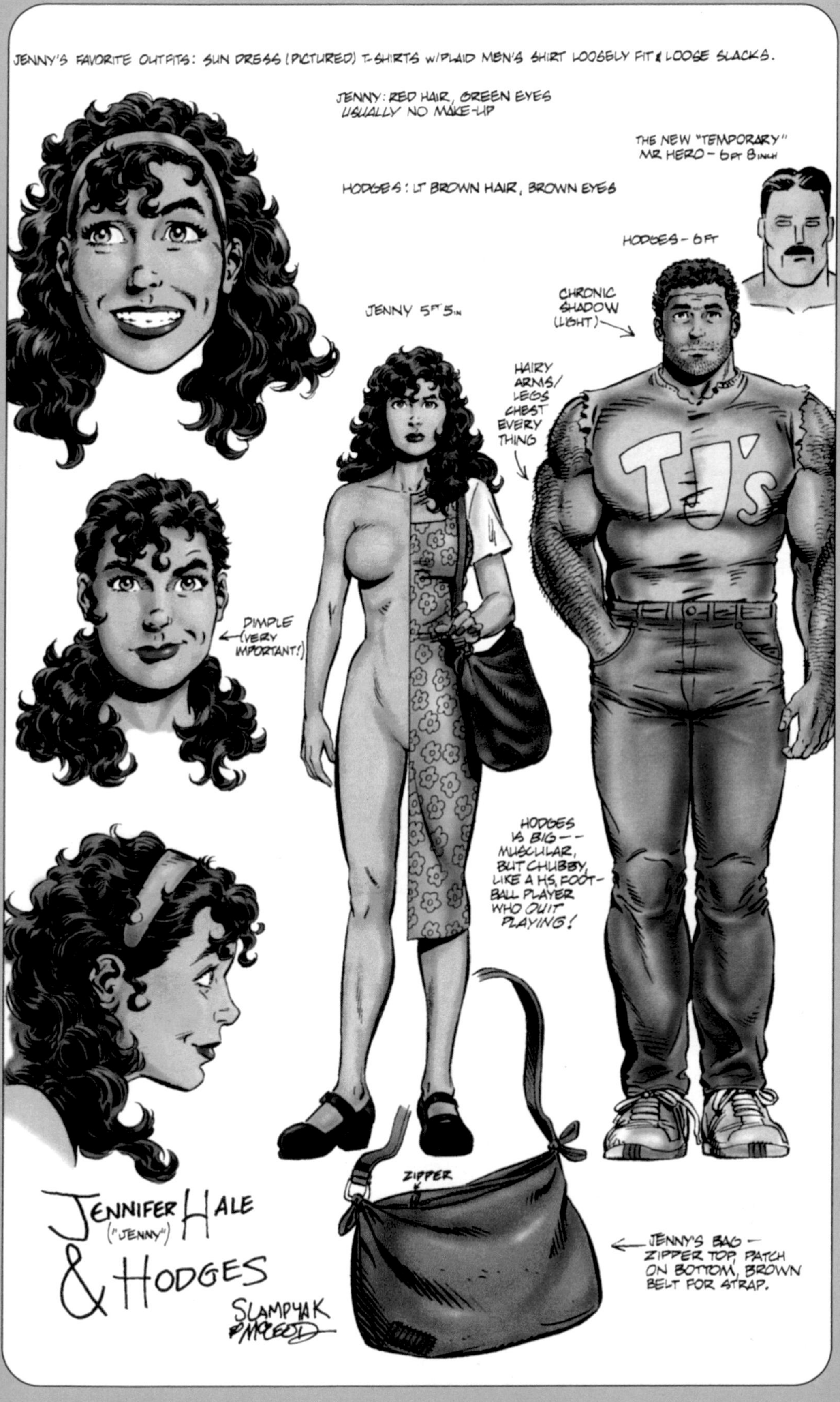
JENNY'S FAVORITE OUTFITS: SUN DRESS (PICTURED) T-SHIRTS W/PLAID MEN'S SHIRT LOOSELY FIT & LOOSE SLACKS.
JENNY: RED HAIR, GREEN EYES
USUALLY NO MAKE-UP
THE NEW "TEMPORARY" MR HERO - 6FT 8INCH
HODGES: LT BROWN HAIR, BROWN EYES
HODGES - 6FT
CHRONIC SHADOW (LIGHT)
JENNY 5FT 5IN
HAIRY ARMS/ LEGS CHEST EVERY THING
TJ's
DIMPLE (VERY IMPORTANT!)
HODGES IS BIG -- MUSCULAR, BUT CHUBBY, LIKE A H.S. FOOT-BALL PLAYER WHO QUIT PLAYING!
ZIPPER
JENNIFER ("JENNY") HALE & HODGES
JENNY'S BAG - ZIPPER TOP, PATCH ON BOTTOM, BROWN BELT FOR STRAP.
SLAMPYAK & MCLEOD

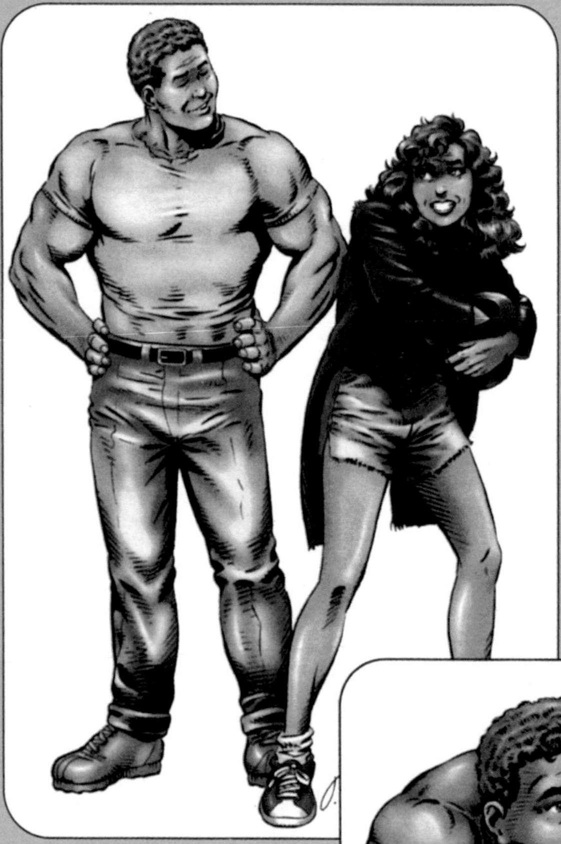

Jennifer Hale— The fun-loving, carefree girl who discovered Mr. Hero. Jenny used to fill her days with simple pleasures, miming on street corners for small change and working at the New Egyptian Hall Magic Club & Museum. But now that Mr. Hero is in her life, things just aren't the same. She's faced genetically-altered monsters and invisible hit men, she's traveled to Monte Carlo, London and even other planets. With more than a lifetime of experiences, Jenny remains the wide-eyed, curious young woman who's willing to go that extra mile for her friends.

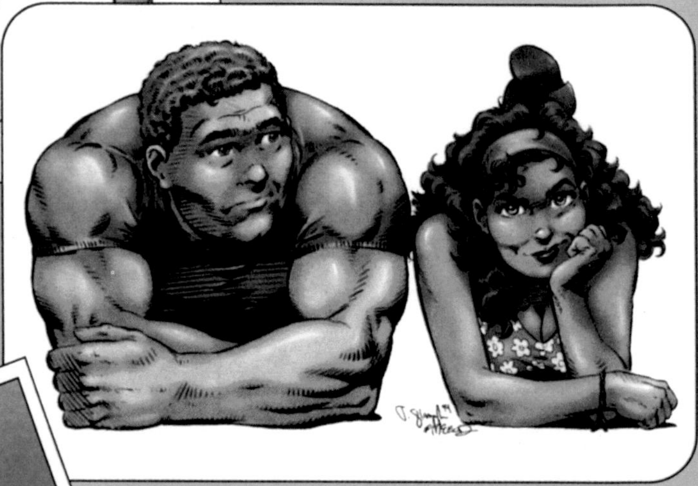

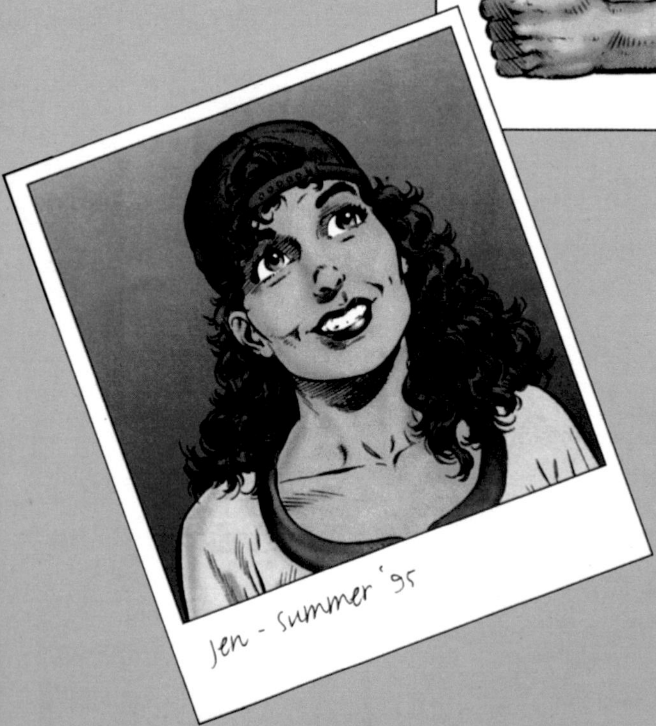
Jen - Summer '95

Hodges— Jenny's B-movie and pizza buddy, Hodges is a big, burly bear of a guy. Before Hero came around, Hodges would do anything for Jenny, whether it be helping her out at the museum or loaning her his last nickel. Since Hero's arrival on the scene, Hodges has had to take a back seat, and that doesn't sit too well with him. But his severe mood swings aren't just a bruised ego talking-Hodges been under the influence of Teknophage's remote brainwashing technique.